Microeconomics

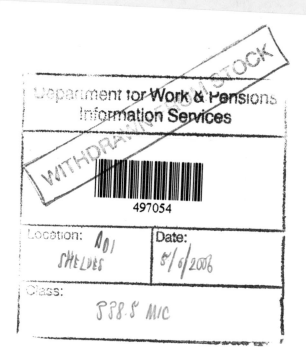

Modern economics

Series editor: David W Pearce

Microeconomics

Hugh Gravelle and Ray Rees

Longman

London and New York

Longman Group UK Limited
Longman House, Burnt Mill, Harlow,
Essex CM20 2JE, England
and Associated Companies throughout the world

*Published in the United States of America
by Longman Inc., New York*

First published 1981
Sixth impression 1987

British Library Cataloguing in Publication Data

Gravelle, Hugh
  Microeconomics. — (Modern economics).
  1. Microeconomics.
  I. Title II. Rees, Ray
  338.5   HB171.5   78 — 40871

ISBN 0-582-44075-0

Produced by Longman Group (FE) Ltd
Printed in Hong Kong

Contents

Preface

* More difficult material – see Preface p. xi.

* More difficult material—see Preface p. xi.

* More difficult material–see Preface p. xi.

* More difficult material–see Preface p. xi.

* More difficult material–see Preface p. xi.

Preface

This textbook in the theory of microeconomics has been written for three kinds of reader. First, for the student who has completed an introductory course in economics at about the first-year undergraduate level and who is now embarking upon a more specialized course in microeconomic theory. The core of this book is an exposition of the topics he will need to cover at the level appropriate for an economics specialist. In this exposition we have made liberal use of a fairly restricted set of mathematical methods. The following can therefore be thought of as prerequisites:

1. The idea of a set and set inclusion; union, intersection and partitions of sets.
2. The meaning of necessary and sufficient conditions and of $\Rightarrow$ and $\Leftrightarrow$ notations.
3. Vectors as arrays of numbers and their association with points in the appropriate coordinate space; addition, subtraction, and inner products of vectors; convex combinations of vectors.
4. Functions.
5. Limits of sequences and continuity of functions.
6. Differentiation of functions of $n \geq 1$ variables.
7. Unconstrained maximization and minimization of functions of $n \geq 1$ variables.

These topics are usually covered in introductory 'maths for economists' courses and several excellent textbooks exist which cover the material. No particular facility with these mathematical prerequisites is assumed. This is something which itself should develop as the reader works carefully through the book.

Because methods of constrained maximization are the foundation for most of microeconomics at this level, Chapter 2 should be worked through at some time. This chapter tries to give an elementary exposition of optimization theory which, though requiring no previous knowledge other than that contained in the prerequisites just described, will help the reader to a better understanding of the subsequent analysis. Where further mathematical ideas are required, such as those of mappings, fixed points and distance functions, they are covered in appendices to the chapters where they are applied.

On each major topic – the theories of the consumer and the firm, competitive and non-competitive markets, general equilibrium and welfare economics – there are chapters or sections of chapters which extend the basic material in a way we hope will be useful for the second kind of reader, the final year undergraduate economist. Here we have sought to provide expositions of such topics as the 'characteristics' approach to consumer theory, the theory of time allocation, search theory, non-profit maximizing theories of the firm, market failure and the second best, and the theory of choice under uncertainty. Our intention was to provide concise but reasonably comprehensive treatments of these topics, which could then be filled out by journal readings and applications to problems. This material has been used by us and our colleagues over the past few years on third-year courses in advanced economic theory, public sector economics, mathematical economics and the theory of business decisions. The more difficult of this material is indicated by an asterisk on the title of the chapter or section in which it is presented. The reader is advised to cover the unasterisked core material thoroughly before going on to the asterisked sections.

Finally, we hope this book will prove useful to the graduate student just embarking on a 'taught master's' course, partly as a means of revision and partly as an introduction to some of the topics he will later cover with greater rigour and depth. It is mainly to this reader that the chapters on general equilibrium theory and exchange under uncertainty, as well as the later sections of several other chapters, are directed.

Broadly speaking, we hope that the student could take up this book when he has completed his studies at the introductory level and will find it a useful basis for his work in microeconomics throughout and possibly beyond his time as an undergraduate.

In writing this book we had two aims: to help the student to a good understanding of the nature and purpose of microeconomic theories and models and the way they all fit together; and to develop the basic tools and concepts of analysis with as much clarity and rigour as is possible at this level. We have tried to avoid what we regard as the two undesirable extremes: a treatment which emphasises tools and techniques without consideration of their underlying purpose and rationale; and a description of microeconomics which leaves the student without a firm grasp of methods of analysis with which he can then solve problems of application.

The exercises at the end of each section should be regarded as an integral part of the book. They are of two kinds: short sharp questions designed to test the reader's understanding of specific points, often by asking him to explain the consequences of changing the assumptions (which has the further advantage of saving space in the text); and the 'starred' questions which might well form the subjects (as they have in our own teaching) of small-group tutorial sessions and written assignments. These latter questions are starred not only because they may be intrinsically more difficult but also because they will usually require a little effort from the student and some discussion with the teacher. Further reading may also often be necessary for which the references at the end of each chapter give a preliminary guide.

For reading and commenting on various parts of various drafts of this book and/or for helpful discussions of many points, we would like to thank Bernard Corry, Mike Danes, Eli Katz, Clive Southey, Francis Tapon, Alf Vanags and Bill Wells. Ian Walker read through the entire manuscript and made many helpful comments and suggestions. The errors and solecisms which remain are no fault of anyone but ourselves. David Pearce has been an exceptionally tolerant and helpful editor. Special thanks go to Norma Venn, who rescued us from a secretarial impasse and did a splendid job of typing the manuscript, and to Pat Watson, who re-typed large parts of the final draft. We are also grateful to several generations of graduate and undergraduate students at Queen Mary College, London, who helped us develop the material contained in this book, and who latterly have commented on several of the chapters.

H.S.E.G.
R.R.

To Maggie and Denny

Chapter 1

The nature and scope of microeconomics

A. Concepts and methods

Microeconomics consists of a set of theories with one aim: to help us gain an understanding of the process by which scarce resources are allocated among alternative uses in a modern economy, and of the role of prices and markets in this process. In its purest form, it is therefore essentially a philosophical inquiry into the processes of resource allocation. However, with understanding usually comes the ability to predict and to control, and this has been the case in microeconomics. The concepts and relationships economists have developed in their attempt to understand the workings of the economy provide the basis for the design of policies by governments wishing to influence the outcome of this process, or alternatively for a critique of the actions governments might take. Through the development of 'operations research', 'management science' and 'business economics', concepts from microeconomics have been applied to assist rational decision-taking in business, suggesting that Nature does indeed imitate Art.

A good way of providing an introductory overview of micro-economics is to set out its basic elements.

1. Goods and services or commodities

These are the central objects of economic activity, since 'economic activity' consists of the production and exchange of commodities. We distinguish commodities from each other by one or more of three characteristics: their *physical* nature and attributes, which determine the way in which they meet the needs of consumers and producers; the *location* at which they are made available; and the *date* at which they are made available. For example, coal and crude oil are physically different commodities, as are the services of a hairdresser and those of an accountant (though in each case, the broad category of resource from which the commodities derive – 'land' in one case and 'labour' in the other – is the same). Equally important is the fact that crude oil in Dubai available tomorrow is a different commodity from crude oil available tomorrow at a refinery in Western Europe; while coal in London today is a different commodity from coal in London this time next year. The basis of the distinction between commodities is that they cannot be regarded as perfect substitutes in production or consumption – a businessman who goes along to his accountant for advice on a tax problem would not be just as happy to be offered a haircut instead. In most of microeconomics we assume that there is a *finite* set of possible physical bundles of attributes, a finite set of possible locations – we do not regard geographical space as continuous, but rather divided up into small areas – and a finite set of dates. We do not regard calendar time as continuous, but rather divided up into equal discrete time intervals, and moreover not as extending indefinitely far into the future, but instead we assume some definite, though possibly very distant, time horizon. These assumptions ensure that there is a finite number of commodities to be taken into account in our theories. Alternatively, we could assume a *continuum* of commodities: given any one commodity, we could always define another which is as close as we like to the first in attributes, location and time. Moreover this commodity continuum need not be bounded – we could picture commodities as points on a line which stretches to infinity, since we could always define commodities available later in time. The methods of analysis required for an economy with such a commodity continuum differ sharply from those conventionally used in economics. Since the assumptions required to establish a finite set of commodities do not seem to do serious injustice to reality, while considerably simplifying the analysis, we gladly adopt them.

2. Prices

Associated with each commodity is a price, which may be expressed in one of two ways. First, we may choose one commodity in the economy as a *numeraire*, i.e. as the commodity in terms of which all prices are to be expressed. For example, suppose we choose gold. Then the price of each commodity is the number of units of gold which exchange for one unit of that commodity. The price of gold of course is 1. In general, we are free to choose *any* commodity as numeraire, so that prices could just as well be expressed in terms of the number of units of some kind of labour service which exchange for one unit of each other commodity. It might be argued that in reality different commodities may have different degrees of suitability for use in market transactions. Commodities which are not easily divisible, and which are bulky and subject to physical decay, will tend not to be used as a means of payment. However, it is important to note that a numeraire is not intended to represent a *means of exchange*, or 'money', in this sense. We are simply using it as a *unit of account*, or a *unit of measurement* for prices in the economy, and *nothing need be implied about the mechanism by which transactions actually take place*. Given the choice of numeraire, prices are effectively *commodity rates of exchange* – they express the rate at which the numeraire exchanges for each other commodity. They have the dimension (units of the numeraire/units of the commodity). They are therefore not independent of the units in which we measure commodities. For example if we double the unit in which we measure each commodity *except* for the numeraire we would have to double prices (explain why).

The second way in which prices might be expressed does not involve a numeraire. Instead, we suppose there to be some unit of account which is not a quantity of some physical commodity, but an abstract unit used in making bookkeeping entries. If one unit of a commodity is sold, the account is credited with a certain number of units of account, while if the commodity is bought, the same number of units is debited from the account. The price of the commodity is then the number of units debited or credited per unit of the commodity. We find it useful to give this unit of account a name, and so we could call it the £ sterling, or the US $, for example. If different accounts are kept in different units, then rates of exchange between units of account must be established before transfers from one account to another can be made. Clearly, there is no physical substance corresponding to the unit of account, say the £ sterling. A cheque made out for £x is an instruction to credit one account and debit another, i.e. to transfer x units of account between accounts. Notes and coin have no intrinsic worth (until perhaps they cease to be used in exchange and acquire intrinsic worth – become commodities themselves – to numismatists), but are simply tokens representing numbers of units of account which are passed around directly and form part (usually a relatively small part) of the credit side of one's accounts.

The somewhat abstract way of expressing prices in terms of units of account therefore corresponds to the way prices are expressed in reality, and has come about because of the development of the modern banking system. There is, however, a straightforward correspondence between prices expressed in terms of units of account and prices expressed as commodity rates of exchange. Thus, suppose we have the set of prices expressed in £ sterling: $p_1, p_2 \ldots p_n$. Then, by taking any one such price, say the nth, and forming the n ratios:

$$r_1 = p_1/p_n; \qquad r_2 = p_2/p_n; \qquad \ldots r_n = p_n/p_n = 1 \qquad \text{[A.1]}$$

we can interpret each r_j, $j = 1, 2, \ldots n$, as the number of units of commodity n which will exchange for one unit of commodity j, i.e. as commodity rates of exchange with n as the numeraire. Each r_j will be in dimensions (units of good n/units of good j) as we can see from:

$$p_j/p_n = (\pounds/\text{units of good } j \div \pounds/\text{units of good } n) = (\text{units of good } n/\text{units}$$
$$\text{of good } j), \qquad j = 1, 2, \ldots, n \qquad \text{[A.2]}$$

Thus, each r_j in effect tells us the number of units of good n we could buy if we sold a unit of good j and spent the proceeds (p_j units of account) on good n.

3. Markets

The everyday notion of a market is as a specific place where certain types of commodities are bought and sold, for example a cattle market, or a fruit and vegetable market. The concept of a market in economics is, however, much more general than this: a market exists whenever two or more individuals are prepared to enter into an exchange transaction, regardless of time or place. Thus, if two poachers meet in the middle of a forest in the dead of night, one with a catch of salmon and the other with a bag of pheasants, and they decide to negotiate an exchange of fish for fowl, we would say that a market exists. The word 'market' denotes an exchange situation. The central problem in microeconomics is the analysis of how markets operate, since we view the process of resource allocation as a market process – a resource allocation is brought about by the workings of markets. For every commodity, therefore, a market does or will exist, and something which cannot be exchanged upon a market is not, from the point of view of microeconomics, a commodity.

It is important to distinguish between *forward* and *spot* markets. On a spot market, an agreement is made under which delivery of a commodity is completed within the current period; on a forward market, delivery will be made at some future period (some markets may do both, e.g. the market in leasehold accommodation, where what may be sold is a flow of housing services over a possibly very large number of years). We could envisage an economy in which at a given point in time there exists a market for every commodity, which means there is a complete system of spot and forward markets. In such an economy, contracts would be entered into for all future exchanges of commodities as well as for all current exchanges, and so market activity could cease entirely after the first period: the rest of time would be spent simply fulfilling the contracts already concluded. Real economies, of course, do not possess such complete market systems. In any one period, markets exist for delivery of commodities within the period, and some forward markets exist for future delivery, but only relatively few. Hence, at any one time only a relatively small subset of all commodities can be exchanged. We then get a sequence of market systems, one in each period, and exchange activity takes place continually.

This picture of the economy raises a number of interesting questions. How will the outcomes on markets at one period be influenced by expectations about the outcomes in later periods? What will be the relationship, if any, between spot prices of commodities with the same physical attributes but different dates of delivery (e.g. the price of crude oil now and its price this time next year)? Can income (which we can take here to be the proceeds of sales of commodities, including of course labour services) be transferred between time periods and, if so, how? What are the consequences of the fact that the future cannot be known with certainty?

The analysis of the full implications of the view of the economy as a time sequence of market systems is complex and still incomplete. One approach to it (that followed in this book) is to take it in three stages. We first of all analyse an 'atemporal economy', which could be thought of as an economy existing for just a single time period. We then extend the analysis to an 'intertemporal economy' by considering an economy which will exist over more than one period, but make the assumption of *complete certainty* – all relevant facts about the future are fully known at each point in time. We then take the final step of relaxing this certainty assumption and allowing incomplete information about data relating to the future. It is the analysis of this last kind of economy which is not yet really complete. Interestingly, as long as we assume complete certainty, analysis of an intertemporal economy can be made formally identical to that of the atemporal economy, or, alternatively, identical to that of the kind of economy in which there is a complete system of spot and forward markets existing at any one time (see Ch. 15). At a more advanced level of analysis, it is usual to merge stages one and two, and analyse an economy which could be interpreted either atemporally or intertemporally. Indeed, on certain quite strong assumptions it is possible to do the same for the economy with uncertainty (see Ch. 20). However, in this book we shall take one stage at a time.

4. Economic agents

The basic units of analysis in microeconomics are the individual economic agents or decision-takers (hence the term *micro*economics), who are usually classified either as *consumers* or *firms*. A consumer is regarded as an individual who may own initially certain stocks of commodities, his 'initial endowment' (counted as part of his wealth), and who has to choose an amount of each commodity (which may of course be zero) to consume. This amount, in conjunction with his initial endowment, will determine the quantity of each commodity he will want to buy or sell on the relevant market. An alternative and less general formulation is to ignore the selling side of the consumer's activities, and assume his initial endowment takes the form of 'income', expressed in units of account or in terms of some numeraire. We then analyse simply his consumption (equals purchasing) decision, assuming also that he holds zero stocks of all the goods he might want to consume. This somewhat restrictive view of the consumer's activities is useful as a way of developing certain tools of analysis, but clearly can only be provisional, if we also want to say anything about the supply of commodities such as labour services.

A firm is also usually regarded as an individual decision-taker, undertaking the production of commodities by combining inputs in technological processes. These inputs will usually themselves be commodities, some of which the firm may own as part of its initial endowment, and some of which it may buy on the relevant markets. In certain cases, however, important inputs may not be commodities, e.g. sunshine in the production of wine. The crux of the distinction between consumers and firms is the nature of their economic activity: consumers buy and sell commodities in order to consume; firms buy inputs and produce commodities in order to sell.

Of course, in reality the counterparts of these theoretical abstractions are more complex. 'Consumer units' are usually groups of two or more people comprising a 'household' and decisions on purchases and sales may well be group decisions. Microeconomics might find itself accused of taking an old-fashioned (even sexist!) view of the world in assuming a single directing intelligence (the head of the household?) as the consumer. The point is of course that we are not trying to model in any detail the organization of a household. Provided that the household acts in its decision-taking in a way which corresponds reasonably closely to certain principles of rationality and consistency, it is *enough for the purposes of our theory* to regard it as a single abstract decision-taker, 'the consumer'. If the organization of the household were shown to be such as to lead to significant departures from these principles of rationality and consistency, and to make our theories seriously misleading when used to explain and predict consumption decisions then we would have to reconstruct our theory of the consumer to take account of this.

In the case of the firm, the empirical counterpart of the theoretical entity may be thought even less like a single individual. Although many owner-controlled or *entrepreneurial* firms exist, economic activity is dominated by large corporations, with complex structures of organization and decision-taking. We can apply the same argument as before: it is a simplifying theoretical abstraction to ignore the organisational characteristics of firms for the purpose of our analysis of the general resource allocation process, which is defensible as long as the explanations and predictions we make about the decisions of firms in this process are not shown to be false by the evidence of firms' behaviour. Much more so than in the case of the household, however, there is a great deal of argument and a little evidence to suggest that certain aspects of the organizational structure of firms *do* lead them to behave differently from the predictions of the theory of the firm as a single decision-taker. Accordingly, we devote a good deal of space in Chapters 6 and 13 below to examine theories which take some account of the organisational characteristics of modern corporations.

The classification of the set of economic agents into consumers and firms reflects the basic distinction between the activities of production and consumption. However, we can quite easily choose a less rigid separation between types of economic agents. For example, if the decision-taker controlling the firm is a person, the *entrepreneur*, then he is necessarily a consumer as well as a producer. We could then construct a theory which has the producer taking consumption decisions as well as production decisions. This leads to a view of an economy as consisting basically of consumers, at least some (and possibly all) of whom have access to production possibilities – they possess the knowledge, skills and initial endowment of commodities (including probably 'capital goods') which enable them to produce as well as exchange. Such an economy is quite amenable to analysis by the methods developed for the economy in which we preserve the distinction between consumers and producers and indeed, if we make the assumption that inputs of 'managerial services' can be bought and sold on a market, there is no essential difference between the two economies.

An alternative way of blurring the distinction between consumers and producers is to regard the consumer as in fact a kind of producer. At the simplest level, we could view him as 'producing' labour services, using as inputs the commodities he buys, and with these labour services being supplied to firms which use them in conjunction with other commodities to produce commodities which are supplied to consumers . . . and so on. The point of interest in this kind of economy is to study the conditions under which the economy can sustain or *reproduce* itself – will the flow of commodities as outputs be just sufficient to produce the labour services and other commodities necessary again to produce that same flow? We could also examine the way in which such an economy might grow over time by producing in each period more commodities than are required simply to reproduce themselves. A more sophisticated model of the consumer as a producer regards him as buying market goods and services, and combining them with his own time and effort, to 'produce' certain consumption services, which are the real objects of consumption. For example a rail journey from A to B involves the purchase of a transportation service on the market, together with an input of the traveller's time, to produce the consumption service of a trip from A to B. The method of analysis developed for production by firms is then used to analyse the consumer's choices of market commodities when they are regarded as inputs into the production of consumption services. Such models have wide applications, for example in the analysis of markets for transport services of various kinds, where the duration of travelling time is an important aspect of the choice, and also to help us understand why, as real incomes increase, consumers appear to substitute time- and labour-saving commodities for others. In other words, such models are useful whenever we want to bring to the forefront of the analysis the fact that time is a scarce resource.

5. Rationality

In whatever way we break down the distinction between consumers and producers in microeconomic models, two central elements remain. First is the adoption of the individual decision-taker as the basic unit of analysis. Second is the hypothesis that this decision-taker is *rational*. The concept of rationality is so pervasive that its meaning must be clearly expressed. We would say that rational decision-taking takes the following form:

(*a*) The decision-taker sets out *all* the *feasible* alternatives which are open to him, rejecting any which are not feasible;

(*b*) He takes into account whatever information is readily available, or worth collecting, to assess the consequences of choosing each of the alternatives;

(*c*) In the light of their consequences he ranks the alternatives in order of preference, where this ordering satisfies certain assumptions of completeness and consistency (discussed in Ch. 3 below);

(*d*) He chooses the alternative highest in this ordering, i.e. he chooses
the alternative with the consequences he prefers over all others
available to him.

These 'requirements of rationality' seem to be quite consistent with the
everyday sense in which rationality is used. People *can* behave irrationally
in this sense: in taking a decision, they may ignore *known* feasible alternatives, they may allow themselves to be influenced by infeasible alternatives,
they may ignore or not bother to collect information on the consequences of
their decisions, they may contradict themselves in the ranking of the
alternatives, and they may even choose an alternative whose consequences
they have already told us they regard as less attractive than those of another
alternative. That is to say, the assumption of rationality is an *hypothesis*,
rather than a *tautology* – we can quite well conceive of its being false for a
particular decision-taker.

However, it is not always as easy to conclude that a decision-taker is
behaving irrationally as may be supposed. The important principle here is
(*b*) above, relating to the use and acquisition of information. The collection
of information, and the process of decision-taking itself, absorbs resources
and therefore imposes costs. Given that all the information which could
possibly be relevant to a decision is not readily and costlessly available, we
may often observe behaviour which is rational on the basis of principles
(*a*)–(*d*), but may be labelled irrational by a careless observer (or one
determined to prove that *homo economicus* does not exist). For example, a
housewife may habitually use the same supermarket rather than shopping
around other supermarkets to find better bargains. This might appear to
violate principle (*a*), but could be explained by the arguments that habit is
essentially a way of economizing on time and effort, and that her expectation of the gain she would make by shopping around does not seem to her to
justify the cost and bother involved.

The danger in this kind of explanation is apparent in the example:
with a little ingenuity, just about any kind of behaviour could be made to
appear rational. This is a danger we have to avert, if the concept of
rationality is not to become an empty tautology – we have to accept that
people may at times be irrational. The general point can be put in the
following way. We do observe in economic behaviour a tendency for the
consistent pursuit of well-defined objectives. Consumers' 'habits' have often
been shown to be very easily changed by sufficiently large price changes; the
growth of the tax avoidance industry is a prime example of the rationality
with which individuals calculate and organize when the returns make it
worthwhile. We also observe instances of apparent irrationality which may
or may not be convincingly explained away. This therefore suggests that it is
very difficult to test the hypothesis of rationality by actually observing
individuals as they go through *the process* of decision-taking. For many
purposes we may not even require that *every* individual act rationally, as
long as in the aggregate enough people act with enough rationality to make
our theories of the behaviour of these aggregates (e.g. all the buyers in a

market) applicable. This suggests that the best *practical* test of the rationality hypothesis is by testing the further hypotheses which are derived from it, especially those further hypotheses which could not be derived from a postulate of 'irrationality' (somehow specified).

To summarize the discussion of this chapter so far, the basic elements of microeconomics are: *rational* individual decision-takers, usually classified as consumers and firms, commodities, markets, prices.

6. Method of analysis

The core of microeconomic theory follows through a systematic line of development. We begin with models of the individual decision-takers, a 'typical' or representative consumer and a 'typical' or representative firm. The assumption of rationality implies that these models take the form of *optimization problems*: the decision-taker is assumed to seek the *best* alternative out of the feasible set of alternatives open to him. By specifying fairly closely the nature of these optimization problems and then solving them, we are able to attribute certain characteristics and properties to the decision-taker's choices. Moreover, by examining the way in which his optimal choices may vary with changes in underlying parameters of the decision problem (especially prices), we can trace out *behaviour relationships* such as the demand and supply curves with which the reader is probably already familiar.

A major purpose of the models of individual decisions is to allow us to place certain restrictions on these behaviour relationships, or at least to clarify the assumptions under which particular restrictions (e.g. that demand curves have negative slopes) can be placed.

The next step in the development of the theory is to aggregate the individual behaviour relationships over groups of economic agents – usually the set of buyers in a market on the one hand and the set of sellers in a market on the other, where these can be separately identified. This latter qualification is necessary because, as we shall see, in some market models an individual may be a buyer at some prices and a seller at others, so that no hard and fast distinction can be drawn between buyers and sellers, and aggregation takes place over *all* economic agents. These aggregated relationships then form the basis for an analysis of the operation of a single market taken in isolation, and also of systems of several interrelated markets. At the most general, we consider the system of markets for the economy as a whole, and analyse the way in which a resource allocation is determined by the simultaneous interaction of this market system.

The method of analysis is the same throughout, and can be described as the *equilibrium methodology*. The equilibrium of a system is defined as a situation in which the forces determining the state of that system are in balance, so that there is no tendency for the variables of the system to change. (*Note*: Strictly speaking, this is the method of *static* equilibrium analysis. We could allow variables and parameters to vary with time, and look for *equilibrium time-paths*, in a dynamic analysis. Since in this book we use static methods throughout, we do not need the qualification.) An equilibrium of a system of economic agents (which may be a single market or a whole economy) will exist when two conditions are satisfied:

    (a) individual decision-makers have no wish to change their planned decisions or reactions;

    (b) the plans of decision-makers are consistent or compatible and hence can be realized.

The significance of the equilibrium concept is that it provides us with a *solution principle*. Once we have defined the forces operating within a given economic system, for example a model of a single market, we naturally ask the question: what will the outcome of the interaction of those forces be? The answer is provided by the concept of equilibrium: we find the characteristics of the equilibrium state of the system, and take this as the outcome we seek. But if we want to use the equilibrium state as a prediction of the outcome of the workings of the system, we first have to answer a number of fundamental questions, namely:

    (a) *Existence.* Does the system in fact *possess* an equilibrium state, i.e. given the forces operating within the system, is there in principle a state in which they would be in balance, or is it the case that no such state of balance is possible? Clearly, if a system does not possess an equilibrium, we cannot describe its outcome as an equilibrium state.

    (b) *Stability.* Suppose that an equilibrium state does exist. Then, given that the system may not initially be in this state, would it tend to converge on it? If it does, then we call the system stable. Clearly, the equilibrium state loses much of its interest if the system is not in this sense stable, since it is unlikely ever actually to be attained.

    (c) *Uniqueness.* A system may possess more than one equilibrium state, and the different possible equilibria may have different properties and implications, and so it is of interest to know for a given system whether there is only one possible equilibrium state which needs to be described.

    These questions of the existence, stability and uniqueness of an equilibrium state are necessarily raised by use of an equilibrium methodology, and so we shall find that we shall be considering them in a number of contexts throughout this book.

    These introductory remarks have been concerned with describing the basic concepts of microeconomics, the overall structure of the theory and its method of analysis. Full understanding of these can only be achieved, of course, by a thorough study of the theory itself. Before embarking upon this, we conclude this introductory chapter with some comments on the view of the economic and social system which is implicit in modern microeconomic analysis.

B. The economic and social framework

The type of economic analysis with which this book is concerned has been criticized, often by social scientists working outside economics, for appearing to ignore the institutional, political and legal framework of society. This criticism has a point, but is wrongly focussed. At one level microeconomics *implicitly assumes* a certain type of framework and is concerned with analysing the major economic forces which operate within it. Not a great deal appears to be said directly about the framework itself. However, at a deeper level, microeconomics has a great deal to say about certain kinds of institutional frameworks and also shows something which is equally important. Some fundamental problems of economic life exist whatever the institutional system and one means of comparing systems (not of course the only means) is in terms of the ways in which they deal with these problems.

The type of economic system with which microeconomics is immediately concerned is a *decentralized private ownership economy*. It is decentralized in two senses. First, each economic agent is assumed to know only the information relevant to his own personal decision problem: his own preferences and initial endowments (which may represent skills and aptitudes as well as physical commodities) if he is a consumer; the relevant technological conditions and initial endowments (especially of capital goods) if he is a firm. In addition, each is usually assumed to know the prevailing prices, at least on the spot markets on which he may trade (though some models may start with the weaker assumption that the decision-taker has only an expectation of these prices and go on to analyse the search process by which the economic agent obtains more information). Secondly, within the constraints imposed by initial endowments, technology (for a firm) and market conditions, each economic agent is assumed to take his own decisions. Thus we view the economy as both *informationally decentralized* (decision-takers know only 'their own' information), and *decisionally decentralized*. We could then rephrase the central question of microeconomics in the form: how do the movements of prices in response to market forces bring about consistency among the plans and decisions of the individuals in this doubly decentralized system? In seeking an answer to this question, we are in effect examining *the implications of a particular institutional framework of the economy*, one that can be contrasted with, say, a centrally planned economy in which information on technology, resource availability, and possibly preferences is collected at the centre and resource allocation decisions are also taken there.

The system is called a *private ownership economy* because it is implicitly assumed that there exists a system of *property rights* under which individuals can be said to *own* commodities and the assets of firms. This presupposes in turn the existence of an entire legal infrastructure by which the rights of ownership of property are *defined* and *enforced*. Moreover, if exchange is to take place, there must be a system of law which regulates the transfer of ownership of property. In other words, we can regard exchange not simply as the physical transfer of commodities, but also as the transfer of property rights in those commodities – exchange of property rights is an essential precondition for exchange of physical commodities, in order that exchange is not robbery (the nature and significance of property rights are further considered in Ch. 18).

Thus, microeconomics is immediately concerned with a society with a particular institutional framework, in which individuals take their own decisions within the constraints of market and technological conditions and in which the rights of ownership and exchange of private property are defined and upheld. The role of the state is minimal: we could regard it as implicitly having the responsibility of providing and enforcing the basic legal framework and the institutions which this requires – civil and criminal courts, the police force, etc., and no real role beyond this is envisaged by the main body of microeconomic theory.

However, it is doubtful that microeconomics would have the interest and relevance it does if it only had something to say about such an individualistic, *laissez-faire* economy. Its applicability is very much broader than this, for two main reasons:

1. Microeconomics takes as its starting point two facts of economic life which are virtually universal, namely the degree of *specialization* in the roles individuals play in the production process and the *relative scarcity* of resources. The first of these has taken place essentially because of the productivity gains which result from the specialization by individuals in particular kinds of activity. The second stems from the observation that however abundant in absolute terms are the resources possessed by an economy, it seems to be a trait of human nature to want to consume more goods and services than can be produced with those resources. If this ever ceased to be the case, microeconomics would cease to be relevant, since it is founded on the assumption of relative scarcity. Given these facts, every economic system is faced with the problems of organizing exchange – as specialized individuals trade at least some of the returns to their effort for goods and services produced by others – and of coordinating the separate individual decisions in both production and consumption. Every economic system is also faced with the problem of allocating resources among competing uses.

Now although the study of the market mechanism as a means of solving these problems arises quite naturally in a decentralized private ownership economy, the understanding of the roles played by prices and markets thus derived can be applied to solve those problems in economies in which no private property rights exist (a purely 'collectivist' state); or in which there exists a mixed system of private property rights, state ownership of property, and a prerogative of the state to amend or abrogate private property rights (a 'mixed economy'). Important areas of application of microeconomic theory are the theory of 'price-guided' central planning procedures and the theories of public finance and public enterprise production in a mixed economy. More fundamentaly the methods of micro-economics can be applied to the analysis of all economies, whatever their institutional characteristics.

2. Economists have not only been interested in understanding how the economic system works, but in evaluating how well it works. Since at least the time of Adam Smith, there has been a strong body of opinion among economists that the market mechanism operating in a decentralized private ownership economy brings about a higher level of welfare for the people in that society than other mechanisms, for example a system of detailed state regulation. This proposition has been subjected to rigorous examination in the course of which has been developed the idea of 'market failure' – a situation in which the outcome of the market mechanism appears in principle at least to be capable of improvement, possibly by state intervention. Many economists, though not without strong opposition, have seen cases of market failure as providing an economic role for the state which goes well beyond that of providing the legal infrastructure for the economy – the 'rules of the game'. A good deal of analysis – *using the concepts and tools of microeconomics* – has been applied to the problem of determining the *optimal* policies for the state in these respects. In analysing the sources of market failure, our understanding of the economy's institutional framework has been greatly increased: for example, the nature and significance of property rights themselves have become better understood. A thorough discussion of the issues raised by market failure is presented in Chapter 18.

C. Conclusions

In this introductory chapter we have given a broad overview of microeconomics: its basic concepts, its mode of analysis, and its implicit institutional framework. We have also tried to suggest that the understanding gained by the study of microeconomics is applicable to types of economy other than the decentralized private ownership economy, though to understand fully the process of resource allocation in just this kind of economy would be achievement enough!

References and further reading

C. J. Bliss. *Capital Theory and the Distribution of Income*, North-Holland Publishing Co., Amsterdam. Oxford, 1975, Ch. 1.

J. Hirschleifer. *Investment, Interest and Capital*, Prentice-Hall, Inc., Englewood Cliffs, N.J., 1970, Ch. 1.

These two readings give a useful general picture of the substance of microeconomic analysis. A general statement on the nature of microeconomics is given by:

O. Lange. 'The scope and method of microeconomics', *Review of Economic Studies*, vol. XIII, No. 19, 1945/6.

A clear and critical discussion of the concept of rationality in economics can be found in:

> **H. A. Simon.** 'Theories of bounded rationality', Ch. 8 in C. B. McGuire and R. Radner (eds), *Decision and Organisation*, North-Holland Publishing Co. Ltd., London, 1972.

The paper:

> **J. Parry Lewis.** 'Dimensions in economic theory', *Manchester School of Economic and Social Studies*, 31, 1963,

gives a good discussion of the question of the dimensions of economic variables, a subject lightly touched upon in this chapter and often neglected – at the cost of frequent confusion – in economics.

Chapter 2

Optimization*

As the previous chapter has suggested, the idea of rationality in economics implies, among other things, that a decision-taker tries to find the best alternative out of those available to him. In other words he tries to *optimize*. For this reason the idea of optimization is fundamental to microeconomics and optimization problems occur repeatedly throughout this book. Although the particular economic context of the problems may vary – a consumer's choice of consumption bundle, a firm's production decision, a planner's choice of resource allocation in the economy, for example – they tend to have a common basic structure. It is therefore efficient and illuminating to invest some time in considering optimization problems in general, abstracting from any particular context.

The reader with a little mathematics and a taste for abstraction may find it useful to work through this chapter before going on to the economic models of subsequent chapters. In this way he will be aware of the nature of these models as *optimization problems* when he encounters them. An equally good strategy, however, would be to take up this chapter after studying the models in Chapters 3, 7, 8, 9, 15 and 17, when the need may well be felt for a general discussion of their common structure.

An understanding of the material in this chapter is not strictly *necessary* for the study of the economic models presented later in this book. A reader who has worked through these models, however, may well be struck by the underlying similarities in their structure. He may also be intrigued by the fact that when quite reasonable changes are made in the way curves are drawn, apparently odd things happen to the nature of the results. For example, it is not unreasonable to suppose that a consumer's indifference curves are in the positive quadrant everywhere steeper than his budget line – nothing in the axioms set out in Chapter 3 rules this out. But what then happens to the cherished 'tangency solution' for consumer equilibrium, and the 'necessary condition' that marginal rate of substitution *equal* price ratio? These latter may be preserved, but only at the expense of allowing negative consumption of one good (draw the diagram). Does this make sense?

An examination of the general theory of optimization problems puts the standard models of economics in context. It makes us aware of the assumptions which have been quietly slipped into the analysis to ensure that a certain set of properties are possessed by the results, and enables us to reformulate the answers when these implicit assumptions have been removed. At the very least it greatly increases our awareness of the nature and meaning of the economic models themselves.

A. The structure of an optimization problem

So far we have defined optimization simply to mean the act of choosing the 'best' alternative out of whatever alternatives are available. It is a description of how decisions (choices among alternatives) are or should be taken. We now go beyond this simple idea and examine in some detail the questions we can ask about optimization problems and the concepts which have been developed to answer them.

All optimization problems consist of three elements:

1. Choice variables

These are the variables whose optimal values have to be determined. For example:

  (i) A firm wants to know at what level to set output in order to achieve maximum profit. Output is the choice variable.

 (ii) A firm wants to know what amounts of labour, machine time and raw materials to use so as to produce a given output level at minimum cost. Choice variables are labour, machine time, raw materials.

(iii) A consumer wants to buy that bundle of commodities which he can afford and which makes him feel best off. Here the choice variables are quantities of commodities.

In economics the amount of any choice variable is almost always assumed to be measurable as a real number. There may be any finite number of choice variables in a particular problem. Usually, we shall be discussing one- and two-variable problems, because problems with more than two choice variables cannot easily be represented in two-dimensional diagrams. The loss of generality is usually more apparent than real.

2. The objective function

This gives a mathematical specification of the relationship between the choice variables on the one hand and some variable whose value we wish to *maximize* or *minimize* on the other. Thus, in the three examples just discussed, the objective functions would relate:

  (i) profit to the level of output;

 (ii) cost to the amounts of labour, machine time and raw materials;

(iii) an index of the consumer's satisfaction to the quantities of the commodities he may buy.

In (i) and (iii) the functions are to be maximized, and in (ii) minimized, with respect to the relevant choice variables.

The reader has, we hope, sensed a difference between the third of these objective functions and the first two. Profit and cost are money magnitudes, the measurement of which seems to present no problem. What however, do we mean by 'an index of satisfactions'? Satisfactions are internal subjective things, and it is not immediately obvious that they are susceptible of representation by a numerical index. In the next chapter we shall consider at some length a set of assumptions which, if they hold, allow us to conclude that in the consumer's problem, we *can* define a numerical objective function which he is taken to maximize. Ultimately all objective functions, even those which appear at first sight to involve readily measurable magnitudes like profit and cost, are numerical representations of preference orderings. A businessman aims to maximize profit because he *prefers* more profit to less, in terms of the uses to which it may be put. He seeks to minimize cost because he *prefers* to pay out less rather than more, given the other things he may spend money on. These two objective functions in fact correspond to a rather special case, in which the decision-taker is interested in only a single measurable outcome of the decision (profit or cost), and his preference ordering over values of this is of a particularly simple form – he always prefers more to less, or less to more. In such a special case, we can ignore the order of preference and operate in terms of the single outcome directly. If, on the other hand, more than one outcome of the decision were to be relevant (e.g. both profit and the effort the businessman must put in), then we cannot ignore the more fundamental preference ordering. One alternative may involve more of one variable and less of the other than a second alternative, and so some kind of relative evaluation is inescapable.

For the rest of this chapter, we shall simply take it that we wish to maximize some magnitude which is a real number, and which is a given function of the choice variables in the problem. The foregoing discussion, however, gives us a useful interpretation of the objective function: we can view it as placing alternative values of the choice variables in order of preference so that we can find those preferred.

3. The feasible set

So far we have talked loosely about 'the available alternatives'. An essential part of any optimization problem is a specification of exactly what alternatives are available to the decision-taker. The available set of alternatives is called the 'feasible set'. Since the alternatives are usually regarded as 'points', feasible sets are usually what are referred to in mathematics as 'point sets'.

There are three ways in which the feasible set may be specified:
(a) By direct enumeration, i.e. by a statement which says: the alternatives are $A, B, C, \cdots$. Clearly, if the choice set contains one alternative, or none, the optimization problem is trivial.

(b) By one or more inequalities which *directly* define a set of alternative values of the choice variable(s).

(c) By one or more *functions* or equations which define a set of alternative values.

Examples of the last two of these can be found in the problems discussed earlier. Thus, in problem (i), we would rule out negative outputs, but would expect any positive outputs to be possible. Hence we would say that output must be greater than or equal to zero, i.e. $y \geq 0$, where y is output. The feasible set is here directly defined by a *weak inequality*.

In the second problem, we are told that only those combinations of inputs which yield the desired output level can be considered. In this case the feasible set is generally defined by a function. Thus, suppose we have the *production function*: $y = f(L, M, R)$ where y is output, L, M, R, are labour, machine time and raw materials respectively. Now let y^0 be the required output level. Then the equation:

$$y^0 = f(L, M, R) \qquad [\text{A.1}]$$

defines a set of values of L, M, R, which are feasible. In addition, note that it may be possible for equation [A.1] to be satisfied by negative values of one or more of the choice variables, implying that such negative values may be chosen. We would not regard negative values of these variables as making sense, however, and so we wish to exclude them. Thus, we would add the direct constraints:

$$L \geq 0 \qquad R \geq 0 \qquad M \geq 0 \qquad [\text{A.2}]$$

which, in conjunction with [A.1] define the feasible set.

In the example of the consumer's problem we can say first of all that it is impossible to consume negative amounts of goods. Then, if we let $x_1 x_2 \cdots x_n$ represent the quantities of the goods which the consumer could buy, we have immediately the n inequalities:

$$x_1 \geq 0, \qquad x_2 \geq 0, \qquad x_3 \geq 0, \qquad \cdots x_n \geq 0 \qquad [\text{A.3}]$$

But there is another limitation on the feasible set implicit in the problem. Each good has a price. Let these prices be $p_1, p_2, \cdots p_n$, for $x_1 x_2, \cdots x_n$ respectively. Then, the consumer's total expenditure for some set of quantities of the goods, will be:

$$p_1 x_1 + p_2 x_2 + \cdots + p_n x_n = \sum_{i=1}^{n} p_i x_i \qquad [\text{A.4}]$$

The consumer will have a given income, M, and this consumption expenditure cannot exceed this. Hence, in the problem, the feasible set is given by

$$p_1 x_1 + p_2 x_2 + \cdots + p_n x_n \leq M \qquad [\text{A.5}]$$

together with the inequalities in [A.4].

Thus, in each of the problems used as examples, as in any optimiza-tion problem, it is necessary to define in an exact way the available set of alternatives. The functions and inequalities written out above which limit or constrain the alternatives which can be considered in defining the feasible set are known as 'constraints'. If no constraints exist in a problem then the feasible set consists of the entire n-dimensional space of real vectors (where n is the number of choice variables) and the problem is called 'unconstrained'; the existence of constraints confines the feasible set to a subset of the whole space.

To summarize: an optimization problem consists of choice variables, an objective function, and a feasible set. The problem is to choose the preferred alternative in the feasible set, and our theory in general allows us to represent this as the problem of finding the maximum or minimum of the objective function with respect to the choice variables, subject to constraints. For this reason, optimization is taken to be synonymous with constrained maximization or minimization.

Exercises 2A

1.* Describe the choice variables, objective functions and feasible sets in the following optimization problems:
 (i) You may go from college to home on foot, by bus, or by train. You know with certainty how long it takes by each mode, and what it will cost. The problem is to choose the 'best' way of going home.
 (ii) You want to go on a diet which will involve as few calories as possible, subject to a certain minimum, and which will ensure that you consume at least minimum amounts of vitamins. You also cannot exceed your weekly food expenditure budget. You know the price, calorie count, and vitamin content of one unit of every foodstuff. There also exists a calorie-free but expensive all-vitamin tablet. How do you choose the 'best' diet?
 (iii) A housewife may shop at market A, which is very close to her home, or take a bus ride and shop at market B, at which prices are relatively lower. The problem is to choose whether to shop at market A, market B, or both.

2.* Draw graphs of the feasible sets defined by the following constraints:
 (i) $x_2 + 2x_1 \leq 4$

 (ii) $x_2 + 3x_1 < 6$
 $x_1 \geq 0 \qquad x_2 \geq 0$

 (iii) $x_2 + 2x_1 \leq 4$
 $x_2 + 4x_1 \leq 6$
 $x_1 \geq 0 \qquad x_2 \geq 0$

 (iv) $x_2 + 2x_1 = 4$
 $x_2 + 3x_1 = 7$

 (v) $x_2 + 2x_1 = 4$
 $x_2 + 3x_1 = 7$
 $x_1 \geq 0 \qquad x_2 \geq 0$

 (vi) $x_2 - 2x_1^2 \leq 0$
 $x_2 \geq 0 \qquad x_1 \geq 0$

 (vii) $x_2 + x_1^2 = 4$

 (viii) $x_2 + x_1^2 = 4$
 $x_1 \geq 0 \qquad x_2 \geq 0$

 (ix) $x_2 + x_1^2 \leq 4$
 $x_2 + 3x_1 \leq 6$
 $x_1 \geq 0 \qquad x_2 \geq 0$

 (x) $x_2 + x_1^2 = 4$
 $x_2 + 3x_1 = 6$

B. Solutions: questions and concepts

A *solution* to an optimization problem is that vector of values of the choice variables which is in the feasible set and which yields a maximum or minimum of the objective function over the feasible set. It is useful here to introduce some notation. We present the objective function as:

$$f(x_1, x_2, \cdots x_n) = f(x) \qquad [\text{B.1}]$$

where x is the n-component vector of choice variables. For convenience, we assume that the problem is always to *maximize* f.[1]† We denote the feasible set of x vectors by S. Then a solution to the problem is a vector of choice variables, x^*, having the property:

$$f(x^*) \geq f(x) \quad \text{all} \quad x \in S, \quad x^* \in S \qquad [\text{B.2}]$$

which is another way of saying that x^* maximizes f over the set S. By definition of the problem, we are interested in finding such a vector x^*.

There are certain important general questions we can ask about the solution to any optimization problem:

Existence

How can we be sure, in advance of trying to solve a particular problem, that a solution to it actually exists? After all, we have no grounds for supposing that every problem *must* have a solution. In economic theory, we spend a great deal of time analysing solutions to optimization problems. We therefore have to take care that our theories provide for their existence, otherwise our analysis is internally inconsistent.

Local and global solutions

A *global* solution is one which satisfies the condition [B.2]; at that point, the objective function takes on a value which is not exceeded at any other point within the feasible set. It is therefore the solution we seek. A local solution, on the other hand, satisfies the condition:

$$f(x^{**}) \geq f(x) \quad \text{all} \quad x \in N^{**} \subset S \qquad [\text{B.3}]$$

where N^{**} is a set of points in a *neighbourhood* of x^{**}. Figure 1 illustrates the difference. We assume only one choice variable, so that the vector becomes the scalar x. The feasible set is defined only by the direct inequalities: $x \geq 0$, $x \leq x^0$. The objective function $f(x)$ has two peaks, one at x^* and the other at x^{**}. Neighbourhoods of these points are shown as N^* and N^{**} respectively. Clearly, both points satisfy [B.3], but only x^* satisfies [B.2]. Thus, x^* is a global maximum, while x^{**} is not.

The difficulty is that *all the methods we have for finding solutions to optimization problems locate only local maxima*. We are therefore interested in the question: under what conditions will every local maximum we locate

† Superior numerals (in parentheses) are references to Notes at the end of the chapter.

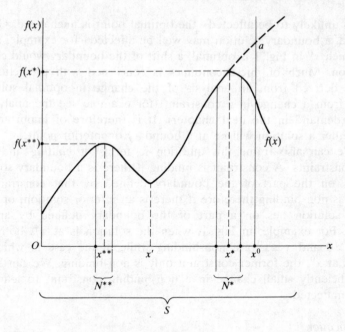

Fig. 1

also be a global maximum? From Fig. 1 we see that this must have something to do with the shape of the objective function (suppose, for example, that the function had only a single peak); we shall explore this question in more detail below.

Uniqueness

It is conceivable that more than one global maximum may exist (e.g. suppose the first peak in Fig. 1 is as high as the second, or that the function has a horizontal segment over the set N^* of values of x). Economists have tended to assume unique solutions, and so it is of interest to consider conditions under which this is the case.

Interior solutions

We take the distinction between an interior and a boundary point of a set as understood for the moment. Thus, in Fig. 1, the points $x = 0$ and $x = x^0$ are boundary points, while all other points in the set are interior points. Then an *interior solution* is an interior point which satisfies condition [B.2], while a *boundary solution* is a boundary point which satisfies that condition. In Fig. 1, x^* is an interior solution. If, however, the function f took the shape indicated by the dotted line in the diagram, then there would be a boundary solution at x^0. The importance of the distinction relates to the question of the consequences of a change in a constraint (which in general changes the location of a boundary of the feasible set – refer back to Question 2 of Exercise 2A). For a small change in a constraint, an interior solution is unlikely to be affected – the optimal point is unchanged. On the other hand, a boundary solution may well be affected – for example, in the case in which x^0 in Fig. 1 is optimal, a shift of the boundary would change the solution. Much of microeconomics is concerned with predictions of behaviour derived from an analysis of the change in optimal solutions following from a change in a constraint (for example see the analysis of consumer demand in the next chapter). It is therefore of importance to know whether a solution will be at a boundary or interior point.

We can also frame this question in terms of *binding* and *non-binding* constraints. A constraint is binding if there is a boundary solution which lies on the part of the boundary defined by that constraint. A constraint is non-binding therefore if there is an interior solution, or if the boundary solution lies on a part of the boundary defined by another constraint. For example, in Fig. 1, when the solution is at x^*, both constraints $x \geq 0$ and $x \leq x^0$ are non-binding while in the case in which the solution is at x^0, the former constraint only is non-binding. We can always find a sufficiently small change in a non-binding constraint to leave the solution unaffected.

Location

Given that a solution exists, we would like to find it. In solving a practical problem we would obtain numerical values for the objective function and constraints and then try to devise computational procedures which will find a solution as quickly and cheaply as possible. In the theoretical context however, we work only with general functions, usually specifying little more than the signs of their first and second derivatives. As a result, the problem is not actually to *compute* solutions but rather to *describe* their essential general characteristics in the analytically most useful way.

This description is made in terms of *necessary and sufficient conditions*: we first of all state certain conditions which must be satisfied by every optimal point (though they may also be satisfied by points which are not optimal), and so these are necessary conditions; we then add a further set of conditions, framed in such a way that every point which satisfies both these and the necessary conditions must be an optimal point. Then, these two sets of conditions taken together are both necessary and sufficient.

To illustrate: take the case of unconstrained maximization, and suppose that in Fig. 1 no constraints on the feasible values of x exist. Then, at the value x^*, the derivative $f'(x^*) = 0$, and we can show that this must be true at all local maxima. However, it is also true that $f'(x') = 0$, but the function takes on a local minimum at x'. Hence, the condition that the first derivative be zero is satisfied at all local maxima but at other points also and so is necessary but not sufficient. We further note that as x increases through x^*, the derivative $f'(x^*)$ passes from positive to negative values, i.e. is decreasing, and that this is only true at a local maximum. It follows that a necessary and sufficient condition for a local maximum is that $f'(x^*) = 0$ *and*

$f''(x^*)<0$, since these are simultaneously satisfied at *all* local maxima, and *only* local maxima.[2] Note that the conditions are defined as necessary and sufficient only for local maxima, since, as the diagram makes clear, they cannot discriminate between points x^* and x^{**}. Hence our earlier concern with local and global optima as a separate issue. To describe an optimal point in terms of necessary and sufficient conditions is to 'locate' that point in terms of its general characteristics rather than its numerical value. Rather surprisingly perhaps, we are often able to say a very great deal on the basis of such a general description.

In discussing these questions concerning solutions to optimization problems, we make use of certain very general properties of objective functions and feasible sets. We shall first set out these properties, and then proceed to answer the questions.

Continuity of the objective function

A function $y = f(x)$ is continuous if there are no breaks in its graph, or crudely, if it can be drawn without taking the pen from the paper. In Fig. 2 the functions drawn in (*b*) and (*c*) are not continuous, while that in (*a*) is continuous. In (*b*) $f(x)$ becomes arbitrarily large at x^0 (tends to infinity) and in part (*c*) $f(x)$ jumps from y^1 to y^2 at x^0. When there is more than one variable in the objective function the intuitive idea of continuity is still valid: there should be no jumps or breaks in the graph of the function, but it becomes more difficult (impossible when there are three or more variables in the function) to illustrate.

Concavity of the objective function

In Fig. 3 we show graphs of four kinds of function. A function with the curvature shown in (*a*) of the figure would generally be called *concave*, that in (*c*) *convex*, while that in (*b*) is of course linear and that in (*d*) neither convex nor concave. If we wanted to find a non-geometrical way of defining the concave function one possibility would be in terms of the function's second derivative $f''(x)$. We note that as we draw successive tangents to the curve in (*a*) of the figure, at increasing values of x, these tangents have flatter and flatter positive slopes and then steeper and steeper negative ones, implying that the first derivative of the function, $f'(x)$, is decreasing. Thus

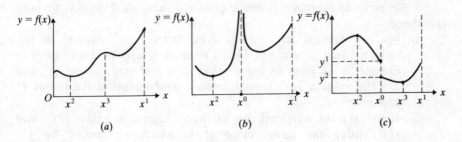

(a)   (b)   (c)

Fig. 2

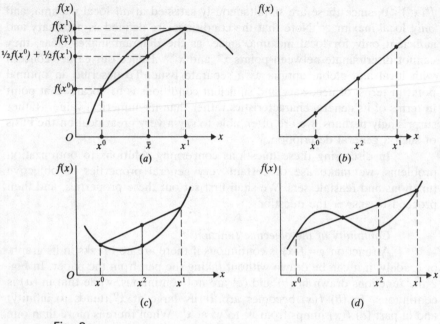

Fig. 3

we could express concavity by the condition $f''(x) < 0$. By a similar argument, convexity could be expressed by the condition $f''(x) > 0$ (supply the reasoning). There is, however a drawback to this. A function may not be differentiable at some point(s), because it possesses a kink or cusp there, and so the definition cannot be applied (draw an example).

To overcome this drawback we define concave and convex functions in terms of an obvious general property they possess. Note that in (a) of the figure, if we take any two points such as x^0 and x^1, and join the corresponding function values $f(x^0)$ and $f(x^1)$ by a straight line (a *chord* to the function), then the graph of the function between these values lies everywhere above the line. For the convex function, the graph lies entirely below the line. In the linear case of course the graph of the function coincides with the line while in (d) of the figure it moves from above to below it.

In order to express this simple geometric idea algebraically, we note two things:

(i) We can express any x-value lying between x^0 and x^1 as the weighted sum $\bar{x} = kx^0 + (1-k)x^1$, where k is a positive fraction. For example $k = \frac{1}{2}$ gives us the x-value lying mid-way between x^0 and x^1. The value $\bar{x}$ is called the *convex combination* of the points x^0 and x^1.

(ii) If we take the weighted sum of the two function values $f(x^0)$ and $f(x^1)$ using the *same* value of k, which we denote by $\bar{f} = kf(x^0) + (1-k) f(x^1)$, then this value is found as the co-ordinate of the point on the chord directly above $\bar{x}$. For example, for $k = \frac{1}{2}$, $\bar{f}$ would lie at a point on the chord directly above $\bar{x} = \frac{1}{2}x^0 + \frac{1}{2}x^1$.[(3)]

For a concave function a point on the curve at any $\bar{x}$ between x^0 and x^1 lies above the chord joining $f(x^0)$ and $f(x^1)$. It therefore follows from (ii) that in this case $f(\bar{x}) > \bar{f}$, for all $\bar{x}$ lying between x^0 and x^1. For a convex function we have $f(\bar{x}) < \bar{f}$ at each $\bar{x}$ between x^0 and x^1. When the function is linear $f(\bar{x}) = \bar{f}$ as Fig. 3(b) shows.

It turns out that some important propositions which are true when objective functions are shaped as in Fig. 3(a) are also true when they are linear or have linear segments. It is useful therefore to define *concave functions* as functions which have the property

$$f(\bar{x}) \geq \bar{f} \qquad \qquad \text{[B.4]}$$

where $\bar{x} = kx^0 + (1-k)x^1$, and $\bar{f} = kf(x^0) + (1-k)f(x^1)$, $0 \leq k \leq 1$, so that linear functions, or functions with linear segments, may also be regarded as concave. A function which satisfies [B.4] as a *strict* inequality is then called *strictly* concave, and so this is the term which would be applied to the function show in Fig. 3(a). Likewise a *convex function* satisfies:

$$f(\bar{x}) \leq \bar{f} \qquad \qquad \text{[B.5]}$$

with a *strictly* convex function satisfying this as a strict inequality. Note that [B.4] and [B.5] taken together imply that a linear function is *both* convex and concave, though neither strictly convex nor strictly concave.

Quasi-concave functions

Given a function $y = f(x_1, x_2, \cdots x_n) = f(x)$, we can choose some number c, and let:

$$f(x) = c \qquad \qquad \text{[B.6]}$$

This defines a set of values of the vector x having the property that they all yield the same value c of the function; in other words, they are solutions to the equation in [B.6]. Now a contour on a map is a set of points of equal height. Hence a useful terminology would be to say that [B.6] defines a *contour of the function* $f(x)$ and to call the set of x-values which satisfy [B.6] a *contour set*, since they correspond to equal values of the function. It turns out that for many purposes we are mainly interested in the *properties of contours of the objective function* and so we now want to consider the most important of these.

It is most convenient to take the two-variable case, so we assume that $x = (x_1, x_2)$. Thus, we have the contour:

$$f(x_1, x_2) = c \qquad \qquad \text{[B.7]}$$

The advantage of taking the two-variable case is that we can graph the contour set satisfying [B.7] in two dimensions. A wide range of shapes is of course possible, and in Fig. 4 we present two examples. It is understood that all the points on a contour line c are vectors x which satisfy an equation for

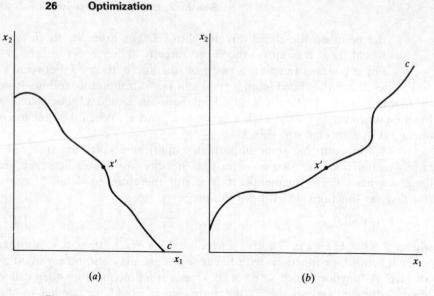

Fig. 4

a contour such as [B.7], and so belong to a given contour set. The diagram illustrates one important property of a contour of a function, namely that of continuity. Just as before, continuity can be thought of intuitively as the absence of breaks, gaps, or jumps in the graph. Continuity of a function and of its contours are closely related: it can be shown that continuity of the function implies continuity of its contours.

To explore further the properties of contours, let us go beyond continuity and assume that the function $f(x)$ is differentiable. Then differentiating [B.7] totally:

$$df = f_1 \, dx_1 + f_2 \, dx_2$$
$$= 0 \quad \text{since } c \text{ is a constant.} \qquad\qquad [\text{B.8}]$$

Note that the differentials dx_1 and dx_2 must be such as to keep the value of the function unchanged at c. Rearranging [B.8] gives:

$$\frac{dx_2}{dx_1} = -f_1/f_2 \quad (f_2 \neq 0) \qquad\qquad [\text{B.9}]$$

The ratio of differentials on the left can be interpreted as the slope of the contour at a point, since they meet the restriction that their values are such as to leave the value of the function unchanged. Thus [B.9] shows that we can evaluate the slope of the contour at a point such as x' in Fig. 4(a) directly from the values of the partial derivatives of the function at that point. Equation [B.9] also allows us to determine the direction of slope of the contour from the signs of the derivatives of the function. If the derivatives have the same sign, the slope of the contour must be negative as in (a) of Fig. 4; while if they have opposite signs, the contour must have a positive slope, as in (b) of the figure.

In optimization theory the continuity of its contours is an important general property which any given function may or may not possess. A second very important property is that of the *concavity* of contours. To examine this, we first restrict ourselves to functions whose derivatives f_1 and f_2 are positive; it follows from this that given two vectors x' and x, $x > x' \Rightarrow f(x) > f(x')$. Figure 5 illustrates concavity of contours for such a function. The property can be described as follows: choose two points, such as x' and x'' in the figure, which lie on the same contour. That is, $f(x') = f(x'') = c$. Choose any point on the straight line joining x' and x'', such as $\bar{x}$ in the figure. Then, the contour is said to be concave if:

$$f(\bar{x}) \geq f(x') = f(x'') = c \qquad \text{[B.10]}$$

In words, a convex combination of any two points on a contour yields at least as high a value of the function and so lies on the same or a higher contour. A function whose contours satisfy this definition is said to be a *quasi-concave function*. The functions whose contours are shown in (a) and (b) of Fig. 5 are quasi-concave, while that in (c) is not. To see this, note that in (a) and (b), part of each contour passes through the shaded area southwest of $\bar{x}$, implying that some points on the contour have smaller values of both x_1 and x_2 than at $\bar{x}$. Since decreasing x_1 and x_2 must reduce the value of the function $(f_1, f_2 > 0)$, it follows that the value of the function must be smaller on the contour than at x, and so [B.10] is satisfied. In (c) on the other hand, this is not the case; part of the contour lies in the area northeast of $\bar{x}$, and so contains points at which both x_1 and x_2 are greater than at x. Hence, the value of the function is greater along the contour. Note the role played in this discussion by the assumption that the partial derivatives of the function are positive. In a later exercise, the reader is asked to generalize this.

A further distinction can be drawn by considering (a) and (b) of the figure. In (a), it is clear that for *any* two points on the contour, the line joining

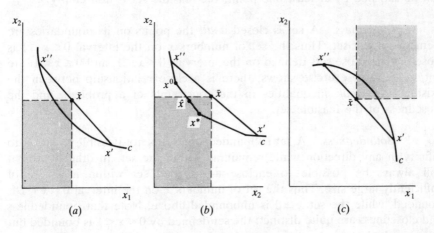

(a)   (b)   (c)

Fig. 5

them will always lie wholly above the contour, implying that the value of the function at a point such as $\bar{x}$ will always be *strictly* greater than that on the contour. Such a function is called *strictly quasi-concave*. This is not however true for the contour in (b). For example, if we take points x_0 and x^* on the contour, then a point such as $\hat{x}$ on the line joining them also lies on the contour, and so:

$$f(\hat{x}) = f(x^*) = f(x_0) = c \qquad\qquad\qquad [\text{B}.11]$$

Hence, a function possessing such contours, though quasi-concave, is not *strictly* quasi-concave.[4]

Note finally that changing the value of the constant c will change the contour of the function. Given $f_1, f_2 > 0$, increasing c will shift the contours in Fig. 5 rightward, since for any given value of x_2, a greater value of x_1 will be required to satisfy the equation defining the contour (and conversely). It follows that in an optimization problem the higher the contour attained, the greater the value of the objective function, so that *we can regard the aim of maximizing the objective function as equivalent to getting onto the highest possible contour.*

Properties of the feasible set

There are four important properties of sets which are of interest from the point of view of optimization theory.

Non-emptiness. A set is non-empty if it contains at least one element, the empty set being the set with no elements. Recall that the feasible set in a problem is the set of points or vectors x which satisfy the constraints. An empty feasible set implies that no such points exist: the constraints are such as to rule out all possible solutions. If the constraints can be satisfied by at least one point, the feasible set is non-empty.

Closedness. A set is closed if *all* the points on its boundaries are elements of the set. Thus the set of numbers x on the interval $0 \le x \le 1$ is closed, while those sets defined on the intervals $0 < x < 1$, and $0 \le x < 1$, are not. As a later exercise shows, there is a close relationship between the existence of *weak* inequalities in the constraints of a problem, and the closedness of the feasible set.

Boundedness. A set is bounded when it is not possible to go off to infinity in any direction while remaining within the set. In other words, it will always be possible to enclose a bounded set within a sphere of sufficiently large size. Thus the set of numbers x on the interval $0 < x < 1$ is bounded, while the set $x \ge 0$ is unbounded above. Note that boundedness and closedness are quite distinct: the set defined by $0 < x < 1$ is bounded but not closed; the set of values $x \ge 0$ is unbounded and closed.

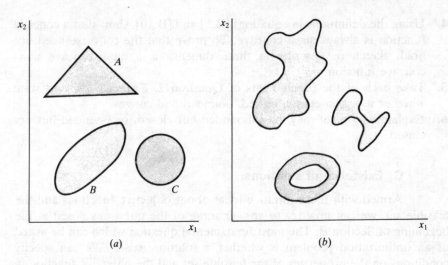

Fig. 6

Convexity. A set is convex if *every* pair of points in it can be joined by a straight line which lies entirely within the set. If two points in the set can be found such that the line joining them lies at least in part outside the set, then the set is non-convex. In Fig. 6, (*a*) shows a number of convex sets, and (*b*) a number of non-convex sets. If, when *any* two boundary points of a convex set are joined with a line, the whole of the line except its end points is in the interior of the set, then the set is *strictly convex.* If two points can be found such that the line joining them coincides at least in part with the boundary, then the set is not strictly convex. In Fig. 6(*a*), the sets *B* and *C* are strictly convex, while *A* is not.

Exercise 2B

1. (*a*) Prove that any global maximum must also be a local maximum.
   (*b*) Prove that if for a given problem more than one global maximum exists, the value of the objective function must be the same at each.
   (*c*) Show that a linear function is both convex and concave, but neither strictly convex nor strictly concave.

2.* For each of the cases:

   (a) $f_1, f_2 < 0$ (b) $f_1 > 0, f_2 < 0$ (c) $f_1 < 0, f_2 > 0$

   where f_1 and f_2 are the partial derivatives of the function $f(x_1, x_2)$, define and draw contours of quasi-concave, strictly quasi-concave and non-quasi-concave functions. Indicate in each case the direction in which higher contours are attained.

3.* Given some point x' on the contour of a function $f(x)$, define the 'better set' B' as that set of points which have the property: $f(x) \geq f(x')$. Can you frame definitions of quasi-concavity and of strict quasi-concavity of the function in terms of a property of this set B'?

4.* Using the definitions in equations [B.5] and [B.10], show that a concave function is always quasi-concave. To prove that the converse need not hold, sketch or describe in three dimensions a quasi-concave non-concave function.

5.* Take each of the feasible sets of Question 2, Exercise 2A, and state whether it is non-empty, closed, bounded and convex.

6. Explain why a set may be unbounded but closed, or bounded but not closed.

C. Existence of solutions

Armed with these intuitive ideas about objective functions and the feasible set, we can now try to answer some of the questions posed at the beginning of Section B. The most fundamental question which can be asked of an optimization problem is whether a solution exists. We can specify conditions on the properties of the feasible set and the objective function in an optimization problem which ensure that there is a solution to that problem. These conditions are embodied in the *Existence Theorem*:

An optimization problem always has a solution if:
    (i) the objective function is *continuous;* and the feasible set is:
    (ii) *non-empty*
    (iii) *closed,* and
    (iv) *bounded*

This theorem, first proved by the mathematician K. Weierstrass, is based on the fact that the set of values of the function $f(x)$, which results when we plug into it the x-values in the feasible set, is itself non-empty, closed and bounded, given that the conditions of the theorem are satisfied. That is we have a set of real numbers which do not exceed some number y_{max} and which are not less than some number y_{min} (boundedness), and moreover these numbers y_{max} and y_{min} belong to the set (closedness). Hence the function $f(x)$ takes on a maximum y_{max} and a minimum y_{min} over the feasible set.

A very simple illustration of the roles played by conditions (i)–(iv) in the theorem is given in Fig. 7. We take a one-variable problem, where the objective function is given by $f(x)$, x a scalar, and the feasible set by the set of values on the interval $0 \leq x \leq x'$. This feasible set is non-empty, closed, and bounded. In (a) of the figure the function $f(x)$ is continuous and a solution to the problem of maximizing f over the feasible set is found at x', the upper boundary of the feasible set. In (b) on the other hand, the function is discontinuous at x^0. In that case there is no solution to the maximization problem; by letting $x \rightarrow x^0$, we can go on increasing the value of the function, since $\lim_{x \rightarrow x_0} f = \infty$. The condition of continuity rules out such cases as (b).

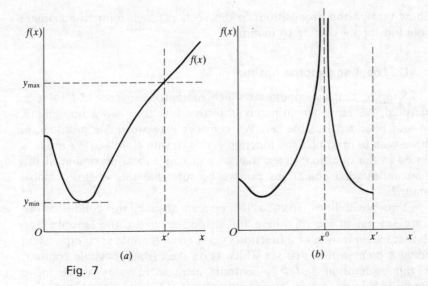

Fig. 7

To see the importance of closedness, suppose that the feasible set is defined by the interval $0 \le x < x'$, so that the upper boundary x' is not in the set. Then, in (a), if we let $x \to x'$, we can go on increasing the value $f(x)$ without end, since we can let x get closer and closer to x' without ever attaining it. In other words y_{max} is not an element of the set of values of $f(x)$. Thus the maximization problem has no solution.

Boundedness is important because in its absence we again have the possibility that the value of the objective function can be made to increase without limit. Thus suppose that the feasible set in the problem is given simply by the constraint $x \ge 0$, and also that the objective function is monotonically increasing for $x > x'$ in Fig. 7(a). Then clearly there will be no maximum. Boundedness of the feasible set rules out this kind of case.

It should be noted that the conditions of continuity of the objective function and closedness and boundedness of the feasible set are *sufficient but not necessary* conditions for existence of a solution. In other words, solutions *may* exist if they are not satisfied, but solutions may also not exist. Satisfaction of the conditions, however, rules out all possible cases of non-existence. Note finally that the condition of non-emptiness of the feasible set is a necessary condition for existence of a solution: any problem in which no point is feasible cannot have a solution.

Exercise 2C

1. Draw variants of Fig. 7 which show that solutions may exist when the objective function is discontinuous, and the feasible set open and unbounded. From this, explain what is meant by the statement that the conditions of the existence theorem are sufficient but not necessary.

2. Explain why the only condition of the existence theorem which is necessary is that the feasible set be non-empty.

3.* Show that all the propositions in this section which refer to maximum solutions apply equally to minima.

D. Local and global optima

Suppose that the conditions which guarantee existence of a solution are satisfied; we have a continuous objective function, and a non-empty, closed and bounded feasible set. We consider a two-variable problem, in which we wish to maximize the function $f(x_1, x_2)$, with $f_1, f_2 > 0$. We are now interested in the question: given that we can find a local maximum of this function under what conditions can we be sure that this is also a global maximum?

Two possibilities, from which we can abstract the conditions we seek, are set out in Fig. 8, where the shaded areas are the feasible sets. Recall that maximization of a function over a given feasible set is equivalent to finding a point within that set which is on the highest possible contour. Given the assumption $f_1, f_2 > 0$, contours increase in value as we move northeastwards in the figure. Then both (a) and (b) show examples of cases in which two local optima exist, only one of which is a global optimum. In (a) the objective function is strictly quasi-concave and the feasible set is non-convex. There is a local maximum at x^* and also at x', since relative to a small neighbourhood of points within the feasible set around them, they are on the highest possible contours. By inspection, we can see that x^* only is a global maximum. In (b), the feasible set is convex, and the objective function is not quasi-concave: there are local optima at x^* and x', but only x^* is a global maximum.

Consider now the problem of framing sufficient conditions for any local optimum also to be global. Figure 8 helps us to see intuitively that they must depend on the shapes of the feasible set *and* of the contours of the

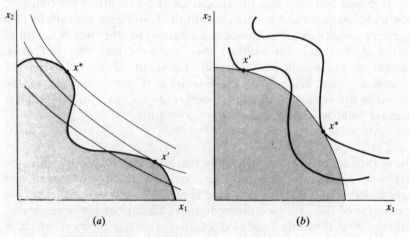

(a)   (b)

Fig. 8

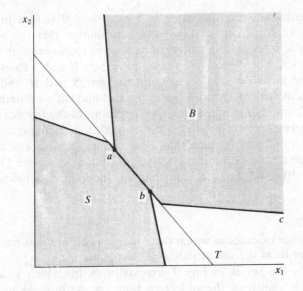

Fig. 9

function. As (*a*) shows, it is not sufficient that the function be quasi-concave; and (*b*) shows that it is not sufficient that the feasible set be convex. However, taking both together, we can state the theorem:

> A local maximum is always a global maximum if:
> (i) the objective function is quasi-concave, *and*
> (ii) the feasible set is convex.

To get some intuitive understanding of this theorem consider Fig. 9. The feasible set S is convex, and the objective function, with contour c, is quasi-concave. This latter implies that the set B, consisting of those points *along and above* the contour c, is also convex. The solutions to the problem consist of the points on the segment ab, since these are the points in S on the highest possible contour. Since these points lie on the same contour they yield the same value of the objective function; each is a global as well as a local maximum. Now consider the line T, part of which is coincident with the segment ab. Because S is a convex set, and the segment ab lies along its upper boundary, the set S must lie on or below T – no point in S can lie above T. Likewise because B is a convex set (as a result of the quasi-concavity of the objective function) and ab lies along its lower boundary, the entire set B must lie on or above T – no point in B can lie below T. But B is the set of points which yield at least as high a value of the objective function as the points along ab. Thus we have the conclusion that no points in B can possibly also be in S except those along the segment ab. But this in turn implies that the points along ab must be global as well as local optima.

The difference between the cases in Figs. 8 and 9 is that in the former the absence of convexity or quasi-concavity implies that the set B may intersect with the set S at points other than a given local optimum, and so that optimum may not be global. Convexity of the sets B and S rules this out. In this case the line T is said to *separate* the sets S and B, and the importance of the convexity of B and S lies in the fact that such a separating line can always be found. Note that, again, the conditions of the theorem are sufficient but not necessary: even if they do not hold, the configuration of contours and feasible set may be such that local optima are also global.

Finally, since a concave function is always quasi-concave (see Question 4 of Exercise 2B), we can conclude that the theorem also holds for concave functions.

Exercise 2D

1. (a) Draw examples of cases in which the conditions of the theorem are not met, but local optima are also global optima.
   (b) Explain why the set B in Fig. 9 consists of points which yield at least as high values of the objective function as those along the segment *ab*.
2. Suggest what happens to the solution illustrated in Fig. 9 if the feasible set S is not closed.
3.* Consider the adaptation of the theorem of this section to the case in which it is desired to minimize the function $f(x_1, x_2)$ [*Hint:* review the definition of quasi-convexity in Note 3].
4. Adapt the discussion of Fig. 9 to the case in which the set B is strictly convex.

E. Uniqueness of solutions

From a normative or prescriptive point of view the question of the uniqueness of solutions is not very important: by definition one global optimum is as good as another. However, if we are using the optimization problems for positive or predictive purposes, the question of whether the decision maker has a unique best decision or a number of equally good decisions is of more relevance. It relates primarily to the nature of the relationships we construct to show the way in which decisions change in response to changes in the constraints defining the feasible set. Where the optimal solution is unique for each given feasible set we can specify functions which relate the optimal values of the choice variables to the parameters in the constraints. For example, this is how we derive demand, cost and supply functions in economics. If, on the other hand, the solution is not unique, then we have a more general relationship between optimal *sets* of values of the choice variables and the constraint parameters, known as a *correspondence*. Though this presents no insuperable obstacles to analysis, it does require us to change our procedures and approach. Since economics (at the level covered by this book) usually deals with functions rather than

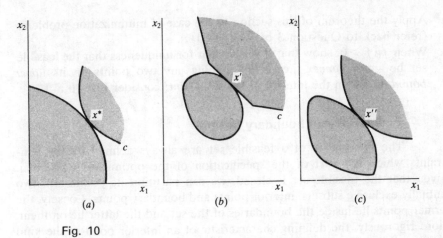

Fig. 10

with correspondences, it is worthwhile to be aware of the precise circumstances in which it is valid to do this. These circumstances exist when the solutions to the relevant optimization problems are unique.

In Fig. 9 of the previous section we saw a case in which there were multiple global optima; there was an infinite number of optimal points on the line segment *ab*. In that case the feasible set was convex, but not strictly convex; and the objective function was quasi-concave, but not strictly quasi-concave. Consider now Fig. 10, where we show three unique global optima, respectively x^*, x' and x''. In the first the objective function is strictly quasi-concave but the feasible set not strictly convex; in the second we have the reverse; and in the third the objective function is strictly quasi-concave and the feasible set strictly convex. These figures illustrate the *Uniqueness Theorem*:

> Given an optimization problem in which the feasible set is convex and the objective function quasi-concave, a solution is unique if:
>   (i) the feasible set is strictly convex, or
>   (ii) the objective function is strictly quasi-concave, or
>   (iii) both

This theorem implies that a necessary condition for multiple optima is that *neither* strict convexity of the feasible set, *nor* strict quasi-concavity of the objective function exists. As usual, the theorem gives only sufficient conditions: it is possible that a unique solution will exist even when the conditions are not satisfied, but we cannot be sure.

Exercise 2E
1. Draw examples in which the optimum is unique even though the conditions of the theorem are not met.

2.* Apply the theorem of this section to the case of minimization problems (refer back to Question 3 of Exercise 1D).

3. When $f_1, f_2 > 0$, show that it is sufficient for uniqueness that the feasible set be *upper convex*, i.e. a line joining any two points on its *upper boundary* lies in the interior of the set. (*Hint*: consider Fig. 10(a).)

F. Interior and boundary optima

The boundaries of a feasible set are always defined by the constraints which are part of the specification of the optimization problem. Given that the feasible set is closed, we can partition its points into two mutually exclusive subsets, interior points and boundary points. Loosely, the former points lie inside the boundaries of the set and the latter lie on them. More rigorously, the defining characteristic of an interior point of the kind of set we are considering is that we can find a (possibly very small) neighbourhood around it which contains *only* points in the set. A boundary point, on the other hand, has the property that *all* neighbourhoods around it, however small, contain points which are and points which are not in the set (draw diagrams to show that these definitions are consistent with your intuition).

Recall why we are interested in the distinction between interior and boundary points. In general a solution to an optimization problem which is at an interior point of the feasible set is unaffected by small shifts in the boundaries of the set, while a solution at a boundary point will be sensitive to changes in at least one constraint. Since much of microeconomics is concerned with predicting the changes in solutions to optimization problems resulting from shifts in constraints, the question of whether such solutions are at interior or boundary points is fundamental.

In parts (*a*) and (*b*) of Fig. 11 the feasible sets are initially the areas $0ab$. In (*a*) we have an interior optimum at x^*, and in (*b*) and (*c*) we have boundary optima also denoted x^*. The solution in (*a*) is unaffected by a *small* shift in the constraint, e.g. to $a'b'$; that in (*b*) *is* affected; that in (*c*) is changed by a shift in constraint cd but not by that in ab, as illustrated.

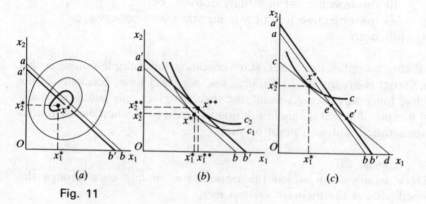

(a)   *(b)*   *(c)*

Fig. 11

The absence of response of the solution in (a) is due to the assumed existence of a *bliss point* at x^* (the 'peak' of the 'hill' whose contours are drawn in the figure), i.e. a point at which the objective function takes on a maximum. The occurrence of a bliss point in the interior of the feasible set is clearly necessary for there to be an interior maximum and so we can characterize cases of boundary maxima as ones in which no bliss points exist (but see Question 1 of Exercise 2F). One such class of cases is that in which the objective function is monotonically increasing, i.e. every $f_i > 0$, where f_i is the ith partial derivative of the function. In these cases we can go further and say that the solution must be on the *upper* boundary of the feasible set (explain why). In terms of the contours of the function, this would imply that higher contours are reached as we move rightwards in the diagram. Clearly however it is not necessary, if we want to rule out bliss points, that the partial derivatives are all positive, or even that the objective function is differentiable. It is simply necessary to assume that at any point in the feasible set it is always possible to find a small change in the value of at least one variable which will increase the value of the objective function. Note that at *optimal* points such a change would have to take us outside the feasible set (explain why), and so the domain of the function must be wider than the feasible set.

Parts (b) and (c) of the figure show two kinds of boundary optima. In (b) there is only one upper boundary and, given the assumption that $c_2 > c_1$, the boundary shift changes the optimum. In (c), the initial feasible set is taken to be the area $0ceb$ defined by two weak linear inequalities and non-negativity constraints on x_1 and x_2. The initial optimum is on the boundary at x^*. At such a point the constraint defined by the line ab is satisfied as a strict inequality (explain why). This constraint is effectively inoperative *at the solution* and so is non-binding. Once we know where the solution lies, a non-binding constraint can be dropped from any analysis concerned with movements around a small neighbourhood of the optimum, and this can often greatly simplify such analysis. *Before* solving the problem, however, it is impossible to know which constraints will turn out to be non-binding (given that we have eliminated constraints which lie *wholly* outside other constraints and so could not possibly be binding) and so all must be retained. Moreover, in a general theoretical analysis we do not have enough information to conclude that some constraint will turn out to be non-binding and so all solution possibilities have generally to be considered. In Fig. 11(a) there are three such solution possibilities – point out the two not shown. What can be said in the latter two cases about the responsiveness of the solution to shifts in the constraints?

Exercise 2F

1. Draw an example of a case in which a bliss point exists, but the solution *is* affected by *some* kinds of constraint shifts.
2.* The theory of 'satisficing' says that given a feasible set, an individual chooses not the *best* alternative but a 'satisfactory' one. Explain why, in

terms of the discussion of this section, this theory may fail to yield predictions about economic behaviour.

3. Given a feasible set such as that in Fig. 11(a), where would you expect the solution to be in the cases:
    (i) $f_1 > 0, f_2 < 0$
    (ii) $f_1 < 0, f_2 > 0$
    (iii) $f_1, f_2 < 0$
    (iv) $f_1 = 0, f_2 > 0$
    where $f(x_1, x_2)$ is the objective function and f_i, $i = 1, 2$ its partial derivatives.

4.* If all consumers in an economy possessed bliss points, what would be the relevance of microeconomics?

5. Explain what is wrong with the following attempt to rule out bliss points: we assume that given any point in the feasible set we can always find another feasible point which yields a higher value of the objective function.

G. Location of the optimum

As suggested earlier, in general theoretical models we do not have numerical information with which to find solutions to optimization problems. Instead, we seek to describe the characteristics or properties the solution possesses in terms of general conditions which it satisfies. In this book we are usually concerned only with necessary conditions, i.e. conditions which are satisfied by all points which are optimum solutions (but which may also be satisfied by points which are not optimal). The further question of sufficiency will only be considered when it is of particular interest or importance.

The reader is assumed to be familiar with the necessary condition for the point $x^* = (x_1^*, x_2^*, \ldots x_n^*)$ to yield a maximum of the function $f(x)$ when no constraints are present, viz.

$$f_i(x^*) = 0 \qquad i = 1, 2, \cdots n \qquad \text{[G.1]}$$

that is, that each partial derivative of the function, evaluated at x^*, must be zero. On the face of it a simple application of this would be to the theory of the profit maximizing firm's choice of outputs. Suppose $R(x)$ and $C(x)$ are the firm's revenue and cost functions respectively, where x is a vector of outputs (we have a multi-product firm). Then the firm's objective function is profit: $f(x) = R(x) - C(x)$. The unconstrained profit maximizing output vector is characterized by:

$$f_i(x^*) = R_i(x^*) - C_i(x^*) = 0 \qquad \text{[G.2]}$$

which yields the familiar description of the profit maximizing output in terms of the equality of each output's marginal revenue ($R_i(x^*)$) with marginal cost ($C_i(x^*)$).

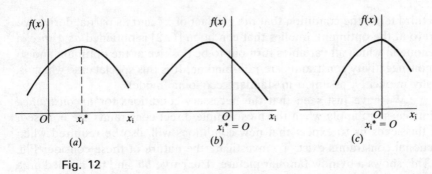

Fig. 12

But is this problem really unconstrained? Given the inadmissibility of negative outputs we should impose the constraints:

$$x_i \geq 0 \qquad i = 1, 2, \cdots n \qquad \text{[G.3]}$$

A perhaps surprising result of this is that the conditions in [G.2] are *no longer necessary conditions for a maximum*. To see this consider Fig. 12. In each part of the figure profit $f(x)$ is plotted holding all variables except the ith constant, at their optimal values. In (a) we have the case implicitly envisaged by the conditions in [G.2]. The ith output's optimal value $x_i^* > 0$ and the constraint in G.3 is non-binding at the optimum. It follows that the usual argument applies – the derivative of profit must be zero at x_i^* since otherwise x_i could be varied so as to increase the value of f. However, in (b) of the figure the highest feasible value of profit occurs at $x_i^* = 0$, i.e. none of the ith output should optimally be produced since positive outputs actually reduce profit $(C_i(x) > R_i(x)$ when $x_i > 0$ and all other outputs are at their optimal values). But at $x_i^* = 0$, the slope of the profit function is negative, not zero, implying that [G.2] is not a necessary condition for an optimum, since an optimal point exists at which it is not satisfied. In the case shown the constraint [G.3] is binding, since without it the firm would seek to increase profit by producing negative x_i. In (c) on the other hand we have a case in which it just so happens that at the optimal $x_i^* = 0$ the profit derivative is zero.

From this discussion we make the following generalization. In a problem in which non-negativity constraints are imposed, the 'necessary conditions' in [G.2] are no longer strictly correct. The correct conditions can be deduced from Fig. 12 (where $f(x)$ now represents any objective function and x_i^* the optimal value of x_i) as:

(i) if $x_i^* > 0$ then $f_i(x^*) = 0$
(ii) if $x_i^* = 0$ then $f_i(x^*) \leq 0$ $\qquad i = 1, 2, \cdots n \qquad \text{[G.4]}$

Condition (ii) ensures that $f(x)$ cannot be increased for *permissible* changes, i.e. increases, in x_i. A more concise way of writing [G.4] is:

$$f_i(x^*) \leq 0 \qquad x_i^* \geq 0 \qquad x_i^* \cdot f_i(x^*) = 0 \qquad i = 1, 2, \cdots n \qquad \text{[G.5]}$$

The third term, the condition that the product of x_i^* and its partial derivative be zero at the optimum, implies that condition [G.2] is obtained *as a special case*, one in which all variables turn out to be positive at the optimum and so all non-negativity constraints are non-binding. It is this special case which is, usually implicitly, assumed in standard economic models.

We have just seen that the necessary conditions for *unconstrained* optima cease to apply when the most simple direct constraints are imposed, and this leads us to expect that new conditions will also be required when functional constraints exist. To investigate the nature of these consider Fig. 13. This shows a by now familiar picture. The curve bb' and the shaded area beneath it in the figure show the set of points which satisfy the constraints:

$$g(x_1, x_2) \leq b \qquad\qquad [\text{G.6}]$$

where the points *on* the curve satisfy $g(x_1, x_2) = b$. Assuming $f_1, f_2 > 0$, the optimum is at x^* on the contour $f(x_1, x_2) = c$. We have built into the diagram the assumptions which ensure that x^* exists, and is a unique global boundary optimum. How then can it be characterized in terms of a set of necessary conditions?

The essential fact about x^* in the figure is that it is a point of tangency. That is, at x^*, the contour of the objective function f and the contour of the constraint function g have a slope equal to that of the common tangent T. We have already shown (see equation [B.9]) that the slope of any contour is given by:

$$\frac{dx_2}{dx_1} = \frac{-f_1}{f_2} \qquad\qquad [\text{G.7}]$$

By an exactly similar argument (supply the details) we can show that the slope of the constraint contour is:

$$\frac{dx_2}{dx_1} = \frac{-g_1}{g_2} \qquad\qquad [\text{G.8}]$$

It follows that the optimal solution x^* satisfies the conditions:

(i) $\dfrac{f_1}{f_2} = \dfrac{g_1}{g_2}$ $\qquad\qquad\qquad\qquad\qquad$ [G.9]

(ii) $g(x_1^*, x_2^*) = b$

Note that (ii) is an important part of these conditions. (i) simply states that the slopes of contours must be the same, but does not precisely locate the optimum point – the single equation cannot determine values of both x_1 and x_2. The addition of (ii) closes the system, and ensures that what we have is actually the point of tangency. (Note that the condition $f(x_1^*, x_2^*) = c$ would do just as well provided we know the value of c at the optimum).

Taking (i), it can clearly be expressed as:

$$\frac{f_1}{g_1} = \frac{f_2}{g_2} = \lambda^* > 0 \qquad\qquad [G.10]$$

where λ^* is simply a number representing the common value of the ratios f_i/g_i, $i = 1, 2$ at the optimum. But [G.10] then implies the two equations:

$$f_1 = \lambda^* g_1 \qquad f_2 = \lambda^* g_2 \qquad\qquad [G.11]$$

which are then logically equivalent to (i) of [G.9]. Given that $\lambda^* \neq 0$ and $g_i(x_1^*, x_2^*) \neq 0$, $i = 1, 2$, [G.11] implies that at the optimum $f_i \neq 0$, $i = 1, 2$. Thus, as we conjectured, the conditions in [G.2] (which in this case would simply be $f_i = 0$) are *not* necessary for a *constrained* maximum. The optimum x^* in Fig. 13 has been shown, in [G.11] and [G.9], to satisfy conditions which can be written as:

$$f_1 - \lambda^* g_1 = 0$$
$$f_2 - \lambda^* g_2 = 0 \qquad\qquad [G.12]$$
$$g(x_1^*, x_2^*) - b = 0$$

As is always the case with geometrical reasoning, we have built into the analysis a number of very restrictive assumptions simply by drawing a particular picture. In particular we have assumed only two choice variables, no non-negativity conditions, and only one functional constraint. However, the way of writing the necessary conditions in [G.12] suggests a major step in generalizing the results, by means of a procedure first formulated by the mathematician J. L. Lagrange. Given the problem illustrated in Fig. 13, we formulate the
Lagrange function:

$$L(x_1, x_2, \lambda) = f(x_1, x_2) - \lambda[g(x_1, x_2) - b] \qquad\qquad [G.13]$$

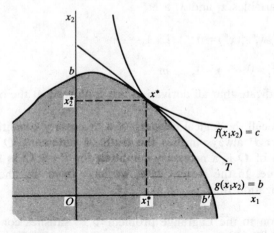

Fig. 13

In words: we take the constraint constant over to the lefthand side, multiply the resulting term by the variable λ (correspondingly termed the *Lagrange multiplier*) and subtract this product from the original objective function f. The point of this procedure is that *if we now carry out the unconstrained maximization of the Lagrange function L with respect to its three variables* x_1, x_2 *and* λ, *we obtain precisely the necessary conditions for an optimum shown in* [G.12]. (Confirm! Note that we have to multiply the third partial derivative by -1. To avoid this we could have formed the Lagrange function by taking $g(x_1x_2)$ over to the *right*hand side of the constraint, multiplying by λ, and *adding* to f. Confirm that nothing significant is affected thereby. You will encounter both methods.)

One way of regarding Lagrange's procedure is as follows. We are initially faced with a problem we do not know how to solve, that of maximizing f subject to a constraint. However, we *do* know how to solve unconstrained problems, and so the trick is to turn the constrained problem into an unconstrained one. This is precisely what Lagrange's procedure achieves. We now show a little more rigorously *why* the procedure works.

Suppose we have the general problem:

$$\max f(x_1, x_2, \cdots x_n) \quad s.t. \quad g^1(x_1, x_2, \cdots x_n) = b_1$$
$$g^2(x_1, x_2, \cdots x_n) = b_2 \qquad \text{[G.14]}$$
$$\cdots\cdots\cdots\cdots\cdots$$
$$g^m(x_1, x_2, \cdots x_n) = b_m$$

where, it is assumed, the constraints $g^j(x) = b_j$, $j = 1, 2, \cdots m$ are such as to allow a non-empty feasible set and $m < n$. Then the generalized Lagrange function is

$$L(x, \lambda) = f(x) - \sum_j \lambda_j[g^j(x) - b_j] \qquad \text{[G.15]}$$

and the resulting necessary conditions for its *unconstrained* maximization with respect to the variables x_i and λ_j are:

$$L_i = f_i(x^*) - \sum_j \lambda_j^* g_i^j(x^*) = 0 \qquad i = 1, \cdots n \qquad \text{[G.16]}$$

$$L_j = g^j(x^*) - b_j = 0 \qquad j = 1, \cdots m \qquad \text{[G.17]}$$

where the asterisks indicate that all derivatives are evaluated at the optimal point (x^*, λ^*).

Now briefly recall the logical meaning of a 'necessary condition'. If the truth of statement P always implies the truth of statement Q, i.e. if $P \Rightarrow Q$, then the truth of Q is a necessary condition for P— if Q is false P cannot possibly be true. In the present case, we have from the theory of unconstrained maximization that:

x^* is a solution to the Lagrange problem $\Rightarrow x^*$ satisfies conditions [G.16] and [G.17] which is why the latter are called necessary conditions. Now we can show that:

x^* a solution to the initial constrained problem in [G.14] $\Rightarrow$ x^* is a solution to the Lagrange problem

and so x^* satisfies conditions [G.16] and [G.17] and these are then necessary conditions for a solution to the constrained problem. To prove the second statement, note first that x^* a solution to the original constrained problem implies:

$$f(x^*) \geq f(x) \tag{G.18}$$

for all x which satisfy the m constraints

$$g^j(x) - b_j = 0 \qquad j = 1, \cdots m \tag{G.19}$$

But then for all such x, we must have:

$$\sum_j \lambda_j^*[g^j(x) - b_j] = 0 \tag{G.20}$$

and so subtracting this from both sides of the inequality in [G.18] gives:

$$f(x^*) - \sum_j \lambda_j^*[g^j(x^*) - b_j] \geq f(x) - \sum_j \lambda_j^*[g^j(x) - b_j] \tag{G.21}$$

which is simply the statement:

$$L(x^*, \lambda^*) \geq L(x, \lambda^*) \tag{G.22}$$

for all x which satisfy [G.19]. But we know from the necessary conditions [G.17] that any x which does not satisfy the constraints in [G.19] cannot maximize the Lagrange function. Hence [G.22] tells us that x^* is a solution to the Lagrange problem. Note that we require that the vector $\lambda^* = [\lambda_1^*, \cdots \lambda_m^*]$ exist, something taken for granted in the above discussion.

Interpretation of the Lagrangean multipliers

We derived necessary conditions for an optimal vector x^* by introducing the Lagrange multipliers λ_j .and forming the Lagrangean function. The multipliers are, however, more than an ingenious mathematical device, and turn out to have an interpretation which is of great interest in specific economic contexts. To show this, we revert to the two-variable problem in Fig. 13. Given the necessary conditions for an optimal solution in [G.12], we can regard these as three equations in the three 'unknowns' x_1^*, x_2^* and λ^*, with the constraint value b as an exogeneous parameter which determines the solution. Under certain conditions, we can solve for the unknowns as functions of this parameter, i.e. we may write:

$$\begin{aligned} x_1^* &= h_1(b) \\ x_2^* &= h_2(b) \\ \lambda^* &= h_\lambda(b) \end{aligned} \tag{G.23}$$

which express the idea that the solution values depend upon the parameter b. We define the *optimized value*, v^*, of the objective function as the value it takes on at the optimal point, i.e.

$$v^* = f(x_1^*, x_2^*) \tag{G.24}$$

Clearly, therefore, v^* depends on b, and so we can write, using [G.23];

$$v^* = f(h_1(b), h_2(b)) = v^*(b) \tag{G.25}$$

Consider the derivative dv^*/db. This gives the rate at which changes in the constraint parameter b cause changes in the optimized value of the objective function, via its effect on the solution values x_1^* and x_2^*. The significance of λ^* stems from the fact that it is possible to prove:

$$\frac{dv^*}{db} = \lambda^* \tag{G.26}$$

In other words, λ^* measures the rate at which the optimized value of the objective function varies with changes in the constraint parameter. To prove this, note first that, from [G.25]:

$$\frac{dv^*}{db} = f_1 \frac{dx_1^*}{db} + f_2 \frac{dx_2^*}{db} \tag{G.27}$$

Since all derivatives are evaluated at the optimal point, we have from the conditions G.11 that $f_1 = \lambda^* g_1$ and $f_2 = \lambda^* g_2$, and so:

$$\frac{dv^*}{db} = \lambda^* \left(g_1 \frac{dx_1^*}{db} + g_2 \frac{dx_2^*}{db} \right) \tag{G.28}$$

Now since the constraint is satisfied at the optimal point, we have:

$$g(x_1^*, x_2^*) = b \tag{G.29}$$

so:

$$dg = g_1 \, dx_1^* + g_2 \, dx_2^* = db \tag{G.30}$$

and so:

$$\frac{dg}{db} = g_1 \frac{dx_1^*}{db} + g_2 \frac{dx_2^*}{db} = 1 \tag{G.31}$$

Then, substituting from [G.31] into [G.28] gives the equality in [G.26]. We can interpret this result with the help of Fig. 14. Initially, the constraint is defined by $g(x_1, x_2) = b$, and the solution is at x^*. Now suppose the constraint becomes $g(x_1, x_2) = b'$, with $b' > b$, and the curve in the figure shifts outward. There will be a new solution at x^{**}, with optimal values x_1^{**}, x_2^{**}. The change in b has caused a change in the optimized value of the objective function, given by:

$$f(x_1^{**}, x_2^{**}) - f(x_1^*, x_2^*) = v^{**} - v^* \tag{G.32}$$

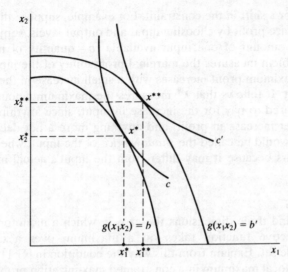

Fig. 14

Thus, we can take the ratio of these changes:

$$\frac{\Delta v^*}{\Delta b} = \frac{v^{**} - v^*}{b' - b}$$ [G.33]

which relates to a finite change in b. Then, in the usual way, we can take:

$$\lim_{\Delta b \to 0} \frac{\Delta v^*}{\Delta b} = \frac{dv^*}{db}$$ [G.34]

Thus, we can think of the constraint shifting infinitesimally and the derivative dv^*/db then measures the rate at which v^* changes, given that an optimal point is always chosen.

In economics, derivatives are usually designated by the term 'marginal this or that'. The equality in [G.26] implies that λ^* can be thought of as the marginal change in the optimized value of the objective function with respect to changes in the constraint. Then, in specific contexts, this leads to useful interpretations of the Lagrangean multipliers. For example, in the case in which the consumer maximizes utility (the objective function) subject to a budget constraint (b = income), λ^* would measure, the marginal utility of income at the optimal point. In a problem in which costs were to be minimized subject to a fixed output constraint (b = output), λ^* would measure marginal cost at the optimal point. In any problem, there exists an interpretation of the multiplier which is of interest to economists.

A further interpretation of the Lagrangean multiplier can be made, as a kind of price. Since its value at the optimum measures the change in value of the objective function caused by a slight shift in the constraint, it can be interpreted as measuring the maximum 'payment' which would be made *in exchange* for a shift in the constraint. For example, suppose that the problem is to maximize profit by choosing input and output levels, subject to a limitation on the amount of one input available (b = quantity of input). Then λ^* in this problem measures the marginal profitability of the input, or the rate at which maximum profit increases with a small increase in the fixed amount of the input. It follows that λ^* measures the maximum amount the firm would be prepared to pay for the increase in input, since anything less would result in a net increase in profit, and anything more a net decrease. For this reason, λ^* would be called the *shadow price* of the input, where the word 'shadow' occurs because it may differ from the input's actual market price.

Exercise 2G

1. Sketch in two and three dimensions the case in which a monotonically increasing objective function takes on a maximum over a closed, bounded feasible set. Explain from this why the condition in [G.1] is not necessary for a local maximum in a constrained maximization problem.

2. Suggest reasons why we assume that m, the number of constraints, is less than n, the number of choice variables, in defining the optimization problem in [G.14] (*Hint*: suppose that the constraint functions are linear, and $m > n$, for $n = 1, 2$. What problems then arise? Explain why such a restriction is unnecessary when the functional constraints involve inequalities.)

3.* Explain why the conditions in [G.16] and [G.17] are also necessary for a solution to the problem:
$$\min f(x) \quad s.t. \quad g^j(x) - b_j = 0 \qquad (j = 1, \cdots, m)$$
and why therefore these conditions are necessary but not sufficient for a maximum.

4.* Interpret in economic terms the Lagrange multipliers which would be associated with the constraints in the following optimization problems:
   (i) A central planner in a developing country wishes to maximize GNP, subject to the constraints that the balance of payments deficit may not exceed a given figure, and that a fixed amount of skilled labour is available.
   (ii) A firm wishes to choose a set of investment projects which maximize its profitability, subject to the constraint that the total amount it spends on investment does not exceed a fixed amount of funds available.

5.* Consider the problem:
$$\max_{x_1 x_2} f(x_1, x_2) \quad \text{where} \quad f_1, f_2 > 0$$
$$s.t. \quad a_{11}x_1 + a_{12}x_2 \leq b_1$$
$$a_{21}x_1 + a_{22}x_2 \leq b_2$$

The objective function f is strictly quasi-concave, and the a_{ij}, $i, j = 1, 2$, are all positive.

(a) Draw in a diagram the feasible set, assuming

$$\frac{a_{11}}{a_{12}} > \frac{a_{21}}{a_{22}}, \quad \text{and} \quad \frac{b_1}{a_{12}} > \frac{b_2}{a_{22}}$$

Find the points at which a solution may be found, and suggest their main characteristics, in terms of whether they imply zero or non-zero variable values, and binding or non-binding constraints.

(b) Recalling the interpretation of Lagrangean multipliers, give an economic interpretation of the case $\lambda_1^* = 0$.

6.* Show that as well as (x^* a solution to the constrained problem) $\Rightarrow$ (x^* a solution to the Lagrange problem), the reverse implication can be proved, and that therefore x^* is a solution to the constrained problem *if and only if* it is a solution to the Lagrange problem.

H. Further generalizations

In the previous section we generalized the Lagrange procedure to $n \geq 2$ variables and $m \geq 1$ constraints, but we hope the reader will have noticed that two special assumptions remained. First, we did not consider direct constraints of the form $x_i \geq 0$. Secondly, we assumed in the formulation of the problem in [G.14] that the constraints were expressed as equalities, which is not only a rather restrictive formulation, but also one which may lead to difficulties, as Question 2 of Exercise 2G will have shown. We now consider generalizing both these assumptions.

The consequences of introducing the non-negativity conditions can immediately be deduced from the discussion with which Section G began. Recall that if a function $f(x_1, x_2, \cdots, x_n) = f(x)$ is being maximized subject to the constraints $x_i \geq 0$ for at least one i, then the true necessary conditions for variable i become:

$$f_i(x^*) \leq 0 \quad x_i^* \geq 0 \quad x_i^* \cdot f_i(x^*) = 0 \qquad \text{[H.1]}$$

where $f_i(x^*)$ is as before the ith partial derivative evaluated at the optimal point. Now we showed that where *function* constraints are imposed, we can replace the constrained maximization problem with an appropriately formulated unconstrained maximization problem using the Lagrange procedure. Therefore if non-negativity conditions exist we simply impose them on the maximization of the Lagrange function to obtain as necessary conditions:

$$L_i = f_i(x^*) - \sum_j \lambda_j^* g_i^j(x^*) \leq 0 \qquad x_i^* \geq 0 \qquad x_i^* \cdot L_i = 0$$

$$i = 1, 2, \cdots n \quad \text{[H.2]}$$

$$L_j = b_j - g^j(x^*) = 0 \qquad j = 1, 2, \cdots m \qquad \qquad \text{[H.3]}$$

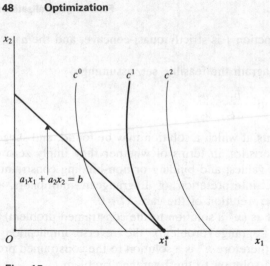

Fig. 15

That is, the Lagrange function $L(x, \lambda)$ simply replaces the function f in the conditions [H.1]. Note that no need has arisen for similarly constraining the Lagrange multipliers and so the conditions [H.3] are exactly as before.

To illustrate, consider the two-variable problem:

$$\max f(x_1, x_2) \ s.t. \ a_1x_1 + a_2x_2 = b \qquad x_1, x_2 \geq 0 \qquad f_1, f_2 > 0 \qquad [\text{H.4}]$$

where f is taken to be strictly quasi-concave. However, we assume that the contours of the objective function are everywhere steeper than the constraint line. Fig. 15 illustrates. The Lagrange function for the problem is:

$$L(x_1, x_2, \lambda) = f(x_1, x_2) - \lambda[a_1x_1 + a_2x_2 - b] \qquad [\text{H.5}]$$

and so the counterparts to conditions [H.2] and [H.3] are:

$$L_1 = f_1 - \lambda^* a_1 \leq 0 \qquad x_1^* \geq 0 \qquad x_1^* \cdot [f_1 - \lambda^* a_1] = 0 \qquad [\text{H.6}]$$

$$L_2 = f_2 - \lambda^* a_2 \leq 0 \qquad x_2^* \geq 0 \qquad x_2 \cdot [f_2 - \lambda^* a_2] = 0 \qquad [\text{H.7}]$$

$$-L_\lambda = a_1x_1^* + a_2x_2^* - b = 0 \qquad [\text{H.8}]$$

Now suppose, as in the figure, that at the optimum $x_1^* > 0$ and $x_2^* = 0$. From [H.6] we must have (explain why):

$$f_1 = \lambda^* a_1 \qquad \text{so that} \ f_1 - \lambda^* a_1 = 0 \qquad [\text{H.9}]$$

while from [H.7] we have:

$$f_2 \leq \lambda^* a_2 \qquad \text{so that} \ L_2 = f_2 - \lambda^* a_2 \ \text{is} \ \leq 0 \qquad [\text{H.10}]$$

Dividing each side of [H.10] into the corresponding side of [H.8] gives

$$f_1/f_2 \geq \frac{a_1}{a_2} \qquad [\text{H.11}]$$

which is simply the condition that, at the optimum, the contour of the objective function must be at least as steep as the constraint line. This is in fact all that *can* be said in characterizing an optimum when non-negativity constraints exist and one is binding at the optimum. Note that if at the optimum $x_1^* > 0$, $x_2^* > 0$, then we have of course the necessary conditions in the form given in G.

Turning now to the case of inequalities in the functional constraints, we can note first that in single-constraint problems the non-existence of bliss points makes this generalization unnecessary. Since in this case a solution will always lie on the boundary, we might as well express the constraint in equality form, as in the problem [H.4]. The generalization does, however, become important in problems of two or more constraints.

The general problem is

$$\max f(x) \ s.t. \ g^j(x) \le b_j \qquad x \ge 0 \qquad (j = 1, \cdots, m) \qquad \text{[H.12]}$$

Suppose that x^* solves [H.12] and let λ_j^* denote the marginal value of a relaxation of the jth constraint i.e. an increase in b_j. Then

$$g^j(x^*) = b_j \Rightarrow \lambda_j^* \ge 0 \qquad \text{[H.13]}$$

To prove this suppose that $\lambda_j^* < 0$. Then a decrease in b_j to b_j' will result in a new solution $x^{*\prime}$ and an increase in the maximized value of f from $f(x^*)$ to $f(x^{*\prime})$. But

$$g^j(x^{*\prime}) = b_j' < b_j \qquad \text{[H.14]}$$

and hence if the constraint can be satisfied as an inequality when b_j is at its initial level x^* cannot be the solution to H.12. This contradiction establishes [H.13]. As λ_j^* is the rate at which the maximized value of f increases with increases in b_j we also have

$$g^j(x^*) < b_j \qquad \lambda_j^* = 0 \qquad \text{[H.15]}$$

i.e. marginal relaxations in non-binding constraints are of no value.

Putting [H.13] and [H.15] together yields

$$b_j - g^j(x^*) \ge 0; \qquad \lambda_j^* \ge 0; \qquad \lambda_j^*[b_j - g^j(x^*)] = 0 \qquad \text{[H.16]}$$

as a necessary condition for the solution of [H.12].

This suggests that we can again adapt the Lagrangean procedure to find necessary conditions for a solution to the general optimization problem [H. 12]. The Lagrangean function from [H. 12] is

$$L(x, \lambda) = f(x) - \sum \lambda_j[g^j(x) - b_j] \qquad \text{[H.17]}$$

and necessary conditions for a solution to [H.11] are

$$L_i = \frac{\partial L}{\partial x_i} = f_i - \sum \lambda_j^* g_i^j \le 0; \qquad x_i^* \ge 0; \qquad x_i^* \cdot L_i = 0 \qquad (i = 1, \ldots, n)$$

[H.18]

$$L_j = \frac{\partial L}{\partial \lambda_j} = b_j - g^j(x^*) \ge 0; \qquad \lambda_j^* \ge 0; \qquad \lambda_j^* \cdot L_j = 0 \qquad (j = 1, \ldots, m)$$

[H.19]

where [H.18] is merely [H.2] and [H.19] is [H.16]. By the same arguments we used in discussing the maximization of $f(x)$ s.t. $x \ge 0$, it is apparent that $L(x, \lambda)$ is being maximized with respect to the x_i and minimized with respect to the λ_j, subject only to the constraints that $x \ge 0$ and $\lambda \ge 0$. (When $L_j > 0$, λ_j is set as small as possible, i.e. zero.) It is possible to show rather more rigorously that the necessary conditions for solving the Lagrangean problem subject to the non-negativity constraints on x and λ are also necessary for a solution to [H.11], but the above intuitive account will suffice for our purposes.

To illustrate the above procedure consider the problem:

$$\max f(x_1, x_2) \ s.t. \ a_1 x_1 + a_2 x_2 \le b_1$$
$$c_1 x_1 + c_2 x_2 \le b_2 \qquad f_1, f_2 > 0, \qquad \text{[H.20]}$$

where for simplicity we ignore non-negativity constraints. The problem is illustrated in Fig. 16. It is assumed that the constraints are such as to intersect in the positive quadrant. The feasible set is then the shaded area. Points α, β and γ correspond to possible types of solution for different assumptions about the contours of the objective function.

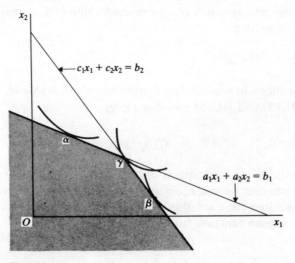

Fig. 16

The Lagrange function is:

$$L(x_1, x_2, \lambda_1, \lambda_2) = f(x_1, x_2) - \lambda_1[a_1x_1 + a_2x_2 - b_1] - \lambda_2[c_1x_1 + c_2x_2 - b_2]$$
[H.21]

and the necessary conditions are:

$$f_1 - \lambda_1^*a_1 - \lambda_2^*c_1 = 0 \tag{H.22}$$

$$f_2 - \lambda_1^*a_2 - \lambda_2^*c_2 = 0 \tag{H.23}$$

$$a_1x_1^* + a_2x_2^* - b_1 \le 0; \quad \lambda_1^* \ge 0; \quad \lambda_1^*[a_1x_1^* + a_2x_2^* - b_1] = 0 \tag{H.24}$$

$$c_1x_1^* + c_2x_2^* - b_2 \le 0; \quad \lambda_2^* \ge 0; \quad \lambda_2^*[c_1x_1^* + c_2x_2^* - b_2] = 0 \tag{H.25}$$

Let us now establish the connection between the solution possibilities in the figure and the conditions in [H.22]–[H.25]. In case of a solution at α, we have that the b_2 constraint is non-binding. It follows therefore that $\lambda_2^* = 0$ (intuitively, the shadow price of a non-binding constraint is zero). Therefore the terms involving λ_2^* in [H.22] and [H.23] drop out and we have the conditions for

$$case\ \alpha \quad f_1 - \lambda_1^*a_1 = 0 \quad f_2 - \lambda_1^*a_2 = 0 \quad a_1x_1^* + a_2x_2^* = b_1 \tag{H.26}$$

These are the standard conditions resulting from applying the Lagrange procedure to the appropriate single-constraint problem, i.e. that with only the b_1 constraint expressed as an equality.

Consider now case β. Here, the b_1 constraint is non-binding. Therefore small shifts in it have no effect on the optimum and $\lambda_1^* = 0$. In that case we have the conditions for:

$$case\ \beta \quad f_1 - \lambda_2^*c_1 = 0 \quad f_2 - \lambda_2^*c_2 = 0 \quad c_1x_1^* + c_2x_2^* = b_2 \tag{H.27}$$

Again therefore we obtain the appropriate conditions from applying the Lagrange procedure to the appropriate single-constraint problem.

In the third case *both* constraints are binding at the optimum, and are satisfied as equalities (but see Question 9* of Exercise 2H). Strictly speaking conditions [H.24] and [H.25], the solution of which determines the point (x_1^*, x_1^*), are in the present case sufficient to solve the problem. From [H.22] and [H.23] we see that:

$$f_1/f_2 = \frac{\lambda_1^*a_1 + \lambda_2^*c_1}{\lambda_1^*a_2 + \lambda_2^*c_2} \tag{H.28}$$

i.e. at the optimum the slope of the contour of the objective function is *not equal* to the slope of either constraint, but rather lies between these slopes (see Question 9* of Exercise 2H).

We can draw the following conclusions from this discussion. The necessary conditions which follow from applying the Lagrange procedure *as if* the problem involved only equality constraints are valid only for the

special case in which all constraints turn out to be binding at the optimum –
a case which may not exist even as a logical possibility if the set of points
satisfying the constraints as equalities is empty. The other solution possibilities are then systematically explored by considering all the possible
combinations of non-binding constraints and by examining the conditions
with the appropriate constraints and terms deleted. Thus the Lagrange
procedure can be used to handle more general optimization problems than
those for which it was initially developed.

Exercise 2H

1.* Re-work the formal argument used to justify the Lagrange procedure in
section G, to show that conditions [H.2] and [H.3] are indeed the
necessary conditions for the problem:

$$\max f(x) \quad s.t. \quad g^i(x) = b; \quad j = 1, \cdots m, \quad and \quad x_i \geq 0, \quad i = 1, \cdots n$$

2.* Explain why condition [H.7] *does not* justify the statement: $x_2^* = 0 \Rightarrow$
$f_2 < \lambda^* a_2$. How would you interpret the case in which $x_2^* = 0$ *and*
$f_2 = \lambda^* a_1$?

3.* After reading Chapter 3, return to this problem and discuss the interpretation of the case analyzed in Fig. 15 as a problem in consumer demand.
Is the type of solution, with one good's optimal consumption zero,
plausible in reality? What if we were talking (realistically) about
thousands of goods and not just two?

4.* Introduce into the problem in [H.20] the direct constraints $x_1 \geq 0$ $x_2 \geq 0$.
Show, in Fig. 16, two further solution possibilities which as a result are
of interest. Use conditions [H.6] and [H.7] in conjunction with conditions [H.24] and [H.25] to analyze these two further cases. From this
discuss the generalization of the Lagrange procedure to problems in
which both non-negativity conditions and inequalities in functional
constraints occur.

5.* Suppose that instead of the direct constraints $x_i \geq 0$ we had $x_i \geq b_i$, $b_i \neq 0$.
Show how the Lagrange procedure can be modified to handle this case
(*Hint*: either re-define the variables x_i so as to put the direct constraints
in non-negativity form, or treat the new constraints as a special form of
functional constraints.)

6.* Suppose that we added to the problem in [H.20] the further constraint
$e_1 x_1 + e_2 x_2 \leq b_3$. Discuss the solution possibilities and necessary conditions for this problem along the lines of the analysis of cases α, β and γ
in this section.

7.* *Points rationing.* First read Chapter 3 and then return to this question.
In the problem in [H.20], we interpret a_1 and a_2 as money prices of the
respective goods and b_1 as money income; while c_1 and c_2 are numbers
of ration coupons which must also be paid per unit of each good and b_2
is the consumer's initial endowment of these ration coupons. f is a
utility function. Give an economic interpretation of the problem and of
the three solution possibilities shown in Fig. 16. What would you expect

to happen if some consumers are at α-type equilibria and others are at β-type equilibria?

8. Show that if λ_1^*, $\lambda_2^* > 0$, the value of the ratio $\lambda_1^* a_1 + \lambda_2^* c_1 / \lambda_1^* a_2 + \lambda_2^* c_2$ must lie between the values a_1/a_2 and c_1/c_2.

9.* In Fig. 16 two somewhat odd cases could occur. The solution could be at $.\gamma$, but the contour of the objective function could be (a) tangent to the b_1 constraint, or (b) tangent to the b_2 constraint, at that point. What happens to the conditions [H.21–H.25] in such a case? (*Hint:* consider what happens in case (a) if the b_2 constraint shifts outward and inward, and in case (b) if the b_1 shifts. What can be said about the relevant Lagrange multiplier in each case?)

I. Conclusions

In this chapter we have discussed the main elements of the general theory of optimization problems. The approach was intuitive rather than rigorous: propositions were in the main asserted and illustrated rather than proved. It is hoped however that as a result the reader will have a good understanding of the most important ideas – the relevant properties of sets and functions, the questions we ask about solutions, and the Lagrange procedure for finding necessary conditions. With this understanding should come greater insight into the nature of the economic models presented elsewhere in this book, and a greater ability to use them in the analysis of economic problems.

Notes

1. This is not restrictive. Suppose the problem is to minimize some function $h(x)$. Then, this is equivalent to the problem of maximizing $f(x) = -h(x)$, since a solution to the latter problem solves the former. Making use of this, all the statements made in the present chapter about maximization problems can be applied directly to problems of minimization.

2. This statement is not entirely rigorous: problems may arise when $f''(x^*) = 0$ at a local maximum x^*, so that proper necessary and sufficient conditions have to be stated in terms of higher order derivatives. For discussion of this see R. G. D. Allen: *Mathematical Analysis for Economists*, Macmillan, 1938, Chapter XIV.

3. The fact that $\bar{f}$ lies on the chord vertically above $\bar{x}$ stems from the essential property of straight lines. Thus, given two points $(x_1 y_1)$ and $(x_2 y_2)$ the points on the straight line joining them, are given by:

$$(\bar{x}, \bar{y}) = k(x_1, y_1) + (1 - k)(x_2, y_2)$$

$$= (kx_1 + (1 - k)x_2, ky_1 + (1 - k)y_2) \quad \text{for} \quad 0 \le k \le 1$$

In the present discussion we simply have $y_1 = f(x_1)$ and $y_2 = f(x_2)$ for some function x.

4. Again, a function $h(x)$ is said to be quasi-convex, if $f(x) = -h(x)$ is quasi-concave. The reader should draw a contour of a quasi-convex function, on the assumption that all its partial derivatives are strictly positive. Show in two dimensions that if the function $g(x_1, x_2)$, with $g_1, g_2 > 0$, is quasi-convex, then the set of points satisfying: $g(x_1, x_2) \leq b$ is a convex set.

References and further reading

The reader with a good background in mathematics will find a rigorous treatment of the material presented in this chapter in:

    M. D. Intriligator. *Mathematical Optimisation and Economic Theory*, Prentice-Hall, Englewood Cliffs, N.J., 1971, Chs. 2–4

and

    H. Nikaido. *Introduction to Sets and Mappings in Modern Economics*, North-Holland, Amsterdam, 1970, Chs. 2, 4, 5, 6.

A less heavily mathematical approach, which also suggests wider applications of the concepts of this chapter, can be found in:

    T. Koopmans. *Three Essays on the State of Economic Science*, McGraw-Hill, London, 1957, Ch. 1.

and an excellent account of the structure, properties and uses of optimization problems in economics is:

    A. Dixit. *Optimization in Economic Theory*, Oxford University Press, 1976.

Chapter 3

The theory of the consumer

The central assumption in the theory of the consumer is that the consumer confronts an optimization problem: given the feasible set of consumption bundles open to him, he chooses the one he prefers. The purpose of the theory is first to describe or characterize the bundle of goods which will be chosen in terms of certain conditions it must satisfy, and secondly to predict how the optimal choice will change in response to changes in the feasible set.

In analysing the consumer's optimal choice, we proceed in three steps. We first construct a model of the consumer's preferences, which allows us to specify certain important properties of the consumer's ranking of consumption bundles in terms of 'better', 'worse' or 'as good as'. We then examine how the prices of commodities in conjunction with the consumer's income (or his initial endowment of commodities in a more general model) together determine his feasible set of consumption bundles. Finally, by applying the model we have constructed of the consumer's preference ordering to the feasible set, we are able to determine and define the characteristics of the optimal choice.

A. The preference ordering

A consumption bundle will be denoted by a vector:

$$x = (x_1, x_2, \ldots, x_n)$$

where x_i, $i = 1, 2, \ldots, n$, is the amount of the ith good in the bundle. Each x_i is assumed to be non-negative – the consumer can consume only zero or a positive quantity of each good – and also is taken to be perfectly divisible – goods do not come in lumpy discrete amounts.

The meaning of the terms 'preference' and 'indifference' is taken as understood; we do not define them in terms of other concepts, but simply take it for granted that everyone knows what is meant by the statement, 'I prefer this to that', or, 'I am indifferent between this and that'. In the present case, we assume that the consumer can make statements such as, 'I prefer consumption bundle x' to x''', or, 'I am indifferent between x' and x''''. To put it more formally, we introduce the symbol $\gtrsim$ which is read 'is preferred or indifferent to', or 'is at least as good as', or 'is no worse than', and we let $x' \gtrsim x''$ stand for the statement that the consumer regards x' as at least as good as x'', and $x'' \gtrsim x'$ for the converse. Since this symbol is a way of relating pairs of consumption bundles, it is called the *preference–indifference relation*.

Recall the view we have of the way the consumer chooses: he will rank the consumption bundles in the feasible set in order of preference, and choose the one which comes highest in the ranking (assuming there is only one). This preference ranking can be thought of as being arrived at by repeated application of the preference–indifference relation to successive pairs of consumption bundles. For the purpose of our theory, we want the preference ranking to have certain properties, which give it a particular, useful structure. We build these properties up by making a number of assumptions, first about the preference–indifference relation itself, and then about some aspects of the preference ranking to which it gives rise. We now go on to examine these assumptions.

As a preliminary, suppose the consumer told us that:

$$x' \gtrsim x'' \quad and \quad x'' \gtrsim x'$$

in words, 'x' is preferred or indifferent to x'''', and 'x'' is preferred or indifferent to x''''. Since we would regard him as talking nonsense – violating the meaning of the word 'preferred' - if he told us that x' is preferred to x'' *and* x'' is preferred to x', this must mean that x' is indifferent to x''. We write 'x' is indifferent to x'''', as $x' \sim x''$. Suppose alternatively the consumer told us that:

$$x' \gtrsim x'' \quad and \ not \quad x'' \gtrsim x'$$

This must mean that x' is preferred to x'' (explain why) and this is written $x' > x''$. Thus we have as implications of the meaning of the preference–indifference relation:

(a) $x' \gtrsim x''$ and $x'' \gtrsim x'$ implies $x' \sim x''$
(b) $x' \gtrsim x''$ and *not* $x'' \gtrsim x'$ implies $x' > x''$.

We can now proceed to the assumptions which give the desired properties to the consumer's preference ordering.

Assumption 1. Completeness.   For *any pair* of bundles x' and x'', either $x' \gtrsim x''$ or $x'' \gtrsim x'$ (or both).

This assumption says in effect that the consumer is able to express a preference or indifference between any pair of consumption bundles however alike or unalike they may be. This ensures that there are no 'holes' in the preference ordering, points or areas to which it does not apply. It also implies that given some bundle x', every other bundle can be put into one of three sets:

(i) the set of bundles preferred or indifferent to x', which could be called the 'better set' for x';

(ii) the set of bundles indifferent to x', which is called the indifference set of x';

(iii) the set of bundles to which x' is preferred or indifferent, which could be called the 'worse set' for x'.

These sets, and especially (ii), play an important part in what follows. Note that a bundle may be in both (i) and (ii) or (ii) and (iii) but not in (i) and (iii).

Assumption 2. *Transitivity.* For any three bundles x', x'', x''', if $x' \gtrsim x''$ and $x'' \gtrsim x'''$ then $x' \gtrsim x'''$.

Intuitively, this is a consistency requirement on the consumer. Given the first two statements, if the third did not hold, so that $x''' > x'$, we would feel there was an inconsistency in his preferences. If the consumer finds a pint of beer and a pork pie at least as good as a glass of Beaujolais and a piece of Camembert, which in turn he finds at least as good as a glass of water and a slice of bread, we would confidently predict that he would find the beer and pie at least as good as the bread and water, and feel he was being inconsistent if he told us that in fact he preferred the latter. The assumption has an important implication for the 'indifference sets' (ii) just defined, in that it implies that no bundle can belong to more than one such set. For suppose that $x' \sim x''$, so that x'' belongs to the indifference set of x'; and also that $x'' \sim x'''$, so x'' belongs to the indifference set of x'''. If $x' \sim x'''$, then there is no problem, since all three bundles are in the same indifference set. But suppose $x''' > x'$. Then x'' must be in two indifference sets, that of x' and that of x'''. But we then have:

$$x' \sim x'' \quad \text{and} \quad x'' \sim x''' \quad \text{but} \quad x''' > x'$$

which violates the assumption of transitivity (explain why). Thus given this assumption, no bundle can belong to more than one indifference set. A way of putting this is to say: *The transitivity assumption implies that indifference sets have no intersection* (since the intersection of two sets consists of the points common to both of them).

Assumption 3. *Reflexivity.* $x' \gtrsim x'$.

In words, any bundle is preferred or indifferent to itself. Since we can interchange the two sides of the relation, the assumption has the implication that a bundle is indifferent to itself, which seems trivially true. However, its implication is less trivial: it ensures that every bundle belongs to at least one indifference set, namely that containing itself, if nothing else.

These three properties of the preference–indifference relation allow us to conclude that every bundle (completeness) can be put into one indifference set (reflexivity) and no more than one indifference set (transitivity). Thus we can *partition* any given set of consumption bundles, by use of the relation, into non-intersecting indifference sets, which provide us with a useful way of representing a particular preference ordering. The indifference sets can be ranked in order of preference on the basis of the ranking of the bundles they contain. From now on, the assumptions we make about the consumer's preferences will be framed in terms of the indifference sets, and in fact are chiefly designed to give these sets a particular structure.

Assumption 4. Non-satiation. A consumption bundle x' will be preferred to x'' if x' contains more of at least one good and no less of any other, i.e. if $x' > x''$.

This assumption establishes a relationship between the quantities of goods in a bundle and its place in the preference ordering – the more of each good it contains the better. Moreover, this is held to be true however large the amounts of the goods in the bundle, hence the term 'non-satiation' – the consumer is assumed never to be satiated with goods. This assumption is much stronger than we need to make in two respects. It first implies that none of the goods is in fact a 'bad', a commodity such as garbage or aircraft noise which one would prefer to have less of. Secondly it assumes that the consumer is never satiated in *any* good. We could generalize by allowing some goods to be bads, and by assuming non-satiation only in at least one good, without changing anything of significance in the results of the theory. For simplicity however we adopt the stronger assumption here.

The non-satiation assumption has two important consequences for the nature of indifference sets, which are best expressed geometrically. In Fig. 1, x_1 and x_2 are goods, and $x' = (x'_1, x'_2)$ is a consumption bundle. Because of assumption 4, all bundles in the area B (including the boundaries, except for x' itself) must be preferred to x', and all points in the area W (again including the boundaries except for x') must be inferior to x' (explain why). The first consequence of the assumption is then that points in the indifference set for x' (if there *are* any besides x'), must lie in areas A and C. In other words, if we imagine moving between bundles in the indifference

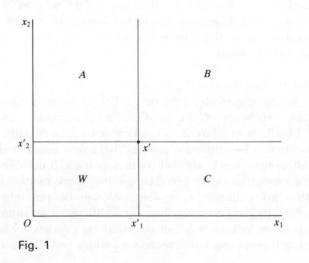

Fig. 1

set, we can only do so by *substituting* or *trading off* the goods – giving more of one good must require taking away some of the other good in order to stay within the indifference set. The second consequence is that an indifference set is never 'wider' than a single point – its geometric representation can never be an area or band, though it may be a single point, an unconnected set of points or a curve. For suppose x' was contained in an indifference set which was a band. Then some bundles indifferent to it must lie in areas B and W, which violates assumption 4. Thus the assumption implies that an indifference set cannot be thick at point x', or, by extending the argument, at any other point contained in it.

None of the assumptions we have made so far however implies that there must be more than one point in an indifference set, or, if there is more than one point, that these make up a continuous line or curve. For example, as is shown in the appendix to this chapter, the so-called *lexicographic ordering* satisfies assumptions 1 to 4, but its indifference sets each consist of only one point. We know that from the point of view of solving optimization problems continuity is a very important property (section 2C), and since we shall in effect be using indifference sets (or their geometric representation: indifference surfaces and, in the two-good case, indifference curves) to model the consumer's problem, it is a property we should like them to possess. Hence we make the assumption of continuity.

Assumption 5. Continuity. The graph of an indifference set is a continuous surface.

This implies that the surface, or curve in two dimensions, has no gaps or breaks at any point. In terms of the consumer's choice behaviour, what we are saying is this: given two goods in his consumption bundle, we can reduce the amount he has of one good, and however small this reduction is, we can always find an increase in the other good which will exactly compensate him, i.e. leave him with a consumption bundle indifferent to the first. The reader should confirm diagrammatically that this is possible only if the indifference surface is everywhere continuous.

We now want to place some restrictions on the shape of the indifference surfaces or curves. From assumption 4 we already know that they must be negatively sloped, and so now we have to say something about their curvature. Recall the earlier definition of the better set of a point x', as the set of bundles which are preferred or indifferent to x'. Then we make the assumption:

Assumption 6. Strict convexity. Given any consumption bundle x', its better set is strictly convex.

Figure 2 illustrates for the two-good case. The better set for the point x' is the set of points on the indifference curve I' and in the shaded area, and this is drawn as strictly convex. There is an important technical reason for making this assumption: we know (from Ch. 2, section E) that, given also that the feasible set is convex, the consumer's optimal point will

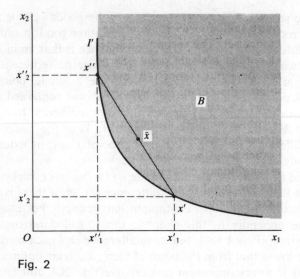

Fig. 2

as a result be a unique local – and therefore a global – optimum, and this is of considerable value when we come to analyse the consumer's responses to changes in the feasible set.

There is also a basis for the assumption in terms of economic behaviour, which can be expressed in two ways. From Fig. 2 it is clear that if we move the consumer along his indifference curve leftward from point x', reducing the quantity of x_1 by small, equal amounts, we have to compensate, to keep him on the indifference curve, by giving him larger and larger increments of x_2. In other words, the curvature implies that the smaller the amount of x_1 and larger the amount of x_2 held by the consumer, the more valuable to him are marginal changes in x_1 relative to marginal changes in x_2. For example, the greater the amount of bread and smaller the amount of cheese he has, the more bread he would have to be given to compensate for a small reduction in the amount of cheese. It is argued that this is a common feature of consumer preferences.

A second way of rationalising the curvature is as follows. In Fig. 2, $x' \sim x''$. Consider the straight line joining these two points. Any point on this line, for example $\bar{x}$, is a particular kind of combination of x' and x'', in that it can be expressed as:

$$\bar{x} = kx' + (1-k)x'' \qquad 1 > k > 0 \qquad [A.1]$$

i.e. the bundle $\bar{x}$ contains an amount of x_1 given by $kx_1' + (1-k)x_1''$, and an amount of x_2 given by $kx_2' + (1-k)x_2''$. So for example if $k = \frac{1}{2}$, $\bar{x}$ lies halfway along the line, and contains half of x_1' *plus* half of x_1'', and half of x_2' *plus* half of x_2''. We now call such a *convex combination* a *mixture* of x' and x''.

It follows from the strict convexity assumption that any mixture along the line will be preferred to x' and x'' (in fact this is the formal *definition* of strict convexity of the better set – see Ch. 2, section B). Thus, what we are saying is that the consumer always prefers a mixture of two consumption bundles which are indifferent to each other, to either one of those bundles. For example, if he is indifferent between three slices of bread and an ounce of cheese, and one slice of bread and three ounces of cheese, the assumption says that he prefers to either of them two slices of bread and two ounces of cheese (or $1\frac{1}{2}$ slices of bread and $2\frac{1}{2}$ ounces of cheese, or $2\frac{1}{2}$ slices of bread and $1\frac{1}{2}$ ounces of cheese, or ...) Again it is argued that this preference for mixtures is a commonly observed aspect of consumer behaviour.

A weaker convexity assumption than assumption 6 can be made: we could assume that the better set is convex but not strictly convex. This means that we allow the possibility of linear segments in the indifference curves, as Fig. 3 illustrates. The better sets for points x', x'' and x''' respectively are each convex but none is strictly convex. Linearity in the indifference curve over some range implies that within this range, the valuation of marginal decreases in one good relative to marginal increments in the other remains constant – successive equal reductions in the amount of one good are compensated by successive equal increases in the amount of the other. Alternatively, a mixture of two indifferent bundles, in the sense just defined, is indifferent to the two, rather than preferred to them. The reason for excluding such linearity by the strict convexity assumption is, as we shall see, to ensure that the solution to the consumer's problem is a unique point and not a set of infinitely many points.

As a result of these six assumptions, we can represent the preference ordering of the consumer by a set of continuous convex-to-the-origin indifference curves or surfaces, such that each consumption bundle lies on one and only one of them. Moreover, as a result of assumption 4 we can say that bundles on a higher indifference surface are preferred to those on a lower. Thus, the best consumption bundle open to a consumer is the one

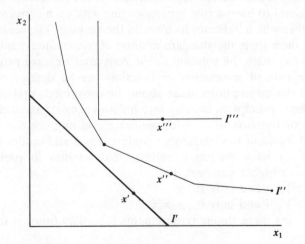

Fig. 3

lying on the highest possible indifference surface. We therefore have part of the analytical apparatus we need to solve the consumer's choice problem. It is however of interest to examine at this point a somewhat different way of representing the consumer's preference ordering.

The utility function

Historically the word 'utility' was used in economics to denote the subjective sensations – satisfaction, pleasure, wish-fulfilment, cessation of need, etc. – which are derived from consumption, and the experience of which is the object of consumption. However, the economists in the late 19th century who were concerned with constructing a theory of consumer choice went further than this definition and regarded utility as something which could be measured as an absolute quantity, in the same way as, say, weight can be measured. They thought it possible to speak of the total quantity of utility derived from consuming a given bundle of goods, of subtracting such quantities from each other, and discussing how these differences changed as consumption varied. Thus was developed the 'law of diminishing marginal utility'. However, even then some of these economists were unhappy about this measurability assumption and it came increasingly under attack as the theory developed. The position which is generally accepted now is that the subjective sensations grouped under the name utility are not capable of being treated as quantities in this sense. An important reason for the adoption of that position was the demonstration that for the purpose of constructing a theory of consumer choice, not only the measurement of utility, but the very concept itself, is unnecessary. As we have seen, we can base a theory of choice on the concepts of preference and indifference, and *nothing more is needed* for the theory than the set of indifference curves (or surfaces) with their assumed properties.

However, for some methods of analysis it is useful to have a function which provides a numerical representation of the preference ordering. That is, it is useful to have a rule for associating with each consumption bundle a real number which indicates its place in the ranking. The reason for this is that we can then apply the standard method of constrained maximization of a function to obtain the solution to the consumer's choice problem.

A suitable rule of association or function can be defined in the following way. On the assumptions made about the consumer's preferences we can partition the consumption bundles into indifference sets and can rank these sets. A rule or function $u(x)$ which assigns a real number u to each bundle x is said to *represent* the consumer's preferences if all bundles in the same indifference set have the same number and bundles in preferred indifference sets have higher numbers, i.e.

(a) $u(x') = u(x'')$ if and only if $x' \sim x''$
(b) $u(x') > u(x'')$ if and only if $x' > x''$

Any function satisfying these simple requirements is a *utility function* for the consumer.

A utility function is merely a way of attaching numbers to the consumer's indifference surfaces or sets such that the numbers increase as higher or more preferred surfaces are reached. It reflects the *ordering* of the bundles by the consumer and so is an *ordinal* function. Since, for the purposes of the theories examined in this and the two following chapters, we only require that the consumer can rank or order bundles and the utility function is a numerical representation of this ordering, no significance attaches to size of the difference between numbers attached to different bundles. We are concerned only with the *sign* of the difference, i.e. whether $u(x') \gtreqless u(x'')$ or whether x' is preferred or indifferent to x'' or x'' preferred to x'.

There are a very large number of ways of attaching numbers to bundles which are consistent with the requirements (a) and (b) above: the utility function is not unique. For example, given four consumption bundles x', x'', x''', x'''' such that $x' \sim x'' > x''' > x''''$, any one of the columns in the following table is an acceptable numerical representation of the preference ordering:

	$u(x)$	$v(x)$	$w(x)$
x'	3	1000	500
x''	3	1000	500
x'''	2	2	499
x''''	1	1.5	1.9

where $v(x)$ and $w(x)$ denote functions which obey the rule in (a)–(b) above, but which differ from $u(x)$. A way of putting this more formally is as follows. We could regard the function $v(x)$ as being derived from $u(x)$ by applying, at each x, some *rule of transformation*, such as, for example, 'When $x = x'$ multiply $u(x')$ by $333\frac{1}{3}$ to obtain $v(x)$'. That is in general we write:

$$v(x) = T[u(x)] \tag{A.2}$$

where $T[\ \ ]$ denotes the rule of transformation we devise. The only restriction we place on this transformation rule is that when u increases, v must increase, because then v will correctly represent the preference ordering. Such a transformation is called '*positive monotonic*', because v must always increase with u. Hence, we say that the function $u(x)$ is *unique up to a positive monotonic transformation* meaning that we can always derive another permissible representation of the preference ordering by applying some positive monotonic transformation T to $u(x)$. Examples of such transformations are:

$$v(x) = [u(x)]^2$$
$$v(x) = 3 + 2u(x) \tag{A.3}$$
$$v(x) = 5 + \log u(x)$$

where the transformation T is defined by a simple function. As the table above showed, we do not *have* to define T in such a simple way. The reader might find it useful to write out a set of instructions to define the transformation $w(x) = T[v(x)]$.

So far we have taken it for granted that a function $u(x)$ which gives a numerical representation of a preference ordering actually does exist. This is something which we should consider explicitly. In the four-consumption bundle example just set out no problem seems to arise, but the general case is where there is an infinity of consumption bundles. Can we be sure that the function $u(x)$ exists in this case? Or, to rephrase the question, what do we have to assume in order to ensure that the function exists? Consider first assumptions 1–3 above, on completeness, transitivity and reflexivity. Recall that they resulted in a family of indifference sets such that every consumption bundle belonged to one and only one set. We might then reason intuitively that since the $u(x)$ function effectively assigns numbers to indifference sets, there can be no problem. We would, however, be wrong. It can be shown that we may have a preference ordering satisfying assumptions 1–3 (and even 4), but for which no numerical representation exists – we cannot apply to it the rule for assigning numbers to consumption bundles that we set out earlier. An ordering for which this is true is the so-called lexicographic ordering discussed in the appendix. The existence of this counter-example tells us that assumptions 1–3 are not sufficient to guarantee existence of a numerical representation of a preference ordering. The further assumption which solves the problem is that of continuity. It can be shown that if assumption 5 holds, so that the indifference surfaces are continuous, a numerical representation $u(x)$ can always be constructed for the preference ordering. Moreover, the function can also always be made continuous.

Since better bundles have higher utility numbers assigned to them, the consumer's optimization problem can be described as the maximization of his utility function subject to certain constraints. The utility function is the objective function for this problem and, as we have seen, the restrictions on its form are very weak. By way of contrast consider the firm's profit maximization problem, in which profit is the objective function. Profit is measured in money terms e.g. in £ or $. The problem can be meaningfully formulated as the maximization of profit measured in any monetary unit, so that there are a large number of profit functions which can be used as the objective function. However all these functions are related in a very restricted way. If f and g are profit functions (defined on output) then they are related by

$$g = b \cdot f$$

where b is a constant. For example, if f is measured in £ and g in $ then b is the rate of exchange ($ per £); if f is measured in £ and g in pence then b is 100 pence per £. The profit function is said to be *unique up to a proportional transformation* and as such belongs to the class of *cardinal* functions.

There are other significant differences between (say) a profit function and a utility function. The former is *measurable* in that it is theoretically possible to calculate the profit attached to any given course of action by a firm by reference solely to *observable* phenomena, such as prices, outputs and inputs. It is not possible to do this in this case of a utility function, which is essentially *subjective*. No amount of observation will enable us to calculate the utility number attached to particular bundles by a specific numerical representation of a consumer's preferences. We will only be able to infer from the consumer's actions in some cases that the utility number of one bundle exceeds that of another. Utility functions are also *personal* in that statements of the form 'Individual A has a higher utility number for bundle than individual B', are meaningless. Since the utility function of an individual is unique only up to a monotone transformation it will always be possible to find a utility function for B which falsifies the statement. Interpersonal comparisons cannot be based on the ordinal functions satisfying conditions (a) and (b). For the same reason statements of the form 'The increase in utility to an individual from consuming x' rather than x'' exceeds the increase in utility from consuming x'' rather than x''''', are also meaningless: only the sign, not the size, of utility differences is preserved by transformations of the functions which represent the consumer's preferences.

We can now consider the relation between the function $u(x)$ and the indifference sets, which are the fundamental expressions of the consumer's preference ordering. Suppose we consider the set of consumption bundles which satisfy:

$$u(x) = u^0 \qquad\qquad\qquad [A.4]$$

where u^0 is some given number. Since these consumption bundles yield the same value of the function they must, by the definition of the function, constitute an indifference set. A set of values of the independent variables in a function which yield a constant value of the function is said to define a *contour* of that function. Hence the indifference sets are contours of the function $u(x)$, and the assumptions 4 and 6 which define the shape of the indifference sets can just as well be interpreted as defining the properties of the contours of $u(x)$. This implies that $u(x)$ is what we called in Chapter 2, section B, a *strictly quasi-concave* function. In addition, we know that a consumption bundle which yields a higher value of the function than another will always be preferred, and so we can interpret the desire to choose the preferred alternative in some given set of alternatives as equivalent to maximising the function $u(x)$ over that set. Thus we can represent the consumer's choice problem as one of constrained maximization of a strictly quasi-concave function.

In formulating the consumer's choice problem in this way, it is useful if we can use methods of differentiation to find solutions. However, none of the assumptions made so far implies differentiability: for example, Fig. 4 shows a contour which satisfies all the assumptions but is not differentiable at x' – the slope of the contour is not uniquely defined at that point, which is a corner. To rule out such cases, we make the assumption of differentiability.

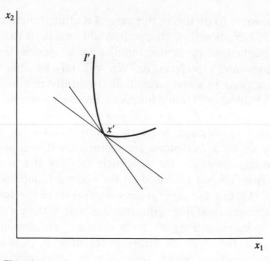

Fig. 4

Assumption 7. Differentiability. Utility functions are differentiable to any required order.

This assumption, which is required only when we want to use techniques of differentiation to solve the constrained maximization problem, rules out cases in which the slope of an indifference surface or curve makes a sudden jump, as in the case shown by Fig. 4. We now have to examine more closely the interpretation of the slope of an indifference curve.

Recall that in discussing assumption 6 we used the idea of successive small reductions in x_1 being compensated by small increments in x_2 just enough to stay on the indifference curve. That is, we defined a sequence of changes in x_1, $\Delta_1 x_1, \Delta_2 x_1, \Delta_3 x_1, \ldots$ and a corresponding sequence of changes in x_2, $\Delta_1 x_2, \Delta_2 x_2, \Delta_3 x_2, \ldots$, around the indifference curve. We could then define the sequence of ratios,

$$\frac{\Delta_1 x_2}{\Delta_1 x_1}, \frac{\Delta_2 x_2}{\Delta_2 x_1}, \frac{\Delta_3 x_2}{\Delta_3 x_1}, \ldots$$

any one term of which shows the change in x_2 required *per unit* of the change in x_1, to stay on the indifference curve. This can be thought of as a 'required rate of compensation', whose (absolute) value increases as we move leftward along the indifference curve. As usual with ratios of *finite* changes, there is an ambiguity arising out of the arbitrariness of the size of the change, and so we find it useful to go to the limit and define the derivative:

$$\left. \frac{dx_2}{dx_1} \right|_{u \text{ constant}} = \lim_{\Delta x_1 \to 0} \left(\frac{\Delta x_2}{\Delta x_1} \right) \qquad [\text{A.5}]$$

where the notation on the lefthand side is intended to emphasize that we are moving along an indifference curve, and so are constraining the changes in

x_1 and x_2 to be such as to keep a constant value of the function u. In effect, we view the indifference curve as defining x_2 as a function of x_1, which could be called an 'indifference function' or 'contour function'. Then the derivative we have defined above is the slope of this function at a point. Figure 5 illustrates. The slope of the tangent L to the indifference curve at x' gives the value of the above derivative at x'. This is (given the differentiability assumption) always uniquely and unambiguously defined. As we take points leftward along the indifference curve, the absolute value of the derivative increases. The figure also shows a sequence of finite changes; the ratio $\Delta x_2 / \Delta x_1$ gives the *average* rate of change of x_2 with respect to x_1 over an arc of the curve, and its value will depend on the size of the change Δx_1.

Important derivatives in economics are always called the marginal something or other, and this is no exception. We define the *marginal rate of substitution* of good 2 for good 1, written MRS_{21}, as:

$$MRS_{21} = -\frac{dx_2}{dx_1}\bigg|_{u \text{ constant}} \qquad [A.6]$$

The negative sign occurs because we wish MRS_{21} to be positive. Assumption 6 implies that MRS_{21} varies inversely with x_1. We also define the marginal rate of substitution of good 1 for good 2, written MRS_{12}, as:

$$MRS_{12} = -\frac{dx_1}{dx_2}\bigg|_{u \text{ constant}} \qquad [A.7]$$

which refers to the slope of an indifference curve relative to the x_2-axis. Since the two are reciprocals of each other, it is enough to work always with just one of them, and MRS_{21} will usually be taken.

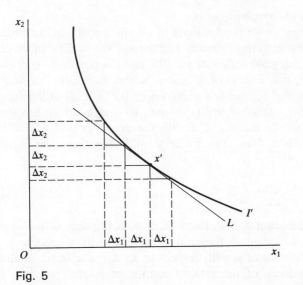

Fig. 5

We now have to consider the relation between the MRS_{21} and the function $u(x)$. Along an indifference surface we have:

$$u = u(x) = u^0$$

where u^0 is a given constant. Assumption 7 allows us to differentiate u totally to obtain:

$$du = u_1\, dx_1 + u_2\, dx_2 + \ldots + u_n\, dx_n = 0 \qquad [\text{A.8}]$$

where u_i, $i = 1, 2, \ldots n$, is the partial derivative $\partial u/\partial x_i$, or the *marginal utility* of good i. This equation constrains the differentials dx_i to be such as to maintain $u = u^0$. Let us assume that the quantities of all goods other than the first two are held constant, i.e. $dx_i = 0$, $i = 3, \ldots n$. Then, by rearranging we have:

$$\left. \frac{-dx_2}{dx_1} \right|_{u\ \text{constant}} = \frac{u_1}{u_2} = \mathrm{MRS}_{21} \qquad [\text{A.9}]$$

Thus the marginal rate of substitution at a point can be expressed as the ratio of marginal utilities at that point. Since u_1 and u_2 are in general functions of all n goods, so is MRS_{21}. Clearly, the above procedure can be used to derive the marginal rate of substitution for any pair of goods.

Note that useful though it is to have this relationship between marginal rates of substitution and partial derivatives of $u(x)$, in a sense it is the former which are more fundamental. The preference ordering of the consumer uniquely determines the indifference sets and hence the marginal rates of substitution. The partial derivatives, on the other hand, depend on the particular function used to represent the consumer's preferences i.e. to label the indifference sets.

Properties of marginal utility

If x_i increases with the amounts of all other goods held constant the consumer achieves a better bundle and hence the utility number must increase, so that marginal utility of the ith good is positive: $u_i(x) > 0$. The *sign* of the marginal utility of a good is the same for all numerical representations of the consumer's preferences (i.e. for all utility functions) but the *size* of the marginal utility is not. If u is a utility function and $v = T[u(x)]$ is a transformation of u with the property that $T' = dT/du > 0$ i.e. v increases with u, then $v(x)$ is also a utility function. The partial of v with respect to x_i is

$$\frac{\partial v}{\partial x_i} = v_i = T' \cdot \frac{\partial u}{\partial x_i} = T' u_i \qquad [\text{A.10}]$$

and, since by assumption $T' > 0$, the sign of v_i is the sign of u_i but $v_i \neq u_i$.

The rate of change of marginal utility of x_i with respect to x_i is the second partial derivative of u with respect to x_i: $u_{ii} = \partial^2 u/\partial x_i \partial x_i$. Neither the *sign* nor the magnitude of the rate of change of u_i are the same for all representations of preferences. For example with the function v considered in the previous paragraph.

$$v_{ii} = \frac{\partial^2 v}{\partial x_i \partial x_i} = \frac{\partial}{\partial x_i}(T' \cdot u_i) = T' \cdot u_{ii} + T'' \cdot u_i.$$

Hence the sign of v_{ii} is the same as the sign of u_{ii} for all T only if $T'' = d^2 T/du^2 = 0$, but the only restriction on T is that $T' > 0$. Statements about increasing or diminishing marginal utility are therefore meaningless, because we can always find a function to represent the consumer's preferences which contradicts the statement.

[A.9] makes the important point that ratios of marginal utilities are invariant to permissible transformations of the utility function since they must all equal the marginal rate of substitution, which is determined by the consumer's preferences. Using the utility functions u and v above and [A.10], we see that

$$MRS_{ij} = \frac{v_j}{v_i} = \frac{T' \cdot u_j}{T' \cdot u_i} = \frac{u_j}{u_i} \qquad [A.11]$$

Our warnings about the meaninglessness of statements about the *size* of changes in utility are valid for the preferences which satisfy the assumptions of this chapter but, as we will see in Chapter 19, if certain additional restricting assumptions about an individual's preferences are made, it becomes sensible to talk of the rate of change of marginal utility. However these extra assumptions are unnecessary for our present purposes and so we do not adopt them until they are needed, when we study decision-making under conditions of uncertainty.

Exercise 3A
1. Show that if indifference curves intersect the consumer is inconsistent.
2.* Construct a set of indifference curves which satisfy all the assumptions of this section, *except*:
   (a) one of the 'goods' is in fact a bad; or
   (b) the consumer may reach a point at which he is satiated with one good but not the other; or
   (c) the consumer may reach a point at which he is satiated with both goods (a 'bliss point'); or
   (d) there is a quantity for each good up to which it is a good, and beyond which it is a bad.
   Give concrete examples of goods which may fit each case.
3.* Discuss the relationship between the non-satiation assumption and the idea of scarcity which underlies microeconomics.
4.* Draw indifference curves relating to:
   (a) red and blue matches with identical incendiary properties;
   (b) left and right shoes of the same size, quality, design etc; and state whether the corresponding utility function is strictly quasi-concave. Comment on the way in which the MRS_{21} varies along these indifference curves.

5. Mr A's indifference curves for water and diamonds satisfy the assumption of strict convexity, and he is endowed with a great deal of water and very few diamonds. Which of the following does this imply?
   (a) diamonds are more valuable to him than water;
   (b) he would give up a lot of water to get one more diamond;
   (c) he would give up more water for an extra diamond than would be the case if he had a combination, indifferent to the first, of less water and more diamonds.

B. The feasible set

We will initially assume that the consumer has a given money income M, that he faces constant prices for all of the goods in his utility function and that he cannot consume negative quantities of any good. Then, recalling section 2A, the consumer's feasible set defined by these assumptions is the set of bundles satisfying

$$p_1x_1 + p_2x_2 + \ldots + p_nx_n = \sum p_ix_i \leq M \qquad [\text{B.1}]$$
$$x_1 \geq 0, \qquad x_2 \geq 0, \ldots, x_n \geq 0$$

where p_i is the price of good i.

The feasible set in the two-good case is shown in Fig. 6 as the triangular area $Ox_1^0x_2^0$. $x_1^0 = M/p_1$ is the maximum amount of x_1 that can be bought with income M at a price of p_1. x_2^0 is analogously defined. The budget constraint is $p_1x_1 + p_2x_2 \leq M$ in this two-good case, or:

$$x_2 \leq (M - p_1x_1)/p_2 \qquad [\text{B.2}]$$

which is satisfied by all points on or below the line B from x_1^0 to x_2^0. B, the upper boundary of the feasible set, is known as the consumer's *budget line* and is defined by

$$x_2 = (M - p_1x_1)/p_2 \qquad [\text{B.3}]$$

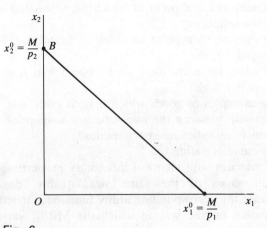

Fig. 6

The slope of the budget line is therefore

$$\frac{dx_2}{dx_1}\bigg|_{M \text{ constant}} = -\frac{p_1}{p_2} \qquad\qquad [B.4]$$

where the notation on the lefthand side is to remind us that this is the rate at which a consumer with fixed income can exchange x_1 for x_2 on the market. A one-unit reduction in purchases of x_1 reduces expenditure by p_1, and so, since 1 unit of x_2 costs p_2, the consumer can buy p_1/p_2 extra units of x_2. Therefore 1 unit of x_1 exchanges for p_1/p_2 units of x_2.

As a preparation for the next section let us examine the consumer's feasible set in terms of the concepts introduced in section 2B. The feasible set is:

(i) *bounded*, from below by the non-negativity constraints on the x_i and from above by the budget constraint, provided that M is finite and no price is zero. If, for example, $p_1 = 0$ then the budget line would be a line parallel to the x_1 axis through the point $x_2^0 = M/p_2$, and the feasible set would be unbounded to the right: since x_1 would be a free good the consumer could consume as much of it as he wished.

(ii) *closed*, since any bundle on the budget line B or the quantity axes is available.

(iii) *convex*, since for any two bundles x' and x'' in the feasible set, any bundle $\bar{x}$ lying on a straight line between them will also be in the feasible set. Since $\bar{x}$ lies between x' and x'', and they both satisfy the non-negativity constraints, $\bar{x}$ will also satisfy these constraints. $\bar{x}$ will cost no more than the consumer's income: lying between x' and x'' it must cost no more than the more expensive of them, say x'. But since x' lies within the feasible set, so must $\bar{x}$. Hence $\bar{x}$ is in the feasible set.

(iv) *non-empty*: provided that $M > 0$ and at least one price is finite the consumer can buy a positive amount of at least one good.

We will consider here the effects of changes in M and p_i on the feasible set, in preparation for section D where we examine their effects on the consumer's optimal choice. If money income increases from M_0 to M_1, the consumer's feasible set expands as the budget line moves outward parallel with its initial position, as in Fig. 7(a). With $M = M_0$ the intercepts of the budget line B_0 on the x_1 and x_2 axes respectively are M_0/p_1 and M_0/p_2 and with $M = M_1$ they are M_1/p_1 and M_1/p_2. A doubling of M for example, will double the value of the intercepts, since $M_1/p_2 = 2M_0/p_2$ when $M_1 = 2M_0$. The slope of the budget line is $-p_1/p_2$ and this is unaffected by changes in M.

Consider next an increase in p_1, as shown in Fig. 7(b). Since M and p_2 are unchanged the budget line will still have the same M/p_2 intercept on the x_2 axis. An increase in p_1 will cause the budget line to pivot about M_0/p_2 and become more steeply sloped as p_1/p_2 becomes larger. In Fig. 7(b) a rise

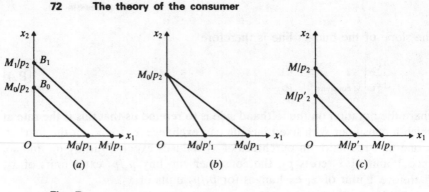

Fig. 7

in p_1 to p_1' shifts the x_1 intercept from M_0/p_1 to M_0/p_1' where $M_0/p_1 > M_0/p_1'$ since $p_1 < p_1'$.

Equal proportionate changes in all prices will cause the budget line to shift inwards towards the origin as in Fig. 7(c). Suppose p_1 and p_2 increase from p_1 and p_2 to kp_1 and kp_2 where $k > 1$. Then the slope of the new budget line is unchanged: $-kp_1/kp_2 = -p_1/p_2$ and the new intercepts are $M/kp_1 < M/p_1$ and $M/kp_2 < M/p_2$.

Finally, if all prices and M change in the same proportion the budget line is unchanged. The intercept on the ith axis after all prices and M change by the factor k is $kM/kp_i = M/p_i$ so the intercept is unaffected, as is the slope, which is $-kp_1/kp_2 = -p_1/p_2$.

Exercise 3B

1.* Suppose that the price of one of the commodities bought by the consumer rises as he buys larger quantities. What effect will this have on his feasible set? What interpretation can be given to the slope of his budget line? Can you show in the diagram the relationship between the average price (expenditure divided by quantity bought) and the marginal price?

2.* Many public utilities sell their products on multi-part tariffs. The consumer must pay a connection charge for the right to consume (say) electricity, irrespective of the amount consumed. The price paid for the first n units will exceed the price paid for any units consumed in excess of n. Draw the feasible set for the consumer, with electricity on one axis and a composite consumption good on the other. Distinguish between the average and marginal prices of electricity and investigate the effects of changes in the connection charge and the price of electricity.

3. Draw the feasible set of the consumer in Exercise 3A, Question 2a, assuming that the 'bad' is garbage and that there is a given price per bag of garbage removed, and a given amount of garbage produced per period by the consumer.

C. The consumption decision

Given the assumptions of the previous two sections, the consumer's problem of choosing the most preferred bundle from those available to him can be formally stated as

$$\max_{x_1,\ldots,x_n} u(x_1, x_2, \ldots, x_n)$$

$$s.t. \sum_i p_i x_i \le M; \qquad x_i \ge 0 \qquad (i = 1, \ldots, n)$$

[C.1]

We can derive the equilibrium conditions which the solution to this problem must satisfy by a diagrammatic analysis of the two-good case. We will leave to the latter part of this section a brief confirmation of our results using the more rigorous methods of Chapter 2.

From the assumptions of section A we can represent the consumer's preferences by a utility function which has indifference curves or contours like those of Fig. 8. All commodities are assumed to have positive marginal utility so that bundles on higher indifference curves are preferred to those on lower indifference curves. This assumption (a consequence of assumption 4 in section A) also means that the consumer will spend all his income since he cannot be maximizing u if he can buy more of some good with positive marginal utility. The consumer will therefore choose a bundle on his budget line B.

In Fig. 8 there is a *tangency solution* where the optimal bundle x^* is such that the highest attainable indifference curve I_1 is tangent to the budget line and the consumer consumes some of both goods. The slope of the indifference curve is equal to the slope of the budget line at the optimum:

$$\frac{dx_2}{dx_1}\bigg|_{u \text{ constant}} = \frac{dx_2}{dx_1}\bigg|_{M \text{ constant}}$$

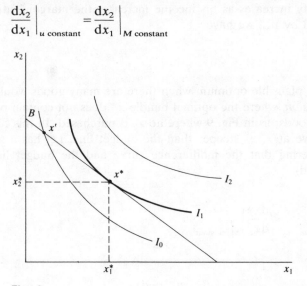

Fig. 8

But the negative of the slope of the indifference curve is the marginal rate of substitution MRS_{21}; and the negative of the slope of the budget line is the ratio of the prices of x_1 and x_2. Hence the consumer's equilibrium condition can be written as

$$MRS_{21} = \frac{u_1}{u_2} = \frac{p_1}{p_2} \qquad \text{[C.2]}$$

The consumer is in equilibrium (choosing an optimal bundle) when the rate at which he *can* substitute one good for another on the market is equal to the rate at which he is just content to substitute one good for another.

We can interpret this property of the optimal choice in a somewhat different way. If the consumer spent an extra unit of money on x_1 he would be able to buy $1/p_1$ units of x_1. $u_1 \Delta x_1$ is the gain in utility from an additional Δx_1 units of x_1. Hence u_1/p_1 is the gain in utility from spending an additional unit of money on x_1. u_2/p_2 has an analogous interpretation. The consumer will therefore be maximizing his utility when he allocates his income between x_1 and x_2 so that the marginal utility of expenditure on x_1 is equal to the marginal utility of expenditure on x_2:

$$\frac{u_1}{p_1} = \frac{u_2}{p_2} \qquad \text{[C.3]}$$

This is exactly the condition obtained by multiplying both sides of [C.2] by u_2/p_1.

If the consumer's income were increased by a small amount he would be indifferent between spending it on x_1 or x_2: in either case his utility would rise by $u_1/p_1 = u_2/p_2$. Hence, if we call the rate at which the consumer's utility increases as his income increases the marginal utility of income, denoted by u_M, we have

$$\frac{u_1}{p_1} = \frac{u_2}{p_2} = u_M \qquad \text{[C.4]}$$

A more plausible optimum when there are many goods would be a *corner point solution*, where the optimal bundle x^* does not contain positive amounts of all goods; as in Fig. 9 where no x_2 is purchased. In this case the indifference curve at x^* is steeper than the budget line, i.e. has a smaller slope, (remembering that the indifference curve and the budget line are negatively sloped).

Hence

$$\left. \frac{dx_2}{dx_1} \right|_{u \text{ constant}} < \left. \frac{dx_2}{dx_1} \right|_{M \text{ constant}} \qquad \text{[C.5]}$$

and therefore

$$\left. \frac{-dx_2}{dx_1} \right|_{u \text{ constant}} = MRS_2 = \frac{u_1}{u_2} \frac{p_1}{p_2} > \left. \frac{-dx_2}{dx_1} \right|_{M \text{ constant}} \qquad \text{[C.6]}$$

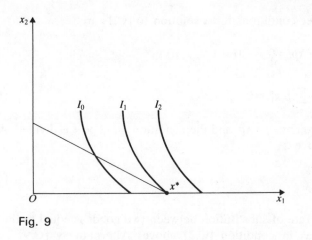

Fig. 9

Rearranging, this equilibrium condition can be written

$$u_M = \frac{u_1}{p_1} > \frac{u_2}{p_2} \qquad\qquad [C.7]$$

The marginal utility of expenditure on the good purchased, x_1, is greater than the marginal utility of expenditure on x_2, the good not purchased. Because of the higher marginal utility of expenditure on x_1 than on x_2 the consumer would like to move further down the budget line substituting x_1 for x_2 but he is restrained by the fact that he cannot consume negative amounts of x_2.

A more formal analysis*

Since the consumer's preferences satisfy the assumptions of section A, the objective function in problem [C.1] above is continuous and strictly quasi-concave. From section B we see that the feasible set for the problem, defined by the budget and non-negativity constraints, will be nonempty, closed, bounded and convex. From the Existence, Local–Global and Uniqueness Theorems of Chapter 2 the consumer's optimization problem will have a unique solution and there will be no non-global local solutions.

Since there is at least one good with positive marginal utility the consumer will spend his entire income and hence the budget constraint can be written as an equality constraint: $M - \sum p_i x_i = 0$. If we assume that the solution will be such that some of all goods will be consumed ($x_i^* > 0$ ($i = 1, \ldots, n$) where x_i^* is the optimal level of x_i), then the non-negativity constraints are non-binding and we have a problem to which can be applied the method of Lagrange outlined in Chapter 2, section G. The Lagrange function derived from [C.1] is

$$L = u(x_1, \ldots, x_n) + \lambda[M - \sum p_i x_i] \qquad\qquad [C.8]$$

and the first-order conditions for a solution to [C.1] are

$$\frac{\partial L}{\partial x_i} = u_i - \lambda p_i = 0 \qquad (i = 1, \ldots, n) \tag{C.9}$$

$$\frac{\partial L}{\partial \lambda} = M - \sum p_i x_i^* = 0 \tag{C.10}$$

If [C.9] is rewritten as $u_i = \lambda p_i$ and the condition on good i is divided by that on good j, we have

$$\frac{u_i}{u_j} = \frac{p_i}{p_j} \tag{C.11}$$

or: the marginal rate of substitution between two goods is equal to the ratio of their prices as in condition [C.3] above. Alternatively [C.9] can be rearranged to give

$$\frac{u_1}{p_1} = \frac{u_2}{p_2} = \cdots = \frac{u_n}{p_n} = \lambda \tag{C.12}$$

which is of course the n-good extension of the condition [C.4] derived earlier.

In Chapter 2 we demonstrated that the value of the Lagrange multiplier λ was the rate at which the objective function increased as the constraint parameter was increased. In this case the objective function is the utility function and the constraint parameter is the individual's money income so that λ is the rate at which utility increases as money income increases:

$$\lambda = \frac{\mathrm{d}u^*}{\mathrm{d}M} = u_M \tag{C.13}$$

The Lagrange multiplier can be interpreted as the marginal utility of money income. This interpretation is supported by [C.12] since, as we argued above, u_i/p_i is the rate at which utility increases as more money is spent on good i.

Corner solutions

If the assumption that $x_i^* > 0$ for all i is dropped, the first order conditions for [C.1] are derived by maximization of the Lagrangean [C.8] subject to the direct non-negativity constraints on the choice variables. Reference to section 2H indicates that the conditions which must be satisfied by a solution to C.1 are

$$\frac{\partial L}{\partial x_i} = u_i - \lambda^* p_i \leq 0, \qquad x_i^* \geq 0, \qquad x_i^* \cdot (u_i - \lambda p_i) = 0$$

$$i = 1, 2, \ldots n. \tag{C.14}$$

plus condition [C.10].

If [C.14] is rearranged to give

$$\lambda^* \geq \frac{u_i}{p_i}, \qquad x_i^* \geq 0, \qquad x_i^* \cdot \left(\frac{u_i}{p_i} - \lambda^*\right) = 0 \qquad \text{[C.15]}$$

it can be given a straightforward economic interpretetion: if the marginal utility of expenditure on good i, (u_i/p_i), is less than the marginal utility of money at the optimal point, λ^*, then good i will not be bought since the consumer will get greater utility by expenditure on other goods. The same result can be derived from [C.7], where $x_2 = 0$, since $u_1/p_1 = u_M > u_2/p_2$, or $u_2 - u_M p_2 < 0$.

Exercise 3C

1.* If a consumer buys electricity on a multi-part tariff, as in Exercise 3B, Question 2, are the conditions of the Existence, Local–Global and Uniqueness Theorems satisfied?
2.* Derive and interpret the equilibrium conditions for the types of preferences postulated in Exercise 3A, Questions 2 and 4.
   (*Note*: what must be assumed about the price of a 'bad'?).
3. Explain why a consumer would:
   (a) not choose a point inside his budget line;
   (b) not choose the bundle x' in Fig. 8.
4.* Suppose that, as well as paying a price per unit of a good, the consumer has to pay a 'transactions cost' for using a market. Analyse the implications for the consumer's optimal choice of assuming:
   (a) the transactions cost is paid as a lump sum;
   (b) the transactions cost is proportional to price but independent of the quantity bought;
   (c) the transactions cost is charged per unit of the good bought, but decreases the greater the amount bought.
5. Is the marginal utility of money income, λ^* or u_M, uniquely defined?

D. The comparative statics of consumer behaviour

The solution to the consumer's optimization problem, as we saw, depends on his preferences, the prices he faces and his money income. We can write this solution, which we call his *demand for goods*, as a function of prices and money income

$$x_i^* = D_i(p_1, p_2, \dots, p_n, M) = D_i(p, M) \qquad (i = 1, \dots, n) \qquad \text{[D.1]}$$

where $p = (p_1, p_2, \dots, p_n)$ is the vector of prices, and the form of the *demand function* D_i depends on the consumer's preferences.

The discussion in Chapter 2 on the properties of feasible sets and the objective function, and the assumptions made about those defined in this chapter, enable us to place restrictions on the form of the demand functions. First, provided that p, M are finite and positive, the optimization problem must have a solution, since the requirements of the

Existence Theorem are satisfied. Hence the demand functions *exist* for all plausible (p, M) combinations. Secondly, the differentiability of the indifference curves and the linearity of the budget constraint imply that the optimal bundle will vary continuously in response to changes in prices and income, and that the demand functions are *differentiable*. Thirdly, the conditions of the Uniqueness Theorem are satisfied and so the demand relationships are functions rather than correspondences. A *unique* bundle is chosen at each (p, M) combination.

Prediction of the bundle chosen in a given situation will require precise knowledge of the consumer's preferences, and hence our results so far are not very useful if we wish to test the model. We will now consider the *comparative statics* properties of the model to see if they yield predictions which do not require information we do not have. We wish to investigate the effects of changes in the exogenous variables (prices, money income) on the equilibrium values of the endogenous variables (the consumer's demand for goods). In other words we want to predict what happens to the optimal bundle $x^* = (x_1^*, x_2^*, \ldots, x_n^*) = (D_1, D_2, \ldots, D_n)$ as the feasible set varies.

We consider first changes in the consumer's money income. In Fig. 10 B_1 is the initial budget line, x^* the initial bundle chosen. An increase in M, with p_1, p_2 constant, will shift the budget line outward parallel with itself, say to B_2 where x' is chosen. A further increase in M will shift the budget line to B_3 where x'' is chosen. The *income consumption curve* or *Engel curve* is the set of optimal points traced out as income varies in this way, with prices constant. In the case illustrated both x_1 and x_2 are *normal goods*, for which demand increases as money income rises. However with different preferences the consumer might have chosen x^0 or x^+ on B_2. If x^0 had been chosen (if I_4 and not I_2 had been the consumer's indifference curve) then the demand for x_1 would have fallen as money income rose. x_1 would then be

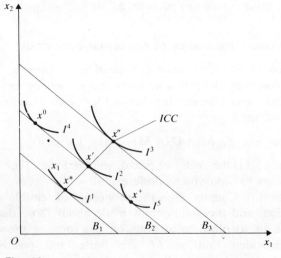

Fig. 10

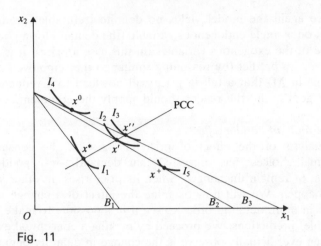

Fig. 11

known as an *inferior good*. It is clear that a rise in M may lead to a rise, a fall, or no change in the demand for a good. Without knowledge of preferences we cannot predict whether a particular good will be inferior or normal. The theory of consumer behaviour cannot be tested by considering the effect of changes in M on the demand for a single good, since any effect is compatible with the theory.

The theory does predict however that *all* goods cannot be inferior. If the consumer reduces his demand for all goods when his income rises he will be behaving in a way incompatible with our model: he will be behaving inconsistently. To show this, let x^* be the bundle chosen with an initial money income of M_1 and x' the bundle chosen when money income rises to M_2. If $x' < x^*$ i.e. if the demand for all goods is reduced, then x' must cost less than x^* since prices are held constant. x' was therefore available when x^* was chosen. But when x' was chosen x^* was still attainable (since money income had increased). The consumer therefore preferred x^* over x' with a money income of M_1 and x' over x^* with money income $M_2 > M_1$. He is therefore inconsistent: his behaviour violates the *transitivity assumption* of section A, and our model would have to be rejected.

If we now turn to the effects of changes in prices on the consumer's demands, Fig. 11 shows the implications of a fall in the price of x_1 with money income held constant. B_1 is the initial budget line, x^* the initial optimal bundle. A fall in p_1, say from p_1 to p'_1 causes the budget line to shift to B_2. x' is the optimal bundle on B_2, x'' the optimal bundle on B_3, which results from a further fall in p_1 from p'_1 to p''_1. The *price consumption curve* (PCC) is traced out as the set of optimal bundles as p_1 varies. In this case the demand for both goods increases as p_1 falls. However, with different preferences the optimal bundle might have been x^0 or x^+ on B_2. If x^0 was the optimal bundle with $p_1 = p''_1$ then x_1 would be a *Giffen good*, the demand for which falls as its price falls. We conclude that the demand for a good may fall, rise or remain unchanged as a result of a change in a price facing the consumer. Once again the model yields no definite (refutable) prediction about the effect on a *single* endogenous variable (the demand for a good) of a change in *one* of the exogenous variables (in this case a price). It is again possible, however, to predict (by reasoning similar to that employed in the case of a change in *M*) that a fall in price will not lead to a reduction in demand for *all* goods, and the reader should supply the argument.

Income and substitution effects

The analysis of the effect of price changes on the consumer's demands (optimal choices) has suggested that demand for a good may increase, decline or remain unchanged, when its price rises; in other words anything may happen. We will now examine the effect of a change in the price of good 1 in more detail in order to see if it is possible to make more definite (refutable) predictions. We proceed by making a conceptual experiment. All we can ever actually observe is the change in quantity demanded following a price change. However, in order to say something more interesting about price-responses than we have been able to do so far, we carry out a purely theoretical analysis which decomposes the overall demand change into two components. We then use this decomposition to say something more definite about consumer behaviour.

In Fig. 12, it can be seen that the fall in price of good 1 does two things:

(i) it reduces the expenditure required to achieve the initial utility level I_1, allowing the higher utility level I_2 to be achieved with the same expenditure. Following J. R. Hicks, we then say that there has been an increase in the consumer's real income;

(ii) it changes the relative prices facing the consumer.

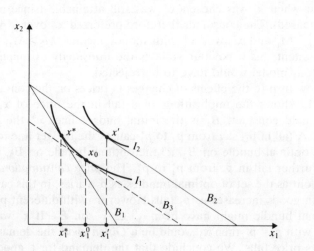

Fig. 12

In Fig. 12 we accordingly break down the change in demand for x_1 into:

(a) *the income effect*, which is the change resulting solely from the change in real income, with relative prices held constant; and

(b) *the own substitution effect*, which results solely from the change in p_1 with real income held constant

x^* and x' are the optimal bundles before and after the fall in p_1, B_1 and B_2 the corresponding budget lines. The *compensating variation* in money income is that change in M which will make the consumer just as well off after the price fall as he was before. In other words there will be some reduction in M after the price fall which will 'cancel out' the real income gain and return the consumer to his initial indifference curve I_1. The budget line is shifted inwards (reducing M) parallel with the post-price fall budget line B_2 until at B_3 it is just tangent to the original indifference curve I_1. If the consumer were confronted with this budget line he would choose bundle x^0. The difference between x^* and x^0 is due to a change in relative prices with real income (utility) held constant. The difference between x^0 and x' is due to the change in money income with relative prices held constant. x_1^*, x_1' and x_1^0 are the amounts of x_1 contained in the bundles x^*, x', x^0 and

(i) $x_1^0 - x_1^*$ is the own substitution effect,

(ii) $x_1' - x_1^0$ is the income effect,

(iii) $(x_1^0 - x_1^*) + (x_1' - x_1^0) = x_1' - x_1^*$ is the total *price effect*.

The purpose of carrying out this experiment in hypothetical compensation is to isolate the fact that the own substitution effect will always be positive in the case of a price fall and negative for a price rise. The (absolute value of the) slope of the indifference curve declines from left to right, i.e. as more x_1 and less x_2 is consumed the curve flattens. The fall in p_1 flattens the slope of the budget line, and hence the budget line B_3 *must* be tangent with I_1 to the right of x^*, i.e. at a bundle containing more x_1.

The income effect happens also to be positive in this particular case: x_1 is a normal good. If x_1 is inferior then the income effect is negative, x' contains *less* x_1 than x^0 and the price effect is smaller than the substitution effect. In Fig. 13(a) the income effect partially offsets the substitution effect

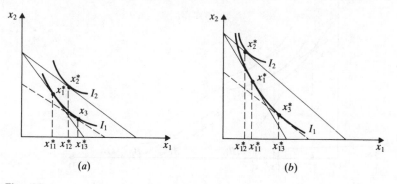

(a)   (b)

Fig. 13

but the price effect is still positive: a fall in p_1 still leads to a rise in the demand for x_1. In Fig. 13(b) the negative income effect more than offsets the positive substitution effect and x_1 is a Giffen good. Hence inferiority is a necessary, but not sufficient, condition for a good to be a Giffen good.

This decomposition of the price effect has generated two further predictions:

(i) *A normal good cannot be a Giffen good.* Hence, if we observe that a consumer increases his demand for a good when his money income rises (other things including prices being held constant), we would predict that if its price should fall, he will want to buy more of it. If we observe that he reduces his demand for the good when its price falls (and all other prices are constant and his money income is reasonably close to its original level), then the optimising model of consumer behaviour has yielded a false prediction.

(ii) *The own substitution effect is always of opposite sign to the price change.*

The above decomposition of the price effect into an income and substitution effect is based on the definition, made by J. R. Hicks, of unchanged *real income* as an unchanged *utility level.* E. Slutsky suggested an alternative definition of a constant real income as the ability to purchase the bundle of goods bought before the price change. This *constant purchasing power* definition has the advantage that it does not require detailed knowledge of the consumer's indifference map.

Figure 14 reproduces Fig. 11 with some additions to show the relationship between the Hicks and Slutsky definitions of a constant real income. The budget line B_4 just enables the consumer to buy x^*, the initially optimal bundle, at the lower price of p_1. Confronted with this budget line, the consumer actually chooses x^+. The price effect has been decomposed into an income effect $(x_1' - x_1^+)$ and an own substitution effect

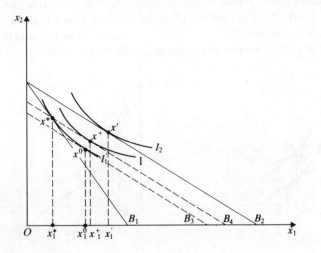

Fig. 14

$(x_1^+ - x_1^*)$. The income effect will again be positive, negative or zero depending on the form of the indifference map. The substitution effect will, as in the Hicksian case, always lead to a rise in demand for a good whose price has fallen. x^+ cannot lie to the left of x^* on B_4 because this would mean that the consumer is now choosing x^+ when x^* is still available, having previously rejected x^+ in favour of x^*. The transitivity assumption would be violated by such behaviour. The Slutsky definition yields a prediction (the sign of the substitution effect) which can be tested without specific knowledge of the consumer's indifference map to 'cancel out' the income effect.

Our consideration of the comparative static properties of the model has shown that it does not yield refutable predictions about the overall change in demand for individual goods induced by *ceteris paribus* changes in a price or money income. In other words

$$\frac{\partial x_i^*}{\partial p_j} = \frac{\partial D_i}{\partial p_j} \gtreqless 0 \qquad i, j = 1, 2, \ldots n.$$

and

$$\frac{\partial x_i^*}{\partial M} = \frac{\partial D_i}{\partial M} \gtreqless 0 \qquad i, j = 1, 2, \ldots n.$$

for every good and price. Only by considering the effect of changes in p_j or M on *all* goods, or by considering the effect of changes in p_j *and* M on a single good or by making more specific assumptions about the consumer's preferences can definite predictions be generated.

Consider, however, the consequences of equal proportionate changes in all prices and M. Suppose M increases to kM ($k > 1$) and prices to kp_1 and kp_2. The slope of the budget line will be unaffected. The intercept on the x_1 axis is M/p_1 before the changes in M and prices and $kM/kp_1 = M/p_1$ after the changes. Similarly for the intercept on the x_2 axis. Hence the equal proportionate changes in M and all prices alter neither the slope nor the intercepts on the budget line and so the feasible set is unaltered. If the feasible set is unchanged then so is the optimal bundle.

The model therefore predicts that the consumer will not suffer from *money illusion*; he will not alter his behaviour if his purchasing power and relative prices are constant, irrespective of the general level of prices and money income. More formally the demand function D_i for every commodity is *homogeneous of degree zero* in prices and money income, since we have:

$$x_i^* = D_i(kp, kM) = k^0 D_i(p, M) = D_i(p, M) \qquad \text{[D.2]}$$

Though it is difficult to test the general theory of consumer behaviour outlined above in which the consumer is considered to maximize a general, unspecified utility function subject to his budget constraint it is possible to derive more easily testable predictions by assuming that the utility function has a particular form i.e., by making more specific assumptions about his preferences. For example, consider the assumption that the consumer's attitude to any good is determined solely by his consumption of that good and is unaffected by the level of consumption of any other good. Assume, in other words, that the utility function has an *additive separable* form:

$$u = u(x_1, x_2, \ldots, x_n) = f_1(x_1) + f_2(x_2) + \ldots + f_n(x_n) \qquad [D.3]$$

with $f_i' > 0$ and $f_i'' < 0$ for all goods. f_i' is the derivitive of $f_i(x_i)$ and is the marginal utility of x_i, hence $f_i' = u_i$. The equilibrium conditions in the tangency solution are

$$\frac{f_1'}{p_1} = \frac{f_2'}{p_2} = \ldots = \frac{f_n'}{p_n} = u_M. \qquad [D.4]$$

Suppose M is increased. The increase in M must be spent on at least one of the goods, say the nth, in which case f_n'/p_n becomes smaller. From the equilibrium conditions all the f_i'/p_i must become smaller. But this can only happen (with prices constant) if f_i' declines. f_i' can decline only if x_i increases. Hence the demand for all goods must increase if income rises: no good is inferior – an unambiguous prediction of the model.

By making similar specific restrictive assumptions about u it is possible to derive a number of clear predictions which can be used to test the particular version of the model being considered. One may in this way be able to rule out a large number of types of preferences, but one cannot thereby refute the general theory based on the assumptions made in this section. There are an infinite number of possible preference orderings (and hence utility functions) satisfying assumptions 1 to 7.

Demand curves

We will complete this section on comparative statics by deriving the demand curve from the utility maximization model. The individual's *demand curve* for a good shows how his desired or planned purchases of it vary as its price varies, other prices and income being held constant. As we have seen, a distinction can be drawn between constant *real* and constant *money* income and there are also two possible definitions of constant real income. Figure 15 shows the derivation of the three demand curves, corresponding to the different assumptions about what is held constant, from the consumer's indifference map. The upper part of Fig. 15 is Fig. 14 with two additions. The *PCC* (price consumption curve) shows the bundles chosen as p_1 varies with M constant (i.e. as the budget line pivots through x_2^0). The constant purchasing power consumption curve (CP) shows the bundles chosen as p_1 varies, with the consumer's money income varying so as just to enable the consumer to purchase the original bundle x^* (i.e. the Slutsky definition of constant real income is adopted and so the budget line pivots through x^*). The indifference curve I_1 shows how consumption varies as p_1 varies, with M varying to keep the consumer's utility level constant (i.e. the Hicks definition of constant real income is adopted and so the budget line slides round I_1). These three curves therefore show the change in the

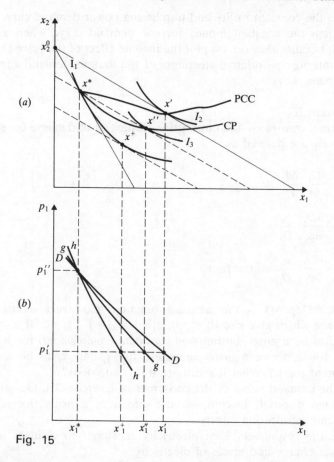

Fig. 15

demand for x_1 (and x_2) as p_1 changes with income (variously defined) and p_2 held constant. The lower half of the figure uses the information contained in the three curves to plot demand curves for x_1.

The *constant money income demand curve DD* shows the effect of changes in p_1 with M (and p_2) held constant. It plots the information contained in the price consumption curve. For example a fall in p_1 from p_1'' to p_1' with M constant causes the consumer to shift from bundle x^* to x' and his demand for x_1 to rise from x_1^* to x_1'.

The *constant purchasing power demand curve gg* corresponds to the CP curve. The fall in p_1 from p_1'' to p_1' with purchasing power constant causes the consumer to shift from x^* to x'' and his demand to increase from x_1^* to x_1''.

The *constant utility demand curve hh* is derived from the indifference curve I_1. The fall in p_1 with utility constant at its initial level $u(x^*)$ causes the consumer to shift from x^* to x^+, and his demand to increase from x_1^* to x_1^+.

The constant money income demand curve plots the whole price effect and the other two curves plot only the two versions of the substitution effect. Hence the constant utility and purchasing power demand curves will be steeper than the constant money income demand curve when x_1 is a normal good, because they do not plot the income effect of the price change. When x_1 is inferior the relative steepness of the various demand curves is reversed (explain why).

Exercise 3D

1. The income, own-price and cross-price elasticities of demand for good i respectively are defined as:

$$e_M^i = \frac{\partial D_i}{\partial M} \cdot \frac{M}{x_i}$$

$$e_i^i = -\frac{\partial D_i}{\partial p_i} \cdot \frac{p_i}{D_i}$$

$$e_j^i = -\frac{\partial D_i}{\partial p_j} \cdot \frac{p_j}{D_i} \qquad (i \neq j)$$

where $x_i = D_i(p, M)$ is the demand function. Construct indifference curve maps which give rise to $e_i^i = 0$, $e_i^i = 1$, $e_M^i = 1$, $e_M^i = 0$. If $e_j^i > (<)0$ x_i is said to be a *gross consumption substitute* (*complement*) for x_j. Is it possible for x_i to be a gross substitute for x_j and x_j to be a gross complement for x_i? What if there are only two goods?

2. Derive the demand curve of the consumer of Exercise 3B, Question 3, for garbage disposal. Decompose the effects of a price change into income and substitution effects.

3.* Examine the responses of an electricity consumer to changes in the connection charge and prices of electricity.

4.* Show that the following restrictions on the demand elasticities must hold:

(a) $\sum_i e_M^i \cdot s_i = 1$

(b) $\sum_j e_j^i = e_M^i$

(c) $\sum_i e_j^i \cdot s_i = s_j$

where s_i is the proportion of the budget spent on the ith good.

5.* Examine the income and substitution effects in the cases given in Exercise 3A, Question 4.

6. Explain the difference between the Hicks and Slutsky definitions of real income, and apply this to explain why, in Fig. 15, the demand curve hh is steeper than the demand curve gg.

7. Why do we decompose the price effect into income and substitution effects?

8. Explain why the demand curves derived in this section show relationships between price and *planned* or *desired* demand, and not necessarily the consumer's actual purchases.

9.* Examine the properties of the demand functions of a consumer with the following utility functions:

(a) $u(x) = x_1^{\alpha_1} \cdot x_2^{\alpha_2} \ldots x_n^{\alpha_n}$ $(\alpha_i > 0$, all i; $\Sigma \alpha_i = 1)$ (Cobb–Douglas)

(b) $u(x) = (x_1 - k_1)^{\alpha_1}(x_2 - k_2)^{\alpha_2} \ldots (x_n - k_n)^{\alpha_n}$ $(\alpha_i > 0$, all i; $\Sigma \alpha_i = 1$; $k_i > 0$, all i) (Stone–Geary)

(c) $u(x) = \Sigma_i f_i(x_i)$ (Additive separable)

What interpretation can be given to the k_i in case (b)?

E. Offer curves and net demand curves

We now consider the case of a consumer who has preferences satisfying the assumptions of section A, and is endowed, not with a given money income, but with fixed amounts of commodities which he can consume or sell on the market in order to finance purchases of other commodities. The feasible set is defined by the non-negativity requirements on consumption and by the constraint that the market value of the bundle consumed cannot exceed the market value of the consumer's initial endowments. His budget constraint is therefore:

$$\sum p_i x_i \le \sum p_i \bar{x}_i = W \qquad i = 1, 2, \ldots n \qquad \text{[E.1]}$$

where $\bar{x}_i$ is his *initial endowment of good i*. $\sum p_i \bar{x}_i = W$ is the market value of the initial endowment, or the proceeds which could be obtained if the consumer sold all his initial endowments at the ruling market prices. Since W is a stock of value owned by the individual, we could think of it as his wealth.

If x_i (the amount of commodity i *consumed*) exceeds $\bar{x}_i$, i.e. if:

(a) $\hat{x}_i = x_i - \bar{x}_i > 0$, then the consumer buys commodity i; and if

(b) $\hat{x}_i = x_i - \bar{x}_i < 0$, then he sells the commodity

where $\hat{x}_i$ is defined as the *net demand* for commodity i. This suggests that we can re-write the budget constraint as:

$$\sum p_i \hat{x}_i = \sum p_i \cdot (x_i - \bar{x}_i) \le 0 \qquad i = 1, 2, \ldots n \qquad \text{[E.2]}$$

which can be interpreted to mean that the sum of his expenditures on the quantities of goods he buys (which will be a positive component of the overall sum) cannot exceed the sum of the proceeds from the quantities of goods he sells (a negative component of the overall sum).

In the two-good case shown in Fig. 16 the budget line B is defined by

$$p_1 x_1 + p_2 x_2 = p_1 \bar{x}_1 + p_2 \bar{x}_2 = W \quad \text{or} \quad p_1(x_1 - \bar{x}_1) + p_2(x_2 - \bar{x}_2) = 0 \quad \text{[E.3]}$$

and has a slope of $-(p_1/p_2)$. B must pass through $\bar{x} = (\bar{x}_1, \bar{x}_2)$, the endowed bundle, since whatever prices he faces the consumer will always have the possibility of consuming his endowment, i.e. neither buying nor selling on

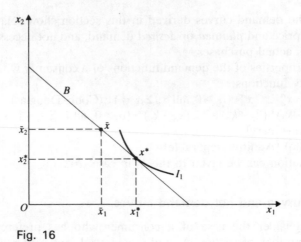

Fig. 16

the market. The feasible set is similar in shape to the case of the consumer endowed with a fixed money income M, but there are several significant differences as regards the effect of changes in prices:

(i) the market value of the endowment $W = \sum p_i \cdot \bar{x}_i$ will increase or decrease as the price of a commodity increases or decreases.

(ii) Since the consumer is always able to consume his initial endowment vector $\bar{x}$, a change in a single price will cause the budget line to pivot through $\bar{x}$, rather than through an intercept on one of the axes.

(iii) An equal proportionate change in all prices leaves the budget line unaffected, though the value of the endowments varies in the same proportion. The budget line must still pass through $\bar{x}$, and its slope will be unaffected by such price changes and hence its position is unchanged. Only changes in *relative* prices or in the initial endowments will alter the consumer's feasible set and therefore the consumer's demand or supply of a commodity. In the terminology of part D his demand functions will again be *homogenous of degree zero in prices*.

It is clear from the way in which the budget constraint E.1 was written that the consumer's optimization problem in this case is formally identical with that considered previously, so we will not dwell on the equilibrium conditions and the possibility of corner solutions. We will restrict ourselves to examining the comparative static properties of tangency solutions and the derivation of supply and demand curves.

In Fig. 16, $x^* = (x_1^*, x_2^*)$ is the optimal consumption bundle on B, where the indifference curve I_1 is tangent to the budget line. Since $\bar{x}_1 < x_1^*$ and $\bar{x}_2 > x_2^*$ the consumer is maximizing his utility by selling (supplying) commodity 2, which gives him receipts of $p_2 \cdot (\bar{x}_2 - x_2^*)$, and buying (demanding) commodity 1 at a cost of $p_1 \cdot (x_1^* - \bar{x}_1)$.

Increases in p_1 relative to p_2 will make the budget line pivot clockwise about $\bar{x}$ and the optimal bundle will vary as p_1/p_2 changes, as the upper half of Fig. 17 illustrates. With the budget line at B_2 the optimal bundle is the endowed bundle $\bar{x}$, and the consumer does not trade at all on the market. A further increase in p_1/p_2 will shift the budget line to B_3 where the optimal bundle is x' and the consumer is now selling commodity 1 and buying commodity 2.

The line FF in Fig. 17 is the locus of optimal bundles traced out as p_1/p_2 varies with $\bar{x}$ fixed and is called the *offer curve*, since it shows the amounts (positive or negative) of the two goods which the consumer offers on the market at different relative prices. The consumer's *consumption demand curve DD* in the lower half of Fig. 17, which plots the consumption of x_1 as a function of p_1/p_2, is derived from the offer curve. As p_1 increases relative to p_2 the consumer reduces his consumption of commodity 1, from x_1^* to $\bar{x}_1$ and then to x_1' as he moves along FF from x^* to $\bar{x}$ and x'. $(p_1/p_2)_1$, $(p_1/p_2)_2$ and $(p_1/p_2)_3$ are the price ratios at which x^*, $\bar{x}$ and x' are chosen.

The $\hat{D}\hat{D}$ curve in part (b) of Fig. 17 is the consumer's *net demand curve* and plots the net demand $\hat{x}_1 = x_1 - \bar{x}_1$, the amount of commodity 1 that he buys or sells on the market, against (p_1/p_2). It is derived by taking the horizontal distance between the DD curve and a vertical line through

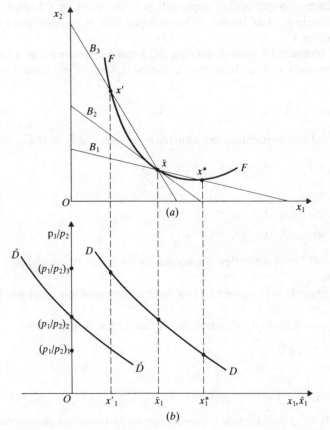

Fig. 17

$x_1 = \bar{x}_1$ at each price ratio. Notice that when $(p_1/p_2) > (p_1/p_2)_2$ the consumer's net demand is negative: he supplies commodity 1 to the market.

In the illustrations above the effect of a fall in the relative price of a commodity was to increase the consumer's demand for it. However with a different indifference map the DD and $\hat{D}\hat{D}$ curves could have been positively sloped, indicating that rises in the relative price of commodity 1 reduce the amount of the commodity supplied to the market. Hence a *ceteris paribus* change in a single price may increase, decrease or leave unchanged the individual's consumption of any single commodity. Similarly a *ceteris paribus* change in the initial endowment may increase, decrease or leave unchanged the consumption of commodity i. The comparative static properties of this model are so similar to those of the model in section C that we will leave their derivation to the exercises at the end of the section.

The consumption decision in terms of net demands*

The consumer's optimization problem studied earlier had the levels of consumption $(x_1, \ldots, x_n)$ as choice variables, but it is possible to formulate the problem with the consumer's net demands $(\hat{x}_1, \ldots, \hat{x}_n)$ as the choice variables. Since this particular approach will be used in Chapter 16 on general equilibrium, it is useful to show here that it is equivalent to the model of section C.

The consumer's utility function $u(x)$ can be rewritten as a function of the net demands $\hat{x}_i$ since from the definition $\hat{x}_i \equiv x_i - \bar{x}_i$ we have $x_i \equiv \hat{x}_i + \bar{x}_i$ and so

$$u(x_1, \ldots x_n) = u(\hat{x}_1 + \bar{x}_1, \ldots, \hat{x}_n + \bar{x}_n) \tag{E.4}$$

Since the initial endowments $\bar{x}_i$ are constants, u varies only as the x_i vary:

$$u(\hat{x}_1 + \bar{x}_1, \ldots, \hat{x}_n + \bar{x}_n) = \hat{u}(\hat{x}_1, \ldots, x_n) \tag{E.5}$$

and

$$\frac{\partial \hat{u}}{\partial \hat{x}_i} = \frac{\partial u}{\partial \hat{x}_i} = \frac{\partial u}{\partial \hat{x}_i} \frac{\partial \hat{x}_i}{\partial x_i} = \frac{\partial u}{\partial x_i} \tag{E.6}$$

$\hat{u}$ will have all the properties possessed by u such as continuity, quasi-concavity, etc.

The feasible set can also be rewritten in terms of the $\hat{x}_i$, as was shown in [E.2].

The non-negativity constraints on the x_i are replaced by

$$x_i = \hat{x}_i + \bar{x}_i \geq 0 \tag{E.7}$$

or

$$\hat{x}_i \geq -\bar{x}_i \qquad (j = 1, \ldots, n)$$

i.e. the supply of a good cannot exceed the endowment of that good. The consumer's optimization problem can now be written in terms of the net demands as (compare [C.1]):

$$\max \hat{u}(\hat{x}_1, \ldots, \hat{x}_n)$$
$$\text{s.t.} \sum p_i \hat{x}_i \leq 0 \qquad\qquad\qquad\qquad\qquad [E.8]$$
$$\hat{x}_i \geq -\bar{x}_i \qquad (i = 1, \ldots, n)$$

Proceeding, as in section C, to assume that the direct constraints [E.7] do not bind at the solution, the Lagrange function of the problem may be written

$$L = \hat{u}(\hat{x}_1, \ldots, \hat{x}_n) + \lambda [0 - \sum p_i \hat{x}_i]$$

or

$$L = \hat{u}(\hat{x}_1, \ldots, \hat{x}_n) - \lambda \sum p_i \hat{x}_i$$

First order conditions are

$$\frac{\partial L}{\partial \hat{x}_j} = \hat{u}_i - \lambda p_i = 0 \qquad (i = 1, \ldots, n) \qquad\qquad [E.9]$$

$$\frac{\partial L}{\partial \lambda} = -\sum p_i \hat{x}_i = 0 \qquad\qquad\qquad\qquad [E.10]$$

and from [E.6] we see that [E.9] is identical to [C.7], so that we would be able to derive exactly the same equilibrium conditions and comparative static properties as in section C.

This reformulation of the problem in terms of net demands rather than consumption bundles is, in terms of the diagrammatic analysis of Fig. 17, equivalent to shifting the origin to $\bar{x}$ so that $\hat{x}_1 = x_1 - \bar{x}_1$ and $\hat{x}_2 = x_2 - \bar{x}_2$ are measured along the axes. The budget line now passes through the new origin and the consumer's indifference map is unaffected. The reader should redraw Fig. 15 and the upper part of 16 in this way to convince himself that nothing of substance is affected by the relabelling.

Exercise 3E
1.* Show that all the predictions of sections 3C, 3D hold when the analysis is recast in terms of net demands.
2. How would you interpret the slope of the consumer's offer curve?
3. Explain why, at every point on the offer curve, there is a tangency between an indifference curve and the budget line generating that point.
4.* Discuss the relevance of the model examined in this section to:
  (a) a market in stocks and shares;
  (b) a market in new and secondhand cars;
  (c) the case where x_1 is bread and x_2 is leisure time, with $\bar{x}_1 = 0$ and $\bar{x}_2 = 24$ hours per day.

Appendix: The lexicographic ordering*

The significance of the lexicographic ordering is that it can be used to show the need for an assumption such as the continuity assumption, if we wish to work with a numerical representation of the consumer's preference ordering, i.e. with a utility function. The lexicographic ordering can be shown to satisfy the first three assumptions set out in section A (indeed the first four) but to be incapable of being represented by a utility function. On the other hand, it can be shown to give rise to perfectly well-defined demand functions, which implies that the continuity assumption is certainly not necessary for the existence of these.

The ordering takes the following form. Suppose consumption bundles consist only of two goods, i.e. $x = (x_1, x_2)$. Then the consumer's preferences are such that, given two bundles $x' = (x'_1, x'_2)$ and $x'' = (x''_1, x''_2)$:

(a) $x'_1 > x''_1$ implies $x' > x''$
(b) $x'_1 = x''_1$ and $x'_2 > x''_2$ implies $x' > x''$

In other words: the consumer always prefers a bundle with more of the first good in it, regardless of the quantity of the second good; only if the bundles contain the same amount of the first good does the quantity of the second matter. An illustration would be the case of a drunkard who would always prefer a combination of beer and bread with more beer in it to one with less, regardless of the amount of bread, but if the amounts of beer are the same, well he will prefer the one with more bread. It is called a 'lexicographic ordering' because it is analogous to the way words are ordered in a dictionary: A always comes before B, but if two words begin with A then the second letter determines the order they are placed in. Here the goods play the role of letters.

The indifference sets corresponding to this ordering are found with the help of Fig. 18. Take the bundle $x' = (x'_1, x'_2)$, and ask: what points are preferred to it, and to what points is it preferred? The area A, *including* the points on the solid line above x', must all be preferred to x', since points to the right of x' contain more x_1, while points along the solid line contain as much x_1 and more x_2. The area B, *including* the points on the broken line below x', must all be such that x' is preferred to them, since points to the left of x' contain less x_1, while points on the broken line contain as much x_1 but less x_2. But if all the points in A are preferred to x', and x' is preferred to all the points in B, there can be no other points indifferent to x', and so the indifference set for x' consists only of this single point. Since x' was chosen arbitrarily, this is true for every point in the space: each lies in an indifference set consisting only of itself.

The lexicographic ordering therefore does not satisfy the assumption of continuity, since the indifference set is a point and not a continuous surface. If we reduce the amount of x_1 in the bundle, by however small an amount, we can find no amount of x_2 to compensate for the change (the drunkard cannot be bribed by any amount of bread to give up even a sip of beer).

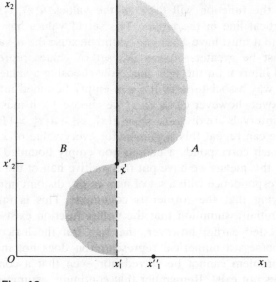

Fig. 18

An intuitive explanation of why this ordering cannot be represented by a utility function is as follows. The utility function has to associate with each bundle a real number. Consider the vertical line drawn through x' and extending indefinitely upwards and associate the real number $u(x')$ with x'. No point on this line is indifferent to any other, and so each must be given a different utility number. This would 'use up' all real numbers greater than $u(x')$. But if we increase x_1 from x'_1 to x''_1, we have another set of bundles, all preferred to the first set of bundles, and so all requiring higher real numbers. But none is available, because we used them up on the first line. In other words, there just aren't enough positive real numbers to provide a different utility number for each consumption bundle (= indifference set).

A more rigorous statement can be made as follows. First, we know that if we divide the real line-up into non-empty, non-overlapping (i.e. disjoint) bounded intervals, the set of these intervals is *countable*. That is, we can put them into a one-to-one correspondence with the set of positive integers, $\{1, 2, 3, \ldots\}$ so that even if we go on indefinitely, we can count them. On the other hand, the points on the real line itself or some interval of it, e.g. its positive half, are *not* countable; the line is infinitely dense and if we designate any two points as numbers n and $n+1$ there is always an infinite number of points in between which we have left out of our count. It follows that any argument which leads to the conclusion that the positive half of the real line is countable must be false. What we can show is that the assumption that a utility function exists for the lexicographic ordering does just that.

Suppose then that a utility function $u(x_1, x_2)$ exists, which gives a numerical representation of the lexicographic ordering. Refer back to Fig.

18. Setting $x_1 = x'_1$, the function will take on the values $u(x'_1, x_2)$ for all $x_2 \geq 0$ along the vertical line in the figure. This set of values has a lower bound at $u(x'_1, 0)$, and it must have an upper bound because the u-values for any $x_1 = x''_1 > x'_1$ must be greater. Hence this set of values represents a non-empty bounded interval on the real line. Now choosing a value $x''_1 > x'_1$ we can in the same way associate with it a non-empty bounded interval of real numbers. Moreover, however close to x'_1 we choose x''_1, it must always be the case that the intervals are disjoint, since $u(x''_1, x_2) > u(x'_1, x_2)$ for every x_2, since $x''_1 > x'_1$. We can repeat this argument for every value of x_1 on the horizontal axis: to each corresponds a unique non-empty bounded interval on the real line. But this means we have put the positive half of the real line into one-to-one correspondence with a set of non-empty disjoint intervals of the real line, implying that the former is countable. This is false, and therefore so is the initial assumption that the utility function exists.

As we suggested earlier however, the fact that the lexicographic ordering does not possess a numerical representation does not mean the consumer's choice problem cannot be solved nor even that a continuous demand function does not exist. Remember that continuity assumptions are usually sufficient rather than necessary. Thus in Fig. 19, B_1 is an initial budget constraint for a consumer with lexicographic preferences. It follows that his preferred choice is the bundle $x^* = (x^*_1, 0)$ – he spends all his income on x_1. If the price of good 1 falls so as to define the successive budget lines B_2 and B_3, he chooses the bundles $x' = (x'_1\ 0)$ and $x'' = (x''_1\ 0)$ respectively – he *always* spends all his income on x_1. It follows that his demand functions are:

$$x_1 = M/p_1, \qquad x_2 = 0$$

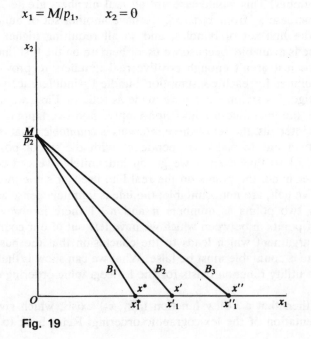

Fig. 19

which are perfectly well-defined and continuous. The first is, of course, a rectangular hyperbola in the (x_1, p_1) space, the second the vertical axis in the (x_2, p_2) space.

Exercise
1. Suppose that the consumer has lexicographic preferences as described in this appendix, but must consume a minimum level of x_2 for subsistence. Show how this affects the analysis of Fig. 19.
2. Likewise, show how the analysis is affected by the assumption that the consumer reaches a satiation level for x_1, beyond which only the marginal utility of x_2 is positive.
3. Generalise the statement of the lexicographic ordering to n goods. What would be the demand functions with and without subsistence and satiation levels of each good?
4. How plausible do you find the assumption that a consumer has a lexicographic preference ordering with respect to:
   (a) each good taken separately;
   (b) groups of goods, e.g. food, clothing, shelter, entertainment?

References and further reading

A general introduction to the theory of consumer behavior and its application is:
   H. A. J. Green. *Consumer Theory*, Macmillan, London, 1976.
The preferences of the consumer are considered in some detail in:
   P. Newman. *The Theory of Exchange*, Prentice-Hall, Englewood Cliffs, N.J., 1965, Ch. 2,
and at a more advanced mathematical level in:
   G. Debreu. *Theory of Value*, John Wiley, New York, 1959, Ch. 4.
An excellent and lucid account of the history of utility theory is:
   G. J. Stigler. 'The development of utility theory', *Journal of Political Economy*, August, October 1950.
The approach set out in this chapter has been criticized by:
   E. J. Mishan. 'Theory of consumer behavior: a cynical view', *Economica*, 1961;
   S. Mohun. 'Consumer Sovereignty', in F. Green and Petter Nore (Editors), *Economics: An Anti-Text*, Macmillan, London, 1977.

Chapter 4

Consumer theory: extensions and applications*

In this chapter we analyse two new concepts: (a) the expenditure function, which relates the minimum expenditure necessary to achieve a specified utility level to the prices faced by the consumer; and (b) the consumer's indirect utility function, which shows the dependence of utility on prices and income. These two concepts are introduced for three reasons. First, they can be used to confirm in a more rigorous way some results derived graphically in the previous chapter. Secondly, they provide some new results without the use of some rather tedious mathematics with little intuitive economic appeal. Finally the two concepts help to answer an important practical problem: how can the benefits (or losses) to consumers arising from changes in prices be measured?

A. The expenditure function

The expenditure function is derived from what appears to be the rather artificial optimization problem of minimizing the total expenditure necessary for the consumer to achieve a specified level of utility u^0:

$$\min_{x_1,\ldots,x_n} \sum p_i x_i \quad s.t. \quad \text{(i)} \quad u(x_1,\ldots,x_n) \geq u^0$$

$$\text{(ii)} \quad x_i \geq 0 \quad (i = 1,\ldots,n) \tag{A.1}$$

If all prices are positive the first constraint in [A.1] will be satisfied as an equality in the solution, since if $u(x) > u^0$ expenditure can be reduced without violating the constraint. If it is further assumed that all x_i are strictly positive in the solution, we can write the Lagrange function for the problem (with μ as the Lagrange multiplier) as

$$L = \sum p_i x_i + \mu[u^0 - u(x_1,\ldots,x_n)] \tag{A.2}$$

and the necessary conditions for a minimum of L will also be the necessary conditions for a minimum of [A.1].

The necessary conditions are

$$\frac{\partial L}{\partial x_i} = p_i - \mu u_i = 0 \qquad (i = 1, \ldots, n) \qquad \text{[A.3]}$$

$$\frac{\partial L}{\partial \mu} = u^0 - u(x_1, \ldots, x_n) = 0 \qquad \text{[A.4]}$$

The conditions on the x_i bear a striking resemblance to [C.9], [C.10] in Chapter 3. Writing them as $p_i = \mu u_i$ and dividing the condition on x_i by the condition on x_j gives

$$\frac{p_i}{p_j} = \frac{u_i}{u_j} \qquad \text{[A.5]}$$

which is identical with Chapter 3 [C.2]: the ratio of prices is equated to the marginal rate of substitution. This is not surprising as examination of the two-good case in Fig. 1 indicates. The indifference curve I_0 shows the combinations of x_1 and x_2 which give a utility level of u^0 and the feasible set for the problem is all points on or above I_0. The lines m_0, m_1, m_2, are isoexpenditure lines similar to the budget lines of earlier diagrams. m_0, for example, plots all bundles costing m_0, i.e. satisfying the equation $p_1x_1 + p_2x_2 = m_0$. The problem is to find the point in the feasible set which is on the lowest isoexpenditure line. This will, in the tangency solution shown here, be where the indifference curve I_0 is tangent to the isoexpenditure line m_0. The problem confronting the utility maximizing consumer is to move along his budget line until the highest indifference curve is reached. The expenditure minimizing problem is to move along the indifference curve until the lowest isoexpenditure line is reached.

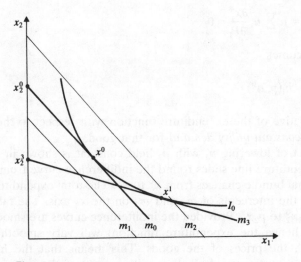

Fig. 1

The optimal x^* in problem [A.1] will depend on the prices and the utility level u^0:

$$x_i^* = h_i(p_1, \ldots, p_n; u^0) = h_i(p; u^0) \qquad (i = 1, \ldots n) \qquad \text{[A.6]}$$

and $h_i(p, u^0)$ is the *constant utility demand function* for x_i. (We have already considered the graphical derivation of the constant utility demand curve in section 3D.) Substituting the optimal values of the x_i in $\sum p_i x_i$ gives

$$\sum p_i x_i^* = \sum p_i h_i(p, u^0) = m(p, u^0). \qquad \text{[A.7]}$$

$m(p, u^0)$ is the *expenditure function*, showing the minimum level of expenditure necessary to achieve a given utility level as a function of prices and the required utility level.

We can consider the comparative statics properties of the model by examining the effect on m and x^* of changes in prices. The effect of *ceteris paribus* change in p_i on m is found by partially differentiating m with respect to p_i

$$\frac{\partial m}{\partial p_i} = \frac{\partial}{\partial p_i}\left(\sum p_j x_j^*\right) = \sum p_j \frac{\partial x_j^*}{\partial p_i} + x_i^* \qquad \text{[A.8]}$$

From the first-order conditions (with all $x_i^* > 0$), $p_j = \mu u_j$ so that

$$\sum p_j \frac{\partial x_j^*}{\partial p_i} = \mu \sum u_j \frac{\partial x_j^*}{\partial p_i}$$

When p_i varies the x_j^* must vary in such a way that the utility level is maintained at $u(x_1, \ldots, x_n) = u^0$

i.e. $\quad \dfrac{du}{dp_i} = \sum u_j \dfrac{\partial x_j^*}{\partial p_i} = 0$

Hence

$$\sum p_j \frac{\partial x_j^*}{\partial p_i} = \mu \sum u_j \frac{\partial x_j^*}{\partial P_i} = 0$$

So that [A.8] becomes

$$\frac{\partial m}{\partial p_i} = x_i^* = h_i(p, u^0) \qquad \text{[A.9]}$$

The partial derivative of the expenditure function with respect to the price of a good is the *constant utility demand* for that good.

The effect of lowering p_1 with p_2 held constant is shown in Fig. 1. The optimal expenditure line slides round the indifference curve from m_0 to m_3 and the optimal bundle changes from x^0 to x^1. The total expenditure can be read off from the intercepts of m_0 and m_3 on the x_2 axis. The fall in p_1 lowers m from $p_2 x_2^0$ to $p_2 x_2^3$. Provided the indifference curves are smooth the optimal x_i (and hence the expenditure function) will vary smoothly and continuously with the prices of the goods. This means that the $h_i(p, u^0)$ functions will have continuous derivatives with respect to the prices.

These derivatives have an interesting economic interpretation. $\partial h_i / \partial p_i$ is the change in x_i induced by a change in p_i *with utility held constant*. It is the *own substitution effect* of a price change which we first came across in Chapter 3 section D. Analogously we can describe $\partial h_i / \partial p_j$ as the *cross-substitution effect*.

Now if some function $f(x, y)$ has continuous cross partial derivatives $f_{xy} = \partial(\partial f/\partial x)/\partial y$ and $f_{yx} = \partial(\partial f/\partial y)/\partial x$, then $f_{xy} = f_{yx}$. From [A.9] we see that $\partial h_i / \partial p_j$ is the cross partial of $m(p, u^0)$, and it is continuous. Hence

$$\frac{\partial^2 m}{\partial p_i \, \partial p_j} = \frac{\partial h_i}{\partial p_j} = \frac{\partial h_j}{\partial p_i} = \frac{\partial^2 m}{\partial p_j \, \partial p_i} \qquad [A.10]$$

By considering the comparative static properties of the expenditure minimizing problem we have been able to deduce a general result of the consumer's utility maximization problem: *the cross-substitution effects are equal*:

$$\left. \frac{\partial x_i^*}{\partial p_j} \right|_{u=u^0} = \left. \frac{\partial x_j^*}{\partial p_i} \right|_{u=u^0}$$

Concavity of the expenditure function

Suppose that a single price p_i increases from p_i^0 to p_i^1. The consumer can maintain the same utility level by continuing to consume the same bundle as before the price change and if he does so his expenditure will have to increase by $(p_i^1 - p_i^0) \cdot h_i(p^0, u^0)$, i.e. in proportion to the change in p_i or linearly with p_i. But the consumer will usually be able to do better (i.e. spend less) than by consuming his original bundle when p_i varies, as Fig. 1 indicates. Hence expenditure will increase less than in proportion to p_i. The possibility of substitution suggests that the expenditure function is concave in p. This can in fact be established rigorously, provided that u satisfies the assumptions of the previous chapter.

The concavity of m in p can be used to establish another result derived in section 3C by other means. Since m is concave in p

$$\frac{\partial^2 m}{\partial p_i^2} = \frac{\partial h_i}{\partial p_i} < 0 \qquad [A.11]$$

Hence *the own substitution effect is negative*.

Exercise 4A

1. What is the economic interpretation of μ in A3? What is the relationship between μ and λ $(= u_M)$ in section 3C?

2.* If $\hat{e}_j^i = (-\partial h_i / \partial p_j)(p_j / h_i)$ $(j = 1, \ldots, n)$ is the constant utility elasticity of demand for good i with respect to the jth price, show that

   (a) $\sum_j \hat{e}_j^i = 0$

   (b) $\sum_i \hat{e}_j^i \cdot s_i = 0$ $(s_i = p_i h_i / m)$

3.* If $\hat{e}_j^i > (<)0$ goods i and j are said to be *Hicks–Allen complements (substitutes)*, does $\hat{e}_j^i = \hat{e}_i^j$? If i and j are Hicks–Allen substitutes are they also gross consumption substitutes (Exercise 3D, Question 1)?

4.* Show that the expenditure function for the Cobb–Douglas utility function (Exercise 3D, Question 9) in the two-good case is

$$m = \delta u^\delta \left(\frac{p_1}{\alpha_1}\right)^{\alpha_1/\delta} \left(\frac{p_2}{\alpha_2}\right)^{\alpha_2/\delta}$$

where $\delta = \alpha_1 + \alpha_2$. If the price of good 1 doubles by how much must the consumer's income increase to keep his utility constant?

B. The indirect utility function

The indirect utility function is derived from the consumer problem of maximizing $u(x_1, \ldots, x_n)$ subject to the budget $(\sum p_i x_i \leq m)$ and non-negativity constraints. We saw in section 3D that the x_i which are optimal for this problem will be functions of the p_i and M: $x_i^* = D_i(p_1, \ldots, p_n, M) = D_i(p, M)$. The *maximized* value of $u(x_1, \ldots, x_n) = u(x_1^*, \ldots, x_n^*)$ will therefore also be a function of the p_i and M:

$$u(x_1^*, \ldots, x_n^*) = u(D_1(p, M), \ldots, D_n(p, M))$$
$$= u^*(p, M) = u^*(p_1, \ldots, p_n, M) \qquad [\text{B.1}]$$

u^* is known as the *indirect utility function* since utility depends indirectly on prices and money income via the maximization process, in contrast to the normal utility function $u(x_1, \ldots, x_n)$ where u depends directly on the x_i. We can use u^* to investigate the effects of changes in prices and money income on the consumer's utility.

From the definition of u^*:

$$\frac{\partial u^*}{\partial M} = u_1 \frac{\partial x_1^*}{\partial M} + \ldots + u_n \frac{\partial x_n^*}{\partial M}$$

and from the equilibrium conditions for an interior solution (see section 3C) $u_i = \lambda p_i$ so

$$\frac{\partial u^*}{\partial M} = \lambda p_1 \frac{\partial x_1^*}{\partial M} + \ldots + \lambda p_n \frac{\partial x_n^*}{\partial M} = \lambda \sum p_i \frac{\partial x_i^*}{\partial M} \qquad [\text{B.2}]$$

When M varies the budget constraint $\sum p_i x_i^* = M$ must still be satisfied despite the changes in the optimal x_i, hence

$$\frac{d}{dM} \left(\sum p_i x_i^*\right) = \frac{dM}{dM}$$

or

$$\sum p_i \frac{\partial x_i^*}{\partial M} = 1$$

Therefore, by substituting this in [B.2] we obtain

$$\frac{\partial u^*}{\partial M} = \lambda \qquad \qquad [B.3]$$

a result that we discussed at some length in section 3C and which does not require further discussion.

The effect of a change in p_i on u^* can be found by a similar procedure. Differentiating u^* with respect to p_i:

$$\frac{\partial u^*}{\partial p_i} = \sum u_k \frac{\partial x_k^*}{\partial p_i} = \lambda \sum p_k \frac{\partial x_k^*}{\partial p_i} \qquad \qquad [B.4]$$

The budget constraint must still be satisfied so that

$$\frac{d}{dp_i} \left(\sum p_k x_k^* \right) = \frac{dM}{dp_i} = 0$$

and so

$$\sum p_k \frac{\partial x_k^*}{\partial p_i} + x_i^* = 0$$

or

$$-x_i^* = \sum p_k \frac{\partial x_k^*}{\partial p_i}$$

Substitution of this in [B.4] gives Roy's Identity:

$$\frac{\partial u^*}{\partial p_i} = -\lambda x_i^* \qquad \qquad [B.5]$$

The expression on the righthand side of [B.5] can be given an intuitive justification. An increase in p_i is a reduction in the purchasing power of the consumer's money income M, and since he spends $p_i x_i^*$ on good i his purchasing power falls at the rate $d(p_i x_i^*)/dp_i = x_i^*$ (or rises at the rate $-x_i^*$) as p_i varies. λ is the marginal utility of money income. The product of λ and $-x_i^*$ is the rate at which utility varies with money income, times the rate at which (the purchasing power of) money income varies with p_i, and so this product yields the rate of change of utility with respect to p_i.

The Slutsky equation

We can now use the expenditure and indirect utility functions to obtain a result which would otherwise require more technical pieces of mathematics. We set the utility level constraint u^0 in the expenditure minimization problem equal to the maximized level of u derived from the utility maximization problem:

$$u^0 = u^*(p, M). \qquad \qquad [B.6]$$

Then the x_i optimal for the expenditure minimization problem will be the x_i optimal for the utility maximization problem:

$$x_i^* = h_i(p, u^0) = D_i(p, M) \qquad \text{[B.7]}$$

(It will also be true that the minimized level of expenditure $m(p, u^0)$ will equal M.)

Now consider the effect of changes in p_j on the utility maximizing consumer's demand for x_i. Changes in p_j will cause the consumer's utility level u^* to alter. Hence as p_j varies h_i will alter because (a) h_i depends directly on p_j and (b) our requirement that $u^0 = u^*$ ensures that changes in u^* cause changes in u^0 and hence in h_i. We can see this if [B.6] is substituted in [B.7] to give

$$h_i(p, u^*(p, M)) = D_i(p, M). \qquad \text{[B.8]}$$

In the expenditure minimization problem u^0 is held constant as p_j varies whereas in this case we allow u^0 to vary with u^* because we want to examine the effects of changes in p_j on the *utility maximizing* demand for x_i, rather than on the *expenditure minimizing* demand.

Differentiating both sides of [B.8] with respect to p_j yields

$$\frac{\partial h_i(p, u^*(p, M))}{\partial p_j} = \frac{\partial h_i}{\partial p_j} + \frac{\partial h_i}{\partial u^0} \cdot \frac{du^0}{du^*} \frac{\partial u^*}{\partial p_j} = \frac{\partial D_i}{\partial p_j} \qquad \text{[B.9]}$$

In other words the utility maximizing demand for x_i varies in two ways as p_j varies. Firstly there is the direct effect of p_j on x_i due solely to the change in relative prices with utility held constant. This is the *partial* derivative of $h_i(p, u^*)$ with respect to p_j, i.e. $\partial h_i/\partial p_j$ and is the *cross substitution* effect. Secondly changes in p_j change the consumer's utility level when M is fixed, and the effect of this is shown by the second expression in the middle term of [B.9]. $\partial h_i/\partial u^0$ is the rate at which the demand for x_i varies when the required utility level changes *with prices held constant*. du^0/du^* is the rate at which the required utility level changes as the maximized level of utility alters and from [B.6] $du^0/du^* = 1$. Finally, in this expression $\partial u^*/\partial p_j$ is the rate at which the maximized value of utility changes as p_j increases.

[B.9] can be simplified by using the result obtained by differentiating [B.8] with respect to M:

$$\frac{dh_i(p, u^*(p, M))}{dM} = \frac{\partial h_i}{\partial u^0} \cdot \frac{du^0}{du^*} \cdot \frac{\partial u^*}{\partial M} = \frac{\partial D_i(p, M)}{\partial M} \qquad \text{[B.10]}$$

Now from [B.5] we have $\partial u^*/\partial p_j = -\lambda x_j$ and from [B.3] $\partial u^*/\partial M = \lambda$ so that in [B.9] we can write:

$$\frac{\partial h_i}{\partial u^0} \cdot \frac{du^0}{du^*} \cdot \frac{\partial u^*}{\partial p_j} = -\frac{\partial h_i}{\partial u^0} \cdot \frac{du^0}{du^*} \lambda \cdot x_j$$

$$= -\frac{\partial h_i}{\partial u^0} \cdot \frac{du^0}{du^*} \cdot \frac{\partial u^*}{\partial M} \cdot x_j = -\frac{\partial D_i}{\partial M} \cdot x_j \qquad \text{[B.11]}$$

and substituting [B.10] in [B.11], [B.9] can be written

$$\frac{\partial h_i}{\partial p_j} - \frac{\partial D_i}{\partial M} \cdot x_j = \frac{\partial D_i}{\partial p_j} \qquad \text{[B.12]}$$

This expression is known as the *Slutsky equation*. As we argued in discussing [B.5], $-x_j$ is the rate at which the purchasing power of money income increases as p_j increases, $\partial D_i / \partial M$ is the effect of changes in money income on the demand for x_i, and so $-x_j \cdot \partial D_i / \partial M$ is the *income effect* of a change in p_j on the demand for x_i: the rate at which demand for x_i changes as a result solely of the induced change in the consumer's real income. We have therefore again decomposed the effect of a change in price on demand into the income and substitution effects, but this time using a more exact mathematical method rather than the earlier geometrical reasoning.

Notice that the income effect is zero (when $x_j^* > 0$ and the consumer is not satiated so that $\partial u^* / \partial M > 0$) if and only if $\partial h_i / \partial u^0 = 0$. This requires that the consumer's indifference curves be vertically parallel: a change in the required utility level will have no effect on the optimal amount of x_j^* if the slopes of the indifference curves are equal at a given level of x_j, since the tangency between an isoexpenditure line and the required indifference curve will occur at the same level of x_j irrespective of the utility level (draw the diagram).

Exercise 4B
1. Express the Slutsky equation in elasticity form.
2.* Derive the indirect utility function for the Cobb–Douglas utility function (Exercise 3D, Question 9) and use it to test the properties of indirect utility functions discussed in this section.

C. Measuring the benefits of price changes

We often wish to measure the benefit to consumers of a change in the price of a commodity. The price change may result, for example, from changes in duties on imported goods, or alterations in the rate of purchase tax and we may want to estimate the effects of these on consumers' welfare for public policy purposes. We know that a change in a price will alter the feasible set confronting a consumer, that a new optimal bundle of goods will result, and that the consumer will be on a new indifference curve. In the case of a price fall the consumer will be better off in the sense that he prefers the new bundle to the initial one. How can we measure this benefit to the consumer? One suggestion might be the change in the utility level of the consumer. This suffers from a number of serious drawbacks. Firstly, it is not objective, in that we cannot observe utility levels. Secondly, because the utility function is only unique up to a positive monotone transformation (recall section 3A), a utility measure of the benefits would be affected by the choice of utility function used to represent the preferences of the consumer. In other words, as we saw in section 3A, no significance attaches to the size of utility differences, only to their *sign*. This means that a utility measure would be essentially arbitrary. Furthermore, any utility measure would not be comparable amongst different individuals and we could not add utility differences for a measure of total benefit to all consumers.

A measure which at least avoids this last problem is the consumer's own monetary valuation of the price change. Since the measure is expressed in terms of money, individual measures are at least commensurable and could *in principle* be added to form a measure of the aggregate benefit to all consumers of the good.

We stress 'in principle' because if the aggregate monetary measure is to be used for policy purposes, an important value judgement must be made before the individual monetary measures can be summed. This is that an extra £1 of benefit to an individual has the same social significance to whichever individual it accrues. This becomes particularly important in cost-benefit analysis when some individuals gain and others lose as a result of particular decisions. Then we have to make the value judgement that £1 of benefit to one individual can offset £1 of loss to another.

Figure 2 illustrates the effect of a fall in the price of good 1 from p_1^0 to p_1^1 with money income and the price of good 2 held constant. The consumer's initial bundle is A on I_0 and the bundle chosen after the fall in p_1 is B on I_1. The consumer is better off, but what is his monetary valuation of this change in his utility? One answer is the amount of money he would be prepared to pay for the opportunity of buying good 1 at the new price rather than at the old price. This is the *compensating variation* (*CV*) measure and is defined formally as the amount of money which must be taken from the consumer in the new situation in order to make him as well off as he was in the initial situation. It is identical to the compensating variation in money income used in section 3D to decompose the price effect into income and substitution effects. Notice that the definition used here applies equally well to price rises, in which case the compensating variation will be negative: the consumer becomes worse off and must be given money to make him as well off with the new prices as he was with the old.

Unfortunately the *CV* measure is not the only plausible monetary measure of the gain to the consumer of a change in the price of a good. The *equivalent variation* (*EV*) is the amount of money which would have to be given to the consumer when he faces the initial price to make him as well off as he would be facing the now lower price with his initial income. Again the definition allows for a rise as well as a fall in price. Both the *CV* and *EV* definitions allow for more than one price to change at the same time, but we will restrict ourselves for the moment to the case of a single price change to keep the exposition simple.

The *EV* and *CV* are shown in Fig. 2(a). *CV* is the change in M required to shift the budget line from B_2 to B_3 so that the consumer's utility level after the price fall is the same as it was before. *CV* is equal to p_2 times the difference in the x_2 intercept of B_2 and B_3. *EV* is the change in M required to shift the budget line from B_1 to B_4 so that facing the initial prices he can just achieve

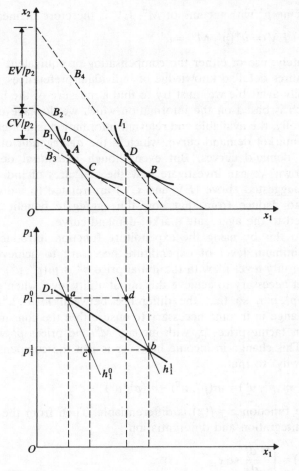

Fig. 2

the utility level he would have had with the new prices. EV is equal to p_2 times the difference in the x_2 intercept of B_1 and B_4. Notice that CV is not equal to EV in this example.

The distinction between EV and CV may be made clearer if we use the indirect utility function introduced in section B. In the initial situation the consumer faces prices $p^0 = (p_1^0, \ldots, p_n^0)$ with income M^0 and his maximized utility is $u^*(p^0, M^0) = u^0$. With the new prices $p^1 = (p_1^1, \ldots, p_n^1)$ and the same income his maximized utility becomes $u^*(p^1, M^0) = u^1$. CV is the change in money income necessary to make his utility when he faces p^1 equal to the initial utility level when he faced p^0 with an income of M^0. Hence CV is defined by

$$u^*(p^0, M^0) = u^*(p^1, M^0 - CV) = u^0 \qquad [C.1]$$

EV is the change in M necessary to make his utility when facing p^0 equal to his utility when facing p^1 with income of M^0. EV is therefore defined by

$$u^*(p^0, M^0 + EV) = u^*(p^1, M^0) = u^1 \qquad \text{[C.2]}$$

Unfortunately, use of either the compensating or equivalent variation measures requires detailed knowledge of individual preferences. Since these are not usually available we must try to find a measure of the benefit to consumers which is based on the information which we do have or can readily find. Generally, the available and relevant information is limited to a knowledge of the market demand curve, which is the *aggregation* of individual consumers' demand curves. But even though *individual* demand curves are not known we can investigate how the measures of individual consumer benefit suggested above (EV and CV) are related to individual demand curves and deduce from that how the aggregate benefit to all consumers is related to the aggregate market demand curve.

We can do this by using the expenditure function introduced in section F. The minimum level of expenditure necessary to achieve the consumer's initial utility level u^0 with the initial price p^0 is $m(p^0, u^0) = M^0$. The minimum level necessary to achieve this initial utility level when prices alter to p^1 is $m(p^1, u^0)$, so that the difference between $m(p^0, u^0)$ and $m(p^1, u^0)$ is the change in income necessary to ensure that the consumer is indifferent between facing prices p_0 with income M^0 and prices p^1 with a different income. This change in income however is just the compensating variation (explain why) so that:

$$CV = M^0 - m(p^1, u^0) = m(p^0, u^0) - m(p^1, u^0) \qquad \text{[C.3]}$$

Suppose that some function $z = f(x)$ is differentiable. Then from the relationship between integration and differentiation

$$f(x_0) - f(x_1) = \int_{x_1}^{x_0} \frac{df}{dx} \cdot dx$$

Applying the same idea to [C.3] gives

$$m(p^0, u^0) - m(p^1, u^0) = \int_{p_1^1}^{p_1^0} \frac{\partial m}{\partial p_1} \cdot dp_1$$

But we saw in section A that $\partial m/\partial p_1 = x_1^* = h_1(p, u^0)$ and so

$$CV = m(p^0, u^0) - m(p^1, u^0) = \int_{p_1^1}^{p_1^0} h_1(p, u^0) \, dp_1 \qquad \text{[C.4]}$$

$h_1(p, u^0)$ is the constant utility demand function for x_1, and if all other prices are held constant we can draw, as in Fig. 2(b), the constant utility demand curve h_1^0, showing the relationship between p_1 and x_1 when utility is constant at $u = u^0$. In Fig. 2(b) CV is the area between the price lines p_1^0 and p_1^1 and the constant utility demand curve h_1^0.

The consumer's market demand curve for x_1 is not, however, his constant utility demand curve but rather his constant money income demand curve, D_1, so the h_1^0 curve is unobservable. But we also saw in section 3D that since the constant utility demand curve plots the substitution effect of a price change and the constant money income demand curve plots the whole price effect (i.e. the substitution *and* income effects) the two curves will coincide if and only if the income effect is zero. Equivalently, as we saw in section A, the consumer's indifference curves must be vertically parallel.

When D_1 and h_1^0 coincide CV can be measured and is the area between the price lines p_1^0 and p_1^1 under the consumer's market demand curve. If the income effect is non-zero then what we *can* measure (the area under the consumer's market demand curve between the price lines) will not be equal to what we *wish* to measure (CV). In particular if x_1 is a normal good ($\partial D_1/\partial M > 0$) then D_1 *will exceed* h_1^0 for all $p_1 < p_1^0$ and the area under the D_1 curve between the price lines will exceed CV, as Fig. 2(b) illustrates.

Points A, B, C, in Fig. 2(a) correspond to points a, b, c, in Fig. 2(b) and D_1 cuts h_1^0 at a. If x_1 had been an inferior good then D_1 would have been below h_1^0 for $p_1 < p_1^0$ and CV would have been overestimated by the area under the D_1 curve between the price lines.

So far we have looked at the relationship between CV and the consumer's market demand curve, but a similar approach can be used for EV and D_1. The value of the expenditure function $M^1 = m(p^1, u^1)$ is the minimum expenditure necessary to achieve the *new* post-price change utility level and $m(p^0, u^1)$ is that necessary to achieve the *new* level of utility with the *initial* prices. Hence $EV = m(p^0, u^1) - m(p^1, u^1)$, and we can show that

$$EV = \int_{p_1^1}^{p_1^0} h_1(p, u^1)\, dp_1 \qquad\qquad \text{[C.5]}$$

In Fig. 2(b) h_1^1 is the constant utility demand curve for $u = u^1$ and EV is the area under h_1^1 and between the price lines p_1^0, p_1^1. Since the income effect is non-zero, h_1^1 and D_1 intersect at b and the area under D_1 between the price lines is an *underestimate* of EV.

The area under the aggregate market demand curve between the price lines is the sum of the corresponding areas under the individual consumer's constant money-income demand curves. Consumers will have different preferences and if for some of them x_1 is normal and for others inferior, income effects may tend to offset each other. In other words, the *algebraic* sum of the income effects rather than the sum of their absolute values is what determines the size of the error involved in using the area under the aggregate market demand curve between the price lines as an approximation to the EV or CV measures.

The magnitude of the individual income effects will depend upon the size of the price change and the importance of x_1 in the consumer's budget. For small price changes, and for goods which account for a small proportion of the consumer's expenditure, the area between the price lines and the market demand curve will provide a reasonably accurate measure of the benefits from the price change.

Multiple price changes

The same procedure as that just outlined can be used to measure the benefits of a change in more than one price. Consider Fig. 3. This shows the effect of lowering the prices of two goods which are gross complements in the sense that the demand for good 1 rises when the price of good 2 falls and *vice versa*. D_1^0 is the consumer's constant money income demand curve for good 1, given that the price of good 2 is at its initial level p_2^0. D_1^1 is the demand curve for good 1 given the now lower price of good 2 at p_2^1. D_2^0, D_2^1 are similarly interpreted for good 2, given the initial (p_1^0) and now lower (p_1^1) price of good 1. Suppose that income effects are zero for both goods. If p_2 is held constant at p_2^0 then the benefit to the consumer of the reduction in p_1 from p_1^0 to p_1^1 is the area A_1 between the price lines and D_1^0. The fall in p_1 shifts D_2 to D_2^1 from D_2^0. Now lower p_2 from p_2^0 to p_2^1 with p_1 constant at p_1^1. The benefit is again measured by the area between the price lines and relevent demand curve (D_2^1) and is the sum of A_2 and A_3. Hence the total benefit obtained from lowering p_1 and then lowering p_2 is

$$A_1 + A_2 + A_3 \qquad\qquad [C.6]$$

But suppose we had lowered p_2 first, with $p_1 = p_1^0$, and then lowered p_1? The benefit of lowering p_2 would have been A_2, since the consumer was on D_2^0. Lowering p_2 shifts D_1 to D_1^1. If p_1 is now lowered from p_1^0 to p_1^1 the benefit is the area between the price lines and D_1^1: $A_1 + A_4$. The total benefit from lowering p_2 and then p_1 is therefore

$$A_1 + A_2 + A_4 \qquad\qquad [C.7]$$

The measure of total benefit from multiple price changes *should be path-independent*: because the prices may *actually* change simultaneously the *notional* order in which we change them to calculate the benefit *should not affect the total benefit figure*. This requires that [C.6] and [C.7] be equal or that

$$A_3 = A_4$$

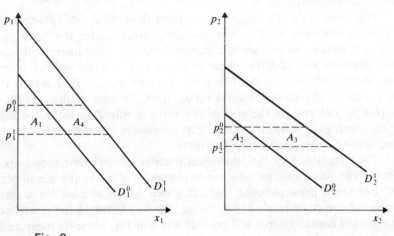

Fig. 3

But are these areas equal? If the price changes are not too large the demand curves may reasonably be regarded as linear over the range of prices considered. This means that A_3 and A_4 are parallelograms with areas

$$A_3 = \Delta p_2 \Delta x_2$$
$$A_4 = \Delta p_1 \Delta x_1 \qquad\qquad\qquad\qquad\qquad\qquad\text{[C.8]}$$

where Δp_i is the price change and Δx_i is the change in the consumption of x_i that results from the shift in D_i, with p_i constant. But D_i shifts because p_j has changed and so (provided Δp_j is not too large)

$$\Delta x_i = \frac{\partial x_i}{\partial p_j} \Delta p_j \qquad i, j = 1, 2. \qquad\qquad\qquad\text{[C.9]}$$

Substituting in C.8 we see that

$$A_3 = \Delta p_2 \frac{\partial x_2}{\partial p_1} \Delta p_1$$

$$A_4 = \Delta p_1 \frac{\partial x_1}{\partial p_2} \Delta p_2$$

so that $A_3 = A_4$ if

$$\frac{\partial x_1}{\partial p_2} = \frac{\partial x_2}{\partial p_1} \qquad\qquad\qquad\qquad\qquad\qquad\text{[C.10]}$$

i.e. the cross effects of price changes on demand are equal. In general the cross price effects are the sum of the income effect and the cross-substitution effect. (Recall the discussion of the Slutsky equation [B.12].) In order to use the area between the price lines and the constant money income demand curves as a measure of benefit we have assumed that income effects are zero for the goods being considered. Therefore the cross price effects consist solely of the cross-substitution effects, and in section A (equation [A.10]) we showed that cross-substitution effects are equal. Hence [C.10] is satisfied, A_3 *is* equal to A_4 and our measure of benefit is path-independent.

We must be careful however not to extend the measure too far. Recall from section 3D that not all goods can have zero income effects. If income effects are non-zero then what we *can* measure will not be what we *want to* measure and the benefit figure will not be independent of the order in which prices are assumed to be varied. Our measure is essentially partial: it cannot be used when we are considering changes in *all* prices. We must restrict it to situations in which only a relatively small number of prices are altered by the policy decisions we are examining.

Consumer surplus

This section has analysed the benefits to consumers of changes in the price of a good they are already consuming, but the results obtained can be extended fairly easily to the problem of measuring the benefits to consumers of having a good available at a given price as compared to a situation in which none of the good is available for consumption. This benefit is known as the *consumer's surplus* since consumers would in general be prepared to pay for the quantity currently being consumed an amount over and above their actual total expenditure on the good. The non-availability of a good is formally equivalent to having the good available at an arbitrarily high price, so that the benefit to consumers of having the good available at a given price is the *CV* or *EV* of a fall in price from some arbitrarily high price at which none is consumed to the given price at which some is consumed.

In Fig. 2(a) the initial indifference curve would be that through the intercept of B_1 on the x_2 axis indicating that no x_1 was consumed initially. The *CV* would then be the change in M required to return the individual to the initial indifference curve. In Fig. 2(b) the corresponding constant utility demand curve would be that with the same intercept on the p_1 axis as the constant money income demand curve D. The benefit to consumers of having x_1 available at p_1^1 is then the whole area above the p_1^1 price line and underneath the constant utility demand curve. When income effects are zero the consumer's surplus is the area between the price line and the market demand curve.

The measures of consumer benefit examined in this section enable us to quantify the effects of price changes on consumers but their usefulness depends crucially on the satisfaction of two conditions. First, since our information is (at best) limited to the market demand curves, what we wish to measure and what we can measure will coincide only if income effects are zero. This is a positive question to be settled by reference to the demand functions in any particular case, but the use of the measures will often have to be restricted to situations where only fairly small price changes are considered and not many prices change. Secondly, in order for it to be meaningful *to compare and add* the measures for different consumers (implicit in working with *market* demand curves) we must make the normative judgement that £1 has the same marginal social value irrespective of which individual gains or loses it. These two conditions mean that our measures are essentially both partial and value-loaded.

Exercise 4C
1. Show diagrammatically that the *EV* for a given price change is equal to the *CV* for a reversal of the price change.
2.* Suppose the consumer *sells* a good. How would you measure the gain to him of a rise in its price? How would the measures be related to his supply curve for the good? (Refer back to section 3E or forward to 5B.) How is the total benefit to the consumer of his ability to sell the good at the ruling price related to his supply curve? (This benefit is known as *economic rent* and is analogous to the consumer surplus.)
3. Is the change in expenditure on a good as a result of a change in its price a useful measure of the benefit to the consumer of the price

change? Is the change in the individual's earned income resulting from a change in the wage rate a useful measure of the benefit to him of the wage change?

4. If the individual is initially consuming x_1^0 of good 1 and its price falls by Δp_1, is $x_1^0 \Delta p_1$ an over- or under-estimate of the compensating variation? What does the size of the error depend on?

5. What is the analogous measure of the benefit to the consumer of a rise in the wage rate? How is it related to the compensating variation measure of the benefit of a wage rise?

6.* Let x_1^0 be the initial quantity of good 1 bought by a consumer before a change in the price of good 1, Δp_1 be the change in the price and Δx_1 be the change in quantity bought of good 1. Under what circumstances will $x_1^0 \Delta p_1 + \frac{1}{2}\Delta p_1 \Delta x_1$ equal the compensating variation?

7.* What, if anything, does the constancy of the marginal utility of money income imply about the income effect of price changes and hence the accuracy of measures of consumer surplus based on the constant money income demand curve?

8.* Suppose the consumer has the utility function $u = f(x_1, \ldots, x_{n-1}) + kx_n$, where k is some positive constant. Show that in this case $CV = EV$ for changes in p_i $(i = 1, \ldots, n-1)$ and that both can be measured by reference to the constant money income demand curve.

9.* Consider a consumer with a Cobb–Douglas utility function for goods 1 and 2 (Exercise 3D, Question 9) with α_1 and α_2 both equal to $\frac{1}{2}$. Assume that his income is £100 and that initially $p_1 = £10$ and $p_2 = £20$. Calculate the CV and EV for a rise in p_1 to £20. Compare the CV and the estimate based on the consumer's constant money income demand curve. How large is the error from using the constant money income demand curve as a proportion of the CV and of the consumer's income?

References and further reading

The first two sections of this chapter were concerned with what is known as 'duality' in consumer theory. For a thorough, though mathematically quite advanced, treatment of this topic see:

> **W. E. Diewert.** 'Applications of duality theory', in M. D. Intriligator and D. A. Kendrick (eds), *Frontiers of Quantitative Economics*, North-Holland, Amsterdam, 1974, Vol. II.

The vast literature on applications of consumer surplus as a welfare measure is surveyed in:

> **J. M. Currie, J. A. Murphy and A. Schmitz.** 'The concept of economic surplus and its use in economic analysis', *Economic Journal*, December 1971.

For a demonstration that the market demand curve can be used to provide a close approximation to the CV and EV measures see:

> **R. D. Willig.** 'Consumer's surplus without apology', *American Economic Review*, September 1976, pp. 589–97.

Chapter 5

Alternative models of consumer behaviour*

A. Revealed preference

We emphasized in Chapter 3 that utility functions are convenient numerical representations of preferences and that neither they nor the consumer's preferences are directly observable. This subjectivity of the foundations of consumer theory stimulated interest in the development of a theory of demand based solely on observable and measurable phenomena, namely the bundles actually bought by a consumer and the prices and money incomes at which they were bought. The emphasis in this approach is on assumptions about the consumer's *behaviour*, which can be *observed*, rather than on his preferences, which cannot.

As in the utility theory of Chapter 3, we will assume that the consumer faces a given price vector, p, and has a fixed money income, M. Our first behavioural assumption is that the consumer spends all his income, which has similar implications to assumption 4 of section 3A.

The second assumption is that only one commodity bundle x is chosen by the consumer for each price and income situation. In other words, confronted by a particular p vector and having a particular M, the consumer will always choose the same bundle.

The third assumption is that there exists one and only one price and income combination at which each bundle is chosen. It is assumed, therefore, that for a given x there is some p, M situation in which x will be chosen by the consumer and that situation is unique.

The fourth and crucial assumption is that the consumer's choices are consistent. By this we mean that, if a bundle x^0 is chosen and a different bundle x^1 could have been chosen, then when x^1 is chosen x^0 must no longer be a feasible alternative.

To amplify this, let p^0 be the price vector at which x^0 is chosen. Then if x^1 could have been chosen when x^0 was actually chosen, the cost of $x^1, p^0 x^1$, must be no greater than the cost of x^0, which is $p^0 x^0$. This latter is also the consumer's money income $M_0 = p^0 x^0$ when x^0 is chosen.

Similarly, let p^1 be the price vector at which x^1 is chosen. Then x^0 could not have been available at prices p^1, otherwise it would have been chosen. That is, its cost $p^1 x^0$ must exceed the cost of x^1, $p^1 x^1$, which equals the consumer's money income M_1 when x^1 is chosen. Hence this fourth assumption can be stated succinctly as

$$p^0 x^0 \geq p^0 x^1 \quad \text{implies} \quad p^1 x^1 < p^1 x^0 \qquad \text{[A.1]}$$

when x^0 is chosen at p^0, M_0 and x^1 at p^1, M_1. If x^0 is chosen when x^1 is purchasable x^0 is said to be *revealed preferred to* x^1. The statement [A.1] is usually referred to as the *weak axiom of revealed preference*.

This set of mild behavioural assumptions will generate all the utility based predictions of section 3D concerning the consumer's demand functions. Consider first the sign of the substitution effect. Figure 1 shows the consumer's initial budget line B_0, defined by price vector p^0 and money income M_0. The bundle chosen initially on B_0 is x^0. B_1 is the budget line after a fall in p_1 with M unchanged, and x^1 the new bundle chosen on B_1. Our behavioural assumptions do not place any restrictions on the location of x^1 on B_1 (explain). (Neither do the preference assumptions of section 3A, as section 3D shows.) As in section 3D, it is useful to partition the price effect (x^0 to x^1) into a change in x due solely to relative price changes (the substitution effect) and a change due solely to a change in real income. Since we have forsworn the use of utility functions in this section we cannot use the indifference curve through x^0 to define a constant real income. Instead we adopt the constant purchasing power or Slutsky definition of constant real income (see section 3D). Accordingly, the consumer's money income is lowered until, facing the new prices, he is just able to buy the initial bundle x^0. In Fig. 1 the budget line is shifted inward parallel with B_1, until at B_2 it passes through x^0. The consumer confronted with B_2 will buy the bundle x^2 to the right of x^0. Therefore x^0 to x^2 is the substitution effect and x^2 to x^1 the income effect of the fall in p_1.

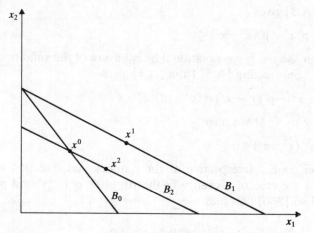

Fig. 1

We can now prove that if the consumer satisfies assumption [A.1] the substitution effect must always lead to an increase in consumption of the good whose price has fallen. This is easily done in the two-good example of Fig. 1. x^2 must lie on B_2 (by the assumption that all income is spent) and hence there are three possibilities: x^2 can be to the left or the right of, or equal to, x^0. x^2 cannot be to the left of x^0 on B_2 because these bundles are inside the consumer's initial feasible set and were rejected in favour of x^0. x^2 cannot equal x^0 because the prices at which x^2 and x^0 are chosen differ and, by our second assumption, different bundles are chosen in different price-income situations. Therefore x^2 must contain more x_1 than (i.e. be to the right of) x^0.

This result can be extended to the n-good case, and the proof is instructive because similar arguments will be used in section 9D to derive comparative statics predictions in the theory of the firm. We can generalize the steps in the analysis of Fig. 1 as follows. p^0, x^0 are the initial price vector and consumption bundle, p^1 and x^1 are the new price vector and consumption bundle. The consumer's income is adjusted until at M_2 he can just purchase x^0 at the new prices, p^1, so that $p^1 x^0 = M_2$. Faced with price vector p^1 and the compensated money income, M_2, the consumer chooses x^2 and because he spends all his money income we have that $p^1 x^2 = M_2$. Hence the compensating change in M ensures that

$$p^1 x^0 = M_2 = p^1 x^2 \qquad \text{[A.2]}$$

Now x^2 is chosen when x^0 is still available (i.e. they are both on the same budget plane) so that by our consistency assumption [A.1] we have

$$p^0 x^0 < p^0 x^2 \qquad \text{[A.3]}$$

or: x^2 was not purchasable when x^0 was bought. Rearranging [A.2] gives

$$p^1 x^0 - p^1 x^2 = p^1 (x^0 - x^2) = 0 \qquad \text{[A.4]}$$

and similarly [A.3] gives

$$p^0 x^0 - p^0 x^2 = p^0 (x^0 - x^2) < 0 \qquad \text{[A.5]}$$

(The reader can use the $\sum p_i x_i$ notation if he is unsure of the validity of these manipulations.) Subtracting [A.5] from [A.4] gives

$$p^1 (x^0 - x^2) - p^0 (x^0 - x^2) = (p^1 - p^0)(x^0 - x^2) > 0$$

and multiplying by (-1) we have

$$(p^1 - p^0)(x^2 - x^0) < 0 \qquad \text{[A.6]}$$

This prediction applies irrespective of the number and direction of price changes, but in the case of a change in the jth price *only*, p^1 and p^0 differ only in p_j and so [A.6] becomes

$$\sum_i (p_i^1 - p_i^0)(x_i^2 - x_i^0) = (p_j^1 - p_j^0)(x_j^2 - x_j^0) < 0 \qquad \text{[A.7]}$$

Hence when p_j changes the substitution effect $(x_j^2 - x_j^0)$ is of opposite sign to the price change. The constant purchasing power demand curve will therefore slope downwards.

We can also derive the Slutsky equation of section 4B from the behavioural assumptions. Since $M_2 = p^1 x^0$ and $M_0 = p^0 x^0$ the compensating reduction in M is

$$\Delta M = M_0 - M_2 = p^0 x^0 - p^1 x^0 = (p^0 - p^1) x^0 = -(p^1 - p^0) x^0$$

and in the case of a change (Δp_j) in p_j only we have

$$\Delta M = -\Delta p_j x_j^0 \qquad [A.8]$$

The price effect of p_j on x_j is $(x_j^1 - x_j^0)$ and this can be partitioned into the substitution $(x_j^2 - x_j^0)$ and income $(x_j^1 - x_j^2)$ effects:

$$x_j^1 - x_j^0 = (x_j^2 - x_j^0) + (x_j^1 - x_j^2)$$

Dividing this by Δp_j gives

$$\frac{x_j^1 - x_j^0}{\Delta p_j} = \frac{x_j^2 - x_j^0}{\Delta p_j} + \frac{x_j^1 - x_j^2}{\Delta p_j} \qquad [A.9]$$

But from [A.8] $\Delta p_j = -\Delta M / x_j^0$ and substituting this in the second term on the righthand side of [A.9] yields

$$\frac{x_j^1 - x_j^0}{\Delta p_j} = \frac{x_j^2 - x_j^0}{\Delta p_j} - x_j^0 \cdot \frac{(x_j^1 - x_j^2)}{\Delta M}$$

$$\left.\frac{\Delta x_j}{\Delta p_j}\right|_M = \left.\frac{\Delta x_j}{\Delta p_j}\right|_{px} - x_j^0 \cdot \left.\frac{\Delta x_j}{\Delta M}\right|_p \qquad [A.10]$$

The $|_M$ notation indicates that money income is held constant in evaluating the rate of change of x_j with respect to p_j, and the similar notation on the righthand side that purchasing power px and price vector p are being held constant in evaluating the rate of change of x_j with respect to p_j and M. [A.10] is the discrete purchasing power version of the Slutsky equation of section 4B.

It is possible to show that the utility maximizing theory of the consumer and the revealed preference theory are equivalent: all the predictions derived from the assumption about preferences in section 3A can also be derived from the assumptions about behaviour made in this section. A consumer who satisfies the preference assumptions will also satisfy these behavioural assumptions. Similarly, if the consumer satisfies the behavioural assumptions from his behaviour we can construct curves which have all the properties of the indifference curves of section 3A and so he can be thought of as acting as if he possessed preferences satisfying the preference assumptions. (Strictly the weak axiom needs to be strengthened slightly.) Since the two theories are equivalent we will not consider any more of the predictions of the theory of revealed preference but will instead use the theory to investigate some properties of price indices.

Price indices

As we noted in section 4C, it is often useful to be able to measure the benefits to consumers of changes in prices of goods. The *CV* and *EV* measures suggested in section 4C suffer from the drawback that they can be precisely measured only if the goods whose prices have changed have zero income effects. This means that the measures are of little use in situations where there are many and large price changes. For example a government may wish to pay state pensions which ensure at least a constant level of utility to its pensioners in a period when most prices of goods bought by pensioners fluctuate. The pensions i.e. money incomes, must therefore be adjusted as prices vary, but by how much?

Let x^0, x^1 be the bundles of goods bought by a consumer with incomes M_0, M_1 at price vectors p^0, p^1 respectively. (So that $p^0 x^0 = M_0$ and $p^1 x^1 = M_1$.) The superscripts and subscripts can be thought of as referring to particular periods, so that 0 denotes the initial or base period and 1 the current period. Suppose the consumer satisfies our behavioural assumptions (or equivalently the preference assumptions of section 3A). Under what circumstances can we say that he is better off in one price-income situation than another?

Suppose first that

$$p^1 x^1 \geq p^1 x^0 \qquad\qquad [A.11]$$

so that x^1 is revealed preferred to x^0, in that x^1 was chosen when x^0 was available. Dividing both sides of [A.11] by $p^0 x^0$ gives

$$MI = \frac{p^1 x^1}{p^0 x^0} \geq \frac{p^1 x^0}{p^0 x^0} = LP \qquad\qquad [A.12]$$

The lefthand side of [A.12] is an index of the consumer's money income and the righthand side is an index of prices with base period quantities as weights, known as the *Laspeyre* price index. Hence if the money income index is at least as large as the Laspeyre price index the consumer will be better off. Note that if the inequality in [A.12] was $<$ rather than $\geq$ nothing could be inferred from the relationship of the two indices.

Now assume that

$$p^0 x^0 \geq p^0 x^1 \qquad\qquad [A.13]$$

so that x^0 is revealed preferred to x^1. [A.13] is equivalent to

$$\frac{1}{p^0 x^0} \leq \frac{1}{p^0 x^1}$$

and hence to

$$MI = \frac{p^1 x^1}{p^0 x^0} \leq \frac{p^1 x^1}{p^0 x^1} = PP \qquad\qquad [A.14]$$

where *PP* is the *Paasche* current weighted price index. If the money income index is less than the Paasche price index the consumer is definitely worse off in the current period than in the base period. Again if $<$ replaces $\geq$ in [A.13] (so that $>$ replaces $\leq$ in [A.14]) nothing can be said about whether the individual is better or worse off.

In some circumstances therefore comparisons of price and money income indices do tell us whether a consumer is better or worse off as a result of changes in prices and his income, without requiring detailed information on his preferences.

Price indices are not, however, calculated for each individual using his consumption levels as weights. The weights used are either total or average consumption bundles for particular groups (e.g. all pensioners, or the inhabitants of particular regions). Suppose that the Laspeyre price index and the money income index are calculated using the sum of consumption bundles and money incomes:

$$MI = \frac{\sum_s M_1^s}{\sum_s M_0^s} = \frac{\sum_s p^1 x^{s1}}{\sum_s p^0 x^{s0}} = \frac{p^1 \sum_s x^{s1}}{p^0 \sum_s x^{s0}} \qquad [A.15]$$

$$LP = \frac{p^1 \sum_s x^{s0}}{p^0 \sum_s x^{s0}} \qquad [A.16]$$

where M_0^s, x^{s0}, M_1^s, x^{s1} are the bundle and income of individuals in the base and current periods. What can be inferred from the relationship between [A.15] and [A.16]? Assume that MI exceeds LP and multiply both indices by $p^0 \sum x^{s0}$ to give

$$p^1 \sum_s x^{s1} > p^1 \sum_s x^{s0} \qquad [A\,17]$$

which, taking a case involving two consumers, *a* and *b*, for simplicity, can be written

$$p^1 x^{a1} + p^1 x^{b1} > p^1 x^{a0} + p^1 x^{b0} \qquad [A.18]$$

Now [A.18] does *not* imply that $p^1 x^{a1} > p^1 x^{a0}$ and $p^1 x_1^{b1} > p^1 x^{b0}$, but merely that *at least one* of these inequalities holds, so that at least one of the consumers is better off in the current period. It is possible, however, that one of the consumers may be worse off. Hence $MI > LP$ does not imply that *all* members of the group for whom the indices are calculated are better off, merely that *some* of them are.

In some circumstances [A.18] will imply that *a and b* are better off in the current period. Suppose that the bundles bought by the consumers at given prices are proportional, i.e. that $x^{a1} = kx^{b1}$ and $x^{a0} = kx^{b0}$. Hence

[A.18] is equivalent to

$$(1+k)p^1x^{b1} > (1+k)p^1x^{b0} \qquad\qquad [A.19]$$

and so

$$p^1x^{b1} > p^1x^{b0} \qquad\qquad [A.20]$$

so that consumer b is better off. But multiplying both sides of [A.20] by k gives

$$p^1kx^{b1} = p^1x^{a1} > p^1x^{a0} = p^1kx^{b0}$$

and consumer a is better off as well. If the consumers in a group have preferences which ensure that each spends the same proportion of his/her income on the same good then price and money income indices can tell us, for some price and income changes, whether *all* consumers in the group are better or worse off. In order for the consumers to have equal proportionate expenditure patterns for all price vectors one of two conditions must be satisfied:

(i) Consumers have identical preferences and identical incomes so that they buy identical bundles. ($k = 1$ in the above example)

(ii) Consumers have identical preferences of a special form which give rise to income consumption curves or Engel curves (see section 3D) which are straight lines from the origin when plotted in goods-space. This means that each good will have the same proportion of the consumer's income spent on it irrespective of the size of his income. The income elasticities of demand for all goods will be unity.

The group of consumers for whom the indices are calculated must satisfy one of the above conditions if the indices are to be of use. This suggests that there may need to be many such indices and that the indices should be frequently updated. This latter suggestion implies that the periods being compared should be not too far apart, in order to minimize the errors from non-unitary income elasticities which can arise if incomes differ even though groups have identical tastes.

Exercise 5A

1. Show that a consumer who satisfies the preference assumptions of section 3A will also satisfy the behavioural assumptions. Can you relate the assumptions in the two sections? Which behavioural assumption, for example, plays a similar role to the transitivity assumption of section 3A?

2. Draw diagrams to show that $MI < LP$ and $MI > PP$ tell us nothing about which situation is preferred.

3. Suppose that the actual weights used in a price index are average consumption bundles for the group of consumers. Under what conditions does $MI > LP$ imply that *all* consumers are now better off?

4. Do the remarks in the last part of the section and the results obtained in question 3 hold for Paasche price indices?

5.* Laspeyre and Paasche quantity indices have the form

$$LQ = \frac{p^0 x^1}{p^0 x^0} \qquad PQ = \frac{p^1 x^1}{p^1 x^0}$$

If $LQ \geq 1$ or $PQ \leq 1$ can anything be said about whether the individual consuming x^0 and x^1 is better or worse off? Suppose the quantities were the total consumption of all members of an economy. Could anything be said about changes in standards of living using the indices?

6. Suppose that the government increases the income of its pensioners in proportion to the rise in the Laspeyre price index. Will they be better or worse off? What if the government used a Paasche price index? What if prices fell?

B. Consumption technology

In this section we outline an alternative approach to the conventional theory of consumer behaviour of the previous chapters, which has been developed by K. Lancaster. The conventional theory is adequate for many purposes but there are some phenomena which can only be incorporated into the theory with great difficulty. Consider for example the introduction of a new good. One method of handling this would be to assume that when there are n goods the consumer has a preference ordering defined with respect to those n goods and on the introduction of a new good his preference ordering is now defined with respect to the $n + 1$ goods. This procedure does not tell us how the two preference orderings are related and hence what the effect of the introduction of the new good will be on the demand for the other goods. Alternatively we could assume that the consumer has a preference ordering defined with respect to *all* goods: those which exist now *and* those which will exist in the future. The introduction of a new good then corresponds to the reduction of the price of that good from an arbitrarily high level. This procedure is unsatisfactory in that it assumes a rather large amount of knowledge on the part of the consumer.

A second source of dissatisfaction with the conventional theory is that it provides no *objective* reason why, for example, butter and margarine should be close substitutes for each other (in the sense of having high cross price elasticities of demand) but not butter and clothing. The only answer the conventional theory can offer is *subjective*: butter and margarine are close substitutes because consumers' *preferences* are such that they have high cross price elasticities. Most people would feel intuitively that this answer is unsatisfactory: that the classification or grouping of goods could be objective in the sense that it is related to some inherent characteristics of the goods themselves and not to the individuals' preferences.

Lancaster's approach is to focus on the intrinsic qualities of goods and to regard the goods bought by consumers as inputs into a process of consumption which transforms the bundle of goods bought into a bundle of *characteristics.* For example the consumer buys different types of food and combines them to produce an array of characteristics: different flavours, calories, vitamin levels and so on. Different mixtures of foods will produce different mixtures of these characteristics. The second stage in the theory is to assume that consumers have preferences for *characteristics* of goods rather than for the goods themselves. The consumer's optimization problem then becomes the choice of a bundle of goods which will yield the preferred bundle of characteristics. This choice is constrained first by his budget constraint, which limits the bundles of goods from which he can choose, and secondly by the *consumption technology*, i.e. the relationship between bundles of goods (inputs into the consumption process) and bundles of characteristics (the outputs of the process).

More formally, let $A = (a_1, \ldots, a_r)$ denote a bundle of characteristics. Then, provided the consumers' preferences as regards characteristics obey the assumptions we made in section 3A for goods, we can represent these preferences by a utility function $u = u(A)$, which has exactly the same properties with respect to A as the function $u(x)$ of Chapter 3 has with respect to x. The amount of each characteristic will depend on the bundle of goods chosen and again denoting a bundle of goods by $x = (x_1, \ldots, x_n)$ we can express this as

$$a_i = f^i(x_1, \ldots, x_n) = f^i(x) \qquad (i = 1, \ldots, r) \qquad \text{[B.1]}$$

Notice that we do not place any restriction on the relation between the number of goods n and the number of characteristics r. Usually one would expect that there are more goods than characteristics $(n > r)$. Notice also that we have allowed for the possibility that each good appears in more than one of the consumption technology constraints $a_i = f^i(x)$. This means that in general each good produces, or is used in the production of, more than one characteristic. Bread, for example, produces such characteristics as calories, proteins, vitamins and flavour. We will assume that the consumption technology is objective in the sense that for a given bundle of goods we can predict the bundle of characteristics which would be produced and that the technology is perceived to be the same by and for all consumers (think about this assumption).

The consumer's budget constraint on the goods he can buy has exactly the same form as in section 3B: $\sum_j p_j x_j \leq M$. If we assume that the consumer is not satiated in characteristics (i.e. will prefer, other things being equal, more of at least one characteristic) and an increase in at least one of the goods will produce more of a desired characteristic, then the consumer will always spend his entire money income M on goods.

The consumer's optimization problem is therefore

$$\max_{x_1, \ldots, x_n} u(a_1, \ldots, a_r) \quad \text{s.t.} \quad \text{(i)} \ \sum p_j x_j = M \qquad x_j \geq 0 \ (j = 1, \ldots, n)$$

$$\text{(ii)} \ a_i = f^i(x_1, \ldots, x_n) \qquad \text{[B.2]}$$

$$(i = 1, \ldots, r)$$

We now proceed to derive the necessary conditions for utility maximization for this problem, and consider how the optimal bundle x^* would vary in response to changes in prices, income *and* the consumption technology. However, to simplify the analysis we will assume (as did Lancaster) that the consumption technology is *linear*. By this is meant that one unit of a good j produces α_{ij} units of characteristic i where α_{ij} is a constant independent of the level of good j or of any other good. The total amount of characteristic i produced from a bundle of goods is the sum of the amounts produced by each good:

$$a_i = \alpha_{i1}x_1 + \alpha_{i2}x_2 + \ldots + \alpha_{in}x_n = \sum_j \alpha_{ij}x_j \qquad (i = 1, \ldots, r) \qquad [\text{B.3}]$$

and so [B.3] replaces (ii) in [B.2].

Rather than solve [B.2] (by use of the Lagrange procedure or other techniques) we will adopt the following *two-stage optimization* procedure: (a) first we consider the problem of an *efficient* choice of goods. By efficient is meant that it is impossible to increase the amount of one characteristic without at the same time reducing the amount of some other characteristic. The bundle of goods which solves [B.2] *must* be efficient (explain why). The set of efficient goods bundles will depend solely on the consumption technology, the prices of the goods and the consumer's money income. It will *be independent of the consumer's preferences:* no information on preferences is required for deciding whether a bundle is efficient or not.
(b) The second stage involves choosing the best or *optimal* bundle from the efficient set and this *does* require knowledge of preferences, since consumers with different preferences, but the same incomes, will choose different bundles.

Efficient combinations of goods

We can, without much loss in generality, concentrate on a model with only two characteristics and two or three goods. Figure 2 has the two

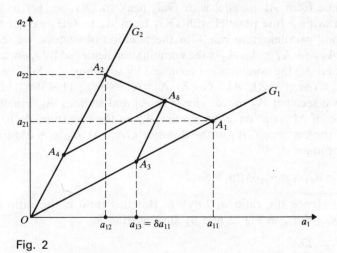

Fig. 2

characteristics a_1, a_2 measured along its horizontal and vertical axes. Purchase of one unit of good 1 will produce α_{11} units of characteristic 1 and α_{21} units of characteristic 2, and so x_1 units of good 1 produce $\alpha_{11}x_1$, $\alpha_{21}x_1$ units of the characteristics.

Purchase of x_1 of good 1 will therefore correspond to a bundle of characteristics or a point in Fig. 2. Since good 1 produces the two characteristics in the fixed proportion α_{21}/α_{11}, the ratio of the characteristics in the bundles of characteristics generated by different levels of x_1 will be constant. In other words, when only good 1 is bought, the ray OG_1 in the figure shows the combinations of a_1, a_2 produced by varying the level of x_1. Since α_{11}, α_{21} have been assumed constant, doubling x_1 will double the levels of a_1 and a_2. Hence points further from the origin along OG_1 correspond to larger quantities of x_1. OG_2 similarly shows combinations of characteristics generated by varying the level of good 2 with x_1 set equal to zero. Notice that good 2 has a higher ratio of a_2 produced to a_1 produced than does good 1.

Now suppose the consumer spends his entire income M on good 1. He will be able to buy M/p_1 units of x_1 and so produce $\alpha_{11}M/p_1 = a_{12}$, $\alpha_{21}M/p_1 = a_{21}$ units of the two characteristics. Hence if only x_1 is bought and all income spent the consumer will be at $A_1 = (a_{11}, a_{21})$ in the figure. Similarly if M is spent only on good 2, M/p_2 units of good will be bought, putting the consumer at $A_2 = (a_{12} = \alpha_{12}M/p_2, a_{22} = \alpha_{22}M/p_2)$ on OG_2.

The assumptions about the consumption technology imply that if two bundles of characteristics A' and A'' are feasible then any *convex combination* of them; $\delta A' + (1-\delta)A''$ $(0 \leq \delta \leq 1)$ is also feasible (see section 2B). Hence all points in the area OA_1A_2 are feasible. In particular, by spending all his income in various proportions on the two goods the consumer can achieve any characteristics combination along A_1A_2.

Conversely, given any point on this line A_1A_2, we can find the mixture of x_1 and x_2 required to attain it. Thus consider A_δ in Fig. 2. By drawing a line from A_δ parallel with OG_2 back to OG_1 we get to A_3 on OG_1. By drawing a line parallel with OG_1 from A_δ to OG_2 we get to A_4. Recalling the "parallelogram rule" for the addition of vectors, we see that the sum of A_3 and A_4 is A_δ. A_3 is the combination achieved by spending δM on good 1 and A_4 the combination achieved by spending $(1-\delta)M$ on good 2: $A_3 = \delta A_1 = (\delta a_{11}, \delta a_{21})$, $A_4 = (1-\delta) A_2 = ((1-\delta)a_{12}, (1-\delta)a_{22})$. By increasing δ we see that A_3 moves closer to A_1 and so does A_δ. Finally, the proportion δ of M spent on x_1 at a point A_δ on the line from A_1 to A_2 is the ratio of the distance OA_3 to the distance OA_1. At A_3, $x_1 = \delta M/p_1$ units of good 1 produce

$$a_{13} = \alpha_{11}x_1 = \alpha_{11}\delta M/p_1 = \delta a_{11}$$

units of a_1. Hence the ratio $a_{13}/a_{11} = \delta$. But this ratio is the ratio of the distances Oa_{13}/Oa_{11} in Fig. 2 and by similar triangles

$$\frac{Oa_{13}}{Oa_{11}} = \frac{OA_3}{OA_1} = \delta \qquad\qquad\qquad \text{[B.4]}$$

We can also show that $OA_4/OA_2 = (1 - \delta)$.

Interpretation of the slope of the boundary of the feasible set

The feasible set in Fig. 2 is OA_1A_2, the set of all combinations of characteristics which can be produced from the two goods given their prices and the consumer's money income M. In section 3B we saw that the slope of the boundary of the feasible set in goods space, i.e. the budget line, was the ratio of the prices of the two goods. But what interpretation can be given to the slope of the upper boundary of the choice set in characteristics space, i.e. the line A_1A_2?

The slope of A_1A_2 shows the rate at which the consumer can substitute a_1 for a_2 by varying his purchases of goods 1 and 2. Any movement along A_1A_2 must satisfy both the consumption technology and budget constraints. Hence the rate at which a_2 can be transformed into a_1 (by buying more x_1 and less x_2 in the case shown in Fig. 2) is (from [B.3])

$$\frac{da_2}{da_1} = \frac{\alpha_{21}\,dx_1 + \alpha_{22}\,dx_2}{\alpha_{11}\,dx_1 + \alpha_{12}\,dx_2} = \frac{\alpha_{21} + \alpha_{21}\cdot dx_2/dx_1}{\alpha_{11} + \alpha_{12}\cdot dx_2/dx_1} \qquad [B.5]$$

From the budget constraint any change in x must satisfy

$$p_1\,dx_1 + p_2\,dx_2 = 0 \qquad [B.6]$$

Using [B.6] to substitute $-p_1/p_2$ for dx_2/dx_1 in [B.5] gives

$$\frac{da_2}{da_1} = \frac{\alpha_{21} - \alpha_{22}\cdot p_1/p_2}{\alpha_{11} - \alpha_{12}\cdot p_1/p_2} = \frac{\alpha_{21}/p_1 - \alpha_{22}/p_2}{\alpha_{11}/p_1 - \alpha_{12}/p_2} \qquad [B.7]$$

Since a unit of x_1 costs p_1, a unit of money (say £1) spent on x_1 will buy $1/p_1$ units of x_1, and since one unit of x_1 produces α_{11} units of a_1, £1 spent on x_1 must produce α_{11} times $1/p_1 = \alpha_{11}/p_1$ units of a_1. But spending £1 extra on x_2 means spending £1 less on x_2. This reduces the number of units of x_2 bought by $1/p_2$ and since one unit of x_2 produces α_{12} units of a_1, the £1 reduction in expenditure on x_2 causes a reduction in a_1 of α_{12} times $1/p_2 = \alpha_{12}/p_2$. Hence the increase in a_1 per £1 change in expenditure is

$$\frac{\alpha_{11}}{p_1} - \frac{\alpha_{12}}{p_2}$$

To increase a_1 by one unit the consumer must therefore switch

$$k_1 = \frac{1}{\dfrac{\alpha_{11}}{p_1} - \dfrac{\alpha_{12}}{p_2}} \qquad [B.8]$$

of expenditure from x_2 to x_1. k_1 has the dimension of units of money per unit of a_1 and can therefore be interpreted as the price of a_1. To emphasize that a_1 is not a good which can be bought directly on the market, but a characteristic which must be produced from goods, we will label k_1 the *implicit price* of a_1.

To increase a_2 the consumer must switch expenditure from x_1 to x_2, the good which produces a_2 most intensively. By a similar process of reasoning we can therefore derive the *implicit price* of a_2

$$k_2 = \frac{1}{\dfrac{\alpha_{22}}{p_2} - \dfrac{\alpha_{21}}{p_1}} \qquad [\text{B.9}]$$

as the amount of expenditure which must be switched from x_1 to x_2 to increase a_2 by one unit.

From [B.8] and [B.9] we see that [B.7] can be expressed as

$$\frac{da_2}{du_i} = \frac{-k_1}{k_2} \qquad [\text{B.10}]$$

We have shown that the slope of the upper boundary of the feasible set in characteristics space (the line A_1A_2), which is the rate at which a_2 can be transformed into a_1 by varying the expenditure on x_1 and x_2, is the negative of the ratio of *implicit prices* of a_1 and a_2. There is clearly an analogy with the slope of the budget line in section 3B (see also the discussion of the relation between state-contingent income claims and shareholdings in Ch. 20).

Effects of prices and income changes

If the consumer's income increases he will be able to buy more of both goods and so the upper boundary of the feasible set will move outwards from the origin. Since prices are constant there will be no change in the slope of the boundary, as Fig. 3 shows for a doubling of M. The boundary shifts from A_1A_2 to A_3A_4.

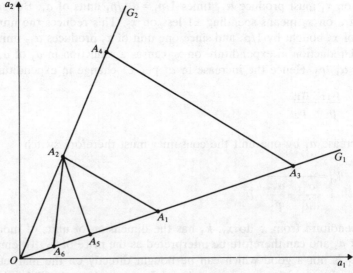

Fig. 3

When prices alter, with M constant, the slope of the boundary will alter. If, for example, the price of x_1 doubles, then the maximum amount of it that can be bought is halved. The point on OG_1 in Fig. 3 corresponding to spending all of M on x_1 will therefore shift inwards from A_1 to A_5, halfway between O and A_1. Notice that if p_1 rises sufficiently, or p_2 falls sufficiently, the slope of the boundary will become positive, as in Fig. 3 where a further doubling of p_1 shifts the boundary to A_6A_2. Since we have assumed that the consumer prefers more of either characteristic to less he will always choose a bundle of goods which takes him to A_2. Since A_2 is on OG_2 he will spend his entire income on good 2. Hence if the boundary is positively sloped the efficient bundle of goods is the one consisting only of good 2. If the boundary is negatively sloped then in this two-good case all bundles of goods which cost the consumer his entire income are efficient, i.e. all bundles of goods which produce a bundle of characteristics on the upper boundary are efficient.

Efficient combinations with three goods

If there is a third good x_3 which produces the two characteristics, Fig. 4 replaces Fig. 2. OG_3 shows the quantities of characteristics produced by spending varying sums of money entirely on good 3. If the consumer's entire income is spent on good 3 the point $A_3 = (M\alpha_{13}/p_3, M\alpha_{23}/p_3)$ is reached. If the consumer divides M between goods 1 and 3 all points on the line A_1A_3 can be reached. For example spending $M/2$ on each good produces the combination A_4. Similarly, dividing M solely between goods 2 and 3 generates the combinations along A_2A_3. Finally spending M only on goods 1 and 2 produces combinations along A_1A_2.

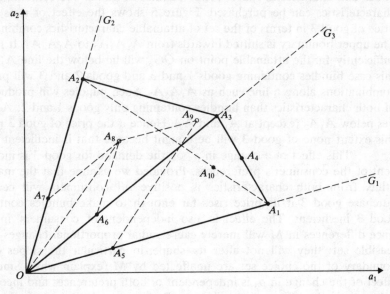

Fig. 4

What happens if the consumer buys some of all three goods? Suppose he spends $M/3$ on each of the goods. $M/3$ spent on x_1 produces A_5, on x_3 produces A_6 and on x_2 produces A_7. The sum of A_7 and A_6 is A_8, and of A_8 and A_5 is A_9. A_9 is, however, an inefficient combination since by rearranging expenditure it is possible to increase the amount of at least one characteristic without reducing the other. For example spending *all* of M on good 3 produces A_3, which contains more of both characteristics than A_9. This is not a result of the specific proportions of M spent on the three goods. Any bundle of goods containing all three goods will be inefficient: it will be possible to increase the amount of characteristic without reducing the other. When all three goods are bought a point *below* the line $A_1A_3A_2$ will be produced. Hence efficient bundles of goods contain at most two goods. This result can be generalized: *if there are* r *characteristics and* n *goods and* $n > r$, *efficient bundles of goods will contain at most* r *goods.*

In our two characteristics case at most two goods will be bought, but which two? In the example shown in Fig. 4 the answer is either goods 1 and 3 or goods 2 and 3. Goods 1 and 2 can only produce combinations along A_1A_2 and hence for any bundle containing goods 1 and 2 it is possible to find a bundle containing goods 1 and 3 or 2 and 3 which produces more of both characteristics. For example the bundle of goods 1 and 2 producing A_{10} is inefficient because by spending $M/2$ each on goods 1 and 3 A_4, containing more of a_1 and a_2, can be reached. Hence the efficient bundles of goods are those (i) on which the consumer spends all his income and (ii) contain either only goods 1 and 3 or only goods 2 and 3.

Suppose that the price of good 3 is increased. The effect will be to shift the upper boundary of the consumer's feasible set inwards in both goods and characterics space: fewer bundles of goods and combinations of characteristics can be purchased. Figure 5 shows the effect of rises in the price of good 3 in terms of the set of attainable characteristics combinations. The upper boundary is shifted inwards from $A_1A_3A_2$ to $A_1A_4A_2$. If p_3 rises sufficiently far the attainable point on OG_3 will lie below the line A_1A_2. In this case bundles containing goods 1 and 3 and goods 2 and 3 will produce combinations along a line such as $A_1A_5A_2$. Such bundles will produce less of both characteristics than bundles containing only goods 1 and 2: $A_1A_5A_2$ lies below A_1A_2 (except at A_1 and A_2). Hence if the price of good 3 rises to this extent none of good 3 will be bought because that is inefficient.

This effect of a change in p_3 on the demand for good 3 is independent of the consumer's preferences. Provided we assume that the marginal utility from both characteristics is positive *all* consumers will cease to purchase good 3 if its price rises far enough to make bundles containing good 3 inefficient. The effect is also independent of consumers' incomes since differences in M will merely cause radial proportional changes in the feasible set: they will not alter its shape, in particular the slopes of the boundary of the choice set are unaffected by M (explain why). Since this effect of the change in p_3 is independent of both preferences and incomes it is known as the *efficiency substitution effect.*

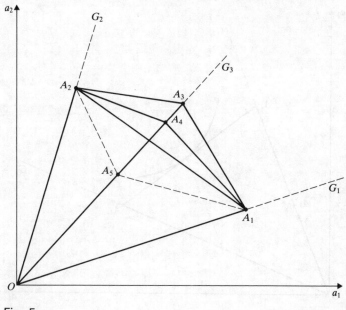

Fig. 5

Figure 5 can also be used to examine the effect of the introduction of a new product. Assume there are initially only goods 1 and 2 and that good 3 is now introduced onto the market. If it has a low price then it will extend the consumer's feasible set, pushing the upper boundary out from A_1A_2 to $A_1A_3A_2$. Previously some consumers bought goods 1 and 2, now some buy 1 and 3 and attain points along A_1A_3, others buy goods 2 and 3 and attain combinations along A_2A_3. If good 3 is introduced at a high price giving rise to a line like $A_1A_5A_2$ then it will be quickly withdrawn from the market since no consumer will buy it.

Choice of the optimal bundle

The first stage of the consumer's problem was finding all efficient bundles of goods which generate the upper boundary of his feasible set in characteristics space. No information on preferences or incomes is required for this part of the problem, but solving it does not yield a unique bundle of goods (except when the efficient set of bundles consists of a single bundle). The second part of the problem is choosing the best or optimal bundle from the set of efficient bundles and for this we require information on the consumer's preferences. Since we have assumed that the consumer's preferences over characteristics satisfy the assumptions of section 3A relating to preferences over goods, we can analyse the consumer's choice by superimposing his indifference map on Fig 2 to give Fig. 6. Each indifference curve shows the combinations of characteristics which are equally valued by the consumer. Since he is assumed to prefer more of both characteristics to

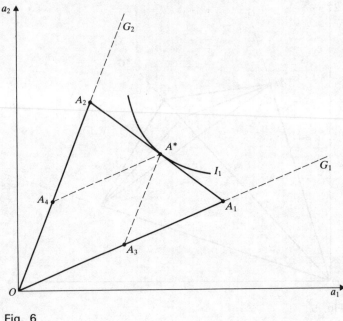

Fig. 6

less (they have positive marginal utility), the indifference curves are negatively sloped, and higher curves denote preferred combinations.

The optimal combination of characteristics is A^* where the highest indifference curve I_1 in the feasible set OA_1A_2 is reached. The optimal bundle of goods which produces A^* is found by drawing lines parallel to OG_1, OG_2 back from A^* to OG_2 and OG_1 at A_3, A_4. The amount of x_1 in the optimal bundle is then proportional to the distance OA_3 and x_2 is proportional to OA_4.

In this particular solution I_1 is tangent to A_1A_2. We have shown that the slope of A_1A_2 can be interpreted as the negative of the ratio of the implicit prices k_1, k_2 of the characteristics. The consumer's preferences can be represented by a utility function $u(a_1, \ldots, a_r) = u(A)$ and so the slope of the indifference curve is

$$\left.\frac{da_2}{da_1}\right|_{du=0} = -\frac{u_1}{u_2} = \mathrm{MRS}^a_{21}$$

where u_i is marginal utility of characteristic i and MRS^a_{21} is the marginal rate of substitution between characteristics 1 and 2: the rate at which the consumer is prepared to substitute characteristic 2 for characteristic 1. Hence the tangency solution to the consumer's problem satisfies

$$\mathrm{MRS}^a_{21} = \frac{u_1}{u_2} = \frac{k_1}{k_2} \qquad\qquad\qquad [\text{B.11}]$$

As in Chapter 3 there may also be a corner solution where [B.14] does not hold. For example, the highest attainable indifference curve may touch the feasible set at A_1. In this case only good 1 is bought.

The reader should superimpose the indifference map on the three good case illustrated in Fig. 4 and examine the different types of solution. With a tangency solution (along A_1A_3 or A_2A_3) two goods are bought, but with a corner solution (at A_1, A_2 or A_3) only one good is bought. Notice that some consumers will choose bundles with goods 1 and 3 and some bundles with goods 2 and 3 depending on their indifference map but none, irrespective of their preferences will buy goods 1 *and* 2.

Comparative statics

As in the conventional model of Chapter 3 the bundle of goods chosen by the consumer will depend on his preferences, which determine his indifference map, and on his money income M and the prices of the goods, which determines the set of purchasable bundles. But, unlike the conventional model, his choice is also affected by the consumption technology which determines the combinations of characteristics producible from a given bundle of goods. The consumer's demand functions are therefore of the form

$$x_i = D_i(p_1, \ldots, p_n, M, a_{11}, \ldots, a_{rn}) \qquad (i = 1, \ldots, n)$$

The effect of changes in prices, income and technology on the demand for characteristics and hence goods can be established by making the appropriate changes in the feasible set and examining the consumer's possible responses with different types of preferences (indifference maps). The results are similar to those of Chapter 4 and are left as an exercise for the reader.

Exercise 5B

1.* The assumptions about $u(x)$ in section 3A ensure that the demand functions for x in section 3D are continuous and single valued (only one bundle maximizes u at each p, M combination). The $u(A)$ function used in this section also reflects the assumptions of section 3A. Does this imply that the demand functions for goods derived from the analysis here are continuous? Draw diagrams to illustrate the consumer's response to income and price changes in which the demand for good 1 varies (a) continuously and (b) discontinuously with M and p_1.

2. Under what circumstances will the introduction of a new good raise, lower or leave unchanged the demand for an existing good?

3. The degree of substitutability between two goods could be defined, without reference to preferences, in terms of the angle between the rays in characteristics-space generated by the two goods. The smaller the angle the closer the substitutes. How will the degree of substitutability affect the answer to the previous question?

4. Show how the introduction of a new good may drive some existing goods off the market. Since the consumer now has fewer goods to choose from is he worse off?

5.* Discuss critically the assumption that the bundle of quantities of characteristics represented by one unit of a good is capable of objective measurement and is the same for all consumers. Illustrate your answer with examples of real consumer goods.

6.* Show that the following comparative static results can be established by simple diagrammatic analysis:
   (a) The demand for characteristics and for goods may rise, fall or remain constant in response to changes in prices and income;
   (b) The elasticity restrictions on the demand for goods of Exercise 3D, Question 4, continue to hold;
   (c) The demand for goods and for characteristics is homogeneous of degree zero in prices and income;
   (d) Demand for all characteristics will increase in response to a sufficiently large increase in income;
   (e) Normality of all characteristics does not imply that all goods are also normal;
   (f) Some goods may be Giffen goods even though no characteristics are Giffen characteristics.

7.* Show how the consumption technology model can be used to examine the cost imposed on the consumer by misleading advertising which causes the consumer to overestimate the ouput of characteristics from a good.

C. The consumer as a labour supplier

Our analysis in this and the two previous chapters has been concerned with the consumer's allocation of income among goods and has ignored the question of how the consumer allocates the time available in a given period. The problem is important first because one of the main sources of the income spent on the goods consumed is the sale of the consumer's time in return for a wage. Second, time is a scarce resource and the consumption of goods requires an input of time as well as of money. In this section we will examine a simple model in which the consumer chooses the amount of time spent at work. In the following section we will enquire more closely into how the time not spent at work ('leisure' time) is allocated to the consumption of different goods and how this affects the consumer's labour supply decision.

The consumer's utility function is assumed to depend on the bundle of goods consumed (x) and the amount of non-work time or leisure (L).

$$u = u(x, L) \qquad\qquad [\text{C}.1]$$

Since more leisure is assumed to be preferred to less, the marginal utility of leisure u_L is positive. The consumer is constrained in two ways. First he cannot spend more than his income M

$$\sum p_i x_i \leq M = wz + \bar{M} \qquad [C.2]$$

where z is the length of time spent at work, w is the wage rate (assumed constant) and $\bar{M}$ is non-work income from shares in firms, bond interest, government subsidies etc. Since the marginal utility of every good is always positive (non-satiation assumption), [C.2] will be treated as an equality.

Second, the consumer in any given period of length T is constrained by his 'time budget'

$$T = z + L \qquad [C.3]$$

which says that the time he has available is divided between work and leisure. The consumer's problem is to maximize $u(x, L)$ subject to [C.2] and [C.3] by choice of x, L and z. In order to concentrate on the labour supply problem we will adopt the following two-stage approach. Assume that L and M are fixed and that the consumer maximizes $u(x, L)$ subject to [C.2] by choice of x. The optimal x in this first-stage problem will depend on the prices of the goods and levels at which M and L are fixed. Assuming that the prices of the goods are constant we can write the optimal x as depending only on the levels of M and L

$$x^* = x(M, L) \qquad [C.4]$$

Substituting [C.4] in [C.1] gives the maximum value of u in this first stage problem

$$u_{\max} = u(x^*(M, L), L) = u^*(M, L) \qquad [C.5]$$

With constant goods prices utility will depend on the amount of leisure and the consumer's income.

The second-stage problem is to choose L and z to maximize $u^*(M, L)$ subject to [C.2] and [C.3]. Now from [C.3] we see that $L = T - z$ and substituting for L in u^* gives

$$u^*(M, T - z) = u^{**}(M, z) \qquad [C.6]$$

and the marginal utility of work time is the negative of the marginal utility of leisure time

$$\frac{\partial u^{**}}{\partial z} = u_2^{**} = u_L^* \frac{dL}{dz} = -u_L^* \qquad [C.7]$$

We can solve the second stage problem, of the optimal allocation of time between work and leisure, either by maximizing u^* s.t. [C.2] by choice of L, or by maximizing U^{**} s.t. [C.2] by choice of z. We will use the latter approach to emphasize the labour supply decision.

Figure 7 shows the consumer's feasible set in terms of z and M. The upper boundary of the feasible set is the *wage line* $\bar{M}M_1$, which plots income as a function of labour supplied: $M = \bar{M} + w_1 z$, given the wage rate w_1. We also have to impose the direct constraints that the consumer cannot supply

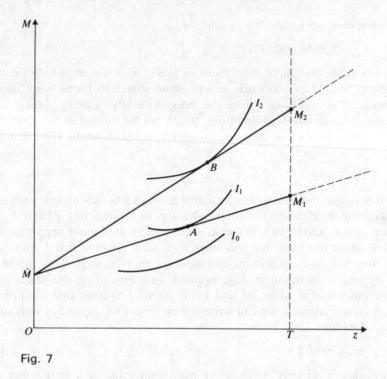

Fig. 7

negative amounts of his labour ($z \geq 0$) and cannot supply more than the total time in the period, ($z \leq T$). With a larger wage rate w_2 ($>w_1$) the wage line becomes $\bar{M}M_2$. The slope of the wage line is the wage rate

$$\frac{dM}{dz} = w$$

so that rises in w steepen the slope of the wage line. Increases in unearned income $\bar{M}$ shift the intercept of the wage line upwards but do not affect its slope.

The consumer's preferences as regards x, L are to satisfy the assumptions of section 3A. This means that *both $u(x, L)$ and $u^*(M, L)$ have all the convenient properties of section 3A*. In particular the indifference curves showing combinations of M and L with equal utility have the same general form of indifference curves of section 3A. But since $L = T - z$ with T fixed, to each value of L there is a corresponding value of z, and variations in L imply variations in z. Corresponding to the M, L combinations which yield a particular level of utility, therefore, there are combinations of M and $z = T - L$ which yield the same utility. The slope of the M, L indifference curve is

$$\left. \frac{dM}{dL} \right|_{du^* = 0} = \frac{-u_L^*}{u_M^*} < 0 \qquad \text{[C.8]}$$

where u_M^* is the marginal utility of income. Now from [C.6] and [C.7] $u_M^* = u_M^{**}$ and $u_L^* = -u_z^{**}$, so that the slope of the M, z indifference curve is

$$\left.\frac{dM}{dz}\right|_{du^{**}=0} = \frac{-u_z^{**}}{u_M^{**}} = \frac{u_L^*}{u_M} > 0 \qquad [C.9]$$

Hence the slopes of M, z indifference curves are the negative of the slopes of the corresponding M, L indifference curves. The indifference map in M, z space is the mirror image of the M, L indifference map. A rise in M must be accompanied by a fall in L and hence a rise in z to keep utility constant.

The lines I_0, I_1, I_2 in Fig. 7 are the individual's indifference curves. Notice that since utility increases with money income M for given z ($u_M^* = u_M^{**} > 0$) higher indifference curves correspond to larger levels of utility. The indifference curves also reflect the physiological fact that individuals must have some leisure (for sleeping, eating and so on) since they never intersect the line $z = T$ but increase in steepness as z increases. In other words (see [C.9]) the marginal utility of work time tends to minus infinity as z tends to T; or the marginal utility of leisure tends to plus infinity as L tends to zero.

Point A, where the highest attainable indifference curve is reached, is the solution to the consumer's labour supply problem when $w = w_1$. In this interior solution the indifference curve I_1 is tangent to the wage line:

$$\frac{-u_z^{**}}{u_M^{**}} = w = \frac{u_L^*}{u_M^*} \qquad [C.10]$$

The amount of money the consumer is *willing* to accept for the loss of a unit (minute) of leisure (the marginal rate of substitution between income and leisure) is equal to w, which is the amount of money he will *actually* receive for the unit reduction in leisure (increase in work time).

We can check the diagrammatic analysis by using the Lagrange procedure to maximize u^{**} s.t. $M = wz + \bar{M}$. (Remember that [C.3] has been eliminated by using $L = T - z$ to derive u^{**}.) Alternatively we can use the constraint to substitute for M in u^{**} so that utility now depends only on the amount of work time z

$$u^{**}(\bar{M} + wz, z)$$

Variations in z now affect utility in two ways: indirectly, they change M and so change utility; they also change utility directly, since less z is preferred to more for given M. The total rate of change of utility with respect to z is

$$\frac{du^{**}}{dz} = \frac{\partial u^{**}}{\partial M}\frac{dM}{dz} + \frac{\partial u^{**}}{\partial z}$$

$$= u_M^{**} \cdot w + u_z^{**} = u_M^* \cdot w - u_L^*. \qquad [C.11]$$

Setting this equal to zero for a maximum and rearranging gives [C.10].

Comparative statics: the labour supply curve

Variations in w and $\bar{M}$ will alter the feasible set and hence the optimal position. For example in Fig. 7 a rise in w to w_2 shifts the optimal position to B where more z is supplied (less L consumed). With the indifference map shown, the consumer's supply curve, plotting the wage rate against z supplied, will be positively sloped (Explain why). With different preferences the chosen point on $\bar{M}M_2$ could have contained less z than A (Draw the diagram). In this case the labour supply curve would be backward bending: rises in w lead to a fall in the supply of labour. Changes in unearned income will shift the wage line but leave its slope unaltered and the labour supplied at a given wage may rise or fall as $\bar{M}$ rises depending on the individual's preference map (Illustrate). In terms of the labour supply curve changes in $\bar{M}$ lead to *shifts* of the curve rather than movements along it.

The effect of changes in w on z supplied can be decomposed into income and substitution effects, as in the earlier analysis of the effect of changes in p_i on x_i demanded in section 3D. The 'wage effect' is the movement from A to B in Fig. 8. The wage line is shifted downward parallel with itself until it is tangent to the initial indifference curve I_1 at C. The substitution effect AC shows the change due solely to the variation in w with utility held constant. CB is the income effect, showing the change due to the rise in utility with w held constant. $\Delta \bar{M}$ is the compensating variation in unearned income which will leave the consumer just as well off after the wage rise as he was before with his initial unearned income $\bar{M}$. The substitution effect of a wage rise is always to *increase* the supply of labour.

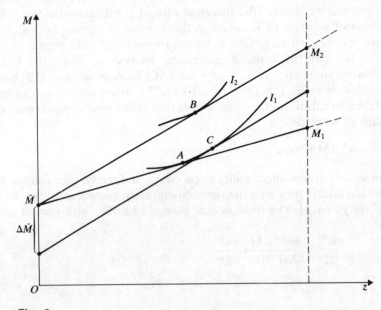

Fig. 8

The wage line becomes steeper, and since the slope of I_1 rises as z rises, the point of tangency C between the wage line with slope w_2 and I_1 must be to the right of A.

No such restriction can be placed on the income effect. B may be to the right or (as in the figure) to the left of C. If B is to the left of C then z falls as income rises with constant w, or equivalently L rises as income rises, so that *leisure is a normal good*. Notice that if the supply of labour declines as w rises B must be to the left of A. Since A is always to the left of C the supply of labour *must* fall (L rise) as income rises with constant w. Hence leisure a normal good is a necessary, but not sufficient, condition for a backward bending, negatively sloped supply curve of labour. It is not a sufficient condition because, as the diagram shows, the substitution effect of a wage rise, in reducing leisure and increasing work, may more than offset the income effect, which increases leisure (compare the discussion of Giffen goods in Chapter 3).

This model of the consumer as a supplier of labour can be extended in a number of ways.

Preference for work
We have assumed that the consumer dislikes work ($u_z^{**} < 0$) but some individuals may like work (up to a certain number of hours per day). In this case $u_z^{**} > 0$ for low levels of z and the indifference curves are U-shaped. Allowing for this possibility in fact makes little difference to the analysis (except to rule out the no-work corner solution), as the reader should check by drawing the appropriate diagrams. This is because the optimum position will still be one where a U-shaped indifference curve is tangent to the wage line and since the wage line is positively sloped so must be the indifference curve at the point of tangency.

Taxes, overtime, unemployment insurance, fixed hours of work
All of these alter the feasible set confronting the labour supplier and can be analysed by superimposing the indifference map on the appropriately revised feasible set. With income taxes at the rate θ the individual's net after-tax income is $M = (1 - \theta)(\bar{M} + wz)$ (Explain why). If the tax rate θ is independent of income, i.e. if it is a proportional tax rate, the tax shifts the intercept of the wage line on the M axis downward and reduces its slope to $dM/dz = (1 - \theta)w$.

Overtime payments, where the worker is paid at the rate $(1 + k)$ $w, (k > 0)$ for work supplied above some minimum amount z^0, kink the wage line upwards at z^0.

If the individual receives unemployment insurance he gets a sum M_u if he works less than some specified amount z^1. The wage line is $\bar{M} + M_u + wz$ for $z \le z^1$ and $\bar{M} + wz$ for $z > z^1$, so that it is discontinuous at z^1.

If firms employ only individuals who are prepared to supply at least z^2 hours of work and the state fixes a maximum of $z^3 > z^2$ the wage line is only defined at $z = 0$ and $z^2 \le z \le z^3$.

The reader should examine the effect of these changes in the feasible set on the amount of labour supplied by superimposing the indifference map on the feasible set. He should prove that:

(i) Income taxation may raise or lower z.

(ii) If the initial optimal $z = z^*$ is less than z^0, introducing overtime payments cannot reduce the labour supply. If $z^* > \bar{z}^0$ no definite answer emerges.

(iii) If $z^* \geq z^1$ unemployment insurance cannot increase the supply of labour; if $z^* < z^1$ the supply may rise or fall.

(iv) If $z^* > z^3$ z falls to z^3, if $z^* < z^2$ z may increase to z^2 or fall to zero.

Job choice

Individuals who are concerned only with income and the length of time at work, irrespective of the kind of work, will clearly choose the job with the highest wage rate. For most people, however, the pleasantness or otherwise of working conditions in different jobs will affect their choice of occupation. We can use the Lancaster model of consumer behaviour from section B to examine the implications of this observation.

Let the pleasantness of work be measured by some index a (for amenity). Then an hour spent in a particular job of type i yields w_i of income (the money wage) and a_i of amenity (the 'amenity wage'). Hence if T_i is the length of time spent in job i total earned income is $T_i w_i$ and total amenity is $T_i a_i$. An hour spent in a job can be thought of as producing the utility-yielding characteristics income and amenity, just as in the consumer technology model, £1 spent on a good will produce utility yielding charac-teristics. The 'job technology' assuming constant w_i, a_i, is perhaps unduly simple but it does focus attention on some interesting aspects of job choice.

The individual's preferences are described by the utility function $u = u(M, L, a)$ and the marginal utilities of M, L and a are positive. The constraints on the individual are $a = \sum T_i a_i$, $M = \sum T_i w_i$ and $L + \sum T_i = T$. To concentrate on job choice, assume that L is fixed and consider Fig. 9. The ray OJ_1 shows the combinations of amenity and income attainable by spending different amounts of time in job 1. OJ_2 is the corresponding ray for job 2. The slope of OJ_1 is w_1/a_1 and similarly the slope of OJ_2 is w_2/a_2. With fixed L, the total working time is also given as $(T-L)$ and A_1, A_2 are the income-amenity combinations reached by spending all work time at each of the two jobs (i.e. by setting $T_1 = T - L$ or $T_2 = T - L$). Notice that $a_1 > a_2$ but $w_2 < w_1$ in this case, i.e. allocating all work time to job 1 yields more amenity but less income than job 2. If one job, say job 2 had a higher money wage *and* a higher 'amenity wage' than the other then no individual with the preferences assumed would choose job 1. Hence if all jobs required the same quantity of labour those with lower 'amenity wages' would pay larger money wages.

The income-amenity combinations along $A_1 A_2$ are reached by varying the proportions of total work time spent in each job. The individual's preferences can be represented by indifference curves with the usual

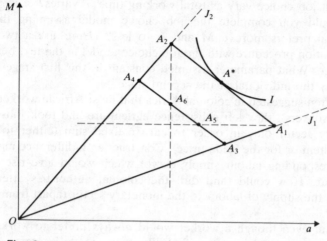

Fig. 9

properties. Depending on the individual's preferences he will either choose to work only in one job or, as in Fig. 9 at A^*, he will attain an optimal amenity-income combination by a mixture of jobs.

It will often be the case that there are costs involved in performing more than one job which will make it more likely that individuals will specialise in one job. Suppose for example that because jobs 1 and 2 are spatially separated a certain length of time is required to transfer between them. The effect of this will be to shift the income-amenity combinations attainable by a *mixture* of jobs inwards. In Fig. 9 for example, the assumption that the transfer time is a fifth of total working time causes the upper boundary of the feasible set to shift down to A_3A_4 where A_3 and A_4 are $\frac{4}{5}$ of the way along OJ_1 and OJ_2. The individual will now choose either A_1, or A_2 or any point between A_3A_4. Given that both a and M have positive marginal utilities the individual will, if he chooses a mix of jobs, limit himself to mixes which produce income amenity combinations between A_5A_6. The larger is the transfer time the more likely is it that there is specialization in one job. With a large enough transfer time all individuals will specialize irrespective of their preferences because A_2 or A_1 will contain more of a and M than points generated by a mix of jobs.

Exercise 5C

1.* Prove the assertions (i)–(iv) on the implications of taxes, overtime, unemployment insurance and fixed hours of work.
2.* What is the effect of replacing a proportional income tax with a progessive income tax which yields the same tax revenue?
3. How will job choices respond to changes in wage rates? Will a rise in the wages paid for a job necessarily attract more labour to the job? Does the answer depend on the transfer time?

4. How will job choice vary as total working time T varies?

5.* How could you complete the job choice model assuming that the individual prefers more a, M and L to less? (*Hint:* use a two stage maximisation procedure with the job choice model in the text being the first stage. What parameter assumed constant in this first stage can be varied by the individual at the second stage?)

6.* It was often suggested in colonial Africa that most African workers were 'target workers': they left subsistence agriculture and took jobs in the monetary sector only in order to earn a fixed sum (either to buy a specific item or for the bride price). Construct an indifference map (and the corresponding labour supply curve) which would give rise to this behaviour. How could (and did) the colonial authorities attempt to increase the supply of labour to the monetary sector (apart from forced labour)?

7.* Show that even though a worker would *always* prefer to work rather than not to work, he must still dislike work at the margin, given a positive wage rate. (*Hint:* assume that work is a good rather than a bad over some initial range, and indifference curves approach vertical lines at $z = 0$ and $z = T$ asymptotically.)

8.* Use the analysis of this section to explain why amateur sports become professionalized.

D. Consumption and the allocation of time

In our discussions of the consumption decision so far we have assumed that the only requirement for the consumption and enjoyment of goods was money to purchase the goods. We now examine the implications of recognizing that the consumption of goods requires an input of the consumer's time, and that time is a scarce resource. Watching a film in a cinema, eating a meal or merely resting all require, in addition to the expenditure of money on cinema tickets, food or an armchair, an expenditure of time. Consumption decisions are therefore constrained by the time needed in the various consumption activities as well as by the consumer's money income. Increasing the time spent working will increase his money income but will reduce the amount of time available for use in consuming the goods. The consumer's problem is therefore to allocate his time *and* his money income. We will consider a model which simultaneously examines the consumer's labour supply and consumption decisions.

The consumer's utility depends in the usual way on x, the bundle of goods consumed: $u = u(x)$. The consumption decision is constrained in two ways. First the bundle of goods consumed cannot cost more than the consumer's income: $\sum p_i x_i \leq M = \bar{M} + wz$. Secondly there is a time constraint: $T = \sum T_i + z$, where T_i is time spent consuming good i and z is work time. For simplicity we assume that there is a proportional relationship between the amount of good i and the length of time used in its consumption

$$T_i = t_i x_i \tag{D.1}$$

t_i is the 'time price' of good i: the number of minutes required for consumption of one unit of good i.

We will assume that the budget constraint $\sum p_i x_i \leq M$ is always binding as an equality. In Chapter 3 we did not have to *assume* this since it was a *consequence* of the positive marginal utility of goods. Here however the equality in the constraint is not implied by the non-satiation assumption because of the fact that the consumer is now subject to two constraints and it is possible that the time constraint would bite before the budget constraint, leaving the latter satisfied as an inequality. The present assumption rules this out. T/t_i is the maximum consumption of x_i permitted by the time constraint, and if all time is spent consuming good i the maximum consumption allowed by the budget constraint is M/p_i. Our assumption that the budget constraint *always* binds implies that $T/t_i > M/p_i$ for all goods, so that the time constraint is 'further out' than the income constraint.

The consumer's problem is (ignoring the non-negativity constraints)

$$\max_{x} u(x) \quad s.t. \quad (i) \ \sum p_i x_i = \bar{M} + wz$$

$$(ii) \ \sum t_i x_i + z = T \tag{D.2}$$

Notice that the T_i and z are not choice variables; this is because the proportionality assumption [D.1] implies that choice of a bundle of goods determines the length of time spent consuming each good and hence also determines $z = T - \sum t_i x_i$. It would be possible to relax the proportionality assumption for many goods and allow for time spent in consuming goods to enter the utility function directly. We could also use the Lancaster consumption technology model and assume that utility yielding characteristics are produced by consumption activities which use time and goods as inputs. These developments would however make the model rather complex and so we will limit ourselves to examining the implications of our very simple assumptions.

We can proceed quite a long way by diagrammatic analysis of a two-good version of [D.2]. Using the time constraint in [D.2] we have $z = T - \sum t_i x_i$ and substituting in the budget constraint gives

$$\sum p_i x_i = \bar{M} + w(T - \sum t_i x_i)$$

or

$$\sum p_i x_i + w \sum t_i x_i = \sum (p_i + w t_i) x_i = \bar{M} + wT \tag{D.3}$$

t_i is the time necessary for consumption of a unit of good i and w is the money earned in a unit of time so that wt_i is the opportunity cost of the time used in consuming a unit of good i. p_i is the money price of a unit of the good and so $p_i + wt_i$ can be defined as the *full price* of good i, i.e. the sum of the usual *explicit* money cost and the *implicit* time cost of a unit of good i. wT is the income which could be earned if all time was used for working and so $\bar{M} + wT$ is the consumer's maximum potential income or *full income*. [D.3] is then the *full budget* or resource constraint: the full cost of the bundle of goods bought must be equal to the full income of the consumer.

In the two-good case the constraint is, from [D.3]:

$$(p_1 + wt_1)x_1 + (p_2 + wt_2)x_2 = \bar{M} + wT$$

or

$$x_2 = [\bar{M} + wT - (p_1 + wt_1)x_1]/(p_2 + wt_2)$$

and so the slope of the full budget line F is

$$\frac{dx_2}{dx_1} = \frac{-(p_1 + wt_1)}{(p_2 + wt_2)} \qquad [D.4]$$

The full budget line is drawn as F in Fig. 10. We can also draw the money and time budget constraints in the figure. For example B' shows all bundles costing $\bar{M} + wz'$ and B'' all bundles costing $\bar{M} + wz''$, where $z'' > z'$. Similarly all bundles along L' require a total time input in consumption of $T - z'$ and those along L'' a total consumption time input of $T - z''$. The B and L lines can be thought of as iso-expenditure and iso-leisure contours. F is the locus of bundles satisfying both time and expenditure constraints simultaneously. For example, x' is on both B' and L' and x'' on both B'' and L''.

As in Chapter 3, the slope of the iso-expenditure lines is $-p_1/p_2$. Since, for given z along the L lines, variations in x_1 and x_2 must satisfy

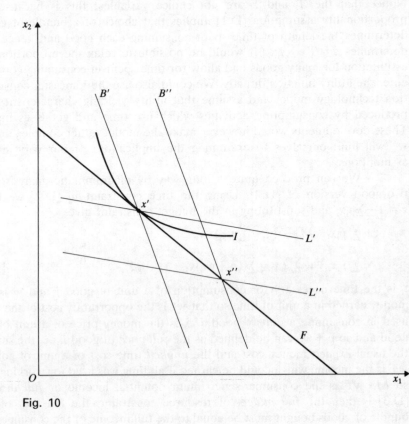

Fig. 10

$t_1 \, dx_1 + t_2 \, dx_2 = 0$, the slope of the iso-leisure lines is $-t_1/t_2$. Fig. 10 has been drawn so that

$$\frac{t_1}{t_2} < \frac{p_1}{p_2} \qquad \qquad \text{[D.5]}$$

Good 1 is in this case relatively less expensive in terms of time than good 2 but relatively more expensive in terms of money. Alternatively we can define the *time intensity* of the ith good as the proportion of the full price accounted for by the time cost; $wt_i/(p_i + wt_i)$. Writing [D.5] as $t_1/p_2 < t_2/p_1$, adding $t_1 wt_2$ to both sides and multiplying through by w yields

$$\frac{wt_1}{p_1 + wt_1} < \frac{wt_2}{p_2 + wt_2} \qquad \qquad \text{[D.6]}$$

so that in Fig. 10 good 1 is less time-intensive than good 2. As the consumer moves down F he substitutes the less time-intensive x_1 for the more time-intensive x_2. He thereby consumes bundles with a greater money cost but with a smaller leisure time input, leaving him more time to earn the extra income required to pay for the more costly bundles.

Equilibrium of the consumer

The consumer is assumed to have preferences which satisfy the assumptions of section 3A and so we can analyse his choice by superimposing his indifference map on his feasible set as in Fig. 10. In the tangency solution at x' shown here the slope of the indifference curve I is equal to the slope of the full budget line, or

$$\frac{u_1}{u_2} = \frac{p_1 + wt_1}{p_2 + wt_2} \qquad \qquad \text{[D.7]}$$

The consumer's marginal rate of substitution is set equal to the ratio of full prices, rather than the ratio of money prices as in the model of Chapter 3. Choice of $x' = (x_1', x_2')$ determines total time spent on consumption $(t_1 x_1' + t_2 x_2')$ and at work $(T - t_1 x_1' - t_2 x_2' = z')$ and the amount of income earned (wz'), which together with unearned income is just sufficient to buy the bundle chosen $(\bar{M} + wz' = p_1 x_1' + p_2 x_2')$.

Comparative statics

The bundle of goods chosen will depend, given the consumer's preferences, on the time and money prices, the wage rate and unearned income:

$$x_i = D_i(p_1, p_2, t_1, t_2, w, \bar{M}) \qquad (i = 1, 2)$$

or in terms of the full prices and full income

$$x_i = H_i(p_1 + wt_1, p_2 + wt_2, \bar{M} + wT) \qquad (i = 1, 2)$$

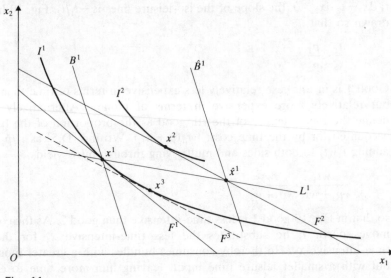

Fig. 11

As in section 3D, we are primarily interested in how the optimal bundle varies in response to changes in all the exogeneous variables $(p_1, p_2, t_1, t_2, w, \bar{M})$.

Let us consider as an example of the comparative static properties, the effect of a rise in the wage rate w. A rise in w will affect the feasible set in two ways. First, it shifts the full budget line F outwards over at least some of its range, thus permitting the consumer to achieve a higher indifference curve. A rise in w will not affect the position of the iso-leisure lines but it will permit a larger expenditure $(\bar{M} + wz)$ for a given z. Hence all the iso-expenditure lines will shift outward, with constant slope. At the consumer's initial equilibrium x^1 in Fig. 11 he will no longer be spending all his money income. He could therefore, without altering z, move down the initial iso-leisure line L^1 to its intersection with the money budget line $\hat{B}^1$ where, at the initial level of z the consumer is again just spending all his income. This point $\hat{x}^1$ is a point on the new full income budget constraint F^2 since it satisfies both the time constraint and the new money income budget constraint. The rise in w, as might be expected, makes the consumer better off, since $\hat{x}^1$ must lie above the initial indifference curve I^1. (Explain why.)

The second effect of the rise in w is to change the slope of the full budget constraint. In Fig. 11 F^2 is flatter than the initial full income line F^1. This is because the diagram is drawn to reflect the assumption that good 1 is less time intensive than good 2. Because good 1 has a lower time price relative to the money price than good 2 the opportunity cost of time used in consuming a unit of good 1 (wt_1) is a smaller proportion of the full price than is the case with good 2. Hence a rise in w will raise the full price of good 1 by proportionately less than for good 2.

The consumer's new optimum bundle on F^2 is x^2, where more of both goods is consumed. The consumer's money income is larger at x^2 than at x^1 but x^2 lies on iso-leisure line above L^1 indicating that more time is devoted to consumption and the consumer's supply of labour has been reduced by the rise in w. Only if the optimum was to the right of $\hat{x}^1$ on F^2 would the rise in w lead to an increased supply of labour as the consumer chose a less time-consuming consumption bundle.

As in Chapter 3, the comparative static responses to changes in the exogeneous variables such as the wage rate will depend on the consumer's preferences. However, we can use Fig. 11 to decompose the effect of the change in w into an income effect and a substitution effect. As in previous analysis we move the new (full) budget line inward until the consumer can just achieve his initial level of utility on I^1. Since the new budget line is flatter than the initial one the compensated demand for goods will be to the right of the initial equilibrium at x^3 where F^3 is tangent to the initial indifference curve. Hence we can establish that the substitution effect of a rise in the wage rate will be to increase the demand for the less time intensive good x_1. This compensated change in w will lead to a rise in the amount of labour supplied (since x^3 is on a lower iso-leisure line than L^1).

This analysis of the effect of a rise in the wage rate suggests some tentative explanations for two phenomena associated with rising real wages, i.e. with w rising faster than the money prices of goods. First the substitution effect will lead to the substitution of goods which are less time-intensive for goods which are more time-intensive. Consumers will spend money in order to save time by buying higher-priced goods which have a smaller time cost. Examples include the growth of 'convenience' foods which require less time for preparation and greater use of domestic appliances to economize on time. Secondly, the secular decline in the average number of hours worked per worker may be ascribed to the strength of the income effect of rising real wages. This more than offsets the substitution effect and leads to an increase in leisure time used for consumption of the larger baskets of goods bought with the rising full income.

Exercise 5D
1.   Prove that a rise in w will indeed flatten the full budget line if and only if good 1 is less time intensive than good 2, as asserted in the text. (*Hint*: differentiate the slope of F with respect to w and use [D.6].)
2.   What will be the effect on the feasible set of changes in unearned income, money prices and time prices?
3.* Using the results of the previous question, examine the changes in the supply of labour and the demand for goods caused by changes in $\bar{M}$, p_i and t_i.
4.* Would you expect the consumer's money price elasticity of demand for a good to be smaller the larger was his wage rate?
5.   Use the model of this section to explain why convenience foods have high income elasticities of demand.
6.* How would you evaluate a commuter's willingness to pay for a small reduction in the length of time it takes him to get to work?

E. Search and information

Our models of the consumer so far have been based on the assumption that he has complete information about the prices and qualities of goods that he is considering buying. In many circumstances this assumption may be misleading, as anyone who has bought a new or secondhand car or some other consumer durable, or has bought, sold or rented accommodation will testify. The consumer may act in conditions of *technological uncertainty* in that the quality, performance, durability, or safety of goods bought cannot be known at the time of purchase. He may also face *market uncertainty*: the goods he wishes to buy may be offered for sale on different terms (particularly at different prices) by different sellers and the consumer does not know which seller offers the most favourable terms (lowest price). The existence of uncertainty or incomplete information will affect the consumer's behaviour in two ways. First, it may change the bundle of goods bought, i.e., the decision that he actually takes. We will defer investigation of this effect of uncertainty until Chapters 19 and 20, where we also consider the nature of uncertainty in more detail. Second, a reduction in uncertainty or an improvement in the information available to the consumer at the time he takes his decision will enable him to make a better decision. Hence the consumer will be prepared to invest some of his resources (time and money) in acquiring additional information. He may buy information produced by others (newspapers containing advertisements, reports of tests by consumers' associations) or he may produce information himself. In this section we will examine the factors influencing the consumer's decision to produce information for his own use. We will construct a very simple model of *search* by a consumer who faces a range of prices for a particular good but does not know which sellers offer the lowest price. We will specify the benefits and costs of search and how they are related to the level of search, and so define the optimal amount of search. We then investigate how this will be affected by changes in the consumer's environment.

Search may be either simultaneous or sequential. *Simultaneous search* involves the consumer in producing a predetermined amount of information before deciding from which seller to buy. For example, a consumer who wants to have his house painted will search simultaneously if he asks *n* painters to give him an estimate before he decides which of these to choose. Simultaneous search is analogous to picking *n* numbered balls from an urn before examining them to see which has the lowest number printed on it. The decision variable in simultaneous search is the sample size *n* since the expected minimum price will decline (but at a decreasing rate), and the costs will rise, with *n*.

In *sequential search* the consumer samples one seller at a time and decides, after discovering each seller's price, whether to accept the offer or to continue searching. The analogy here is picking and examining one numbered ball at a time from an urn, with examined and rejected balls not being replaced in the urn. The decision variable in sequential search is the *acceptable price* p_a, defined as the highest price at which the consumer is prepared to buy. The lower p_a the lower will be the expected price paid and the greater the expected length of time the consumer spends searching. The consumer must therefore trade off expected search costs against the expected price he will have to pay, and this will result in an optimal choice of a maximum acceptable price at or below which he stops searching and buys.

The consumer-searcher will often have some control over the method of search to adopt and indeed could use a mix of the two methods, for example by conducting a sequence of samples of size n. The particular method adopted will depend on which promises to yield the largest excess of benefit over cost and the choice of the method of search will therefore be an economic decision. We will not examine the choice of method except to point out that simultaneous search is more likely to be used when there will be a significant length of time between the consumer requesting information and a seller providing it, because sequential search may then take a very long time. Hence we would expect simultaneous search to be used when the consumer requires a highly specific good or service, as for example in house construction or repairs, since this will involve the seller in making a different estimate of the cost for each customer. When all consumers buy the same type of good the seller can quote his price quickly to any consumer-searcher and so sequential search is more likely. We will concentrate on the sequential search decision and leave the simultaneous search model to the exercises, since it produces broadly similar results.

The consumer is assumed to know in advance the distribution of prices that he faces, though not of course which seller offers which price. He *does not revise* his beliefs about the price distribution in the process of searching. To keep the model simple, let us suppose that the probability distribution of prices is rectangular, with p^0 and p^1 being the minimum and maximum possible prices of the good, and all p ($p^0 \leq p \leq p^1$) being equally probable.

If the consumer is prepared to buy from the first seller who offers a price of p_a (the acceptable price) *or less*, the price he will pay will be between p_a and p^0. Since we have assumed that the distribution of prices is rectangular all prices between p_a and p^0 are equally likely and so the *actual expected price*, p_α, paid by the consumer-searcher will be

$$p_\alpha = (p_a + p^0)/2 \qquad\qquad [\text{E}.1]$$

Assuming, again for simplicity, that only one unit of the good will be purchased whatever the price, [E.1] also shows the expected cost of the good to the consumer, and this will increase at a constant rate as p_a increases from p^0 to p^1. This is plotted in Fig. 12 as a function of p_a by the line labelled p_α. The dotted line is the 45° line and is the locus of points such that $p_a = p_\alpha$.

If p_a exceeds p^1 (the consumer's maximum acceptable price exceeds the actual maximum price he will be offered) then the consumer is not really searching at all. He will accept the first offer he receives and on average will

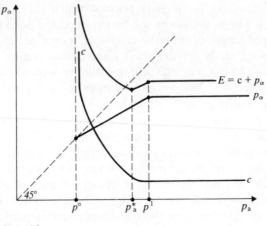

Fig. 12

pay $(p^1 + p^0)/2$. If on the other hand $p_a < p^0$ the p_α line is undefined because the consumer will never receive an acceptable offer. He will therefore not engage in search. We shall analyze here the only interesting case, in which $p^1 \geq p_a \geq p^0$.

The main cost of search to the consumer is assumed to be his time, and we will assume that the length of time required to discover any one seller and evaluate his offer is independent of the total number of sellers investigated. The length of time on average spent searching (or equivalently the average number of sellers who must be investigated) will increase as the acceptable price is lowered and will increase at an increasing rate. (See exercises for a proof). Hence the expected total cost of search is plotted in Fig. 12 as the curve c, which is constant for $p_a \geq p^1$, since just one offer is investigated and accepted, and rises at an increasing rate as p_a is lowered. The consumer is assumed to wish to minimize the total expected cost of the good, which is the sum of the expected purchase price and the expected search cost. (This assumption, that the consumer is only concerned with expected cost and is unaffected by the variability of costs, implies, as we will see in Chapter 19, that the consumer is indifferent to risk and that his utility function has a special form). In Fig. 12 the curve E plots expected total cost, given by the vertical sum of the p_a and c curves. E is at a minimum at p_a^*. In this case the consumer's maximum acceptable price is below the actual maximum price p^1 and the expected search time will be positive.

This model of search is very simple but it yields a number of predictions about the consumer's search activity:

(a) The acceptable price will rise, and hence the average search time fall, with increases in the marginal cost of search. The reader should satisfy himself of this by redrawing Fig. 12 with steeper search cost (c) curves, and should also show that the consumer may not search at all (i.e., he sets $p_a^* = p^1$) if marginal search costs are sufficiently large. If the main cost of search is the opportunity cost of the time involved we would expect, *ceteris paribus*, that individuals with higher wage rates will do less 'shopping around' than those with lower wage rates. A further implication, following from the discussion in section D, is that those with higher wage rates will be more likely to buy information (subscribe to consumer associations, magazines and so on) rather than produce it themselves by search, which is a relatively time-intensive method of acquiring information.

(*b*) The average amount of search will be larger and the optimal acceptable price (p_a^*) lower, the larger the quantity of the good purchased. If x units are to be bought (where x is independent of p) the expected actual purchase cost to the consumer will be

$$p_\alpha x = \frac{(p_a + p^0)x}{2} \qquad [\text{E.2}]$$

and expected search cost is

$$c = c(p_a) \qquad [\text{E.3}]$$

with $c' < 0$ and $c'' > 0$. The total expected cost E is $c + p_\alpha x$ which is minimized by choice of p_a when

$$\frac{\text{d}}{\text{d}p_a}(c + p_\alpha x) = \frac{x}{2} + c'(p_a^*) = 0 \qquad [\text{E.4}]$$

Now an increase in the number of units to be bought (x) means that $c'(p_a)$ must decrease to satisfy [E.4]. Since $c'' > 0$, p_a^* must *fall* to decrease c'. So the larger is x the smaller will be p_a^* and the greater the average search time. In terms of Fig. 12 increases in the number of units bought will shift the expected purchase cost line upward and increase its slope. The economic rationale of our result is straightforward: the more of a good that is bought the greater are the rewards from searching for a lower price.

Our discussion also indicates that behaviour which is apparently sub-optimal in terms of models which assume certainty is in fact optimal in an uncertain environment. Consumers who are prepared to buy at a particular price when they know that the same good is being sold at a lower price by some other seller are, on the face of it, acting irrationally. However, once it is recognized that information is both incomplete *and* costly to acquire (the consumer does not know *which* seller is offering a lower price and investigating additional sellers involves expenditure of time and money) the use of an acceptable price decision rule does not imply sub-optimal behaviour.

Our search model is clearly very simple and we will conclude by indicating how it would be possible to make it more realistic (and more complicated). We could change our assumption about the probability distribution of prices: production costs will set a lower limit to the price of a good but it is not obvious that there is an upper limit. We could allow for the consumer becoming more efficient at discovering sellers as he searches; or for his grouping sellers and assigning different probability distributions of prices to different groups (supermarket prices may be differently distributed from corner shop prices). A more fundamental extension of the models would be to recognize that when the consumer starts searching he is unlikely to know accurately the actual probability distribution of prices. He will start with an estimate of the distribution together with a decision rule (p_a^*, the optimal acceptable price), and as he searches, the information generated (the sequence of prices offered) may lead him to revise his estimate of the distribution. This in turn will lead to changes in his decision rule p_a^*. If, for example, he initially correctly believes the distribution to be rectangular but underestimates its mean he will set a p_a^* which is too low given the actual distribution. He will find that he is searching for longer than initially expected and getting higher than anticipated offers. The consumer will adjust his estimate of the mean and increase his acceptable price. This type of behaviour under uncertainty differs from the behaviour we have investigated in this section (and in Chapters 19 and 20) in two fundamental ways:

(*a*) there is a *learning process*, whereby the consumer generates additional information which leads him to change his probability beliefs.

(*b*) as a consequence of the learning process the consumer changes his decision rule (p_a^*). His behaviour is *adaptive* in that it changes in response to the new information acquired as more sellers are investigated.

We cannot examine the implications of these extensions because of a binding length constraint on this book, but the interested reader should follow up the references at the end of the chapter.

Exercise 5E

1. (*a*) In the model of sequential search in the text let $q = q(p_a)$ be the probability that a particular seller's price is acceptable. What is the form of the function $q(p_a)$?

   (*b*) Show that the probability that the first acceptable price is that of the nth seller is $(1-q)^{n-1} \cdot q$, i.e. that the number of unsuccessful searches follows the geometric distribution.

   (*c*) Hence show that the mean number of searches is $[(1-q)/q]+1 = 1/q$ and prove the assertion in the text that the mean number of sellers investigated increases and at an increasing rate as the acceptable price is lowered.

   (*d*)* What will be the effect on the acceptable price and the average amount of search of

   (i) an increase in the maximum possible price p^1?

   (ii) an increase in the dispersion of prices with a constant mean price $(p^1 + p^0)/2$?

References and further reading

Revealed preference theory is discussed and its relationship with utility theory examined in

P. Newman. *The Theory of Exchange*, Prentice-Hall, Englewood Cliffs, N.J., 1965, Chapter 6,

and its usefulness for making aggregate welfare judgements in:

P. A. Samuelson. 'Evaluation of real national income', *Oxford Economic Papers*, 1950, pp. 1–29.

Price indices are considered in detail in

R. G. D. Allen. *Index Numbers in Theory and Practice*, Macmillan, London, 1975.

Consumption technology theory and its applications are set out in:

K. Lancaster. *Consumer Demand: A New Approach*, Columbia University Press, New York 1971,

and the relationship between the consumer's preferences as regards characteristics and his demands for goods is discussed in:

R. G. Lipsey and **G. Rosenbluth.** 'A Contribution to the New Theory of Demand: A Rehabilitation of the Giffen Good', *Canadian Journal of Economics*, 1971.

The seminal work on the economics of time is:

G. S. Becker. 'Theory of the Allocation of Time', *Economic Journal* 1965.

and the time and household production models are integrated in:

R. T. Michael and **G. S. Becker.** 'On the new theory of consumer behaviour', *Swedish Journal of Economics*, 1975.

Both the preceding references are reprinted, along with other papers applying the same kind of models to a wide variety of behaviour, in:

G. S. Becker. *The Economic Approach to Human Behaviour*, University of Chicago Press, Chicago, 1976.

Two of the earliest contributions to search and information in economics are:

G. J. Stigler. 'The Economics of Information', *Journal of Political Economy*, June 1961;

G. J. Stigler. 'Information in the Labor Market', *Journal of Political Economy*, October 1962,

and there is a collection of papers on various aspects of the subject in:

E. S. Phelps *et al. Microeconomic Foundations of Employment and Inflation Theory*, Macmillan, London, 1970.

Chapter 6

The firm

A. Introduction

In the last three chapters we have examined the theory of the consumer at some length. Our interest in this was partly to explain and predict consumer behaviour as such, and partly to derive some general results which will be used in Chapters 10 and 16 as building blocks in constructing a theory of markets and of resource allocation in the economy as a whole.

A *pure exchange economy* is one in which economic agents have given endowments of goods and exchange goods among themselves to achieve preferred consumption patterns. In analyzing the determination of prices and quantities exchanged in such an economy, it would be sufficient to use the consumer theory so far constructed – the model of section 3F would be directly applicable (see Ch. 10, where an example is given). However, the pure exchange economy lacks an important aspect of real economies, namely that of *production*. Production is the activity of combining goods and services called *inputs*, in technological processes which result in other goods and services called *outputs*. In the pure exchange economy, although each consumer can transform his endowed bundle of goods into some other bundle through exchange, this is not true for the group as a whole: the sum of consumptions of each good cannot exceed the sum of initial endowments of it. The existence of production possibilities adds another dimension to economic activity: it permits transformations of endowed bundles of goods into other bundles for the economy as a whole. Clearly, any attempt at explaining resource allocation is incomplete unless it takes production into account. Theories of *the firm* arise out of the need to incorporate production into our theory of resource allocation.

B. The nature of the firm

At a primitive stage in economic development production can be wholly individualistic, being carried on by one person working with tools and raw materials. Some goods and services are still produced in this way, for example, writing (though not publishing) a book, giving someone a haircut, painting a picture, but the overwhelming majority of goods and services (including some books, haircuts and paintings) are produced by *co-operating groups* of individuals. The reasons for this are not hard to find: specialization of individuals in parts of the production process can be carried further within a group than if one individual undertakes the whole process and, in many processes, there are gains from *teamwork* – the total output of a group when working as a team is greater than the sum of outputs of individuals working separately. However, the 'firm' as it has been traditionally conceived of in economics is more than simply a co-operating group of producers; it is a group with a particular *organizational structure*, and a particular set of *property rights*. For example, it is possible to conceive of a 'producers' co-operative' in which assets are owned in common – no individual has the right to exclusive use or disposal of any of the equipment, output, cash reserves, etc. of the co-operative and decisions are taken by majority vote. This would clearly not be a 'firm' as traditionally conceived. The essence of the latter is the existence of a central figure, the owner, employer or *entrepreneur*, who:

(*a*) enters into a contract with each of the individuals who supply productive services which specifies the nature and duration of those services and the remuneration for them;

(*b*) either takes decisions, or has the right to insist that decisions are taken, in *his* interests, subject to his contractual obligations;

(*c*) has the right to the *residual income* from production, i.e. the excess of revenue over payments to suppliers of productive services made under the terms of their contracts;

(*d*) can transfer his right in the residual income, and his rights and obligations under the contracts with suppliers of productive services, to another individual;

(*e*) has the power to direct the activities of the suppliers of productive services, subject to the terms and conditions of their contracts;

(*f*) can change the membership of the producing group not only by terminating contracts but also by entering into new contracts and adding to the group.

The essential feature of the 'classical firm' is therefore a central figure, with whom all contracts are concluded, and who controls and directs in his own interests, subject to constraints arising out of the terms of the contracts he has made.

Since we can conceive of different ways of organizing co-operating productive groups, it is of interest to ask why this particular form, the entrepreneurial firm, developed into the dominant form of organization of production. It is possible to give an historical account of this: in the transition from the feudal, largely agrarian economy of the late Middle Ages to the capitalist industrial economy of the nineteenth and twentieth centuries, an important role was played by wealthy men who had accumulated their wealth through trade, inheritance of land, or by being successful skilled craftsmen. These were able to respond to important developments in transport and production technology, especially mechanization and the use of steam power, by investing in plant and machinery, grouping workers together into factories, entering into contracts of employment with them, and financing production in advance of sales. Thus their ownership of wealth was translated into their ownership of the assets of the producing group and they became the buyers of labour power. The advent of the 'capitalist entrepreneur' thus shaped the organization of the producing group into that of the classical firm just described.

However, though this historical account may give a description of what happened, it does not constitute a complete explanation because it does not fully explain why it was this and not other forms of organization which came to dominate. Other organizational forms were certainly known and attempted, for example the early socialist experiments of Robert Owen. In addition, as R. Coase (1937) has emphasized, an alternative to organization within the firm which is always available is that of *organization through the market*. 'Organization through the market' means the co-ordination of the myriad separate, individual decisions by the 'impersonal workings' of the price system. In this process there is no 'central planning' but only the self-interested planning of *individual* economic decision-takers, which interacts through the system of prices and markets to determine a resource allocation. In a phrase borrowed from D.H. Robertson, Coase describes the firm as 'an island of conscious power' in this 'ocean of unconscious co-operation'. Within the firm there is centralized economic planning and administrative co-ordination replaces the price mechanism, although, of course, the firm is embedded in an external system of market forces which condition its operations. The question then is: why does the firm, viewed as a centrally planned system, replace co-ordination through the market, and become the dominant form of organization of the producer group?

An *explanation* of the dominant position of the classical firm in the organization of production must rest on a demonstration of the advantages which it has over other forms of organization, including that of the market. Thus Coase has argued that the firm superseded market organization because there are costs associated with use of the price mechanism and that administrative organization within the firm is, up to a point, less costly. The major types of costs involved in effecting market transactions are those of acquiring information about prices and terms under which trade takes place; the costs of negotiating and concluding contracts; and the uncertainty which may exist about the conditions on markets in the future, given that the world is not continually in long-run static equilibrium. In some kinds of activities and markets these costs might be minor, but in others they could greatly exceed the costs of organizing production within a firm, in which case we would expect the latter to dominate.

A second important reason for the dominance of the classical firm, not only over organization through the market but also over other forms of organization such as that of the 'producer co-operative' has been advanced by A. Alchian and H. Demsetz (1972). When the producing group works as a team, there is the problem of measuring and rewarding each member's effort in such a way as to reward high productivity and penalize 'shirking'. In the absence of such measurement and reward, the presumption is that it pays any one individual to minimize his effort, since the costs of doing so, in terms of reduced output, are spread over all the members of the team – this is similar to the 'free rider problem' of Chapter 18. Then it is argued that the system under which a central individual monitors performance and apportions rewards stimulates productivity, as the retention by that individual of the residual income of the group provides an incentive for him to perform the monitoring function efficiently. To this we might add that in terms of the speed with which decisions are arrived at, the costs absorbed in the decision-taking process, and the flexibility of response to changed circumstances, a system based on central direction rather than multilateral consultation and voting procedures is likely to have an advantage (see the discussion in Ch. 18 on the problems of common access resources and voting procedures, and relate it to the question of the likely efficiency of a 'producers' co-operative'). It can therefore be argued that the classical 'entrepreneurial firm' emerged as the dominant form of organization of production not only because the historical conditions were appropriate, but also because it had advantages of efficiency and productivity over other forms of organization, whether they were the market or formal organizations with different systems of decision structure and property rights.

The characteristics of the 'classical firm' described above have determined the form of the 'theory of the firm' in economics, and hence the representation of how production is carried on in a private ownership economy. The firm is viewed as being faced with an optimization problem (see Ch. 2). Its choice variables are input and output levels and possibly other variables such as advertising and expenditure on research and development. Its objective is to maximize profit, defined as the excess of revenue over all opportunity costs, including those associated with the supply of capital and the managerial functions of planning, organizing and decision-taking. This formulation of the objective function appeared quite natural, since the individual controlling the firm receives the profit as his income (over and above payment for his supply of productive services), and, viewing him as a consumer, his utility from consumption is greater the greater the income available for it (but see Ch. 13, where this somewhat naïve view is challenged).

The constraints in the problem are of two types. First, the conditions on the markets which the firm enters as a seller of outputs or buyer of inputs will determine, through prices, the profitability of any production plan (i.e. a particular set of quantities of inputs and outputs), and hence also the way in which profits vary with the production plan. Another way of putting this is to say that market conditions determine the terms of the contracts into which the firm enters with buyers and suppliers of goods and productive services, and hence determine the amount of the residual income, or profit, which can be made. Second, the state of technology will determine which production plans are feasible, i.e. what amounts of inputs are required to produce given output levels, or conversely what outputs can be produced with given input levels. Thus, market conditions on the one hand, and the nature of technology on the other, determine the constraints in the firm's optimization problem.

The classical theory of the firm, therefore, operates at a high level of abstraction, at least equivalent to that of the theory of the consumer in Chapter 3. In its basic formulation, the firm is assumed to know with certainty the market conditions and state of technology. The theoretical problem is then to formalize the firm's optimization problem; examine the nature of its solution and the way in which this solution varies with changes in the parameters of the problem; and then translate the results into explanations and predictions of the firm's behaviour. Before going on to examine all this in detail in the next three chapters, we consider in the next section some criticisms of this approach.

Exercise 6B

1. Until fairly recently, employment in the UK ports industry was subject to the 'casual system'. Twice each day, dock-workers and employers would assemble at a particular place at each port, and employers would hire the men they wanted for a specific job, the men being paid off once the job was completed, possibly the same day or a little later. Explain why this system of allocating labour resources in the ports industry could be called 'co-ordination by the market'. Why do you think it existed in the ports industry when in most other industries workers are employed on a regular weekly basis? Why was it ended?

2. On Oxford Street, a major shopping thoroughfare in London's West End, the only department store which does not open on a Saturday afternoon (a busy time for the stores) is the John Lewis Partnership. This store is a form of producers' co-operative: employees share in profits and many major decisions, e.g. on opening hours, are subject to vote. The other Oxford Street stores are conventional 'firms'. Discuss as analytically as you can the reasons why the difference in organization leads to the difference in opening times. Relate this example to the discussion of this section.

3. Set out as fully as possible the probable advantages and disadvantages of the producers' co-operative as compared to the conventional firm in the cases of:
    (i) a group of six potters producing handmade pottery;
    (ii) a group of two hundred workers producing motorcycles;
    (iii) a group of four thousand workers producing a range of electrical and non-electrical components for motor cars.

4. What view of human nature underlies the Alchian–Demsetz rationale for the firm, outlined in this section? Do you agree with it?

C. Critique of the classical theory of the firm

If we were to compare a factual description of a modern firm with the rather abstract description implied by the 'orthodox' view of the firm set out at the end of the previous section, we would find several marked differences. There appear to be many features of real firms which simply do not have counterparts in the theory:

(i) Ownership structure: a firm may be owned by a single individual or by a small group, with each owner liable for the debts of the firm to the complete extent of his wealth. Alternatively, the firm may be owned by any number from a few to several thousands of people, with the liability of each limited only to the value of his ownership shares, exchangeable on a stock market. Part or all of the shares may be held by other firms, or financial organizations such as pension funds and insurance companies.

(ii) Control structure: where the firm is owned by one individual or a small group, it is likely that overall control will be exercised by someone with a significant ownership share. Where the ownership is dispersed over many individuals, overall control is exercised by a group, the 'board of directors', acting in principle as representatives of the owners, and comprising employees of the firm (senior executives) and 'outside directors'. Where the firm is partly owned by another firm or financial organization, some members of this group will often represent it on the board. If ownership is total, then control will usually be exercised by having the senior executives directly responsible to executives of the owning firm.

(iii) Organization: a hierarchical structure will exist between the people who directly carry out the basic activities of production, selling output and buying inputs, on the one hand, and the people exercising overall control, on the other. This is intended to fulfil a number of functions: to translate broad policy objectives formulated by controllers into specific plans; to co-ordinate the separate activities at lower levels and ensure consistency of plans; to monitor performance and transmit information on this up to controllers; and to provide information with which overall policy objectives can be formulated. The larger the scale and greater the diversity of the basic production and selling activities of the organization, the more extended and complex this hierarchical structure will be.

(iv) Information: the normal operations of the firm will generate information (reports from salesmen on demand conditions, performance of production processes, etc.) and also activities will be undertaken to acquire it (market research, technological research and development) and this information must be transmitted to the points in the firm at which it is required for decision-making. This information will rarely be complete, so that decisions will generally be taken under varying degrees of uncertainty.

(v) Conflict: objectives, plans and decisions will generally be formulated or taken by more than one individual. Conflicts may arise between these individuals, for one or both of two reasons: (a) because of lack of objective information, beliefs may differ about possible outcomes of decisions and the relative likelihoods of these, or (b) preference orderings of the individuals over the outcomes of the decision may differ. This latter source of conflict is in turn due to the fact that a given outcome of a decision may benefit different decision-takers in different ways, so that conflict would be avoided in this case only if they subordinated their own self-interest to some common objective, possibly that of the firm's shareholders. Moreover, although the direct participants in decision-taking are usually the executives of a firm, there will usually be other groups who can influence certain decisions by their behaviour. For example, workers can refuse to work if decisions about wages, hours and conditions of work do or do not take a certain form; shareholders can sell their shares if profits are low, and so on. The conflicts which exist among such groups will be reflected in decision-taking.

The description of the firm implicit in the profit maximization theory seems to include little of this. Nothing is said about control or organization structures and a very restricted view is taken of the nature of ownership. It seems to be assumed that whatever these may be, the firm will act in the best interests of its owners, i.e. the recipients of the 'residual income', and that there is no organizational problem in translating this objective into decisions. Moreover, no conflict is seen to exist: all decisions are taken in a way consistent with the objective of the firm. In all its decisions, including even inter-temporal ones, the firm has complete information, and there is no uncertainty. Thus, the theory clearly does not seem to take into account many features of reality.

Is this alone sufficient, however, for rejecting the theory? The answer to this question must stem from some view of what theories are, what they are required to do, and under what circumstances they should be rejected. That is, we have to consider issues raised by the 'methodology' of economics. (At this point, the reader might find it useful to review the discussion of rationality in section A of Ch. 1.)

We summarize briefly what appears to be the most widely accepted position. In formulating the basic assumptions, axioms or postulates of a theory, it is always necessary to abstract from many of the factual details of the real situation. Indeed, note that the 'description' of the firm just given is still a highly selective one, ignoring many features of real firms, and concentrating on quite a small number of 'facts'. The ground for rejection of a theory is not, then, that it omits aspects of reality in its formulation, but rather that the statements it makes about reality are proved wrong. Implicitly, the theory of profit maximization is saying that the specific facts of ownership, control and organization structure are not really relevant to the decisions taken by the firm, and that the dominant motive in firms' decision-taking is profit-making. To refute this theory, we would have to provide evidence of decision-taking by firms which was inconsistent with it, for example details of instances in which firms chose a particular decision alternative when they knew of others which would generate greater profit. Such evidence might also suggest the directions in which we could modify the axioms of the theory, so as to make the implications we draw from those axioms consistent with reality.

In the light of this, we might expect that criticism of the theory of profit maximization is based on carefully researched evidence which shows that the actual behaviour of firms cannot be deduced from the premise that they maximize profit. Not so. Most of the criticism is based on *a priori* reasoning and casual observation, and amounts to the counter-assertion that some of the characteristics of firms from which the theory abstracts *are* important, and lead them to behave in a different way. Of course, anyone is free to make his own abstractions, formulate his own axioms and show that their implications differ from those of the profit maximization theory. But this in itself does not refute the theory; we still have to gather evidence on firms' behaviour, and see which theory 'fits the facts'.

The *a priori* reasoning which forms the basis of the rejection of the profit maximization theory, and its suggested replacement by other theories, revolves around the idea of the 'divorce of ownership from control' and the concept of *managerial capitalism* (see R. Marris [1964]). As we saw in the previous section, the classical theory of the firm is based upon the idea of a central individual who owns the firm's assets, which he finances by saving and borrowing; receives as his income the profits of the business; employs the inputs; bears the risks; and controls the firm. Since the work of Berle and Means (1944) a different view of the nature of capitalism has become general, receiving impetus from the ever-increasing size of firms and con-centration of economic activity. Though owner-controlled firms may still form the majority of business units, the bulk of economic activity is controlled by large corporations, the distinguishing characteristic of which is a divorce of ownership from control. The owners of the firm are the shareholders, who may number thousands, and each of them has a very small proportion of the total equity of the company. They bear the risks, in the sense that fluctuations in the profits of the company imply fluctuations in their income – dividends – from it. They also supply the risk capital for new investment, either by buying new issues of shares, or, more usually, by 'agreeing' to forego profits which are then ploughed back into the business. On the other hand, by diversifying their shareholdings across a number of companies (or having experts do this for them, in unit trusts or investments trusts), they reduce the riskiness of the overall portfolio, until the main element of this may simply be the variability in general business conditions. A consequence of this is that shareholders take only a very general interest in the running of any one company. In exceptional circumstances, poor performance by a company could lead to 'stormy shareholders' meetings', and 'acrimonious debate', but the mechanisms of direct shareholder control are rarely effective. Rather, dissatisfied shareholders vote with their feet: they sell their shares, thus reducing the company's share price. This may in fact represent the most effective ·control on management, first because managers may like a high stock market valuation (share price × number of shares issued) for its own sake, but probably more importantly because a valuation which is low relative to the earning power of the assets of the company raises the threat of takeover by another company after which the present senior managers, at least, could lose their jobs. Hence there is some constraint on managers to take account of shareholders' interests.

In principle, the board of directors of a firm are meant to be the 'stewards' for the shareholders, to oversee the operations of the company on the shareholders' behalf. However, these boards are usually dominated by the senior executives of the company. Hence, if there were to be a conflict of interest between management and shareholders, it is far more likely that the board would espouse the interests of the former. Thus, the senior executives of the company rather than shareholders effectively control the decision-taking activities of the firm (subject to the organizational problems which they themselves may have in ensuring that their decisions are actually implemented). It follows that these executives are essentially carrying out all except one of the entrepreneurial functions of the capitalist, and so we have the term managerial capitalism. The one function which they do not perform is that of supplying the risk capital of the business, and to that extent they would prefer their position to that of the capitalist in the traditional story (note that of course the executives still have certain things at risk, such as income and possibly some wealth, as well as social prestige, which may depend on performance of the company).

The first thing deduced from this picture of managerial capitalism is that if managers' and shareholders' interests were in conflict, the divorce of ownership from control *permits* managers to pursue their own interests rather than those of shareholders, to an extent determined by the sanctions possessed by shareholders. The second step is to argue that the interests of managers and shareholders *do* conflict. It is suggested that managers derive their satisfactions from: their salaries; amounts of additional perquisites such as expense accounts, company cars, subsidized food and drink (which also have tax advantages); status, prestige, power and security. Although these things may depend on a profit performance which keeps shareholders happy, they do not necessarily vary directly with profit, but rather may vary with other dimensions of the firm's performance. To complete the argument, then, the third step is the proposition that, as we usually assume in economics, people take decisions in their own self-interest. This means in the present case that managers will choose output and input levels, and investment plans, in the light of their effects on the determinants of their own satisfactions, taking account of shareholders' interests only insofar as they represent an externally imposed constraint. The main problem for any theory based on this view is *to set up an analytical connection between the decision variables of the firm* – outputs, inputs, advertising and investment – on the one hand, and *those things which provide satisfaction for managers*, on the other.

A major aspect of managerial capitalism, then, is the ability of managers to pursue their own interests, subject only to a constraint imposed by the interests of the owners. It is crucial to the theories stemming from this view that this constraint should be satisfied by less than maximum profit.

If this were not the case, then all that is being said is that managers would like to pursue their own interests but cannot, and the profit maximization theory would be justified in ignoring the institutional detail of the divorce of ownership from control.

Still remaining at the level of *a priori* reasoning, there are several cases in which the profit constraint would be for maximum profit. First, if a firm operates in competitive output markets, then at least in the long run, profit maximization is a condition of survival. Potential entrants are assumed to know the costs of production and prices prevailing in the market and so would enter, increasing supply, until the maximum profit a firm could earn would be normal profit. Hence, profit maximization and long-run survival become synonymous. A necessary condition for managerial capitalism therefore, at least in the long-run, is the existence of market imperfections.

At least as important are capital market conditions. To fix ideas, suppose that there is complete information about the profit-making *possibilities* of every firm and that the capital market is perfect, in the sense that any amount can be borrowed or lent by anyone, at the same given interest rate. In this case, the takeover mechanism mentioned earlier would mean that every firm would have to maximize profit. The argument is as follows: the market value of the company's shares (which is what an acquirer would have to pay to gain 100% control of the company, though this degree of control would certainly not be necessary) will be equal to the present value (see Ch. 15) of the profit time stream which will result from the decisions of the managers. Should this fall below the maximum possible present value, *anyone* (including an employee of the company) could immediately borrow a sum equal to the company's current market value, buy up the company, change its policies, and thereby increase his wealth. Hence, if they did not want to lose their jobs, the managers would have to adopt policies which maximized shareholders' wealth.

Although this picture is simplistic, it concentrates attention on the two crucial factors: availability of information on the firm's profit opportunities; and existence of buyers able to command finance for acquisition. Now the central question concerns the degree to which real capital markets approximate to this ideal. Is there *sufficient* information, and are there potential acquirers with *sufficient* access to funds for the approximation to be close? Casual observation points to plenty of takeover activity, followed by 'asset-stripping', 'pruning' of activities, and so on. However, this does not provide hard evidence to conclude either that firms are thereby constrained to maximize profits or that they are not. We must still regard the case as 'not proven'; despite the attractive plausibility of the description of firms inherent in the doctrine of managerial capitalism, we still need evidence which establishes that firms' decisions could not be deduced from the premise of profit maximization.

Finally, it has been argued that the doctrine of managerial capitalism itself overstates the extent of the divorce of ownership from control. Individuals or families may own a significant portion of the shares of even very large companies, and may take part in running the company. So may other institutions, such as pension funds and insurance companies. Moreover, managers themselves may be shareholders, having received remuneration through options to buy the company's shares at favourable prices, and for this reason, as well as for socio-economic reasons such as 'class solidarity' may pursue shareholder interests. It is impossible on *a priori* grounds to decide whether these factors are sufficient to imply that firms will maximize profits. Again, the only test is the evidence on the decisions which firms actually take.

Exercise 6C

1. Is the observation that, after a takeover, profits of the firm taken over are increased while the labour force and managerial staff are reduced consistent with the proposition that the objective of firms is to maximize profit?
2. Describe the ways in which (a) shareholders and (b) other firms acquire informaton about the profit-making *possibilities* of a particular firm.
3. What is the relevance to the doctrine of managerial capitalism of the fact that equity ownership is increasingly dominated by 'institutional investors' such as pension funds and insurance companies,
4. Provide explanations, in terms of (a) the theory of the profit-maximizing firm and (b) the doctrine of managerial capitalism, of why the sales of expensive cars (Rovers, Jaguars, Rolls-Royces, etc) are almost entirely to companies rather than to private individuals.
5. What would be the effects of having workers' representatives on the board of directors, in a world of (a) perfect markets, and (b) imperfect goods and capital markets, as compared to the situation in which the board consisted entirely of managerial executives?
6. How are the facts that firms are organized hierarchically and information dispersed and costly to acquire and transmit likely to affect the behaviour of firms?

D. Conclusions

The purpose of this chapter was to give a general picture of the concept of 'the firm' in economic theory. Seven of the next eight chapters go on to develop the theory of the firm at some length. At many points, the analysis becomes detailed and technical, but, important as it is that the reader should master these details, the overall nature and purpose of the theory should not be lost sight of, and this chapter is designed to help in this. Six of the next seven chapters are concerned with developing the theory of the profit-maximizing firm: the optimization problem with which the firm is assumed to be confronted is examined in detail, under a range of assumptions about market conditions and technology, and a wide set of hypotheses about firms' behaviour is derived. In Chapter 13 we consider some 'alternative' theories of the firm, which derive very largely from the concept of 'managerial capitalism' discussed in this chapter.

References and further reading

The fundamental paper on the question of why firms exist is:

R. Coase. 'The nature of the Firm', *Economica* N.S. vol. IV, Nos. 13–16, 1937.

More recent contributions to the debate are:

A. Alchian and **H. Demsetz**. 'Production, information costs, and economic organization', *American Economic Review*, December 1972.

G. B. Richardson. 'The organisation of industry', *Economic Journal*, September 1972.

O. E. Williamson. 'Markets and hierarchies: some elementary considerations'. *American Economic Review*, May 1973.

O. E. Williamson. 'The vertical integration of production: market failure considerations', *American Economic Review*, May 1971.

The best articulated criticisms of the orthodox theory of the firm can be found in:

R. M. Cyert and **J. G. March**. *A Behavioural Theory of the Firm*, Prentice-Hall, Engelwood Cliffs, N.J., 1963, Chs. 1, 2.

R. Marris. *The Economic Theory of Managerial Capitalism*, Macmillan & Co. London, 1964, Chs. 1, 2.

The empirical research which provided a foundation for these theoretical developments is:

A. A. Berle and **G. C. Means**. *The Modern Corporation and Private Property*, Macmillan, London 1944.

Chapter 7

Production

The starting point for an analysis of the firm's production decision is the problem of minimizing the cost of producing a given level of output subject to technological constraints. This problem is an incomplete model of the firm because the level of output is taken as given, but it is still important for two reasons. First, minimization of production cost is a necessary condition for the maximization of the objective functions of several important models of the firm, and the analysis will be valid for firms which seek to maximize profits, sales or growth. Secondly, as we shall see in Chapter 17, least-cost production is a necessary condition for the efficient allocation of resources, and hence our results provide criteria for making judgements about the efficiency of resource allocations. In this chapter we examine in some detail the technological constraints in the firm's cost minimization problem, and leave the analysis of the problem itself to the next chapter.

A. The production function

The firm will in general transform a large number of inputs into a number of outputs, but to simplify the analysis we will initially restrict ourselves to the case of a firm using two inputs (z_1, z_2) to produce a single output y. It is possible to describe the technical constraints on the firm's production in a variety of ways. In most of this chapter we will use a *production function* to relate the firm's output to its inputs, but in the final section we will generalise this by introducing the *production set* as an alternative description of the feasible input and output combinations.

In Chapter 3 we gave a set of assumptions about the consumer's preferences which ensured that they could be numerically represented by a function and which restricted the form of that function. We will follow here the same procedure for the firm's technical relations of production. To begin with we restrict y, z_1 and z_2 to be non-negative. (In section D below we show how, by suitable redefinition of the variables, this restriction becomes unnecessary.)

Assumption 1.   Inputs and outputs are divisible.

This assumption has been made formally (unlike the analogous assumption on the divisibility of consumption goods which is simply taken as given in the assumptions of section 3A) because it is not a harmless simplification. The implications of dropping it are examined in sections 7E and 8B.

Assumption 2.   Corresponding to every input combination (z_1, z_2) there is a maximum feasible output y_{max}, which is given by the *production function*:

$$y_{max} = f(z_1, z_2). \hspace{3cm} [A.1]$$

Thus the function f shows the largest output which can be produced from any input pair (z_1, z_2).

Assumption 3.   Wasteful production is possible: for all (z_1, z_2) pairs, all output levels in the interval $0 \le y \le y_{max}$ are feasible.

In other words the firm may choose to produce a smaller-than-maximum output from a given input combination. If the actual output y is equal to y_{max} the firm is said to be *output efficient.* The possibility of output inefficiency $(y < y_{max})$ is allowed primarily in order to investigate the circumstances under which the firm *will choose* to be output efficient. Assumption 3 means that the technological constraints on the firm are described by the *production correspondence* (see Ch. 16, Appendix I on the distinction between functions and correspondences):

$$y \le f(z_1, z_2) = y_{max}, \hspace{1cm} y \ge 0 \hspace{2cm} [A.2]$$

If $y > y_{max} = f(z_1, z_2)$, then y is called *technically infeasible*: given the state of technology it is impossible to produce an output as large as y from the input combination (z_1, z_2).

Assumption 4. $y > 0$ implies either $z_1 > 0$, or $z_2 > 0$

This states formally the uncontroversial assumption that the firm cannot produce output without using some of at least (the 'or' in the assumption is inclusive) one of the inputs. The assumption can be given in terms of [A.1] by $f(0, 0) = 0$.

Assumption 5.   The production function is twice continuously differentiable.

This assumption, unlike the previous one, is a rather strong restriction on the production function and we adopt it to simplify the derivation of our results. The *marginal product, MP_i* of input i in the production of y is the rate at which the maximum output of y changes in response to a change in z_i with the other input held constant. It is therefore the partial derivative of $y_{max} = f(z_1, z_2)$ with respect to z_i:

$$MP_i = \frac{\partial f(z_1, z_2)}{\partial z_i} = f_i(z_1, z_2), \qquad (i = 1, 2) \qquad \text{[A.3]}$$

The second-order partial derivatives of f are the rates at which the marginal products of the inputs change as one of the inputs is varied. $\partial^2 f / \partial z_1 \, \partial z_2 = f_{12}$ is for example the rate of change of the marginal product of z_1 with respect to variations in z_2. Assumption 5 states that the first-order $[f_i \, (i = 1, 2)]$ and second-order $[f_{ij} \, (i = 1, 2; j = 1, 2)]$ partial derivatives exist and are continuous functions of (z_1, z_2) and that $f_{12} = f_{21}$. We have therefore assumed that the production function is continuous and that its slope is well-defined at every point.

The effect of the remaining restrictions on the firm's technology we have to make will be illustrated by introducing the *isoquant,* which is defined as the *set of input combinations which will produce a specified output level when used output efficiently,* i.e. when the output from each combination of inputs is maximized. More formally, the isoquant I_0 for the output level y^0 is the set

$$I_0 = \{(z_1, z_2) \mid f(z_1, z_2) = y_{max} = y^0\} \qquad \text{[A.4]}$$

If the reader refers back to the discussion of the implications of assuming the continuity and differentiability of the utility functions in Chapter 3 he will see that assumption 5 ensures that the set I_0 contains no breaks or gaps, and is not a collection of separated points. However, to ensure that isoquants are not thick areas we must adopt an assumption similar to assumption 4 of section 3A:

Assumption 6. The marginal product of at least one input is always positive.

Or: a small change in one of the inputs, the other held constant, will always increase output. The reader should apply the discussion of section 3A to confirm that this assumption ensures that isoquants, like the indifference sets of that section, must be curves rather than areas. Note that this assumption does not rule out the possibility that an input's marginal product may become negative at some point, only that they never both do simultaneously.

An isoquant is clearly a *contour* of the production function, since it satisfies the relation:

$$y_{max} = f(z_1, z_2) = y^0 \qquad \text{[A.5]}$$

Given assumption 5, we can differentiate this totally to get:

$$dy_{max} = f_1 \, dz_1 + f_2 \, dz_2 = 0$$

which constrains the changes in z_1 and z_2 to be such as to move along the isoquant. By rearranging therefore we have:

$$\frac{-dz_2}{dz_1}\bigg|_{y_{\max} \text{ constant}} = f_1/f_2 = \frac{MP_1}{MP_2} \qquad [A.6]$$

The lefthand side of this expression, which gives the negative of the slope of the isoquant at a point, has the interpretation that it shows the rate at which z_2 must be substituted for z_1 so as to keep output constant. It is therefore called the marginal rate of technical substitution of input 2 for input 1, and denoted by $MRTS_{21}$. It is clearly directly analogous to the MRS_{21} in consumer theory. The important difference here is that the utility function is an *ordinal* function, whereas the production function involves a measure of output which is *cardinal* – we are only free to change the units of measurement. This gives the marginal products f_i and their rates of change f_{ij} a significance which the marginal utilities did not possess. On the other hand, just as the MRS_{21} was independent of the units in which we 'measured' utility, so the $MTRS_{21}$ is independent of the units in which we measure output (Prove this).

The cost minimization problem consists of choosing an input combination so as to minimize the cost of producing some specified output level. The feasible set Z^0 for this problem is the set of input combinations which will produce *at least* the desired output y^0:

$$Z^0 = \{(z_1, z_2) \mid f(z_1, z_2) \geq y^0\} \qquad [A.7]$$

Note that it is possible to partition the input pairs which can produce y^0 into two groups: those which produce y^0 output efficiently (those input combinations for which $f(z_1, z_2) = y^0$) and those which can produce a larger output than y^0 ($f(z_1, z_2) > y^0$) and so produce y^0 by output-inefficient use of inputs.

The feasible set for the cost minimization problem is closed because of the weak inequality in [A.7], and we now assume that it is strictly convex.

Assumption 7. For any output level y^0 the set of input pairs Z^0 capable of producing that output level is strictly convex.

Referring back to Question 3 of Exercise 2B we see that this is equivalent to assuming that the production function, like the utility function, is strictly quasi-concave.

The implication of all these assumptions is shown in Fig. 1. I_0, I_1 and I_2 are isoquants for successively higher output levels y^0, y^1 and y^2. They are drawn convex to the origin because of assumption 7: for example, the set of input pairs which can produce *at least* the output y^0 consists of the points on and above the isoquant I_0, and by assumption this is a strictly convex set. Unlike indifference curves, the isoquants are drawn as having positive as well as negative slopes. We expect the latter when the quantities of z_1 and z_2 are such that both inputs have positive marginal products (since from [A.6] the slope of the isoquant at a point is the negative of the ratio of marginal products at that point). So the former must occur when one (and

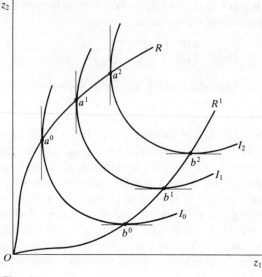

Fig. 1

only one) of the marginal products is negative (not ruled out by assumption 6).

The positively-sloped portions of the isoquants can be explained in the following way. As we move, say, leftward along an isoquant, substituting z_2 for z_1, we are increasing the ratio of z_2 to z_1 or making production more z_2-intensive. Intuitively we are reducing the amount of z_1 which each unit of z_2 has available to work with. There comes a point when a further increase in this ratio adds nothing to output, and these points are shown by a^0, a^1 and a^2 at output levels y^0, y^1 and y^2 respectively, in the figure. If the ratio were increased by reducing z_1 and increasing z_2 still further, output would fall because the marginal product of z_2 has become negative (of which the adage 'too many cooks spoil the broth' is a homely but apt description). It follows that as we increase z_2 we must now *increase* z_1 in order for the negative marginal product of z_2 to be offset by the positive marginal product of z_1, so that output can be held constant. Hence the slope of the isoquant becomes positive. The reader should extend this explanation for rightward movements along the isoquants.

The curves OR and OR^1 in the figure, connecting the points at which MP_2 and MP_1 respectively become zero, are called *ridge lines*. The region on or inside the ridge lines is known as the *economic region*, because a cost-minimizing firm would always choose a point within it and never a point outside it. This can easily be seen in the figure. For example for every point on the isoquant I_2 (corresponding to output y^2) outside the economic region, there is a point on the isoquant inside the region representing less of *both* inputs (Demonstrate). Hence, as long as input prices are non-negative, a firm will incur lower costs by producing output y^2 within the region.

The reason we bother to show the non-economic region outside the ridge lines is in part one of generality (our theory permits the region to exist) but also the region may be relevant in theories where the firm may not be cost-minimizing, e.g. if the firm has a preference for using one kind of input (see Ch. 13 and the discussion of the 'expense preference' theory of the firm there).

Finally, consideration of the non-economic region of production tells us that although an input combination may be what we have called output-efficient, in that the output in question is the maximum it is capable of producing, it may not be *technically efficient*, because there may be input combinations which produce the given output with less of at least one input and no more of any other. The economic region shows the set of input combinations which are technically efficient in this sense, therefore, while points in the non-economic region are not technically efficient.

Exercise 7A
1. Explain what is meant by (*a*) technically efficient input combination and (*b*) an output-efficient input combination and show that for an input combination to be technically efficient it is necessary but not sufficient that it be output-efficient.
2. Why do isoquants have positively sloped regions while indifference curves do not? (*Hint:* compare assumption 4 in Chapter 3 with assumption 6 here.)
3. Why can we adopt an assumption of diminishing marginal products when we could not adopt an assumption of diminishing marginal utility?
4.* *Fixed Proportions Technology*
   (*a*) Process 1 uses at least β_{11} units of z_1 *and* β_{12} units of z_2 to produce one unit of output. Draw the isoquant for $y = 1$, and distinguish between the technical and output efficient (z_1, z_2) points. Suppose that at least $y \cdot \beta_{11}$ units of z_1 *and* $y \cdot \beta_{12}$ units of z_2 are required to produce y units of output, so that the production function for process 1 is

$$y = \min \left(\frac{z_1}{\beta_{11}}, \frac{z_2}{\beta_{12}} \right)$$

   Draw the isoquant map for the process. What does the economic region look like? (*Note:* min (. . .) is read: 'the smaller of' the terms in brackets.)
   (*b*) Suppose that y can also be produced from process 2, which requires at least $y \cdot \beta_{21}$ of z_1 and $y \cdot \beta_{22}$ of z_2 and that processes 1 and 2 are *additive* in that the output from one process is independent of the level at which the other process is used. Under what circumstances would it never be technically efficient to use process 2? A given level of y could be produced by different mixtures of the two processes using different total amounts of the inputs. Derive the isoquant for mixtures of the two processes (where a mixture uses

$k\beta_{11} + (1-k)\beta_{21}$ of z_1, *and* $k\beta_{12} + (1-k)\beta_{22}$ of z_2 to produce 1 unit of output, with $0 \le k \le 1$). A mixture is a convex combination of processes. (Compare the analysis of the Lancaster consumption technology model in section 5B.)

(c) Let there be three, four, ... n processes satisfying the above assumptions. Investigate the circumstances in which particular processes are never used. Show that as the number n of technically efficient processes becomes large the isoquant tends to the smooth shape assumed in section A.

5.* The *Cobb–Douglas* production function is

$$y = z_1^{\alpha} z_2^{\beta} \qquad \alpha > 0, \qquad \beta > 0$$

Show that $MP_1 = \alpha y/z_1$, $MP_2 = \beta y/z_2$

What is the $MRTS_{21}$? How does it vary with: (a) y; (b) z_2/z_1?

Draw the isoquant map.

6.* The *CES* production function is

$$y = A(\delta_1 z_1^{-\alpha} + \delta_2 z_2^{-\alpha})^{-1/\alpha}, \qquad \delta_1 + \delta_2 = 1, \qquad \alpha > -1, \qquad A > 0.$$

Show that

$$MP_i = \frac{\delta_i}{A^{\alpha}} \left(\frac{y}{z_i}\right)^{1+\alpha}.$$

What is the $MRTS_{21}$? How does it vary with: (a) y; (b) z_2/z_1?

(*CES* stands for constant elasticity of substitution, a term to be defined in the next chapter.)

B. Variations in scale

The assumptions made in section A do not place very great restrictions on the relationships between output and inputs and so in this and the next section we will examine further the responses of y to changes in the input combinations (z_1, z_2), as a preparation for the investigation in Chapter 8 of the relationship between output and cost-minimizing input pairs.

The firm can produce changes in output in two ways (we consider only the economic region since the firm is assumed to wish to minimize costs). It can:

(i) change the scale of production by varying all inputs in the same proportion;

or

(ii) change relative input proportions.

The first corresponds to movements along a ray through the origin such as OA or OB in Fig. 2, the second to a movement from one ray to another. For example the firm can increase y by moving from z^0 on I_0 to the higher I_2 isoquant, either by doubling both inputs and so moving to z^2, or by varying the relative input proportion and moving to z^3, where z_2 has fallen relative to z_1. In this section we will consider variations in scale and in the

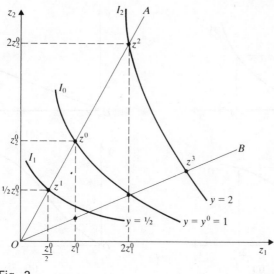

Fig. 2

next an important case of variations in input proportions resulting from varying one input with the other held constant.

In Fig. 2 I_0 is taken to be the *unit isoquant* – the set of all input combinations which will produce *one unit* of output. $z^0 = (z_1^0, z_2^0)$ is a point on I_0: $f(z_1^0, z_2^0) = 1$. Multiplying each input by $s \geq 0$ will be equivalent to a movement along the ray OA through z^0. If $s = \frac{1}{2}$ then the point $z^1 = (z_1^0/2, z_2^0/2)$ is reached and if $s = 2$, $z^2 = (2z_1^0, 2z_2^0)$ is reached. For $s < 1$ there is a movement along OA towards the origin and for $s > 1$ a movement away from it. Movements along the ray correspond to changes in all inputs in the same proportion and hence s is known as a *scale parameter*. Any point on OA can be written in the form (sz_1^0, sz_2^0) by selecting the correct value for s. Hence, *along the ray* the output level y can be thought of solely as a function of the scale parameter s:

$$y = f(sz_1^0, sz_2^0) = y(s)$$

The *elasticity of production E* is defined as the proportionate change in y divided by the proportionate change in the scale of production i.e. the proportionate change in s:

$$E = \frac{dy}{y} \cdot \frac{s}{ds} = \frac{d\dot{y}}{ds} \cdot \frac{s}{y} \tag{B.1}$$

It is a measure of the responsiveness of output to equal proportionate changes in all inputs. Output is increasing more or less proportionately with scale as E is greater or less than 1.

Increasing, constant or decreasing *returns to scale* are said to exist as $E > 1$, $E = 1$, or $E < 1$. Figure 2 shows that it is possible for the ray OA to exhibit constant returns and another, OB, increasing returns. It is also

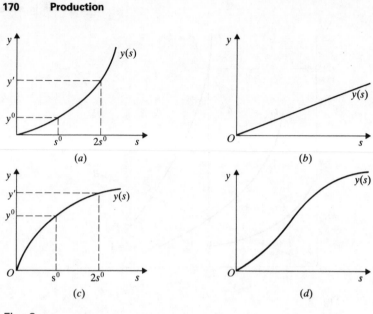

Fig. 3

possible for there to be different returns along different parts of the same ray. Figure 3 has output plotted against the scale parameter s and illustrates some of the possibilities. Part (a) shows increasing, (b) constant, (c) decreasing and (d) variable returns to scale. In (a) output increases more than proportionately with s (doubling s more than doubles output); in (b) output increases proportionately with s; in (c) output increases less than proportionately with s (doubling s less than doubles output).

Homogeneous production functions*
Much attention has been paid in the literature to production functions which are *homogeneous of degree one* or *linear homogeneous*. A production function is homogeneous of degree n if multiplying all inputs by the factor s causes output to increase by s^n,

i.e. if $f(sz_1, sz_2) = s^n \cdot f(z_1, z_2) = s^n \cdot y$.

If $n = 1$ then f is linear homogeneous. Many models adopt the assumption of linear homogeneity because linear homogeneous production functions have a number of properties which greatly aid analysis.

(i) From the definition of linear homogeneity, $y = f(z_1, z_2) = f(sz_1^0, sz_2^0) = sf(z_1^0, z_2^0) = s$ (recalling that $f(z_1^0, z_2^0) = 1$). Hence, $E = dy/ds \cdot s/y = 1$ irrespective of either factor proportions or the scale of production: *the linear homogeneous production function has constant returns to scale at all points on all rays.*

(ii) *The marginal product of an input depends only on the relative input proportions and not on the absolute levels of the inputs.*

This follows from the definition of a linear homogeneous function

$$f(sz^0) = sf(z^0) \tag{B.2}$$

which must hold as we vary z_i^0. Hence

$$\frac{\partial f(sz^0)}{\partial z_i^0} = \frac{\partial sf(z^0)}{\partial z_i^0} \tag{B.3}$$

But $z = sz^0$ or $z_i^0 = z_i/s$, so that

$$\frac{\partial f(z)}{\partial z_i} = \frac{\partial f(sz^0)}{\partial z_i^0} \cdot \frac{dz_i^0}{dz_i} = \frac{\partial f(sz^0)}{\partial z_i^0} \frac{1}{s} \tag{B.4}$$

and using [B.3] to substitute in [B.4] gives

$$\frac{\partial f(z)}{\partial z_i} = \frac{\partial f(z^0)}{\partial z_i^0} \tag{B.5}$$

More formally, a function which is homogeneous of degree n has partial derivatives which are homogeneous of degree $n-1$. Hence the marginal products of a linear homogeneous production function are homogeneous of degree zero. A doubling of all inputs for example will not alter the marginal product of any of the inputs. *The marginal product is therefore independent of scale*, and depends only on the ratio of input quantities. f_1 (and also f_2) will be constant along a ray from the origin.

(iii) It follows from this that the slope of the isoquants (equal to $-f_1/f_2$) will also depend only on the input ratio and will be constant along a ray from the origin. Every isoquant is, therefore, a radial expansion or contraction of any other isoquant.

(iv) Differentiating [B.2] with respect to the scale coefficient s and remembering that $f(z^0) = 1$ gives

$$\frac{dy}{ds} = \sum_i f_i(z) \frac{dz_i}{ds} = \sum_i f_i(sz^0) \frac{dsz_i^0}{ds} = \sum_i f_i(sz^0)z_i^0 = 1$$

(since $y = s$). Multiplying the last equation above by s ($= y$) gives

$$y = \sum_i f_i(sz^0)sz_i^0 = \sum_i f_i(z)z_i \tag{B.6}$$

This is the *adding-up* property of linear homogenous production functions: output is equal to the sum of the marginal products of the inputs times the level of use of the input.

Exercise 7B

1.* What is the degree of returns to scale for the Cobb–Douglas production function of Question 5, Exercise 7A? Under what circumstances are there decreasing, constant or increasing returns?

2. Are the fixed proportions processes of Question 4, Exercise 7A, linear homogeneous?

3.* What is the degree of returns to scale for the *CES* production function (Question 6, Exercise 7A)?

4. Do all homogeneous production functions of whatever degree have (a) marginal products and (b) marginal rates of technical substitution which are independent of the level of output?

5.* Show that when the production function is linear homogeneous it is possible to express the second order partial derivatives f_{ii} in terms of the cross partial derivatives f_{ij}

$$f_{ii} = \frac{-z_j}{z_i} f_{ij}$$

(*Hint:* use the fact that [B.6] must hold as z_i varies.)

C. Variations in input proportions

Figure 4 illustrates the effects of changes in input proportions when one input (z_2 in this case) is held fixed and the other is free to vary. In part (a) the isoquant map is shown and z_2 is assumed fixed at z_2^0. Variations in z_1 will lead to a movement along the line through z_2^0 parallel to the z_1 axis, and the output of y produced with $z_2 = z_2^0$ for different levels of z_1 can be read off from the isoquants. Part (b) plots the total product curve $y = f(z_1, z_2^0)$ which results. If part (a) can be thought of as the contour map of the total product hill then part (b) shows a vertical slice through the hill at $z_2 = z_2^0$. Holding z_2 at different levels will give rise to different total product curves. Part (c) shows the average and marginal product of z_1 as a function of z_1 and is in turn derived from the total product curve of part (b).

The *average product* of z_1, $AP_1(z_1, z_2^0)$ is total product divided by z_1: y/z_1. Consider in part (b) a ray from the origin to a point on the total product curve, for example the line OB. The slope of this line is the vertical distance BC divided by the horizontal distance OC. But $BC = y^0$ and $OC = z_1$ and hence: slope $OB = BC/OC = y^0/z_1 = AP_1(z_1, z_2^0)$. The AP_1 curve is, therefore, derived by plotting the slope of a ray from the origin to each point on the total product curve.

The marginal product curve MP_1 is derived by plotting the slope of the total product curve. Notice the relationship between the AP_1 and MP_1, with the MP_1 cutting the AP_1 from above at the point z_1' where AP_1 is at a maximum. It can be demonstrated that this relationship is no accident of draughtsmanship. The definition of the average product is:

$$AP_1 = \frac{y}{z_1} = \frac{f(z_1, z_2^0)}{z_1}$$

[C.1]

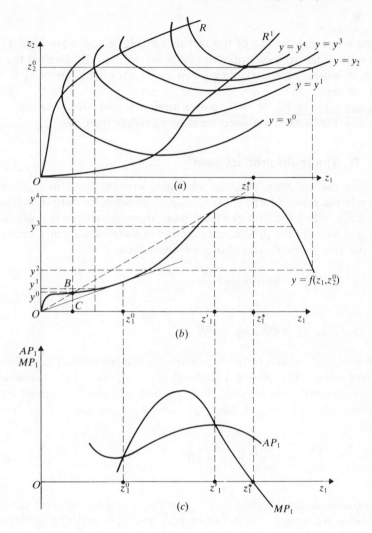

Fig. 4

Differentiating and setting equal to zero as a necessary condition for maximization yields

$$\frac{\mathrm{d}}{\mathrm{d}z_1}[AP_1] = \frac{1}{(z_1)^2}\left[\frac{\partial f}{\partial z_1}\cdot z_1 - f\right] = 0 \qquad [\text{C.2}]$$

$$= \frac{1}{z_1}\left[f_1 - \frac{f}{z_1}\right] = \frac{1}{z_1}[MP_1 - AP_1] = 0 \qquad [\text{C.3}]$$

Hence $MP_1 = AP_1$ is a necessary condition for AP_1 to be maximized.

Exercise 7C

1. What is the significance of the fact that in Fig. 4, the input level z_1^* is at the same time (*a*) a co-ordinate of a point on the ridge line (*b*) the value of z_1 at which y is a maximum given $z_2 = z_2^0$, (*c*) the value of z_1 at which MP_1 is zero?

2. Explain why, in Fig. 4, AP_1 is at a minimum and $MP_1 = AP_1$ at z_1^0.

3. Redraw Fig. 4 taking a fixed level of z_1 rather than z_2.

D. The multi-product case*

In the previous sections we have written the firm's production function in the *explicit* form $y = f(z_1, z_2)$, or, allowing for output inefficiency, $y \leq f(z_1, z_2)$. When the firm produces more than one output it is often more convenient to write the production function in its *implicit* form. Corresponding to the two explicit cases above we could have

$$y - f(z_1, z_2) = g(z_1, z_2, y) = 0$$

or

$$y - f(z_1, z_2) = g(z_1, z_2, y) \leq 0$$

The implicit and explicit forms are clearly equivalent ways of describing the firm's technology. The marginal products of the inputs and the marginal rate of technical substitution between them are derived from the implicit form by the implicit function rule of differentiation. Applying the rule we have for example

$$\frac{dy}{dz_1} = \frac{-g_{z_1}}{g_y} = -\left(\frac{-f_1}{1}\right) = f_1 = MP_1$$

It is also convenient in many cases to adopt a slightly different notational convention. We have so far talked of y as an output and z_i as an input and restricted both outputs and inputs to being non-negative. But what is an input for one firm may be an output for another, or a firm may change from producing a good to using it as an input, or it may use part of an output as an input (a power station uses electricity for lighting in producing electricity). To save relabelling the good when this happens it is easier to use the concept of the firm's *net output* of a good. (*Note*: This is quite different from the meaning of the term net output as it occurs, say, in national income accounting, namely as the difference between a firm's revenue and cost of bought-in inputs.) If the net output is positive the firm is producing the good, if it is negative the firm is 'consuming' it or using it as an input. The firm's net output of a good *i* will be written as the variable y_i which is not constrained to be non-negative. If $y_i > 0$ good *i* is produced or supplied by the firm, if $y_i < 0$ good *i* is 'consumed' by the firm and if $y_i = 0$ the good is neither produced nor consumed. Using this labelling we can rewrite the implicit production function with $y_i = -z_i$ and $y_3 = y$ as:

$$g(y_1, y_2, y_3) = 0$$

Notice that an *increase* in y_i means that if good i is an input ($y_i < 0$) the use of the input has been *reduced*: y_i is measured along the negative axis of any diagram if it is an input.

The multiproduct function can now be written simply as

$$g(y_1, y_2, \ldots, y_n) = g(y) \leq 0 \qquad \text{[D.1]}$$

where y is now the net output vector. $g_j > 0$ indicating that when $g(y) = 0$ it is not technically possible to increase an output or reduce an input, *ceteris paribus*. Again using the implicit function rule on $g(y) = 0$ and allowing only y_i and y_j to change, we have:

$$\frac{dy_i}{dy_j} = \frac{-g_j}{g_i} \qquad i, j, = 1, 2, \ldots n \qquad \text{[D.2]}$$

and this can be given a number of interpretations depending on whether y_i and y_j are positive or negative:

(a) $y_i < 0$ and $y_j < 0$. Both goods are inputs so that dy_i/dy_j is the rate at which one input can be substituted for another when all other goods (inputs and outputs) are held constant. It is therefore the (negative of) the marginal rate of technical substitution, i.e. it is the slope of the isoquant, which in the multi-product case is the boundary of the set of y_i, y_j combinations which will just produce a given level of the firm's outputs with all other inputs held constant. For example, in the single output-two input case considered in previous sections we have (remembering that an *increase* in y_i means a *decrease* in z_1):

$$\frac{dy_2}{dy_1} = \frac{g_1}{g_2} = \frac{-f_1}{f_2} = -MRTS_{21} \qquad \text{(D.3)}$$

Figure 5(a) shows the isoquant for given levels of $y_3, \ldots, y_n$ for a particular production function which has the convexity and smoothness properties of the explicit function of previous sections. Again all points in the shaded area are technically possible ($g(y) \leq 0$) but only points on the boundary of it are output efficient ($g(y) = 0$)

(b) $y_i > 0$, $y_j < 0$. Good i is an output, j an input, so that dy_i/dy_j is the rate at which the output of i changes when input j is reduced with all other outputs and inputs held constant. It is therefore the negative of the marginal product of input j in the production of output i. Using our single output, two input example and remembering that $y_1 = -z_1$

$$\frac{dy_3}{dy_1} = \frac{-g_1}{g_3} = -f_1 = -MP_1 \qquad \text{[D.4]}$$

Figure 5(b) shows the relationship between an input (good 1) and an output

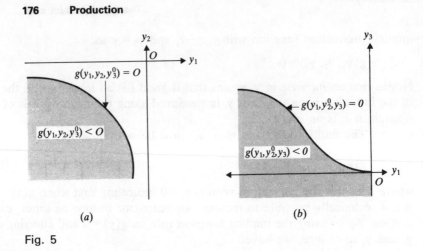

Fig. 5

(good 3) and corresponds to the total product curve of Fig. 4(b). All points in the shaded area are technically possible but only points on the upper boundary (the total product curve) are output efficient.

(c) $y_i > 0$, $y_j > 0$. Both goods are outputs and so dy_i/dy_j is the rate at which the output of i varies as the output of j is increased when all inputs and all other outputs are held constant. This is the negative of the *marginal rate of transformation* of i into j or MRT_{ij}. In Fig. 6 both good 1 and 2 are outputs, and the shaded area is the set of all technically possible combinations. The upper boundary of this shaded area is the set of output efficient points and is known as the *transformation curve*. Increases in y_j require reductions in y_i. Different transformation curves are generated by fixing the other net outputs at different levels. A reduction in any other net output shifts the transformation curve out from the origin. In other words decreases in other outputs or increases in inputs allow more of both good 1 and 2 to be produced. We have assumed that the technology allows

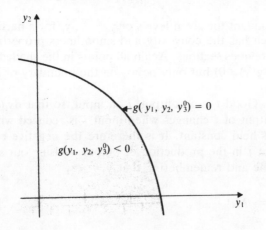

Fig. 6

substitutability of outputs so that the transformation curve is negatively sloped. If the outputs must be produced in fixed proportions (as for example in some chemical processes) the transformation curves would be rectangular, indicating that an increase in the output of one good requires an increase in the level of inputs and cannot be made by reducing the output of the other good.

Joint products

In some cases where a firm produces more than one output it may be possible to relate the output of each product to a specific part of the bundle of inputs used by the firm, so that the firm has a production function for each output. For example if y_1 and y_2 are the levels of the firm's outputs and z_i^j is the amount of input i used in production of good j the firm's production possibilities could be written explicitly as

$$y_1 \leq f^1(z_1^1, z_2^1)$$
$$y_2 \leq f^2(z_1^2, z_2^2)$$

[D.5]

or implicitly as

$$y_1 - f^1(z_1^1, z_2^1) \leq 0$$
$$y_2 - f^2(z_1^2, z_2^2) \leq 0$$

[D.6]

When it is possible to describe the technical constraints on the firm in this way the production function is *separable*. If the firm is producing several products and inputs *cannot* be assigned to outputs in this way the firm is said to be producing *joint products*. Notice that it is the way in which the inputs relate to outputs, *not* the number of products, which is the defining characteristic of joint production. When the production function is separable the firm could be regarded as the sum of several single-product plants, and if each of the constituent plants acts to minimize cost of its own production, total costs are minimized. Production can be *decentralized* without increasing cost. When there is joint production decentralization (instructing each product division to minimize cost) will not lead to minimum total cost because of the interdependence between the costs of each product. This point will be elaborated in the exercises in Chapter 9.

E. The production possibility set*

An alternative and more general way of describing the technological constraints on the firm is by its *production set, PS*, which is the set of all possible input–output combinations. In the terminology of section D the *PS* is the set of all feasible net output bundles, or of all feasible *activities*. An *activity* of the firm is the firm's net output bundle: $y = (y_1 \ldots y_n)$. The production function $g(y) \leq 0$ and the *PS* are equivalent descriptions of the technological constraints in the sense that the statement that y^0 is in the *PS* is equivalent to the statement $g(y^0) \leq 0$. If the activity y^0 is not technically possible then it is not in the *PS* and $g(y^0) > 0$. In terms of the figures in section D, the shaded areas (including their boundaries) can be thought of as slices through the *PS* and all points in the shaded areas are in the *PS*. The upper boundary of the *PS* is the set of points with the property that it is not possible to increase the net output of any good without reducing the net output of some other good (i.e. reducing an output or increasing an input). This upper boundary is therefore output-efficient and satisfies the equation $g(y) = 0$.

In section A we proceeded to make assumptions about the technology open to the firm by placing restrictions on the production function. Here we will discuss the implications of certain assumptions about the shape of the *PS*.

(i) The *PS* is assumed to include the null activity $(0, 0, \ldots, 0)$, i.e. it is always possible for the firm to do nothing. This ensures that the *PS* is non-empty.

(ii) We have already assumed that the *PS* is closed, i.e. points on the boundary are technically possible.

(iii) The firm's *PS* is assumed to be *bounded above* in the sense that if all but one of the firm's net outputs are held constant then there is a maximum level of the remaining net output which can be produced. To ensure that the set is a bounded set in the sense of section 2C however we have to specify more than this. Figure 7(a) illustrates. The *PS* is the shaded area together with its boundary points. Increasing y_2 with y_1 held constant will eventually lead to an infeasible point outside the *PS* so that the *PS is* bounded above. It is, however, possible to increase y_2 indefinitely provided more of the input is used, i.e. we can move indefinitely far to the left in the figure. Hence it is impossible to enclose the shaded area within a circle of finite radius and so it is, strictly speaking, an unbounded set.

(iv) The reader may notice in Fig. 7, which shows some two-good *PSs* that the shaded area extended below the y_1 axis and appeared to include the whole of the negative quadrant of the diagram. In this quadrant the net outputs of both goods are negative, indicating that when there are

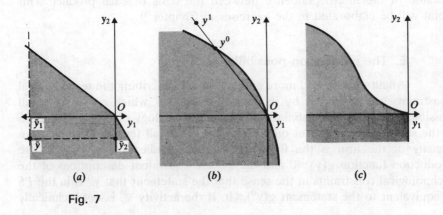

(a)   (b)   (c)

Fig. 7

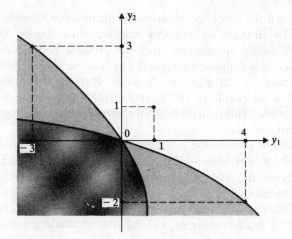

Fig. 8

only two commodities the firm is using up commodities and not producing positive net outputs of any commodities. More importantly, the firm is able to use up or dispose of unlimited amounts of a commodity without requiring the use of additional units of the other commodity. We have therefore, by drawing the *PS* so as to include the whole of the negative quadrant in the two-good case, made the assumption of *free disposal*.

The free disposal assumption is unrealistic for many situations but it is made in order to simplify the analysis because it implies that prices of goods cannot be negative. If the price of (say) good 1 is negative then the economic agent (an individual or firm) who wishes to *reduce* his holding of good 1 must pay someone to take it from him. If free disposal were possible the individual or firm could reduce his holding of the commodity without cost. Hence no one will pay the negative price and so free disposal ensures that no price is negative. The analysis is complicated, but the results are not essentially altered, by dropping the free disposal assumption.

(v) The reader will also notice that in the two-good examples illustrated in Fig. 7 the shaded areas of the *PS*s do not extend into the positive quadrant. If activities in this quadrant were feasible the firm would be able to produce positive amounts of all goods, i.e. outputs without using inputs. The assumption that *each firm's PS* does not include any activities with all goods produced in positive amounts is not however sufficiently strong. In Fig. 8, for example, we have the *PS*s of two firms, neither of which includes activities in the positive quadrant. But suppose that firm 1 chooses the activity $y^1 = (-3, 3)$ and firm 2 the activity $y^2 = (4, -2)$. *Neither* firm is producing without using inputs but *together* they are producing positive amounts of both goods: $y^1 + y^2 = (1, 1)$. To rule out this possibility we adopt the assumption that production is *irreversible*: if the net output vector y for the whole economy, (i.e. the sum of the net output vectors (activities) of all the firms in the economy) is technically feasible, then the net output vector $-y$ for the whole economy is *not* technically feasible. This assumption combined with the assumption of free disposal (iv) rules out the possibility that the economy or any firm in it can produce positive output from no inputs. To see this suppose that $y>0$ was feasible. Then irreversibility would imply that $-y<0$ was not feasible. But the free disposal assumption means that all points in the negative quadrants in the figures (where $y<0$) are feasible. Hence irreversibility and free disposal together imply that $y>0$ is not feasible.

The irreversibility assumption is a reasonable one to make when it is remembered that our concept of inputs and outputs in this section is a very general one and covers the case where output (say a ton of grain) is produced tomorrow by using input (say a ton of fertilizer) today. If production were reversible then it would be possible to produce a ton of fertilizer today by using a ton of grain tomorrow, i.e. the output would precede the input! Irreversibility is also implied by the fact that there is at least one good (labour) which cannot be produced in positive quantities but which is needed for the production of positive quantities of all other goods. In the two good example if the first good is labour the *PS* cannot extend into the positive and 'south-east' quadrants.

(vi) Finally, let us examine the relationship between the *PS* and returns to scale. To do so we need to refine our concept of the convexity of a set slightly. The *upper boundary* of the *PS* is the set of net output vectors such that it is impossible to increase the net output of any good without reducing the net output of some other good, i.e. by having less of some good produced in positive quantity or more of some input. The *PS* is said to be *upper convex* if all convex combinations of points on its upper boundary are feasible, i.e. in *PS*. *PS* is *strictly upper convex* if y' and y'' being on its upper boundary imply that all points $ky' + (1-k)y''$ $(0<k<1)$ on the straight line between them are in *the interior* of *PS*. In terms of Fig. 7 the *PS* in part (*a*) is upper convex but not strictly upper convex, that in part (*b*) is strictly upper convex and that in part (*c*) is not upper convex.

If the *PS* is strictly upper convex as in Fig. 7(*b*) the production function (which, remember, defines the upper boundary of the *PS*) will exhibit decreasing returns to scale: proportionate increases in inputs (a reduction in y_1) cause less than proportionate rises in output. Movements along a ray from the origin in a north-westerly direction indicate equal proportionate changes in inputs and outputs. If we take any activity on the upper boundary of the *PS* in Fig. 7(*b*) such as y^0, then activities such as y^1 beyond y^0 and along the line Oy^0 are not feasible, indicating that a proportionate·increase in inputs causes a smaller proportionate increase in output along the upper boundary of the *PS*.

In Fig. 7(*a*) the *PS* is upper convex, but not strictly upper convex, and there are constant returns to scale: proportionate changes in inputs cause equal proportionate changes in output. In this case the technology is said to be linear in the sense that if an activity y is feasible so are all activities ky $(0 \le k)$. All activities lying on the ray through any feasible

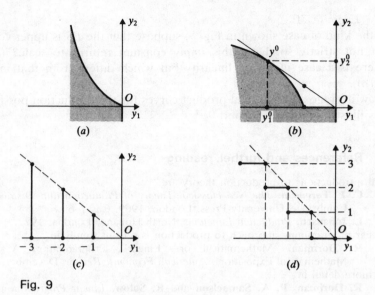

Fig. 9

activity and the origin are feasible. (See also Question 1 of Exercise 7E.)

Figure 9 shows some non-upper convex PSs. In (a) of the figure there are increasing returns to scale over the entire range of the PS. In (b) there are increasing returns up to y_1^0 and decreasing returns thereafter (Explain why). This case arises when a minimum input of good 1 is required before any of good 2 can be produced: for example time spent travelling between home and work, or fuel required to bring ovens up to a specific temperature before baking can start. In (c) good 1 is not divisible while good 2 is, so that the PS becomes a set of vertical lines at $y_1 = -1$, $y_1 = -2$ etc. In (d) good 1 is divisible but good 2 is not. In these cases where one of the goods is not divisible returns to scale are defined only if we restrict ourselves to proportionate changes in scale which do not lead us to activities involving fractions of indivisible goods. The elasticity of production of section B must also be redefined in terms of discrete changes rather than derivatives. If this is done then in Figs. $9(c)$ and $9(d)$ there are *discrete* constant returns to scale even though the PS is not convex.

An activity y is *divisible* if all activities on the line between y and the origin are feasible, i.e. if all activities ky $(0 \leq k \leq 1)$ are in the PS. The PS is divisible if all activities in it are divisible and is *indivisible* if some feasible activities are not divisible. Examination of Figs. 7 and 9 should convince the reader that if PS is convex it is also divisible and that if it is indivisible it is not convex. It is important to distinguish carefully between goods and activities in this context. Divisibility of goods is a necessary but not sufficient condition for an activity to be divisible, as Fig. 9 illustrates. We see therefore that if goods are divisible but activities are not there are increasing returns to scale but if goods are indivisible there may be constant, increasing or decreasing discrete returns to scale.

Exercise 7E

1. In the kind of case shown in Fig. 7, suppose that the *PS* is upper convex but not strictly so. Does this *imply* constant returns to scale? (*Hint:* There is a case involving linearity but which differs from that in Fig. 7(*a*).)

2. Draw average and marginal product curves for the production possibility sets illustrated in Figs. 7 and 9.

References and further reading

General introductions to production theory are:

C. E. Ferguson. *The Neo-classical Theory of Production and Distribution*, Cambridge University Press, London, 1969, Chs 1–6;

L. Johansen. *Production Functions*, North-Holland, London, 1972.

The linear programming approach to production is set out simply in:

R. Dorfman. 'Mathematical or "Linear", Programming: A Non-Mathematical Exposition', *American Economic Review*, December 1953, and in more detail in:

R. Dorfman, P. A. Samuelson and **R. Solow.** *Linear Programming and Economic Analysis*, McGraw-Hill, London, 1958, Chs 1, 6, 9, 10.

There is a very clear exposition of the properties of homogeneous functions and an account of some economic applications in:

R. G. D. Allen. *Mathematical Analysis for Economists*, Macmillan, London, 1938, Chs 12, 13, 14.

The following references examine in depth the properties of production sets and their implications for general equilibrium theory:

*K. J. Arrow** and **F. H. Hahn.** *General Competitive Analysis*, Oliver & Boyd, Edinburgh, 1971, Ch. 3;

*G. Debreu.** *Theory of Value*, John Wiley, New York, 1959, Ch. 3.

Chapter 8

Cost

A. Introduction

Time dimension of production

In the previous chapter we did not consider in any detail exactly what is meant by 'inputs' and 'outputs' and in particular we did not discuss the time dimension of the firm's production function, preferring instead to talk loosely of 'levels' of outputs and inputs, in order to concentrate on the technical relationships involved. Output, however, is a *flow* and so must always have a time dimension: it is meaningless to say that a firm produces so many tons of a particular good unless we also specify the period of time (hour, day, month or year) over which the output was produced. y therefore has the dimension of a rate of flow of units of the good *per unit of time* or *per period*.

Input levels must be similarly interpreted. This is straightforward with inputs such as raw materials which are transformed or consumed by the firm. z_i would then have the dimension of the flow of the quantity of raw material of type i per period. Durable assets, however, such as machines, are, as the term implies, not consumed by the firm. In these cases we can think of the asset itself as embodying a *stock of productive services* and z_i is the flow of productive services of the asset used per period of time. For example with a machine of type i, z_i would be machine hours (the number of hours the machine is used) per day. The *capacity* of an asset is the maximum possible flow of productive services which can be used per period. In the example above the capacity of the machine is 24 machine-hours per day (assuming no time has to be taken for cooling down, maintenance etc.). As we will see in section C it is often necessary to distinguish carefully between capacity and actual usage.

In this chapter, an 'input' will always be measured as a rate of flow, either of some physical good (coal, crude oil, cotton) or of the *services* of some factor of production which is not itself used up in the production process (labour, machinery).

Long- and short-run decision-making

We concentrate in this chapter on a two-input model and we assume that z_1 is a *variable input*: it can be varied at will by the firm. The firm can decide at the start of period 0, the 'present' time period, to use any level of z_1 in production in period 0 and can implement that decision. The other input z_2 on the other hand takes time to vary: it is assumed to take one period to make available an increment of z_2, for example the flow of services from a machine or type of skilled labour. A decision taken 'now' at the start of period 0 to increase the amount of z_2 by Δz_2 will result in that increment becoming available for use in producing y at the start of period 1. As far as production of y in period 0 is concerned z_2 is a *constrained input*. The amount of z_2 used in production *in period 0* certainly cannot be increased beyond the amount available at the start of period 0. On the other hand the firm may or may not be able to *reduce* the amount of z_2 it uses in period 0. If the input is divisible the firm will be able to use less than the maximum amount unless there is some contractual limitation. Since contracts usually stipulate the amount of an input which will be *paid for* rather than the amount which must be used, divisibility will usually imply the possibility of using an input below capacity. For example, a firm may hire labour on a monthly contract, and be unable to increase or reduce the number of workers to whom it must pay a guaranteed weekly wage within that period, but it may *if it chooses* use less than the maximum possible number of man-hours.

The distinction between fixed and variable inputs has a crucial implication for the firm's decision-making. The firm is located in time at the start of period 0 and at that moment of time it must make two types of decision. First, given the desired output level for period 0, it must choose an *actual* level of z_1 for period 0, remembering that maximum z_2 is fixed in production of y in period 0. (When z_2 can be less than its maximum level the firm must also choose an *actual* level of z_2 to be used in period 0.) Second, given the planned or desired output level for period 1, it must *formulate a plan* specifying desired levels of z_1 *and* z_2 to be used in period 1. If the desired amount of z_2 in period 1 in the plan differs from the level of z_2 held by the firm at the start of period 0 it must begin to organize the required change at the start of period 0, so that it is available at the start of period 1. Thus the choices *implemented* by the firm in period 0 are first on the input levels actually used in period 0, and second on the change in the fixed input available for the next period.

In order to predict how the firm's behaviour will vary in response to changes in the desired output levels in periods 0 and 1 or changes in the costs of inputs, we must construct a model of the two kinds of decision taken by the firm at the start of period 0. In section B, therefore, we consider the problem of finding desired levels of z_1 and z_2 to minimize the cost of producing the planned period 1 output. Both inputs are variable in this problem since the firm will be able to bring about any planned change in z_2 by the start of period 1. This is referred to as the *long-run* cost minimization problem. In section C we model the problem of setting z_1, with a fixed maximum z_2, so as to minimize the cost of producing the required period 0 output. This is the *short-run* cost minimization problem.

Adjustment costs

We assumed above that it was *impossible* to increase z_2 within period 0 but that z_1 was freely variable. This distinction is a crude recognition of the fact that in general there are differing *adjustment costs* for different types of inputs. Let us look at the question of adjustment costs in general terms. Adjustment costs are those costs which arise solely from a *change* in the level of use of an input. For example if a firm wishes to hire more labour it may have to advertise for new workers, but once the new workers are employed the advertisements are no longer necessary. This advertising cost is an adjustment cost: it is incurred solely because the firm wishes to hire more men, since no advertisement is needed to retain men already employed. In general firms must shop around, search, and collect information just as do consumers. Moreover, changes in input quantities have to be planned and organized over and above the management of 'ongoing' activities. All this absorbs resources and hence imposes costs of adjustment.

If actual input levels differ from cost minimizing levels the firm will gain from changes in input levels. These changes will, however, in themselves involve adjustment costs and so the firm has a problem of finding the *optimal rate of adjustment* by balancing the benefits (reduced production costs) against the adjustment costs of the changes. In a single-period model determination of the optimal change in decision variables will require a comparison of the marginal benefits and costs of adjustment within the single period. For example, let $\bar{z}$ be the initial level of the firm's decision variable and z the new level chosen by the firm. The objective function is $B(z) - A(z - \bar{z})$ where B is sales revenue less production costs, a function of the *chosen* or *desired* level of z; and A is adjustment cost, which depends on the size of the change in z: $z - \bar{z}$. The firm sets z to satisfy $B' - A' = 0$. This level of z will differ from the level which would be chosen if marginal adjustment costs A' were zero, since then z would satisfy $B' = 0$. The firm will not in general adjust fully within the period because there are positive marginal costs of adjustment and the decision taken (actual increment in z in this period) will depend on the *initial* level of the decision variable. In other words what the firm does this period will depend on what it did last period.

In general the firm's problem is multiperiod: its objective function is of the form[1]

$$\sum_{t=0}^{T} B_t(z_t) - A_t^{\bullet}(z_t - z_{t-1}) \qquad [\text{A.1}]$$

where B_t, A_t, z_t are benefits, total adjustment costs and the decision variable in period t respectively. The firm must now plan at $t = 0$ a *sequence* of levels of the decision variable $(z_0, z_1, \ldots, z_T)$ to maximize [A.1], given the initial value of $\bar{z}$. Changes in z_t, the decision variable in period t, will have *three* effects on [A.1]. Firstly they alter B_t, secondly they alter A_t and thirdly they alter A_{t+1}, i.e. they also affect adjustment costs in the next period. Given z_{t+1} and z_{t-1}, a rise in z_t will raise adjustment cost in period t and lower adjustment cost in period $t + 1$. The optimum level of z_t cannot be decided in isolation from the decisions on z_{t+1} and z_{t-1} because z_{t+1} and z_{t-1} determine the marginal benefit and adjustment costs of changes in z_t.

If there were zero marginal adjustment costs there would be no need for the firm to plan an optimal *sequence* of the decision variable. In each period z_t could be costlessly adjusted, irrespective of z_{t-1}, so as to maximize $B_t(z_t)$. Each z_t could be chosen without examining the implications of z_t for future adjustment costs because these are zero. The firm could follow the *myopic decision rule* of setting z_t at period t, with reference only to period t benefit. To put things crudely: when there are no adjustment costs every decision is a long-run decision. When there are adjustment costs the firm's decision problem is *dynamic*: it must plan now a sequence or time path of z values, allowing for the effect of z_t on A_{t+1}.

Such problems are complicated (though not impossibly so) and we will therefore adopt here the crude simplification of regarding fixed and variable inputs as *polar cases* of adjustment costs. Variable inputs can be thought of as having zero adjustment costs and fixed inputs as having infinite adjustment costs for changes within period 0. The reader should remember when he sees the terms 'long run' and 'short run' that they are based on these polar cases and that the rate of adjustment of inputs by the firm is not solely technologically determined: it depends on an economic decision balancing the benefits and costs of adjustment. More complete but complex models can always be formulated by choosing a case intermediate between these extremes.

Opportunity costs

Before we can analyse the firm's cost minimization problems we must define the 'cost' of an input to the firm. The *marginal opportunity cost* of an input is the value of the alternative forgone by the use of an additional unit of that input by the firm. If the additional unit used is not already owned or hired by the firm then it must be bought or rented, and the marginal opportunity cost is the market price or rental of the input. If the additional unit used is already owned or rented there is no additional cash outlay by the firm, but, since the unit could have been sold on the market, the market price is the value of the alternative (selling the unit rather than using it) which is forgone. If for example the firm has a stock of raw materials then the marginal opportunity cost of raw material to it is the ruling market price of that raw material, since the firm has the option of selling the raw material rather than using it in production.

In the analysis of this chapter we will interpret the 'cost' of an input as its marginal opportunity cost and assume that this is measured for variable inputs by the market price of the input. This assumption may not be valid for a number of reasons:

(i) If the market price of the input to the firm varies with the amount purchased then if the price rises (falls) as the firm buys larger quantities of the input the marginal opportunity cost of the input is greater (less) than its market price to the firm. The reason is that cost to the firm of an extra unit consists of the market price for that unit *plus* the effect of the rise in price on the total cost of the units which the firm has already decided to buy. If $p_1^0 z_1^0$ is the total cost of z_1^0 units of input 1 and $(p_1^0 + \Delta p_1) \cdot (z_1^0 + 1)$ the cost of $(z_1^0 + 1)$ units, the marginal cost of the extra unit is

$$(p_1^0 + \Delta p_1)(z_1^0 + 1) - p_1^0 z_1^0 = (p_1^0 + \Delta p_1) + \Delta p_1 z_1^0 = p_1^1 + \Delta p_1 z_1^0$$

where $p_1^1 = p_1^0 + \Delta p_1$ is the market price after the purchase of the additional unit. We will leave to a later chapter the analysis of this case and assume throughout this chapter that input prices are fixed as far as the firm is concerned.

(ii) The firm may face different market prices for the input depending on whether it wishes to buy or sell it. Purchase taxes may cause the buying price to exceed the selling price. Markets may be costly to use because of the costs of acquiring information, negotiation, etc., so that a seller may receive a net price below that paid by a buyer. These *transactions costs* may also include fees and commissions paid to agents and brokers. The contract under which an input was hired or bought may create a gap between buying and selling prices. For example a firm may rent warehouse space under a contract which forbids the firm to re-let. The selling price is therefore zero but the purchase price of additional space is the market price. Again, consider a firm which hires labour under a contract which gives each worker the right to a month's notice of dismissal, so that his wage is an inescapable cost over this period. The *marginal opportunity cost* of the input in the short-run decision problem in such cases is the selling price (zero in the two examples above) for quantities less than the amount already owned or rented and the buying price for larger quantities. In the long run (a month in the labour contract example) the marginal opportunity cost is the market price irrespective of the quantity the firm wishes to use.

We see therefore that the marginal opportunity cost of an input depends on the quantity of it which the firm wishes to use, the quantity of it which is already owned or contracted for, the costs of using the input market, and the terms of the contracts under which inputs are traded. As the last two examples above indicate, *it will also depend on the time horizon of the decision for which the cost calculations are required*, i.e. on whether the decision is short- or long-run, or whether the input is fixed or variable. In the rest of this chapter we shall adopt the simplifying assumption that the marginal opportunity cost of an input when it can be varied without constraints is its market price; while that of an input subject to a maximum capacity constraint – a 'fixed' input, is zero. More realistic and complicated analyses are therefore clearly possible.

Exercise 8A

1.* If the firm can borrow and lend at the interest rate r per annum what is the opportunity cost of using an infinitely durable asset for one year, with and without a secondhand market in the durable asset? How would significant transaction costs (due to the need to dismantle and transport the asset each time it is sold) affect your answer? Suppose the asset had a finite life?

B. Long-run cost minimization

The firm's long run cost minimization problem is to formulate a *plan* (an input combination) which will minimize the cost of producing *a specified output* during some period sufficiently far into the future for inputs to be considered freely variable. The firm is assumed to be able to buy inputs or sell inputs that it already owns, at a constant positive price, so that total cost to be minimized is $\sum p_i z_i$. The production function constraining the minimization is assumed to have all the properties discussed in section 7A. The long run cost minimization problem is

$$\min_{z_1, \ldots, z_n} \sum p_i z_i \quad s.t. \quad \begin{aligned}&\text{(i)} \ \ y = f(z_1, \ldots, z_n) \geq y^0 \\ &\text{(ii)} \ \ z_i \geq 0 \qquad (i = 1, \ldots, n)\end{aligned} \qquad \text{[B.1]}$$

where y^0 is the required output level.

Figure 1 illustrates a two input version of the problem. The lines C_1, C_2, C_3 are *isocost* lines which show the combinations of the two inputs which have the same total cost. The C_1 line, for example, graphs the equation

$$p_1 z_1 + p_2 z_2 = C_1$$

or

$$z_2 = \frac{C_1}{p_2} - \frac{p_1}{p_2} \cdot z_1$$

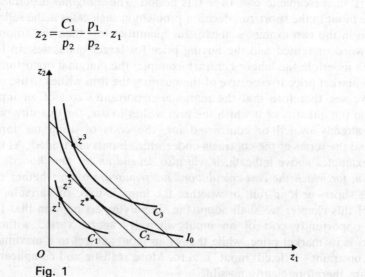

Fig. 1

The slope of each isocost line is

$$\frac{dz_2}{dz_1}\bigg|_{dC=0} = \frac{-p_1}{p_2} \qquad \text{[B.2]}$$

and in this case, where the prices of the inputs are independent of the amounts of the inputs bought by the firm, the isocost lines are parallel.

The further from the origin the higher are the total costs represented by the lines: z^2 on C_2 is an input bundle containing more of both inputs than z^1 on C_1. It must therefore cost more, and since all points on the same isocost line have the same total cost, all points on C_2 cost more than all points on C_1. I_0 is the isoquant for $y = y^0$ and, as we argued in section 7A, the solution must be on this isoquant when input prices are positive. The problem is to choose the point on I_0 which has the lowest cost, i.e. is on the lowest isocost line. In this case the least cost input combination is z^* where I_0 is tangent to C_2. Combinations along lower isocost lines such as C_1 cost less than z^* but do not produce enough y: they are on lower isoquants. Combinations on higher isocost lines such as z^3 on C_3 satisfy the output constraint but have higher costs.

The slope of the isoquant is the negative of the marginal rate of technical substitution between z_1 and z_2 and, in the interior solution illustrated here, cost is minimized where

$$\frac{-p_1}{p_2} = \frac{dz_2}{dz_1}\bigg|_{y=y^0} = -MRTS_{21} = \frac{-f_1}{f_2}$$

or

$$\frac{p_1}{p_2} = \frac{f_1}{f_2} \qquad \text{[B.3]}$$

The ratio of input prices is equal to the ratio of the marginal products. Rearranging this expression yields

$$\frac{p_1}{f_1} = \frac{p_2}{f_2} \qquad \text{[B.4]}$$

as a necessary condition for cost minimization. Now f_1 is the marginal product of z_1: the rate at which y increases as z_1 increases, and $1/f_1$ is the rate at which z_1 must increase to increase y; it is the number of units of z_1 required to increase y by one unit. p_1 is the cost of an additional unit of z_1. p_1 times $1/f_1$ is therefore the cost of increasing the output of y by one unit by increasing the input of z_1. p_2/f_2 has a similar interpretation. When costs are minimized the firm would be indifferent between increasing y by increasing z_1 or z_2.

The effect on total cost is the same whichever input is varied so as to increase output by one unit, when inputs are chosen optimally. $p_1/f_1 = p_2/f_2 = LMC$ is therefore the *long-run marginal cost* of extra output to the firm: the rate at which cost increases as y increases when cost is minimized for every level of y and all inputs are variable.

In section 7A we introduced two distinct but related definitions of efficiency (output efficiency and technical efficiency) and we now introduce a third: *economic efficiency*. An input combination is economically efficient when it minimizes the cost of producing a given output. It is important to be clear about the relationships of these three types of efficiency: economic efficiency implies technical efficiency, which implies output efficiency, but none of the converse implications hold.

Method of Lagrange in the cost minimization problem*

Since the solution to [B.1] will satisfy $y^0 = f(z_1, \ldots, z_n)$ on our assumptions about input prices and technology, we can, if we also assume that all inputs are used in positive quantities in the solution, analyse the solution to [B.1] by forming the Lagrange function

$$L = \sum p_i z_i + \lambda [y^0 - f(z_1, \ldots, z_n)] \qquad [B.5]$$

First order conditions for a minimum of L are

$$\frac{\partial L}{\partial z_i} = p_i - \lambda f_i = 0 \qquad (i = 1, \ldots, n)$$

$$\frac{\partial L}{\partial \lambda} = y^0 - f(z_1, \ldots, z_n) = 0 \qquad [B.6]$$

and by writing the conditions on z_i as $p_i = \lambda f_i$ and dividing the ith condition by the jth we have the n-input extension of [B.3]:

$$\frac{p_i}{p_j} = \frac{f_i}{f_j} \qquad (j = 1, \ldots, n, j \neq i) \qquad [B.7]$$

We can, as in all economic problems using Lagrange techniques, give an economic interpretation to λ. Recall section 2F, in which it was shown that the optimal value of λ is the rate at which the optimized value of the objective function increases as the constraint parameter is increased. In [B.1] the objective function is total cost and the constraint parameter is output, so that the optimal value of λ is the rate at which cost increases as output increases, i.e. long run marginal cost (LMC) so that

$$\lambda = \frac{\partial C}{\partial y^0} = LMC \qquad [B.8]$$

where C is the minimized value of $\sum p_i z_i$. This interpretation is supported by writing the conditions [B.6] as

$$\frac{p_1}{f_1} = \ldots = \frac{p_n}{f_n} = \lambda$$

and using the previous discussion of the two-input case in [B.4].

Comparative statics: *effect of output changes*

The optimal (cost minimizing) input combination will be a function of the prices of the inputs and the output level produced i.e.

$$z_i^* = z_i^*(p_1, \ldots, p_n, y) = z_i^*(p, y) \qquad (i = 1, \ldots, n) \qquad [B.9]$$

and so will the minimized total cost:

$$C = \sum_i p_i z_i^* = \sum_i p_i z_i^*(p, y) = C(p, y) = C(p_1, \ldots, p_n, y) \qquad [B.10]$$

Just as in Chapter 3, we are here interested in the comparative static properties of our model: the response of the endogenous variables (the optimal z_i) to changes in the exogenous variables (the input prices and the level of output), and in the effect of changes in the exogenous variables on the optimized value of the objective function C. In Fig. 2 the effects of changes in y on the optimal input levels are illustrated. z^0, z^1, z^2 are optimal input combinations for producing y^0, y^1, y^2 at least total cost of C_0, C_1, C_2. The *expansion path EP* is the locus of optimal input combinations traced out as the output level changes, with input prices held constant. In this case *EP* is positively sloped indicating that increases in y cause increases in both inputs. However with a different production function the expansion path might be negatively sloped over part of its range, as in Fig. 3. Here, as y increases from y^0 to y^1, the amount of z_1 declines from z_1^0 to z_1^1. Over this range z_1 is an *inferior* input and z_2 is *normal*.

So far the analysis is reminiscent of the effect of changes in income on the consumer's demand for goods: no prediction can be made without knowledge of the form of the production function in this instance, just as was the case with the consumer's utility function. There is an important distinction, however, in that utility functions satisfying the assumptions of Chapter 3 are not objectively verifiable since utility cannot be measured. Output can be measured, and so definite predictions can be made on the basis of empirically verifiable restrictions on the production function.

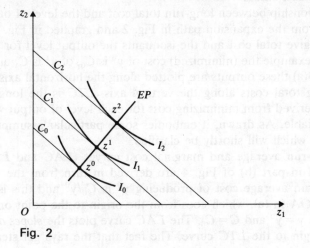

Fig. 2

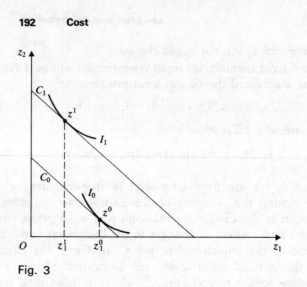

Fig. 3

Suppose, for example, that the firm's production function is linear homogeneous. The necessary condition for cost minimization is

$$p_1/p_2 = f_1/f_2$$

A change in y will lead to a new input bundle at which this condition will be satisfied. Since p_1, p_2 are constant, f_1/f_2 must be unchanged in the new position. But f_1/f_2 is constant along any ray from the origin only if $f(z_1, z_2)$ is linear homogeneous (see section 7B). Therefore the expansion path will be a positively sloped straight line through the origin. Increases in output will lead to both inputs increasing so that the relative input proportions are constant. Only changes in relative input prices will lead to changes in the ratios of inputs.

Long-run cost curves

The relationship between long-run total cost and the level of output can be read off from the expansion path in Fig. 2 and graphed in Fig. 4(a). The isocost lines give total cost and the isoquants the output level for each point on *EP*. For example the (minimized) cost of y^0 is C_0, of y^1 is C_1 and of y^2 is C_2. In Fig. 4(a) these outputs are plotted along the horizontal axis and the corresponding total costs along the vertical axis. *LTC* is the long-run total cost curve derived from minimizing cost for each level of output when all inputs are variable. As drawn, it embodies some particular assumptions about technology which will shortly be clarified.

The long-run average and marginal cost curves (*LAC* and *LMC*) which are plotted in part (b) of Fig. 4 are derived in turn from the *LTC* curve. The long-run average cost of producing y^0 is C_0/y^0 and this is the slope of the line *OA* in (a), which goes from the origin to the point on the *LTC* curve where $y = y^0$ and $C = C_0$. The *LAC* curve plots the *slopes of the rays* from the origin to the *LTC* curve. The fact that the rays get steadily flatter up to point B, and then steeper, accounts for the U-shaped *LAC* curve.

Since long-run marginal cost is the rate at which long-run total cost increases as output increases ($LMC = \partial LTC/\partial y$) the *LMC* curve is derived by plotting the slope of the *LTC* curve for each level of output. Notice that the *LMC* curve cuts the *LAC* curve from below at the point where *LAC* is at a minimum, since at output y^2 the ray from the origin *OB* is also tangent to the curve. It can be shown that this relationship must always hold by the same reasoning as was applied to the relationship between average and marginal product curves in section 7C. (See Question 1 of Exercise 8B.) Note also that the output y^1 at which *LMC* is a minimum is the point of inflexion of the *LTC* curve, and that *LAC* is decreasing through this point (the rays in (*a*) are still getting flatter). Again the curvature of the *LTC*

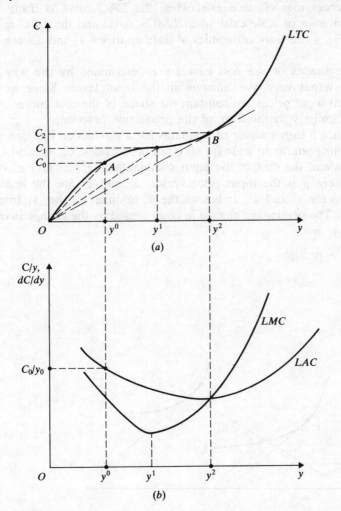

(*a*)

(*b*)

Fig. 4

curve in (a), with its slope, though always positive, at first falling and then rising, implies the U-shaped *LMC* curve in (b).

Economies of scale

The *elasticity of cost with respect to output* is a measure of the responsiveness of cost to output changes. It is defined as the proportionate change in cost divided by the proportionate change in output:

$$\frac{\partial LTC}{LTC} \bigg/ \frac{\partial y}{y} = \frac{\partial LTC}{\partial y} \cdot \frac{y}{LTC} = \frac{LMC}{LAC} \qquad [\text{B.11}]$$

since $\partial LTC/\partial y = LMC$ and $LTC/y = LAC$. The cost curve is said to exhibit *diseconomies of scale* if $LMC/LAC > 1$ and *economies of scale* if $LMC/LAC < 1$. Since $LMC > LAC$ implies that LAC is increasing with output, diseconomies of scale exist when the LAC curve is rising. Conversely economies of scale exist when $LMC < LAC$ and the LAC curve is falling. In Fig. 4 there are economies of scale up to $y = y^2$ and diseconomies thereafter.

The shapes of the cost curves are determined by the way input prices and output vary with changes in the input levels. Since we have assumed that input prices are constant the shape of the cost curves will be determined entirely by the form of the production function.

Figure 5 shows a pair of isoquants for a production function which has *diminishing returns* to scale for all input proportions. C_0, C_1 and C_2 are isocost lines and the cost of the input combinations z^0, z^1 and z^2 is pz^0, pz^1, pz^2 where p is the input price vector. z^0 and z^1 are the least cost combinations for y^0 and y^1. z^2 lies on the y^0 isoquant on the ray from the origin to z^1. The percentage change in costs caused by the change in output from y^0 to y^1 is

$$(pz^1 - pz^0)/pz^1$$

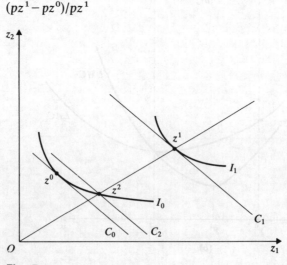

Fig. 5

The percentage change in costs caused by moving from z^2 to z^1 is

$$(pz^1 - pz^2)/pz^1 = p(z^1 - z^2)/pz^1$$

but z^2 lies on the same ray as z^1 and so $z^2 = kz^1$ $(k < 1)$. Hence $(pz^1 - pz^2)/pz^1 = 1 - k$, and since z^2 lies on a higher isocost curve than z^0

$$(pz^1 - pz^0)/pz^1 > 1 - k \qquad [\text{B.12}]$$

Since there are decreasing returns to scale a *reduction* in scale will cause a *smaller* percentage fall in output, i.e. $f(kz) > f(z)k$ if $k < 1$. Hence,

$$f(z^1) - f(z^2) = f(z^1) - f(kz^1) < f(z^1) - f(z^1)k = f(z^1)(1 - k)$$

so that the percentage change in output between z^2 and z^1 is

$$\frac{f(z^1) - f(kz^1)}{f(z^1)} < \frac{f(z^1)(1 - k)}{f(z^1)} = 1 - k$$

But, because z^2 and z^0 are on the same isoquant

$$\frac{f(z^1) - f(z^0)}{f(z^1)} = \frac{f(z^1) - f(z^2)}{f(z^1)} < 1 - k \qquad [\text{B.13}]$$

Comparing [B.12] and [B.13], we see that there are *diseconomies of scale* since the percentage change in cost ([B.12]) exceeds the percentage change in output ([B.13]) when output increases from y^0 to y^1. Hence, if the production function has diminishing returns to scale there are diseconomies of scale.

By means of similar arguments for the cases of constant and increasing returns we can show that these imply constant *LAC* and declining *LAC* (economies of scale) respectively (see Question 1 of Exercise 8B).

Comparative statics: effect of input price changes

We now hold output constant and consider the effect of variations in input prices on the firm's use of inputs. At first glance the effect appears obvious. Suppose the firm is minimizing the cost of producing y^0 as illustrated in Fig. 6. With input prices at their initial levels z^0 is the cost-minimizing input combination, where the isoquant I_0 is tangent to the isocost line C_0. Let the price of z_1 rise. The isocost lines will pivot about their intercepts on the z_2 axis and will become steeper. The new optimal bundle is z^1 where the isocost line C_1 is tangent to I_0. The effect of the rise in p_1 is to reduce the amount of z_1 used. We can use the argument of Chapter 3 concerning the sign of the substitution effect in consumer theory to show that a rise (fall) in an input's price will always reduce (increase) the firm's use of that input when output is held constant. The price rise makes the isocost line steeper and the isoquant becomes steeper as z_1 is reduced (z_2 substituted for z_1). The necessary condition for cost minimization (in the interior solution case) is that the isocost line and the isoquant are tangent. Hence a rise in p_1 must lead to a fall in z_1. This definite prediction of the

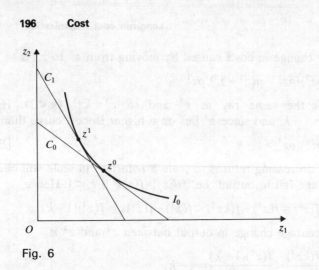

Fig. 6

sign of the 'input substitution effect' is not, however, of much consequence to empirical tests and applications because of the nature of the model which generates it. As was pointed out in the opening paragraph of Chapter 7, the cost minimization model is essentially incomplete because no attention is paid to the determination of the firm's output level. A change in input prices will cause a change in the firm's cost curves and hence in general a change in the optimal *output* level. The total change in input use will therefore consist of the 'substitution effect' (the effect of a change in p_1 with y constant) plus an 'output effect' (the effect of a change in y, caused by a change in costs, on input use). Without knowledge of the firm's production function and its objectives it is impossible to sign the 'output' effect. For example if z_1 is a strongly inferior factor *and* if the rise in costs causes the optimal output to fall then the total effect of the rise in the price of p_1 may be to increase its use by the firm (Explain why). Figure 7 illustrates this possibility, z^0, z^1

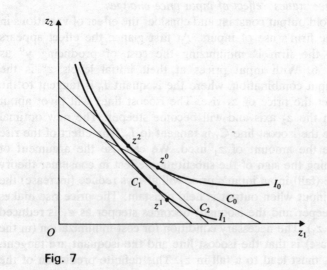

Fig. 7

being the initial and new optimal input choices on the initial and new optimal isoquants I_0, I_1. C_0 is the initial isocost line and C_1, C_2 are new isocost lines after the rise in p_1. z^0 to z^2 is the 'input substitution effect', z^2 to z^1 the 'output effect'. It is also possible to construct examples in which the 'output effect' reinforces the 'input substitution effect'.

The definite prediction concerning the input substitution effect is of little empirical use because we would not expect a change in input prices to leave output unaltered and if output does vary the substitution effect will be disguised by the output effect. We must leave consideration of the general relationship between input prices and the firm's demand for inputs until we have a complete model which treats output as an endogenous rather than, as here, an exogenous variable. So far we have only examined the effect of changes in *relative* input prices but similar remarks apply to equal proportionate input price changes. The slopes of the isocost lines are unaltered and therefore at each level of output the input bundles chosen are unaltered. The change in costs will, however, usually induce a change in the optimal output level and once again we have to specify a model which treats output as endogenous before definite predictions are possible.

Elasticity of substitution

We will return to the effect of input price changes on the demand for the inputs in Chapter 14, but in preparation we will examine the relationship between the firm's production function and the input substitution effect in more detail. It is clear from Figure 6 that the effect of changes in relative input prices on the cost minimizing input combination depends on the curvature of the isoquant. Cost minimization requires that the *MRTS* be equal to the input price ratio. Hence the smaller the rate of change of the slope of the isoquant as the input ratio varies the greater will be the change in the input ratio required to re-establish the equality of *MRTS* and the price ratio after a change in that ratio.

The elasticity of substitution is defined in the two-input case as

$$\sigma = \frac{\%\ \text{change in } z_2/z_1}{\%\ \text{change in } MRTS_{21}}$$

For a cost minimizing firm $MRTS_{21} = p_1/p_2$ so that an equivalent formulation is

$$\sigma = \frac{\%\ \text{change in } z_2/z_1}{\%\ \text{change in } p_1/p_2} = \frac{\mathrm{d}(z_2/z_1)}{\mathrm{d}(p_1/p_2)} \cdot \frac{(p_1/p_2)}{(z_2/z_1)}$$

σ will be smaller the greater the change in *MRTS* in response to a change in the input ratio. It is a natural measure of the degree of substitutability in production since it indicates how responsive the input mix is to changes in relative input prices. The greater σ is the greater will be the responsiveness of the input mix chosen by a cost minimizing firm to produce a given output to a change in relative input prices, i.e. the greater will be the input substitution effect.

*Input price changes and cost curves**
If all input prices increase in the same proportion then the total cost
of any *given* output must rise in the same proportion, *because there is no
change in the optimal input combination* (Supply the reasoning). Thus:

$$\frac{\Delta LTC}{LTC} = \frac{\sum \Delta p_i z_i^*}{\sum p_i z_i} = \frac{\sum k p_i z_i^*}{\sum p_i z_i} = k$$

where $k = \Delta p_i / p_i (i = 1, \ldots, n)$ is the proportionate change in input prices. The
LAC will also rise by k:

$$\frac{\Delta LAC}{LAC} = \frac{\Delta(LTC/y)}{LTC/y} = \frac{\Delta LTC}{LTC} = k$$

as will *LMC*. Since $LMC = p_i/f_i$ (for $z_i^* > 0$) we have:

$$\frac{\Delta LMC}{LMC} = \frac{\Delta(p_i/f_i)}{p_i/f_i} = \frac{\Delta p_i/f_i}{p_i/f_i} = \frac{\Delta p_i}{p_i} = k$$

The proportionate increase in input prices will have the effect of shifting the
LTC, *LAC* and *LMC* curves vertically in the proportion k for each level of
output, as Fig. 8 illustrates. LAC_0 and LAC_1 are the long-run average cost
curves before and after the proportionate price rise, and LMC_0, LMC_1,
LTC_0, LTC_1 have similar interpretations.

The effects on the cost curves of non-proportional price increases
are less easy to predict without detailed knowledge of the production
function. The reason for this can be shown by considering a rise in a single
input price p_1, all other input prices remaining constant. When the relative
input prices change, as they do in this case, the cost minimizing input bundle
will also change, as in Fig. 9. The rise in p_1 causes the isocost lines to pivot
about their intercepts on the z_2 axis, so that C_1 and C_3 represent sets of
input combinations with the same total cost before and after the rise in p_1.
At the intercept on the z_2 axis, $z_1 = 0$ so that total cost is $p_2 z_2$; this is
unaffected by the rise in p_1, and hence by definition of the isocost lines, all
input bundles on C_1 and C_3 have the same total cost. With y constant the
new optimal input combination is z^2 on C_2 and, since C_2 is further from the
origin than C_3, total cost is higher at z^2 than z^1 by p_2 times the difference
in the C_2, C_3 intercepts on the z_2 axis.

The conclusion that a rise in p_1 leads to a rise in total cost for each
level of output (an upward shift in the *LTC* curve) is unsurprising but we
have no indication of how sensitive total cost is to a rise in an input price.
Let us define the *elasticity of total cost with respect to p_i* in the usual way as

$$E_{p_i}^c = \frac{\partial C}{C} \bigg/ \frac{\partial p_i}{p_i} = \frac{\partial C}{\partial p_i} \cdot \frac{p_i}{C} \qquad \text{[B.14]}$$

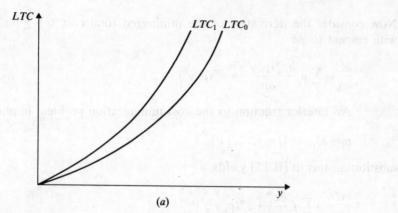

(a)

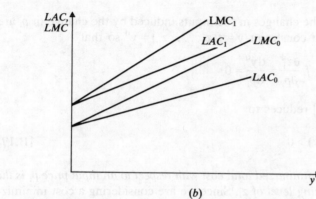

(b)

Fig. 8

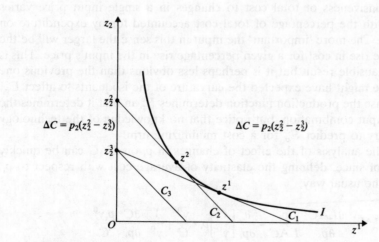

$$\Delta C = p_2(z_2^2 - z_2^3) \qquad \qquad \Delta C = p_2(z_2^2 - z_2^3)$$

Fig. 9

Now consider the derivative of the minimized total cost $C = \sum p_i z_i^*(p, y^0)$ with respect to p_i:

$$\frac{\partial C}{\partial p_i} = \sum p_j \frac{\partial z_j^*(p, y^0)}{\partial p_i} + z_i^*(p, y^0) \qquad [\text{B.15}]$$

An interior solution to the cost minimization problem implies that

$$p_j = \lambda f_j \qquad (j = 1, \ldots, n)$$

substituting this in [B.15] yields

$$\frac{\partial C}{\partial p_i} = \lambda \sum_j f_j \frac{\partial z_j^*}{\partial p_i} + z_i^*(p, y^0) \qquad [\text{B.16}]$$

But remember that the changes in the inputs induced by the change in p_i are subject to the output constraint $y = f(z_1, \ldots, z_n) = y^0$ so that

$$\frac{dy}{dp_i} = \frac{df}{dp_i} = \sum f_j \frac{\partial z_j^*}{\partial p_i} = \frac{dy^0}{dp_i} = 0$$

and therefore [B.16] reduces to

$$\frac{\partial C}{\partial p_i} = z_i^*(p, y^0) > 0 \qquad [\text{B.17}]$$

The derivative of the minimized total cost with respect to an input price p_i is the optimal cost minimizing level of z_i. Since we are considering a cost minimizing firm we can substitute [B.17] for $\partial C/\partial p_i$ in [B.14] so that

$$E_{p_i}^c = \frac{\partial C}{\partial p_i} \cdot \frac{p_i}{C} = \frac{z_i^* \cdot p_i}{C} \qquad [\text{B.18}]$$

The responsiveness of total cost to changes in a single input price varies directly with the percentage of total cost accounted for by expenditure on that input. The more 'important' the input in this sense the larger will be the percentage rise in cost for a given percentage rise in the input's price. This is again a plausible result but it is perhaps less obvious than the previous one in that one might have expected the curvature of the isoquants to affect $E_{p_i}^c$. In one sense the production function determines $E_{p_i}^c$ in that it determines the optimal input combination, but notice that no knowledge of the technology is necessary to predict $E_{p_i}^c$ for a cost minimizing firm.

The analysis of the effect of changes in p_i on LAC can be quickly disposed of since, defining the elasticity of average cost with respect to p_i, $E_{p_i}^{LAC}$ in the usual way,

$$E_{p_i}^{LAC} = \frac{\partial LAC}{\partial p_i} \cdot \frac{p_i}{LAC} = \frac{\partial}{\partial p_i}\left[\frac{C}{y^0}\right] p_i \cdot \frac{y^0}{C} = \frac{1}{y^0} \cdot \frac{\partial C}{\partial p_i} \cdot \frac{p_i y^0}{C}$$

$$= E_{p_i}^c$$

The effect of a given rise in p_i on the LTC and LAC curves will be to shift the LTC and LAC curves upward vertically by an amount dependent on the proportion of total cost which is spent on z_i. This does *not* mean that the curves shift by the same proportion for all output levels since the proportion of C spent on z_i may well vary with the output level. The effect of the change in p_i may be to increase or lower the output level at which LAC is a minimum and to increase or decrease the slope of the LAC curve at any output level. The precise effects will depend on the production function. For example if it has linear expansion paths ($MRTS$ constant along rays from the origin) then the proportion of total cost spent on the ith input will be constant since input proportions are constant along all expansion paths. Hence the LTC and LAC curves will shift vertically upward in the same proportion for all output levels and the output at which LAC is at a minimum will be unchanged.

The effect on the firm's LMC curve is less easy to predict without knowledge of the production function. The reason for this can be shown in Fig. 10. The initial input prices give rise to isocost lines C_0, C_2 and optimal input bundles z^0, z^2 for outputs of y^0 and y^1. The new higher price of p_1 gives isocost lines C_1, C_3 and optimal input bundles z^1, z^3 for outputs of y^0 and y^1. The change in total cost for the change in output $\Delta y = y^1 - y^0$ with the initial lower price of z_1 is $\Delta C = C_2 - C_0$ and this can be measured in the diagram by p_2 times the distance AB. Similarly with the higher price of z_1 the change in cost caused by a change in output from y^0 to y^1 is $\Delta C' = C_3 - C_1$ and is measured by p_2 times the distance DC. In Fig. 10 $\Delta C' > \Delta C$ and thus the effect of the rise in p_1 is to increase the marginal cost of Δy. However, with a differently shaped isoquant it is possible that $\Delta C' < \Delta C$. (Draw the diagram). Hence it is impossible to predict the effect of a rise in p_i on marginal cost without knowledge of the production function.

Use of the cost function enables us to establish what information is required to show the effect of changes in p_i on marginal cost. Given the smoothness of the production function the cost function $C(p_1, p_2, y)$ will also

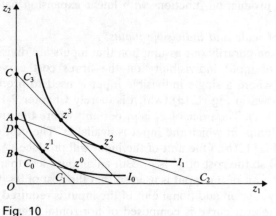

Fig. 10

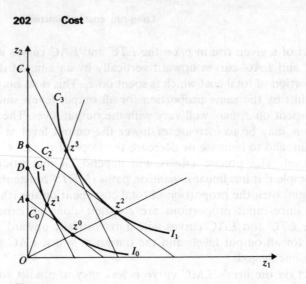

Fig. 11

be a smooth function of its arguments and in particular the second order cross partials with respect to y and p_i will be continuous and therefore equal. Hence, using [B.17],

$$\frac{\partial^2 C}{\partial y\, \partial p_i} = \frac{\partial^2 C}{\partial p_i\, \partial y} = \frac{\partial z_i}{\partial y} \qquad \text{[B.19]}$$

But $\partial z_i / \partial y$ is the rate at which z_i varies as output varies and is positive if z_i is a normal input and negative if z_i is inferior. Hence *a rise in p_i will raise marginal cost if and only if z_i is a normal input.*

   If the expansion paths are linear (and so both inputs are normal), as in Fig. 11, then marginal cost must increase. In the figure the ratio of the distance from z^0 to z^2 to the distance from the origin to z^0 is equal to the ratio of the distance from z^1 to z^3 to the distance from the origin to z^1. Then (by similar triangles) $AB/OB = CD/OC$ and since $OA < OC$ it must be the case that $AB < CD$. Hence marginal cost increases when p_i rises, for every level of y, for production functions with linear expansion paths.

Economies of scale and indivisible inputs*

   Let us drop temporarily our assumption that inputs are divisible and consider the effect of input indivisibility on the firm's cost curves. The simplest case is one where a single indivisible input is used to produce the firm's product, as shown in Fig. 12(a) (which is merely Chapter 7 Fig. 9(c) with $-y_1 = z_1$ and $y_2 = y$). The price of z_1 is p_1 per unit where the unit is the smallest indivisible 'lump' in which the input is available. The cost curve is the step function in Fig. 12(b). One unit of the input will produce y^1 units of output (and $y^n = ny^1$) so the cost of y^1 is p_1. But an amount less than y^1 can be produced only if a unit of the input is used so that the cost of $0 < y \le y^1$ is p_1. To produce $y^1 < y \le y^2$ an additional unit of the input is required and the cost is $2p_1$. Hence the cost curve is composed of horizontal segments.

The average cost curve is shown in Fig. 12(c). The average cost of $0 < y \leq y^1$ is p_1/y, which declines with y to the limit p_1/y^1. The average cost of $y^1 < y \leq y^2$ is $2p_1/y$ which declines from $2p_1/y^1$ to $2p_1/y^2 = 2p_1/2y^1 = p_1/y_1$ as y increases. In general the average cost of $y^n < y \leq y^{n+1}$ is $(n+1)p_1/y$ which declines from $(n+1)p_1/ny^1$ to p_1/y^1 as y increases. The average cost curve is a series of disconnected segments each of which exhibits economies of scale but with the degree of economies decreasing with successive segments. With a large number of segments (large number of input units) the average cost curve will be nearly horizontal. The importance of the economies caused by input lumpiness will depend, therefore, on the

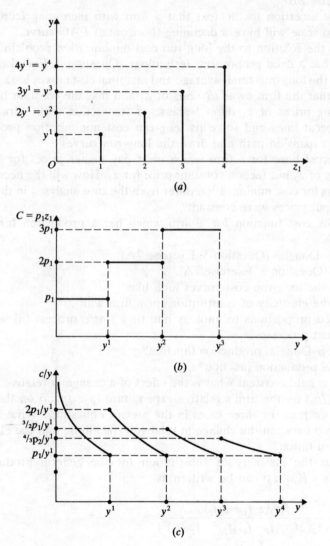

(a)

(b)

(c)

Fig. 12

ratio of the maximum output of a unit of the input to the total output of the firm or industry. Economies of scale arising from the indivisibility of spades will be less significant than those arising from the indivisibility of bulldozers.

    The marginal cost curve arising from the total cost curve of Fig. 12(b) will also be discontinuous. The marginal cost of one unit of output is p_1 but the marginal cost of successive units up to $y = y^1$ is zero. When $y = y^1$ the marginal cost of an extra unit is again p_1 but zero for successive units. Generally marginal cost is zero for $y \neq y^n$ and p_1 for $y = y^n$. Hence the marginal cost curve is the y axis for $y \neq y^n$ and the points p_1 for $y = y^n$.

Exercise 8B

1. Prove the assertion in the text that a firm with increasing (constant) returns to scale will have a declining (horizontal) *LAC* curve.
2. Illustrate the solution to the long-run cost minimization problem when the firm has a fixed proportions technology (Question 4, Exercise 7A). What do the long-run total, average and marginal cost curves look like?
3. Assume that the firm owns z_1^0 units of z_1 and that the constant buying and selling prices of z_1 differ because of transaction costs. Draw the firm's isocost lines and solve its long-run cost minimization problem. Show its expansion path and draw the long-run curves.
4. Draw isocost lines for a firm which must pay higher prices for larger purchases of z_2 but faces a constant price for z_1. How will the necessary conditions for cost minimization differ from the case analysed in the text where input prices were constant?
5.* Derive the cost function for a firm which has a production function which is
    (a) Cobb–Douglas (Question 5, Exercise 7A);
    (b) *CES* (Question 6, Exercise 7A).
    What do the long-run cost curves look like?
6.* What is the elasticity of substitution for a firm with:
    (a) a fixed proportions technology and (i) a single process (ii) several efficient processes?
    (b) a Cobb–Douglas production function?
    (c) a *CES* production function?
7.* If output is held constant what is the effect of a change in relative input prices (p_1/p_2) on the firm's relative expenditure $(p_2 z_2/p_1 z_1)$ on the two inputs in each of the three cases in the previous question? What is the relationship between the change in relative expenditure and the elasticity of substitution?
8.* Show that the elasticity of substitution for the general production function $y = f(z_1, z_2)$ can be written as

$$\sigma = \frac{f_1 f_2 (z_1 f_1 + z_2 f_2)}{z_1 z_2 (2 f_{12} f_1 f_2 - f_{11} (f_2)^2 - f_{22} (f_1)^2)}$$

where f_{ij} refers to the second-order partial derivatives of f. Show that this expression simplifies to

$$\sigma = \frac{f_1 f_2}{y f_{12}}$$

provided that the production function is linear homogeneous (section 7B and Question 5, Exercise 7B).

9.* What plausible intuitive grounds are there for supposing (correctly) that the long-run cost function $C(p, y)$ is concave in p? (*Hint*: recall the discussion of the expenditure function in section 5A). What does the concavity of C in p imply about the sign of the input substitution effect?

C. Short-run cost minimization

The short-run cost minimization problem is that of choosing a (z_1, z_2) pair to minimize the cost of a given output, when there are constraints on the adjustment of the fixed input z_2. The short-run cost function and associated curves show the relationship between y and minimized cost and are derived from the minimization problem. The constraints on z_2, and hence the short-run cost function, may take a variety of forms (see section A). We will assume that the constraint is of the form $z_2 \leq z_2^0$. There is a fixed ceiling on the amount of z_2 available in the period but, since inputs are assumed divisible, the firm *can* choose to use less if it wants to. To bring out the circumstances under which it *would* or would not choose to, we consider the following two cases:

(i) The firm faces a quota or ration on z_2 and pays the market price p_2 for units of z_2 bought, up to a maximum of z_2^0 units. The marginal opportunity cost of z_2 is p_2 for $z_2 \leq z_2^0$ and effectively infinite for $z_2 > z_2^0$. Short-run total cost is $p_1 z_1 + p_2 z_2$ and the short-run isocost lines have a slope (the negative of the ratio of marginal opportunity costs) of $-p_1/p_2$ for $z_2 < z_2^0$. An example of this case would be where the firm has a leasing agreement under which it may lease units of z_2 up to some stipulated maximum per period, and *it only pays for what it uses*. Since inputs are assumed divisible, this implies that it is free to *use and pay for* less z_2 than the maximum z_2^0.

(ii) The firm has contracted to pay $p_2 z_2^0$ for the fixed input regardless of whether it uses less of it than z_2^0 or not. Equivalently, the firm may own z_2^0 units of z_2 and transactions costs or the absence of a market may prevent the firm from selling those units of z_2 it does not want to use. Hence, unlike case (i), the *existence of a fixed input creates a fixed cost*. This is the essence of the difference between cases (i) and (ii), and reflects the fact that a 'fixed input', i.e. one which is subject to a maximum level of use, *need not imply a fixed cost* – it all depends on the nature of the relevant contract into which the firm has entered. Here, the short-run total cost is $p_1 z_1 + p_2 z_2^0$, where $p_1 z_1$ is *total variable cost* and $p_2 z_2^0$ is *total fixed cost*. Since changes in z_2 below the capacity level z_2^0 cause no change in costs, the marginal

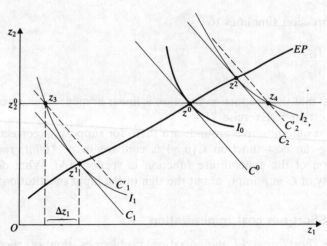

Fig. 13

opportunity cost of z_2 is zero for $z_2 < z_2^0$, and is effectively infinite for $z_2 > z_2^0$ (no more can be had at any price).

The derivation of the short-run cost curves for cases (i) and (ii), and their relation to the long-run cost curve, are shown in Figs. 13 and 14. In Fig. 13, the curve EP again represents the expansion path – the locus of points of tangency of price lines of slope $-p_1/p_2$ with isoquants. The cost/output pairs lying along EP are then plotted as the long-run total cost curve in Fig. 14. In the figures we show just three such points. Output y^1, corresponding to isoquant I_1, and the associated minimized cost C_1; output y^0, corresponding to isoquant I_0, and its minimized cost C_0; and output y^2 with cost C_2. We now consider the analysis for the short run.

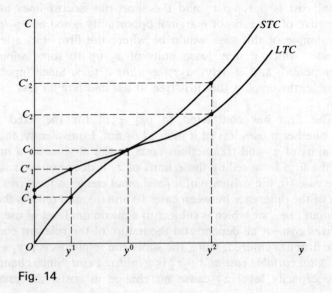

Fig. 14

Take first case (i). For $z_2 < z_2^0$, the marginal opportunity cost of z_2 is identical to that in the long run. For example, if the firm wished to produce output y^1 then the solution to its cost-minimizing problem is point z^1 in the figure (supply the details of the argument). Thus at such an output the firm would choose to use less than z_2^0, the maximum available. A similar result holds for all outputs up to and including y^0, corresponding to isoquant I^0 (Again, supply the argument). Thus for case (i) the expansion path *coincides with EP* up to and including the point z^0. It follows immediately that over the corresponding range of outputs the short-run total cost curve coincides with the long-run total cost curve in this case.

For outputs greater than y^0, however, the picture changes. To move further along *EP* would require amounts of $z_2 > z_2^0$, which are unavailable to the firm. For example output y^2 corresponding to isoquant I_2 would require an amount of z_2 which is the coordinate of point z^2 in the figure. To produce y^2, the best the firm can do is to choose point z^4, using the fixed input to capacity at z_2^0, and a greater amount of the variable input z_1, than at z^2.

It necessarily follows that at such an output the total production cost in the short run will be greater than that in the long run. Point z^4 lies on the iso-cost line C_2', indicated in the diagram, and $C_2' > C_2$. Hence, for all outputs greater than y^0 in Fig. 14, the short-run total cost lies above the long-run total cost. The capacity constraint on z_2 is binding and causes a departure in the short run from the optimal input combination for producing each output level.

In case (ii), recall that $p_2 z_2^0$ is a fixed cost and the marginal opportunity cost of z_2 is zero. Since z_2 is divisible, the portion of the expansion path *EP* to the left of point z^0 in Fig. 13 is still available to the firm, but the important fact now is that the firm will *not choose* to be on it. The firm's *chosen* expansion path will now be the horizontal line $z_2^0 z^3 z^0 z^4$. To see this, suppose the firm were to choose point z^1 to produce output y^1 on isoquant I_1. By moving along I_1 to z^3, it reduces the amount of z_1 by Δz_1 and therefore saves costs equal to $p_1 \Delta z_1$. There is no corresponding increase in cost due to the increased use of z_2 because its marginal opportunity cost is zero: all costs associated with z_2 are fixed and do not vary with the level of use. Hence it always pays the firm to use z_2 to capacity even when it has the (technological) option of not doing so.

This argument can be repeated at all outputs up to y^0. For outputs above y^0 the earlier argument again holds – no more than z_2^0 can be used to produce any such output. Thus in case (ii) the entire short-run expansion path is the horizontal line through z_2^0. (This conclusion may have to be qualified where this line intersects a ridge line. See Question 3 of Exercise 8C.)

The implications of this for the *STC* curve in case (ii) are easy to see. At all outputs below y^0 total costs, though minimized *given the capacity constraint*, are higher than in the long run. At a zero output the fixed cost $p_2 z_2^0$ must still be paid, and the intercept *OF* of the *STC* curve in Fig. 14 represents this. As output increases *STC* lies above *LTC* (compare C_1', the cost of input combination z^3, with C_1 in Fig. 13) but converges to it. At y^0

long-run and short-run total costs are equal. This is because y^0 is the unique output level with the property that the fixed input level z_2^0 is actually the *optimal* long-run z_2-level for the output. For outputs above y^0 input combinations are again sub-optimal in the short run, STC lies above LTC and diverges steadily from it.

Thus we conclude that in case (i) given the input constraint $z_2 \leq z_2^0$, the short-run total cost curve coincides with the long-run total cost curve up to output y^0 (the unique output for which z_2^0 is in fact optimal) and then is the STC curve shown in Fig. 14. In case (ii), on the other hand, the short-run total cost curve is the entire STC curve.

Short-run average and marginal cost

We can now derive the short-run average and marginal cost curves from Fig. 14 for case (ii), leaving the simpler case (i) (in which there are no fixed costs) to the reader. The short-run average and marginal curves are derived in the same way as for the long-run curves in section B and are shown in Fig. 15 together with the long-run curves. SAC is the short-run average cost, SMC the short-run marginal cost curve. Notice that SMC cuts SAC from below at the output at which SAC is at minimum. SAC lies above LAC for outputs other than y^0 since short-run total cost exceeds long-run total cost for outputs other than y^0. Letting $S(y)$ be short-run cost we have $S(y) \geq C(y)$ and hence $S(y)/y \geq C(y)/y$, or short-run average cost is never less than long-run average cost. SAC is tangent to LAC at y^0 because $S(y)$ is tangent to $C(y)$ at y^0. Differentiating $SAC = S(y)/y$ with respect to y gives

$$\frac{1}{(y)^2}\left[\frac{dS}{dy}\cdot y - S\right],$$

but at y^0, dS/dy equals dC/dy and $S = C$, so that the slope of SAC equals the slope of LAC. Note also that the tangency of S and C at y^0 implies that

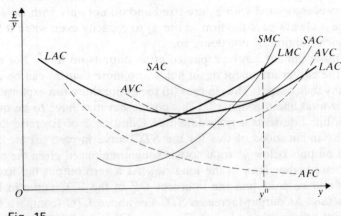

Fig. 15

SMC equals LMC at y^0, since short- and long-run marginal costs are the slopes of the short- and long-run total cost curves respectively.

In case (ii) short-run cost is the sum of variable cost (VC) and fixed cost (FC):

$$S = VC + FC = p_1 z_1 + p_2 z_2^0 \qquad\qquad [C.1]$$

where z_1 varies with y. In Fig. 15 the dashed AVC curve plots *average variable cost* $p_1 z_1/y$ and the AFC curve *average fixed cost* $(p_2 z_2^0/y)$ which is a rectangular hyperbola. z_1/y is the average product AP_1 of z_1 (see section 7C) and so

$$AVC = \frac{p_1 z_1}{y} = \frac{p_1}{AP_1} \qquad\qquad [C.2]$$

By similar arguments to those used in the long-run case

$$SMC = \frac{p_1}{f_1} = \frac{p_1}{MP_1} \qquad\qquad [C.3]$$

The reader should compare the relationship between the short-run average and marginal cost curves shown in Fig. 15 with that between the average and marginal product curves of Chapter 7, Fig. 4.

The envelope property

Fixing the z_2 constraint at different levels will generate different short-run cost curves, each of which, in case (ii), will lie above the long-run curve except where they are tangent to it at the output for which the constrained level of z_2 is the long-run cost minimizing level. If the expansion path is upward sloping as in Fig. 13 the short-run and long-run cost curves will touch at higher levels of output as the fixed level of z_2 is increased. This is illustrated in (a) of Fig. 16 where S^0, S^1, S^2 are short-run cost curves for z_2 constraints of $z_2^0 > z_2^1 > z_2^2$. As the constrained level of z_2 varies, more short-run cost curves are generated and we can see that the long-run cost curve C is the lower boundary or *envelope* of the short-run curves, in that all of them lie above C except at the output at which they are tangent to it. In part (b) of the figure are shown the average and marginal curves derived from part (a). The SAC^0, SAC^1, SAC^2 and SMC^0, SMC^1, SMC^2 curves are the short-run average and marginal cost curves derived from S^0, S^1, S^2 Each of the SAC curves lies above the LAC curve except at the output for which $S = C$, where they are tangent to it. Hence the LAC curve is the envelope of the SAC curves. The SMC curves however *cut* the LMC curve at the outputs for which their respective SAC curves are tangent to LAC, and so the LMC curve is not the envelope of the SMC curves. Short-run marginal cost may be greater *or* less than long-run depending on the output and the level of the fixed input. When the fixed input is at the long-run cost minimizing level for a particular output level SMC equals LMC. In the neighbourhood of this point for larger outputs SMC will exceed LMC,

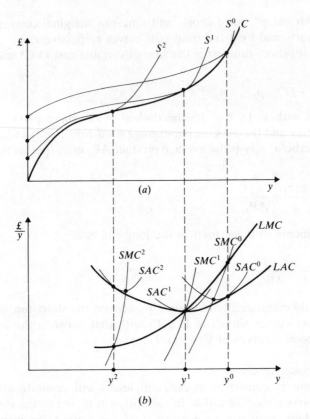

Fig. 16

indicating that it will cost more in the short run to expand output than in the long run. On the other hand at *smaller* outputs than that for which the fixed z_2 is optimal, short-run marginal costs are below long-run marginal costs. This is because output expansion over this range is improving the rate of utilization of the fixed input – the short-run input combinations are converging toward the long-run input combination (cf. Fig. 13).

This relationship between *SMC* and *LMC* is derived from that between the *STC* and *LTC* curves in the neighbourhood of the output level at which the fixed input is at its optimal long-run level. Since the *STC* curve is tangent to the *LTC* curve from above at y^0 the slope of the *STC* curve (*SMC*) must be less than that of the *LTC* curve (*LMC*) for $y \le y^0$ and greater for $y > y^0$ for some neighbourhood of y^0. However it is possible to construct *LTC* and *STC* curves with the envelope property but having $SMC > (<)LMC$ for some $y < (>)y^0$ outside the immediate neighbourhood of y^0 (Show this). The implications of the relationship between *SMC* and *LMC* for the firm's response to output price changes in the short and long runs is examined in the next chapter in Exercise 9B, Question 4.

Comparative statics in the short run

We have already considered the effect of variations in output on short-run cost and input use in deriving the firm's short-run cost curves. Let us now briefly examine the effect of changes in the price of the variable input on the firm's cost curves. In case (i) defined above the firm's short-run expansion path is its long-run expansion path up to $y = y^0$ and the $z_2 = z_2^0$ line thereafter. Hence changes in p_1 will cause the expansion path for $y \leq y^0$ to alter in the same way as the long-run path and so all the remarks relevant to the long-run case apply. For $y > y^0$ the expansion path is identical to the case (ii) path, to which we now turn.

In case (ii) the expansion path is the $z_2 = z_2^0$ line for all outputs. This path is the same for all levels of p_1 so that *the optimal short-run input combination is independent of p_1*. Variable cost is $p_1 z_1$ and average variable cost is $p_1 z_1 / y$, so a given percentage change in p_1 will shift the *VC* and *AVC* curves upward in the same proportion. Since the optimal input bundles do not change when p_1 alters $MP_1 = f_1(z_1, z_2)$ will also be unaffected and so $SMC = p_1/f_1$ will vary proportionately with p_1. Compare the analogous results for the long run where the effect of changes in p_1 on *LMC* could not be predicted without detailed knowledge of the production function.

Exercise 8C

1.* Solve the short-run cost minimization problem and draw the short-run cost curves for a firm with a multiprocess fixed proportions technology. Why does the short-run marginal cost curve become vertical?

2.* Repeat Question 1 for the case of a Cobb–Douglas production function. Does the *SMC* curve become vertical? Why, or why not?

3. What happens in Fig. 13 if part of the ridge line lies below the horizontal line at z_2^0? How will the short-run expansion path and cost curves differ?

4. Assume that the firm wishes to produce a given output next month, has already contracted to hire z_2^0 units of labour at a price of p_2 per unit and cannot fire workers without giving them a month's notice, i.e. without paying them for the time they would have worked during the month. Additional labour can, however, be hired for next month at a price of p_2, though the firm cannot resell the labour hours it has already contracted for. Solve the short-run cost minimization problem for a firm with one other freely variable input and draw the short-run cost curves. How do the results obtained differ from those in the text?

D. Cost minimization with several plants

Many firms possess more than one plant capable of producing their product and hence face the problem of allocating a required total output amongst their plants so as to minimize the cost of producing that output. The problem can be solved in two stages. First each plant solves the problem of producing a given output level at least cost in that plant, subject to the production function for that plant, by choosing a plant cost minimizing input bundle. Each plant then has a cost function derived in the usual way. In the two-plant problem the plant cost function is

$$C_i = C_i(y_i) \qquad (i = 1, 2)$$

where C_i is total cost in plant i, y_i is the output in plant i (y_1 and y_2 are the same goods but produced in different plants) and the input prices have been omitted from the cost functions. C_i may be the short- or long-run cost function depending on the constraints on the adjustment of inputs. The second stage of the problem is

$$\min_{y_1, y_2} C = C_1(y_1) + C_2(y_2) \quad \text{s.t.} \quad \begin{array}{l} \text{(i)} \ \ y_1 + y_2 \geq y^0 \\ \text{(ii)} \ \ y_i \geq 0 (i = 1, 2) \end{array} \qquad \text{[D.1]}$$

Assuming for simplicity that marginal costs (MC_i) are increasing with y_i, we can analyse the solution by using Fig. 17 where MC_1 and MC_2 in parts (a) and (b) are the MC curves of plants 1 and 2. The required total output is y^0. Total cost is minimized when y^0 is allocated between the plants so as to equalize marginal costs in the two plants. Suppose MC_1 exceeds MC_2 under an alternative allocation. Costs cannot be minimized because if y_2 is increased by one unit and y_2 reduced by one unit total cost rises by MC_2 and falls by MC_1 and since $MC_2 < MC_1$ by assumption, the net effect is to reduce total cost. Similarly with an allocation for which $MC_1 > MC_2$. Hence producing y_1^* in plant 1 and y_2^* in plant 2 minimizes the cost of $y^0 = y_1^* + y_2^*$.

The rule of equating marginal costs does not, however, give a complete answer to least cost multi-plant production. First, as is shown in Question 3 of Exercise 8D, the rule may not work if marginal costs are declining over some output ranges. Secondly the least-cost solution, even when MC_i curves are upward sloping, may require production to be concentrated in one plant. For example, in Fig. 17 for required outputs of y^1 or less

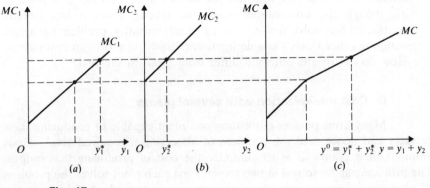

Fig. 17

only plant 1 is used, since for $y_1 < y^1$ its marginal cost is less than the marginal cost of the first unit produced in plant 2. The firm's marginal cost curve (MC in part (c) of Fig. 17) is MC_1 for $y \le y^1$ and the horizontal sum of the MC_1 and MC_2 curves for $y > y^1$.

Formal analysis of the problem*

On the plausible assumption that marginal cost is positive the firm will never produce more than the required amount so that the output constraint in [D.1] can be written as an equality: $y_1 + y_2 = y^0$. This means that [D.1] can be treated as a one-variable optimization problem: choice of y_1 determines y_2 since $y_2 = y^0 - y_1$. Hence [D.1] can be rewritten as

$$\min_{y_1} C = C_1(y_1) + C_2(y^0 - y_1) \quad s.t. \quad 0 \le y_1 \le y^0 \qquad \text{[D.2]}$$

and

$$\frac{dC}{dy_1} = \frac{dC_1}{dy_1} + \frac{dC_2}{dy_2}\frac{dy_2}{dy_1} = MC_1 - MC_2.$$

Now recall section 2G, in which we discussed the solutions to an optimization problem when there are direct constraints on the choice variable. There are three possibilities:

(i) $dC/dy_1 = 0$, so that $MC_1 = MC_2$ and $0 < y_1 < y^0$, so that both plants are used. (We ignore the possibility that $dC/dy_1 = 0$ at $y = 0$ or $y = y^0$.) In this case both plants are used and output is allocated so that marginal costs are equalized.

(ii) $dC/dy_1 < 0$ and $y_1 = y^0$. MC_1 at $y_1 = y^0$ is less than MC_2 at $y_2 = 0$ and so output is produced entirely in plant 1.

(iii) $dC/dy_1 > 0$ and $y_1 = 0$. MC_1 at $y_1 = 0$ is greater than MC_2 at $y_2 = y^0$ so that output is produced entirely in plant 2.

Exercise 8D

1. Draw the LTC and LAC curves for the two plant firm whose LMC curve is shown in Fig. 17.

2. Suppose that a firm has n different plants each of which embodies a different fixed proportions process and that each plant has a maximum output rate which cannot be exceeded in the period because of constraints on the fixed input in each plant. Derive the short-run marginal cost curve for the firm and the *merit order* of plants which shows the order in which plants are brought into production as the required output level increases.

3. Assume that the marginal cost curve of one of the firm's two plants is downward sloping over some initial range of output and then is positively sloped (i.e. one of the plants has a U-shaped MC curve). How will the firm allocate different required total output levels between its two plants? Why will the use of calculus techniques to minimize the total cost function lead to the wrong answer?

E. Multi-product cost functions*

If the firm produces two outputs, y_1 and y_2, its problem is to minimize the cost of producing specified levels, y_1^0 and y_2^0 of its products. The production function constraint is written in the implicit form $g(y_1, y_2, z_1, \ldots, z_n) \leq 0$ of section 7D. If input prices are positive the firm will produce exactly the specified levels of outputs $(y_1 = y_1^0, y_2 = y_2^0)$ and in a technically efficient way: $g(\ldots) = 0$. The cost minimization problem therefore, is

$$\min_{z_1,\ldots,z_n} \sum p_i z_i \quad \text{s.t.} \quad \text{(i)} \ g(y_1^0, y_2^0, z_1, \ldots, z_n) = 0$$
$$\text{(ii)} \ z_i \geq 0 \ (i = 1, \ldots, n) \qquad \text{[E.1]}$$

The Lagrange function is

$$L = \sum p_i z_i + \lambda g(y_1^0, y_2^0, z_1, \ldots, z_n)$$

and the first order conditions on the inputs are in an interior solution

$$\frac{\partial L}{\partial z_i} = p_i + \lambda g_i = 0 \qquad (i = 1, \ldots, n) \qquad \text{[E.2]}$$

Writing the conditions as $p_i = -\lambda g_i$ and dividing the ith condition by the jth gives

$$\frac{p_i}{p_j} = \frac{g_i}{g_j} \qquad \text{[E.3]}$$

In section 7D it was demonstrated that g_i/g_j is the marginal rate of technical substitution between the two inputs so that the necessary condition for cost minimization in the multi-product case is identical with that in the single-product case.

The Lagrange multiplier λ has a somewhat different interpretation in the multi-product problem [E.1]. λ is attached to the production function constraint rather than to the output constraint as in the single output problem. It measures the rate at which the minimized cost of production is reduced if the production function constraint is relaxed slightly, i.e. if it is possible to produce the specified outputs with smaller inputs.

The cost function and joint costs

As in the single output case the optimal input levels will be functions of input prices and the required output levels:

$$z_i^* = z_i(y_1, y_2; p)$$

and substitution in $\sum p_i z_i$ gives the multi-product cost function which shows the minimized cost of production as a function of the output levels and input prices:

$$C = \sum p_i z_i^* = C(y_1, y_2; p) \qquad \text{[E.4]}$$

The marginal cost of additional quantities of good 1 or 2 is the derivative of C with respect to y_1 or y_2.

[E.4] indicates that total cost depends jointly on the amounts of the two goods produced. Is it possible to write the cost function in the *separable* form

$$C = C_1(y_1; p) + C_2(y_2; p),$$

where the cost of producing a given amount of one good does not depend on the amount of the other good produced? Since we have assumed that input prices are constant as far as the individual firm is concerned the form of its cost function is determined by the form of its production function. The cost of producing say good 1 will be unaffected by the output of good 2 only if the input levels required to produce good 1 are unaffected by the output of good 2, that is if the production function is separable. When y_1 and y_2 are joint products in the sense of section 7D the cost function is non-separable and it is meaningless to talk of the total or average cost of producing one of the goods. The *marginal* cost of a joint product is well defined, however, as the derivative of the cost function with respect to that product.

In some cases the cost function may be partially separable:

$$C = H(y_1, y_2; p) + H_1(y_1; p) + H_2(y_2; p).$$

For example the two goods might be jointly produced by one stage of the productive process at a joint cost of H and then require further processing, packaging or transportation at the separate costs of H_1 and H_2. Any attempt to assign the joint cost H to the two products (for example in proportion to their prices, sales revenue or separate costs), as accountants are prone to do, is mere arithmetical manipulation without any economic significance. The cost function is determined by technology and the cost minimization problem. Accounting conventions may apportion joint costs to outputs by various arbitrary procedures but the resulting relationships between outputs and cost will provide no information useful for decision-making. Any attempt to decentralize production by instructing different product divisions to maximize the 'profit' on their products will lead to sub-optimization because, since costs cannot sensibly be assigned to products, the 'profit' figures will be equally meaningless. We return to this question in the next chapter.

F. Inventories*

Firms will often hold stocks of inputs or finished goods but nothing in our analysis so far explains why they should do so. In this section we will examine the way in which inventories can reduce the cost of producing a given output. In Chapter 9 we will consider other motives for storage of inputs and outputs.

Input inventories

In order to explain the holding of stocks of inputs by a firm it is necessary to drop the assumption that the cost of an input to the firm is

measured solely by its price and to recognize that there are additional costs .
involved in the use of a market. These *transaction costs* include the costs of
finding and communicating with suppliers and the administration and bookkeeping involved in processing the order. Transaction costs may be assumed
to be incurred each time additional supplies of an input are purchased and
to be independent of the number of units of the input bought on each
transaction. Suppose that z units of an input are required by the firm in a
period, that the market price of the input is p and that the fixed cost per
transaction is b. Then the cost of z to the firm in the period is

$$bn + pz \qquad\qquad [F.1]$$

where n is the number of transactions.

Clearly if there were no other costs involved the firm would
minimize [F.1] by setting $n = 1$, i.e. buying its entire requirement of z in one
transaction. However if the firm uses the input *at a constant rate* over the
period it will have a store of unused input. If the input is bought in n
transactions the quantity bought in each transaction is z/n. The quantity
stored will decline to zero at a constant rate as the input is used up, and
when the stock is fully depleted a new order is placed and the stock rises to
z/n again. Hence the *average* quantity stored is

$$s = \frac{z}{n} \cdot \frac{1}{2} \qquad\qquad [F.2]$$

Assuming that the costs of storing are proportional to the average
quantity stored, storage costs are

$$sc = \frac{cz}{2n} \qquad\qquad [F.3]$$

where c is storage cost per unit. The total cost of the z units is therefore the
sum of purchase and inventory costs

$$bn + pz + \frac{cz}{2n}$$

or, in terms of the average stock $(s = z/2n)$

$$\frac{bz}{2s} + pz + cs \qquad\qquad [F.4]$$

Hence purchase costs fall with s but storage costs rise, so that the optimal
stock level is found by balancing these two effects of s on total costs.

Differentiating [F.4] with respect to s and setting equal to zero as a
necessary condition for a minimum gives $-bz/2s^2 + c = 0$ and solving for s

$$s = \sqrt{\frac{bz}{2c}} \qquad\qquad [F.5]$$

Hence the average stock held will increase with rises in the level of transactions costs and the total requirement of the input and fall with rises in the costs of storage.

Output inventories

As in the case of input inventories the cost minimization model of the firm must be broadened to explain the holding of a stock of output by the firm. One possible extension is to consider a firm which wishes to sell *different* quantities in two consecutive periods and which has the marginal cost curve C' in Fig. 18. C' is derived from the firm's cost function $C(y)$ where $C(y)$ may be the long-run or short-run cost function depending on how long it takes the firm to adjust all its inputs. $\bar{y}_1$ and $\bar{y}_2$ are the amounts the firm wishes to sell and y_1, y_2 its actual output in periods 1 and 2. If $\bar{y}_1 \leq \bar{y}_2$, as in the figure, then the firm can meet its sales targets by producing more output than sales in period 1, storing the excess and supplementing period 2 output from the stock, so that period 2 sales can exceed period 2 output. If the firm produces and sells at a constant rate in each period and $y_1 > \bar{y}_1$ (i.e. output exceeds sales in the first period) then it will have a stock of $y_1 - \bar{y}_1$ units at the end of the first period. Having started with a zero stock, its average stock is $(y_1 - \bar{y}_1)/2$ in the first period. In the second period output can be less than sales because of the stock held at the beginning of the second period. Period 2 production will therefore be less than sales by $\bar{y}_2 - y_2 = y_1 - \bar{y}_1$. Since the initial period 2 stock is $y_1 - \bar{y}_1$ and the final stock is zero, the average period 2 stock is $(y_1 - \bar{y}_1)/2$. If the cost of holding a stock is c times the average stock then total inventory cost over the two periods is

$$c(y_1 - \bar{y}_1)/2 + c(y_1 - \bar{y}_1)/2 = c(y_1 - \bar{y}_1). \qquad [\text{F.6}]$$

Now if y_1 is increased from $\bar{y}_1$ by one unit, period 1 production cost rises by marginal cost of period 1 production, $C'(\bar{y}_1)$, storage costs rise by c

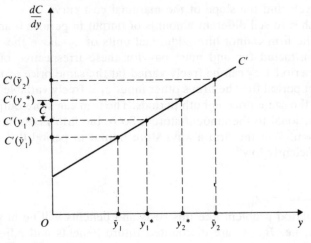

Fig. 18

and y_2 can fall below $\bar{y}_2$ by one unit, thus *reducing* period 2 production cost by $C'(\bar{y}_2)$ (marginal cost of period 2 production). The net effect of this substitution via storage of period 1 for period 2 production is

$$C'(\bar{y}_1) + c - C'(\bar{y}_1) \qquad\qquad [\text{F.7}]$$

If this is negative the firm will have reduced total (production plus inventory) costs over the two periods by means of storage. If on the other hand [F.7] is positive so that

$$c > C'(\bar{y}_2) - C'(y_1) \qquad\qquad [\text{F.8}]$$

then the firm will not store any period 1 output because the marginal storage costs exceed the reduction in costs obtained. If [F.7] is negative the firm will continue increasing its stock of y until no further cost reductions are possible, where

$$C'(y_1) + c - C'(y_2) = 0 \qquad\qquad [\text{F.9}]$$

In other words the firm will increase its inventory until the difference in period marginal production costs equals marginal storage cost. This is illustrated in Fig. 18 where the optimal y_1^* and y_2^* satisfy [F9] and the optimal average inventory is $y_1^* - \bar{y}_1$.

The size of the stock of finished output held by the firm will depend on the marginal cost of storage, and the magnitude of production cost savings which inventories permit, which will depend in turn on the difference in sales levels, and the steepness of the marginal cost curve.

Exercise 8F

1. Suppose that the price of z varies with the amount bought. How does this affect the optimal average stock?
2. Draw diagrams to illustrate the remarks at the end of section E on the relationship between s and the marginal cost of storage, the difference in sales levels and the slope of the marginal cost curve.
3.* A firm wishes to sell different amounts of output in periods 0 and 1. In period 0 the firm cannot hire additional units of z_2 above the number already contracted for and must pay for these irrespective of actual usage. In period 1 z_2 can be freely varied (at the same price as the firm is paying in period 0). The firm's other input z_1 is freely variable in both periods at the same price in both periods. The firm can store output at a cost proportional to the amount stored. Solve the firm's cost minimization problem. Will the firm always store output in period 0 if storage cost is sufficiently low?

Notes

1. In a multi-period problem like this costs and benefits will be in present value terms, i.e. B_t, A_t are discounted future benefits and adjustment costs. See Chapter 15 on inter-temporal optimization.

References and further reading

Rather different concepts of cost to those developed in this chapter are examined in:

A. Alchian. 'Costs and outputs', in M. Abramovitz et al, *The Allocation of Economic Resources*, Stanford University Press, California, 1959;

J. M. Buchanan. *Cost and Choice: An Enquiry into Economic Theory*, Markham, Chicago, 1969.

Adjustment costs are considered in:

*****F. Brechling**. *Investment and Employment Decisions*, Manchester University Press, Manchester, 1975.

Various aspects of least-cost production and investment in public utilities with many plants of different ages and types are considered in:

S. C. Littlechild. 'Marginal Cost Pricing with Joint Costs', *Economic Journal*, June 1970;

R. Turvey. *Economic Analysis and Public Enterprises*, George Allen & Unwin, London, 1971, Ch. 6;

R. Bates and **N. Fraser**. *Investment Decisions in the Nationalized Fuel Industries*, Cambridge University Press, London, 1974.

There is a good short discussion of the elasticity of substitution in:

R. G. D. Allen. *Mathematical Analysis for Economists*, Macmillan, London 1938, Ch. 13.

The relationship between cost and production functions is examined in:

*****D. McFadden**. 'Cost, revenue and profit functions', in M. Fuss and D. McFadden (eds), *Production Economics: a Dual Approach to Theory and Applications*, North Holland, Amsterdam, 1978, Vol. 1.

and at a very rigorous level in:

*****R. W. Shephard**. *Theory of Cost and Production Functions*, Princeton University Press, Princeton, N.J., 1970.

Chapter 9

Supply

The discussion of the technological constraints on the firm in Chapter 7 required no mention of the firm's objectives and even for the derivation of the cost functions and curves of Chapter 8 all that was required was the assumption that the firm wished to produce each output level at least cost. Nothing was said about how that output level was determined. It is now necessary to make some assumptions about the objectives of the firm. We can then proceed to analyse the firm's output decision and its responses to changes in the environment. The assumption we will adopt is that the firm wishes to maximize its profits. This assumption has not gone unchallenged, as we saw in Chapter 6, and the implications of some suggested alternatives are considered in Chapter 13.

The existence of adjustment costs means that the firm must make two kinds of decision at any point in time: it must choose an output level that it will produce in the current period and it must *plan* the outputs to be produced in future periods. This plan of future outputs will imply a sequence of future input levels and this in turn will imply a programme of actions by the firm, to be implemented over time, beginning in the current period, to increase or decrease input levels to the planned future levels.

As in Chapter 8, we will not analyse this problem in its full generality but will instead consider a two-period approximation to it. At the start of period 0 the firm will choose (*a*) an output level for the current period (period 0) given the constraints on the adjustment of the fixed input and (*b*) a planned output level for period 1, given that all inputs are variable. Problem (*a*) is the short-run profit maximization problem which is analysed in section B and problem (*b*) the long-run profit maximization problem analysed in section A.

These two sections are concerned with the case of a single output y and two inputs z_1 and z_2. Sections C and D examine the multiproduct firm. In these first four sections the firm is assumed to operate in competitive markets in the sense that it is faced with prices of inputs and outputs which it takes as unaffected by its actions: prices are treated as parameters by the firm. The final section E is a discussion of the implications of uncertain or varying demand.

A. Long-run profit maximization

The firm's long-run decision problem is to *plan* an output and input combination to maximize profit, π, where profit is revenue $R = py$ *minus* cost $\sum p_i z_i$, and p, p_i are the prices of y and z_i respectively. Formally the problem is:

$$\max_{y, z_1, z_2} \pi = py - \sum p_i z_i \quad \text{s.t.} \quad y \leq f(z_1, z_2)$$

$$y \geq 0, \qquad z_1 \geq 0, \qquad z_2 \geq 0 \qquad \text{[A.1]}$$

This problem can be reformulated in two equivalent ways:

(i) For any output, profit cannot be maximized unless cost is being minimized. Hence, we can make use of the earlier analysis of cost minimization, and work with the long-run cost function $C(p_1, p_2, y)$, derived there. The profit maximization problem can be expressed as:

$$\max_{y} py - C(p_1, p_2, y) \quad \text{s.t.} \quad y \geq 0 \qquad \text{[A.2]}$$

In other words the firm simply chooses the output level which maximizes profit given its revenue function py and cost function C.

This two-stage optimization procedure (minimizing costs to derive the cost function and then maximizing the difference between the revenue and cost functions) has thus reduced the profit maximization problem to a single decision variable problem and, as we will see below, this makes the analysis of the model based on this problem fairly easy.

(ii) Alternatively we can state the problem as follows: since prices are positive the profit maximizing firm will never produce in an output-inefficient way. If $y < f(z_1, z_2)$ then either y can be increased holding z_1 and z_2 constant, or one or both of the inputs can be reduced with y constant, and so profit cannot be at a maximum if $y < f(z_1, z_2)$. Hence the production constraint on a profit maximizing firm can be written as $y = f(z_1, z_2)$. Since a choice of z_1 and z_2 determines y, there are only two independent decision variables: the two input levels. The firm's profit maximization problem is therefore:

$$\max_{z_1, z_2} \pi = p \cdot f(z_1, z_2) - p_1 z_1 - p_2 z_2 \quad \text{s.t.} \quad z_1 \geq 0, \quad z_2 \geq 0 \qquad \text{[A.3]}$$

The equilibrium conditions of this model are derived by setting the partial derivatives of π with respect to z_1 and z_2 equal to zero. It is left for the reader to extract these and to show that they are equivalent to those derived from the first statement of the problem in [A.2]. We will concentrate here on [A.2] because it yields its comparative static results more easily.

Differentiating [A.2] with respect to y we have the following first order condition for y^* to provide a maximum of the profit function:

$$\frac{d\pi}{dy} = p - \frac{\partial C}{\partial y} \leq 0, \qquad y^* \geq 0, \qquad y^* \cdot \frac{d\pi}{dy} = 0 \qquad \text{[A.4]}$$

Since nothing has been assumed about the shape of the profit function [A.4] is a necessary but not a sufficient condition for y^* to yield a maximum. [A.4] may be satisfied by a number of local maxima or minima as Fig. 1 illustrates. The total cost, revenue and profit functions are plotted in part (a) and the marginal cost, revenue and profit and average cost functions in part (b).

It is clear from Fig. 1(a) that y^* is the global profit maximizing output and that y^* satisfies [A.4]. But consider two other output levels: $y = y^1$ and $y = 0$. At $y = 0$, $d\pi/dy = p - \partial C/\partial y < 0$ so that [A.4] is satisfied and this is a local profit maximum since profit is larger (loss is smaller) than at neighbouring feasible outputs. At y^1, $d\pi/dy = 0$ but π is at a minimum. To distinguish *interior* local maxima and minima (when $y > 0$) a second-

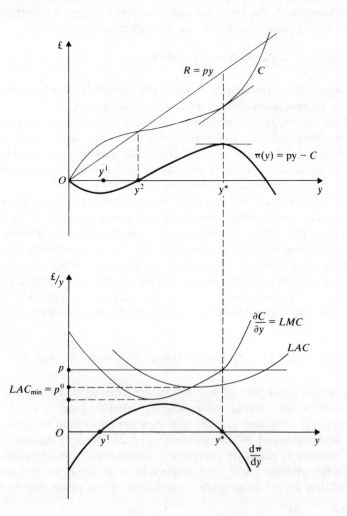

Fig. 1

order condition is required:

$$\frac{d^2\pi}{dy^2} = \frac{-\partial^2 C}{\partial y^2} < 0 \quad \text{i.e.} \quad \frac{\partial LMC}{\partial y} > 0 \qquad [\text{A.5}]$$

This condition is satisfied at y^* but not at y^1, and hence distinguishes between *interior* points $(y > 0)$ which satisfy the necessary condition in [A.4] but which may be minima or maxima. Condition [A.5] is however *not applicable* at $y = 0$. The zero output position is a true *local* maximum because small permissible changes (i.e. increases) in y from $y = 0$ reduce profit (refer to Fig. 1(a)) even though *LMC* is falling at that point. We have in fact a case where there are multiple local optima and the global optimum can only be found by direct comparison of these – profit or loss at $y = 0$ must be compared with profit or loss at $y = y^*$. In the Figure y^* is clearly superior, but it is easy to re-draw the curves in such a way that total cost is everywhere above total revenue and the interior point at which profit is maximized (loss is minimized) is inferior to $y = 0$ (draw the diagram).

In terms of the discussion of local and global optima in section 2D, the problem has arisen here because the conditions of the relevant theorem are not satisfied. The theorem states that if the feasible set is convex and the objective function is quasi-concave *every* local optimum is a global optimum, and so all local optima must yield equal values of the objective function. Here the feasible set defined by $y \geq 0$ is convex (explain why) but the objective function is *not* quasi-concave. To see this, take two points at which profit is equal, say $y = 0$ and $y = y^2$ in Fig. 1(a) (where profit is zero). The definition of quasi-concavity requires that, for *any* pair of points at which profit is the same, the profit yielded by an output on the straight line joining them must be at least as great as that yielded by the two points. But, clearly, at all outputs on the straight line joining $y = 0$ and $y = y^2$ profit is less than zero and so the profit function is *not* quasi-concave. We cannot then be sure that every local maximum will be a global maximum and indeed we have just seen that, in the case shown in Fig. 1(a), one will not be.

Of course, as pointed out in section 2D, the conditions of the theorem are sufficient but not necessary. The reader is invited to re-draw Fig. 1(a) in such a way that $y = 0$ and $y = y^*$ are equally good. (*Hint:* look for a point of tangency.) The point is of course that this is a special case and in general we cannot conclude that a local optimum is a global optimum when the profit function is not quasi-concave.

Interpretation of the conditions

Assuming that $y^* > 0$, conditions [A.4] and [A.5] can be given a familiar interpretation. Condition [A.4] states that it is necessary, for profit to be maximized at y^*, that a small change in output adds as much to cost as it does to revenue, i.e. marginal revenue (which is equal to the price of the output in a competitive market) must equal marginal cost. Condition [A.5] requires that the marginal cost be increasing with y so that the marginal cost curve cuts the price line from below. The firm will maximize its profit by moving along its marginal cost curve until price is equal to marginal cost.

This result means that changes in the price of y will cause the firm to move along its long-run marginal cost curve as long as price exceeds long-run average cost. The portion of the *LMC* curve above *LAC* is therefore the *long-run supply curve* of the competitive firm. It shows the *maximum quantity* which the firm *plans* to supply at any given price, or alternatively the *minimum price* at which the firm would *plan* to supply any given quantity. As a result some of the comparative static properties of the model (in the sense of changes in the firm's plans in response to changes in exogenous variables) are easily derived (others are left to section D):

(i) Increases in the price of y will cause an increase in the planned supply. The firm will move along the marginal cost curve until $p = \partial C/\partial y$ and since $\partial C/\partial y$ is increasing with y at the optimum a rise in p must lead to a rise in y.

(ii) Changes in cost conditions which lead to a rise in the long-run marginal cost of all output levels will lead to a reduction in the planned supply of y for any given p. The supply curve will have shifted upward.

When the optimal y is zero these results are changed. Clearly the firm makes a loss at a positive output level if price is less than the long-run average cost of that output. Letting LAC_{min} denote the minimum level of *LAC*, the firm will plan to produce a zero output next period if it expects $p < LAC_{min}$. A greater profit (of zero) would be earned by producing nothing at all. In Fig. 1(b) a price of less than p^0 will cause the firm to plan to cease production, since p^0 is the lowest price at which *LAC* can be covered.

In this case result (i) above should be modified to: an increase in p will not cause a reduction in y, but rather will leave y unchanged at zero, whenever it leaves $p < LAC_{min}$. In general, therefore, the firm's long-run supply curve is the vertical axis (i.e. nothing is supplied) for $p < LAC_{min}$ and the *LMC* curve for $p \geq LAC_{min}$. If, as in Fig. 1(b), LAC_{min} is at a positive output, i.e. there are economies of scale over some initial range of outputs, the long-run supply curve is discontinuous at $p^0 = LAC_{min}$. If, on the other hand, the *LAC* curve exhibits everywhere diseconomies of scale the supply curve will be continuous.

Exercise 9A

1. Solve problem [A.3], interpret its equilibrium conditions and show that they are equivalent to those derived from [A.2].
2. Show how proposition (ii) just given would be changed at a price $p < LAC_{min}$.
3. Explain why strictly diminishing returns to scale at all output levels would eliminate the discontinuity in the firm's long-run supply function.
4.* What *decisions* or *actions* must the firm take now, in period 0, if it expects $p < LAC_{min}$ next period and so plans a zero output for that period? How important is the assumption here that the firm is *certain* about the future price?

B. Short-run profit maximization

The firm's short-run problem is to choose output and input levels for the current period which will maximize its current period profits, given that there are constraints on the adjustment of some of the inputs. Since inputs are chosen so as to minimize cost for any given output level the problem can be reduced to choosing current period output, y, so as to maximize the difference between revenue and short-run cost:

$$\max_{y} \pi = py - S(p_1, p_2, z_2^0, y) \quad \text{s.t.} \quad y \geq 0 \qquad [\text{B.1}]$$

where the constraint on the adjustment of z_2 is assumed to be an upper limit on the use of z_2 and the firm must pay for z_2^0 units irrespective of use. (See section 8C on the firm's short-run cost function.)

The first- and second-order conditons for this problem are very similar in form and interpretation to [A.4] and [A.5]. The firm will either produce where $p = \partial S/\partial y = SMC$ and where the SMC curve cuts the horizontal price line from below; or the firm will produce nothing if price is less than short-run average opportunity cost (average variable cost) at all positive outputs.

In the short run the maximized level of profit may be negative, even if p exceeds minimum AVC. In Fig. 2, for example, which is based on Chapter 8 Fig. 15 the firm makes a loss if $p < SAC_{\min}$ since fixed costs $(p_2 z_2^0)$ are not covered. If p is less than $AVC_{\min}$ the firm will set $y = 0$ since positive y implies that revenue does not cover variable cost, and so a loss is made on these which must be added to the loss on fixed costs. Conversely if p exceeds $AVC_{\min}$ then revenue is made over and above variable costs, so that some of the fixed costs are recovered by producing and selling some output. The firm may still make a loss but this is lower than the loss at zero output, which is equal to the fixed cost incurred whatever the output level.

The firm's *short-run supply curve*, which shows the output it wishes to produce given the prevailing constraints on the adjustment of its inputs,

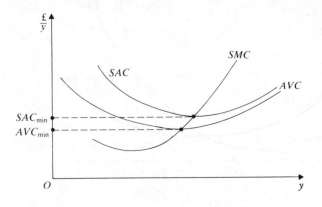

will be the *SMC* curve for $p \geq AVC_{min}$ and the vertical axis at $y = 0$ for $p \leq AVC_{min}$. The firm's short-run supply curve, therefore, is discontinuous when the minimum of the *AVC* curve does not occur at $y = 0$.

The relationship between long- and short-run profit maximization

We pointed out in the introduction to this chapter, and in section 8A, that the firm makes two kinds of decisions at the start of each period: (*a*) it chooses the actual output level for that period, given the constraints on the adjustment of its inputs; (*b*) it *plans* an output level for the next period, when all inputs are freely variable (provided the decision to change them is made at the start of the current period). The first decision is the short-run, and the second the long-run, problem. We will now investigate in more detail how the two types of decision are related.

Some new notation is needed to distinguish between actual and planned, and between actual and forecast, magnitudes:

y_a^t: actual output in period t.

y_p^t: planned output in period t, decided upon in period $t - 1$.

p_a^t: actual price of output in period t.

p_f^t: forecast of price of output in period t made in period $t - 1$.

Since all inputs are freely variable after the current period, plans and expectations need only be made one period ahead, so that as indicated y_p^t refers to a plan made at period $t - 1$ and p_f^t to the firm's forecast of p_a^t made at period $t - 1$. It is assumed for simplicity that input prices and technological conditions are constant over all periods and that they are correctly anticipated at all times, so that actual and expected cost curves coincide and are the same in each period. To make the analysis more concrete let us take z_2 to be a measure of *plant size*.

Initially, at the start of period 0 the firm has a given plant size (z_2^0) which it cannot vary in period 0. Its short run cost curves are shown in Fig. 3 as SMC^0 and SAC^0. In period 0 the firm maximizes its profits by

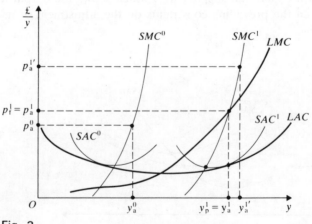

Fig. 3

equating short-run marginal cost to the known, current price of y (p_a^0) and so produces y_a^0. At the same time the firm *plans* an output for period 1. Since the level of z_2 for period 1 can be varied if the decision to do so is made at the start of period 0, the relevant cost curves for planning the next period's output are the long-run curves *LMC* and *LAC* in Fig. 3. (Recall that these curves are derived from a cost minimization problem in which all inputs are freely variable.) At the start of period 0 the firm *expects* the period 1 price to be p_f^1 and so it *plans* to maximize period 1 profit by producing y_p^1, where $p_f^1 = LMC$. The planned period 1 output in turn implies that the period 1 level of z_2 is z_2^1. To ensure that z_2^1 is actually available at the start of period 1, the firm must, at the start of period 0, order and install the additional plant required. Hence the decisions taken in period 0 are (*a*) to set the actual output in period 0, on the basis of the actual price p_a^1 and actual plant size z_2^0; (*b*) to choose the plant size z_2^1 for period 1, on the basis of planned period 1 output, which in turn depends on the forecast period 1 price.

At the start of period 1 the firm's actual plant is z_2^1, giving rise to the short run cost curves SMC^1, SAC^1. Suppose that the actual price is p_a^1. Period 1 profit is maximized by equating SMC^1 to the actual price. In this case the firm's forecast was correct and $p_a^1 = p_f^1$. This means that actual and planned period 1 output are equal: $y_a^1 = y_p^1$. Note that at this output level $SMC^1 = LMC$, indicating that the actual plant (z_2^1) is the optimal plant for producing that output level.

The firm will also plan in period 1 an output for period 2, based on its forecast p_f^2 of the period 2 price, and this will imply a period 1 decision on the actual plant for period 2 (z_2^2). If the firm expects p_f^2 to equal p_a^1 then $y_p^2 = y_a^1$ and there is no need to adjust plant size ($z_2^2 = z_2^1$). The firm will then be in *long-run equilibrium*: it will be maximizing profit for the current period (1) and its current plant will be optimal for the next period (2), given the firm's forecast of the next period's price (and ignoring depreciation).

Suppose, however, that at time 0 the firm had made the wrong price forecast, i.e. the actual and forecast period 1 prices differ (e.g. actual period 1 price is $p_a^{1'} > p_f^1$). The firm would find that its actual period 1 plant (z_2^1) was not optimal for the market price $p_a^{1'}$. In order to maximize period 1 profit, given z_2^1 and the corresponding SMC^1 curve, the firm will set $SMC^1 = p_a^{1'}$ and produce the output $y_a^{1'}$. At the same time it will plan to produce y_p^2, given its price forecast p_f^2, and it will adjust its plant if $p_f^2 \neq p_f^1$, i.e. if *its forecast* of the price has changed (rather than if $p_a^{1'} \neq p_f^2$. Explain why).

The output that the firm *plans* to produce in the next period, based on its forecast of the next period's price, determines the actual plant in the next period, but if the forecast is incorrect actual output next period will in general differ from that planned. The plan made commits the firm to a particular plant size next period, but *not* to a particular output level. When the firm chooses its current output at the start of a period it is *always* 'in the short-run': its plant size is fixed by the plan made in the previous period and is unalterable in the current period. Hence the firm will *always* produce where $p_a^t = SMC^t$ in order to maximize current period profit. If the past forecast was correct then the current plant is optimal and the firm will be producing where $LMC = SMC^t = p_a^t = p_f^t$. If the past forecast was incorrect then the firm will not produce where $LMC = SMC^t$ and the existing plant will not be optimal. Short-run marginal cost and *actual* price determine *actual* output in the current period. Long-run marginal cost and the *forecast* price determine *planned* output and *actual* plant in the next period.

The relationship between forecast and actual, and planned and actual magnitudes can be represented in the following way:

$$p_f^t \rightarrow y_p^{t+1} \rightarrow z_2^{t+1} \rightarrow SMC^{t+1}$$
$$\searrow y_a^{t+1}$$
$$\nearrow$$
$$p_a^{t+1} \dashrightarrow p_f^{t+2} \rightarrow y_p^{t+2} \rightarrow z_2^{t+2} \rightarrow \cdots$$

This emphasises that a model which attempts to predict the firm's *actual* behaviour must include a sub-model of the way in which the firm makes its price forecasts. In the diagram above for example the dashed line from actual price to the forecast of the next period's price indicates that the forecast may depend on the actual current price. We will return to this point in section *E*.

Exercise 9B

1. Adapt Fig. 3 to show that period $t+1$ profit is larger if the firm's expectation of period $t+1$ price is correct, than if it is incorrect.
2. Will the firm have a larger profit if its expectation of p_f^t is 10% larger than p_a^{t+1}, or 10% smaller?
3.* Analyse the relationship between the short- and long-run decisions if the actual and forecast output prices are equal and constant, but the firm's forecast of the price of its variable input may differ from its actual price.
4.* Assume that the firm has correctly forecast current price and believes that next period's price will be the same as this period's. Suppose that this forecast is incorrect and the actual price in period $t+1$ is less than forecast, but that the firm correctly forecasts that the price in period $t+2$ will remain at the actual level for period $t+1$. Show that for *small* changes in the actual price the long-run response exceeds the short-run, i.e. that the long-run supply curve is *more* elastic than the short-run. Draw *SMC* and *LMC* curves and the corresponding total cost curves which will lead to the long-run supply elasticity being (*a*) more and (*b*) less than the short-run for *large* price changes.

C. The multi-product firm*

In this and the next section we will not use the two-stage optimization procedure (deriving a cost function and then maximizing the difference between revenue and cost) of the previous sections. We will instead adopt the single-stage procedure of simultaneous choice of input and output levels. These two sections are also concerned with the firm's *long-run* decision or plan, it being assumed that there are no constraints on the adjustment of inputs. It is also assumed that the actual and forecast price are always equal and constant.

The notation of sections 7D, 7E will be adopted in this section, so that the firm's decision variables are its *net* output levels $y = (y_1, \ldots, y_n)$. Recall from that section that if $y_i < 0$ good i is an input and so $p_i y_i$ will be negative and measure the outlay on good i by the firm. If $y_i > 0$ good i is an output so that $p_i y_i > 0$ is the revenue from the sale of i. Since profit π is the difference between revenues and costs the firm's profit is

$$\pi = \sum p_i y_i = py.$$

The reader should also recall from sections 7D, 7E that the firm's technologically feasible net output bundles can be described either by means of the implicit production function $g(y) \leq 0$, or the concept of the production set (*PS*). If all goods are divisible profit π will be a continuous function of the firm's net outputs and, if the *PS* is assumed to be non-empty, closed and bounded, the Existence Theorem of section 2B applies. As was implied in section 7E, the assumptions about the *PS* necessary for the existence of a profit maximizing net output bundle are not very strong. (What further theorems of Chapter 2 can be applied if the *PS* is also strictly convex?)

When all prices are positive the firm will never choose a bundle y where $g(y) < 0$ (The reader should apply the argument of section A for the single output, two input case to convince himself of this.) Hence the firm's decision problem is

$$\max_y \pi = py \quad \text{s.t.} \quad g(y) = 0 \tag{C.1}$$

There are of course no non-negativity constraints on the y_i because the notational convention of this section gives an economically sensible interpretation to the negative net output levels as inputs, or goods demanded by the firm. The Lagrange function for [C.1] is $\pi + \lambda g(y)$ and the first-order conditions are

$$p_i + \lambda^* g_i = 0 \quad (i = 1, \ldots, n) \tag{C.2}$$
$$g(y) = 0$$

Rearranging the condition on good i gives $p_i = -\lambda g_i$ and dividing by the similarly rearranged condition on good j gives

$$\frac{p_i}{p_j} = \frac{g_i}{g_j} \quad (i = 1, \ldots, n; \, i \neq j) \tag{C.3}$$

This general condition succinctly summarizes a number of familiar results for the three logically possible cases:

(i) Both goods i and j are inputs. In this case g_i/g_j is the marginal rate of technical substitution between two inputs (see section 7D) and for profit maximization this must be equated to the ratio of the inputs' prices. This is the same condition as that required for cost minimization in section 8B, which is to be expected since cost minimization is a necessary condition for profit maximization.

(ii) When i is an input and j an output g_i/g_j is the marginal product of i in the production of good j: MP_i^j. Rearranging [C.3] yields

$$p_j = \frac{p_i}{MP_i^j}$$

But p_i/MP_i^j is the marginal cost of good j (see section 8B) so that [C.3] states that **for profit maximization the output of a good should be set at the level at which its marginal cost is equal to its price**, thus confirming the results of section A. This is illustrated in Fig. 4 where y_1 is the firm's sole input and y_2 its sole output. The shaded area is the PS, π_1 is an iso-profit line satisfying the equation $\pi_1 = p_1 y_1 + p_2 y_2$ or $y_2 = (\pi_1 - p_1 y_1)/p_2$, and π_2, π_3 are derived in a similar way. The profit maximizing net output bundle is $y^* = (y_1^*, y_2^*)$ where the highest attainable iso-profit line, π_2, is tangent to the upper boundary of the firm's PS. The negative of the slope of the iso-profit line is p_1/p_2 and the negative of the slope of the boundary of the PS is the rate at which y_2 increases as y_1 decreases (the input 1 is *increased*) or the marginal product of the input 1 in production of output 2: MP_1^2. Hence condition 3 is satisfied at y^*: $p_1/p_2 = MP_1^2$, or $p_2 = p_1/MP_1^2$, so that price is equated to marginal cost. The firm's profit is $\pi_2 = p_1 y_1^* + p_2 y_2^* = py^*$ or, measured in terms of the output y_2, by the intercept of the iso-profit curve on the y_2 axis: π_2/p_2.

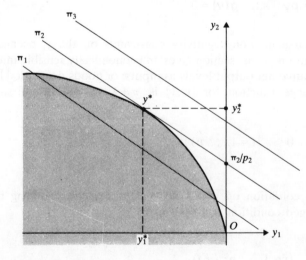

Fig. 4

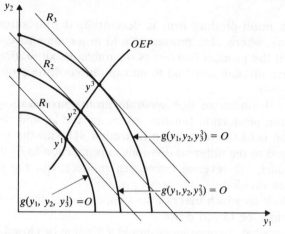

Fig. 5

(iii) If both i and j are outputs g_i/g_j is the marginal rate of transformation between them (MRT_{ji}), so that when the firm produces more than one output it will maximize profit by producing where the MRT between two outputs is equal to the ratio of their prices. This is illustrated in Fig. 5 where the firm produces two outputs (y_1, y_2) from the single input, good 3. The three transformation curves show the varying combinations of the outputs that can be produced from different fixed input levels. The $g(y_1, y_2, y_3^1) = 0$ curve, for example, shows the combinations of goods 1 and 2 that can be produced in a technically efficient way when good 3 (the input) is fixed at y_3^1. As the input level is increased the transformation curve shifts outward.

R_1, R_2 and R_3 can be called *iso-revenue lines*. They show output bundles which will produce the same total revenue: $p_1 y_1 + p_2 y_2 = R_j$, $j = 1, 2, 3$ where R_j is a given constant, $R_1 < R_2 < R_3$. Thus the lines have the equation $y_2 = (R_j - p_1 y_1)/p_2$, $j = 1, 2, 3$.

For a given level of the input y_3, its costs are given and so the firm maximizes profit by choosing an output combination which *maximizes revenue*. If, for example, $y_3 = y_3^1$ the firm will choose the output bundle y^1, where the highest attainable iso-revenue line R_1 is tangent to the transformation curve generated by $y_3 = y_3^1$. If $y_3 = y_3^2$ or $y_3 = y_3^3$ the firm chooses y^2 or y^3 where the respective transformation curves are tangent to iso-revenue lines. *OEP* is the *output expansion path*: the locus of points such as y^1, y^2, y^3, generated by the transformation curve shifting as the input level varies. The firm's profit varies as it moves out along *OEP* since its revenue is increasing (higher iso-revenue curves are reached) and so is its cost (larger inputs are required to reach higher transformation curves). The firm will choose the point on *OEP* where the difference between revenue and cost is at a maximum. If for example this is y^2 the firm's profit is $p_1 y_1^2 + p_2 y_2^2 + p_3 y_3^2 = R_2 + p_3 y_3^2$ (where of course y_3^2 is negative since good 3 is an input).

Exercise 9C

1.* Suppose that a multi-product firm is decentralized into autonomous product divisions, where each product is sold in a competitive market.

   (a) Show that if the product function is separable, maximization of the profit of each division will lead to maximization of the profit of the firm as a whole.

   (b) Conversely, demonstrate that separate profit maximization is not optimal if the production function is not separable, and the firm's cost function is of the form given in section 8D with the joint cost being charged to the different divisions in proportion to (i) the price of the product; (ii) revenue from each product; (iii) the separate costs of each division.

   (c) Should a division which makes a loss under one of the above joint cost allocations be closed down?

   (d) If not, under what circumstances should a division be closed down?

D. Comparative statics: the firm's net supply functions*

The solution to the firm's optimization problem is a vector or bundle of net outputs $y^* = (y_1^*, \ldots, y_n^*)$ which maximizes its profit. Some of the y_i^* will be positive, indicating that the firm supplies good i; some will be negative, indicating that the firm demands good i as an input, and some (perhaps the majority, given that there is a large number of goods) will be zero. The optimal net output of each good will depend on the prices which the firm faces and upon the technological constraints on its actions. The firm's net output can be written, therefore, as functions of prices of the goods.

$$y_i^* = y_i(p_1, \ldots, p_n) = y_i(p) \qquad (i = 1, \ldots, n) \qquad [\text{D.1}]$$

The forms of the *net supply* functions $y_i(p)$ depend on the firm's *PS*. For example:

   (i) If the *PS* is strictly upper convex (i.e. the production function has diminishing returns – see section 7E) the solution to the firm's optimization problem is unique: for a given set of prices only one net output bundle yields the maximum profit (c.f. Fig. 4).

   (ii) If the *PS* has a smooth upper boundary then the optimal y_i^* will vary continuously with prices.

   Prediction of the bundle which will be chosen at a given set of prices will require detailed information about the firm's *PS* and, while it is possible to acquire such information, the comparative static properties of the model yield predictions which are more easily testable. We will consider how the equilibrium profit maximizing values of the endogenous variables (net outputs) of the model vary when the exogenous variables alter. The results which will be derived will be very general in that it will not be necessary to assume that goods are divisible, or that the *PS* is strictly upper convex, or that the production function is differentiable. The only assumption necessary for the results below is that there is a unique profit maximizing net output bundle for any given vector of prices. (If the maximum profit bundle is not unique slightly weaker results can be derived.)

Equal proportionate changes in prices '

For a given vector of prices p the profit maximizing net output bundle y^* is defined by

$$\sum p_i y_i^* = py^* > \sum p_i y_i = py, \text{ all } y \text{ and } y^* \text{ in } PS \qquad [D.2]$$

If all prices are multiplied by the factor k then the new price vector is $(kp, \ldots, kp_n) = kp$, and multiplying prices by k will also multiply the profit from any net output bundle by k. If both sides of [D.2] are multiplied by a positive number k the inequality will still hold:

$$kpy^* > kpy$$

so that if y^* was optimal at p it will be optimal at kp. Hence the *absolute* level of prices has no effect on the firm's net output decision; only changes in *relative* prices can lead to changes in the net supply of a good. In the language of section 3D *the net supply functions are homogeneous of degree zero in prices:*

i.e. $y_i(kp_1, \ldots, kp_n) = k^0 y_i(p_1, \ldots, p_n) = y_i(p_1 \ldots p_n)$ \qquad [D.3]

Note that the net supply functions cannot be homogeneous in *input prices alone,* a fact already suggested by the analysis in section 8D.

Changes in a single price

Turning to changes in relative prices, let us consider how the firm's net supply of a good alters when the price of that good alters, all other prices being held constant. Let y^0 be the profit maximizing bundle when $p = p^0$ and y^1 that when $p = p^1$, where $p^0 = (p_1^0 \ldots p_k^0 \ldots p_n^0)$ and, since only one price (say that of good k), alters $p^1 = (p_1^0 \ldots p_k^1 \ldots p_n^0)$. It is assumed in this case that $y^0 \neq y^1$, i.e. that there are no kinks in the upper boundary of the PS which cause the same bundle to be optimal at more than one set of relative prices. From the definition [D.2] of an optimal bundle:

$$p^0 y^0 > p^0 y^1 \quad \text{and} \quad p^1 y^1 > p^1 y^0 \qquad [D.4]$$

or y^1 yields less profit when $p = p^0$ than y^0 and vice versa. Subtracting the r.h.s. of each inequality from its l.h.s. gives

$$p^0 y^0 - p^0 y^1 = p^0 \cdot (y^0 - y^1) > 0 \qquad [D.5]$$

$$p^1 y^1 - p^1 y^0 = p^1 \cdot (y^1 - y^0) > 0 \qquad [D.6]$$

(The reader should substitute $\sum p_i y_i$ for py if he is doubtful about the validity of these manipulations.) Multiplying p^1 and $(y^1 - y^0)$ by (-1) means that [D.6] can be rewritten as

$$-p^1 \cdot (y^0 - y^1) > 0 \qquad [D.7]$$

Adding [D.7] to [D.5] gives

$$p^0 \cdot (y^0 - y^1) - p^1 \cdot (y^0 - y^1) > 0$$

or

$$(p^0 - p^1) \cdot (y^0 - y^1) > 0 \qquad\qquad [\text{D.8}]$$

Writing Δp_i for $p_i^0 - p_i^1$ and Δy_i for $y_i^0 - y_i^1$ and expanding [D.8], we have

$$\sum \Delta p_i \Delta y_i > 0$$

Since only p_k alters (so that $\Delta p_i = 0$ when $i \neq k$) this reduces to

$$\Delta p_k \Delta y_k > 0 \qquad\qquad [\text{D.9}]$$

This means that if p_k rises ($\Delta p_k > 0$) so must y_k ($\Delta y_k > 0$) and if the price of good k falls ($\Delta p_k < 0$) the firm's net supply of it will be reduced ($\Delta y_k < 0$). We have, therefore, established that *the firm's net supply of a good will always vary positively with its price.*

If the good is an output we have confirmed the result arrived at in the special single-output case of section A: the supply curve has a positive slope. When the good is an input a rise in its price causes the firm to demand less of it (an increase in y_k when $y_k < 0$ corresponds to a reduction in its use as an input). This result can therefore be restated in the case of an input as: *the firm's demand curve for an input is always negatively sloped.* This result is valid whether the input is normal or inferior. (Compare this with the discussion in section 8B where by looking only at the cost minimizing problem we could not come to any conclusions about the effect of changes in input prices on input demands.)

This result is very general but it is important to remember that it holds only for changes in a single price and only for the good whose price has changed. Little can be said, without more restrictive assumptions on the firm's production function, about the effects of *multiple* price changes or of the cross-effect of single price changes on the net supply of other goods. If the upper boundary of the *PS* had been kinked, so that the same bundle could have been optimal at more than one set of relative prices, we would have had to allow for the possibility that $y^0 = y^1$. In this case, our result [D.9] would be $\Delta p_k \Delta y_k \geq 0$. In other words, when the technology does not give rise to a *PS* with a smooth upper boundary, the input demand and output supply curves may contain completely inelastic segments, where changes in p_k have no effect on the supply or demand for good k.

Corporation taxes

Suppose that the firm must pay a percentage tax on its profits. The net of tax profit is $(1-t)py$ where t is the percentage rate of corporation tax. (Since in the long run the firm can always earn a zero profit by ceasing production, py can be safely considered to be non-negative.) If both sides of [D.2.] are multiplied by $(1-t)$ we get

$$(1-t)py^* > (1-t)py$$

If y^* maximizes pre-tax profit it will also maximize after-tax profit. Hence the *rate of corporation tax will have no effect on the profit maximizing firm's net supply decisions.*

The reader is warned that this result applies to a tax levied on what economists usually define as profit, namely the difference between revenue and *all opportunity costs.* Most of the taxes which are in practice called 'profits' taxes or corporation taxes, however, are taxes on the difference between revenue and the costs *allowed by the tax authorities.* If there is any difference between opportunity costs and the allowable costs a 'profits' tax *may* lead to a change in the firm's behaviour, as we will see in Fig. 7 below.

Two kinds of divergences between opportunity and allowable costs are likely to be important. First, the funds invested by the owners in a firm will have an opportunity cost (the return which could have been earned in alternative uses of the funds) but, unlike say interest charges on bank loans to the firm, this opportunity cost is not usually counted as an allowable cost in calculating the taxable profit. Secondly, in a rapid inflation the recorded cost of inputs used by the firm, which is the allowable cost of the inputs for tax purposes, will be less than their opportunity costs if there is any appreciable lag between purchase and use of the inputs. In either of these cases some of the opportunity costs will be disallowed for calculation of the taxable profit, which will therefore exceed the true profit.

It should also be noted that the tax authorities' definition of revenue may also differ from that of the economist and this will be a further reason why we would expect actual 'profits' taxes to alter the behaviour of firms.

Lump-sum taxes and fixed costs
Let T be some lump sum tax or fixed cost that the firm must pay whatever its output level. Then the firm's net profit is $py - T$ and if T is subtracted from both sides of [D.2] we have

$$py^* - T > py - T$$

and if py^* maximizes profit before tax or the fixed cost it will maximize net profit after the tax or fixed cost. *The level of lump-sum taxes will have no effect on the firm's decisions.* This result is critically dependent on T being independent of py. Suppose, for example, that the firm had to pay a licence fee to in order to operate. This licence fee is *not* a lump sum tax or fixed cost because if the firm does not operate, i.e. $y = (0, \ldots, 0)$ it does not have to pay the fee. The fee therefore varies discontinuously with the firm's net output decision. If for example the firm's optimal bundle is $y^* > (0, \ldots, 0)$ raising T from $0 < T < py^*$ to $T > py^*$ will cause the firm to switch from y^* to $(0, \ldots, 0)$: it will go out of business.

These results are illustrated in Fig. 6 for a single-product firm. π is the non-negative part of the pre-tax profit curve in the figure. Pre-tax profit is maximized at y_1^*. A proportional profit tax of t will give rise to the after-tax profit curve π_t which plots $(1-t)\pi$. The proportional tax flattens

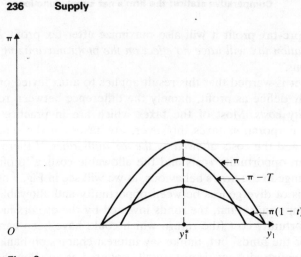

Fig. 6

the profit curve, as (except where $d\pi/dy = 0$) the slope of π_t is $(1 - t)\,d\pi/dy < d\pi/dy$. y_1^* also maximizes after-tax profit and so changes in t do not affect the output at which π_t is maximized. They alter the shape of π_t but not the level of y at which π_t reaches a maximum. Lump sum taxes T shift the profit curve vertically downward to π_T which plots $\pi - T$. Again, no change in after-tax profit maximizing output is caused by changes in T.

Figure 7 illustrates our remark about the importance of the distinction between opportunity and allowable costs. $\hat{\pi}$ plots taxable profit, which differs from π because some opportunity costs are not recorded or are disallowed. If a tax is levied on taxable profits $\hat{\pi}$ the firm's tax bill is $t\hat{\pi}$, which is also plotted in Fig. 7. The firm's after-tax pure profit, which it wishes to maximize, is $(\pi - t\hat{\pi})$ which is drawn as the dashed line. The tax on taxable profit will therefore alter the firm's output from y_1^*, which

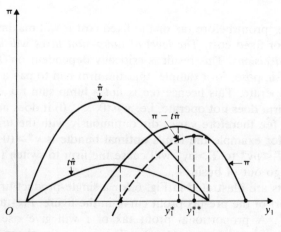

Fig. 7

maximizes before-tax pure profit, to y_1^{**}, which maximizes after-tax pure profit $(\pi - t\hat{\pi})$. Similarly changes in t will change the $(\pi - t\hat{\pi})$-maximizing output.

Exercise 9D
1.* Draw diagrams of the firm's *PS* in the single input, single output case to illustrate the circumstances under which
   (*a*) the profit maximizing y is not unique,
   (*b*) the same y is optimal at different relative prices.
   What do the firm's net supply curves look like in these two cases?
2.* Suppose that in the time between the firm's purchase and use of inputs *all* prices (including the price of its output) double. How, if at all, will recorded profit (revenue minus the purchase cost of the inputs) differ from actual or pure profit? Does a percentage tax on recorded profit lead to a rise or fall in the firm's output? (Assume that the firm realizes that the tax is levied on recorded profit and it correctly anticipates the rate of inflation.)

E. Uncertainty: forecasting and adjustment*

In making its long-run decision (i.e. choosing now a plant size for use in production in a later period) the firm faces *market uncertainty* in that it must base its decision on *its forecast* of the price in the later period, since the actual price is unknown. (See sections 5E, 19A on definitions of different types of uncertainty.) In the previous two sections we have assumed away market uncertainty by supposing that the firm always believes that its forecasts will be correct, but we will conclude this chapter by examining some of the ways in which firms respond to market uncertainty.

The better the firm's forecast of the next period's price the more nearly optimal will be the actual plant installed for the next period, given the actual price next period. This means that the firm may benefit from devoting resources to improving its forecasts of future prices, i.e. from reducing its uncertainty. In the same way the consumer of section 5E benefits from reducing his uncertainty by searching: better information enables better decisions to be taken. The firm may use one of a variety of forecasting methods. The crudest is that the price next period will be equal to this period's actual price: $p_f^{t+1} = p_a^t$. More sophisticated methods use the information on the previous periods' prices, in order to decompose the series of actual prices into a time trend, seasonal fluctuations and a residual element. Alternatively, the forecast price may be a weighted average of past values, possibly with more recent prices being given more weight than less recent. The forecast price may be related to variables other than prices in an attempt to find *leading indicators* of the price, observation of which will yield information about next period's price. Given that more accurate forecasts will generally require more calculation and information and so will be more costly, we may expect there to be an optimal method of forecasting.

Since the cost of information is not independent of the rate at which it is acquired, the firm may start with a very crude, low information requirement forecast (e.g. $p_f^{t+1} = p_a^t$) and adapt its forecast method as more information is acquired. It will, in other words, learn about its environment and adapt its behaviour in the light of the additional information.

An explicit model of the firm's forecasting behaviour would be rather complicated, so here we will merely emphasize the relationship between adjustment costs, forecasting and uncertainty. When there are no adjustment costs (which, in the models in this chapter, means when all inputs are freely variable in the current period) the firm has no need to forecast future prices: it can adjust its inputs in each period in the light of the actual prices ruling in that period without incurring any additional costs. With zero adjustment costs future prices are irrelevant because the firm has no need to plan future output and capacity in the current period. Decisions made in the current period are therefore concerned solely with current input and output levels. The larger are the costs of adjustment the greater are the benefits from accurate forecasts, since the firm will then need to make smaller changes in its decision variables.

Devoting resources to improving its forecasts is not, of course, the only possible response by the firm to market uncertainty. It may use more flexible (but more costly) equipment. It may attempt to remove its market uncertainty completely by selling its output on the futures market for the product, if one exists. It may also resort to storage. We saw in section 8E that storing part of one period's output to help meet the sales of the next period may reduce the firm's total cost. In section 8E the required sales levels in the two periods were known with certainty. We will now see how the ability to store one period's output may increase profit when the firm faces an uncertain future price of its output (and hence an uncertain future output).

To keep the analysis simple we will assume that the next period's price is a random variable with a known distribution, independent of the current period's price. The firm is assumed to wish to maximize in each period the expected value of profit resulting from its decisions in that period. (This implies that the owners of the firm have a particular type of attitude to risk, as we will see in Chapter 19.) Since the distribution of future prices is known and constant over time, the firm will choose the same optimal plant size in each period. With the given plant the firm will be faced with the SMC curve shown in Fig. 8. The firm can store its current period output (y^t) for one period only, after which it is unsaleable. This means that the firm *must* sell its stock next period at whatever is the actual market price. (Allowing for non-perishability, or only partial decay, evaporation, spoilage or obsolescence means that we would have to formulate an optimal decision rule concerning the decision to sell or hold the stock held at the start of each period. This would complicate the derivation of our results but would not alter them substantially.) Hence the revenue from a stock s^t built up during period t is $p^{t+1}s^t$. The cost of holding the stock is $C(s^t)$ and $C' > 0$, $C'' > 0$

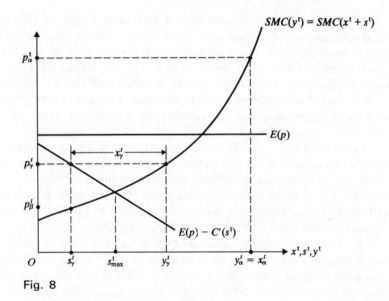

Fig. 8

so that increases in stocks increase storage costs more than proportionately. Finally, revenue earned in period t is $p^t x^t$ where $x^t = y^t - s^t$ is the amount sold to consumers in period t. The profit resulting from period t decisions on x^t, s^t, y^t is

$$\pi = p^t x^t + p^{t+1} s^t - C(s^t) - S(y^t) \qquad \text{[E.1]}$$

where $S(y^t)$ is the cost of current output, given the optimal decision on plant size. The firm wishes to maximize at each period the expected value of [E.1] and so, using $y^t = x^t + s^t$, its objective function is

$$E(\pi) = p^t x^t + E(p) s^t - C(s^t) - S(x^t + s^t) \qquad \text{[E.2]}$$

which depends only on x^t and s^t. $E(p)$ is the average (expected) price in period $t+1$. (Actual revenue earned in period t will include the proceeds of the sale of any stock carried over from period $t-1$, but, since s^{t-1} is *not* a decision variable in period t and the firm will sell s^{t-1} at *whatever* is the current price p^t, we can safely ignore this revenue in determining the optimal levels of s^t and x^t.) We must also impose the non-negativity restrictions $x^t \geq 0$, $s^t \geq 0$.

The various types of solution to the firm's problem can be illustrated in Fig. 8. (The reader is asked to derive the same results by the techniques of section 2G in the Exercises). The firm has two kinds of decision to make:
- (*a*) any given output must be divided optimally between storage and sales;
- (*b*) output must be set optimally.

With y^t given, $S(y^t)$ is fixed and so maximization of [E.2] requires maximization of

$$p^t x^t + E(p) s^t - C(s^t) \qquad \text{[E.3]}$$

Now $p^t x^t$ is revenue from current period sales and $E(p)s^t - C(S^t)$ is the expected revenue, net of storage cost, from storage. Hence [E.3] is the total revenue from a given y^t. The marginal revenue from x^t is p^t and the net expected revenue from s^t is $E(p) - C'(s^t)$, i.e. the expected price less marginal storage costs. $E(p)$ and $E(p) - C'$ are shown in Fig. 8. The optimal levels of x^t and s^t will depend on their marginal revenues. There are three possible cases depending on the relationship of current price and net expected future price $E(p) - C'$.

(a) $p^t > E(p) - C'(0)$. $E(p) - C'(0)$ is the net marginal revenue from storing one (small) unit of current output. If it is less than the current price it can never pay to store current output instead of selling it. Hence $x^t = y^t$ and $s^t = 0$. Since $x^t = y^t$ the marginal revenue from extra output is p^t and so the optimal level of y^t is where $p^t = SMC$. For example in Fig. 8 if $p^t = p^t_\alpha$ the firm produces (and sells) $y^t_\alpha = x^t_\alpha$ in the current period.

(b) The other extreme case arises if p^t is very low, in which case revenue is maximized by storing all current output: $y^t = s^t$ and $x^t = 0$. In this case marginal revenue from extra y^t is $E(p) - C'(s)$ and [E.2] is maximized by equating $E(p) - C'(s)$ to $SMC(y^t = s^t)$, at $y^t = s^t_{max}$ in Fig. 8, where the $E(p) - C'$ curve cuts the SMC curve. For this case to occur p^t must be less than $SMC(s^t_{max})$, as for example with a current price of p^t_β.

(c) $E(p) - C'(0) \geq p^t \geq SMC(s^t_{max})$.

In this case small amounts of output are stored but as y^t increases and so does s^t, C' gets larger until $E(p) - C'(s^t) = p^t$. As y^t is further increased s^t is held constant and x^t is increased (from zero). Since the marginal revenue from x^t is constant y^t is increased, increasing x^t, until $SMC = p^t = E(p) - C'(0)$. This case is shown in Fig. 8 for a current price of p_γ, which results in optimal output, storage and current sales of $y^t_\gamma, s^t_\gamma, x^t_\gamma$.

This model of storage is simple but it does lead to a number of clear-cut predictions:

(i) The firm's current supply of output will increase with the current price of output;

(ii) The firm's stock will decrease with the current market price.

The rationale of these two results is that x^t and s^t are alternative uses of the firm's output and so the opportunity cost of a unit increase in s^t is (with given y^t) a unit reduction in x^t. The more valuable is the forgone x^t (the higher is p^t) the less the expected net gain $(E(p) - C' - p^t)$ from additional storage. Or: the higher is p^t the less likely is p^{t+1} to exceed p^t and so the less likely is the net gain to be positive.

(iii) Storage decreases with rises in the marginal storage cost function, the reader should check by redrawing Fig. 8 with larger values of C'.

(iv) The possibility of storage reduces the variations in the firm's output: it can never fall below s^t_{max}, whereas with storage infeasible a p^t less than $SMC(s^t_{max})$ will lead to a $y^t < s^t_{max}$.

Exercise 9E

1. Solve the problem of maximizing [E.1] s.t. $x^t \geq 0$, $s^t \geq 0$ using the techniques of Section 2G and show that the results agree with the diagrammatic analysis in the main text.

2. Draw (a) the supply curve of the firm relating *total* current sales $(x^t + s^{t-1})$ to current prices; and (b) the relationship between p^t and s^t. How do variations in p^t affect the supply curve in period $t + 1$? How will a rise in the expected price $E(p)$ affect x^t and s^t?

References and further reading

The classic article on cost and supply curves is:

    J. Viner. 'Cost Curves and Supply Curves', in G. J. Stigler and K. E. Boulding (eds), *Readings in Price Theory*, George Allen and Unwin, London, 1953,

and there is an extensive discussion in:

    C. E. Ferguson. *The Neo-classical Theory of Production and Distribution*, Cambridge University Press, London, 1969, Ch 7.

The various concepts of income and profit are examined in:

    R. H. Parker and **G. C. Harcourt** (eds), *Readings in the Concept and Measurement of Income*, Cambridge University Press, London, 1969.

The following work is an intensive investigation of the competitive firm's production decision under conditions of price uncertainty:

    *****C. A. Tisdell.** *The Theory of Price Uncertainty, Production and Profit*, Princeton University Press, Princeton, N.J., 1968.

Chapter 10

The theory of competitive markets

A. Introduction

In the preceding seven chapters we have considered in some detail a number of models of the optimal choices of consumers and firms. In these models, prices were always taken as parameters outside the control of the individual decision-taker. We now have to examine how these prices are determined by the interaction of the decisions of such 'price-taking' individuals. Since this interaction takes place through markets, we have to examine theories of the operation of markets whose participants act as price-takers, that is, of *competitive markets*. In later chapters we go on to look at theories of markets in which at least one decision-taker is able to – and perceives that he is able to – influence price, so that this becomes a choice variable in his decision problem.

This chapter is organized as follows: we first look at markets in which there is *pure exchange*; that is, in which there is no production. Each consumer is assumed to be endowed initially with a stock of the commodity and exchange on the market brings about a reallocation of these stocks. Examples of such markets would be markets in houses, company shares, antique furniture and paintings by eminent dead artists, i.e. markets in which the flow of *new* supplies is very small in relation to the outstanding stock, and so can be ignored as a first approximation. Though production forms a significant part – if not the whole – of the supply of most commodities, it is useful to begin with a pure exchange market because certain concepts and problems are brought out more simply and clearly in this way. We will then go on to examine the additional and quite difficult problems which are introduced when we take supply to depend on production. The basic mode of analysis is the *equilibrium methodology*: the market outcome in which we are interested is the equilibrium outcome. As discussed in Chapter 1, therefore, we shall find ourselves mainly concerned with the questions of the existence and stability of equilibrium.

B. Equilibrium in a pure-exchange market

The model of the individual decision-taker adopted here is a simple version of that in section 3E. Since we are interested in only one good, we shall not need a subscript for goods to any great extent, and so let x_i be the consumption† of the good x by individual $i = 1, 2, \ldots n$. The ith individual has the initial endowment $\bar{x}_i$ of the good, and $\hat{x}_i = x_i - \bar{x}_i$ is his *net demand* for the good. Recall that we have the conditions:

$$x_i \geq 0, \qquad \bar{x}_i \geq 0, \qquad \hat{x}_i \geq -\bar{x}_i \qquad\qquad\qquad\text{[B.1]}$$

where the last inequality means that the individual cannot sell more than his initial endowment ($\hat{x}_i > 0$ means i buys the good, $\hat{x}_i < 0$ means he sells, $\hat{x}_i = 0$ means he is content to consume his initial endowment). We assume there is a numeraire or unit of account and p is the good's price in terms of this (*note:* in this chapter p is a number rather than a vector). The ith consumer's net demand function is:

$$\hat{x}_i = D_i(p, W_i) \qquad i = 1, 2, \ldots n \qquad\qquad\qquad\text{[B.2]}$$

where all other prices (though not net demands) are assumed constant throughout the analysis and are therefore suppressed and W_i is i's wealth, that is the value of his initial endowment of commodities at their given prices. This is a thoroughly *partial equilibrium* analysis – we are concerned only with variations in the $\hat{x}_i$ and p, not with any other quantities or prices. (To assume the consumer's demands for all other commodities constant however would imply too great a restriction on the form of his net demand function for the good under consideration. Explain why.) The reader who lusts after generality is referred to the analysis of general equilibrium in Chapter 16.

Given the individual consumer net demand functions in [B.2], we can sum them over all consumers to obtain the market net demand function:

$$z = \sum_i D_i(p, W_i) = D(p, W) \qquad\qquad\qquad\text{[B.3]}$$

It is usual to call the 'market net demand' the *excess demand* for good x, and this is denoted by z to be consistent with general usage and Chapter 16. The function D corresponds to the usual procedure of horizontal summation of individual net demand curves: at a given price, individual net demands are aggregated and the price is then varied and the procedure repeated. Note that in the excess demand function D, the vector of individual wealth values $W = (W_1, W_2, \ldots, W_n)$, appears. This is to emphasize that the market demand function depends on the *distribution* of wealth as well as on its total or average value in general. Here, however, since we are assuming other

---

† *Note:* In this context, 'desired holding' would be a better term, since consumption is best thought of as a *flow*, while here we are dealing with *stocks*. However, since consumption is the term usually used, we adopt it here.

prices constant, and initial endowments are given, W can be dropped from the analysis – excess demand will be taken as a function of p alone (though of course a change in p changes each consumer's wealth directly because it changes the value of the initial endowment of good x).

In Figs 1(a) and (b) we show the net demand curves of two 'representative' individuals, $D_1(p)$ and $D_2(p)$, and in (c) the market excess demand curve. These curves are all 'well-behaved' in the sense of being continuous and having negative slopes. We define equilibrium in the market as a price p^* and an excess demand z^* which satisfy:

$$z^* = D(p^*) = 0 \qquad\qquad [B.4]$$

The reason for this definition is that we expect a *non-zero* excess demand to cause changes in price, and therefore consumers would revise their planned purchases/sales, and so the market cannot be in a state of rest or balance. The mechanism by which these disequilibrium adjustments take place will be examined in some detail in later sections. At the price p^*, on the other hand, planned purchases are in the aggregate exactly equal to planned sales, the plans of all consumers can be exactly realized, and so there will be no incentive to change those plans. The characteristic of the market equilibrium is that the total initial stock, $\sum \bar{x}_i$, is exactly equal to the total amount which consumers wish to consume at price p^*, since:

$$z^* = \sum (x_i^* - \bar{x}_i) = \sum x_i^* - \sum \bar{x}_i = 0 \qquad\qquad [B.5]$$

where x_i^* is the planned consumption of each consumer at price p^*.

The zero excess demand market equilibrium is of course consistent with positive, negative or zero net demands of individuals. In the figure, at price p^* consumer 1 is a buyer of the good and consumer 2 is a seller. Many other individuals may be content just to consume their initial endowments (for example the flows of houses, antique furniture, and old masters across

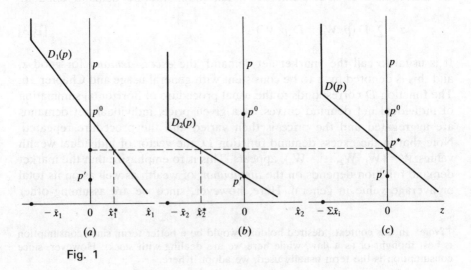

(a)   (b)   (c)

Fig. 1

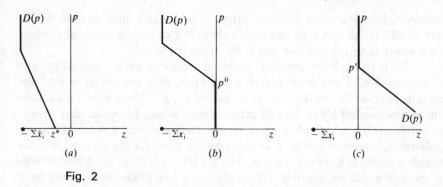

Fig. 2

the market at any one time are a fairly small proportion of the total stocks in existence). It would take a market price above p^0 to induce 1 to become a seller of the good, and it would take a price below p' to induce 2 to become a buyer. Tastes (and wealth) differ. In the aggregate, the sum of demands of individuals like 1 is equal to the sum of supplies (negative net demands) of individuals like 2. (Before leaving Fig. 1, explain why the demand curves become vertical where they do.)

The demand curves in Fig. 1 are well-behaved and a market equilibrium exists with a positive quantity traded. Figure 2 illustrates some other possible excess demand curves which have interesting equilibria. In (a), there is negative excess demand at every price $p \geq 0$, in other words the good is always in excess supply. It follows that its equilibrium price must be zero, since no positive price can be sustained. Such a good is called *a free good*. For example, we are all endowed with the right to breathe in our body's requirement of oxygen from the air around us and these endowments are so plentiful that no-one could succeed in selling us oxygen. If our endowments became sufficiently reduced by atmospheric pollution however, we would expect oxygen (and the associated breathing equipment) to command a positive price. It does now, in fact at locations under the ocean where our endowments do not extend – in other words, oxygen under the ocean is a different commodity from oxygen above the surface, and our endowments of the former are zero, hence aqualungs have a positive price.†

In (b), there is never excess demand for the good. At prices in the range $0p^0$, everyone consumes their initial endowments (or, less interestingly, the net demands of all consumers just happen to sum to zero at all prices over this range), while at prices above p^0 a net supply will be forthcoming on the market. In this case the equilibrium price can be any member of the *set* of prices $0p^0$ and a zero quantity will be traded (Explain why). Since such a market is in effect dormant, any example must be entirely hypothetical. We could take it, not entirely seriously, as the market for

---

† Note that the equilibrium in Fig. 2(a) does not conform to the definition in [B.4], since excess demand is negative at the equilibrium price. Question 10 of Exercise 10B pursues this.

mothers-in-law. However low the price, it is unlikely that anyone would want to add to his stock of mothers-in-law, but at a sufficiently high price (some lower than others) one might be prepared to sell.

In (c), we have positive excess demand at prices below p', but no-one supplies at any price (again a less interesting possibility is that net demands happen to sum to zero at all prices $p \geq p'$). Therefore the equilibrium is represented by the set of prices $p \geq p'$, which is unbounded above, and nothing is traded (Explain why). Again, such a market will be inactive in equilibrium, but there will be a known positive price for the commodity. An example might be a desert town in which each individual is endowed with just enough water for survival. At a sufficiently low price, there would be a demand for water, but at no price would anyone sell his 'subsistence' endowment.

In each of these somewhat odd cases, then, there existed an equilibrium (though it was not always unique). Figure 3 shows two cases in which an equilibrium does not exist. In each case there is a discontinuity in the excess demand function. In (a), there is a break in the function at p^0, with excess demand at that price negative at z^0, but jumping to a strictly positive value z' for any reduction in price, however small, below p^0. (Note that this is *not* the same as saying that the excess demand curve is horizontal at p^0, since in that case z could equal zero at $p = p^0$, and so we would have a unique equilibrium at p^0).

In (b) excess demand tends to, but never reaches, zero as price increases indefinitely (e.g. the excess demand function could have the equation $z = \alpha/p$, $\alpha > 0$). Thus there is always excess demand for such a commodity, at every price, and no equilibrium is possible. (Can a similar example be constructed for $z = -\alpha/p$? Take care with your answer. What has to be assumed?)

It should be noted that in the case shown in Fig. 3(b), there must be an excess supply disequilibrium in at least one other market, at all values of p, given that consumers' planned purchases satisfy their budget constraints.

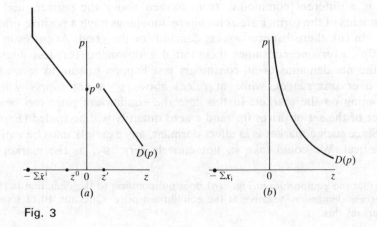

Fig. 3

Thus the ith consumer's budget constraint is:

$$p(x_i - \bar{x}_i) + \sum_{k=1}^{K} p_k(x_{ik} - \bar{x}_{ik}) = 0 \qquad [\text{B.6}]$$

where x_{ik} is his consumption of the kth good other than the one whose market demand is shown in Fig. 3(b). Summing these budget constraints over consumers gives:

$$p\sum_i (x_i - \bar{x}_i) + \sum_k p_k \sum_i (x_{ik} - \bar{x}_{ik}) = pz + \sum_k p_k z_k = 0 \qquad [\text{B.7}]$$

where z_k is the excess demand for the kth good. It follows that an always positive z must mean at least one other good is in excess supply at all values of p. The equation in [B.7] is a form of what is known as *Walras' Law* which can be interpreted to mean that: (a) the value of excess demands at given prices always equals the value of excess supplies; (b) equilibrium on all but one market must imply equilibrium on the remaining market; (c) disequilibrium on any one market must imply disequilibrium on at least one other market, as we have just seen. This law will play a very important part in the analysis of general equilibrium in Chapter 16.

All these diagrams are meant to suggest in a non-rigorous way an important general proposition: in the absence of discontinuities in the excess demand function, a market equilibrium will in general exist (although it may not be unique). Thus, for existence, the kind of good behaviour we require from the underlying net demand functions is that they possess the property of continuity. Fortunately, the assumptions of continuity and convexity we made in constructing the theory of the consumer ensure continuity of the excess demand functions, and so our theory is at least internally consistent, in that it provides for the existence of the solutions to the market process on which we base all our predictions. A rigorous proof of this assertion will be given in Chapter 16.

Exercise 10B

1.* Explain what is meant by the statement: 'Only at an equilibrium of the market are the plans of sellers consistent with the plans of buyers', and reconcile this with the statement: 'A purchase is also of course a sale, and so the quantities bought and sold must be equal at all prices'.

2.* Show that if consumers have identical preferences and identical initial endowments, no trade will take place. (*Hint:* what must be true of the individual net demand curves in this case and what does that imply after aggregation?) Apply this to a discussion of the question of why trade takes place even in a world without production.

3. Suppose x is a normal good for all consumers. What would be the effect on the equilibrium price of x if:
   (a) all consumers had an increase in initial endowments of all goods *except* x;
   (b) all consumers had an increase in initial endowments of x alone.
   (Continue to assume all other goods' prices are constant.)

4. Discuss the effects on the excess demand for x of a redistribution of consumers' initial endowments (a) with the exception of x; (b) of x alone.

5. There are three consumers in the market who have the consumption demand functions for x:

$$x_1 = 3 - p$$
$$x_2 = 8 - 2p$$
$$x_3 = 10 - 3p$$

and who have initial endowments of x of 1, 3 and 5 units respectively. Find the excess demand function and solve for the market equilibrium price and the consumptions, purchases or sales of the three consumers.

6. Explain carefully how the model of this section shows how both the *flows* of purchases and sales of a commodity, and the holdings of the *stocks* of the commodity, are simultaneously determined.

7. Suppose the commodity x is some kind of labour service. How would you interpret the model of this section? In particular, how would you interpret the initial endowment, consumption and a positive net demand?

8.* Suppose the commodity x represents 'houses' (assumed uniform in quality, size and location), which come in indivisible units and can only be bought, not rented. Construct a net demand 'curve' for an individual initially endowed with (a) one, (b) two and (c) no houses. Then discuss the determination of a market equilibrium. Under what conditions will the market excess demand function be smooth? Analyse the consequences of the imposition of a maximum house price below the equilibrium (a) *with* and (b) *without* an accompanying tax on 'second homes'.

9. Explain why a negative slope of the excess demand curve is not *necessary* for the existence of equilibrium. What is the simplest assumption which is *sufficient* for the *uniqueness* of equilibrium?

10. Explain why:

      if equilibrium price is positive, excess demand must be zero;

      if equilibrium price is zero, excess demand may be zero or negative but cannot be positive.

 Express these equilibrium conditions in a succinct formula (*Hint:* what must be true of equilibrium price, of equilibrium excess demand, and of the product of equilibrium price and excess demand?).

C. Stability of equilibrium

The analysis of stability is concerned with the question: if at a given point in time the market price is not at an equilibrium value, will changes take place over time which cause the price to converge to such a value? If the answer is yes, the market is called stable, and if no, unstable. There is a related aspect of stability analysis, which is concerned with the properties of *a particular* equilibrium price. We can ask whether, if price is not equal to that *particular* value, it will tend towards it, and if so, we call that equilibrium stable, and if not, unstable. Clearly, the two aspects of stability boil down to the same thing if there is a unique equilibrium in a market: if it is stable then the market is stable, and conversely. However, where there are multiple equilibria, a particular equilibrium price may be unstable but the market stable, as we shall see. In general, we are interested in the stability of the market, rather than of a specific equilibrium position. A further point of definition: a market is *locally* stable if it tends to an equilibrium when it starts off in a small neighbourhood of one, and it is *globally* stable if it tends to an equilibrium *wherever* it starts off. Global stability implies local stability but not conversely. In general, we are more interested in global stability.

The analysis of stability is concerned with the behaviour of a market *out of equilibrium*, i.e. with its *disequilibrium* behaviour. It follows that we have to formulate a theory of how markets operate out of equilibrium. Any such theory must, implicitly or, preferably, explicitly, assume answers to three fundamental questions:

1. How do the market price or prices respond to non-zero excess demand?
2. How do buyers and sellers obtain information on the price or prices being offered and asked in the market?
3. At what point does trading actually take place, i.e. when do buyers and sellers enter into binding contracts?

These questions are important because answers to them may differ and differences in the answers lead to significant differences in the models of disequilibrium adjustment to which the theories give rise. In questions 1 and 2 we use the phrase 'price or prices' because at this stage we prefer to keep our options open. Some theories may provide for a single price to prevail throughout the market even out of equilibrium, while others allow there to be differences in prices offered by buyers and asked by sellers throughout the market. In fact whether or not a unique price will always prevail depends very much on the answers adopted to questions 2 and 3, as we shall see.

To begin with, we consider a particular theory of market adjustment known as the *tâtonnement process* (tâtonnement can be interpreted to mean 'groping'), which is one of the simplest and best defined theories, and one whose stability properties have been thoroughly explored. We then go on to consider alternative approaches.

The tâtonnement process (TP)

The *TP* is an idealized model of how a market may operate out of equilibrium, in the sense that it may not *describe* the way a market works, but under certain conditions a real market may operate *as if* its adjustment process were a *TP*. It works as follows: there is a central individual, who can be called the market 'umpire', and who essentially has the role of a market coordinator. He announces to all decision-takers a single market price (the answer to question 2), which they take as a parameter in choosing their planned net demands. They each inform the umpire of their net demands, and he aggregates them to find the excess demand at the announced price. He is then bound to revise the announced price by the following rule (the answer to question 1):

$$\Delta p = \lambda z \qquad \lambda > 0 \qquad\qquad\qquad [C.1]$$

that is, he changes the price proportionately to the excess demand, so that if excess demand is positive he raises price and if negative he reduces price, while if it is zero, i.e. the market is at equilibrium, he of course leaves price unchanged. No trading takes place unless and until equilibrium is reached (the answer to question 3) at which time sellers deliver their planned net supply and buyers take their planned net demand. Notice that in this process there need be no contact between a buyer and seller at all – everything is mediated through the umpire.

Before going on to discuss the economics of this process, we consider the formal analysis of the stability of a market to which it is applied. Figure 4 shows three possible cases of market excess demand functions. In (*a*), the excess demand curve has a negative slope. It follows that if initially the umpire announces the price $p^0 < p^*$, excess demand will be positive and he will revise the announced price upward towards p^*; if announced price were above p^* it would be revised downward. Since these movements are always in the equilibrating direction, from *wherever* the process starts, equilibrium will be globally stable.

In (*b*), the excess demand curve has a positive slope, the good is, in the aggregate, a Giffen good (recall Ch. 3). If the announced price is initially at p^0 the umpire will now *reduce* price, since $z < 0$, and hence the *TP* leads away from equilibrium. A similar result would occur if the initial price were above p^*. Hence in this market the equilibrium is globally unstable.

In (*c*) we have a somewhat more complex case. The excess demand curve is *backward-bending*, having a negative slope over one range of prices

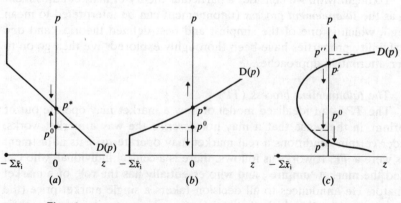

Fig. 4

and a positive slope over another. If in this case the initial price were anywhere in the interval $0 \leq p < p'$, the *TP* would converge to the equilibrium p^* (Explain why). If, however, the initial price were, say, $p'' > p'$, the market would move away from equilibrium, since excess demand is positive over this range and so price would be increased. Therefore the market is not globally stable, since an initial point sufficiently far from the equilibrium p^* would lead away from market equilibrium. This market has two equilibrium positions, one at p^* and one at p', the former is locally but not globally stable, the latter is locally (and therefore globally) unstable.

From this discussion we can deduce the following *stability conditions*, i.e. sufficient conditions for the *TP* to be stable:

(a) under the *TP* an equilibrium is globally stable if the excess demand function has everywhere a negative slope;

(b) under the *TP* an equilibrium is locally stable if the excess demand function has a negative slope in a neighbourhood of it.

These conditions are *sufficient* because they ensure the relevant kind of stability; they are not *necessary* because a portion of the excess demand function could slope vertically, or even positively as long as it did not re-cross the price axis, and equilibrium could still be globally stable under the *TP* (Draw a diagram to illustrate).

This analysis then has told us that whether or not the *TP* leads towards or away from the equilibrium depends upon the slope of the excess demand function. We now return to the question of the economic meaning of the assumptions which define the *TP*. If an umpire actually existed for a market, we might well consider him rather myopic if not downright stupid. As he announced successive prices he would know whether the slope of the excess demand function were negative or positive and could modify the adjustment rule accordingly, so as always to move towards an equilibrium. However, the anthropomorphism underlying the description of the *TP* becomes counter-productive if it leads us into this sort of argument. The short-sighted adjustment rule is adopted because it is thought to represent the actual adjustment processes in markets: excess demand signifies a seller's market, buyers compete amongst each other for the inadequate supplies and bid the price up; excess supply implies a buyer's market, sellers compete by shading prices, offering discounts, etc. Because the market is decentralized in fact it moves myopically and no single central controller tries to find an equilibrium. The device of the umpire is a convenient fiction introduced to bypass two of our three 'fundamental questions', the questions of information dissemination and of when trading takes place, and to concentrate on the answer to the first, the price adjustment question. These two further questions cannot be bypassed indefinitely, however, if we are to have a satisfactory theory of disequilibrium market adjustment.

The empirical relevance of the *TP* does not depend on whether an actual market has an umpire, but rather on whether the mechanisms which exist in that market for disseminating information and organizing transactions work in such a way that all economic agents know the price prevailing on the market in or out of equilibrium and no-one actually transacts out of equilibrium – trade only takes place at an equilibrium price. It is possible perhaps to argue that some highly organized markets in which professional middlemen and brokers 'make the market' approach this situation quite closely. A local housing market in which estate agents disseminate information and bring buyers and sellers together, or the market in stocks and shares, gold, and primary products in which dealers and brokers are active could provide examples. Many economists have felt that the conditions are not very generally met, however, and theories have been developed which try to explore our three questions further.

What is the significance of assuming that trade takes place *only* at equilibrium? The answer is that in that case, consumers' holdings of the good stay unchanged throughout the trading process, until equilibrium is reached. That is, at each 'round' in the *TP*, exactly the same net demand function is applicable for a given consumer, because his endowment of the commodity has not changed – the process is simply sliding around a set of *given* functions. If we allow trading *out of equilibrium* then this no longer holds: at any one round of the process, holdings change in some way as a result of trading at the announced (disequilibrium) price and so at the next round the net demand functions will be different because endowments are different. The adjustment process is therefore fundamentally different and more complex, because we now have to allow for the time-paths of holdings (quantities) as well as prices. Any theory which allows trading out of equilibrium has to specify the process by which consumers' holdings change between successive 'rounds' of the process. This is not easy to do in a convincing way. Consider the difficulties. If the going price is below equilibrium, not all buyers will be able to get what they want, but how is it determined who gets what? What is the rationing mechanism at a disequilibrium price? A variety of different mechanisms are possible, each with possibly differing results for the stability of the system. Moreover, is the basic assumption of a single price and price-taking behaviour tenable? In a seller's market, an individual seller may feel he has some degree of monopoly power as eager buyers compete for supplies. Different sellers may be more or less adept at judging the market and raising price, so that differences in prices in the market may develop. It is fair to say that economists have not yet succeeded in modelling satisfactorily the behaviour of a market when trading takes place out of equilibrium (though a formal treatment of a 'non-tâtonnement process' has been presented; see Negishi, 1962).

The question of information dissemination is also important. If no umpire exists to call out prices, what is the process by which consumers learn of prices and how does this process affect the stability of the market? Indeed, can we think at all of individuals in the market reacting passively to given prices? Actual markets often involve search by buyers and sellers, as they try to find the best deal to make. There may be a certain amount of haggling and bargaining, shopping around, and so on. Here, however,

economists have developed well-specified models which examine the consequences of these aspects of markets. The theory of consumer search,
outlined in section 5E, examines the consequences of assuming that a
consumer (or supplier of labour) enters the market only with an expectation
of price, samples the market to obtain more information about price and
makes a deal when the expected gains from further search are outweighed
by its costs. The reader is referred to section 5E for a fuller treatment.

There is another body of theory which also dispenses with the idea
of an umpire who announces a market price and begins simply with a view
of the market as a situation in which buyers and sellers haggle and do deals.
This is the theory of exchange developed by F. Y. Edgeworth, to which we
now turn.

D. Edgeworth exchange theory

The view of the market which has underlain the analysis so far is
that of individual decision-takers responding to a given market price by
choosing optimal quantities, which then are aggregated into excess demands.
Nothing has been said about *exchange activity* in the market. In the TP, for
example, buyers and sellers need never meet: sellers of the commodity could
simply toss their supply on to a pile and buyers could then come along and
take away their demands, everyone's account being debited or credited with
the appropriate number of units of account (someone of course would have
to be around to make sure no-one cheats). Since supplies and demands are
actually only activated at equilibrium there would be nothing left of the pile
when every buyer had taken exactly what he planned to take.

We shall now examine a theory of markets which takes a more
realistic view of the process. The theory formulated by F. Y. Edgeworth
begins by considering direct exchange between two individuals and proceeds
to analyse a market in which many individuals shop around, bargain, make
tentative deals, look for better ones, and then make contracts with each
other when they think they have found the best deals they can. This theory
has much more of the flavour of the market place about it but, much more
importantly from the point of view of microeconomics, it gives important
insights, introduces powerful concepts, and leads to interesting generaliza-
tions of the theory we have considered so far.

We begin with two individuals 1 and 2. x_i, $\bar{x}_i$ and $\hat{x}_i$ continue to
denote the individual's consumption, endowment and net demand, respec-
tively, of the commodity, with $i = 1, 2$. Likewise, $\bar{x} = \bar{x}_1 + \bar{x}_2$ is the total
endowment of the commodity. In addition, each possesses some amount of a
numeraire commodity, y and y_i, $\bar{y}_i$ and $\hat{y}_i$ are respectively i's consumption,
endowment and net demand for this. Each therefore has the budget con-
straint

$$p(x_i - \bar{x}_i) + y_i - \bar{y}_i = 0 \qquad i = 1, 2$$

where p gives the number of units of y which exchange for 1 unit of x, and
the price of y is 1. However, in this theory, the budget constraints do not

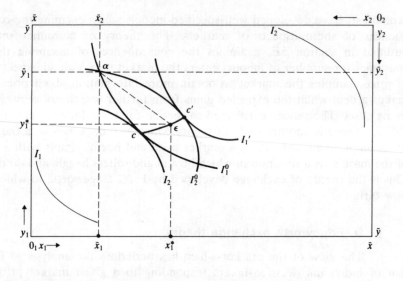

Fig. 5

really play a direct role: we shall only make use of them when we come to relate the conclusions of Edgeworth's analysis to what has gone before.

    The central tool of analysis in this theory is the Edgeworth (strictly, the Edgeworth–Bowley) box diagram, in conjunction with the consumers' indifference maps. Figure 5 shows an Edgeworth box. The length of the horizontal side of the box represents the total endowment $\bar{x}$ of commodity x. The length of the vertical side of the box represents the total endowment $\bar{y} = \bar{y}_1 + \bar{y}_2$ of the numeraire. The usefulness of the diagram stems from the fact that a single point within it shows the four consumption values (x_1, y_1, x_2, y_2) and moreover these values satisfy the *feasibility conditions*:

$$x_1 + x_2 = \bar{x}$$
$$y_1 + y_2 = \bar{y}$$

[D.1]

i.e. the sum of the consumptions of each good exactly exhaust the total endowment, and no more. This is because we measure 1's consumption of x rightward from the origin 0_1 at the bottom lefthand corner of the box, and his consumption of y vertically upward from 0_1; while 2's consumption of x is measured leftward from the origin 0_2 at the top righthand corner of the box, and his consumption of y_2 is measured vertically downward from 0_2. Thus each point in the box has four consumption coordinates. We can draw in 1's indifference curves with reference to origin 0_1, and 2's with reference to origin 0_2 – examples are I_1 and I_2 in the figure. The initial endowment point has the co-ordinates $(\bar{x}_1, \bar{y}_1, \bar{x}_2, \bar{y}_2)$ and is indicated by point α in the figure. The indifference curves I_1^0 and I_2^0 passing through that point are of special significance, as we shall see. The Edgeworth box diagram is used extensively in analysing exchanges of all kinds, and the reader will find it valuable to master its characteristics before proceeding, if he has not already done so. To help in this, question 1 of Exercise 10D should be answered at this point.

The indifference curves of the consumers satisfy the assumptions of Chapter 3 and so are drawn convex to their respective origins. Before trading, the consumers are located at α. We then have the question: will trading take place, and if so, what will its outcome be? The answer is based upon two crucial propositions which we shall call the *Edgeworth hypotheses* (*EH*):

1. The two individuals will always agree to an exchange when at least one of them is better off as a result;
2. Neither individual will ever agree to an exchange which makes him worse off.

These hypotheses appear to us eminently reasonable, though some might argue that 1 should be put in the stronger form:

1′. The two individuals will agree to an exchange if and only if *both* are better off as a result.

In other words one would not exchange if he gained nothing from it, even if the other did. Two problems arise if we want to make this stronger postulate. First, either it contradicts the meaning of the term 'indifference' (since if two points are indifferent why should one object to moving between them?) or it contradicts the implicit assumption that the preference orderings of the consumers are *independent* of each other – 'if he gets better off and I don't this makes me feel worse off and so I won't trade'. Secondly, it leads to a certain set in which we are very interested not having the property of closedness (see Question 2 of Exercise 10D). Of these two problems, the first is the more important. We must retain the concept of indifference and therefore the stronger postulate would require us to allow interdependence of preference orderings. Since we do not wish to do that at this stage we continue to adopt the weaker form of the postulate.

Note also that the first hypothesis rules out a failure to agree. Although of course the parties will haggle and bargain as each tries to do best for himself, we assume that each is sufficiently rational as to end up making some exchange which makes him no worse off and quite probably better off.

Given *EH*, we can say immediately that in the situation shown in Fig. 5 exchange will take place. For example by moving along I_2^0, with 1 giving 2 the numeraire in exchange for x, i.e. with 1 buying x from 2, 1 is making himself better off and 2 is no worse off. Likewise, by moving along I_1^0, with 1 again buying x from 2, but not getting so much x for each payment of y, 2 is getting better off and 1 is no worse off. Clearly *both* can be better off if 1 buys x from 2 with payments falling between those implied by moving along I_2^0, and those implied by moving along I_1^0. Thus, by hypothesis 1, trade will take place. It is left to the reader to confirm that this will always be true when the initial endowment point occurs at an intersection of the indifference curves, i.e. at a point at which the consumers' marginal rates of substitution are unequal and when the set of points which are *both* below I_2^0 and above I_1^0 is non-empty (see Question 4 of Exercise 10D).

We now have to determine the outcome of the exchange process. Consider the curve cc' in the figure. It has the property that it is the locus of *points of tangency of the indifference curves of the consumers in the area bounded above by I_2^0 and below by I_1^0*. Two such points of tangency at c and c' are shown as an illustration. Because of the strict convexity assumption, any given pair of indifference curves for the two consumers will have no more than one tangency point, and so no point off cc' in the area bounded by I_1^0 and I_2^0 can be a tangency point. *All* points off cc' must therefore be points of intersection (see Question 8 of Exercise 10D). But given any point of intersection of indifference curves, it is always possible for one consumer to become better off (by sliding along an indifference curve) if not both (by moving into the lens-shaped area between the indifference curves), as point α has illustrated. Hence no point off cc' can be an outcome of the exchange process, since it does not satisfy hypothesis 1.

On the other hand, a point on cc' cannot be improved upon once reached. A move off cc' must make at least one consumer worse off, since a move in any direction off the curve leads to a lower indifference curve for at least one consumer. Once the exchange process reaches a point on cc', it will not move along this curve 'searching' for another point, because any move from one point to another along cc' makes one consumer worse off. Thus, *all* the points along cc' satisfy hypothesis 1. Since hypothesis 2 rules out any outcome of the exchange process outside the area bounded by I_1^0 and I_2^0 (explain why) it follows that *only* the points on cc' satisfy *both EH*. Therefore the curve cc' is the equilibrium we seek. Edgeworth called this the 'contract curve', because it shows the set of possible contracts for purchases/sales which the individuals will finally make.

Notice that the theory does not specify exactly how the consumers get from point α to a particular point on cc'. Edgeworth himself suggested that this would be determined by 'higgling dodges and designing obstinacy, and other incalculable and often disreputable accidents' (*Mathematical Psychics*, p. 46). In other words we do not say anything specific about the nature of the bargaining process.

However, the two hypotheses are inexorable: if they are satisfied, the bargainers must end up at a point on the contract curve and nowhere else and would not agree to change.

Note also that the theory predicts the equilibrium as a *set of points* rather than as a single point. Economists accustomed to single-point solutions have tended to call this model 'indeterminate' because it results in a *set* of points. (Bargaining theory (see Ch. 14) has developed to try to predict the point in the set at which the parties will arrive in terms of the dynamics of the bargaining process.) To this extent the conclusions of Edgeworth's theory may appear weaker than those of the earlier theory of markets, but it should be remembered that it started from a far more general, and in the two-person case rather more plausible, view of the market. The individuals are not acting as passive respondents to a given market price, but are actively bargaining and dealing until they have found an exchange which cannot be improved upon for both of them (though of course it could be improved upon for one at the expense of the other). This exchange then *implies a price*, as can be seen in Fig. 5. Suppose the process ends up at point ε. Then the line $\alpha\varepsilon$ defines a price ratio. Consumer 1 pays 2 the amount $\bar{y}_1 - y_1^*$ of the numeraire in exchange for $x_1^* - \bar{x}_1$ of x, and so the *implied equilibrium price* of x is $p^* = (\bar{y}_1 - y_1^*)/(x_1^* - \bar{x}_1)$. It follows that the equilibrium could be expressed in terms of a set of prices, defined by the slopes of the lines from α to the curve cc', and bounded above by the slope of αc and below by the slope of $\alpha c'$ (ignoring minus signs in each case). This is quite consistent with our intuitive expectation that since 1 is the buyer of x, the lower the price the better off he is.

We have therefore found the equilibrium solution of the 2-person exchange situation. Furthermore, we can prove that the assumptions of continuity and strict convexity ensure that such an equilibrium always exists – a unique locus of tangency points of indifference curves always exists. We leave further discussion of that issue to the Exercises, and now consider the question of the stability of the equilibrium.

Given that the exchange process begins at a point off the contract curve, do the *EH* ensure, in conjunction with the assumptions underlying the indifference curves, that the bargaining of the individuals will lead them to a point on it? The answer is that they do, but the argument will only be sketched out here. Refer to Fig. 6, and suppose the consumers are at point α. Given *EH*, they can only move in one of three ways: along I_1^0; along I_2^0; or into the lens-shaped area. If they do one of the first two and continue along the curve, then they will necessarily reach point c or c' and stop, so in

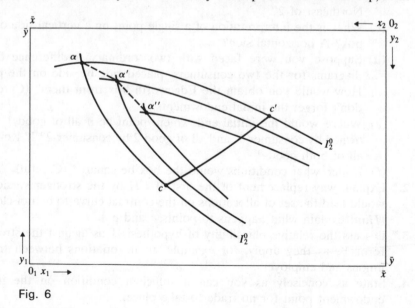

Fig. 6

that case we have stability. If they move along the curve and then *into* the area, the analysis becomes identical to that for the case where they moved into the area to start with. So let us examine the third possibility. If they move into the area, but don't reach cc', they must be at a point of intersection of indifference curves 'closer' to cc' than α, and which we can label α'. They must then be able to make themselves better off, and so they will agree on a second exchange (1 increases his desired purchase of x). In this case, α' replaces α and we repeat the argument we just used to get them either to cc' or a point of intersection α'', which is 'closer' to cc' than α'. Replacing α' by α'' we repeat the above argument and so on. At each step they must move closer to cc', and they stop if and only if they reach it, hence we conclude stability.

We therefore have a satisfactory equilibrium theory for this two-person exchange situation. However, markets in general contain more than two participants, and so we would like to extend the analysis to a situation of exchange among $n > 2$ individuals. We are also interested in going beyond the simple comparison made earlier of the 'size' of the equilibrium solution here as compared with the (possibly) unique equilibrium of the excess demand approach, to examine in some depth the relation between the two approaches. We can in fact achieve both these in one step, introducing in the process some interesting new ideas. This is the subject of the next section.

Exercise 10D

1. (a) What is the implication of the two consumers being at different points in the Edgeworth box?
   (b) What would be implied if 1 was at a point southwest of 2? Northeast of 2?
   (c) What is the interpretation of a single point on a vertical side of the box? A horizontal side?
   (d) Suppose you were faced with two 'ordinary' indifference curve diagrams for the two consumers, placed side by side on the page. How would you obtain the Edgeworth box from them? (Careful – don't forget the initial endowments.)
   (e) Where would the initial endowment point be if all of good 1 were owned by consumer 1, and all of good 2 by consumer 2? If 1 owned all of both goods?
   (f) Under what conditions would the box be square? (Careful)
2.* Explain why replacement of the first of EH by the stronger version $1'$ would lead the set of allocations on the contract curve to be not closed. (*Hint:* explain what happens to points c and c'.)
3.* Discuss the relative plausibility of hypothesis 1 as against the stronger form $1'$, as they apply, for example, to negotiations between trades unions and employers.
4. State as concisely as you can a sufficient condition on the initial endowment point for no trade to take place.

5.* Under what circumstances would the contract curve lie along an edge of the box, and what necessary conditions characterize these equilibrium outcomes?

6.* Consider the locus of points of tangency of the two indifference curves right throughout the box, and explain why it is incorrect to call the whole of this locus 'the contract curve'. What is the only case in which this entire locus would be the contract curve? (*Hint:* think of the indifference curves which follow from the goods as being perfect complements, and consider an initial endowment point at a special place on the box.)

7. Show that if we relax the assumption of *strict* convexity of indifference curves for both consumers the contract curve may widen into an area.

8. Explain why the two consumers' indifference curves can meet *only* in a point of intersection *or* in a point of tangency in the Edgeworth box diagram, so that a point of contact which is not the latter must be the former.

9.* The two-person exchange situation examined in this section has often been called 'bilateral monopoly' in economics (see Ch. 14). Discuss the statement: 'The outcome of bilateral monopoly is indeterminate' in terms of the analysis of this section.

E. Exchange, equilibrium and the core*

The development of the theory of games has had many important implications for microeconomics and one concept which is of importance to that theory is of direct relevance to the theory of markets. This is the concept of the *core* of a game. Here, we shall explain and apply the concept of the core only as it relates to exchange situations, but the reader should be aware that it has a wider definition and field of application than those discussed here.

Consider the two-person exchange situation of the previous section. A way of looking at the situation which is natural to game theorists is in terms of the possible coalitions of the participants in the situation ('players' in the 'exchange game'). There are three possible coalitions: those consisting of each player alone, and that consisting of both of them together. It may seem a little abusive of the language to regard a single individual as a 'coalition', but to do so greatly simplifies all the statements we have to make, and one soon gets used to the idea.

An *allocation* is a specification of a quantity of each good received by each consumer, i.e. a value of the vector (x_1, y_1, x_2, y_2). Hence, if an allocation satisfies the conditions in [D.1], so that it is a feasible allocation, then it is a point in the Edgeworth box. An allocation is said to be *blocked* if a coalition can find a way of *improving upon* it (i.e. make at least one of its members better off and none worse off) by having nothing to do with it and exchanging among themselves (or, if the coalition has just one member, he does not trade at all but keeps what he has).

The *core* is defined as *the set of allocations which is not blocked by any coalition*, i.e. the set of allocations having the property that no coalition could improve upon them by rejecting them and trading among themselves. It is easy to show that the core in the two-person exchange situation is nothing else but the contract curve and so at this point we simply have a new name for an old concept. Thus refer again to Fig. 5. Any allocation outside the lens-shaped area bounded by the indifference curves I_1^0 and I_2^0 can be improved upon by the coalition containing the first consumer only, or that containing the second only, since one or the other would always prefer his initial endowment to such an allocation. Therefore all these allocations are blocked. But in addition, any allocation within the lens-shaped area but not on cc' can be improved upon by the coalition of the two consumers, since they can always find a feasible trade which makes at least one better off and the other no worse off and so these allocations are blocked. Finally, at an allocation on cc', no trade can be found which would make one better off without making the other worse off and so these allocations cannot be improved upon by any coalition, they are not blocked. The definition of the core is equivalent to *EH* and so they yield the same sets of possible solutions to the exchange process. From now on therefore, we shall refer to the contract curve as the core (of this two-person exchange situation). The analysis of the previous section showed that in this case the core is not an empty set, i.e. the two-person exchange game has a non-empty core.

Theorists always find it exciting when a central concept of a body of fairly specialized theory is shown to be a particular case of a central concept in a more general body of theory. The former gains by at once having applied to it more general concepts and more powerful analytical tools, which may not only solve unresolved problems but may also show how empirical phenomena not previously handled can be readily assimilated, thus increasing the scope and interest of the theory itself. The latter gains by having a fresh field of application, which may raise further problems and stimulate developments in the more general theory. If all that had happened in the present case was a change of terminology, from contract curve to core, economists would be right not to get excited. However, both in solution of unsolved problems and in widening the scope of the theory of markets the introduction of the concept of the core has had significant payoffs. We now turn to one important example of this, the relation between the equilibrium of a competitive market as discussed in section C, and the core.

Recall that in a competitive market there is some mechanism by which a price is announced and consumers respond by making optimal choices. An equilibrium occurs when excess demand is zero. To begin with, we will consider how this equilibrium relates to the core in the two-person exchange situation and then generalize to n persons. Recall from Chapter 3 the construction of *the offer curve* of an individual. Figure 7 repeats the construction for the two individuals. In (a) and (b), α is the initial endowment point, and I_1^0 and I_2^0 are the initial indifference curves. The line p^0 in

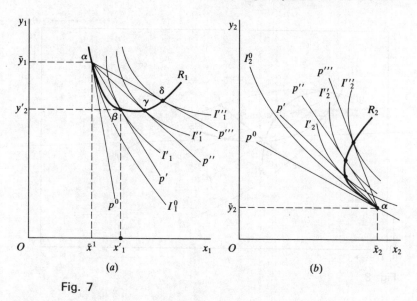

Fig. 7

(a) is defined to be tangent to I_1^0 at α, and similarly p^0 in (b) is tangent to I_2^0 at α (hence in general the two lines have different slopes). As successively lower values of p are announced in (a), we have a sequence of tangency points such as β, γ and δ. The interpretation of each of these is that it shows the amount of y consumer 1 would be prepared to give up, at the prevailing price, for the amount of x read off from the other co-ordinate. For example, at price p', the tangency at point β indicates that consumer 1 would give up $(\bar{y}_1 - y_1')$ units of y in exchange for $(x_1' - \bar{x}_1)$ units of x, with the ratio $(\bar{y}_1 - y_1')/(x_1' - \bar{x}_1)$ of course equal to p'. The locus of all such points of tangency, αR_1 in the figure, is called 1's offer curve, and it shows the trades that 1 would want to make at each market price. The offer curve αR_2 in (b) of the figure is derived in a similar way and the reader should reinforce his understanding by working through its derivation. The two properties of the offer curves which are of central importance are:

(a) They must lie entirely above their respective initial indifference curves I_1^0 and I_2^0 (see Question 1 of Exercise 10E).
(b) A line drawn from α to a point on the offer curve represents a price line to which the consumer's indifference curve is tangent at that point.

The significance of these offer curves is that they provide us with a means other than the excess demand curve of finding a market equilibrium, a means which is more useful than the latter when we are using the Edgeworth box. Thus, in Fig. 8 we reproduce the Edgeworth box of the previous section, but include the offer curves αR_1 and αR_2. Because of property (a) above, both must lie in the lens-shaped area bounded by I_1^0 and I_2^0. It is no accident that their intersection point E lies on the contract curve cc', i.e. is a point in the core. In a competitive equilibrium a single price

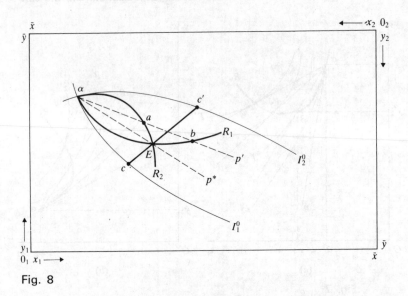

Fig. 8

prevails, it must be tangent to an indifference curve of each consumer and it must be such that the chosen demands and supplies of each good are equal. These three conditions are all satisfied at and only at a point of intersection of the offer curves, as can be shown with the help of the figure. Suppose the price corresponding to the line $\alpha p'$ were announced. Then consumer 2 would choose point a while consumer 1 would choose point b. Therefore this cannot be an equilibrium. At a price corresponding to the line αp^*, however, consumer 1 chooses point E as does consumer 2, and so we have an equilibrium. Moreover, αp^* is tangent to each consumer's indifference curve at E (by definition of the offer curves) and therefore they must be tangent to each other at this point. Since the intersection can only occur within the lens-shaped area, we have that the market equilibrium is a point of tangency of indifference curves within this area and so must be on cc'. Hence, the competitive equilibrium is in the core.

   The meaning of this interesting result can be put in the following way: when the two consumers act as price-takers in a market, passively responding to movements in the market price, they are guided to an equilibrium position which is one of a large number of allocations which they *may* have achieved if instead they had got together, bargained and haggled, and made a contract when they had exhausted all possible mutual gains from trade.

   This will be shown to have important implications for the optimality properties of the competitive market solution (see Ch. 17) but for the time being we are simply interested in the relation between the solution concepts of the two approaches to the analysis of markets.

   The consequence of assuming a competitive market mechanism with passive price adjustment is to collapse the whole set of possible exchange equilibria into a single point (or at most a finite number of points if the offer curves happen to have multiple intersections, a case not considered here). This greater precision of the competitive market theory is bought at a cost: the tâtonnement process by which equilibrium is brought about does not accord well with reality and neither does the assumption that in a market with only two participants we will in fact get passive price-taking behaviour. We may feel that the weaker solution concept of the core is a better reflection of what we are able to say about real two-person markets.

This discussion has raised the important question of the *number* of consumers. After all, the competitive market case really derives its interest from the observation of markets with *many* buyers and sellers, where price-taking behaviour is far more plausible and it seems unfair to criticize it in its application to a two-person exchange situation, which would only be used to *illustrate* the theory. What happens to Edgeworth's theory of exchange and the concept of the core as the number of decision-takers increases and the competitive market theory becomes more relevant?

This question was one of those unresolved problems the solution of which was a major benefit to flow from the application of the concept of the core to Edgeworth's analysis. Edgeworth in fact provided an ingenious analysis which showed how the problem might be solved and correctly conjectured the result, but it was left to the more powerful tools of modern mathematical economics to resolve the issue more or less satisfactorily. The answer can be stated in two propositions:

  I *Regardless of the number of consumers, the competitive market equilibrium is always in the core.*

  II *As the number of consumers increases indefinitely, the set of allocations in the core shrinks until, in the limit, it contains only the competitive market equilibrium allocation (s).*

Broadly speaking, these propositions imply that for markets with large numbers of participants, the solution concepts are equivalent, and whether we view a market as a collection of active, bargaining, wheeling and dealing individuals or as a collection of passive price-takers co-ordinated by some price adjustment mechanism makes no difference in terms of the equilibrium outcome. As we shall see, this implies something of interest about both approaches to the market, but first we consider proofs of the propositions in turn.

Suppose now that there are n individuals, each characterized by his preference ordering and initial endowments. There are now many more possible coalitions than when $n = 2$. There are the n coalitions of one person each, plus the coalition of all of them together, plus the possible group coalitions which could form so that there are $2^n - 1$ possible coalitions altogether (excluding the coalition with no members). An allocation now assigns a quantity of x and y to each individual and it will be blocked if any of the n individuals can get together, trade among themselves and do better, in the usual sense, than under the original allocation. It should be clear that this definition of 'blocking' is again equivalent to *EH*, suitably redefined for any number of consumers. In addition, if people are going to be able to wheel and deal we have to allow them to make tentative contracts which they can break if they find another individual, or group, with whom they can make a better deal, i.e. they have to be free to *re-contract* (Edgeworth's term). Thus, any consumer can set up a tentative trade with one or more others, so that he knows exactly what that would imply for his allocation, but he can then drop out – blocking this allocation – if he can do better elsewhere. The possibility of recontract (which, in terms of the three fundamental questions posed at the beginning of this chapter, specifies at what point binding contracts are made) is an important element of the theory, as we shall see.

To put things a little more formally, let S denote a set of consumer subscripts or indexes, for example $\{1, 3, n\}$, $\{1\}$ or $\{1, 10, 80\}$. Then $i \in S$ is the statement: consumer i belongs to the coalition whose subscripts are shown in the index set S. This notation is obviously a handy way of describing coalitions. Given initial endowments $\bar{x}_i$ and $\bar{y}_i$ for each individual i, the total resources available to a coalition S are:

$$\bar{x}_s = \sum_{i \in S} \bar{x}_i \qquad \bar{y}_s = \sum_{i \in S} \bar{y}_i \qquad\qquad [E.1]$$

i.e. the sum of endowments for members of that coalition. A *feasible* allocation for that coalition is then a set of consumptions (x_i, y_i) for each member such that:

$$\begin{aligned} \sum_{i \in S} x_i &\leq \bar{x}_s \\ \sum_{i \in S} y_i &\leq \bar{y}_s \end{aligned} \qquad\qquad [E.2]$$

So if some particular allocation is blocked by the formation of a coalition whose members do better by trading among themselves, the resulting allocation must be feasible in the sense of [E.2].

We are now in a position to prove proposition *I*. Suppose we have a competitive market equilibrium allocation in which the ith consumer receives the bundle (x_i^*, y_i^*), which by definition of a competitive equilibrium is the bundle he prefers at the equilibrium price p^*. Since his budget constraint must be satisfied, we have that for each i:

$$p^*(x_i^* - \bar{x}_i) + y_i^* - \bar{y}_i = 0 \quad \text{all } i \qquad\qquad [E.3]$$

Now we have to show that this market equilibrium is in the core, which is to say that no coalition S, consisting of anything from 1 to n members, can get together, opt out of the market equilibrium, and find a feasible allocation among themselves which makes at least one better off and no-one worse off. To prove this, we assume that such a coalition does exist, and then show that this implies something which cannot be true – we have a proof by contradiction.

Thus suppose there exists a coalition S such that for *each* individual $i \in S$ we have:

$$(x_i', y_i') \succsim (x_i^*, y_i^*) \qquad \text{[E.4]}$$

and for at least *one* $i \in S$ we have:

$$(x_i', y_i') \succ (x_i^*, y_i^*) \qquad \text{[E.5]}$$

where (x_i', y_i') is a *feasible* allocation for $i \in S$. In other words, the coalition can find a feasible set of exchanges, given their initial endowments, which makes no-one worse off and at least someone better off. Take the individual who is strictly better off. It must be the case for him that:

$$p^* x_i' + y_i' > p^* x_i^* + y_i^* \qquad i \in S \qquad \text{[E.6]}$$

that is, the expenditure on the bundle (x_i', y_i') at the price p^* (remember y is the numeraire) must exceed that on (x_i^*, y_i^*). If this were not true he could have afforded (x_i', y_i') at the competitive equilibrium and so would have chosen it. By the same argument, for all other individuals in the coalition who satisfy [E.4], we must have:

$$p^* x_i' + y_i' \geq p^* x_i^* + y_i^* \qquad i \in S \qquad \text{[E.7]}$$

(here we are allowing $(x_i', y_i') \sim (x_i^*, y_i^*)$ to be consistent with $p^* x_i' + y_i' = p^* x_i^* + y_i^*$). Now, if we sum [E.6] and [E.7] over all the individuals in the coalition, we must have:

$$p^* \sum_{i \in S} x_i' + \sum_{i \in S} y_i' > p^* \sum_{i \in S} x_i^* + \sum_{i \in S} y_i^* \qquad \text{[E.8]}$$

But summing the budget constraints in [E.3] for $i \in S$ gives:

$$p^* \sum_{i \in S} x_i^* + \sum_{i \in S} y_i^* = p^* \sum_{i \in S} \bar{x}_i + \sum_{i \in S} \bar{y}_i = p^* \bar{x}_s + \bar{y}_s \qquad \text{[E.9]}$$

and therefore substituting from [E.9] into [E.8] implies:

$$p^* \sum_{i \in S} x_i' + \sum_{i \in S} y_i' > p^* \bar{x}_s + \bar{y}_s \qquad \text{[E.10]}$$

But from the definition of feasible allocations in [E.2] we have that for any feasible allocation:

$$p^* \sum_{i \in S} x_i + \sum_{i \in S} y_i \leq p^* \bar{x}_s + \bar{y}_s \qquad \text{[E.11]}$$

(since multiplying the first line of [E.2] by $p^* > 0$ and then adding gives [E.11]). Hence the allocations (x_i', y_i') cannot be feasible for the coalition S, and so the assumption that such a coalition exists must be false.

Thus we have that no coalition can do better than a competitive market equilibrium allocation, whatever the number of consumers in the market, and so *that allocation must be in the core*. Note that in this proof the only assumption used was that of the degree of consumer rationality implied by inequalities [E.6] and [E.7].

It is unfortunately not possible in this book to give as complete a proof of proposition II. In fact we shall not go any real distance beyond Edgeworth's original contribution. The proposition is that as the number of consumers in the market increases, the set of allocations in the core shrinks toward the competitive equilibrium allocation(s). What we shall show is that when the market grows from two consumers to four in a particular way a section of the contract curve not containing the competitive equilibrium will no longer lie in the core, and we simply assert that a general proof of the proposition can be constructed on the lines of the argument we shall use. We assume that the size of the market grows in a very special way, by the addition of two more consumers, the first of whom is identical in every economically relevant respect to consumer 1 of this and the previous sections, and the second of whom is identical, in the same sense, to consumer 2.

From the point of view of the market model, there are only two aspects of the consumer which are relevant. The first is his initial endowment and the second is his preference ordering or indifference map. Nothing else matters. Accordingly we shall use the term 'a consumer of type A' for a consumer with initial endowment $(\bar{x}_A, \bar{y}_A)$ and indifference curves $I_A^0, I_A', I_A'' \ldots$ and 'a consumer of type B' for one endowed with $(\bar{x}_B, \bar{y}_B)$ and with indifference curves $I_B^0, I_B', I_B'' \ldots$. In this analysis there are two consumers of each type, denoted respectively by A_1 and A_2 and B_1 and B_2. The total initial endowments available to this economy are:

$$\bar{x} = 2\bar{x}_A + 2\bar{x}_B$$

$$\bar{y} = 2\bar{y}_A + 2\bar{y}_B$$

[E.12]

Any one consumer is free to trade with any other consumer and re-contract is possible. From proposition I we know that the competitive market equilibrium resource allocation in this economy is in the core. The question we are interested in is this: what happens to the set of allocations in the core as the market grows from one consumer of each type to two consumers of each type? What we show is that certain consumption bundles for each consumer which are in the core in the two-person market are no longer in the core in the four-person market and it is in this sense that the core can be said to shrink.

We proceed by showing that certain resource allocations can be excluded from the core, because there exists *some* coalition which can improve upon them. The first kind of allocation we can exclude is any that gives two consumers of the same type a different consumption bundle, i.e. we prove that *in every allocation in the core, consumers of the same type receive the same consumption bundle.* This could be called the *Equal Treatment Principle* (ETP). The way we prove it is to assume an initial allocation at which it does not hold, and then show that a coalition can form having a feasible allocation which improves upon the initial allocation, so no such allocation can be in the core.

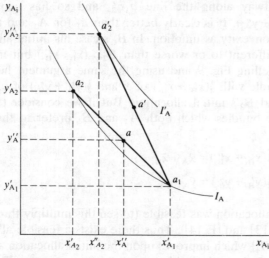

Fig. 9

Thus, note that for a resource allocation to be feasible overall requires:

$$x_{A_1} + x_{A_2} + x_{B_1} + x_{B_2} \leq \bar{x} = 2\bar{x}_A + 2\bar{x}_B \qquad [\text{E.13}]$$

$$y_{A_1} + y_{A_2} + y_{B_1} + y_{B_2} \leq \bar{y} = 2\bar{y}_A + 2\bar{y}_B \qquad [\text{E.14}]$$

Now suppose A_1 and A_2 have different bundles under the initial allocation. Two cases are possible:

(i) the bundles are such as to put the consumers on the same indifference curve, such as I_A in Fig. 9 where point a_1 denotes A_1's bundle and a_2 denotes A_2's bundle. In this case it follows from the strict convexity assumption that A_1 and A_2 could gain by trading along the line $a_1 a_2$, since points on this line have the property that they are feasible re-allocations of the total amounts of goods held by the two at the initial points a_1 and a_2.

For example, suppose A_1 gave $(x'_{A_1} - x''_A)$ to A_2 in exchange for $(y''_A - y'_{A_1})$ where $x''_A = \frac{1}{2}(x'_{A_1} - x'_{A_2})$ and $y''_A = \frac{1}{2}(y'_{A_2} - y'_{A_1})$. This is clearly feasible since the total holdings of the two goods by the two consumers are unchanged, while both are better off at point a. The strict convexity of indifference curves implies that a point such as a *always* exists whenever a_1 and a_2 are separate, and so in that case the coalition $\{A_1, A_2\}$ could always improve upon the allocation. Hence it cannot be in the core.

(ii) The bundles are such that A_1 and A_2 are on different indifference curves. In this case the coalition $\{A_1, A_2\}$ may or may not do better, but we can show that if we take A_1 as being on a lower indifference curve than A_2, and B_1 being on *no higher* an indifference curve than B_2 then the coalition $\{A_1, B_1\}$ can certainly improve upon the initial allocation. We can show this as follows. In Fig. 9 suppose the initial allocation puts A_1 at a_1 and A_2 at a'_2, where, as it happens, A_2 would not want to trade with A_1.

The point a' is halfway along the line $a_1 a_2'$, and so has coordinates $\frac{1}{2}(x_{A_1}' + x_{A_2}'')$ and $\frac{1}{2}(y_{A_1}' + y_{A_2}'')$. It is clearly better than a_1 for A_1 and this will always be so by the convexity assumption. In B_1's case his initial allocation (x_{B_1}', y_{B_1}') may be indifferent to or worse than B_2's (x_{B_2}', y_{B_2}') but in either case simply by re-labelling Fig. 9 and using the same argument he would always prefer the bundle with $\frac{1}{2}(x_{B_1}' + x_{B_2}')$ of x and $\frac{1}{2}(y_{B_1}' + y_{B_2}')$ of y, that is the average of B_1 and B_2's initial allocation. But if we consider the total requirements of these bundles which both A_1 and B_1 prefer to the initial allocation, we have:

$$\frac{1}{2}(x_{A_1}' + x_{A_2}'') + \frac{1}{2}(x_{B_1}' + x_{B_2}') = \bar{x}_A + \bar{x}_B \qquad [E.15]$$

$$\frac{1}{2}(y_{A_1}' + y_{A_2}'') + \frac{1}{2}(y_{B_1}' + y_{B_2}'') = \bar{y}_A + \bar{y}_B \qquad [E.16]$$

given that the initial allocation was feasible (to see this multiply through by 2 and compare to [E.13] and [E.14]). Thus there exists a feasible allocation for the coalition $\{A_1, B_1\}$ which improves upon the initial allocation at which A_1 was worse off than A_2 and so this cannot be in the core. (The acute reader may wonder what happens if in the initial allocation B_1 and B_2 are at the *same point*. See Question 7 of Exercise 10E and show that this presents no obstacle.)

As well as excluding certain points from the core, the proof of the *ETP* has the further advantage that when discussing allocations in the core, we need only consider identical positions for the two A_i and for the two B_i so that a single set of indifference curves suffices for consumers of a given type. This is a useful expositional simplification.

We turn now to the central question, that of the shrinking of the core. Consider the Edgeworth box of Fig. 10. The indifference curves I_A^0, I_A', I_A'' describe the preferences of both A_1 and A_2 and the initial endowment point α is also the same for both. But suppose that the market contains initially *only* consumers A_1 and B_1. The curve cab is a portion of the contract curve (to keep the figure uncluttered, B_i indifference curves are not drawn). We assume that in this two-person market the equilibrium allocation is at point c where A has the allocation $(x_{A_1}^c, y_{A_1}^c)$ – in fact he's managed to emerge with no gains from trade. B_1's allocation at this point is $(x_{B_1}^c, y_{B_1}^c)$ and clearly these allocations are feasible, i.e.

$$x_{A_1}^c + x_{B_1}^c = \bar{x}_A + \bar{x}_B \qquad [E.17]$$

$$y_{A_1}^c + y_{B_1}^c = \bar{y}_A + \bar{y}_B \qquad [E.18]$$

Now suppose we expand the market by adding A_2 and B_2. A_2 'comes in' at point α, the A_i initial endowment point. Consider point c^0 in the figure which is halfway along the line αc. Because of strict convexity this point is preferred to c by A_1 and preferred to α by A_2. Moreover, it can be reached by A_1 and A_2, since if A_1 gives A_2 $\frac{1}{2}(x_{A_1}^c - \bar{x}_A)$ in exchange for $\frac{1}{2}(\bar{y}_A - y_{A_1}^c)$, they will clearly each be at the allocation $(x_{A_1}^0, y_{A_1}^0)$. Thus we have shown that point c cannot be in the core, in the sense that the coalition $\{A_1, A_2, B_1\}$ can

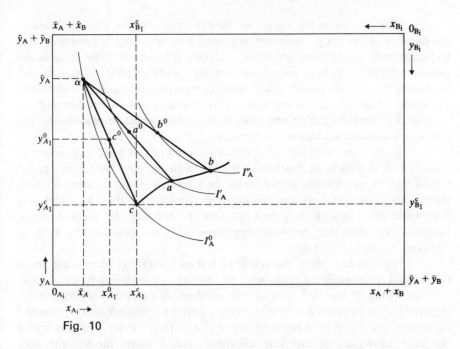

Fig. 10

improve upon it. It may be wondered why B_1 is included in this coalition, since A_1 and A_2 appeared to manage everything between themselves. The point is of course that the coalition $\{A_1, A_2\}$ alone can manage nothing better than their initial endowment point – recall that consumers with identical preferences and initial endowments can get no gains from trade. B_1 was necessary to get A_1 to point c, away from α; once this deal was done A_1 could then set up a mutually advantageous deal with A_2. The allocation as a whole therefore required the coalition $\{A_1, A_2, B_1\}$.

We cannot conclude from this that c^0 is in the core. We might expect B_2 to come along and try to get into the picture and, given re-contract, another coalition might form and a move would be made away from c^0. Our purpose however was to show that a point which was in the core of the two-person market will not, for the same two persons, or indeed for the two 'new entrants' (see Question 8 of Exercise 10E), be in the core of the four-person market – the introduction of new participants *widens* the possibilities for trade, and *narrows* the set of core allocations which the original traders will find themselves in.

As Fig. 10 shows, it is not only the end point of the contract curve which may be removed from the core. For example, suppose that A_1 and B_1 had initially settled on point a when A_2 comes along. Point a^0 is halfway between α and a, and lies above I'_A and I^0_A. Hence again by exchanging x and y along αa until they reach a^0, both A_1 and A_2 can be better off, and so a cannot be in the core. The reader should now supply the argument to decide whether or not point b is in the core, given that b^0 is halfway along αb, and lies on I''_A as does b.

This discussion has suggested how the core may be said to shrink as the number of market participants increases. The argument is essentially due to Edgeworth. Using more advanced methods, it has been shown that as the number of participants of each type increases without limit, though always remaining equal, all points other than competitive market equilibria are excluded. Thus for 'large' markets where the assumptions underlying the competitive market equilibrium analysis have their greatest plausibility, the two solution concepts become equivalent.

There are two points of significance in all of this for the competitive equilibrium approach to markets. First, at such an equilibrium, no group would find it worthwhile to withdraw and trade among themselves. Secondly, for large markets the assumptions underlying that approach are acceptable even though they may not *describe* the way the market works, because, provided that recontracting is possible, in practice the type of outcome is much the same.

We also can apply the result to tell us something of interest about the core. Traditionally in economics we distinguish between types of markets according to a broad view of the numbers of participants – monopoly, oligopoly, monopolistic competition, perfect competition, bilateral monopoly, etc. Each of these is analysed as a distinct model. The concept of the core allows us to integrate all these into a single model: the core provides us with an equilibrium concept for them all, with the particular market outcomes taking the form of different but related cores as the number of market participants changes. Though much of the attractiveness of this kind of generalization may be aesthetic, it is important nevertheless.

Exercise 10E

1. Explain why offer curve OR_i in Fig. 7 must always lie above the indifference curve I_i^0, $i = 1, 2$.
2. Explain why a competitive equilibrium occurs at and only at an intersection point of offer curves.
3.* Suppose that in the analysis of Fig. 8 consumer 2 acts as a passive price-taker, while consumer 1 seeks to make himself as well off as possible given this fact. What is the nature of the resulting equilibrium? Is it in the core? How might it be driven into the core?
4. Explain why a consumption bundle which is preferred to a bundle chosen at price p^* must be more expensive at that price.
5. For the market consisting of $\{A_1, A_2, B_1, B_2\}$ spell out the proof that the competitive market equilibrium is in the core.
6.* Prove that in the competitive market equilibrium in the four-person case consumers of the same type must have the same consumption bundle. What is the role played by *strict* convexity in this proof?
7.* Suppose that B_1 and B_2 have identical consumption bundles but that A_1 has a bundle which makes him worse off than A_2. Show that the coalition $\{A_1, B_1\}$ can block this initial allocation.
8.* Suppose that in an initial allocation A_1 and B_1 have agreed a deal

which puts them at point c of Fig. 10, as have A_2 and B_2. Use the argument of this section to show that the coalition $\{A_1, A_2, B_1\}$ can block this allocation (*Hint:* recall that A_2 can break his deal with B_2).

9.* What is the significance of the fact that in Fig. 10 a^0, b^0 and c^0 are halfway along the lines αa, αb and αc respectively? (*Hint:* think about feasibility.) From this frame a condition which is sufficient to ensure that a point on the contract curve will *not* be in the core.

10.* Adapt the argument of this section to show how point c' in Fig. 5 can be excluded from the core.

F. Markets with production

In the pure exchange market there is a fixed total stock of a good, consumers decide on how much they want to hold at some given price and use the market to dispose of unwanted stocks or expand their stock holdings. An equilibrium exists when everyone is able to make the net purchases or sales which leave him with the stock he wants to hold. As we have seen, certain interesting and important questions concerning existence and stability of equilibrium and the operations of markets can be analysed in this simple context, but the analysis of competitive markets is incomplete until we take account of production. The theory of markets with production is however not a simple extension of the theory of pure exchange. There are some essential differences between the two types of market, so that although analysis of pure exchange is a useful preliminary, we shall have to take care to clarify those aspects of markets with production which lead to these differences.

First we should note the distinction between stocks and flows: production gives rise to a flow of goods per unit time, and so desired or planned supply in this case is also a flow, not just a difference between two kinds of stock – the stock a consumer in a pure exchange market *wishes* to hold and that which he *does* hold. We have to specify the time dimension of the production/supply flow; no flow variable is properly defined until we have done so. Here we shall take *the day* as the smallest time unit, and define supply and production as a *daily* rate of flow. The market is now regarded as a system of flows – demand is a daily flow of the commodity off the market, supply is a daily flow on to the market. The market therefore operates each day to determine a daily price and an equilibrium is the balancing of these flows.

The second important difference is that we have to specify the period over which supply adjustments are assumed to take place. As we saw in Chapters 7–9, this is important in determining the costs of supply and we shall also see that it determines the market adjustment process.

Recall from Chapter 9 the basic view we took of the firm's decision situation. At the beginning of 'time period 0' it had to choose a current output rate, in the light of the known current price and fixed capacity; and it had to *plan* a capacity and output rate for the next period in the light of *expected* or forecast market price. The length of this time period was determined by the possibilities of capacity adjustment, i.e. by the time it takes to be able to vary capacity by any amount. For concreteness, we assume here that this period is a year.

The picture is this: on the first day of the year the firm produces the rate of output which it planned in the previous period, and discovers when it markets this output what price it can get. If this price is different from that expected, it cannot vary its production that day (the day is the *very short run*) and this is true of every firm, so that on the first day supply is fixed. It can vary its next day's production, however, since a day is assumed to be long enough to organize changes in, say, labour and raw material inputs. If equilibrium is not reached on the second day, then production and supply will again be altered on the third, and so on. If and when the market reaches a daily equilibrium, the firm will make a forecast of price for next year, and plan its daily output and capacity for that year accordingly. Clearly, the absolute lengths of the time periods, the day and the year, are not crucial. The difference between the picture of the adjustment process painted here and that of Chapters 6–8 is the introduction of the 'very short run', the day. This period is totally uninteresting from the viewpoint of the theory of production, since no input can be varied and so there is no choice problem (given that we also assume that the commodity is not storable, so there are no stocks and production = supply). In the theory of markets, on the other hand, the very short run plays an important role *out of equilibrium*, as we shall see.

We now let x_i denote the ith consumer's rate of demand per day for the commodity, and define the market demand function:

$$x = \sum_i x_i = \sum_i D_i(p) = D(p) \qquad \text{[F.1]}$$

where p is again market price. We assume that demand adjusts to market conditions *within the day* so that, unlike production, there are no adjustment lags. Let y_j denote the daily rate of production (= supply) of firm j, and:

$$y_j = s_j(p) \qquad j = 1, 2, \ldots m \qquad \text{[F.2]}$$

$$y_j = S_j(p) \qquad j = 1, 2, \ldots m' \qquad \text{[F.3]}$$

are the short- and long-run supply functions, respectively, of firm j. Thus, $s_j(p)$ relates the firm's desired supply on each day in year 0 to expected price and S_j relates the firm's planned supply on each day in year 1 to expected price. Thus s_j is derived subject to fixed capacity, while S_j reflects the relaxation of this constraint. Note that there are assumed to be m firms in year 0 and $m' \gtreqless m$ firms in year 1. This is to allow for the possibility of entry of new firms or exit of existing firms at the start of year 1. Initially, however, we shall be concerned only with short run supply decisions in year 0.

The short run

It might appear that we could proceed to obtain a market supply function by aggregating the firms' supply functions as we did the consumers' demand functions, but this is not in general the case. Recall that in deriving the *firm's* supply function we assumed input prices constant. This was a natural assumption to make, since any one firm in a competitive 'industry' (defined as the set of all producers of a given commodity) could be expected to be faced with perfectly elastic input supply curves. Then, as its output price is raised, the firm could expand its desired production and input levels without raising input prices. This assumption may not be appropriate for the industry as a whole however: as the price at which they can sell their outputs rises for all firms, expansion in production and input demands may raise input prices because the size of demand increase is no longer insignificant, and input supply functions have positive slopes to the industry as a whole.

The consequences for the firm's actual supply are shown in Fig. 11. In the figure, price is assumed to rise from p to p'. The firm's initial supply ($\equiv SMC$) curve is in each case s_j. However, if the effect of simultaneous expansion by all firms is to raise input prices, the marginal cost curves and short run supply curves of each firm must rise. Figure $11(a)$ shows one possible end result of the expansion of firms in response to the higher price. The short run supply curve has risen to s_j^0 and so at price p' the firm will want to supply y'_j and not y_j^0. Hence the points on the firm's supply curve corresponding to p and p', when *all* firms expand, are a and b respectively and $\hat{s}_j$ is the locus of all such price-supply pairs. Clearly, the firm's *effective market supply curve* $\hat{s}_j$ will be less elastic than its *ceteris paribus* supply curve s_j. They would only coincide if input prices were not bid up by simultaneous expansion of output by all firms (and there were no technological externalities – see below).

In (b) of the figure is shown a more extreme case. The increase in input prices causes a sufficient shift in the firm's SMC curve to make the

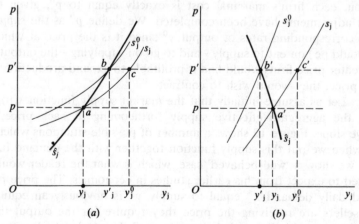

Fig. 11

post-adjustment output y'_j actually less than y_j, and so its effective market supply curve $\hat{s}_j$ has a negative slope. Thus, although the 'law of diminishing returns' ensures that each firm's *ceteris paribus* supply curve has a positive slope (explain why) this is not sufficient to ensure that the firm's effective supply curve has a positive slope, if input prices increase with the expansion of outputs of all firms.

Note a further interesting feature of this analysis. If, at price p, each firm were asked the hypothetical question: 'How much would you produce if price were raised to p'?', it would answer y^0_j, $j = 1, 2, \ldots m$. Aggregating these outputs would, however, give a totally misleading estimate of actual market supply at p', since each firm is basing its estimate on its own *ceteris paribus* supply curve, i.e. on the assumption that input prices remain constant. It is only as firms try to realize this increase in supply that they find that competition is bidding up input prices and the most profitable output expansion is less than they previously thought.

This has important consequences for both theory and policy. In the case of the theory, it suggests that the market supply function must be found by aggregating the *effective* supply functions $\hat{s}_j(p)$, which will incorporate the *actual* output adjustments, rather than the $s_j(p)$, which relate only to hypothetical output adjustments. In the case of policy, it implies that asking firms hypothetical questions about intended output adjustments may be seriously misleading (see Question 5 of Exercise 10F).

Given the effective supply curves $\hat{s}_j(p)$ we can then define the market supply curve as:

$$y = \sum_j \hat{s}_j(p) = s(p) \qquad s'(p) \gtreqless 0 \qquad [F.4]$$

which takes account of input price changes. The slope of this market supply function depends on the extent to which increases in input demands increase input prices and the consequent increases in marginal costs at all output levels. Note that at a market supply $s^0 = s(p^0)$, i.e. a point on this supply function, each firm's marginal cost is exactly equal to p^0, given that all output adjustments have been completed. We define p^0 as the *supply price* of the corresponding rates of output y^0_j since it is the price at which each firm would be content to supply – and to go on supplying – the output y^0_j. At any greater price firms would find it profitable to expand production; at any lower price, they would wish to contract.

Let us assume initially that the market supply function $s(p)$, which shows the aggregate effective supply forthcoming at each price, has a positive slope. Figure 12 shows a number of possible situations which might arise when we put this supply function together with the demand function. In (*a*) we show a 'well-behaved' case, which is what the reader would have been led to expect from his earlier studies in economics. The price p^*, with desired daily demand x^* equal to supply y^* is obviously an equilibrium, since sellers are receiving the price they require for the output they are producing, and this output is being taken off the market by buyers at that

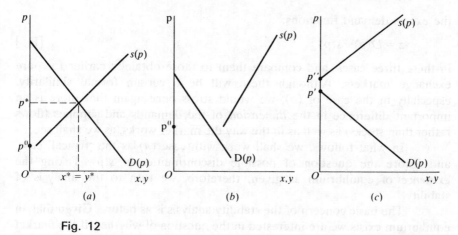

Fig. 12

price. There is no reason therefore either for sellers to change their output (since each $y_j^* = \hat{s}_j(p^*)$ maximizes j's profit at price p^*) or for buyers to change the amount they buy.

Figure 12(b) represents a case which could arise when there is a certain kind of discontinuity in the supply curve $s(p)$. Recall from Chapter 9 that when price falls below average variable cost (AVC) a profit maximizing firm will produce zero output. If all firms have identical AVCs, they will all produce zero output at the same price. Hence, at some critical price, shown as p^0 in the figure, supply may suddenly drop to zero. Thus there is a discontinuity in the short run supply function at p^0. If it happens that the demand curve has the position shown, there is no equilibrium. Individual buyers would be prepared to offer individual sellers prices in excess of p^0 for some output (explain why) but if firms respond by starting up production, they flood the market and price must fall to a level below p^0. As in section B we see that discontinuities, which are perfectly possible in this case, cause problems for the existence of equilibrium. Note however that continuity is sufficient but not necessary: if $D(p)$ were higher and intersected $s(p)$, as in (a) of the figure, the discontinuity at p^0 would present no difficulty.

In (c) we show a further possibility. Suppose that firms do not all have the same AVC, but instead are evenly distributed over a range of AVCs, with the minimum point of the lowest AVC curve being equal to p''. If there are many sellers, and each seller is an insignificant part of the market, we can then take the $s(p)$ curve as continuous, with intercept at p''. However, at price $p' < p''$, demand is zero – no-one would be prepared to pay p' or more for this good. It follows that equilibrium in this market implies a zero output and a price in the interval $[p', p'']$ – the highest price any buyer would pay is insufficient to cover the AVC of the firm with the lowest minimum AVC. Thus the good is a 'non-produced good', a good for which the technology is known, firms would supply if the price were right, but nobody wants to buy. The reader might find it instructive to construct the excess demand functions:

$$z = D(p) - s(p) \tag{F.5}$$

in these three cases, and compare them to those obtained earlier for pure exchange markets. Although there will be a certain formal similarity, especially in the case of (a), we would stress once again that there is an important difference in the *dimension* of the demands and supplies (flows rather than stocks) as well as in the way the market works, as we shall see.

In what follows, we shall work with case (a) as the 'typical' case, and ignore the question of possible discontinuities in $s(p)$. Taking the *existence* of equilibrium as given, therefore, we turn to the analysis of stability.

The basic concern of the stability analysis is as before. Given that an equilibrium exists we are interested in the question of whether, if the market is initially not at an equilibrium, it will tend to converge to one through time. Again, the analysis requires a specification of how the market moves when it is out of equilibrium. An easy answer would be to assume that we can proceed just as before. Taking the excess demand function defined in [F.5], (which in the case shown in Fig. 12(a) would again have a negative slope) we could apply the tâtonnement process (TP) of section C to derive stability conditions.

However, the objections to use of the TP in the case of markets with production are far stronger than in the case of pure exchange, and it can be argued that it should not in the present case be applied at all. The reason is that in a market with production, we would regard quantity supplied as adjusting to differences between the price buyers are prepared to pay for the available output (*the demand price*) and the price sellers are prepared to accept for producing this output (the supply price). This is completely the converse of the TP, where it was envisaged that in a pure exchange market (where, remember, the total available 'supply' or stock of the commodity was fixed), differences in desired demands and supplies would cause adjustments in price (bidding up or down). We have not shown at this stage that this converse view of the adjustment process *would* make a difference to the results of the analysis, but we shall see that in some circumstances it could. Thus, we shall proceed by analysing stability in terms of *quantity adjustment to differences in demand and supply prices*, rather than *price adjustment to differences in desired demands and supplies*.

Given this approach, there still remain a number of alternative specifications of the adjustment process. Thus, suppose that on day 1 of year 0, the rate of supply on the market is y^0 in Fig. 13(a). Demand $D(p)$ has turned out to be higher than firms anticipated when planning their output. The price at which sellers are prepared to maintain this rate of output, the supply price, is p_s^0, while the price buyers are prepared to pay for this supply, the demand price, is p_D^0. Thus, price rises on the market that day to ration off the available supply (in this respect, in the *very short run*, the day, the market can be thought of as operating like a pure exchange market,

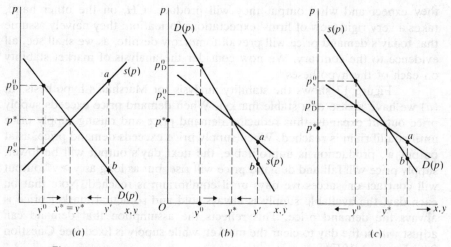

Fig. 13

which gives that model added relevance). Since supply is very profitable, sellers will respond to this higher price by expanding production, so that on the next day supply will be greater. Now the important question is: how exactly does supply respond to the high demand price p_D^0 on the first day? We shall examine two hypotheses which give significantly different answers to this question:

1. *Marshall's hypothesis* (*MH*).   Alfred Marshall, in his analysis of competitive markets, suggested a very general rule. This is simply that *output expands when demand price exceeds supply price and vice versa.* Thus Marshall's hypothesis implies that there will be *some* expansion in supply tomorrow if demand price exceeds supply price today, and some contraction in the converse case, but is very general about the rate at which this takes place.

2. *The cobweb hypothesis* (*CH*).   This is, in contrast to *MH*, a rather stronger hypothesis which says that firms will expect the demand price *today* to continue to prevail tomorrow, and so will expand production up to the point at which their supply price is equal to the demand price. This can be expressed formally as:

$$y_{t+1} = s(p_{Dt}) \qquad t = 1, 2 \ldots \tag{F.6}$$

where p_{Dt} is demand price on day t and y_{t+1} is supply the following day. The stability analysis which results from this hypothesis is rather different to that for Marshall's hypothesis, as we shall see.

The important difference between these two hypotheses concerns the *formation of expectations by firms.* In the case of *MH*, firms simply interpret the high demand price as a sign that a greater output tomorrow will be sold profitably, but the hypothesis does not specify exactly what price they expect and what output they will produce. *CH*, on the other hand, takes a very rigid view of firms' expectations formation: they naively assume that today's demand price will prevail tomorrow despite, as we shall see, all evidence to the contrary. We now consider the analysis of market stability on each of the hypotheses.

Figure 13 shows the stability analysis for Marshall's hypothesis. In (a) we have a case of a stable market. When demand price exceeds supply price output expands, thus reducing demand price and raising supply price until equilibrium is reached. When supply price exceeds demand price, as at output y', production is unprofitable, the next day's output will be lower, supply price will fall and demand price will rise, but as long as $y > y^*$ output will contract on successive days until equilibrium is reached. Note that on each day, the available supply is always sold and so actual market price is always the demand price. This reflects the assumption that demand can adjust *within* the day to clear the market, while supply is fixed (see Question 2 of Exercise 10F).

In (b) of Fig. 13 we have a case in which the market supply function has a negative slope. Again, however, given *MH*, the market is stable. If $y < y^*$, e.g. at y^0, demand price again exceeds supply price and production expands until the discrepancy in demand and supply prices is eliminated. Similarly, if $y' > y^*$, *MH* implies that market supply contracts until equilibrium is reached. Clearly, although the market supply curve has a negative slope, we may still have stability provided that $p_D > p_s$ for $y < y^*$, and $p_D < p_s$ for $y > y^*$, which is satisfied when the demand curve cuts the supply curve *from above*.

Finally, in (c) of the figure, we have an unstable case. At output $y^0 < y^*$, for example, $p_s^0 > p_D^0$, so that output contracts. Conversely, output will expand when $y > y^*$ since the difference between demand and supply prices is positive. Thus, when the demand curve cuts the supply curve *from below*, the market is unstable.

The adjustment process implied by *MH* does not, therefore, always imply a stable market. A *necessary condition* for stability under this process is:

$$\frac{dp_D}{dy} < \frac{dp_s}{dy} \quad \text{all} \quad p \geq 0 \qquad\qquad [\text{F.7}]$$

i.e. that the rate of change of demand price with respect to total output must be less than that of supply price.

This condition can be explained with reference to Fig. 13 as follows. dp_D/dy is the slope of the demand function with respect to the quantity axis. It is always negative. Therefore, when the supply curve is positively sloped, dp_s/dy, the slope of the supply curve with respect to the quantity axis, will necessarily be greater than dp_D/dy. When both are negative, but the demand function is steeper with respect to the quantity axis (it cuts the supply curve from above), the slope of the supply curve is numerically greater (a negative number with a smaller absolute value). Hence cases (a) and (b) of the figure

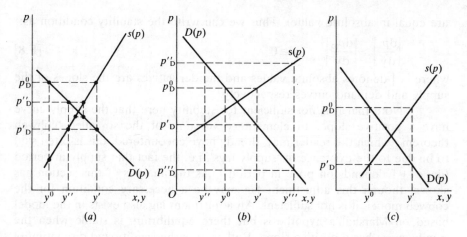

Fig. 14

satisfy the stability condition. Case (c) does not. Note that in Fig. 13(b) the excess demand function is not negatively sloped.

The stability analysis for the cobweb hypothesis is carried out in Fig. 14. Recall that the hypothesis is that the demand price p_D which prevails on a given day will be expected by firms to prevail on the next day, and they will expand production so as to equate supply price with this expected demand price (maximize profit at the expected price). The consequences of this naive behaviour are shown in the figure. In (a), suppose that supply is initially at y^0. Demand price is therefore at p_D^0, and so on the next day supply will be at y'. But in that case demand price falls to p'_D, thus reducing the following day's supply to y'', and so on. Clearly, over time the market will converge on the equilibrium: the changes in price are getting successively smaller, as are the changes in quantity. Price and quantity are fluctuating around their equilibrium values, but the amplitude of the fluctuations is diminishing. In (b) on the other hand, the market is clearly unstable. Beginning at y^0, demand price is initially at p_D^0 and so supply on the next day is at y'. This causes demand price to fall to p'_D and so the following day's supply falls to y'', and so on. In this case, successive changes in price and supply are getting larger. Price and quantity are fluctuating about their equilibrium values with increasing amplitude. Finally, the market shown in (c) of the figure is also unstable. Beginning at y^0, demand price is p_D^0 and so supply on the next day will be y'. This causes demand price to fall to p'_D and so on the following day supply will again be y', and so on. In this case, the market never converges to equilibrium: price and quantity fluctuate around their equilibrium values with constant amplitude.

By examining these three cases, we note that the stable case occurs when the supply curve is steeper than the demand curve, and otherwise there is instability, with widening fluctuations (when the supply curve is flatter than the demand curve) and constant fluctuations (when their slopes are equal in absolute value). Thus we can write the stability condition as:

$$\left|\frac{dp_s}{dy}\right| > \left|\frac{dp_D}{dy}\right| \qquad y \geq 0 \qquad\qquad\qquad \text{[F.8]}$$

where $|\ |$ denotes absolute values and the derivatives are the slopes of the supply and demand curves respectively.

Note that it is not sufficient for stability here that the supply curve have a positive slope. In elementary accounts of the so-called 'cobweb theorem', which the reader may already have encountered, this is often said to be due to the existence of 'supply lags', i.e. the fact that supply in period (day) $t+1$ depends on price in period t. As the analysis of this section has shown, though this adjustment lag may be a necessary condition for the cobweb model, it is not sufficient. An adjustment lag also exists in the model based on Marshall's hypothesis but there equilibrium is stable when the supply curve has a positive slope. Rather, it is the rigidity and discontinuity implied by the *naive expectations* assumption which give the cobweb model its essential character. The assumption that supply adjusts to the difference in demand and supply prices may yield a smooth continuous adjustment process. The assumption that supply adjusts from day to day to the rate which maximizes profit at the previous day's demand price yields a discontinuous adjustment process in which the leaps and bounds of price and quantity adjustment may easily diverge from equilibrium.

It is of course an empirical question as to which hypothesis is more appropriate. It could however be pointed out that the expectations assumption in the cobweb model is *exceedingly* naive. On each day of the adjustment process, firms go on believing that today's price will prevail tomorrow, even though this has been proved wrong every day that the market has been out of equilibrium! Indeed, a clever seller would surely work out that if today's price is low he should expand output tomorrow, and conversely (explain why). If enough sellers behaved like this, the production on day $t+1$ would *not* be the co-ordinate on $s(p)$ of the demand price on day t, and we would indeed have an adjustment process rather better described by Marshall's hypothesis.

Note finally that although the cobweb model is often introduced as an example of price adjustment in agricultural markets (the famous hog cycle), its essential features can just as well be applied to markets in manufactured goods. Adjustment lags exist in both sectors, although in agriculture the 'very short run' is likely to be considerably longer than the 'day' assumed here, being determined by the 'growing period' of whatever commodity is being considered. There is no reason however why the cobweb model should be applied only to agricultural markets, unless it is thought that farmers are more likely to conform to the naive expectations assumption than manufacturers!

The long run
We have so far examined the existence and stability of equilibrium in a market in the short run. That is, firms' output variations from day to day

were made within the constraint of fixed capacity. If the market is stable, a short-run equilibrium will be achieved in which the flow of production on to the market each day is just equal to the amount buyers want at the prevailing price. This price is both the demand price and the supply price (for *short-run* supply decisions). We then have the question: will this daily equilibrium continue to hold indefinitely as long as input prices, technology and consumers' demand functions remain unchanged, or will sellers be planning capacity changes which may disturb this equilibrium once they are put into effect? Here 'sellers' may include not only firms which currently supply the commodity in question but also 'new entrants' to the market. This question can be rephrased: is the market in *long-run* as well as short-run equilibrium? We answer this question by examining the circumstances under which it is profitable to change capacity, since it is profitability which is assumed to determine supply decisions in the long run as well as the short. The first step is to construct the long-run market supply curve, and to examine the nature of 'long-run equilibrium'.

The nature of long-run equilibrium

In Chapter 9 we saw that the *firm's* long-run supply curve is its long-run marginal cost curve. There are several reasons why the market supply curve cannot be obtained simply by summing these supply curves:

(*a*) A reason already familiar from the construction of the short run market supply curve: as *all* firms vary output, we can expect input prices to change, thus causing each firm's cost curves to shift. Its effective long-run supply curve $\hat{S}_j(p)$, $j = 1, 2 \ldots m'$, differs therefore from its *ceteris paribus* supply curve, and represents the locus of actual supply adjustments as prices and cost curves change (review the argument of Fig. 11);

(*b*) In addition to what are often called '*external pecuniary diseconomies*' described under (*a*), there may be *external technological diseconomies* – e.g. congestion, pollution, – or *economies*, – e.g. improvement of common facilities such as transport and communications – which also shift individual firms' cost curves as a result of expansion of scale by all firms;

(*c*) *the number of firms in the market* will in general depend on the price – as price rises firms which previously found it unprofitable to produce the commodity may now find it profitable, and so invest in capacity and add to output. A firm which at the going price just breaks even, with total revenue equal to long run total cost (including the opportunity cost of capital and effort supplied by its owner(s)) is called a *marginal firm* at that price. One which makes an 'excess profit' (total revenue > total long-run opportunity costs) is called an *intra-marginal* firm, and one which would make a loss, but breaks even at a higher price, is called an *extra-marginal* firm. As price rises, marginal firms become intra-marginal and some extra-marginal firms enter (Question 8 of Exercise 10F asks you to consider conditions under which there are no intra- or extra-marginal firms – all possible sellers are marginal).

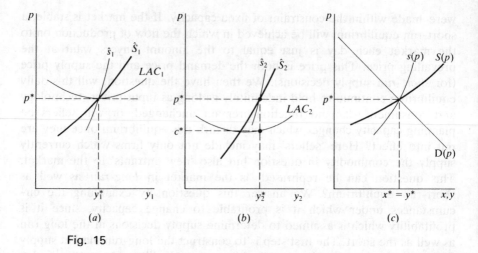

Fig. 15

Given the set of influences which determine how the rate of output changes with price as firms adjust capacity and entry or exit take place, it is by no means assured that the long-run market supply curve will be positively sloped (see Question 9 of Exercise 10F). However, in Fig. 15(c) we assume this to be the case. $S(p)$ shows how the daily rate of output varies with price when capacity is adjusted and the number of sellers may change. It should be noted that underlying this curve is a possibly complex set of adjustments, and the transition from one point on the curve to another is not so smooth and effortless as the curve suggests. It should be interpreted as showing the output which will be forthcoming at each price *after* all these adjustments have been made. Or, alternatively, it shows the price at which a given number of firms would remain in the industry, maintain their capacity and supply in aggregate a given rate of output. The p-coordinate of any point y is then the *long-run supply price* of that rate of daily output.

As we would by now expect, the assumption of continuity of $S(p)$ and $D(p)$ will ensure that a long-run equilibrium will exist, and this is shown in Fig. 15(c) as the point (y^*, p^*). At this point firms are prepared to maintain the daily rate of supply y^*, and consumers are prepared to buy this daily production at price p^*. If, therefore, the short-run supply curve $s(p)$ was as shown in the figure, the short-run equilibrium we have earlier been examining would also be a long-run equilibrium. It would therefore be maintained indefinitely in the absence of any change in demand, input prices or technology.

The other parts of the figure show the implications of the long-run equilibrium for two 'representative firms'. In (a) we show firm 1 as a marginal firm. At market price p^* it chooses a long-run profit maximizing scale of output y_1^*, and it happens that at that output, $p^* =$ its minimum long run average cost. Firm 2, on the other hand, shown in (b) of the figure, is an intra-marginal firm; at its profit maximizing scale of output y_2^*, its long run average cost $c^* < p^*$, and it makes an excess profit equal to $(p^* - c^*)y_2^*$.

However, such 'excess profits', which may be earned temporarily, will not persist indefinitely, but rather should be regarded as true opportunity costs in the long run.

The reasoning is as follows: the fact that the intra-marginal firm's average costs are lower than those of a marginal firm must reflect the possession of some particularly efficient input, for example especially fertile soil or exceptionally skilful management. Since these generate excess profits, we expect other firms to compete for them, so that after a period long enough for contracts to lapse, the firm which currently enjoys the services of these super-efficient inputs will have to pay them what they ask or lose them. The maximum these inputs can extract is the whole of the excess profit $(p^* - c^*)y_2^*$, and so what was a profit during the period when the contract was in force becomes a true opportunity cost to the firm after that time. Such excess profits are therefore called *quasi-rents*, to emphasize that they are not true long-run excess profits, but merely rents accruing to the contractual property rights in certain efficient input services, which become transformed into costs 'in the long run'. Once this transformation has taken place, the 'intra-marginal' firm's *LAC* curve will rise until its minimum point is equal to p^* at output y^*. Hence in the long run *all* firms will be marginal firms.

Stability analysis

This discussion of the nature of long-run equilibrium has of course ignored the question of how the market came to be at that point: this is the question of *long-run stability*, to which we now turn. We can phrase the question in the following way: suppose that on the first day of year 0, the market is in short-run equilibrium (since we have already examined short run stability and do not want to complicate things unduly), but not in long-run equilibrium; will changes take place to lead price, output, capacity and the number of firms toward the long-run equilibrium position, or away from it? This is our usual stability question, the answer to which is found in this case by analysing the interaction of short- and long-run supply decisions. Figure 16 sets out the essentials of the analysis.

Let us first take the case in which capacity output is initially too low. Suppose that in the previous year, the capacity decisions of existing sellers and new entrants (or old quitters), made in the light of their price forecasts for the current year, implied a scale of output per day at y^a. To maintain this output they require a supply price at point a on $S(p)$. However, as it turns out, they seriously under-estimated the strength of demand, and if on the first day of year 0 they supply y^a, they find the high demand price p_D^a. However, for the next 364 days they have fixed capacity which means that the relevant market supply curve for that period is $s(p)$. Ignoring the details of adjustment, we assume that the market quickly finds its short-run equilibrium (within a few days) at an output y^0 and price p_D^0. At this output, there is no difference between *short-run* supply price and demand price, but there is an excess of demand price over *long-run* supply price p_s^0. This

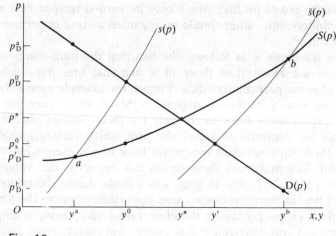

Fig. 16

implies that although it is not profitable to expand output in the short run, firms are in general earning excess profits (draw the diagram for a representative firm), and perceive that it is profitable to *expand capacity*. Thus they will be putting capacity expansion plans into effect, so that at the beginning of year 1, the scale of output would be greater, demand price lower than p_D^0, and supply price higher than p_s^0.

To take a converse case, suppose that in the previous year sellers had overestimated demand and the planned scale of output is y^b in Fig. 16. When this is put on the market on day 1, demand price is found to be p_D^b, no doubt causing some chagrin (particularly on the part of the new entrants who now wish they hadn't). But for this year, since capacity is fixed (by assumption it takes a year to reduce as well as expand capacity) the relevant market supply curve is the short-run curve $\bar{s}(p)$, and this implies a short-run equilibrium at price p_D' and output y'. This price is below the *long-run* supply price of output y' and so sellers will be planning to reduce capacity for next year. On the first day of year 1 we will therefore expect a fall in supply.

This broad account is not however sufficient to resolve the problem of stability: it is clearly necessary to specify the adjustment process which determines by *how much* capacity output is changed in response to a difference between demand price and long-run supply price. But this is familiar territory. We could again postulate Marshall's hypothesis, which would here take the form: *capacity* output y changes according to the value $p_D - p_S$, where p_S is now *long-run supply price*. The analysis of stability, given this hypothesis, is now complicated by the fact that the successive demand prices are determined by the intersections of the short-run supply functions $s(p)$ with the demand function $D(p)$ where the sequence of short-run supply functions is in turn determined by the sequence of capacity outputs. Matters could be complicated indeed if we allowed negatively sloped short-run supply functions in conjunction with negatively or positively sloped long run supply functions. However, the reader should satisfy himself of the following proposition, which should make clear the kind of analysis involved:

If both short- and long-run supply functions are always positively sloped, then long-run market equilibrium is stable under Marshall's hypothesis.

The argument is briefly as follows: given any initial $y < y^*$, the short-run equilibrium demand price must exceed the long run supply price at the short run equilibrium output (e.g. at y^0 in Fig. 16 $p_D^0 > p_s^0$) and so capacity will be expanded until y^* is reached. A similar argument shows that any initial $y > y^*$ will lead to reductions in capacity until y^* is reached. Thus long-run equilibrium in this case is stable.

This is by no means an exhaustive analysis of all the possibilities but it would not be fruitful to pursue all the complexities of the analysis here.

To complete the discussion we consider briefly the cobweb hypothesis of the adjustment process. The naïve expectations assumption now would take the form: given the demand price which is established in the short-run equilibrium, sellers adopt this as their forecast of next year's demand price and adjust capacity accordingly. Thus, we have the adjustment relationship:

$$y_{t+1} = S(p_{Dt})$$

where y_{t+1} is the y co-ordinate on the *long-run* supply curve of the price p equal to the *short-run equilibrium demand price* in year t. Again the previous analysis becomes much more complex because stability not only depends now on the slopes of $D(p)$ and the long-run supply function $S(p)$, but also on the slopes of the short-run supply functions $s(p)$. It is in fact easy to show that where the $D(p)$ and $S(p)$ functions alone would lead long-run equilibrium to be *unstable*, the slopes of the short-run supply functions could be such as to make it stable. Thus consider Fig. 17. $S(p)$ is flatter than $D(p)$

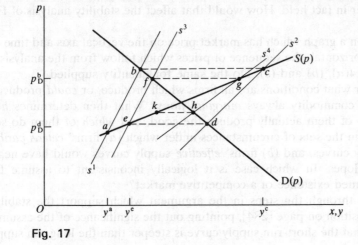

Fig. 17

and so if the short-run supply curves were vertical (as they are in the *very* short run) the market would be unstable. However, given the short-run functions as drawn, equilibrium is stable. Thus, suppose initial output is at y^a, implying short-run supply function s^1. The short-run equilibrium demand price will be at b, implying that next period planned output will be at y^c, the co-ordinate of p_D^b on $S(p)$. But the corresponding short-run supply curve is s^2 implying a short-run equilibrium at d and a demand price p_D^d. This leads to a planned output of y^e next period, a short-run supply function s^3, and so on. Clearly it is possible to construct a sequence of short-run supply curves which lead to convergence on long-run equilibrium over time. Though general stability conditions could be found, they would be more complex than interesting, and we shall not pursue them here.

Exercise 10F

1. Analyse the process of adjustment to short-run equilibrium on the assumption that the very short run is a week rather than a day.
2.* Analyse the process of adjustment to short- and long-run equilibrium on the assumption that it also takes time for buyers to adjust their demands.
3. Will the short run market supply curve ever be negatively sloped if input prices rise as all firms expand output?
4. Derive the short-run market supply curve on the assumption that input prices *fall* as all firms expand output. What could account for this?
5. Suppose that a survey of domestic farmers suggests that if only agricultural prices were a little higher, domestic agricultural production would expand significantly. How does the analysis of this section tell us that we should treat this conclusion with caution?
6.* Discuss the difference between the tâtonnement process, in which price adjusts in response to differences in planned supplies and demands, and the Marshallian adjustment process, in which supply adjusts in response to differences in demand and supply *prices*. Suppose the former in fact held. How would that affect the stability analysis of Fig. 13?
7. Plot on a graph which has market price on the vertical axis and time on the horizontal, the sequence of prices which follow from the analysis in Fig. 14(a), (b) and (c). Do the same for quantity supplied.
8.* Under what conditions are all firms which produce, or *could* produce a given commodity always *marginal firms*? What then determines *how many* of them actually produce the good, and *which* of them do so?
9.* Explain the sets of circumstances under which (a) firms' *ceteris paribus* supply curves, and (b) firms' *effective* supply curves would have negative slopes. In which case is it logically inconsistent to assume the continued existence of a competitive market?
10.* Trace through the steps in the argument which support the stability proposition on page [284], pointing out the significance of the assumption that the short-run supply curve is steeper than the long run supply curve.

11.* Construct an example under the cobweb hypothesis in which the long-run supply curve $S(p)$ is steeper than the long-run demand curve, but the short-run supply curves $s(p)$ are such that long-run equilibrium is unstable.

G. Conclusions

In this chapter we have examined in some depth the existence and stability of equilibrium in competitive markets with and without production. We examined a number of theories based on differing views of how markets actually operate. The reader will most probably have met and used 'simple' supply and demand curves in comparative statics exercises in his previous studies in economics. These 'simple' treatments gloss over a number of difficult problems, which it has been the purpose of this chapter to raise, and for which we have tried to indicate the solutions as far as existing theory permits. But it should be clear that a number of difficulties remain, particularly in relation to the workings of markets out of equilibrium, when trading may take place at disequilibrium prices. Since this is the state markets are usually in, it should be appreciated that the resolution of these difficulties is a major problem of economic research.

References and further reading

On the analysis of pure exchange and the core, excellent treatments can be found in:
> * **W. Hildenbrand** and **A. P. Kirman.** *Introduction to Equilibrium Analysis*, North-Holland, Amsterdam, Oxford, 1976, Ch. 1.
> **P. Newman.** *The Theory of Exchange*, Prentice-Hall, Englewood Cliffs, N.J., 1965, Chs. 3–5.

An interesting descriptive account of a pure exchange economy is given by:
> **R. A. Radford.** 'The economic organisation of a POW camp', *Economica*, Vol. 12, 1945.

On the operation of competitive markets with production, the most thorough treatment is:
> **M. Friedman.** *Price Theory, A Provisional Text*, Aldine Publishing Co., Chicago, 1962, Ch. 5.

For a discussion of the relationship between the Walrasian tâtonnement adjustment process and the Marshallian adjustment hypothesis see:
> **A. Takayama.** *Mathematical Economics*, The Dryden Press, Hinsdale, Ill., 1974, pp. 295–301.
> **D. G. Davis.** 'A note on Marshallian vs. Walrasian stability conditions', *Canadian Journal of Economics and Political Science*, **29,** 1963.

For a discussion of stability in general, though one which is chiefly of relevance to general equilibrium, see:
> * **T. Negishi.** 'The stability of a competitive economy: a survey article', *Econometrica*, 30, 1962.

A seminal article on disequilibrium price and quantity adjustment is:
> **K. J. Arrow.** 'Towards a theory of price adjustment', in M. Abramovitz *et al.*, *The Allocation of Economic Resources*, Stanford University Press, Stanford, California, 1959.

Monopoly

Chapter 11

A. Introduction

It is clear that the assumptions underlying the model of the competitive market, and in particular that buyers and sellers act as price-takers, are often not satisfied in reality. Sellers may perceive that the market price will vary with the amount of output they put on the market: buyers may appreciate that an increase in their purchases will drive the price up. This sort of situation is so widespread that it is important to develop a set of theories about resource allocation under such conditions. This chapter and the next will be concerned with the main elements of theories about the price-setting behaviour of *sellers*; parts of Chapter 14 will be concerned with analysis of cases in which *buyers* have influence over market price.

Given the basic assumption that a seller, usually taken to be a *firm*, perceives that market price and the quantity he sells vary with each other, we obtain two separate types of theory, according to the assumption we make about the nature of the competitive relation with other sellers. If we assume that a firm recognizes that a change in its price will have a significant effect on the demand for the output of one or more other identifiable firms and that changes in these firms' prices have a similar effect on its own demand, then we have the market situation known as *oligopoly*. This will be examined in the next chapter. Here, we shall be concerned with the case in which no such *perceived interdependence* exists: there is no close competitive relationship between the firm in question and one or more other identifiable sellers, and so in setting its price the firm can ignore its effect on other sellers – we have the market situation known as *monopoly*. This characterization of monopoly must however be qualified: although at a given point in time there may be no close competitive relation with another firm, there may be a *potential* competitive relation, since in the long run other firms may be attracted to enter the market and sell in competition with the monopoly. As we shall see, this may place an important constraint on the behaviour of the monopolist, and will affect the outcome of the analysis. In the next two sections we shall proceed as if no such potential competition existed, and in sections D and E we shall examine the consequences of taking into account the threat of new entry.

On the question of definition, note that it is usual to define oligopoly and monopoly in terms of the size distribution of sellers in a market. Monopoly is defined as the case of a 'single seller' of a good, and oligopoly as the case of a 'few sellers'. However, this kind of definition encounters difficulties, arising out of the problem of defining the 'good' or 'a market'. Consider the following cases:

(*a*) A public utility may have a 'monopoly' of the supply of electricity, yet in its sales to domestic consumers, there may be a close competitive relation with the 'firms' which sell oil, coal and gas. The relevant good here is 'energy' or 'heat', and the various 'monopolies' are in a market situation of oligopoly.

(*b*) A cement manufacturer may be one of, say, five sellers in the nationwide cement industry. However, because of high transport costs, he may be able to vary his price over some range to buyers in a region around his cement works, without affecting the demands of any of the other sellers, and the same may be true of them. Each enjoys a 'local monopoly'. Thus what is apparently an oligopolistic market is really a collection of monopoly sub-markets.

(*c*) A restaurant is able to raise its prices relative to those of the other, say, forty restaurants in town, without losing all its customers to them; and is able to lower its prices relative to theirs, without taking all their customers. This is because of differences in quality, location, style of cooking, ambiance, all of which contribute to 'customer loyalty'. If its gains or losses of customers are spread evenly over all other restaurants, then there is unlikely to be a perceived interdependence among the restaurants, and so each restaurant could be regarded as a monopoly (although possibly with a very elastic demand curve). On the other hand, if the customer changes are concentrated on just one or two 'close rivals' (the only other *Chinese* restaurants in town) then the restaurant is in an oligopolistic market situation.

The point of these examples is to show that the appropriate model to use depends not on the size distribution of firms in what may be thought of as 'the market', but on the nature of the competitive relations between sellers. Indeed, the *appropriate definition of the 'market' depends on the nature of the competitive relations*, rather than the other way around. Our definitions of monopoly and oligopoly in this introduction are designed to make this clear from the outset.

B. Price and output determination under monopoly

The 'theory of the firm' (in the sense of Ch. 6) which we adopt in the analysis of monopoly is not essentially different from that which underlay the analysis of competitive markets. The firm is assumed to seek to maximize profit in a stable, known environment, with given technology and market conditions. We continue to assume diminishing marginal productivity of all inputs, and so, in the presence of fixed inputs, the firm's average and marginal costs will at some point begin to rise with the rate of output per unit time. However, we no longer assume that diminishing returns to scale set in at some point: we leave the question open, and permit any one of increasing, constant, or diminishing returns to scale to exist over the range of outputs we are concerned with. The essential difference with the competitive model is the assumption that the firm faces a demand function which relates output inversely to price. We write this demand function in the (inverse) form:

$$p = D(q) \qquad dp/dq < 0 \tag{B.1}$$

where p is price, q is output per unit time, and D is the demand function. Note that we do not in general place restrictions on the second derivative of the function, but restrict its first derivative to be always negative.

The firm's total cost function can be written as:

$$C = C(q) \qquad C'(q) > 0 \tag{B.2}$$

where C is total cost per unit time. We assume that marginal cost is always positive, but again do not place restrictions on the second derivative, the slope of the marginal cost curve. The profit function of the firm is given by:

$$\pi(q) = pq - C(q) \tag{B.3}$$

where π is profit per unit time. The output $q^* > 0$ maximizes the firm's profit if and only if it satisfies the conditions:

$$\pi'(q) = p + q\, dp/dq - C'(q) = 0 \tag{B.4}$$

$$\pi''(q) = 2\, dp/dq + q\, d^2p/dq^2 - C''(q) < 0 \tag{B.5}$$

where [B.4] is the 'first-order' and [B.5] the 'second-order' condition. The term $(p + q\, dp/dq)$ is the derivative of total revenue pq with respect to q (taking account of [B.1]), and so is the *marginal revenue* of output. Thus, [B.4] expresses the condition of equality of marginal cost with marginal revenue. The term $(2\, dp/dq + q\, d^2p/dq^2)$ is the derivative of marginal revenue with respect to output, and so [B.5] is the condition that the slope of the marginal cost curve must exceed that of the marginal revenue curve at the optimal point. If marginal costs are increasing with output while, by assumption, marginal revenue is diminishing with output, [B.5] will necessarily be satisfied, since in that case:

$$C''(x) > 0 > 2\, dp/dq + q\, d^2p/dq^2 \tag{B.6}$$

However, unlike the competitive case, the second order condition may also be satisfied if $C''(q) < 0$ (see Question 1 of Exercise 11B).

More insight into this solution can be gained if we write marginal revenue, MR, as:

$$MR = p(1 + (q/p)\, dp/dq) \tag{B.7}$$

Given the definition of the point elasticity of demand from Chapter 3:

$$e = -p \, dq/q \, dp \qquad [B.8]$$

we can therefore write:

$$MR = p(1 - 1/e) \qquad [B.9]$$

which directly expresses the relationship between demand elasticity and marginal revenue. Clearly, for any finite demand elasticity, $e > 1 \Rightarrow MR < 0$, while $e = 1 \Rightarrow MR = 0$, and $e < 1 \Rightarrow MR < 0$. Combining [B.9] with [B.4], we can write the condition for optimal output as:

$$p(1 - 1/e) = C'(q) \qquad [B.10]$$

This equation then establishes immediately the two propositions:
  (i) the monopolist's chosen price always exceeds marginal cost since his price elasticity is finite;
  (ii) his optimal output is always at a point on the demand curve at which $e > 1$ (given that $C'(q) > 0$).
The reader should use [B.10] to convince himself of these propositions.

Because under competitive conditions market price will be equal to each firm's marginal cost, the extent of the divergence of price from marginal cost under monopoly is often regarded as a measure of the degree of monopoly power enjoyed by the seller. Thus, from [B.10] we have:

$$\frac{p - C'(x)}{p} = \frac{1}{e} \qquad 1 < e < \infty \qquad [B.11]$$

where the lefthand side, the price-marginal cost difference expressed as a proportion of the price, was defined by A. Lerner (1934) as an index of the degree of monopoly power. Thus, as $e \rightarrow \infty$ (the competitive case) monopoly power tends to zero.

The equilibrium position of the firm implied by its choice of output q^* satisfying the above conditions, is illustrated in Fig. 1. In (a) of the figure

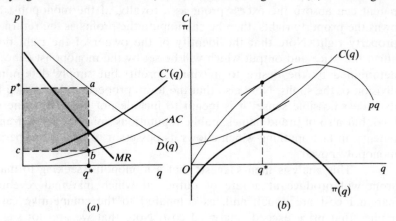

(a)   (b)

Fig. 1

the demand curve is labelled $D(q)$ and the corresponding marginal revenue curve is MR. Given the marginal and average cost curves $C'(q)$ and AC respectively, profit maximizing output is at q^*. Since this must be sold at a market-clearing price, choice of q^* requires the price $p^* = D(q^*)$. We could therefore regard the equilibrium position as a choice either of profit maximizing price p^* or of output q^*, since each implies the other. At output q^*, profit is the difference between total revenue p^*q^* and total cost $AC \cdot q^*$, and so is shown by the area p^*abc in Fig. 1(a). In (b) of the figure the same equilibrium position is shown in terms of total revenue and cost curves. The total revenue curve is denoted pq, and its slope at any point measures marginal revenue at that output. Its concave shape reflects the assumption of diminishing marginal revenue. The total cost curve is denoted $C(q)$, and its convex shape reflects the assumption of increasing marginal cost. The total profit function is the vertical difference between these two curves, and is shown as the curve $\pi(q)$ in the figure. The maximum of this curve occurs at the output q^*, which is also the point at which the tangents to the total revenue and total costs curves respectively are parallel, i.e. marginal revenue is equal to marginal cost.

The 'supernormal profit', i.e. profit in excess of all opportunity costs (including a market-determined rate of return on capital which enters into determination of the average and marginal cost curves), given by the area $q^*(p - a)$, can be imputed as a rent to whatever property right confers the monopoly power *and* prevents the new entry which would compete the profits away. It may be the case that this right is owned by an individual who leases it to the firm. In that case, we would predict that if the supplier is rational and well-informed, he will bid up the price of the lease so as just to absorb the super-normal profit, and so the rent is transformed into an opportunity cost for the monopolist. This would be true, for example, if the monopolist rented a particularly favourable location: then, when the lease is re-negotiated, the lessor can raise the rent to absorb the monopoly profit; or if the monopoly profits are due to some patented invention, the owner of the patent can absorb the excess profit as a royalty. If the monopolist himself owns the property rights, then he can impute the profits as the return on this property right. Note that the identity of the owner of the right does not affect the price and output which will be set by the monopolist (since this is determined by the desire to maximize profit) but simply determines the division of the spoils. Note also that the term 'property right' is used here in its widest possible sense: it is meant to include not only the ownership of land, but also of brand names, public reputations, mineral rights, franchises, patents, in fact anything which allows its possessor to create and perpetuate monopoly power.

This analysis then suggests that a monopolist seeking to maximize profit will produce at a rate of output at which marginal revenue and marginal cost are equal, and, as compared to the competitive case, this implies that price exceeds marginal cost. Note that we are not suggesting that a monopolist (or a competitive or oligopolistic firm) draws the kinds of curves we have used to reach that conclusion, or that he consciously uses concepts such as marginal revenue and marginal cost. We are rather asserting that in the last analysis he cares only about the profitability of his business, that he weighs up the advantages of different amounts of sales or output on the basis of the profit they yield, and chooses that amount at which profit is greatest. Given a concave relationship between profit and output of the kind shown in Fig. 1(b), the profit maximizing output must have the property that to exceed it slightly would add more to costs than it does to revenue. In the language of the theory, we refer to this in terms of marginal revenue and marginal cost, but we should not be surprised to find that businessmen use different language.

Exercise 11B

1. The analysis in the text assumed implicitly that there were constraints on the firm's inputs, so that the short-run cost function of Chapter 8 was the relevant cost function for the firm's decisions. Extend the analysis to take account of the interaction of long-run and short-run decisions (c.f. Ch. 9). Show that the firm will set output so that $SMC = MR$ in each period and will plan to produce next period where $SMC = LMC = MR$.

2. Using diagrams analogous to those in Figs 1(a) and 1(b), illustrate cases in which there are increasing returns to scale.

3.* Show how a monopolist's price and output will be affected by:
   (i) an increase in demand;
   (ii) a specific tax per unit of output;
   (iii) a proportionate 'excess profit' tax.
   Compare these comparative statics results with those for the competitive firm in Chapter 9.

4.* What methods could you use to induce the monopolist to produce at the output at which $C'(q)$ cuts $D(q)$ (i.e. at which price = marginal cost) in Fig. 1(a)? Describe four methods, and assess their advantages and disadvantages.

5.* Discuss, in the light of the theory of this section, the famous comment by Lord Thompson of Fleet, that a franchise to run a commercial television company was 'a licence to print money'.

6. (a) Explain why it is meaningless to talk of 'the supply curve' of a monopolist.
   (b) Is it also meaningless to talk of the demand curve of the monopolist for inputs he uses in production?

7.* Describe as fully as you can the economic consequences of the sudden monopolization of an industry which had previously been competitive. Apply your answer to the analysis of the consequences of introducing 'marketing boards' for agricultural products which had previously been sold under competitive conditions.

8.* Suppose that a good could be produced at equal per unit cost by a monopolist, on the one hand, and a competitive industry, on the other.

Can you give reasoned answers to the following questions:
(a) Would the monopolist invest more in research and development than the competitive industry?
(b) would the good have a higher or lower quality under the monopoly?
(c) would it be more or less durable under the monopoly?
(d) would it be accompanied by more or less advertising under the monopoly?
(e) given fluctuations in demand, would price be more or less stable under monopoly than under competition?

9. Explain why a monopolist with zero marginal cost would produce at an output at which $e = 1$. What is the value of the Lerner index at such a point?

10.* Discuss circumstances in which the owner of a property right leased to a monopolist would not absorb the monopoly profit entirely in the lease rental.

C. Price discrimination

Price discrimination is the practice whereby different buyers are charged different prices for the same good. It is a practice which could not prevail in a competitive market because of *arbitrage:* those offered lower prices would resell to those offered higher prices and so a seller would not gain from discrimination. Its existence therefore suggests imperfections of competition, and we are particularly interested in its practice by a monopolist.

At the extreme, suppose that the monopolist can prevent arbitrage at zero cost, and that he is able to take each buyer separately, and charge him the maximum he is prepared to pay for each unit of the good he buys. In this way, the monopolist is able to appropriate for himself all the consumer's surplus, and his profit will be at the maximum possible.

In practice, however, such perfect price discrimination would not be feasible, and it is more likely that the overall market will be divided into sub-groups, between which arbitrage will be prevented; and prices would be charged which are uniform within but different between groups. Price differentials between groups only constitute price discrimination when they' do not exactly reflect differences in costs of supply (e.g. transport and distribution costs) and so to concentrate on the main point at issue, we assume that costs of supply are identical across groups.

The questions of interest concerning price discrimination are: what determines the breakdown of the market into sub-groups? and, what can be said about the structure of prices which the monopolist will set? We consider the questions in reverse order, taking the market segmentation as given, initially, and considering the determinants of the discriminatory pricing structure.

For simplicity, we assume that the monopolist divides the market into *two* groups. He knows the demand, and therefore marginal revenue, curves, for each group. Let q_1 and q_2 be the quantities sold to the first and second groups respectively, so that total output $q = q_1 + q_2$. Take some *fixed* total output level, q_0, and consider the division of this between the two sub-markets in such a way as to maximize profit. Since the total production cost of q_0 is given, profit from the division of this between the two markets is maximized if revenue is maximized. But revenue is maximized only if q_1 and q_2 are chosen such that the marginal revenues in each sub-market are equal. To see this, let MR_1 be the marginal revenue in sub-market 1, and MR_2 that in 2. Suppose $MR_1 > MR_2$. Then it would be possible to take one unit of output from market 2, and put it in market 1, with a net gain in revenue of $MR_1 - MR_2 > 0$. As long as the marginal revenues were unequal such possibilities for increasing revenue, and therefore profit, would exist. Hence we have that a necessary condition for a profit maximizing allocation of any given total output between the two markets is that marginal revenues in the markets be equal.

In determining the optimal total output level, we are on familiar ground. If $MR_1 (= MR_2)$ differed from marginal cost, it would be possible to vary output in such a way as to increase total profit: by increasing output when $MR_1 > MC$, and reducing it in the converse case. Hence a necessary condition for maximum profit is that $MC = MR_1 = MR_2$.

Now let e_1 and e_2 be the price elasticities of demand in the respective sub-markets. Then, the basic relation given in [B.9] applies in this case, so that we have:

$$MC = p_1(1 - 1/e_1) = p_2(1 - 1/e_2) \qquad [C.1]$$

From this we can immediately find the condition under which price discrimination, i.e. $p_1 \neq p_2$, will take place, and also the relation between the prices. Thus, from the second equality in [C.1] we have:

$$\frac{p_1}{p_2} = \frac{1 - \dfrac{1}{e_2}}{1 - \dfrac{1}{e_1}} \qquad [C.2]$$

If $e_1 = e_2$, then clearly $p_1/p_2 = 1$, and so there will be no discrimination, but as long as the elasticities are unequal at the profit maximizing point, there will be. Moreover, it can be shown that if $e_1 > e_2$, then from [C.2] $p_1 < p_2$, and conversely. (Try it with $e_1 = 2$ and $e_2 = \frac{3}{2}$.)

Thus we conclude that in maximizing profit the monopolist will always set a higher price in the market with the lower elasticity of demand.

The analysis is illustrated in Fig. 2. In (a) of the figure are the demand and marginal revenue curves for sub-market 1 and in (b) those for 2. The curve MR in (c) is the *horizontal sum* of the MR_1 and MR_2 curves, and therefore has the property that at any total output, q^0, the two output levels q_1^0 and q_2^0 which have the same marginal revenues in the sub-markets

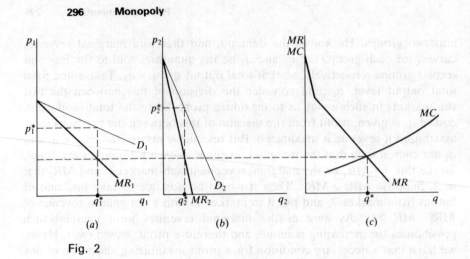

Fig. 2

as that at q^0, sum exactly to q^0, i.e. $q_1^0 + q_2^0 = q^0$. The horizontal summation therefore reflects the first condition derived above, that any total output must be divided between the sub-markets in such a way as to equalize their marginal revenues. The profit maximizing level of total output is shown at q^*, where $MC = MR$. To divide q^* optimally between the sub-markets, we simply take q_1^* and q_2^*, the sub-market outputs which have the appropriate marginal revenues, and which by construction must sum to q^*. We see immediately from the figure that since demand for q_2 is less elastic than that for q_1, we have $p_2^* > p_1^*$.

Thus we have a prediction about the profit maximizing price structure, which can be extended to any number of sub-markets. Given the market segmentation, the structure of prices will be exactly determined by price elasticities of demand, with prices relatively lower in markets with relatively higher demand elasticities. However, how is this market segmentation or division of the overall market into sub-markets achieved?

We can first sketch out a general theoretical answer. Suppose there are n buyers in total. Then, any one way of dividing up *all* these buyers into *non-overlapping* sub-groups can be called a *partition* of the market. There are very many possible partitions of the market, including the extreme cases in which (a) each sub-group consists of only one buyer and (b) there is only one sub-group, consisting of the entire market. Associated with each possible partition will be a profit-maximizing discriminatory pricing structure, worked out on the principles set out above, with a corresponding total profit; and a cost of actually *enforcing* that partition, i.e. ensuring that no arbitrage takes place, and administering the pricing structure. The possible partitions could then be compared on the basis of the difference between maximized profit and enforcement cost, and that partition with the greatest positive difference chosen.

This solution, however, assumes unlimited information and computational ability on the part of the monopolist. In reality, he is unlikely to consider all possible partitions, since that may be a very large number, and some may be ruled out from the start, as having 'infinite enforcement costs' (in other words, it would be impossible to segment the market in that way, e.g. the partition in which each sub-group consists of just one consumer may be impossible since arbitrage could not be prevented). In addition, there may not be sufficient differences in the demand elasticities of particular consumers to warrant the costs of separating them (the returns to price discrimination depend on elasticity differences). In reality, there will probably be a few rather obvious partitions of the market into consumer groups, based on location, or broad characteristics (industrial or domestic consumers, high income or low income, male or female) which provide the basis for significant differences in demand elasticities, and low-cost market segmentation. Thus, price discrimination in practice is unlikely to be very much more complex than that analysed in this section.

Exercise 11C

1.* Academic journals charge different subscription rates to institutions (college libraries, etc.); individual academics; and students. Explain this in terms of the theory of price discrimination. What would you predict about the pattern of relative subscription rates across these groups? Some journals are owned by profit maximizing firms and others by learned societies. What difference, if any, would you expect this to make to (a) the level of their rates and (b) the pattern of price discrimination?

2. Why are sparking plugs sold to car manufacturers as 'initial equipment', to be installed in new cars, at a price just about equal to average production cost, and sold to retailers and garages, for replacement purposes, at a price several times greater than average production cost?

3. Why are the fees charged by solicitors and estate agents, for services provided in buying and selling houses, expressed as percentages of the house price, even though the cost of the services involved is independent of the house price?

4. Why do firms sometimes offer quantity discounts ('one packet for 50p, two for 90p')?

5. Suppose that a monopolist was sufficiently well informed to be able to extract the whole of each customer's consumer surplus. What output would he produce?

6.* Why do most public utilities, whether regulated or unregulated profit maximizers, or nationalized industries, make a connection charge which the customer must pay if he wishes to consume any units at all?

7.* A firm which monopolizes one good may sometimes insist that people wishing to buy that good must also buy their requirements of some other good, which would otherwise be competitively produced, from the monopolist. (Examples have included Kodak and IBM and more prosaically the practice of restaurants of making a corking charge if customers wish to drink their own, rather than the restaurant's, wine.) Why is this *full line force* profitable given that the monopolist can charge a monopoly price for the monopolized good?

D. Entry and potential competition

The analysis of the previous two sections has suggested that in the absence of competition, or the threat of it, from other sellers, a monopolist will earn excess profits. We cannot continue to ignore the possibility of new entry, however, since we would expect the existence of excess profits to create at least a *prima facie* attraction for other sellers. To the extent that the monopolist could conceal the profitability of his business, he might be able to avoid the attentions of firms attracted by returns on capital greater than those to be earned on the market in general. In reality, however, the information channels which exist, and the legal requirement to produce properly audited profit and loss accounts for taxation purposes, make concealment of high profitability difficult, even for companies not quoted on the stock exchange. For companies which *are* quoted on the stock exchange, the high dividends and strong performance of the firm's shares would be a clear signal to other firms. Monopoly power might therefore sow the seeds of its own destruction, and we expect a rational monopolist to take this into account. We now have to carry out an analysis of the implications of the possibility of new entry for the behaviour of the monopolist.

The first crucial question concerns the *condition of entry*, i.e. we have to ask whether *barriers to entry* exist. We distinguish between an *absolute entry barrier*, which rules out, over some time horizon, all new entry whatsoever; and a *relative entry barrier*, which places a new entrant at a disadvantage, but not an insurmountable one. An absolute entry barrier may arise out of some legal impediment, such as a patent or statutory monopoly right, or out of the exclusive ownership of some resource which is indispensable for production. In that case, we interpret the monopoly profits, which will continue for as long as the absolute barrier exists, essentially as rents accruing to the monopoly's holding of the legal rights or privileges.

Relative entry barriers may arise out of: capital market imperfections; specific cost advantages; and consumer loyalty. Capital market imperfections imply that different borrowers pay different interest rates, and also that the interest rate increases with the amount borrowed. This means that an entrant may have to pay a higher interest rate than the well-established monopolist, particularly if the lenders regard the entry as a risky proposition anyway. It takes on particular force if there are significant economies of scale in production of the monopolized good. If the entrant sets up production on a scale smaller than that at which long-run average costs are at a minimum, then he will incur average costs which exceed those of the monopolist (assuming the latter *is* producing at minimum long-run average costs). On the other hand, if he enters on a scale large enough to achieve minimum average costs, the capital expenditure required may be very large, and may again involve him in higher interest costs than those incurred by the monopolist. Indeed, if there is capital rationing in the capital market, then the entrant may not be able to obtain the amount of funds he would require to set up on the optimal scale. If, on the other hand, the capital market were perfect, then both the monopolist and potential entrants would borrow at the same interest rate, and the entrants could borrow as much as they wished at the going rate, so the scale of capital expenditure required would be irrelevant.

'Specific cost advantage' is a cover-all term for things like superior location, availability of marketing outlets, advantageous input supplies, information, expertise, experience and contacts, which are enjoyed by an established firm and make its costs lower, other things being equal, than those of a firm new to the market.

Consumer loyalty, built up and reinforced by advertising, and strengthened perhaps by innate conservatism and risk aversion of buyers, may impose on an entrant higher costs of advertising, packaging, sales promotion and product quality. In order to get his product known and accepted he will have to spend more on these than does the established monopolist, at least in the initial stages.

Each of these relative entry barriers can be converted into a cost, and incorporated into the long-run cost curve of the entrant, which would then lie above that of the monopolist. A consequence of this would be that, since entry takes place only as long as the *entrant* anticipates excess profits, positive monopoly profits are not a sufficient condition for new entry. Then, any excess profits which remain to the monopolist could be imputed as rents to the factors which create the relative entry barrier, and indeed provide a measure of this barrier.

Note that a relative entry barrier depends on the characteristics of *both* the monopoly and the potential entrant. In general, we might expect different potential entrants to have different long-run average costs of producing the good supplied by the monopolist. For example, a large firm, well-established in a market which is closely related to the monopolized one, may have little difficulty in raising cheap capital, may possess information about the market, and may be able to use its reputation in its existing markets to overcome consumer resistance in the new one. Indeed, a great deal of the 'new entry' which takes place is in the form of diversification and integration by already established firms. Thus it is not possible to gauge the extent of relative entry barriers by reference to the characteristics of the monopoly alone; it is also necessary to take account of the characteristics of potential entrants.

At the opposite extreme to the case of an absolute entry barrier is that of the complete absence of a barrier to entry. New firms are able to enter the market and produce at costs identical with those of the existing monopolist. Any excess profit earned by the monopolist can be shared by the new entrant, and so we would predict that new entry will take place until all excess profits have been competed away.

We therefore have three logically possible cases: that of no entry barriers; that of relative entry barriers, which imply higher cost curves for new entrants than for the existing monopoly; and that of absolute entry barriers, where no entry whatsoever can take place. In Fig. 3 we illustrate

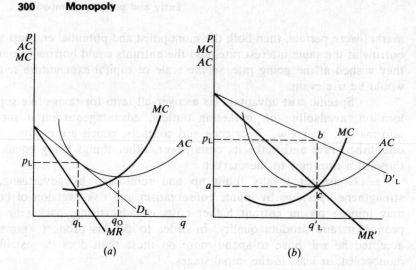

Fig. 3

two alternative post-entry equilibrium situations for the monopolist, corresponding to the first two of these cases. In each case we assume that before entry the monopolist's demand and marginal revenue curves were above those shown in the figure: the effect of entry is to shift down the monopolist's demand and marginal revenue curves and probably to increase their slopes. The 'no entry barriers' case is shown in (a) of the figure. For any post-entry demand curve D_L, the monopolist will continue to choose the profit maximizing output (by hypothesis). It must also be the case that in long-run equilibrium no excess profits are earned. It follows that the equilibrium must be at a point of tangency of demand and average cost curves, since only such a point can satisfy *both* the conditions: marginal revenue equals marginal cost; *and* price equals average cost. Thus, the monopolist's post-entry equilibrium price and output will be p_L and q_L respectively.

Note that in Fig. 3(a) we have implicitly made two assumptions. First we have assumed that the outputs of the new entrants are *not* regarded by consumers as perfect substitutes for that of the monopolist, since we have drawn P_L with a negative slope. If they were perfect substitutes, the demand curve would be a horizontal line and, as in the theory of competitive markets, long-run equilibrium could only occur at the output q_0, at which average costs are a minimum. Thus, in this case, 'entry' means the production by firms of outputs which are much closer, though still imperfect, substitutes to that of the monopolist than any previously existing.

Secondly, we have assumed that the new entry does not transform the market situation into one of oligopoly, so that we are able to draw a well-defined demand curve (for the discussion of the relation between oligopoly and the demand curve, see the following chapter). In other words, the new entrants do not create a situation of *perceived strategic interdependence* with the existing firm.

For example, suppose that forty new firms enter the market, shifting the monopoly's demand down to D_L, and that variations in the (now ex-) monopolist's price cause changes in demand for his output which are spread *uniformly* and *symmetrically* over the other forty firms, this being true also for each of them. No one seller is sufficiently 'close' to another in terms of their competitive relation, for there to be a significant perceived effect on him. Then each seller would have a well-defined demand curve. This corresponds to the kind of market structure which has been termed *monopolistic competition:* each seller of a group of close substitutes has some degree of monopoly power, conferred because of product differentiation (Chinese v. Indian restaurants), or locational factors (the local grocer's shop v. the other grocers' shops in town). There is no significant perceived interdependence and the absence of barriers to entry implies that no excess profit can be made in long-run equilibrium.

Figure 3(a) also shows the central result of the theory of monopolistic competition, namely the existence of *excess capacity*, which in this case means the excess of the output at which long-run average cost is minimized, q_0 in the figure, over the output produced by the firm, q_L. Since the demand curve has a negative slope, zero-profit equilibrium *must* imply positive excess capacity, and so the consequence of free entry in the present model is that firms will not exploit all possible economies of scale – each firm in the market produces at an inefficiently low scale of output. This conclusion has however been challenged, on the grounds that it may not hold when advertising and selling costs are taken into account explicitly – the interested reader is referred to Demsetz (1964).

Figure 3(b) illustrates the case in which relative entry barriers exist, and new entrants exhaust *their* possibilities for excess profits at a share of the market which leaves the monopolist earning excess profits. The post-entry demand curve is at D_L', and excess profits are made, of the amount shown by the area $p_L' acb$. These profits are a measure of the value to the firm of those factors which create the relative entry barrier. Note that implicit in Fig. 3(b) are again the assumptions that new entrants' outputs are not perfect substitutes for that of the monopolist, and that we do not have the creation of an oligopolistic market (the 'uniformity' and 'symmetry' conditions hold). A consequence of the existence of relative entry barriers is that it is no longer true that excess capacity must exist – in fact, the figure shows *as a special case* that profit maximizing output q_L' occurs at minimum long-run average cost. However, consumers are not necessarily better off as a result of this – the equilibrium price with relative entry barriers is likely to be greater than that with no entry barriers, the lower production cost in the former case simply being absorbed as part of monopoly profit.

Although it may happen in practice that the consequence of new entry into a hitherto monopolized market would be the creation of 'monopolistic competition', the case in which the result would instead be an oligopoly appears to be at least as important. In the presence of relative entry barriers especially, there may be a fairly small number of potential entrants who perceive that they could earn excess profits. Thus Fig. 3 does not show all possible post-entry situations. Analysis of an oligopolistic post-entry situation however requires a theory of oligopoly in general, and so is postponed to the next chapter.

The analysis of the consequences of new entry so far has assumed that the monopolist behaves in a passive and rather myopic way. He maximizes short-run profit and allows new entry in the long-run to reduce his market share and reduce or eliminate his excess profits. In his short-run behaviour, he pays no heed to the threat of potential entry and does not resist it when it appears. In the next section we examine two alternatives to this strategy.

Exercise 11*D*

1. Suppose entry takes the form of production of outputs which are perfect substitutes for that of the monopolist, and for each other. Discuss the nature of the post-entry market structure and demand curves in the cases:
   (*a*) there is a large number of new entrants, and the 'uniformity and symmetry' conditions hold;
   (*b*) there is a single new entrant.
2.* Suppose that in the case in which relative entry barriers exist, the post-entry excess profits (as shown in Fig. 3(*b*)) are in the long-run transformed into a cost. Discuss the mechanism by which this might take place. How does it affect the equilibrium position in Fig. 3(*b*) as compared to that in 3(*a*)?
3. Use the analysis of this section to explain why attempts by non-members of the legal profession to supply the services of 'conveyancing' (transfer of legal title to property, especially houses) are usually contested in the courts by the Law Society.
4. Prove the assertion in the text that tangency of the average cost and demand curves implies that marginal revenue and cost are equal.
5.* Why have:
   (*a*) large breweries integrated forward to own public houses?
   (*b*) large oil companies integrated forward to own petrol stations?
   In your answer discuss the significance of (i) licensing laws for public houses and (ii) planning restrictions on the number and location of petrol stations.
6.* Examine the responses of a monopolistically competitive market to changes in the level of purchase and profit taxes. Are there any predictions of the model which differ from those derived from models of a competitive market?

E. Limit pricing and selective response

Rather than setting a price which maximizes short-run profits regardless of new entry, the monopolist could adopt a pricing policy which makes new entry unattractive, in other words he may set a *limit price*. Clearly, an effective limit price would be one which was equal to the monopolist's own long-run average cost, since in that case no excess profit would be made and so no signals would go out to other sellers that opportunities exist for excess profit. However, we assume that the monopolist wishes *to maximize* profit, *subject to the constraint* that no other seller will find it profitable to enter the market. The question then is whether there exists a limit price which yields positive excess profits to the monopolist, and, if so, how is it determined? We now turn to an analysis which shows that *provided the monopolist adopts or threatens to adopt the appropriate post-entry response*, a limit price exists which yields positive excess profits. This is true even in the absence of relative entry barriers, while the existence of such barriers would increase the profitability of the limit-pricing strategy.

Assume:

   (i) the monopolist knows the long-run average cost curve on which a potential entrant will operate (possibly, though not necessarily, because it is identical with his own);

  (ii) he also knows the market demand curve;

 (iii) the entrant's output would be undifferentiated from his own, so that both firms' outputs must sell at the same price;

 (iv) economies of scale exist over a significant range of the entrant's long-run average cost curve.

Assumptions (i) to (iii) are simplifying, although relaxation of them leads to further analysis which is not without interest (see Question 1 of Exercise 11E).

Figure 4 sets out the analysis. D is the market demand curve for the monopolist's output, and AC_E is the potential entrant's long-run average cost curve (incorporating assumption (iv)). The entry-excluding price which maximizes the monopolist's profit is p_m^*, implying an output of q_m^*. It is always assumed that the entrant's costs are such as to make the highest possible limit price less than the price which maximizes the monopolist's short-run profits, otherwise the problem is trivial. p_m^* is the optimal limit price.

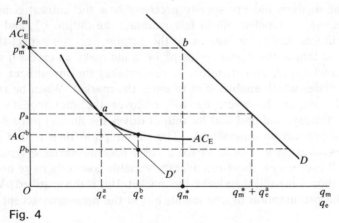

Fig. 4

The reasoning underlying this is as follows: consider the dema
curve D', which is found by shifting D leftward and parallel to itself until
is just tangent to the entrant's average cost curve. This tangency point
labelled a. The price p_m^* is found as the point at which D' cuts the vertic;
axis. Suppose that *the entrant is made to believe that if he enters the marke
the existing seller will maintain his output at* q_m^*, so that total market outpu
will be q_m^* *plus* the entrant's output. Then, he will perceive that price mus
fall along the portion bD of the market demand curve, to an exten
dependent on his own output. In other words, the line p_m^*D' is effectively the
entrant's perceived demand curve, since it shows the price at which he car
sell the various amounts of output he may want to put on to the market. Bu
since this demand curve lies nowhere above the entrant's long-run cos
curve, he will see that he cannot earn excess profits, and so there appears to
be no incentive to enter.

For example, suppose the entrant decided to set up at scale of
output q_e^a. Adding this output to q_m^* implies that market price would fall to
p_a, and so the entrant's revenue would just cover his costs, no excess profit
would be earned, and so there is no incentive to enter. At any other output
he might choose, a loss would actually be incurred. (Supply the reasoning.)
Overall, therefore, a policy of setting the price p_m^* and output q_m^*, together
with the 'declared intention' of maintaining this output in the event of entry
taking place and allowing the entrant's output to 'spoil the market', appears
to offer to the monopolist maximum profit consistent with complete exclusion of new entry.

It is of interest to extend this analysis by considering among other
things the implications of changing assumptions (i) to (iv) above, but this is
left for the reader as an exercise. Here we concern ourselves with the central
aspect of the analysis, the entrant's belief that the monopolist will continue
to produce the output q_m^* in the event of his entry. It is in fact this output,
rather than the price as such, which is the crucial feature of the entry-
excluding strategy – the price p_m^* simply follows from the need to sell this
output on the market – and the theory could perhaps be more aptly described as one of the 'limit output'.

The analysis did not specify precisely how the entrant is made to
accept that the monopolist will in fact maintain the output q_m^*, and indeed
one possibility is that before the event the entrant *does not* expect this. He
may perceive that at the market price p_m^* he could make an excess profit if it
remained unchanged, and therefore he undertakes the investment in production facilities which enables him to enter the market. When he starts to
market the output, however, he will discover the monopolist's entry-
restricting strategy, and find that his output drives the market price down so
as to make production unprofitable. The presumption then is that he will
incur losses until such a time as fixed costs become variable (given that
revenue still exceeds his short-run average variable costs otherwise he would
exit in the short run) and then leave the market. But is this justified? We will
question the presumption in a moment, but in the meantime accept it.

In the situation just analysed, the limit-pricing strategy failed as an *entry-forestalling* device, although, by assumption, it succeeded as a *competitive response* to the new entry which actually takes place. Clearly, for the strategy to *forestall* entry, the potential entrant must anticipate the post-entry response of the monopolist. He might be able to infer this from evidence of past attempts at entry, by himself or other sellers. Alternatively, he may receive the information from the monopolist himself, directly or indirectly. For example, on learning of the intention to enter (from equipment suppliers, market outlets, industrial espionage . . .) the monopolist may let it be known that any attempt at new entry will be met with vigorous price-cutting and maintenance of his rate of output so that entry will inevitably be unprofitable. However, the entrant still has *to believe* this.

Moreover, we have the question just raised of whether the entrant would necessarily be deterred by initial losses, especially when it is remembered that the entry-deterring strategy also may involve the monopolist in losses. For example, suppose that the entrant produces at output q_e^b in Fig. 4. When added to q_m^*, this has the effect of driving market price down to p_b, implying losses for the entrant. However, suppose that the relative entry barriers are minor, so that the monopolist's cost curve is close to that of the entrant. Then the price p_b may also imply losses for the monopolist. In that case, who gives in first? The answer clearly depends on their relative abilities to sustain losses, and, if the entrant is large, well-established, with substantial reserves, he may be able to force the monopolist to accept his presence, end the 'cut-throat competition', and return to 'more orderly' market conditions (for a discussion of what these may be, see the next chapter).

Conversely, high relative entry barriers and a greater ability of the monopolist to sustain losses might imply that the entrant is beaten out of the market. The point remains that the expectation of initial losses need not deter an entrant absolutely; rather, it reduces the present value of the expected profit stream which would follow from entry, and therefore reduces the set of potential entrants who would find entry profitable.

This discussion suggests two points. First, *we cannot ignore the element of strategic interdependence which may exist in the entry situation.* Given that the monopolist can identify the potential entrant, he will be aware that the entry decision will depend on his own actions or threatened actions, and likewise the entrant must try to predict both the short- and long-run reactions of the monopolist to his entry. Threats may be exchanged, bargaining attempted, and the situation bears many resemblances to the case in which two sellers *already* exist in a market, which is considered in the next chapter.

Secondly, the suggestion that observation of the price-output pair p_m^*, q_m^* by the entrant is *alone* insufficient to make him believe that output q_m^* will be maintained after entry, puts in doubt the relevance of the entire limit-pricing analysis. If the monopolist is in any case going to have to issue threats, or demonstrate his willingness to fight by allowing market price to fall after entry, then he will increase his profit, while making no difference to the entry situation, by adopting a *selective response strategy*. That is, in the absence of a threat of new entry, he sets a *profit maximizing* price, and when this attracts a potential entrant, he issues threats which suggest the extent of the losses which would be inflicted upon the entrant. The entrant himself must treat the entry as an investment decision: he must forecast the time-stream of losses and profits which would result from his entry, discount them to a present value (cf. Ch. 15) and take a decision accordingly. In making this forecast, he will have to estimate the size of initial losses which may result from the reactions of the existing producer and also their *duration*. The longer the monopolist maintains his post-entry competitive behaviour, the greater will be the duration of the entrant's losses, and, because of the influence of the discounting procedure, these will play a relatively more important role in determining the present value than the more distant profits which may result if and when the monopolist would become reconciled to the existence of the new firm and agree on a less damaging policy (for which see the next chapter). In estimating the duration and extent of initial losses, the potential entrant must take into account not only the threatened actions of the monopolist, but also the losses which these actions will imply for the monopolist himself, and his ability to sustain them. Clearly, a threatened competitive response will not be credible if it would very quickly bankrupt the monopolist. There would probably be an inescapable element of uncertainty in these estimates and, to the extent that the potential entrant is *risk-averse* (see Ch. 19) this will tend to weaken the incentive to enter.

The limit-pricing analysis does not give a useful prediction of the policy which the monopolist would adopt under this 'selective response' strategy. For suppose he were to adopt the policy of holding output at q_m^* in Fig. 4. Then the entrant could produce at the scale of output q_e^a, at which, although not making profits, he makes no losses either. He could then hope to get a foothold in the market, and eventually persuade the monopolist that they could *both* do better by adopting a more co-operative policy. Thus the present value of the entry decision would certainly be positive. To deter the entrant the monopolist must inflict initial losses large enough to offset the future profits which the entrant expects he might make when 'peaceful co-existence' has been established. This implies that the monopolist must respond to entry by producing an output greater than q_m^*, so that any output the entrant produces, when added to that of the monopolist, forces price strictly below the entrant's average costs and yields a loss.

To summarize this discussion: as an alternative to passive acceptance of new entry by the monopolist, it was suggested that a more profitable strategy might be to accept lower profits in the short run in exchange for greater profits in the long run, by setting a limit price. We then examined the determination of the optimal limit price, i.e. the most profitable price the monopolist could set, consistent with no new entry. In deriving this price, a central assumption was that a potential entrant could be made to believe that the monopolist would maintain his output if entry took place, ensuring that no output produced by the entrant could earn excess profits. Examination of this assumption however suggested the possibility of more complex reasoning by both parties in this situation of strategic interdependence. Furthermore, it can be argued that the limit pricing strategy would be dominated by that of 'selective response', i.e. of maximizing profit in the short run, and responding to the threat of entry with threats of a competitive response which would make the present value of the entry decision negative. In general, this would imply a more vigorous competitive response than is the case under limit pricing, because it would be necessary to inflict definite losses on an entrant, to offset the prospect of positive profits in the period of 'peaceful co-existence' which the entrant might anticipate once the initial period of market warfare is over.

This discussion is intended to be suggestive rather than exhaustive – no rigorous analysis of the precise nature of the *optimal* selective response has been given. However, it is hoped that the general outlines of such an analysis have been made clear. In particular, it should be clear that once potential entry is taken into account, the analysis of monopoly becomes virtually indistinguishable from that of oligopoly, to which we turn in the next chapter.

Exercise 11E

1. Discuss the implications for the analysis of limit pricing of this section, of assuming:
   (a) the monopolist does not know for certain the entrant's long-run average cost curve;
   (b) the entrant's cost curve reflects constant returns to scale at all levels of output.
2. Show how the limit price p_m^* depends on:
   (a) the slope of the market demand curve;
   (b) the rate at which the entrant's average cost falls with output, i.e. the extent of economies of scale.
3. Suppose market demand is growing through time, in such a way that the demand curve D in Fig. 4 shifts outward parallel to itself. What will be the effect on the price-output pair p_m^*, q_m^* over time?
4. Suppose that because of technological change, the entrant's average cost curve lies *below* that of the monopolist. Does a profitable limit price still exist, and, if so, under what conditions?
5.* Extend the limit pricing analysis to the case in which the entrant's output will be a close but not perfect substitute for that of the monopolist.
6.* Suppose more than one potential entrant exists. How can the limit pricing analysis be extended to this case?
7.* Discuss the ways in which a monopolist:
   (a) might become aware of the intentions of a potential entrant;
   (b) communicate his planned post-entry response.
8.* Discuss the factors which will determine the relative profitability to a

monopolist of:

(a) maximizing short-run profits and passively accepting new entry;

(b) maximizing short-run profits and adopting a vigorous competitive policy towards new entry;

(c) adopting the limit pricing policy discussed in this section.

References and further reading

The classic paper on monopoly is:

> **A. P. Lerner.** 'The concept of monopoly and the measurement of monopoly power', *Review of Economic Studies*, Vol. 1, 1934.

On price discrimination:

> **F. Machlup.** 'Characteristics and types of price discrimination' in *Business Concentration and Price Policy*, Princeton University Press, Princeton, N.J. 1955,

gives a thorough taxonomy of possible situations, while for a practical example see:

> **The Monopolies Commission.** *Report on the Supply of Electrical Components to Mechanically Propelled Land Vehicles*, H.M.S.O., London, 1960.

The basic readings on entry barriers are:

> **J. S. Bain.** *Barriers to New Competition*, Harvard University Press, Cambridge, Mass., 1956.

> **H. Hines.** 'The effectiveness of entry by already established firms', *Quarterly Journal of Economics*, 1957.

The market form known as 'monopolistic competition' has received rather brief treatment in this chapter. For a reasonably complete coverage, see:

> **G. C. Archibald.** 'Chamberlin vs. Chicago', *Review of Economic Studies*, Vol. 24, 1961.; plus the responses from Stigler and Friedman and the rejoinder from Archibald in the Feb. 1963 issue.

> **E. H. Chamberlin.** *The Theory of Monopolistic Competition*, Oxford University Press, London, 1937.

> **H. Demsetz.** 'The nature of equilibrium in monopolistic competition', *Journal of Political Economy*, Vol. 67, No. 1, 1959.

> **J. Hadar.** 'On the predictive content of models of monopolistic competition', *Southern Economic Journal*, July 1969.

The questions concerning entry-preventing strategies are well-covered by:

> **J. N. Bhagwati.** 'Oligopoly theory, entry-prevention and growth', *Oxford Economic Papers*, N.S. Vol. XXII, No. 3, 1970.

> **R. F. Harrod.** 'Doctrines of imperfect competition' in *Economic Essays*, Macmillan, London, 1952.

> **F. Modigliani.** 'New developments on the oligopoly front', *Journal of Political Economy*, Vol. 66, 1958.

> ***M. Shubik.** *Strategy and Market Structure*, John Wiley, New York, 1959.

> ***L. Telser.** *Competition, Collusion and Game Theory*, Macmillan, London, 1972.

Chapter 12

Oligopoly

A. Introduction

If a firm believes that the outcome of its decisions depends significantly on the decisions taken by one or more other identifiable sellers, then
we have the market situation known as oligopoly. It is usual to define
oligopoly as the case of a market with 'few sellers' (and indeed the word
'oligopoly' means this), but, as we argued in the previous chapter, a
definition in terms of the number of sellers in a market is not without
ambiguity, and since the essence of the situation is the nature of the
competitive relationships between sellers, it is best to make this the basis of
the definition. Nevertheless, loosely and intuitively we always think of
oligopoly as 'competition among the few'.

Consistent with our theory of the firm, we assume that a seller in
this situation of close interdependence of decision-taking will seek to
maximize profit. The problem he faces is that of assigning a unique profit
outcome to each decision alternative (e.g. alternative production plan), in
order to rank them and find the optimum. Each seller is necessarily involved
in reasoning: 'if I choose A, and he chooses B, then I get X, while if I
choose C, and he chooses D then I get Y . . .', and so on. In this example,
the competitor's reactions $B, D, . . .$ could take one of a number of forms,
and so the seller in question must try to reason out what the response will
be. Thus, before he can come to a ranking of alternative decisions, he must
take some view of the reactions of each of his competitors. The theory of
oligopoly is concerned with understanding and predicting the decisions of
sellers in such situations of 'strategic interdependence', i.e. of interactions
of reasoning and decision-taking among sellers.

A natural way to proceed would seem to be by formulating a
particular hypothesis about the nature of the competitive reactions which
each seller expects and using this to find an equilibrium solution. In other
words, the hypothesis allows us to say that each decision-taker will associate
with his decision A some specific response B; and with his decision C some
specific response D, and so on. Then, by using the basic analytical

framework of cost and demand curves, we arrive at a precise prediction of the market equilibrium position. This approach was indeed the one first adopted by economists. However, a difficulty is that there are several hypotheses about reaction patterns which are possible, each with a different associated equilibrium solution. Thus, rather than having an 'indeterminate' theory of oligopoly, with no solution, we have several possible theories with several different solutions. This in itself need not be a serious cause for concern, since we could presumably use empirical evidence to distinguish among the various hypotheses and find that which appeared to be the best representation of sellers' beliefs about reaction patterns.

A more serious criticism of the approach is that it ignores the possibility of explicit communication and cooperation among sellers. It appears to assume that the sellers remain 'at arm's length', guessing at each other's likely reactions, whereas an obvious possibility is that they would at least consult and quite conceivably co-operate. To quote a famous passage from Adam Smith's *Wealth of Nations:* 'People of the same trade seldom meet together, even for merriment or diversion, but the conversation ends in a conspiracy against the public, or in some contrivance to raise prices. It is impossible indeed to prevent such meetings, by any law which either could be executed, or would be consistent with liberty and justice' (Vol. 1, p. 117, Everyman edition). The modern phenomenon of the expense account lunch fits Smith's description of a meeting 'for merriment or diversion' quite accurately. Admitting the possibilities of communication and cooperation then changes the focus of the analysis. Instead of constructing hypotheses about expected reaction patterns and examining their consequences, we are interested in answers to the questions:

(i) Under what conditions will the sellers agree to cooperate in their decisions?

(ii) If they agree to cooperate, what kinds of price and output policies will result?

(iii) Will their cooperative agreement be *stable*, in the sense of being maintained over time in the face of changing circumstances, and, in particular, are there forces making for the breakdown of the agreement?

An attempt to answer these questions will be made in section C below. In the next section, we look at some of the models which have resulted from the approach of hypothesizing reaction patterns, though we should at this point state our opinion (which might not be universally accepted) that these are of interest mainly in the history of economic thought.

B. Conjectural variations and reaction patterns

To facilitate the analysis, particularly that part of it which will be carried out diagrammatically, we shall assume that we have two firms producing close but not perfect substitutes, with no strategic interdependence with other sellers. This defines the special case of oligopoly known as *duopoly.* Many, though by no means all, of the elements of oligopoly theory can be satisfactorily discussed in this context. In general, we would be interested in the determination of a number of choice variables by each seller, e.g. outputs, investment, advertising and product quality, but again for simplicity we restrict ourselves here to consideration of output and price choices only.

Consider first the firms' demand functions. We write these in inverse form, as:

$$p_i = D_i(q_1, q_2) \qquad i = 1, 2 \tag{B.1}$$

where p_i is the ith firm's price and q_i, $i = 1, 2$, its output. Since the firms' outputs are substitutes, we have:

$$\frac{\partial p_i}{\partial q_j} < 0 \qquad i, j = 1, 2, \qquad i \neq j \tag{B.2}$$

In other words, at a fixed output of firm i, a reduction in firm j's output, brought about of course by an increase in its price, shifts firm i's demand curve upward and therefore increases the price corresponding to the given output. Holding firm j's output (and price) constant, we have as usual:

$$\frac{\partial p_i}{\partial q_i} < 0 \qquad i = 1, 2 \tag{B.3}$$

i.e. the *ceteris paribus* demand curve for each firm has the usual negative slope.

However, if a variation in firm i's output would cause a change in output of firm j, then the partial derivative in [B.3] does not fully capture the rate at which its price will vary with its output. For this we need the *total derivative.* Thus, differentiating [B.1] totally, with $i = 1$, we have:

$$\frac{dp_1}{dq_1} = \frac{\partial p_1}{\partial q_1} + \frac{\partial p_1}{\partial q_2} \frac{dq_2}{dq_1} \tag{B.4}$$

where dp_1/dq_1 is the total derivative of firm 1's price with respect to its output. Only if the second term on the righthand side is zero would the effect of output on price be equal to the slope of the *ceteris paribus* demand curve. This second term has two parts. The derivative $\partial p_1/\partial q_2$ reflects the degree of substitutability between the two outputs, and is objectively determined, as far as the sellers are concerned, by the characteristics of the outputs, consumers' preferences, incomes, etc. The second term, dq_2/dq_1, measures the competitive reaction of firm 2 to the output decision of firm 1, *as subjectively perceived by firm 1*, and it is the determination of this which is the crux of the 'oligopoly problem'. The problem, discussed in the previous section, of second-guessing the competitor's reactions, can be expressed formally as that of specifying a value of the derivative dq_j/dq_i, $i, j = 1, 2, i \neq j$. Since this derivative relates to output *variations*, and since its values must be guessed at or *conjectured* by firm i, it is known in the literature of oligopoly theory as the *conjectural variation* of firm i.

Thus the problem for the firm can be expressed as that of assigning a value to its conjectural variation. Until it does so, the relation between the demand for its output and its price is *indeterminate*, i.e. its effective demand curve (as opposed to its *ceteris paribus* demand curve) cannot be drawn, and so its profit maximizing output choice cannot be made. The problem for the theorist under this approach, as discussed in the previous section, is that of formulating a hypothesis about the value which each firm assigns to its conjectural variation and then analysing the determination of equilibrium. We now consider three models of duopoly, which can be regarded as stemming from three different hypotheses about the values the sellers assign to their conjectural variations.

Cournot's duopoly model

The duopoly model first formulated by the French mathematical economist A. Cournot takes an extreme view of the values the sellers assign to their conjectural variation: the hypothesis is that each sets the conjectural variation equal to zero. That is, each takes the other's output as given, and does not take account of the possibility that it will change as a result of his own decision. In effect, therefore, the hypothesis is that firms ignore their strategic interdependence, and do not even embark upon the guessing game that we regarded as characteristic of oligopoly. Alternatively, we could express the hypothesis as asserting that each firm operates as if its *ceteris paribus* demand curve correctly reflected the relation between its price and its output, ignoring the fact that this may shift as a result of responses made by the competitor.

If $C_i(q_i)$ is the ith firm's total cost function, $i = 1, 2$, its profit function is written:

$$\pi_i = p_i q_i - C_i(q_i) = q_i \cdot D_i(q_1, q_2) - C_i(q_i) \qquad i = 1, 2 \qquad \text{[B.5]}$$

Maximizing the ith firm's profit with respect to its output yields as a necessary condition:

$$p_i + q_i \cdot \left[\frac{\partial p_i}{\partial q_i} + \frac{\partial p_i}{\partial q_j} \cdot \frac{dq_j}{dq_i} \right] = C_i'(q_i) \qquad i, j = 1, 2 \qquad i \neq j \qquad \text{[B.6]}$$

where the lefthand side could be called the 'total marginal revenue' of the firm's output, since it incorporates the total derivative of price with respect to output, the term in square brackets. However, since, in the Cournot model, each firm sets the conjectural variation $dq_j/dq_i = 0$, it chooses its output so as to satisfy:

$$p_i + q_i \frac{\partial p_i}{\partial q_i} = C_i'(q_i) \qquad i = 1, 2 \qquad \text{[B.7]}$$

taking the other firm's output as given and *not liable to change*. This condition is of course the standard one for a profit maximizing monopolist (see section 11B), emphasizing the implication of Cournot's hypothesis that each firm ignores its interdependence with the other and operates only with regard to its *ceteris paribus* demand curve.

Now there is nothing to guarantee that when, say, firm 1 chooses an output $\hat{q}_1$ given firm 2's current output $\hat{q}_2$, firm 2 will actually choose $\hat{q}_2$ given that firm 1 has chosen $\hat{q}_1$. In other words, there is nothing to guarantee that the output choices are mutually consistent. We can define an equilibrium concept in terms of such consistency: an equilibrium pair of outputs (q_1^*, q_2^*) has the property that q_1^* maximizes firm 1's profit when firm 2 chooses q_2^*, and q_2^* maximizes firm 2's profit when q_1^* is chosen by firm 1. It follows that simultaneous choices of q_1^* and q_2^* by the two firms would be consistent with each other, and there would be no tendency for either firm to change its output. From [B.7] and using [B.1], we can say that the equilibrium output pair must satisfy the simultaneous equations:

$$D_1(q_1, q_2) + q_1 \frac{\partial p_1}{\partial q_1} - C_1'(q_1) = 0 \qquad [\text{B.8}]$$

$$D_2(q_1, q_2) + q_2 \frac{\partial p_2}{\partial q_2} - C_2'(q_2) = 0 \qquad [\text{B.9}]$$

since in that case we have that the profit maximizing choices of the firms are consistent.

As usual with equilibrium solutions, we are interested in the questions of first, whether such an equilibrium pair (q_1^*, q_2^*) exists, and secondly, whether it is stable, in the sense that if the firm's output choices were initially out of equilibrium (and therefore inconsistent) changes would take place which would push them toward equilibrium. It is possible to examine these questions entirely in terms of algebra, but we adopt the less rigorous alternative of a diagrammatic analysis.

In Fig. 1(a), we show firm 1's marginal cost curve, MC_1, and a sequence of three marginal revenue curves, derived from different *ceteris*

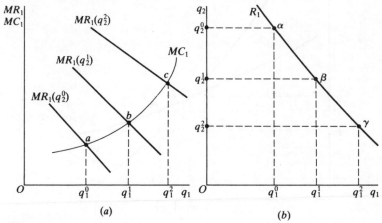

(a)   (b)

Fig. 1

paribus demand curves, each corresponding to a different output level of firm 2. Thus, $MR_1(q_2^0)$ corresponds to firm 2's output q_2^0, shown also on the vertical axis of Fig. 1(b). Given this output (and its associated price), firm 1 maximizes its profit by choosing output q_1^0, i.e. that output at which its marginal revenue and marginal cost are equal. If, on the other hand, firm 2 were to produce output q_2^1, implying that it sets a higher price in its market since $q_2^1 < q_2^0$, then firm 1's marginal revenue curve (and associated demand curve, not shown) would be higher, at $MR_1(q_2^1)$ in Fig. 1(a). In that case firm 1's profit maximizing output would be q_1^1. Likewise, if firm 2's output were even lower, at q_2^2, then firm 1's marginal revenue curve would be higher, at $MR_1(q_2^2)$, and its profit maximizing output choice would be q_1^2. Thus, corresponding to each output choice by firm 2 is a profit maximizing output choice by firm 1. In Fig. 1(b), the curve R_1 represents this relationship. Given an output of firm 2 on the vertical axis, it shows the profit maximizing output of firm 1 on the horizontal. The three points α, β, γ representing respectively the output pairs (q_1^0, q_2^0), (q_1^1, q_2^1), (q_1^2, q_2^2), correspond to the profit-maximizing points a, b and c in Fig. 1(a). The curve in Fig. 1(b) is called firm 1's *reaction curve*, since it shows how firm 1's output choices vary with, or react to, those of firm 2. It should be clear that at each point on it, firm 1 is taking firm 2's output as given, and is not trying to predict the consequences of its *own* output choice. This follows from Cournot's assumption of zero conjectural variation.

In precisely the same way, we can construct a reaction curve for firm 2, showing the profit-maximizing output which firm 2 will choose *given* each possible output choice of firm 1. In Fig. 2 R_2 denotes this reaction curve, and it is superimposed upon firm 1's reaction curve R_1. Given any output q_1, firm 2 will choose the corresponding output q_2 on its reaction curve R_2, and given any output q_2, firm 1 will choose the corresponding output q_1 on *its*

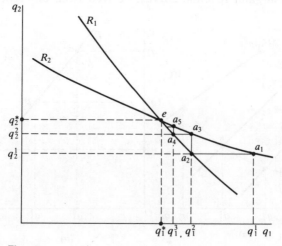

Fig. 2

reaction curve R_1. It follows that there is only one equilibrium position in the figure, and that is at point e, the intersection point of the reaction curves, with associated output pair (q_1^*, q_2^*). This clearly has the property of the equilibrium: given q_2^*, firm 1 chooses q_1^*; and given q_1^*, firm 2 chooses q_2^*. Any output pair which is not on *both* reaction curves cannot be an equilibrium. For example, consider the pair (q_1^1, q_2^1). If firm 1 chooses q_1^1, firm 2 will choose q_2^1, from its reaction curve R_2. But if firm 2 chooses q_2^1, firm 1 will revise its output choice to q_1^2, from its reaction curve R_1. Hence, (q_1^1, q_2^1) was not an equilibrium output pair.

The figure suggests a necessary and sufficient condition for an equilibrium to exist, namely that the reaction curves intersect at least once in the positive quadrant of the (q_1, q_2)-space. This is of course a geometric statement of the requirement that equation [B.9] possesses a solution. It is possible to carry out a deeper analysis of the existence problem by examining conditions which can be placed on the demand and cost functions to ensure a solution, but that will not be undertaken here.

We can also make use of Fig. 2 to examine the question of stability. Thus, again suppose that firm 1 initially chooses output q_1^1, and firm 2 then chooses q_2^1. As just described, this causes firm 1 to revise its choice to q_1^2, since this corresponds to q_2^1 on its reaction curve R_1. But the choice of q_1^2 by firm 1 will then induce firm 2 to choose output q_2^2, since this is the output corresponding to q_1^2 on its reaction curve. But this in turn induces firm 1 to choose q_1^3, and so on. Thus firm 2 moves along its reaction curve through the points $a_1, a_3, a_5, \ldots$, while firm 1 moves through the points $a_2, a_4, \ldots$. Clearly, both sequences are converging on e, the equilibrium point, which is therefore a stable equilibrium (confirm that choosing any other initial output for either firm, e.g. to the left of e, would result in a sequence of output pairs converging to e).

On the other hand, suppose that we had drawn the reaction curves in such a way that the indices were exchanged: R_2 was in fact R_1 and R_1 was R_2. Then the reader should satisfy himself that beginning at any output pair other than e, the process of output revision would actually *diverge* from the equilibrium, implying in this case that the equilibrium is *unstable*. This suggests the *stability condition:* equilibrium is stable if and only if the slope of R_1 is greater in absolute value than that of R_2, i.e. if R_1 cuts R_2 from above.

The intuitive reasoning underlying this stability condition can be illustrated with reference to the figure. If we begin with an output pair (q_1, q_2) on R_2 such that $q_1 > q_1^*$ and $q_2 < q_2^*$, then convergence requires that the first change in q_1 should be a decrease, back towards q_1^*. But this only occurs if R_1 lies to the left of R_2 at such a point. Since this applies to all such points on R_2, stability requires that R_1 lie below R_2 as long as $q_1 < q_1^*$ and $q_2 > q_2^*$. By a similar argument, any point on R_2 such that $q_1 < q_1^*$ and $q_2 > q_2^*$ would require a consequent increase in q_1, and this means that R_1 must lie to the right of R_2 at such a point.

Of course, the precise slopes of the reaction functions depend, as can be seen from the construction of R_1 in Fig. 1 on:

(a) the slopes of the respective marginal cost curves:

(b) the rate at which the marginal revenue curve of output j shifts with changes in output i, that is, on the value of the cross-derivative of demand between the outputs.

Since the two outputs may have marginal cost curves of widely differing slopes, and since

$$\frac{\partial p_1}{\partial q_2} \lesseqgtr \frac{\partial p_2}{\partial q_1},$$

there are no grounds for asserting that equilibrium in Cournot's model is *necessarily* stable. Question 1 of Exercise 12B asks you to explore an example which *is* stable, while Question 2 asks you to provide an example of an unstable equilibrium.

We can now consider the reasonableness of Cournot's model. It seems to embody a low opinion of the intelligence of the sellers in the market. Despite clear evidence to the contrary, each continues to ignore the fact that the other's output depends on his own. Moreover, they are extremely unenterprising: as we shall see below, a seller who realizes that the effect of his own output decision on that of the other is not zero, can make use of this to increase his profit relative to that which he earns at the equilibrium of the Cournot model; while if *both* sellers appreciate their interdependence, they can, by cooperating, both do better than if they ignore this rather obvious fact. We do not therefore find the Cournot hypothesis particularly convincing, though the model itself is of analytical interest, and it provides a useful starting point for further study of oligopolistic markets.

The leader-follower model

The German economist von Stackelberg suggested a model of duopoly which goes a step further than that of Cournot. A 'leader' is defined as a seller who chooses his profit-maximizing output on the assumption that the other seller will accept this output and take it as given in maximizing his own profit. A 'follower' is defined as a seller who reacts passively, accepting the other's output choice and not regarding it as being influenced by his own decision. Thus a follower sets his conjectural variation equal to zero, as in the Cournot model, while a leader does not, but rather bases the value of the conjectural variation on the assumption that the other is a follower. Given two sellers, there are three possible types of situation:

(a) both sellers may act as followers;

(b) both sellers may try to act as leaders;

(c) one may act as a leader, the other as a follower.

In the first case, we have the Cournot model: each firm has a zero conjectural variation and so analysis of the equilibrium proceeds along the lines of the model just examined. In the second case, von Stackelberg argues, we simply have conflict with the outcome indeterminate. Each seller refuses to adopt a passive role, the choices of the sellers are mutually inconsistent, and so neither can successfully play the leadership role – the situation is inherently unstable. Ultimately, out of the struggle, a victor will emerge, who will take as his prize the position of leader, and the loser will become the follower. We here examine in some detail the third case, the 'harmonious' situation in which the leader leads and the follower accepts his passive role.

Let firm 1 be the leader, and firm 2 the follower. Since firm 2 chooses its output by maximizing profit *given* firm 1's output, it follows that its choices can be described by a reaction curve such as R_2 in Fig. 2: given an output q_1, firm 2's *ceteris paribus* demand curve and associated marginal revenue curve are given, and choice of profit maximizing q_2 results in a point on R_2, by construction. Firm 1 is assumed to know this reaction curve, i.e. it knows the output choice of firm 2 which will follow from an output it itself chooses. We would expect firm 1 to be able to take advantage of this knowledge, and Fig. 3 illustrates how. In the figure, the reaction curves R_1 and R_2 are drawn as before, with their intersection at point e. Consider the curve labelled π_1^0. This can be called a *profit contour* for firm 1, and it shows the set of (q_1, q_2) pairs which yield the same value of profit to firm 1. That is, it shows the (q_1, q_2) pairs which satisfy the relation:

$$\pi_1^0 = q_1 D_1(q_1, q_2) - C_1(q_1) \qquad [\text{B.10}]$$

where π_1^0 is a given amount of profit. The inverted U-shape of the profit contour has the following explanation. Given firm 2's output q_2^0, the output q_1^0 yields the maximum profit for firm 1, since it lies on firm 1's reaction curve R_1. We could express this by saying that q_1^0 maximizes π_1 *subject to the constraint* that $q_2 = q_2^0$, and π_1^0 is the resulting maximized profit. Suppose we now vary q_1 away from q_1^0 but change q_2 in such a way as to keep profit constant at π_1^0. We will have to *reduce* q_2, because (*a*) varying q_1 away from q_1^0 must reduce profit, by definition of the maximum, and (*b*) reducing q_2 means increasing the demand, marginal revenue, and profit of firm 1, thus compensating for the effect of varying q_1 away from q_1^0. Of course, this argument only justifies *the slope* of π_1^0 on either side of point b, and not the curvature: the strictly concave nature of the curve must be explained by more detailed assumptions about the cost and demand functions. Without going into this, we shall assume that the profit contours are strictly concave. A further point to note is that in the figure, the *lower* the profit contour the higher the amount of profit it represents: thus, in the figure $\pi_1^* > \pi_1^0 > \pi_1^1$. This can be explained as follows: take firm 1's output as fixed, say at q_1^0. Then, the lower the profit contour, the lower the value of q_2 corresponding to q_1^0, the higher firm 1's demand and marginal revenue curves, and the higher the profit (this again obviously assumes some kind of regularity in the demand relationship).

From this discussion of the profit contours, we can see from Fig. 3 how firm 1 can do better by making use of its knowledge of firm 2's reaction function. The Cournot equilibrium is at point e, and so at that point firm 1

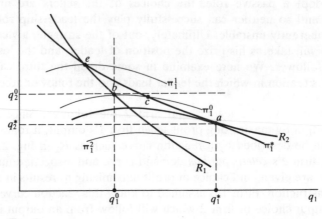

Fig. 3

would earn the profit π_1^1. But by 'moving along' the reaction function R_2, to point c, firm 1 earns the higher profit π_1^0. This move is of course achieved by firm 1's setting its output at the q_1 co-ordinate of point c, in which case it knows firm 2 will set *its* output at the q_2 co-ordinate. This then naturally raises the question: what is the *maximum* profit firm 1 can make? The answer is again shown in the figure. As long as it is constrained to choose points on R_2, the highest profit contour firm 1 can reach is clearly π_1^*, and it does this by choosing q_1^*, leaving firm 2 to choose q_2^*. This solution corresponds to a tangency of the reaction function with the profit contour at point a. There may of course exist higher profit contours, such as π_1^2, but these are not available to firm 1 because they do not meet the reaction function R_2.

We can restate the assumptions of the leader-follower model in terms of conjectural variations. Firm 2 (the follower) has a conjectural variation of zero as in the Cournot model, since it assumes that the other firm will not respond to a change in its output. Firm 1 (the leader), on the other hand, realizes that firm 2 will always remain on its reaction curve R_2. The conjectural variation of the leader is therefore the slope of R_2, which shows how the follower will respond to changes in the leader's output.

We again see therefore that once we assign values to the conjectural variations we can obtain a determinate equilibrium solution. The leader-follower model seems to take a step nearer reality as compared to Cournot's model, since it assumes that one firm at least is acute enough to recognise the interdependence which exists, and is enterprising enough to take advantage of it. However, it is still necessary to *assume* that one of the sellers will be prepared to act as a follower. We have not been able to justify this in terms of some deeper analysis of the duopoly situation, nor to say anything about the case in which neither firm is willing, or can be forced, to become the follower. The model therefore still does not provide an entirely satisfactory analysis of oligopoly.

The kinked demand curve model

This model, proposed by P. Sweezy (1939), is based on a postulated discontinuity in the firm's conjectural variation. Each firm is assumed to expect that an increase in its price and reduction in its output away from the existing price-output pair would not be followed by the other, whereas a cut in its price and increase in its output would provoke a competitive response. For the first type of change from the existing price-output position, therefore, each firm's conjectural variation is zero, while for the second, it is positive. The implication for the ith firm's demand curve, $i = 1, 2$, is shown in Fig. 4. The firm's existing price and output are $\hat{p}_i$ and $\hat{q}_i$ respectively. Since an increase in the firm's price will, by hypothesis, induce no response, the segment ae of the demand curve D_i coincides with the firm's *ceteris paribus* demand curve. However, since reductions in price will be followed, the segment aD_i has a steeper slope, reflecting the fact that a given price reduction will have a smaller impact on demand because the other firm is also reducing its price. The different slopes of the two segments of the demand curve result in a kink at point a. Of major interest in this theory is the marginal revenue curve of the firm, denoted in the figure as MR_i. Because of the kink in the demand curve at output $\hat{q}_i$, there is a discontinuity in the marginal revenue curve at that output, represented in the figure by the vertical segment bc. For a small *reduction* in output at $\hat{q}_i$, revenue changes at a rate shown by the distance $b\hat{q}_i$; while for a small *increase* in output at $\hat{q}_i$, revenue changes at the lower rate shown by the distance $c\hat{q}_i$. More formally, we have:

$$MR_i^- = p_i + q_i \frac{\partial p_i}{\partial q_i} \quad \text{for} \quad q_i \leq \hat{q}_i \qquad \text{[B.11]}$$

$$MR_i^+ = p_i + q_i \left[\frac{\partial p_i}{\partial q_i} + \frac{\partial p_i}{\partial q_j} \frac{dq_j}{dq_i} \right] \quad \text{for} \quad q_i \geq \hat{q}_i \qquad \text{[B.12]}$$

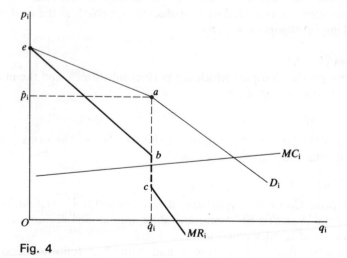

Fig. 4

As a result of the discontinuity of the marginal revenue curve, it is not really appropriate to speak of an *equality* of marginal revenue and marginal cost at the profit maximizing output. Rather, we have as the profit maximizing condition the inequalities:

$$MR_i^- \geq MC_i \geq MR^+ \qquad\qquad\qquad [\text{B.13}]$$

Thus, given the marginal cost curve shown in the figure, $\hat{q}_i$ is the profit maximizing output. A further result of the discontinuity is that quite significant shifts in the marginal cost curve can occur without a change in the profit maximizing output. Thus, in the figure, shifts in MC_i between the limits of points b and c do not cause a change in output. This was a point of great interest in the early discussion of this model, since it was first proposed as an explanation of the apparent 'price rigidity' in oligopolistic markets, i.e. the apparent tendency for prices to change infrequently (but see Stigler (1947), who questions the real extent of such price rigidity).

As a model of oligopoly, the kinked demand curve theory is unsatisfactory in several respects. First is the implausibility of the underlying hypothesis about conjectural variations. If an increase in, say, firm 1's price causes a change in demand for firm 2, surely the profit-maximizing position of the latter will have changed, and so there will be some kind of response? More importantly, the model does not explain how the initial price and output pair $\hat{p}_i$ and $\hat{q}_i$ are determined. They are certainly not determined by the hypothesis about the conjectural variations, since this takes them as given. Recourse might be had to the 'full-cost pricing doctrine', which holds that $\hat{p}_i$ would be determined by some 'conventional' mark-up applied to the cost of production of the good. But this simply redefines the question, since we then have to analyse what determines the mark-up – to suggest that it is more or less arbitrary, and independent both of firms' objectives, and of market conditions, is absurd. Thus, although it has received a good deal of attention in the literature of economics, the kinked demand curve model cannot, in our view, be regarded as a satisfactory approach to the analysis of decision-taking in oligopolistic markets.

Exercise 12B

1.* Two firms produce outputs which are perfect substitutes, and the market demand function is given by:

$$p = a - bq$$

where q is the sum of the outputs of the two firms. The firms possess identical total cost functions, given by:

$$C_i = cq_i \qquad i = 1, 2$$

(a) Adopting Cournot's hypothesis of zero conjectural variation, derive the firms' reaction functions, and show that an equilibrium exists, is stable, and implies equal market shares.

(b) Assuming firm 1 is a leader and firm 2 a follower, find the equilibrium price and outputs. Confirm that this yields a higher profit for firm 1 than under the Cournot model.

(c) Given the hypothesis underlying the kinked demand curve model, discuss the nature of the demand and marginal revenue curves for this case.

2.* Construct an example, using words, graphs or functions, in which equilibrium in the Cournot model is unstable.

3.* Express the leader-follower model of the text mathematically and prove the assertion that the leader's conjectural variation is the slope of the follower's reaction function.

4. To what extent does the leader-follower model involve cooperation between the firms?

C. Collusive oligopoly

The models based on hypotheses about conjectural variations have the common feature that they assume the firms do not communicate and cooperate with each other (though we might perhaps regard the leader-follower model as involving *tacit* co-operation). Yet, as we saw in the introduction to this chapter, since at least the time of Adam Smith it has been known that sellers who recognize their mutual interdependence will tend to do just this. We therefore have to redirect the analysis, to examine the conditions under which cooperation will be achieved and maintained, and the implications for resource allocation of this co-operative or, as it is usually termed in economics, *collusive* behaviour.

The basis for the argument that an incentive always exists for oligopolists to collude can be developed from the observation that the maximum profit which the firms can *jointly* earn would result if they acted as a multi-product monopolist. Let us again take the case of two sellers, with demand and profit functions as set out in [B.1] and [B.6] of the previous section. The *total profit* which can be earned jointly by the two firms is:

$$\pi(q_1, q_2) = \pi_1(q_1, q_2) + \pi_2(q_1, q_2)$$

$$= q_1 D_1(q_1, q_2) + q_2 D_2(q_1, q_2) - C_1(q_1) - C_2(q_2) \qquad [C.1]$$

Maximizing this with respect to q_1 and q_2 yields as necessary conditions:

$$p_1 + q_1 \, \partial p_1/\partial q_1 + q_2 \, \partial p_2/\partial q_1 - C_1'(q_1) = 0 \qquad [C.2]$$

$$p_2 + q_1 \, \partial p_1/\partial q_2 + q_2 \, \partial p_2/\partial q_2 - C_2'(q_2) = 0 \qquad [C.3]$$

which are the usual 'marginal revenue = marginal cost' conditions, but where the marginal revenue of each output now takes account of the effect of changes in that output on demand and revenue of the other. Note that no 'conjectural variation' is involved: the interdependence between the outputs has been 'internalized' by the procedure of maximizing joint profits. In other words, if the firms are colluding so as to maximize joint profits, they are not involved in guessing at each other's reactions. It is assumed that the total

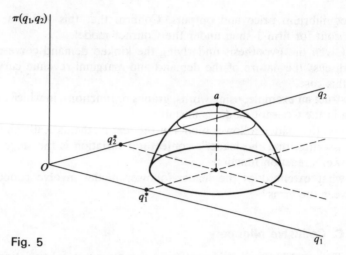

Fig. 5

profit function $\pi(q_1, q_2)$ is strictly concave in both outputs, so that an output pair (q_1^*, q_2^*) which satisfies conditions [C.2] and [C.3] will yield a true maximum. Figure 5 illustrates. The dome-shaped figure is the total profit function $\pi(q_1, q_2)$, the point of maximum profit is at a, and q_1^* and q_2^* are the coordinates of this point. By definition of the maximum, and from the assumption of strict concavity of the profit function, any other output pair produced by the two sellers, whether or not they collude, must yield a smaller profit in total.

Consider now the profit received by each firm from the sale of its optimal output. We have that:

$$\pi(q_1^*, q_2^*) = \pi_1(q_1^*, q_2^*) + \pi_2(q_1^*, q_2^*)$$
$$= \pi_1^* + \pi_2^* = \pi^* \qquad \text{[C.4]}$$

where π_i^*, $i = 1, 2$ denotes the profit received by the i'th firm when each sells its optimal output. However, this need not represent the final distribution of the maximized joint profit, π^*, if *side payments* are possible. Thus, let S denote a lump-sum side payment, with $S > 0$ implying firm 1 pays firm 2 and $S < 0$ implying the reverse. Then the actual profit firm 2 receives is:

$$\hat{\pi}_2 = \pi_2^* + S \qquad \text{[C.5]}$$

while firm 1 receives:

$$\hat{\pi}_1 = \pi_1^* - S \qquad \text{[C.6]}$$

This defines a linear relationship between the profits, inclusive of side payments, received by the firms, which takes the form (by substituting for S from [C.6] in [C.5]):

$$\hat{\pi}_2 = \pi_1^* + \pi_2^* - \hat{\pi}_1 = \pi^* - \hat{\pi}_1 \qquad \text{[C.7]}$$

This relationship, which has a slope of unity, and which must pass through the point (π_1^*, π_2^*) (explain why), is graphed in Fig. 6 as the line $\pi^*\pi^*$.

Clearly, the intercept on each axis must be the total profit π^*, since this is the amount of profit one firm would get if the other received nothing. Point m in the figure corresponds to the profit pair (π_1^*, π_2^*) and so is the point at which the firms would be if no side payment was made. Leftward movements along the line are made by side payments from firm 1 to firm 2, and rightward movements are made by payments from firm 2 to firm 1.

We can now use Fig. 6 to illustrate the gains from collusion. Suppose that initially, the two firms do not collude, but instead pursue an 'arm's length' policy, which, we assume, results in an output pair different from (q_1^*, q_2^*). It follows that the sum of their profits must be less than π^*, and so they cannot be on the line $\pi^*\pi^*$ in Fig. 6 but rather must be at some point below it. For example, suppose that their profits in the non-collusive case are π_1^0 and π_2^0 respectively, so that they are initially at point a in the figure. Then, it is clearly possible for *both* sellers to increase profits by:

(a) agreeing to produce the output pair (q_1^*, q_2^*) thus generating the total profit π^*:

(b) agreeing on a side payment from firm 1 to firm 2, so as to move along the line $\pi^*\pi^*$ to any point on the segment bc, for example a side payment of S^* will result in the profit pair $(\hat{\pi}_1^*, \hat{\pi}_2^*)$ at the point e in the figure.

In other words, the points on the segment bc of the line involve greater profits for both sellers, and therefore there is an inducement to collude. There are clearly strong similarities between this case and the analysis of Pareto optimality in Chapter 17, of the core in Chapter 10 and of bilateral monopoly in Chapter 14. In fact, we could define the set of points on the segment bc as *the core* of this duopoly situation, since movement towards it from a point such as a would not be blocked by a coalition of the two sellers: in other words, such a move can make at least one of them better off and neither worse off. We therefore have an explanation, in modern terminology, of the tendency towards collusion to which Adam Smith drew attention in the *Wealth of Nations*.

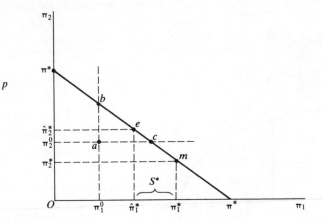

Fig. 6

It may however be objected that the assumption of the possibility of side payments is not tenable. Before considering possible reasons why this may be so, let us consider the consequences for the analysis. If side payments are ruled out, the profit a firm earns can only consist of the proceeds of sale of its own output. Referring again to Figure 6, the point m on the line $\pi^*\pi^*$ is still available to the two firms, since π_1^* results from sale of output q_1^*, and π_2^* from sale of q_2^*.

However, if point m were the only point available, we would not get collusion, because as compared to the existing situation at point a, collusion would involve a loss of profit for firm 2. Only if the existing non-collusive profit pair were in the area southwest of point m would this point be regarded as better by both firms. Can collusion take place in the absence of side payments therefore? We now show that the answer is in general in the affirmative.

Given the initial profit pair (π_1^0, π_2^0), we know that an incentive to collude exists if at least one firm can earn higher profits thereby and the other no lower. We saw that one way of achieving this was by the maximization of joint profits and appropriate side payment. An alternative way, when side payments are ruled out, is simply to find the output pair which maximizes one firm's profit for each given level of profit of the other firm (again note the similarity to the concept of Pareto optimality in welfare economics). Thus, consider the problem;

$$\max_{q_1 q_2} \pi_1 = q_1 D_1(q_1, q_2) - C_1(q_1) \qquad\qquad [\text{C.8}]$$

$$\text{s.t.} \quad \pi_2 = q_2 D_2(q_1, q_2) - C_2(q_2) = \bar{\pi}_2 \qquad\qquad [\text{C.9}]$$

where $\bar{\pi}_2$ is some given value of profits for firm 2. By varying $\bar{\pi}_2$ from zero up to any positive number we like, and solving the problem at each value, we trace out a set of output pairs (q_1, q_2) which are solutions to this problem, and a corresponding set of values of firm 1's profit, π_1. In Fig. 7

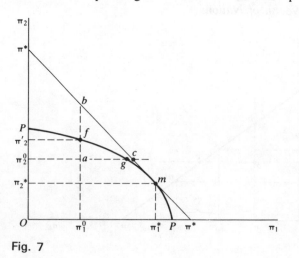

Fig. 7

the curve PP shows the set of pairs of (positive) profits for the two firms which result from this procedure. That is, a point on PP shows the maximum value of π_1 consistent with the co-ordinate value of π_2.

Two things should be noted about this curve. First, it is drawn strictly concave to the origin, reflecting the assumptions that an increase in firm 2's profit must imply a reduction in the maximum level of firm 1's profit, and that successive equal increments in firm 2's profit require increasingly large decreases in that of firm 1. These assumptions are consistent with the shape of the total profit function $\pi(q_1, q_2)$ shown in Fig. 5.

Secondly, the curve PP coincides with the line $\pi^*\pi^*$ (reproduced from Fig. 6) only at point m. This point is common to both because if we set $\bar{\pi}_2 = \pi_2^*$, so that in the problem in [C.8] we wish to find the maximum profit for firm 1 subject to the constraint that firm 2 earns a profit of π_2^*, then this maximum profit is exactly π_1^*. (See Question 2 of Exercise 12C, which asks you to supply the reasoning.) The curve lies below the line at every other point because we can only generate profit pairs other than (π_1^*, π_2^*) by varing output pairs away from (q_1^*, q_2^*), and so the sum of the two firms' profits must fall below π^*, implying profit pairs below the line $\pi^*\pi^*$. Thus when side payments are ruled out, the colluding firms cannot do better, and may do worse, than if they were possible.

However, collusion still is in general better than non-collusion, as can be seen in the figure. Given the initial position at point a, it is possible for both firms to increase their profits by moving to a point on the arc fg of PP. (Why must point a lie on or below PP?) Thus, the core of this oligopoly situation when side payments are ruled out is the set of points on fg. The move to the core would of course be achieved by the firms' agreeing to adjust their outputs (and consequently their prices) to values which constitute a solution to the problem in [C.8] and [C.9], with the $\bar{\pi}_2$ value in that problem being taken at some point on the vertical axis between π_2^0 and π_2' in Fig. 7. The only case in which there would not be an incentive to collude would be that in which the initial non-collusive situation was already in the core; that is, in terms of Fig. 7, point a already lies on the curve PP.

There is then an incentive for oligopolists to collude, which will be greater when side payments are possible than when not, but which nevertheless will still in general exist in the latter case. Of course, this does not in itself establish that firms *will* collude. There are a number of factors which may prevent the realization of a collusive agreement. Chief among these are:

(a) *Failure to agree on terms.* Although it pays firms to cooperate to increase joint profits, the choice of a specific set of outputs, prices and profits involves them also in direct conflict. For example, in the case where side payments are possible, once firms have agreed to maximize joint profits they still have to decide on the amount of the side payment, where their interests are in direct opposition. On the face of it, it would appear irrational if the problem of agreeing on a division of the spoils ruled out their acquisition in the first place. It should be remembered however that in reality firms may have incomplete information and different expectations and beliefs about market conditions. Given that the profits, costs and demand conditions for one firm may not be completely known by the other, it pays each firm to overstate the amount of profit it would get in the absence of collusion, in order to increase its profit share under the collusive agreement. The case might arise therefore where no agreement could satisfy the (inflated) profit demands of the sellers. Firms may also genuinely differ in the profit outcomes they expect to result from given output allocations or pricing decisions, and this may make agreement more difficult. Two further complicating factors are, first, that agreement may have to extend beyond prices and outputs to include product quality, advertising expenditures, investment plans, etc; secondly, that there may be more than just two sellers involved, since this discussion is intended to apply to oligopoly in general and not just duopoly, and we expect that the difficulty in achieving agreement increases with the number of firms. In the latter case, there is the added complication that coalitions of firms may form, which may use their market power to coerce weaker firms to accept an agreement giving them a relatively small share in the excess profits. Little is known in general about the dynamics of the process by which collusive agreements are formed, although it is an important aspect of oligopoly behaviour.

(b) *The legal system.* In most Western industrialized countries legislation exists which is designed to regulate behaviour in oligopolistic markets. In the USA, collusion among sellers is illegal *per se*, so that oligopolists who seek to collude must do so in secret, accepting the risk of penalties such as fines and even imprisonment of executives, if detected. In the UK formal documents embodying collusive agreements have to be registered with the Registrar of Restrictive Practice Agreements, who may then bring an action in a special court, the Restrictive Practices Court, to end a specific agreement. Collusion among sellers is not illegal *per se*, and there are agreements which have been upheld, on the grounds that they operate 'in the public interest'. Even where agreements have been ended, it does not appear to be impossible to collude provided the terms of the collusion are not embodied in a written document. There appears to be no mechanism by which informal collusion can always be detected.

In general therefore the legal system places constraints on the formation of collusive agreements. The mere fact of illegality might lead law-abiding businessmen not to collude, though there is a good deal of evidence to suggest that covert or informal collusive agreements exist. Where collusion does take place, the effect of the legal constraints is to determine its form. Outputs and prices may have to be secretly agreed upon, and more or less elaborate devices for dividing the market may have to be employed. When the need arises to vary prices (usually upward) the sellers may separately announce increases over a couple of weeks, rather than making a common announcement of a simultaneous change. The system of *price leadership* may be employed, whereby one firm initiates all price changes and the others follow. This can be distinguished from the leader-follower model of the previous section in that the price-leader will not be maximizing his own profit subject only to the reaction functions of the other firms, but rather is implementing *agreed* policies which take into account the profit objectives of *all* firms. However, it may often be the case that the price leader is the dominant firm in the market, and, because of its market power, the agreement may represent a point in the core which is relatively more favourable to it.

Given that the difficulties in negotiating an agreement, and the constraints which may be presented by the legal framework, can be overcome, we have the question of the nature of the market equilibrium which will result. The analysis of the incentive to collude which we have just carried out suggests some hypotheses about this. First, if side payments are possible, then the firms will maximize joint profits and the price and output policies are essentially those of a multi-product, multi-plant monopolist. The equilibrium position in the market is described by the necessary conditions in [C.2] and [C.3], at least for the two-firm case, and of course these results can easily be generalized. Where side payments are not possible – perhaps because they would be clear evidence of collusion where this is illegal – then the required profit distribution under the agreement must be achieved by varying prices and outputs away from the joint profit maximizing levels. It has been argued above that the equilibrium will have the property that it maximizes one firm's profit subject to the given level of profit of the other, and so the solution to the problem in [C.8] and [C.9] will be the equilibrium. Necessary conditions for a maximum of firm 1's profit subject to a given profit level for firm 2 are:

$$p_1 + q_1\, \partial p_1/\partial q_1 + \lambda q_2\, \partial p_2/\partial q_1 - C_1'(q_1) = 0 \qquad \text{[C.10]}$$

$$p_2 + q_2\, \partial p_2/\partial q_2 + (q_1/\lambda)\, \partial p_1/\partial q_2 - C_2'(q_2) = 0 \qquad \text{[C.11]}$$

where λ is the Lagrange multiplier associated with the constraint, and can be shown to be positive when the profit constraint is binding. A solution to these conditions will yield a profit pair on the curve *PP* in Fig. 7, but the exact location will depend on the specified level of $\bar{\pi}_2$. This in turn will depend, *inter alia*, on the initial profit position of the two firms, and the bargaining over the precise position within the core to which they agree to move. However, it is possible to make some general statements about the nature of the equilibrium position:

1. since the derivatives of each price with respect to each output are negative, we have:

$$p_1 > p_1 + q_1\, \partial p_1/\partial q_1 + \lambda q_2\, \partial p_2/\partial q_1 = C_1'(q_1) \qquad \text{[C.12]}$$

and similarly for good 2. Thus, prices exceed marginal costs, and so the market equilibrium is closer in nature to monopoly than to competition.

2. However, since in general the equilibrium is unlikely to be at point *m* in Fig. 6 (where, incidentally, $\lambda = 1$), outputs and prices will not be those predicted by joint profit maximization. We can use the case shown in Fig. 7 to illustrate the kind of departure which might arise. At point m in the figure, firm 1 is earning 'too much' and firm 2 'too little' profit relative to points in the core. If firm 1 then raises its price and reduces its output from that at point m, this will cause an increase in demand, output and profit for firm 2. Hence a leftward move around PP can be brought about by reducing firm 1's output and increasing that of firm 2. Thus, in this case, the collusive agreement will involve a greater market share for firm 2 than would exist under joint profit maximization.

This concludes our discussion of the incentive to collusion and the nature of the price output solution which results. We now turn to the third aspect of collusive oligopoly, the question of the stability of the system of collusion.

Stability of collusion

Given that firms reach a collusive agreement, with or without side payments, and establish an equilibrium pattern of prices and outputs in the market, we are interested in the question of whether the collusive system will be maintained over time. A way of developing an answer to this question is to consider the stresses to which the agreement might be subject. We can classify these stresses as either external or internal in origin. One external source of stress has already been mentioned: the legal system of the economy may increase the difficulties of reaching and perpetuating a cooperative equilibrium and may even rule one out. General fluctuations in market demand, and rapid technological change, also pose problems. Significant changes in cost and demand conditions require revisions to the cooperative equilibrium, thus imposing costs and reintroducing the difficulties of negotiation. Falls in demand and the development of excess capacity may induce firms to act irrationally and compete, ('Some fool always panics') the pressures to do so being greater, the lower are average variable costs relative to total costs, and the less elastic is market demand.

The internal threats to the maintenance of collusion stem from a basic property of the collusive equilibrium. As long as all other sellers maintain their agreed prices, any one firm will in general find it profitable to increase its sales at or just below the agreed price, since this will be the marginal revenue of each unit of these sales, and we have just seen that this will exceed marginal cost at the collusive equilibrium. One way in which a firm may try to increase its sales at the collusive price is by advertising and sales promotion, which has been observed to be markedly high in oligopolistic consumer goods markets such as cigarettes, beer, detergents and cosmetics. The problem is that if each firm attempts to increase its sales in this way, there is a competitive cancelling out of each other's efforts (since overall market demand is relatively unaffected), and firms may find they are dissipating their profits in trying to keep up with the general level of marketing activity. Product quality variations and product innovation may also be used in the same way. The existence of 'non-price competition' may

then place strains on the collusive agreement, and may lead to the development of price competition, initiated by companies which are losing out in the
marketing war. It may then be necessary to extend the collusive agreement
to include instruments of competition other than price.

A second source of stress on the collusive agreement, which again
arises out of the profitability, at the collusive price, of increased sales, is the
tendency for excess capacity to develop. Firms may try to increase their
market shares in the long run by investing in greater capacity. However, if all
firms do this then this will lead to over-expansion of total capacity and
subsequent pressures to reduce prices and increase capacity utilization.
Again, therefore, it may be necessary to extend the collusive agreement to
include investment plans and future capacity.

Finally, an important threat to the stability of collusion arises from
the possibility of *secret* price competition, or 'cheating'. Open price competition clearly would break up the collusive agreement and so would lead all
firms to a worse outcome than under collusion. However, if a firm can make
extra sales at a price just below the collusive price without being detected,
then it will increase its profits, provided also that the other sellers are
adhering to the agreement. But if each seller perceives this, then each will
want to cheat, as long as this would go undetected, and we would therefore
have the undermining of the collusive agreement, with all firms worse off
than if no-one cheated. The question then is, can we construct a theory
which will explain and predict the incidence of cheating in an oligopolistic
market? The following are the elements of such a theory.

We can first describe the situation with the help of some concepts
from game theory. Suppose there are just two firms, each of which may
choose one of two courses of action or *strategies:* adhere to the collusive
agreement, or cheat by giving secret discounts. The following *pay off
matrix* illustrates the situation, on the assumption that *some amount of
cheating can be carried out without detection.* The number on the left of each
cell in the matrix shows the profit pay off to firm 1 if both firms choose the
strategies corresponding to that cell, e.g. if both firms adhere to the
agreement firm 1 gets £100. The number on the right is firm 2's profit, e.g. if
both firms adhere firm 2 gets £80.

Table 1

		Firm 2			
		Adhere		Cheat	
Firm 1	Adhere	100	80	75	90
	Cheat	120	50	90	70

The numbers in the matrix, which of course are purely illustrative, embody
the following principles which are fundamental to the situation:
   (a) worst of all is to adhere to the agreement when your competitor
       cheats;
   (b) best of all is to cheat when he adheres;

(c) the payoffs when *both* cheat are lower than those when both adhere.

The reader should confirm that the numbers reflect these principles.

From the payoff matrix, it is clear that the individually rational strategy is to cheat: whatever firm 2 does, firm 1 makes a higher profit by cheating rather than adhering to the agreement, and similarly for firm 2. However, if both adopt the cheat strategy, they are worse off than if they both adhered to the agreement – the payoffs in the top lefthand cell exceed the corresponding payoffs in the bottom righthand cell. This is the dilemma, the conflict between individual and collective rationality, which confronts oligopolists in this situation.† Will cheating then take place? It is quite conceivable that the firms in this situation will act in a collectively 'responsible' way, and choose to adhere to the agreement. For example, the existing system of education and social *mores* may be directed at reinforcing collectively rational rather than individually rational behaviour ('team spirit' as an element in educating the future captains of industry?). However, to oligopolists wishing to maintain a collusive agreement, a more reliable course of action would be to try to change the structure of the payoff matrix by making the profit from cheating (when others adhere) less than that from adhering. This would of course be done by making it likely that cheating would be detected, and devising some kind of penalty which would more than offset the gain from cheating. Let us now consider, therefore, the questions of detection and sanctions to be applied against cheats.

Suppose the oligopolists operate in a world in which in the absence of price competition buyers always buy from the same seller. Then cheating could easily be detected, since a switch by a buyer from one seller to another would be evidence of cheating. However, as G. J. Stigler (1964) has pointed out, in general firms do not operate in such a world. Stigler goes on to construct a model of cheating based on the observation that buyers have a propensity to switch from one seller to another from time to time, in a way which is not predictable with certainty, and this provides scope for profitable cheating.

Thus suppose buyers make purchases from sellers once a week, and that each buyer may, with some given probability, switch from one seller to another from week to week. Then, each seller will expect to lose some of his own past customers each week, and to gain some of the customers of other firms. Moreover, the precise number acquired and lost will, because of random factors, vary from week to week, though each firm will have some idea of the weekly number of buyers it ought to lose and gain *on average*, and of the degree of variability of this number about the average. Using standard methods of probability theory, it can be shown that the greater the propensity of buyers to switch between sellers, the greater will be the

† *Note:* The general structure of the situation corresponds to the game known as the *prisoner's dilemma* in game theory. For an exposition, see Luce and Raiffa (1966), and Rapaport (1960).

variability about the average of the weekly number who switch, and also the greater the average. It is precisely this variability which offers scope to the cheat. He may approach some of his own customers, and also some of his rivals', and offer them secret price cuts if they will stay with or switch to him. Assuming they do so, he will suffer a smaller loss of his own buyers, and a larger gain in those of his rivals, than he could have expected. The other sellers may notice that the firm in question is doing well, but they cannot necessarily infer cheating, since it may have been due to purely random factors. They are in fact involved in a problem of weighing up evidence, or *hypothesis testing*. They have to consider the *probability* that such a pattern of switching would be observed as a result of random variations, and then decide whether it is so unlikely, that cheating must have been going on. Suppose, for example, that they observe a pattern of switching which would be produced by random factors once every hundred weeks (a probability of 0.01). They may decide that this is just too unlikely to have happened by chance, and take it as evidence of cheating. On the other hand, if the switching pattern could be observed once every twenty weeks (a probability of 0.05) they may accept randomness. The more suspicious the sellers are, in the sense that the less unlikely a switching pattern has to be for them to conclude there has been cheating, the less scope there is for profitable cheating. However, as long as they will accept as consistent with random factors *some* pattern of switching which differs from the average, cheating up to this level will be 'undetected' and therefore profitable. Hence, we are back with the dilemma set out above, and it is very likely that the individually rational, but collectively sub-optimal, outcome will result.

However, this highly suggestive analysis glosses over two important points. Clearly, each firm's choice of a critical level of probability for the hypothesis test is crucial for the profitability of cheating, but this choice is not analysed by the theory. In fact, in choosing its critical level, each firm is involved in balancing out two types of error: the lower the critical level, and the less suspicious it is, the greater the losses it will sustain if cheating actually takes place, the greater the profits to the cheat, and so the greater the incidence of cheating in the market. However, the greater the critical level, and the more suspicious the firm is, the more likely it is to accuse someone of cheating when in fact the observed pattern of switching *was* due to random factors. Hence the firm must weigh up the costs of letting itself be cheated, against the cost of false accusation, in setting its critical level. The former can be quite well specified, being the profit on the sales gained by cheating, but the theory says nothing about the latter. This is important, because the theory cannot generate testable predictions about the incidence of cheating in markets if it can say nothing about the critical levels of tests which firms will choose.

The second point is closely related to this: the theory does not provide for the *consequences* of detection of cheating. 'Detection' may exist in two senses. Sellers may obtain unambiguous evidence that one of them has given secret price reductions, e.g. from the buyers themselves, who report it

in order to induce matching price cuts, or when the cheat withdraws his offer†
and from information leaks. Alternatively, they may decide to reject the
hypothesis of randomness and accept that of cheating, even though there is a
chance that it is wrong. This might well occur if the cheat has guessed
wrongly at his rivals' critical level, or 'degree of suspiciousness' (note that it
is in each firm's interest to keep its critical level secret). In case of either
kind of detection, the aggrieved firms must decide what they are going to do
about it, and the form of their retaliation provides the answer to the
question of the cost of a false accusation. We can conceive of two types of
response to detection of cheating, apart from that of 'no response', which is
an invitation to be cheated.

The first would be a quasi-judicial procedure in which the evidence
of cheating could be assessed, the cheat allowed to state his case, and a
penalty in the form of a lump sum 'fine' exacted, The advantage of this
procedure is that it minimizes the cost of the punishment to the enforcer,
and also reduces the risk of false accusation. An example of this kind of
procedure is provided by the law on resale price maintenance in the UK
before its repeal in 1968, where a manufacturer could take a retailer
to a court of law and extract damages if the retailer was pricing his product
below a specified amount. Clearly, this kind of situation requires the
collusive agreement between the duopolists to have actual or quasi-legal
status, a situation which is relatively rare.

The second type of response is the imposition of market sanctions:
the enforcers would cut their prices, thus inflicting losses of profit on the
cheat, and the extent and duration of the price cut would be chosen so as to
punish the cheat adequately. However, the problem here is that this policy
also inflicts losses on the enforcers, and this limits the power of this sanction.
Again the relative ability of the sellers to sustain losses will be an important
determinant of the extent to which cheating can be punished. A large,
diversified firm with strong reserves would find it much easier to inflict
punitive losses on a cheat than vice versa. Hence, other things being equal,
we would expect more cheating in markets in which firms were similar in
their ability to sustain losses, and, where cheating takes place, it is more
likely to be by the stronger partner than by the weaker.

To summarize this attempt at a generalization of Stigler's analysis, a
potential cheat is someone who weighs up the profits from cheating, against
the probability that he will get caught, and the losses that will be inflicted on
him if he is. The probability of detection depends on the likelihood of
information leaks, and the uncertainty of his knowledge about the critical
level chosen by the other firm. The losses which can be inflicted depend on
whether quasi-legal or market sanctions can be imposed and, if it is the
latter, on the losses which these imply for the enforcers, in relation to their

† *Note:* The *duration* of the secret price cuts is obviously important. If the cheat
maintains his offer indefinitely, then a *succession* of 'unlikely' switching patterns will
be clear evidence of cheating to the other sellers. But if the cheat withdraws the offer
the buyers may retaliate by giving him away.

own profits and reserves. Within this framework, we can analyse the circumstances under which the probability of detection, and the magnitude of punishment, can be set in such a way as to make cheating unattractive in a market. Indeed, such an analysis is very close to the analysis of crime and punishment in society, as suggested by G. Becker (1968).

Exercise 12C

1.* Two firms produce outputs which are perfect substitutes, and the market demand function is:

$$p = a - bq$$

where q is total output of the good. The firms have identical cost functions, of the form:

$$C_i = cq_i^2 \qquad i = 1, 2$$

where C_i is total cost and q_i is the ith firm's output.

(a) Find the joint profit maximizing output pair, and show that it implies that production costs of the total output q are minimized.

(b) Assuming that side payments are possible, show in a diagram the set of possible profit pairs which the firms may achieve by collusion

(c) Assuming that side payments are not possible, show the set of possible profit pairs which the firms can achieve by collusion. Take a profit pair which does not correspond to the joint profit maximum, and compare the output pair associated with it to that obtained at the latter. In particular, show that production costs will not be minimized in the absence of side payments.

2. Explain why, in Fig. 7, the point m is common to both $\pi^*\pi^*$ and PP (Hint: show that if $\pi_1^* + \pi_2^*$ is the maximum possible total profit, then maximizing π_1 when $\pi_2 = \pi_2^*$ must yield π_1^*.)

3.* Discuss the formation and subsequent history of the OPEC cartel in the light of the analysis of this section.

4. Explain why, in the presence of excess capacity, the extent of price-cutting in an oligopoly will be greater the lower are average variable costs and less elastic is market demand.

5.* Discuss the similarities and differences between the problems of preventing crime in a modern society, and of preventing cheating in collusive oligopoly.

6.* Many contracts for supplying goods to central or local government are put out to open tender, i.e. firms are asked to submit bids and the bids made are disclosed by the government when the successful tender is announced. The rationale of the procedure is that it reduces the possibility of bribery of the civil servants awarding the tender. Does the analysis of section C suggest any possible disadvantages?

7.* Why are dealers' rings at auctions likely to be stable cartels?

D. Conclusions

This chapter has considered two types of approach to the analysis of price and output determination in situations of strategic interdependence among sellers. The first is based on hypotheses about conjectural variations, i.e. competitors' reactions to the firm's own output decisions, and leads to a number of models with different, though determinate, equilibrium solutions. The second is directed explicitly at an aspect of behaviour disregarded in these models, the tendency for firms to communicate and collude. It leads to an analysis of the incentive to collude and the obstacles to a collusive agreement which may exist; the nature of collusive equilibrium; and the ability of an agreement to survive in the face of internal and external stresses. Several elements of the second approach are still relatively tentative and undeveloped, and, in particular, more needs to be known about the dynamics of the process by which agreements are formed, and the methods by which cheating is controlled. Pursuit of these questions would be rewarding, since the view of ologopolistic markets as essentially collusive seems to have more relevance to reality than that which sees firms guessing at arm's length about each other's reactions.

References and further reading

For a discussion of the kinked demand curve theory see:

> **G. J. Stigler.** 'The kinky oligopoly demand curve and rigid prices', *Journal of Political Economy*, 1947.
>
> **P. M. Sweezy.** 'Demand under conditions of oligopoly', *Journal of Political Economy*, 1939.

An interesting account of actual behaviour in an oligopolistic industry is given in:

> **E. M. Loescher.** *Imperfect Collusion in the Cement Industry*, Harvard University Press, 1959.

Underlying the modern analysis of oligopoly is the theory of games. Excellent expositions of the theory are given in:

> **R. D. Luce** and **D. Raiffa.** *Games and Decisions*, John Wiley, New York, 1966.
>
> **A. Rapoport.** *Fights, Games and Debates*, University of Michigan Press, 1960.

Applications of the theory to oligopolistic markets can be found in:

> **M. Shubik.** *Strategy and Market Structure*, John Wiley, New York, 1959.
>
> **L. Telser.** *Competition, Collusion and Game Theory*, Macmillan, London, 1972.

A rigorous analysis of cheating in oligopoly was presented by:

> **G. J. Stigler** 'A theory of oligopoly', *Journal of Political Economy*, 1964.

A general analysis of cheating in social groups, which we usually call crime, and which has direct applicability to oligopoly theory, can be found in:

> **G. S. Becker** 'Crime and punishment', *Journal of Political Economy*, vol. 76, 1968.

Chapter 13

Alternative theories of the firm

A. Review of the theory of the profit maximizing firm

In the preceding chapters we have analysed and applied extensively the theory of the profit maximizing firm. Let us review briefly the main elements of this theory. The firm is assumed to confront itself with an optimization problem. It wishes to choose the quantities of its outputs and inputs (and possibly other choice variables such as advertising) in such a way as to maximize profits. It is constrained in this on the one hand by market conditions and on the other by the technological possibilities of producing outputs from inputs. If its output and input markets are competitive, they determine for the firm a set of output and input prices, which the firm takes as given in evaluating the profitability of alternative production plans. If it has monopoly power in output markets, or monopsony power in input markets, then it faces given relationships or functions, which it must incorporate into its maximizing procedure (if markets are oligopolistic, then, as we saw in Chapter 12, the decisions of one firm cannot be considered in isolation from those of its close rivals, and indeed the notion of straightforward *maximization* of profits may lose its meaning, though in this chapter we ignore this problem). The technological possibilities can be summarized by the firm's production function, or, more generally, by its production set.

Certain implications follow from this theory, which can be regarded as hypotheses about the behaviour of firms:

(a) The firm will always produce on the boundary of its production set, i.e. it will not use technologically inefficient production techniques.

(b) For any given set of output quantities, it uses those quantities of inputs which minimize costs of production at the prevailing input prices (subject to constraints imposed by the rate at which it is feasible, or profitable, to vary the quantities of inputs, c.f. the distinction between the short run and the long run).

(c) It chooses those output levels which maximize total profits, defined as the difference between revenues and costs (where the latter must include all opportunity costs, whether they exist as outlays or have to be imputed).

(d) If we consider the firm's decisions over time, it must choose a time
path of outputs and inputs (including its stocks of capital goods).
Profit is a flow associated with its choices at any period of time, and
so it is insufficient to stipulate that it maximizes 'profits'. Rather, we
can show (see Ch. 15) that in order to maximize the wealth of its
owners, it chooses time paths of inputs and outputs which maximize
the *present value* of the firm's profit stream, using a market determined discount rate. Thus, although it suffices to talk about the
'profit maximizing firm' when we have in mind an atemporal model,
we should really regard the theory as concerned with owners' wealth
maximization.

These hypotheses concern the equilibrium position of the firm, i.e.
the choices it will make for a given set of underlying data and relationships.
It is then natural to develop a further set of hypotheses, concerned with the
responses of the firm's choices to changes in these data and relationships.
This of course is the problem of comparative statics analysis.

The results of this analysis can be summarized very simply if we
describe the firm's equilibrium position in the following way: at the profit
maximizing position, the marginal profit of each of the firm's decision
variables must be zero, by definition of a maximum. The marginal profit of
an *input* is its marginal revenue product *minus* its marginal buying cost
(= its price in competitive input markets). The marginal profit of an *output* is
its marginal revenue (= its price in competitive output markets) *minus* its
marginal production costs. If any change takes place which causes the
marginal profit of a decision variable to become positive at the initial
optimum, then its quantity will be increased until its marginal profit is again
zero. If the change causes the marginal profit to become negative at the
initial optimum, the variable will be reduced in amount until its marginal
profit is again zero. (These results, of course, are assuming something about
the shapes of the underlying relationships: see Chapters 7–9.) If marginal
profit is left unchanged at the initial optimum, then so will be the chosen
quantity of the variable (subject to a qualification mentioned below). It
follows that we can predict the qualitative effects of some change once we
have found its effects on the marginal profits of inputs.

The comparative statics analysis fulfills two important functions.
First, it enables us to derive general relationships between the underlying
parameters of decisions, especially prices, on the one hand, and the decision
variables of the firm on the other. These then form the bases for further
analyses of single markets, small groups of markets, or the entire general
equilibrium of the economy. These analyses are fundamental to all branches
of microeconomics, whether concerned with 'positive' predictions, practical
policy formation, or the construction of a general theoretical system such as
the Walrasian system of Chapter 16.

Second, it provides us with the main areas in which we may test the
validity of the theory itself. Given that we do not regard the theory as
self-evidently true, we need to ask whether the hypotheses it generates are

refuted or not by the decisions which firms actually take. It will usually be very difficult to test the hypotheses concerning the equilibrium positions of firms, since this would involve quantification of the underlying revenue, cost, and production relationships. (For example, how would you determine whether the marginal profit of a particular output were zero?) Furthermore, this quantification would have to be of the relationships *as perceived by the firm*, since it is these which determine the decisions the firm takes. Given that data are usually in *ex post* form, while the relevant relationships are all *ex ante*, this quantification may be an impossible task.

On the other hand, it may be much easier to observe the way in which firms react to changes in the environment: do firms adjust prices and outputs following an increase in profits tax? Do firms respond to significant changes in relative input prices or technology by changing input mix? Of course, it will still not be easy to answer such questions in a world in which many things often change at once, so that we must disentangle the various effects from the overall resultant change: in other words, the 'other things being equal' assumption on which comparative statics analysis is based is not often fulfilled. Nevertheless, tests of hypotheses about reactions to changes seem to be more feasible than tests relating to equilibrium positions.

The preceding paragraph suggested that the theory of the profit maximizing firm is not self-evidently true: its hypotheses are capable of being refuted, otherwise it would not be a theory. Although it forms the basis of much of microeconomics, there is a long history of criticism of the theory and relatively recently several alternative theories have been proposed. The criticisms were considered in Chapter 6. In this chapter, we examine some of the proposed 'alternative' theories of the firm.

B. The entrepreneurial firm

It has sometimes been argued that the axiom of profit maximization has more plausibility when it refers to owner-controlled, or *entrepreneurial*, firms. The owner receives the firm's profit as income, and hence to maximize his profit is to maximize his income, a reasonable-sounding aim. T. Scitovsky, however, suggests that matters are not so straightforward. The argument is as follows: in generating the firm's 'gross income' (defined as revenue less all costs *except that of his own services*), the entrepreneur must expend *time and effort*. If we regard the amount of effort as constant per unit time, then we can measure the entrepreneur's input in terms of, say, the number of hours per day, up to a maximum of 24, he devotes to the work of the firm. We expect that, at least over some range, the firm's gross income increases with the entrepreneurial input – he devotes more time to getting business and controlling costs – but at a diminishing rate. The curve OP' in Fig. 1 shows the relation between gross income per day (clearly a longer time period could just as well be chosen), measured on the vertical axis, and input, measured in hours per day, along the horizontal (cf. the analysis in Ch. 5 above). It is assumed that up to some point $\hat{E}$, gross income increases,

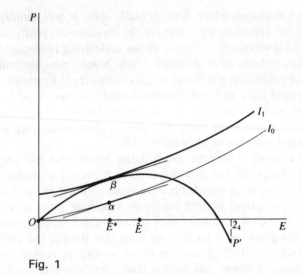

Fig. 1

though at a diminishing rate; after $\hat{E}$, it actually decreases until E reaches its upper limit of 24 hours (the presence of negative marginal profitability is inessential to the argument).

In defining gross income, we excluded any allowance for the entrepreneur's imputation of cost for his own services, which means that this does not correspond to the definition of profit used when we talk about the theory of profit maximization, namely that measured after *all* opportunity costs have been subtracted from revenue. How then do we measure the true profit defined in this latter sense? Consider the indifference curve OI_0 drawn in the figure (The reader should be able to explain its slope and curvature.) The fact that it meets the origin indicates that it represents the set of combinations of gross income and effort which are indifferent to the origin, the point at which the entrepreneur devotes zero effort to the firm. Hence the curve shows the minimum income he must be paid to induce him to supply the corresponding amount of effort *as opposed to doing nothing*. We can therefore impute, as the opportunity cost of his services, that amount of income on OI_0 which corresponds to any given amount of effort (which implies that the foregone alternative is that of doing nothing). This suggests we can calculate his pure profit by subtracting vertically the curve OI_0 from the curve OP, since the corresponding distance at any value of E is the amount of profit over and above his minimum supply price. We then interpret the axiom of profit maximization as implying: the entrepreneur will choose that level of E at which the difference between OP' and OI_0 is greatest. In the figure, this corresponds to the value E^*, since the slope of OI_0 at α is equal to the slope of OP' at β, and the second-order conditions for a maximum are also satisfied.

Now, under what conditions would an entrepreneur actually *choose* E^*? The answer is provided by indifference curve I_1. For E^* to be chosen, there must be tangency between an indifference curve and OP' at point β on OP'. Tangency at some other point implies that the entrepreneur chooses to supply effort which does not maximize profit. But the condition of tangency at β implies an important restriction on the nature of the indifference curves, and hence on the tastes and psychology of the entrepreneur. It implies that at E^* the slope of indifference curve I_1 must be equal to the slope of indifference curve I_0.

That is, the marginal rate of substitution of income for effort must be the same at points α and β.

We can immediately generalize this result. Whatever the precise shape of OP', profit will always be maximized at a value of E at which the slope of OI_0 is equal to the slope of OP'. At this value of E the slope of the indifference curve tangent to OP' must be equal to the slope of OI_0. But this can only be true for *all possible OP'* curves, if, taking any vertical line, the slopes of all indifference curves at their points of intersection with this line are equal to each other and to the corresponding point on OI_0: in other words, all the indifference curves are parallel to, and vertical displacements of, each other. Figure 2 illustrates. Along any vertical line, the slopes of successive indifference curves are equal (the reader should confirm that, for any OP' curve drawn in, profit will be maximized).

To express this technical result in more general language, it means that the money value the entrepreneur places on his marginal unit of effort is independent of his total income, and depends only on his level of effort. The businessman who, as he gets richer, spends more time on the golf course and at the races, even though the marginal return to his effort is the same, cannot be a profit maximizer. So we see that on *a priori* grounds, even for the entrepreneurial firm, profit maximization is something of a special case, since it requires specific restrictions on the indifference map of the

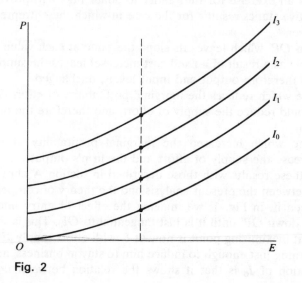

Fig. 2

entrepreneur. The analysis also gives us interesting insights into the psychology of profit maximization: the profit maximizer does not value his time more, at the margin, no matter how rich he becomes (effort remaining constant), nor less if he becomes poor; he does not sell up and retire to the South of France on winning the football pools. We do not wish to discuss the *a priori* plausibility of this kind of psychology, but simply note that the testable implications of the theory of profit maximization have been extended by this analysis to include reactions of the entrepreneur's supply of effort to changes in its marginal returns and in his total income.

We now consider further testable implications of this theory, for the case in which the entrepreneur does in fact seek to maximize profits. First, does the entrepreneur minimize costs? He may in fact appear not to be doing so, though this conclusion would follow from incorrectly ignoring his own opportunity costs. Thus, referring again to Fig. 1, the solution at E^* must be to the left of $\hat{E}$, at which gross income (excluding entrepreneurial opportunity costs) is maximized. How do we account for the increase in gross income between E^* and $\hat{E}$? If the entrepreneur buys inputs and sells outputs in perfect markets, then increased effort may increase his profit by increasing output, and/or by increasing productive efficiency, thus lowering costs. If the latter is the case, then the equilibrium at E^* would imply that there is scope for further efficiency improvements and cost reductions, which would increase gross profit if only the entrepreneur would devote more effort to the business. However, this is ignoring his own costs. The meaning of point E^* is that the marginal cost of increased effort (*when measured by the slope of OI_0*) is greater than the marginal reduction in production cost resulting from that effort (measured by the slope of OP'), and so this implies that when we take into account the entrepreneur's own costs, total costs are indeed minimized.

It is left as an exercise for the reader to adapt Fig. 1 to prove the following comparative statics results: for the case in which the entrepreneur *is* a profit maximizer:

(a) any shift in OP' which leaves its slope the same at each value of E (for example as a result of a fixed cost increase) leaves the supply of effort, and therefore output and input levels, unchanged.

(b) any change which reduces the marginal profitability of effort (slope of OP') would reduce the supply of effort, and therefore the output of the firm.

(c) any change which increased the marginal profitability of effort would increase the supply of effort and the firm's output.

Compare these results with those described in section A above.

The link between the present analysis and the theory of competitive markets can be seen if, in Fig. 1, we imagine the effect of entry into the market as pushing down OP' until it is just tangential to OI_0. This is shown in Fig. 3. The profit maximizing point is now at δ, with effort supply $\bar{E}$. The entrepreneur is earning just enough to induce him to stay in business, and so another interpretation of I_0 is that it shows the relation between *normal*

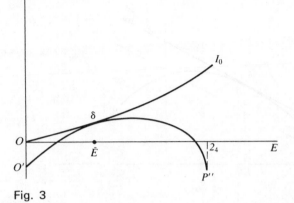

Fig. 3

profit and entrepreneurial effort. If $O'P''$ were to shift down even further, then the entrepreneur would leave the industry. Note also that even if the entrepreneur had not initially been a profit maximizer, his final long-run equilibrium solution would be as shown in Fig. 3, so that *in the long-run, under conditions of free entry, profit maximizers and profit non-maximizers are indistinguishable.*

Suppose now that there exists a competitive market, on which the entrepreneur may buy and sell entrepreneurial inputs at a fixed price. That is, the entrepreneur could run his own business, employ someone else to run it, or become employed by someone to run a business for them, it being assumed that the nature of the work is precisely the same. Moreover, we assume that he feels no particular preference for 'being his own boss', which, though perhaps not typical, simplifies things considerably. Then what effect does this have on the analysis? We find, interestingly enough, that in the most general case, the Scitovsky conclusions become invalid. The reason is that the opportunity cost of the entrepreneur's effort is not now the sum of money required to induce him to work rather than do nothing (retire?) but rather the sum which he could get if he sold his services on the market instead of supplying them to his 'own firm'. Figure 4 illustrates the analysis.

The line OW has slope equal to the going price per unit of entrepreneurial effort, and shows the income-effort combinations open to the entrepreneur if he sold his services *on the market alone.* However, suppose that he can also run his own business, with OP' the curve of gross income, as before. Consider the line $W'W'$, parallel to OW, drawn so that it is tangent to OP' at β. This line shows the income-effort combinations open to the entrepreneur, *once he has fixed the total input of effort into the firm at E^*.* To see this, note that with effort at E^*, the gross income from the firm is given by $E^*\beta$. If, then, the entrepreneur sells *additional* effort on the market, he moves rightward along $W'W'$ from point β. If, on the other hand,

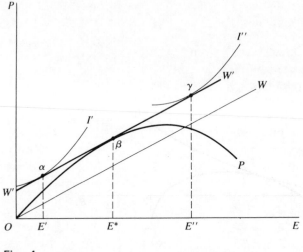

Fig. 4

he keeps the total effort input in the firm fixed at E^*, but *buys in* effort from the market, thus reducing his own contribution, then he moves *leftward* from β along $W'W'$. Thus, the line $W'W'$ becomes the constraint along which he transacts in the 'entrepreneur market', given that he sets the total level of entrepreneurial effort into the firm at E^*. (The analysis here is completely analogous to that of the investment decision in Chapter 15, the reason being that *they belong to the same class of general problems, those in which a decision-taker has both production and exchange opportunities.*) The entrepreneur's final optimal solution depends on his preference pattern. There are three types of solution possible:

(i) Suppose his preferences happen to be such that indifference curve I' is tangent to $W'W'$ at α. Then, this is the highest indifference curve he may reach, and he does so by setting total effort into the firm at E^*, then buying in the amount $E^* - E'$ at the market price, thus putting in his own effort of OE'.

(ii) If his preferences are such that indifference curve I'' is tangent to $W'W'$ at α, then this is the highest indifference curve he may reach. He does this by again setting effort into the firm at E^*, and then selling his own effort on the market in the amount $E'' - E^*$, so that he ends up supplying a total effort of OE'', part of which goes into his own firm, and part into 'outside activities'.

(iii) An indifference curve (not drawn) is tangent to $W'W'$ at β. In this case, it happens that his total effort is OE^*, which goes completely into the business: he neither buys nor sells entrepreneurial effort on the market.

The crucial thing to note about this analysis is that it *establishes a separation* between the entrepreneurial input into the firm on the one hand, and the preferences of the entrepreneur on the other. Whatever the type of solution in the above analysis, the input into the firm is always at E^*. The preferences of the entrepreneur then simply determine the outcome of his market trading. Moreover we must now measure the opportunity cost of effort supplied to the firm by the entrepreneur as the market price, and so pure profits are calculated by subtracting OW from OP in the figure. But then, *whatever* the preferences of the entrepreneur, profit is maximized at E^*, since the distance between OW and OP is maximized at β ($W'W'$ is the tangent to OP at β, and parallel to OW). When the alternative open to the entrepreneur is to buy and sell effort on the market, rather than to produce nothing, we have a reversal of the Scitovsky conclusion; profit maximization is not a special case. The present conclusion can be summarized as follows:

Whatever his preferences concerning income and effort, a utility maximizing entrepreneur will set entrepreneurial effort in his firm at the profit maximizing level; profit is measured net of entrepreneurial opportunity cost, given by the market price of entrepreneurial services.

It follows from this that the Scitovsky analysis is relevant only when there is no market in entrepreneurial services. The reader is invited to use Fig. 4 to prove the following propositions:

(i) If entry into the market were to push OP' down, then the entrepreneur would continue to run the firm until OP' became tangent to OW. If OP' were to fall further, he would close down the firm and offer his services entirely to the market.

(ii) The total entrepreneurial input into the firm always varies inversely with its market price, whatever the preferences of the entrepreneur.

(iii) Any shift in OP' which leaves its slope unchanged at every value of E will leave unchanged the entrepreneurial input into the firm, though it is likely to change the amounts bought or sold on the market. Examples: a fixed cost change, a pure profits tax (i.e. one which allows for deduction of entrepreneurial opportunity costs).

(iv) A change in OP' which increases (decreases) its slope at every E will increase (decrease) the entrepreneurial effort into the firm.

Thus, again we have the usual comparative statics results of the profit maximizing model.

The above analysis was based on several simplifying assumptions; it ignored the constraints on the entrepreneur's choice problem imposed by rigidities in the time which must be allocated to employment (the '8-hour day'), which may obviously affect the solution considerably; it ignored the value which an entrepreneur may attach to 'being his own boss'; and it ignored the fact that in an uncertain world, the risks associated with running your own business are likely to be greater than those of being a salaried executive. The analysis, however, provides a basis for exploration of these questions.

The introduction of a market for 'entrepreneurial services', by which we mean essentially managerial services, raises issues of the separation of ownership from control, which were discussed in Chapter 6. We can in fact extend the analysis of this section to the case of the divorce of ownership from control, to obtain results in this quite simple framework

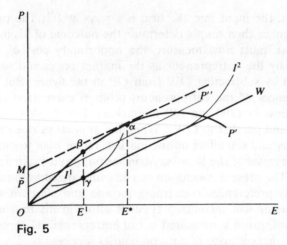

Fig. 5

which anticipate those of the more complex models analysed in later sections.

Thus, suppose that a salaried manager has complete control over the firm, subject to some profit constraint imposed by the owner(s). Then, in Fig. 5, suppose that the indifference curve I^1 is that of a salaried manager, with the slope of the line OW now measuring his salary per unit of time. The curve OP' now represents the relation between the firm's gross income, before subtraction of managerial salary, and the manager's effort. Hence, the income of shareholders (= gross income *less* managerial salary) is measured by the vertical distance between OP' and OW, and achieves a maximum at E^*, since the slope of OP' at α is equal to the slope of OW. However, given his preferences over income and effort combinations, as shown by indifference curve I^1, and the attainable combinations of *his* income and effort, shown by OW, the manager's optimum solution is at E^1, i.e. he prefers to devote less effort to the firm than would be required to maximize profit. (Note, on the other hand, that if his preferences were described by indifference curve I^2, he would devote *more* effort than required to maximize shareholders' income – the increment in profit from increasing effort beyond E^* is less than the increment in the manager's income, and so the firm becomes over-expanded from the shareholders' point of view.)

Whether E^*, E^1, or some other effort level will be selected depends on the extent to which the manager is constrained in his choice. If the shareholders possess all the information contained in the diagram, then they could use their power as owners to ensure that E^* is chosen. In the absence of this the manager may regard himself as faced by a profit constraint, i.e. an obligation to make a certain amount of profit for the owner. In the diagram, it is assumed that this profit is the amount $O\bar{P}$. Then the line $\bar{P}P''$ represents the profit constraint to the manager, since it shows the gross profit he must earn to cover his own salary and the shareholders' profit requirement. The fact that $\bar{P}P''$ intersects with OP' below point β implies that the constraint is non-binding, i.e. by doing what he wanted to do anyway, which is to supply effort E^1 the manager makes more than enough profit to meet the constraint (the distance $\gamma\beta$ is greater than $O\bar{P}$). The reader is invited to show a case in which the profit constraint induces the manager to supply more effort and earn greater profit than at E^1. In the limit, if the profit constraint were OM, then the manager would effectively have to maximize shareholders' income at E^*. This case corresponds to the case of perfect information and a perfect capital market discussed in Chapter 6.

Finally, the role of imperfections in output markets can quickly be shown in the diagram. Let $\bar{P}$ represent normal profit, i.e. the competitive market rate of return on the assets provided by shareholders is just achieved. Then profits greater than $O\bar{P}$ would attract entry, pushing down OP' until it lies everywhere below, and is just tangent to $\bar{P}P''$. But this tangency must be at the level of effort E^*, and so, in the long run the manager must maximize profit in a competitive market. This leads to an interesting interpretation of the behaviour of the manager: in a competitive market, where there are short-run quasi-rents, these are 'appropriated' by the manager, who uses them to generate satisfaction for himself (in this case by working less hard), paying to shareholders only normal profits. In the long run these quasi-rents (assuming they are perceived by potential competitors) will be competed away by new entry. On the other hand, if the market is non-competitive, so that these quasi-rents persist even in the long run, they continue to be appropriated by the manager, unless, as discussed in Chapter 6, the capital market is perfectly competitive.

Exercise 13B

1. Discuss the different concepts of opportunity cost of entrepreneurial effort employed in this section, and comment on their reasonableness.
2.* Suggest how one might incorporate in the analysis of Fig. 4, the following assumptions:
   (a) entrepreneurial activity can only be bought or sold in amounts whose minimum value is 5 hours per day.
   (b) an entrepreneur prefers to be his own boss rather than work for someone else, though a price does exist at which he would be prepared to do the latter.
3.* A physician has a number of 'private' patients, whom he can arrange in order of fee per minute spent in attendance, from highest to lowest. He may also work as a consultant to the state health service, at a given fee per unit time. Adapting Fig. 4, to this case, state necessary and sufficient conditions under which he would attend private patients *and* work for the state health service. Suppose that he is now forced to choose *either* to work privately *or* for the state health service. Analyse the determinants of his choice, indicating also the effects on his income and total supply of effort. Finally, suppose that a special tax is levied on his earnings from private practice, and analyse the consequences as fully as possible.

4.* Suppose that the preferences of Mr *A*, an entrepreneur, are such that at a given effort level, the money value of the marginal unit of effort increases with his income. Using Scitovsky's model, as shown in Fig. 1, derive the comparative statics results of (*a*) a lump sum cost increase, and (*b*) a proportional profits tax, and compare them to the case of the profit maximizing entrepreneur. Explain why the distinction vanishes in the long run, assuming competition and free entry.

C. Revenue maximization

In the discussion of managerial capitalism in Chapter 6, we suggested that the problem for theories of the firm which base themselves on this concept is that of establishing an analytical connection between the firm's decision variables and managerial preferences. We now look at a theory which follows from one particular attempt at this.

It was suggested by W. J. Baumol that the things from which managers derive satisfaction all vary directly with the size of the firm, as measured by sales revenue or turnover. In terms of the model considered at the end of the previous section, income and effort are replaced in the manager's utility function by sales revenue. If this function always increases with revenue, as is assumed, then we can effectively dispense with the utility formulation, and simply regard the firm as wanting to maximize sales revenue subject to a profit constraint.

Given this premise concerning the firm's objective, it is then assumed that demand, input supply and technological relationships are given, known and take the forms familiar from the theory of profit maximization. (Despite the fact that Baumol called his theory a 'theory of oligopoly', nothing is said about interaction of firms, and a determinate demand relation is assumed. It is better to regard the theory as a theory of the firm's decision-taking behaviour, which, though worked out initially for a particular kind of market situation, monopoly, is capable of being applied to others.) In particular, the firm is assumed to operate with a total cost function and cost curves similar in every respect to those in the profit maximizing theory: they are assumed to be derived by minimizing cost for every level of output, using in doing so only technologically efficient input combinations. The reason for this is given below.

Profit enters as a constraint, as we have already seen in the previous section. The managers are assumed to know the minimum amount of profit they must earn to keep shareholders happy. By assumption, output and capital markets are imperfect, so that the profit constraint is for less than maximum profit.

What then are the implications for the behaviour of firms which can be deduced from this theory? First, assume that the firm does not advertise. Then Fig. 6 gives the analysis.

In (*a*) we show the total revenue curve, *TR*, the total cost curve, *TC*, and the implied total profit curve, *TP*, of the firm. It is assumed for

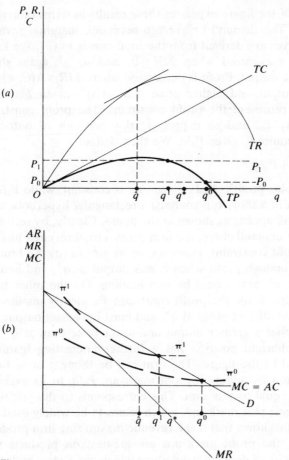

Fig. 6

simplicity that there are constant returns to scale, and that the firm is in the long run, so that the TC curve is a straight line through the origin. Note that the output of maximum profit, $\hat{q}$, must be smaller than the output of maximum revenue, q^*, because the slope of TC (i.e. marginal cost) is positive. Now, in the absence of a profit constraint, the revenue maximizing firm would produce at q^*, and thus at a greater output than would the profit maximizing firm. Suppose there were a profit constraint for the amount OP_0, as indicated by the line $P_0 P_0$. By producing the output q^*, the firm actually makes more profit than is strictly required, and so this constraint is non-binding. On the other hand, if the profit constraint were for the amount OP_1, then the largest total revenue consistent with this is generated by output q^1, so that in this case q^1 is the output the firm will choose. The reader should explain why, for any profit constraint for less than maximum profit, the firm will produce a greater output than that which maximizes profit.

Part (b) of the figure expresses these results in terms of average and marginal curves. The demand (= average revenue), marginal revenue and marginal cost curves are derived from the total curves in (a). We know that total revenue is maximized when $MR = 0$, and so q^* again shows the maximum revenue output. Profit is maximized where $MR = MC$, which must imply a lower output and higher price than at q^*, given $MC > 0$. Now consider how to represent the profit constraint. The profit constraint is a fixed number, say P_0, and so expressing this per unit of output, as an 'average profit required', gives P_0/q. We then define:

$$\pi^0 = AC + P_0/q \qquad\qquad\qquad\qquad\qquad\qquad [C.1]$$

as 'average cost plus profit', ACP. Since AC is constant, while P_0/q is (like average fixed cost in a short-run analysis) a rectangular hyperbola, the curve of π^0 against q will appear as shown in the figure. Clearly, by setting output where π^0 cuts the demand curve, the firm earns a total revenue just equal to total cost plus profit constraint. However, as we saw in (a) the firm actually earns more than enough profit when it sets output at q^*, and hence if the ACP curve were π^0, this would be non-binding. On the other hand, the ACP curve π^1, drawn for the profit constraint P_1, clearly implies that the firm would earn insufficient profit at q^*, and must in fact set output q_1. This, however, still implies a greater output and lower price than at $\hat{q}$.

This equilibrium position has a further interesting feature, most clearly seen in (b) of the figure. The firm can be thought of as finding its equilibrium position by adding a profit mark-up, P_0/q, to its average cost, and setting price equal to this sum. This corresponds to the pricing procedure of 'average cost plus mark-up', which seems to be widely used in firms. Moreover, it can be shown that if the revenue maximizing firm produces two or more outputs, the profit mark-ups are greatest on products with the lowest price elasticity of demand, something which also seems to accord with observation. On the other hand, note that the latter would also be true for a profit maximizing firm, while any price, including one which maximizes profit, can be expressed as the sum of average cost plus *some* mark-up.

We can also use (b) to show why the revenue maximizing firm will minimize costs at each level of output, *as long as its profit constraint is binding*. Thus, suppose the profit constraint is as shown by π^1 in the diagram. Then, the lower are average and marginal costs, the lower will be the curve π^1, and the closer is output to q^*; in other words, the lower are costs, then the greater the revenue the firm can earn, for a given profit constraint. However, note that this argument does not apply if the profit constraint is non-binding, as at π^0. In that case, the firm produces at q^*, and the 'excess' profit it makes is a matter of indifference to it. In that case, costs may well be allowed to increase and swallow up these 'excess' profits.

The main comparative statics results for the theory are quickly derived with the help of Fig. 7. In (a), it is assumed that a proportionate profit tax increase changes the total profit curve from TP to TP'. In the case where the profit constraint OP_1 is binding, this clearly requires the revenue

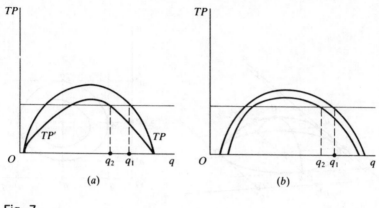

Fig. 7

maximizing firm to reduce output, if it is to continue meeting its profit constraint, whereas a profit maximizing firm would not change its output (Show, on the other hand, that if the profit constraint is and continues to be non-binding, output is unaffected). In (*b*) it is assumed that some change takes place which reduces the slope of the total profit curve at every output (e.g. a fall in demand, an increase in an input's price, a tax on output). This would lead *both* profit maximizing and revenue maximizing firms to reduce output (except that a revenue maximizing firm would not reduce output if its *revenue curve* stayed unchanged, and its profit constraint was non-binding. Prove this). Thus, with exceptions in certain special cases, a revenue maximizing firm differs from a profit maximizing firm in its responses to fixed cost changes, profit tax changes, and indeed any change which shifts the total profit curve, while leaving the *profit maximizing output* unchanged. In addition, we saw that a revenue maximizing firm will produce a larger output at a lower price relative to the profit maximizing position.

The above analysis assumed however that the firm did not advertise, which is not generally true of firms in non-competitive markets. If we introduce advertising, then we find that some of the results just derived change. In particular, given a certain assumption about the marginal revenue of advertising, we find that profit constraints will *always* be binding, but it may happen that the revenue maximizing firm will produce at a smaller output and higher price relative to its profit maximizing position. On the other hand, the differences in comparative statics responses of the firm between the two theories remain broadly as described above.

Let us assume that the marginal revenue of advertising is always positive but diminishing; that is, an increment of advertising always increases revenue (by increasing demand), but by a smaller amount, the greater the level of advertising. This holds for each given level of output. We assume also that advertising is measured in money terms, so that the marginal cost of a unit of advertising is 1, as is its average cost. Now consider the relation between profit, as the dependent variable, and the

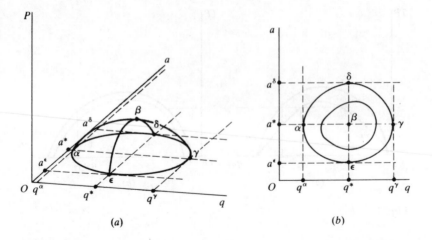

Fig. 8

output and advertising levels chosen by the firm. This can be written as:

$$P(q, a) = R(q, a) - C(q) - a \qquad [C.2]$$

where $P(q, a)$ is the total profit function, $R(q, a)$ is the revenue function, $C(q)$ is the output cost function, and a is advertising. We show the general form of this profit relation in Fig. 8.

In (a), we have a three-dimensional profit hill, representing the function $P(q, a)$. We explain the figure by taking cross sections through it. Choose some given level of a, say a^* in the figure. Then increasing q, from, say q^α, to q^*, leads to steadily increasing profit, as shown by the arc $\alpha\beta$. As output further increases, to q^γ, however, profit falls along the arc $\beta\gamma$. The curve $\alpha\beta\gamma$ has the shape which we have previously assumed to be typical for total profit curves, and follows from the relation between total revenue and cost curves. Taking any other value of a as fixed, and again varying q, would give a similarly shaped total profit cuve. Next, taking some given level of q, say q^*, we can vary a from a^ε through a^* to a^δ, thus tracing out the curve $\varepsilon\beta\delta$. Again, this is assumed first to rise, reach a maximum at β, and then fall, reflecting the assumption that, holding output constant, increasing advertising will first increase revenue by more than cost, but because of the diminishing marginal revenue assumption, this is reversed at some point. (The reader is invited to draw two graphs, one which relates revenue and cost to output for a given level of advertising, and another which relates revenue and cost to advertising for a given output, and which are consistent with the assumptions underlying the total profit surface shown above.) The top of the hill, point β, corresponds to the advertising and output pair (q^*, a^*), and hence these are the levels which would be chosen by a profit maximizing firm.

For our present purposes, it is far more convenient to work in two dimensions, and so (b) of Fig. 8 shows the *contour map* derived from (a).

Each closed curve, drawn between the output and advertising axes, represents a given level of profit, i.e. a given contour of the 'hill' in (a). (b) can be thought of as being derived by projecting the entire hill down onto the 'floor' of (a). Hence, point β is the peak of the hill, and represents maximum profit.

Consider now the relation between revenue as dependent variable and output and advertising, i.e. the revenue function $R(q, a)$. In (a) of Fig. 9 we show total revenue graphed against output and advertising. Again, the shape of the graph can be explained by cross-sections. Fixing a level of advertising, at say a^*, and varying output, we obtain a relation between revenue and output of the usual inverted U-shape. Fixing output at q^* and varying advertising, we trace out a curve which illustrates the assumption that revenue always increases with advertising, but at a diminishing rate. Again, we can translate the figure into two dimensions by taking the contours of the function in (a) and projecting them onto the 'floor' of the figure. The result is shown in (b). The two things to note are that the iso-revenue curves in (b) are convex to the origin, and revenue increases as we move to successively higher curves. These properties can be shown to follow from the nature of the function graphed in (a) (Prove).

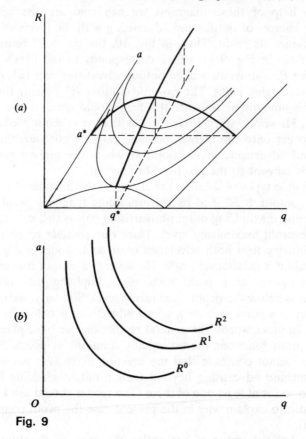

Fig. 9

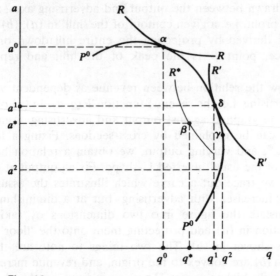

Fig. 10

With the help of these diagrams we can compare the revenue maximizing firm's choices of output and advertising with the levels of them which would maximize its profit. Thus, in Fig. 10, the curve P^0 represents the profit contour (as in Fig. 9(b)) which corresponds to the firm's profit constraint P^0. Point β, with its associated output-advertising pair (q^*, a^*), is again the profit maximizing point. The revenue contour R^* passing through point β shows the amount of revenue the firm would earn at the profit maximizing point. However, since P^0 is for less than maximum profit, and the firm wishes to get onto the highest possible revenue contour, the firm will set output and advertising at the point at which the highest possible revenue contour is tangent to the given profit contour.

Three possible types of solution are shown in the diagram. Consider first the revenue contour $R'R'$, and its corresponding tangency point δ. In this case, the revenue maximizing output-advertising pair is (q^1, a^1), each of which exceeds the profit maximizing level. Thus, one *possible* result is that the revenue maximizing firm both advertises more and produces a greater output than it would if it maximized profit. However, we cannot rule out the possibility of a tangency at a point such as α, implying that revenue maximizing output is below the profit maximizing level. Similarly, we cannot rule out a tangency at a point such as γ, where advertising is below its profit maximizing level. In other words, the general restrictions we have placed on the revenue and profit functions permit equally solutions at points like α, and γ, so that we cannot conclude that the revenue maximizer necessarily carries *both* output and advertising beyond their profit maximizing levels, though he must do so for at least one of them (The reader should use Fig. 10 to say why, and also to explain why in the present case the profit constraint is *always* binding).

Though it has the virtue of presenting the analysis clearly and in

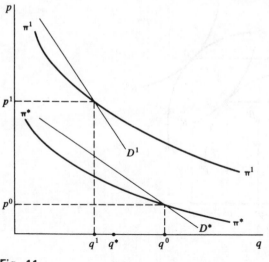

Fig. 11

considerable generality, Fig. 10 does not help intuition in understanding why case α or γ could arise. Therefore consider Fig. 11.

In the figure, suppose that the demand curve D^* is that which corresponds to the profit maximizing advertising level, and q^* is the output which maximizes profit given that demand curve (to keep the figure as clear as possible, marginal cost and marginal revenue curves have not been drawn in). The curve $\pi^*\pi^*$ represents the sum average production cost plus profit required plus advertising costs per unit of putput, so that it shows the amount of revenue which must be earned per unit of output if total costs, plus profit constraint, are to be covered. Now suppose the firm were to increase its advertising beyond the profit maximizing level, and that this generates the new demand curve D^1. It will also increase total cost per unit of output, by the amount of the increase in advertising, and so $\pi^*\pi^*$ becomes $\pi^1\pi^1$. The output q^1 at which the latter intersects the demand curve is below q^*, but revenue is clearly greater at q^1 than at q^0, which was the revenue maximizing output at advertising level a^*. This then illustrates the situation in which the revenue maximizing firm sets advertising above and output below their profit maximizing levels. (Now construct an example of the converse case.)

The derivation of the comparative statics results from Fig. 12 which turn out to be broadly similar to those in the case of no advertising, can be carried out by adapting Fig. 10. In the figure, we assume that some change (increased profits tax, for example) has taken place which leaves the profit maximizing output-advertising pair unchanged, but which reduces the absolute amount of profit at all levels of output and advertising. In particular, the profit contour corresponding to the profit constraint shifts from P^0P^0 to $\bar{P}^0\bar{P}^0$, requiring the revenue maximizing firm to move from point α to point γ. Thus, the change leaves unaffected the profit maximizing position, but causes the revenue maximizing firm to respond by reducing both output and

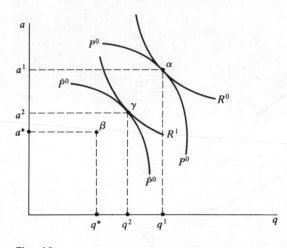

Fig. 12

advertising. Note, however, that it is possible to construct cases in which: (*a*) output would fall but advertising would rise; (*b*) output would rise but advertising would fall, and the reader is asked to do this in Question 1 of the exercise below.

It is also possible to compare profit maximizing and revenue maximizing responses in cases where the profit contours and the profit maximizing point shift, but nothing new is added to the previous analysis. The major difference in the two theories' implications concerning comparative statics responses lies in the effects of the type of change shown in Fig. 12.

The result of this analysis of the revenue maximizing firm is that we obtain significantly different implications for the equilibrium choices and some comparative statics responses of the firm. These differences are points at which evidence can be brought to bear to discriminate between the theories.

Exercise 13C
1. Construct cases in which a revenue maximizing firm will
    (*a*) reduce advertising and increase output
    (*b*) increase advertising and reduce output
    in response to an increase in a lump-sum tax. Rationalize these results, and explain the source of the indeterminacy.
2.* Suppose that a revenue-maximizing firm produces two goods but does not advertise. The two goods are independent in demand and costs. The marginal costs of the goods are constant and equal. Show that the profit margin will be higher on the good with lower demand elasticity. (*Hint:* derive iso-profit and iso-revenue curves for this case, and show that at the optimum the ratios of marginal revenue to marginal cost of the two goods must be equal. Interpret the profit margin as the ratio of price to marginal cost.)

3. Suggest and explain five tests by which it could be determined whether a firm's objective is to maximize profit or revenue.

D. Expense preference

The theory we have just considered postulates that managers generate for themselves the things from which they derive satisfaction – salaries, perquisites, status, security – by maximizing sales revenue. We now consider a somewhat different and more detailed way of setting up the connection between the goals of managers, on the one hand, and the firm's decision variables, on the other. The basis of the approach, first proposed by O. E. Williamson, is the postulate that managers' goals are achieved by incurring certain kinds of expenditure, and thus imply a preference for such expenditures. Hence the term the 'expense preference theory' will be used to denote this approach. By specifying these types of expenditure and relating them to the firm's decision variables, we are able to derive testable implications about the behaviour of firms. Moreover, we find that some of these implications differ significantly from those of all the theories so far considered.

Williamson identifies three kinds of expenditure which would be regarded by managers as generating salary, status, etc. First, we have total expenditure on the staff which they control, denoted by S. There is some ambiguity here, since it is not clear whether what is important is the number of staff, at given salary levels, or the salary levels of a given number of staff, or, indeed, both. The former would imply that managers get satisfaction from the size of their departments, the latter that they do so from having well-paid subordinates. To accept both hypotheses, but not to distinguish between them in measuring S, implies that managers are indifferent between spending £1 more on an extra staff member, salaries constant, or on salaries, with staff constant. The most reasonable resolution seems to be to assume that managers derive satisfaction essentially from staff numbers. This then captures the 'empire-building' phenomenon which is often held to occur in large organizations (see, for example, the famous work 'Parkinson's Law', for many humorous but apt illustrations of the phenomenon). By working to increase the number of his subordinates, a manager increases his salary, perquisites, status and security.

Secondly, expenditure on managerial 'emoluments' other than salaries, is liked by managers. This expenditure provides the expense accounts, company cars, school fees, medical expenses, cheap mortgages and all those goods and services which are a cost to the company, and which yield pleasure to the managers. This is denoted by M.

Finally, managers like to earn 'discretionary profit', denoted by D. When all costs (including S and M) have been subtracted from revenues, and all taxes paid, the resulting profit is divided between dividends to shareholders, and 'additions to reserves'. The essential feature of the latter is that they are under the control of managers, and may be used for purposes of, by and large, their own choosing – expenditure on prestige projects, political contributions, reserves against poor future performance, and so on. Moreover, profits over and above the minimum necessary to keep shareholders happy may in themselves be desirable to managers. Strictly speaking, discretionary profit, D may not entirely be an expenditure, but it would complicate the terminology to recognize this, so we can regard it as, loosely, an expense category for which managers have a preference.

We can see immediately that this statement of the 'goals' of managers is far richer and more specific than that of the revenue maximization theory. It reflects a different view of *the way in which managers appropriate the quasi-rents which result from non-competitive markets.* In the present theory, managers allocate these quasi-rents – the excess of revenues over all opportunity costs of production – among these various categories of expenditure for which they have preferences, paying out to shareholders only the minimum required. In the revenue maximization theory, managers use the quasi-rents essentially to 'buy' increased sales revenue: the firm's scale is expanded until everything is absorbed in output and advertising costs except the profit required by shareholders. It is thereby *assumed* that managers can then get the things they like, while the expense preference theory is looking at these things explicitly. It remains to be seen whether this has significantly different implications for the analysis of firm's behaviour.

Given that there are three goals for the firm, S, M and D, we have to consider how the firm determines their relative importance. The way of doing this which is natural in microeconomics is to assume that the firm's objective function is an ordinal utility function;

$$U = U(S, M, D) \tag{D.1}$$

which it wants to maximize. We assume that each of the three expense categories is always a good to the firm, and apply to this function the assumptions about preference orderings set out in Chapter 3, and so the indifference curves for any two out of the three variables will have the usual convex-to-the origin shape. We now have to relate the variables in the utility function to the decision variables of the firm. In doing this, we initially follow Williamson's treatment.

The profit of the firm is defined as revenue *minus* costs, where costs are separated into staff expenditures, S, managerial emoluments, M, and production costs, C, where

$$C = C(q) \tag{D.2}$$

is the total cost function for output. It is assumed that this possesses the usual properties, and, in particular, that it is derived from a cost-minimizing procedure, for every level of output, and that the most efficient known techniques are used. The revenue function is written as:

$$R = R(q, S) \tag{D.3}$$

where, for a given level of S, the graph of R is assumed to have the usual inverted U-shape, while, for given q, it is assumed that increasing S *always* increases R, though at a diminishing rate. Thus, if the reader replaces a by S in Fig. 8, the assumed form of the revenue function is shown there. Note, therefore, that staff expenditures are here assumed to play an exactly similar role to advertising in both revenue and cost functions. We can write the total profit P, as:

$$P = R(q, S) - C(q) - S - M \qquad [\text{D.4}]$$

i.e. as total revenue *minus* production costs, staff expenditures and managerial emoluments.

The shareholders' profit constraint is again written as P°. Hence, discretionary profit, D, is by definition:

$$D = P - P^\circ = R(q, S) - C(q) - S - M - P^\circ \qquad [\text{D.5}]$$

the amount of profit over and above the minimum required to satisfy shareholders. Note that D is written entirely in terms of q, S and M; once these are chosen, and given P^0, D is also determined. Therefore, for purposes of analysis, we need consider only these three as the decision variables. Also, note that if a positive amount of D is chosen by the firm, this *implies* that $P > P^\circ$, i.e. that the firm earns more than enough profit to pay its shareholders. Hence, if we assume that the preferences of the firm are such that D is always positive (a non-satiation assumption) then the profit constraint is always more than satisfied and so is non-binding. Given this assumption, the problem is one of the unconstrained maximization of the utility function in [D.1], where [D.5] can be used to substitute for D and express the utility function in terms of q, S and M. Thus the problem is to

$$\max U(S, M, R(q, S) - C(q) - S - M - P^\circ) \qquad [\text{D.6}]$$

The necessary conditions for a maximum of U are:

$$\frac{\partial U}{\partial S} + \frac{\partial U}{\partial D}\left[\frac{\partial R}{\partial S} - 1\right] = 0$$

$$\frac{\partial U}{\partial M} - \frac{\partial U}{\partial D} = 0 \qquad [\text{D.7}]$$

$$\frac{\partial U}{\partial D}\left[\frac{\partial R}{\partial q} - \frac{dC}{dq}\right] = 0$$

The first condition implies that:

$$\frac{\partial R}{\partial S} = 1 - \frac{\partial U}{\partial S}\bigg/\frac{\partial U}{\partial D} \qquad [\text{D.8}]$$

Where the partial derivative on the lefthand side is the marginal revenue of staff expenditure, and the ratio of marginal utilities on the righthand side represents the marginal rate of substitution between staff and discretionary profit. An immediate implication of this condition is that staff expenditure is carried beyond the profit maximizing point. To see this, note that both

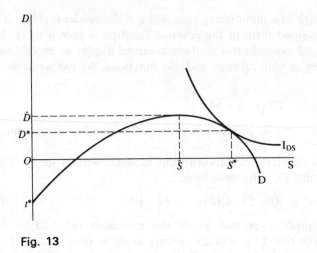

Fig. 13

marginal utilities are assumed always positive (non-satiation), and so

$$1 - \frac{\partial U}{\partial S} \Big/ \frac{\partial U}{\partial D} < 1.$$

But recall that staff expenditure is measured in money terms, so that the marginal cost of £1 more of staff is 1. Hence, [D.8] implies that in equilibrium, the firm uses more staff than is consistent with profit maximization. (Note that, as we expect, this arises because S appears in the utility function meaning that it is desired for its own sake, and not just for generating revenue. If $\partial U/\partial S = 0$, then [D.8] would imply an equality between marginal revenue and marginal cost of staff.) To illustrate this first condition, assume that M and q have been set at their optimal values, so that, using [D.5], we can write:

$$D = R(q^*, S) - S - t^* \qquad\qquad [D.9]$$

where $t^* = C(q^*) + M^* + P^\circ$, and is fixed throughout the analysis. Because of the assumed relation between R and S, the relation between D and S will be as shown by the curve t^*D in Fig. 13. The indifference curve I_{DS} is drawn for $M = M^*$, and is the highest which can be attained given the feasible (S, D) pairs as shown by t^*D. Hence the firm chooses the pair (S^*, D^*) to maximize its utility. The level of S chosen is greater than $\hat{S}$, which maximizes D, and which satisfies the condition:

$$\frac{\partial R}{\partial S} - 1 = 0 \qquad\qquad [D.10]$$

The fact that $S^* > \hat{S}$ clearly reflects the negative sope of I_{DS}. For $\hat{S}$ to be chosen by the utility maximizing firm, the indifference curves would have to be horizontal, which is equivalent to specifying $\partial U/\partial S = 0$. As long as this marginal utility is positive, the chosen staff level S^* always exceeds the staff level which satisfies the condition of equality of marginal revenue and marginal cost of staff.

The second condition implies that M and D are set so that their marginal utilities are equal. To see why this should be so, assume that q and S have been set at their optimal levels q^* and S^*, so that from [D.5] we can write:

$$D = K^* - M \qquad\qquad [D.11]$$

where $K^* = R(q^*, S^*) - C(q^*) - S^* - P^\circ$ is a constant. In other words, we can imagine the firm setting output and staff, and then dividing the resulting revenues, minus the resulting costs and profit constraint, between M and D. Now consider Fig. 14.

The line K^*K^* is the graph of the relation $D = K^* - M$, having intercepts on each axis at K^*, and a slope of -1. £1 more devoted to D must imply, given K^*, £1 less devoted to M. Then, optimal D and M are determined at the point of tangency of K^*K^* and the highest possible indifference curve, shown here as I_{DM} (which is drawn for $S = S^*$). At the point of tangency, the slope of I_{DM}, which we know to be $-(\partial U/\partial M)/(\partial U/\partial D)$, must equal that of K^*K^*, which is -1. Hence, we have:

$$-\frac{\partial U}{\partial M}\bigg/\frac{\partial U}{\partial D} = -1 \Rightarrow \frac{\partial U}{\partial M} = \frac{\partial U}{\partial D} \qquad\qquad [D.12]$$

which is the second condition in [D.7]. The firm is here seen to be allocating a fixed sum (given S^* and q^*), to the two expense categories, and its utility is maximized when that sum is allocated so that their marginal utilities are equal. If this were not so, it would be possible to reallocate expenditure from the category with the lower marginal utility, to that with the higher, and increase total utility.

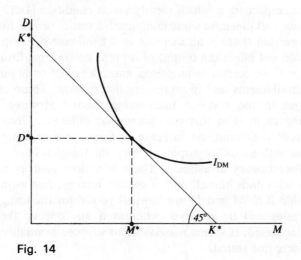

Fig. 14

In the third condition in [D.7], given that $\partial U/\partial D \neq 0$, we must have that:

$$\frac{\partial R}{\partial q} - \frac{dC}{dq} = 0 \qquad \text{[D.13]}$$

i.e. that marginal revenue of output must equal marginal cost of output, which is of course *precisely the condition for maximum profit*. However, this does not imply that the firm chooses the same *output level* as it would choose if its objective were to maximize profit. Recall that the level of S is greater than that which maximizes profit, and that the effect of increasing S is, analogously to advertising, to shift out the firm's demand and marginal revenue curves. Now, the firm is here choosing an output which equates marginal cost to marginal revenue, but with reference to a marginal revenue curve which is higher than that it would face if it chose S to maximize profit. Hence, the output chosen will in general be different from, and possibly higher than, profit maximizing output.

We can note here an important similarity to and an important difference from the theory of the revenue maximizing firm. The similarity lies in the expansion of the scale of the firm beyond the profit maximizing point, the motive in one case being the acquisition of revenue, the motive in the other being the indulgence in staff expenditure. The difference lies in the fact that, *given* its choice of staff expenditures, the firm in the present case then maximizes profit with respect to output, whereas the revenue maximizing firm does not. This difference arises because of the existence of emoluments and discretionary profits, M and D, as desirable things. *Given S*, the greater are profits, the greater may be M and D, and so the firm maximizes the amounts of these which it may have by maximizing profits with respect to output. This is clearly seen if we rewrite [D.5] as:

$$D + M = R(q, S^*) - S^* - P^\circ \qquad \text{[D.14]}$$

Then, for given S^*, the sum $D + M$ is maximized by maximizing the RHS of this expression with respect to q, which clearly yields condition [D.13].

We now state and illustrate some comparative statics results for this model. First, suppose that there is an increase in a fixed cost or lump-sum profit tax. This would not affect the output of a profit maximizing firm, but in the present case will, on certain assumptions, cause a reduction in output, staff expenditure, emoluments and discretionary investments. These effects are similar to those in the revenue maximizing theory. However, the reasoning underlying them is in this case somewhat different. Given the constancy of its profit constraint, an increase in fixed costs or lump-sum taxes leaves the firm with a smaller surplus to 'buy' the things it likes – staff, emoluments and discretionary investment. There is a close analogy to the case of a consumer who finds himself with a smaller income. Just as in that case, so it is here that if S, M and D are 'normal goods' for the firm, then their chosen quantities will be reduced, whereas if any one of them is inferior, it will be increased. It seems reasonable to suppose normality, and so we have the effects just stated.

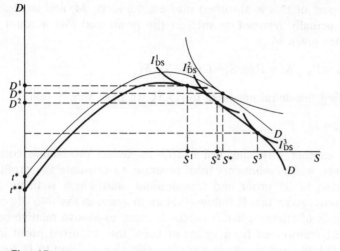

Fig. 15

The main points can be illustrated in Fig. 15, which is based on Fig. 13. Recall that the curve t^*D is drawn for given values of q and M. Holding those values constant, suppose that after the cost or tax change, the curve shifts to $t^{**}D'$, which is simply a vertical displacement of t^*D because the change works on the constant term t^*. Given the initial equilibrium pair (S^*D^*), there are five possibilities for the new position, three of which we show. Given indifference curve I_{DS}^1, then the new pair is (S^1D^1). Given I_{DS}^2, then the new pair is (S^2D^2). While given I_{DS}^3, the new pair is (S^3D^3). The other two possibilities would involve respectively choice of S^* or choice of D^*. Thus, following the change, S and D could increase, decrease, or remain the same. However, if we assume that neither is an inferior good, then both decrease.

The change in q is yet to be explained, and has an interesting rationale. The change in a fixed cost or lump sum tax affects neither the marginal revenue nor marginal cost of output directly. However, the reduction in S which occurs as the firm reallocates its now smaller surplus over the expense categories causes a downward shift in the marginal revenue curve (in the most plausible case) and hence a fall in optimal output. Thus the comparative statics responses in this case differ from those of a profit maximizing firm, though not from those of a revenue maximizing firm.

Consider now the effects of a change in the rate of a proportionate profits tax. In the profit and revenue maximizing theories, we saw that this had the same effects as a change in a lump-sum profit tax, but in the present case there is an interesting difference. A distinction which arises in the present model is that between 'actual' and 'reported' profits. Actual profits are defined as revenue minus production costs and staff expenditure, i.e.

$$P_A = R(q, S) - C(q) - S \qquad\qquad [D.15]$$

However, part of this is absorbed into emoluments, M, and so the profits which are actually *reported* as such in the profit and loss account of the company are given by:

$$P_R \equiv P_A - M = R(q, S) - C(q) - S - M \qquad \text{[D.16]}$$

but, recalling the definition of D in [D.5], we have simply that:

$$P_R = D + P^\circ \qquad \text{[D.17]}$$

To put it another way: the firm is able to deduct production costs, staff expenditures, and emoluments from revenue, to calculate the profit which gets reported in its profit and loss account, and which is liable for the proportionate profits tax. It follows that an increase in the rate of profit tax has two kinds of effects. First, it makes D more expensive relative to S and M, since £1 transferred from either of these into reported profit incurs a larger tax liability and results in a smaller effective addition to D. Secondly, it increases the overall tax liability of the firm, in a way similar to an increase in a lump-sum tax (note the similarity here to the effect of an increase in the price of a good bought by a consumer). The first of these effects implies that, other things being equal, there would be a substitution of staff expenditures and emoluments for discretionary investment, since they are now relatively cheaper ways of generating utility. The second implies that there is a smaller surplus of profit over the profit constraint, available for 'purchase' of utility-generating S, M and D. If the 'substitution effect' is stronger than the 'income effect', S and M will increase, while they will decrease in the opposite case. If D is a normal good, its amount will in every case decrease. Figure 16 illustrates the case for choice between S and D.

    The t^*D curve is as before; assuming that q and M remain unchanged, the effect of a proportionate profit tax is to shift the curve down to aC. At each value of S, the slope of the curve is smaller in absolute value,

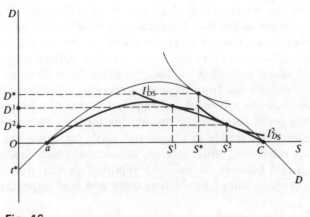

Fig. 16

reflecting the fact that £1 increase in reported profit results in a smaller effective increase in D. Two new equilibrium positions are shown, corresponding to two possible sets of preferences. The choice of pair (S^1, D^1) implies that the 'income effect' of the increase in rate of profit tax outweighs the substitution effect, while choice of pair (S^2, D^2) implies the converse. Note that the latter case is quite consistent with S being a 'normal good', as can be seen by shifting t^*D parallel to itself until it is tangent to I_{DS}^2.

To find the effect of the profit tax change on output, first we note that it does not affect directly the marginal revenue and marginal cost of output. However, since there is a change in S, this will in turn change the marginal revenue curve, and therefore output. Thus, suppose that the substitution effect dominates, so that S increases. Then, given the formulation of the revenue function, the marginal revenue curve will shift out, and output will increase until marginal cost is equated to marginal revenue on the higher curve. Thus we have that the effects of a proportionate profit tax increase, *given the dominance of the substitution effect*, differ in the present case from those in both profit and revenue maximizing theories, since they take the form of *increases* in output and staff expenditures.

There are of course many other kinds of comparative statics effects which could be derived, but the above analysis suffices to show the main features of them, and the way in which they may differ from those of other theories. We now consider a somewhat broader question, that of the relation between the postulates of the theory, and the formal model which was set up in equations [D.1] to [D.5], and on which all the analytical results were based.

We find ourselves in the position of being able broadly to accept the formalization of the goals of the firm, in terms of the three expense categories, as being plausible and potentially fruitful. However, two aspects of the formal model do not accord very well with the postulates on which the theory is based. First is the specification of the revenue function in [D.3], which says that increases in staff expenditure always increase the firm's revenue. If staff expenditure were simply another term for advertising and selling costs, this would be acceptable, but the theory does not say this. The staff expenditure may occur in any branch of managerial operations – finance, purchasing, research, administration – and not only those concerned with marketing. Moreover, it is quite possible to conceive of unproductive staff expenditures, which simply swell the staff numbers at any given level of basic productive activity. In other words, the specification of the revenue function in [D.5] does not really arise from the basic postulates of the theory, and is much more restrictive than these imply.

Secondly, note that the formal model says nothing about input choices, other than staff expenditure. Since the production cost function $C(q)$ is assumed to have the usual properties, we assume that it is derived from cost minimization. However, the relation between staff expenditure and output (as opposed to revenue) is never made explicit, even though we would expect some relation of a production function type: the larger is output, the larger will be the labour force, capital stock, and, we would expect, managerial inputs. Moreover, we would expect there to be possibility of substitution between staff and other inputs, especially capital. For example, the greater the use of business machinery and computers, the smaller the need for staff, other things being equal. We would thus expect a profit maximizing firm to choose its staff just like any other input, by finding the cost minimizing combination of inputs at every output level, and then finding the profit maximizing output level, thus determining inputs. We then get the interesting possibility, not contemplated by the model of this section, that the expense preferring firm may *not* choose cost minimizing input levels, but rather may use more staff relative to other inputs than is economically efficient. This suggests that the implications of the expense preference theory could be greatly extended by adopting a different formal model: one which did not contain the unduly restrictive form of revenue function, and which explicitly analyzed input choices.

Such a model has been analyzed elsewhere (see Rees, 1974). We give here, briefly, its main conclusions. The expense preferring firm may adopt three kinds of behaviour:

(i) it may choose profit maximizing levels of output and advertising, and then divide the resulting surplus of profit over its profit constraint, among S, M and D, in such a way as to equalize their marginal utilities. In its external decisions, the firm acts as a profit maximizer, and this extends to comparative statics responses. However, it employs more staff than is necessary for the given output and advertising levels. This staff is simply surplus; it could be eliminated with no loss of output or advertising.

(ii) it may set staff at the cost-minimizing level for each level of output and advertising (possibly because it is forced to by a parent company), and so indulges its taste for staff by expanding output and advertising beyond their profit maximizing levels. This case has similar results to those of the model considered here, including comparative statics effects.

(iii) the firm chooses input combinations which are biased towards excessive staff use, and which do not minimize costs. In addition, it expands output and advertising beyond the profit maximizing levels. The comparative statics results turn out to be similar to those of the revenue maximizing model.

We find that the comparative statics predictions of these models differ, which presents problems for testing the theory, and for the use of it to predict behaviour of firms. However, it can also be shown that, on very plausible assumptions, the firm achieves the highest utility level by acting as in case (iii), and so, assuming the firm is rational, we could take this model to be the appropriate formalization of the theory.

Exercise 13D

1. * By interpreting S as labour cost and not staff expenditures, discuss the applicability of the analysis of this section to a firm which is controlled by its workers, rather than by management.

2. Suppose we observe that when a firm is taken over, its managerial staff is drastically reduced, but its output and sales expand. Is that consistent with the model set out in this section?

3.* Show on an isoquant diagram, and on a diagram of the production set, the differences between:
   (i) a firm which indulges its taste for excess staff by simply adding more staff at any level of output.
   (ii) a firm which chooses excessively staff-intensive techniques, though not *technologically* inefficient techniques.

E. Conclusions

The theories set out in sections C and D of this chapter have explored some of the implications of managerial capitalism. This is the system in which the productive capital of an economy, though owned by the shareholders of firms, is essentially controlled by the firms' managers. The quasi-rents which are generated because of imperfections in markets for outputs are, because of imperfections in capital markets, appropriated by the managers rather than the owners of capital. These theories have then explored the implications of this for output and input decisions of the firm.

The most striking feature of the theories is that they are all squarely in the tradition of 'neo-classical' microeconomics, with which this book is concerned. The firm is assumed to have a well-defined utility function which it tries to maximize, and so conforms to the basic notion of rationality in economics. As a result, the firm acts in a 'marginalist' way; it weighs up marginal costs, marginal revenues, and, in some cases, marginal utilities, in taking decisions. Moreover, the environment of the firm is static and known with certainty, while conditions of technology, demand, and input supply are essentially those envisaged in the neo-classical theory. The theories explore the consequences of different sets of objectives of the firm, within a utility maximizing framework, and few other concessions are made to the critics of the neo-classical approach.

However, this need by no means be a bad thing. The models we have considered are still relatively simple and tractable, a virtue they possess *because* they have abstracted from many 'realistic' features of firms. What is still necessary is a programme of empirical testing which will tell us whether this degree of abstraction is appropriate, and which will also discriminate between the theories themselves.

References and further reading

The basic reference on the theory of the entrepreneurial firm is:

> **T. Scitovsky.** 'A note on profit maximization and its implications', *Review of Economic Studies*, 1943.

The theory of the revenue maximizing firm is set out in:

W. J. Baumol. *Business Behaviour, Value and Growth*, Macmillan, London, 1959.

For exposition and discussion of the 'expense preference' theory of the firm, see:

O. E. Williamson. *The Economics of Discretionary Behaviour: Managerial Objectives in a Theory of the Firm*, Prentice-Hall, Englewood Cliffs, N.J., 1964.

R. Rees. 'A reconsideration of the expense preference theory of the firm', *Economica*, 1974.

An approach to the firm which rejects the 'neo-classical' orientation of this chapter is developed in:

R. M. Cyert and **R. March.** *A Behavioural Theory of the Firm*, Prentice-Hall, Englewood Cliffs, N.J., 1963.

Chapter 14

Input markets

In this chapter we examine the markets for the inputs used in production by firms, drawing on many of the concepts used in earlier chapters. Section A considers the demand for inputs arising from the firms' profit maximizing problems discussed in Chapters 7–9. The supply of inputs is analysed in section B. Since inputs are supplied both by utility maximizing consumers and profit maximizing firms use is made there of the results of sections 3E, 5C and Chapter 9. In these first two sections it is assumed that input markets are competitive, with input prices treated as parameters by suppliers and users of inputs. (This does not of course mean that a firm buying inputs cannot be a monopolist in its product market.) In the remaining sections some of the simplifying assumptions are removed. Section C considers the determination of the price of an input under monopsony, i.e. when there is only one buyer. In section D we look at the case of a single seller of an input, taking the specific example of unionization of a labour force and using some of the ideas of section 10A and Chapter 11. The problem of formulating an adequate theory of bilateral monopoly (a single seller confronting a single buyer) is discussed in section E.

A. Demand for inputs

We will concentrate on the demand for inputs by a profit maximizing firm facing input prices which it regards as unalterable by its actions. There are assumed to be no adjustment costs involved in varying input levels or, in the terminology of Chapters 7, 8 and 9, the firm's problem is *long-run*: there are no constraints on the adjustment of its inputs. Derivation of the short-run demand for inputs is left to the exercises. To keep the analysis simple it is further assumed that the firm produces a single output y from two inputs z_1, z_2 subject to the constraint $y \le f(z_1, z_2)$, where f is a production function. Since a profit maximizing firm never produces where $y < f(z_1, z_2)$ (explain why) the production constraint can be treated as an equality: $y = f(z_1, z_2)$. The firm faces a demand curve for its output, $p = p(y)$. If $dp/dy = 0$ the demand curve is horizontal and the firm sells y in a competitive market. If $dp/dy < 0$ the demand curve is negatively sloped and the firm is a monopolist. The firm's total revenue is $R(y) = p(y)y$ and since the production constraint is an equality we can write $R(y) = R[f(z_1, z_2)]$. Since choice of z_1, z_2 determines costs and revenue the firm's output need not appear explicitly in its profit maximization problem

$$\max_{z_1 z_2} R[f(z_1, z_2)] - \sum_i p_i z_i \qquad \text{[A.1]}$$

where p_i is the price of z_i. (Compare equation [A.3] in Chapter 9, which relates only to the competitive case.)

Assuming that both inputs are positive at the solution, necessary conditions for a maximum are

$$R'f_i - p_i = 0 \qquad (i = 1, 2) \qquad \text{[A.2]}$$

where $R' = dR/dy$ is marginal revenue and f_i is the marginal product of z_i in the production of y. [A.2] can be rewritten as

$$MR \cdot MP_i = p_i \qquad (i = 1, 2) \qquad \text{[A.3]}$$

The firm will adjust its input levels until the cost of an extra unit of input i, p_i, is equal to the extra revenue generated by the extra unit, $MR \cdot MP_i$. The increase in z_i increases y by MP_i (its marginal product) and a unit increase in output increases revenue by marginal revenue (MR), so that the extra revenue from using an extra unit of z_i is $MR \cdot MP_i$. This is usually called the *marginal revenue product* of z_i and written MRP_i. When the firm sells y in a competitive market

$$MR = \frac{dp}{dy} \cdot y + p = p$$

since dp/dy is zero. In this case the MRP_i is $p \cdot MP_i$ which is known as the *value of the marginal product* and written VMP_i. Given that dp/dy is non-positive we see that $VMP_i \geq MRP_i$.

Recalling from section 8B that p_i/MP_i is marginal cost, if we divide both sides of [A.3] by MP_i we get

$$MR = MC = \frac{p_i}{MP_i} \qquad (i = 1, 2) \qquad \text{[A.4]}$$

and so we have the familiar conclusion that profit maximization requires that marginal revenue be equated to marginal cost.

From the equilibrium conditions we see that the firm's demand for inputs will depend on the prices of the inputs and the parameters of the production and output demand functions. Let us consider how the demand for an input varies with its price. Denote the initial price of z_1 by p_1^0. At this price, and given the price of z_2, the firm chooses the initial optimal combination (z_1^*, z_2^*). If z_2 is held constant at z_2^*, since $MRP_1 = R'[f(z_1, z_2^*)] \cdot f_1(z_1, z_2^*)$ varies only with z_1 we can plot MRP_1 against z_1 in

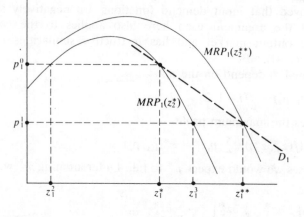

Fig. 1

Fig. 1. This is the curve labelled $MRP_1(z_2^*)$, to indicate that its position depends on the pre-assigned level of z_2. As z_1 varies with z_2 fixed, MRP_1 varies, firstly because more output is produced and this will reduce MR if the firm faces a negatively-sloped demand curve in its output market; and secondly because MP_1 varies with z_1. Now over a range of values of z_1, MP_1 may *rise* with z_1 (see section 7C) and so it is possible that MRP_1 at first rises with z_1 (the increase in MP_1 offsetting any decrease in MR) and then falls (the MP_1 must eventually decline and so reinforce the nonpositive change in MR.) The $MRP_1(z_2^*)$ curve in Fig. 1 reflects this possibility.

The firm chooses its profit maximizing level of z_1 where $p_1^0 = MRP_1$. But MRP_1 equals p_1^0 *at both* z_1^2 and z_1^*. At z_1^2 however the $MRP_1(z_2^*)$ curve cuts the p_1^0 line from below, indicating that an increase in z_1 above z_1^2 will lead to $MRP_1 > p_1$, i.e. an increase in z_1 will generate revenue in excess of its cost. Hence z_1^2 cannot be the optimum. At z_1^* on the other hand, an increase in z_1 will lead to $MRP_1 < p_1$ so that profit is reduced and a reduction in z_1 loses more revenue than cost (since then $MRP_1 > p_1$). Hence the profit maximising level of z_1 must occur where MRP_1 is negatively sloped and cuts the p_1^0 line at z_1^*.

Now suppose that p_1 falls to p_1^1, so that the price line cuts $MRP_1(z_2^*)$ at z_1^3. Is this the new profit maximizing level of z_1? The answer is no, because a change in p_1 will also cause a change in the optimal z_2, to z_2^{**}, so that the MRP_1 curve will shift to the right to $MRP_1(z_2^{**})$. The new optimal level for z_1 is z_1^{**} where $p_1^1 = MRP_1(z_2^{**})$. The demand curve for z_1 is therefore the negatively sloped dashed line D_1: a fall in the price of an input leads to an increased demand for it by the firm.

Since $MRP_1(z_2^{**})$ lies to the right of $MRP_1(z_2^*)$ the demand curve must be negatively sloped, but here we have merely asserted rather than proved that this is the case. It is tedious to show that MRP_1 shifts right as

p_1 falls and so we will support our conclusion that D_1 is negatively sloped by a more direct argument. For a firm selling y on a *competitive* market we have already proved that input demand functions are negatively sloped (section 9D) but the argument used here also applies to the case of monopoly in the output market and has instructive similarities to the methods of sections 4B, 8B.

The optimal z_i depend on the p_i:

$$z_i^* = D_i(p_1, p_2) \qquad (i = 1, 2) \tag{A.5}$$

and hence so does the maximum profit

$$\pi_{max} = R(f(z_1^*, z_2^*)) - \sum p_i z_i^* = \pi^*(p_1, p_2) \tag{A.6}$$

Now as p_k increases we would expect π^* to fall. Differentiating π^* w.r.t. p_k gives

$$\frac{\partial \pi^*}{\partial p_k} = R' \left\{ f_1 \frac{\partial z_1^*}{\partial p_k} + f_2 \frac{\partial z_2^*}{\partial p_k} \right\} - \sum p_i \frac{\partial z_i^*}{\partial p_k} - z_k^* \tag{A.7}$$

But from [A.2], $R'f_i = p_i$ and so rearranging [A.7] gives

$$\frac{\partial \pi^*}{\partial p_k} = \sum_i (R'f_i - p_i) \frac{\partial z_i^*}{\partial p_k} - z_k^* = -z_k^* = -D_k(p_1, p_2) \tag{A.8}$$

which is indeed negative as expected. Profit declines with the price of input k but it is intuitively plausible (and it can be proved rigorously) that the rate of decline of profit with p_k becomes smaller as p_k rises, i.e. π^* is concave in input prices. Hence

$$\frac{\partial^2 \pi^*}{\partial p_k^2} > 0 \tag{A.9}$$

(remember $\partial \pi^* / \partial p_k < 0$ and so it is becoming less negative if the rate of decline is itself declining). But from [A.8]

$$\frac{\partial^2 \pi^*}{\partial p_k^2} = -\frac{\partial D_k}{\partial p_k} > 0$$

and so

$$\frac{\partial D_k}{\partial p_k} < 0 \tag{A.10}$$

We have therefore given a justification for the slope of D_1 in Fig. 1, in terms of the maximum profit function π^*. (Note the similarity to the methods used in sections 4B and 8B: this is a reflection of the similarity of the structures of the corresponding optimization problems.)

We can also use $\pi^*(p_1, p_2)$ to establish another important property of the input demand functions. Recall section 5A, where it was pointed out that if a function possesses continuous second derivatives the second-order cross partials are equal. Applying this to π^*, we see that

$$\frac{\partial^2 \pi^*}{\partial p_1 \partial p_2} = \frac{\partial D_1}{\partial p_2} = \frac{\partial D_2}{\partial p_1} = \frac{\partial^2 \pi^*}{\partial p_2 \partial p_1} \qquad [\text{A}.11]$$

The cross effects of changes in the price of one input on the demand for the other are equal. (Compare the result in section 5A on the equality of cross-substitution effects.) If $\partial D_i/\partial p_k > 0$ the inputs are substitutes and if $\partial D_i/\partial p_k < 0$ they are complements.

Substitution and output effects

The firm's demand for z_1 changes as p_1 changes, first because a *different input combination* will now minimize the cost of any given output and secondly because a *different output level* will now be optimal. We can call these two effects the *substitution* and *output effects* of a change in p_1. In section 8B we showed that the substitution effect of an input price fall always leads to a rise in the use of the input whose price had fallen. We will now use techniques similar to those used in deriving the Slutsky equation of section 5B, to decompose the total effect of a change in p_1 into the substitution and output effects.

From section 8B we know that the *cost minimizing* z_1 depends on the input prices and the level of y:

$$\hat{z}_1 = h_1(p_1, p_2, y) \qquad [\text{A}.12]$$

where $\hat{z}_1$ denotes the cost minimizing z_1. From the firms' profit maximization problem [A.1] we know that the *profit maximizing* z_1 depends on p_1 and p_2, as shown in [A.5], and that the profit maximizing output y^* will therefore also depend on p_1 and p_2 since choice of z_1, z_2 determines y:

$$y^* = f(z_1^*, z_2^*) = y^*(p_1, p_2) \qquad [\text{A}.13]$$

If we set y in [A.12] equal to y^* in [A.13]:

$$y = y^*(p_1, p_2) \qquad [\text{A}.14]$$

and, since profit maximization implies cost minimization it must be true that

$$z_1^* = D_1(p_1, p_2) = \hat{z}_1 = h_1(p_1, p_2, y^*(p_1, p_2)) \qquad [\text{A}.15]$$

Now let p_1 vary but ensure that y in $h_1(p_1, p_2, y)$ varies to maintain the equalities in [A.14] and [A.15]. Hence h_1 will vary, first because with y constant a new cost minimizing input combination is chosen and secondly because varying p_1 will change y^* and therefore y via [A.14]. Hence differentiating [A.15] with respect to p_1 gives

$$\frac{\partial D_1}{\partial p_1} = \frac{\partial h_1}{\partial p_1} + \frac{\partial h_1}{\partial y} \cdot \frac{\partial y}{\partial y^*} \cdot \frac{\partial y^*}{\partial p_1} \qquad [\text{A}.16]$$

where the first term on the righthand side of [A.16] shows how z_1 varies with p_1 when y is constant and so is the substitution effect. The second term is the rate at which z_1 varies indirectly with p_1 because of the effect of changes in p_1 on the optimal output level. This is the output effect. From section 8B we know that

$$\frac{\partial h_1}{\partial p_1} < 0$$

so let us consider the output effect. $\partial h_1/\partial y$ is the rate at which z_1 varies with y along the cost minimizing expansion path and $\partial h_1/\partial y$ may be positive (z_1 is normal) or negative (z_1 is an inferior input). From [A.14], $\partial y/\partial y^* = 1$. The last part of the second term is $\partial y^*/\partial p_1$: the rate at which the profit maximizing output varies with the price of input 1. Now, recalling equation [A.4] above, y^* is determined by the equality of marginal revenue with marginal cost. If a rise in p_1 shifts the marginal cost curve upward then output must fall and, conversely, if the marginal cost curve falls as p_1 rises output will rise. Hence $\partial y^*/\partial p_1$ is positive or negative as MC falls or rises with p_1, i.e. as $\partial MC/\partial p_1$ is negative or positive. But from section 8B, $\partial MC/\partial p_1$ is negative or positive as z_1 is inferior or normal. Hence

$$\frac{\partial h_1}{\partial y} \gtrless 0 \Leftrightarrow \frac{\partial MC}{\partial p_1} \gtrless 0 \Leftrightarrow \frac{\partial y^*}{\partial p_1} \lessgtr 0$$

and therefore

$$\frac{\partial h_1}{\partial y} \cdot \frac{\partial y}{\partial y^*} \cdot \frac{\partial y^*}{\partial p_1} = \frac{\partial h_1}{\partial y} \cdot \frac{\partial y^*}{\partial p_1} < 0 \qquad [A.17]$$

The output effect of a rise in p_1 always reduces the demand for z_1, so reinforcing the substitution effect. We have therefore established by another route that

$$\frac{\partial D_1}{\partial p_1} = \frac{\partial h_1}{\partial p_1} + \frac{\partial h_1}{\partial y} \frac{\partial y^*}{\partial p_1} < 0 \qquad [A.18]$$

i.e. the input demand curve is negatively sloped, irrespective of whether the firm sells its output in a monopolised or competitive market.

From [A.18] we see that the slope of the firm's input demand curve will depend on the magnitude of the substitution and output effects. The substitution effect will in turn depend on the curvature of the firm's isoquants and if the elasticity of substitution (section 8B) is taken as the measure of curvature, the substitution effect is larger the larger is the elasticity of substitution. The output effect is the product of two terms and is larger the greater is the response of the cost minimizing level of z_1 to changes in output and the greater is the response of output to the change in input price. This latter influence will depend on how much marginal cost varies with the price of the input: the bigger the shift in the marginal cost curve the bigger the change in the profit maximizing output. If the firm is a monopolist in the output market the change in y will also depend on the slope of the marginal revenue curve: the steeper this is the smaller will be the change in y as the marginal cost curve shifts. (Draw a diagram to show this.)

The market input demand curve

The market demand curve for a good consumed only by individuals is derived by horizontally summing the individual demand curves. If an input is used only by firms which are monopolists in their respective output markets and these are unrelated in demand then the input market demand curve can be derived in the same way by horizontal summation of the individual firms' demand curves (See Question 4 of Exercise 14A). Apart from this somewhat unlikely case the input market demand curve is *not* the horizontal sum of individual firms' demand curves. The reason for this can be seen if we examine an input used only in production of one type of good which is sold on a competitive market by the many firms producing it. Consider Fig. 2, in which the curve $\sum_j D_1^{j0}$ is the horizontal sum of the individual firms' demand curves for input 1 and, at the initial price p_1^0, $\sum_j z_1^{j0}$ is demanded. Each individual demand curve is like the dashed line D_1 in Fig. 1, which shows how each firm's *ceteris paribus* demand varies with p_1. It is assumed in drawing D_1 that the firm regards the price of output as unalterable by its actions, so that the D_1^{j0} curve of each firm is derived with the price of output held fixed. Hence the $\sum_j D_1^{j0}$ curve is also based on the assumption that the price of output is constant. But when the input price p_1 falls to p_1^1 all firms' average and marginal cost curves alter. In the long run when the number of firms and the size of firms' plants can be varied the change in total output is determined by the change in the firms' average cost curves (see Chapter 10). Average cost curves shift down when the price of the input falls (section 8B) and the long-run supply of the industry will increase. The price of output will therefore fall, shifting the MRP_1, D_1^j and $\sum D_1^j$ curves to the left. This is shown in Fig. 2, where $\sum D_1^{j1}$ is the new horizontal sum of the new individual D_1^{j1} curves and the amount of input

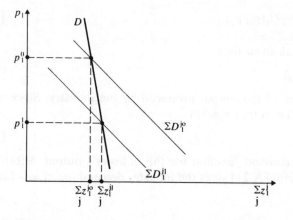

Fig. 2

demanded at p_1^1 is $\sum z_1^1$. We see that the market input demand curve is D, which is steeper than the $\sum_j D_1^j$ curves. (Compare the derivation of the market supply curves in Chapter 10.)

The market input demand curve is therefore determined by the demand conditions in the market for the output produced by the input, the change in firms' cost curves caused by the change in the input price and by the elasticity of substitution amongst the inputs.

Elasticity of market input demand*

It is possible to derive a simple expression for the elasticity of the market input demand function in the case in which all firms have the same constant returns to scale production function. (In this case the size of the individual firm is indeterminate but this does not matter since we are only concerned with the size and hence the input demand of all the firms together.) Since all production functions are identical and all firms face the same input prices, all firms have the same cost function $C(p_1, p_2, y^j)$, where y^j is the output of the jth firm. Because there are constant returns to scale the cost of producing y^j units is merely y^j times the cost of producing one unit. Letting $\tilde{C}(p_1, p_2) = C(p_1, p_2, 1)$ be the cost function for producing one unit, the total industry cost for producing $y = \sum y^j$ is

$$\sum C(p_1, p_2, y^j) = \sum y^j \tilde{C}(p_1, p_2) = y\tilde{C}(p_1, p_2) \qquad [A.19]$$

For industry equilibrium we require that (a) all firms are maximizing their profits, (b) every firm is just breaking even and (c) industry output, i.e. supply, equals demand. Now profit maximization implies cost minimization so that the jth firm's demand for z_1 is

$$z_1^j = C_1(p_1, p_2, y^j) = y^j \tilde{C}_1(p_1, p_2) \qquad [A.20]$$

where $\tilde{C}_1 = \partial \tilde{C}/\partial p_1$, and so the industry demand for z_1 is

$$z_1 = \sum z_1^j = y\tilde{C}_1(p_1, p_2) \qquad [A.21]$$

If all firms just break even then

$$p = \tilde{C}(p_1, p_2) \qquad [A.22]$$

where p is the price of the output produced by the industry. Since supply equals demand in the output market

$$y = D(p) \qquad [A.23]$$

where $D(p)$ is the demand function for the industry's output. Substituting [A.22] and [A.23] into [A.21] gives the industry demand for z_1 as a function of the input prices only:

$$z_1 = D(\tilde{C}(p_1, p_2)) \cdot \tilde{C}_1(p_1, p_2) \qquad [A.24]$$

Differentiation of [A.24] with respect to p gives

$$\frac{\partial z_1}{\partial p_1} = D' \cdot \tilde{C}_1 \cdot \tilde{C}_1 + D \cdot \tilde{C}_{11} \qquad [A.25]$$

where $D' = dy/dp$ and $\tilde{C}_{11} = \partial^2 C/\partial p_1^2$. Multiplying [A.25] through by $-p_1/z_1$ and using [A.21] gives the elasticity of demand for z_1 with respect to its price

$$e_1 = \frac{-\partial z_1}{\partial p_1}\frac{p_1}{z_1} = \frac{-dy}{dp}\frac{p}{y} \cdot \frac{p_1 z_1}{py} - \frac{yp_1}{z_1}\tilde{C}_{11} = e \cdot s_1 - \frac{yp_1}{z_1}\tilde{C}_{11} \qquad [A.26]$$

where e is the price elasticity of demand in the product market and s_1 is the share of total cost spent on z_1. The second term in the expression is less easy to interpret as it stands. However, recalling the discussion of the individual firm's demand and [A.18], $\tilde{C}_{11}$ is the substitution effect, showing how z_1 varies with p_1 with output constant. The second term therefore depends on the shape of the isoquant, i.e. the elasticity of substitution. In fact we can show that the second term can be written as $s_2 \cdot \sigma$, where s_2 is the proportion of cost spent on the second input and σ is the elasticity of substitution. (See Exercise 14A.) Hence the own price elasticity of demand for z_1 can be written as

$$e_1 = s_1 e + s_2 \sigma \qquad [A.27]$$

The own price elasticity of demand for the input by the industry is a weighted average (since $s_1 + s_2 = 1$) of the elasticity of demand for the output produced by the input and the elasticity of substitution. The output effect $s_1 e$ depends on how responsive cost and therefore the price of output is to changes in input prices (recall from Chapter 8 that s_1 is the elasticity of total and average cost and, in the constant returns case, marginal cost to p_1) and on how demand (equals output) varies with market price.

Exercise 14A
1.* Show that the term $-(yp_1/z_1)\tilde{C}_{11}$ in [A.26] can indeed be written as $s_2\sigma$. Generalize [A.27] to the case of the more than two inputs. (See Hicks (1963) and Diewert (1971), and Exercise 8B, Question 8.)
2.* The D curve in Fig. 2 is the long-run market demand curve for the input since it shows how demand varies when all inputs and the number of firms are freely variable. Construct the short-run market demand curve showing how demand varies with the price of the input when the other input is fixed and the number of firms does not alter. Would you expect this curve to be more or less elastic than that in Fig. 2?
3. Suppose that the fall in p_1 leads to a shift in the market demand curve for z_2. Under what circumstances will this change the price of z_2? What effect will this have on the market demand curve for z_1?
4. Explain why, when the buyers of an input are monopolists in markets unrelated to each other in demand, the input market demand curve can

be obtained by horizontal summation of the individual firms' demand curves.

5.* Discuss the problems involved in deriving an input demand curve for an oligopolistic industry, with and without the assumption of collusion.

B. Supply of inputs

Inputs may be supplied either by profit maximizing firms or by utility maximizing individuals. An input supplied by a firm is simply a commodity produced subject to the usual technological constraints, and used by firms to produce other commodities. Since we devoted Chapter 9 to the competitive firm's supply decision, we will concentrate here on inputs supplied by individuals.

The individual is assumed (for the moment) to be endowed with a fixed amount of some good $\bar{z}$ which he may sell at the ruling market price. If $\bar{z}$ does not enter into his utility function then the individual will sell his entire endowment in order to maximize the income available to be spent on goods which do enter his utility function. In this case the supply curve of the individual is a vertical line through his initial endowment: he sells all his endowment at any positive market price.

The main source of income for most individuals is the sale of their labour time and they will not in general be indifferent about the amount of time spent working. We can apply the utility maximizing models of sections 3E, 5C and 5D to derive the supply curves of those inputs (mainly labour time) which do enter the individual's utility function. The models are fairly general in that they can allow for the effect of non-price variables such as pleasantness of working conditions, and for the fact that individuals have different skill levels. The latter complication is easily handled by defining the labour time of individuals with different skill or ability levels as different commodities. Each individual will then be earning income by supplying a particular type of labour time which commands a particular wage. In a competititive input market the price of different types of inputs will be determined in the usual way by the equilibrium of demand and supply. We discussed the market demand curve in section A, and for inputs supplied by individuals the market supply curve is simply the horizontal sum of the individual supply curves derived in the earlier chapters. We will therefore take up here a further problem: what determines the *kind* of labour time supplied by an individual?

Consider the decision whether to acquire a skill. Suppose for the moment that all jobs have equally pleasant working conditions and other non-pecuniary attributes and that the individual would work the same length of time at whatever job he chose. Under these circumstances the decision is made solely on the basis of the income streams earned over the working life of the individual in skilled and unskilled jobs, and the costs of acquiring the skill. In Fig. 3 the unskilled job can be taken up immediately and gives rise to the income stream labelled M_1. Time t_R is the date at which the individual

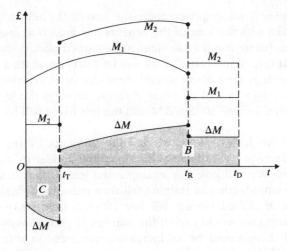

Fig. 3

will retire and t_D the date of his death. The income stream drops at t_R when the individual stops working and receives a pension. We have made the remarkable assumption that the individual knows the date of his death. t_D will in general be a random variable (which may be less than t_R) and may be affected by the type of job chosen by the individual. (The unskilled job may carry a larger probability of a fatal accident, or life expectancy may depend on income through its effect on consumption.) We will ignore these complications, as well as those presented by the possibility of life insurance, in order to isolate the essential features of the skill acquisition decision: we assume that the individual's decision is affected only by his expected life t_D, which is independent of his job.

The curve M_2 in Fig. 3 is the income stream earned if the individual acquires the skill. Acquisition of the skill requires a period of t_T years training during which the income earned is below that which could be earned in the unskilled job. Income during training may be lower because the individual cannot work and train at the same time, or he can only work at lower wages while being trained, or there are direct cash outlays (tuition fees etc.) during training. After t_T years the now skilled worker will earn a larger income and after his retirement will have a larger pension.

The individual is therefore choosing between two income streams M_1 and M_2 and this is an *investment decision*, in that he incurs costs now in order to receive future benefit. We can see this clearly from the curve ΔM in Fig. 3 which plots the difference $(M_2 - M_1)$ between the two income streams. ΔM shows the *net* effect of acquiring a skill on the individual's lifetime income stream. He incurs a net cost over the period up to t_T while he is training and receives the benefits of increased income thereafter. Chapter 15 is devoted to the analysis of intertemporal decision-making and so we will not consider in detail how the individual decides whether the net opportunity costs of training are greater or less than the benefits. We just point out here that in general he will not simply compare the *sum* of the net costs (the area C below the t axis) with the *sum* of the benefits (the area B above the t axis). £1 earned in the future is *not* equivalent to £1 earned now, because if there is a positive real rate of interest £1 now will be worth more than £1 in the future. Future earnings (and costs) should therefore be *discounted,* and the larger is the individual's rate of discount of future earnings the less will he value the incremental income stream ΔM and the less likely will he be to acquire the skill.

Even though we have not examined the mechanics of the individual's investment decision we can use this very simple model to make a number of predictions. We will give one example and leave the rest to the exercises. If the (discounted) costs of training fall then more individuals will train and the supply of skilled labour will rise (after a lag of t_T years). Therefore during a slump we would expect the number of people wishing to train to increase and there would be an increased enrolment in voluntary full-time education. This is because a general depression (which is not expected to be permanent) will either reduce wages or the probability of finding work in skilled and unskilled jobs. This reduces the opportunity cost of full-time training (i.e. the expected unskilled wage forgone which equals the unskilled wage times the probability of getting an unskilled job). Provided the depression is expected to last for no more than the training period the *current* reduction in the skilled wage or the probability of getting a skilled job will not affect the future benefits of training. Hence the costs of training will have declined relative to the benefits and more people will wish to train.

Since training is an investment decision which alters the income earning potential of the individual the models of skill acquisition are usually referred to as *human capital theory.* When training is viewed in this way the concepts of inter-temporal decision-making developed in the next chapter generate many useful insights (as the references at the end of this chapter demonstrate). However, the closeness of the analogy with investment to improve or increase physical capital should not be overstated. There are two main differences.

First, the aim of investment in physical capital is to maximize the net discounted *earnings* of the owner of the capital, whereas the individual considering an investment to change his earning ability is concerned with maximizing his discounted lifetime *utility.* This is so for exactly the same reason that at any point in time the individual (with a given skill level) will not wish to maximize his *earnings.* His utility depends not just on his income but also on the number of hours worked and the pleasantness or otherwise of working conditions. Hence predictions based on the assumption that the individual wishes to maximize income in the period may not hold true. Similarly with predictions based on the assumption of maximization of discounted lifetime earnings. Only if hours worked and all non-wage attributes of jobs are held constant will a job with higher discounted lifetime earnings necessarily yield higher discounted lifetime utility. A consequence of this is that monetary and subjective rates of return from investment in training will differ. It is the subjective rate of return which will be compared with the individual's opportunity cost of funds, and it may in general be greater or less than the monetary rate of return. We should therefore interpret with care the results of studies which calculate the monetary rates of return (social and private) to investment in training and education.

A second important difference between human and physical capital theory is that property rights in the physical asset exist and can be sold but since slavery is illegal only the *services* of human capital (i.e. the individual's labour time) can be sold, and this usually only for limited periods. In other words the only economic agent who can own the labour services embodied in an individual is that individual. This may have important consequences for the supply of funds to finance investment in human capital and hence on the supply of trained labour. An individual who wishes to undertake full-time training to improve his future earning ability will need funds to finance himself while training. If he does not have other assets which he can sell he will need to borrow. He will usually find it more difficult or more expensive to borrow a given sum to finance his training than to borrow the same sum to buy a physical asset. The reason is that the lender will take on a greater risk in financing training because the loan cannot be secured against the human capital which it has financed. If a borrower who acquires a physical asset defaults the lender has a claim on the physical asset: he can legally become the owner of the asset in lieu of repayment and can then sell it to recover part of his initial loan. In the case of a loan to finance human capital formation such a transfer of ownership on default is impossible.

Exercise 14B
1. Extend the skill acquisition model to take account of (a) t_D and (b) t_R varying with skill level.
2. Examine the effect of (a) proportional and progressive income taxes, and (b) increases in state-provided pensions (which are independent of earned income), on the acquisition of skills.
3.* Suppose that the hours worked in the skilled and unskilled job differ but that the two jobs have equally attractive non-wage attributes. The difference in income streams would now reflect both a difference in wage rates and a difference in hours worked so that a comparison of *actual* income streams is not a comparison of like with like. How would you adjust the income streams so that they can be compared (i.e. so that they do reflect the different utility streams)? (*Hint:* refer back to section 4C and the exercise there.) It is common in the training literature to work out the individual's rate of return on the investment in training on the basis of the income streams which may reflect differences in hours worked. Under what circumstances will this procedure over- or under-estimate the true individual rate of return?
4.* How would you attempt to estimate the financial rate of return on university education to the individual student? Is this likely to differ

from the social rate of return (i.e. are there any differences between the private costs and benefits to the student and the costs and benefits to society)? Since the actual number of students is determined by the private rate of return is there 'too much' or 'too little' human capital formation? If there is inefficiency (i.e. a divergence between social and private rates of return) discuss as possible policies which could correct the misallocation of special taxes (positive or negative) on graduates, loan and grant finance and subsidized tuitition. Can you suggest other policies?

5.* How is the theory of human capital formation affected by the fact that individuals are not equally *capable* of becoming carpenters, plumbers, computer programmers or university professors?

6.* Using the text model as a guide, develop a model of the individual's inter-country or inter-regional migration decision. Use the model to analyse the effect of changes in the income tax rate, taxes on emigrants, and reduced transport costs.

7. Return to this section when you have covered the material in Chapter 15, and formulate an expression for the net present value of the investment in skill acquisition. Explain why an increase in the interest rate will reduce the supply of skilled labour.

8.* Comment on the assumptions made in the model of this section of the knowledge the individual is assumed to have about future variables. What are the major uncertainties which in practice exist? Formulate a model which takes account of them (you may find it helpful to read Ch. 19 first). Would your answers to Question 2 above be different as a result?

C. Monopsony

Monopsony is defined as a market in which there is a single buyer of a commodity who confronts many sellers. Each of the sellers treats the market price of the good as a parameter and so there is a market supply curve for the good which is derived in the usual way from the supply curves of the individual suppliers. This means that the single buyer of the good faces a market supply function relating total supply to the price he pays. This can be expressed (in inverse form) as:

$$p_1 = p_1(z_1) \qquad (p_1' > 0) \qquad\qquad [C.1]$$

where [C.1] shows the price of the commodity which must be paid to generate a particular supply. Note that the buyer is assumed to face an upward-sloping supply curve: the price required is an increasing function of the amount supplied.

The market price of the monopsonized input is determined, given the supply function [C.1], by the buyer's demand for z_1. We will assume that the monopsonist is a profit maximizing firm, in which case the demand for z_1 and hence its price is determined by the firm's profit maximizing decision. In the two-input single-output case the firm's problem is

$$\max_{z_1, z_2} = R[f(z_1, z_2)] - p_1(z_1)z_1 - p_2 z_2 \qquad [\text{C.2}]$$

This is very similar to problem [A.1] except that p_1 depends on z_1 because of [C.1]. Input 2 is assumed to be bought on a market in which the firm treats p_2 as a parameter. The firm's output may be sold in a competitive or a monopolized market: monopsony need not imply monopoly. The firm may, for example, be the only employer of labour in a particular area but be selling its output in a market where it competes with many other firms, and labour may be relatively immobile.

Necessary conditions for a maximum of [C.2] are (when both z_1 and z_2 are positive at the optimum):

$$R'f_1 - (p_1 + p_1' z_1) = 0 \qquad [\text{C.3}]$$

$$R'f_2 - p_2 = 0 \qquad [\text{C.4}]$$

[C.4] is identical with [A.2], but [C.3] is not, because of the $p_1' z_1$ term. The firm will adjust its use of an input up to the point at which the additional revenue from a unit of the input equals the extra cost incurred. When the price of the input is independent of the number of units bought the cost of an extra unit is its price. But when the firm faces an upward sloping supply curve for the input it must pay a higher price for *all* units bought to ensure supply for an extra unit. This means that the cost of an extra unit of z_1 is the price paid for that unit *plus* the increased cost of the units already bought, which is the rise in p_1 times the amount of z_1 bought: $p_1' z_1$. Hence writing MRP_i for the marginal revenue product of input i and MBC_i for the marginal cost of z_i to the buyer (marginal buyer cost) the firm maximizes profits by setting

$$MRP_1 = MBC_1 > p_1 \qquad [\text{C.5}]$$

$$MRP_2 = MBC_2 = p_2 \qquad [\text{C.6}]$$

This equilibrium is illustrated for the monopsonized input in Fig. 4. S_1 is the supply curve of z_1 and MBC_1 plots the marginal buyer cost $(p_1 + p_1' z_1)$ of the single buyer. $MRP_1(z_2^*)$ is the marginal revenue product curve for the input given the optimal level of z_2. The firm maximizes profit with respect to z_1 by equating MRP_1 to MBC_1 at z_1^*. To generate this supply of z_1 the firm will set the monopsony price p_1^* where $p_1^* = p_1(z_1^*)$.

The analysis of the single buyer confronting many competitive sellers is rather similar to the analysis in Chapter 11 of the single seller confronting many competing buyers. In each case the firm realizes that it faces a curve relating price to quantity which summarizes the response of the competitive side of the market and the firm sets the quantity or price in the light of this interdependence of price and quantity. In each case the market price overstates the *marginal* profit contribution of the quantity and in each case this overstatement depends on the responsiveness of quantity to changes in

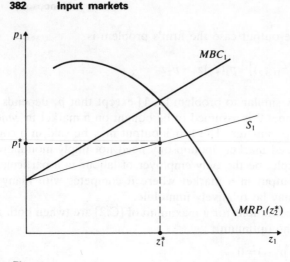

Fig. 4

price. Under monopoly the firm equates $MR = p[1-(1/e)]$ to the marginal cost of output, and the smaller is the elasticity of demand e the greater is the difference between price and marginal cost. [C.5] can usefully be rewritten in a similar way. Defining the elasticity of supply of z_1 with respect to price as

$$e_1^s = \frac{dz_1}{dp_1} \cdot \frac{p_1}{z_1} \tag{C.7}$$

we see that

$$MBC_1 = p_1 + \frac{dp_1}{dz_1} \cdot z_1 = p_1 \left(1 + \frac{1}{e_1^s}\right) \tag{C.8}$$

and so [C.5] becomes

$$MRP_1 = p_1 \left(1 + \frac{1}{e_1^s}\right) \tag{C.9}$$

The less elastic is supply with respect to price the greater will be the difference betwwn MRP_1 and the price of the input. In other words, the less responsive to price the input supply is, the greater the excess of the value of the marginal unit of the input over the price it receives. This could be regarded as a measure of the degree of 'monopsonistic exploitation'.

The effect of monopsony and output monopoly on the input market

When output is produced from two or more inputs the analysis of the effect of both monopsony and output monopoly on the price of one of the inputs is complicated, because the use of the other input is likely to change as well, thus shifting the MRP_1 curve. If the output is produced by a single input this complication does not arise, and it is possible to show the implications of monopsony and output monopoly in a single simple diagram

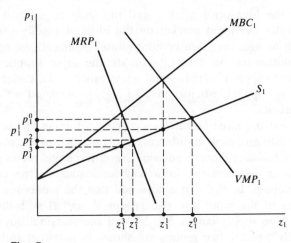

Fig. 5

such as Fig. 5. Since there is a single input z_1 its marginal product depends only on z_1 and so the marginal revenue product MRP_1 and the value of the marginal product VMP_1 curves in Fig. 5 are fixed. S_1 and MBC_1 are supply and marginal buyer cost curves. There are four possible equilibria in this input market, where suppliers treat the price of z_1 as a parameter. If the firm also treats p_1 as given, i.e. if it acts as if it has no monopsony power and if it also treats output price as a parameter then VMP_1 is its demand curve for z_1 and the market price is p_1^0. If the firm uses its monopsony power but continues to treat output price as a parameter it will equate VMP_1 to MBC_1 and set the price p_1^1. If the firm monopolizes its output market but regards p_1 as a parameter its demand curve for z_1 is MRP_1 and the price of z_1 is p_1^2. Finally, if the firm exercises both monopoly and monopsony power it equates MRP_1 and MBC_1 and sets a price p_1^3. We see therefore that the price in an output market is reduced below the competitive level p_1^0 by both monopsony and monopoly power. The less elastic are the demand for output and the supply of input functions, the lower will be the price paid to suppliers of the input.

Discriminating monopsony*

We saw in Chapter 11 that a monopolist will be able to increase his net profit if he can separate his overall market into sub-markets with differing demand elasticities and charge different prices in the sub-markets, provided that the costs of separating the markets do not exceed the resulting increase in profit. The monopsonist has similar opportunities and so may pay different prices to different groups of suppliers. He must be able to prevent arbitrage, i.e. it must be impossible for anyone to buy the input from the suppliers facing the low price and sell in the high price market. This will be easier when the input is physically inseparable from the supplier, as in the labour market. In this case the low-price worker will have to try to sell his labour himself in the high-price market and this may be difficult if the monopsonist separates the input market on the basis of readily verifiable characteristics such as age, sex, race or educational qualifications. In addition the monopsonist must be able to separate the input suppliers into groups with different supply elasticities and again this may be easier in the labour market where supply elasticities may be highly correlated with easily verifiable characteristics.

Provided that the monopsonist can prevent arbitrage and separate the input suppliers into groups with different supply elasticities and provided also that the cost of fulfilling those conditions is not 'too large' prices are set by the discriminating monopsonist in a way analogous to the case of discriminating monopoly. In Fig. 6 it is assumed that the monopsonist can divide the suppliers of the input into two groups A and B with different supply elasticities. The supply curves S_1^A, S_1^B and the marginal buyer cost curves MBC^A, MBC^B of the two groups are shown in parts (a) and (b) of the figure. If the monopsonist wishes to purchase a given small quantity of the input he will buy only from group A, since for small levels of z^A, $MBC^A < MBC^B$. For requirements larger than z_1^A the firm will allocate its purchases between the two groups to satisfy

$$MBC^A = MBC^B \qquad\qquad [C.10]$$

For suppose [C.10] does not hold and in particular that $MBC^A > MBC^B$. Then if the firm buys one unit less from group A and one unit more from group B total cost of z falls by MBC^A and rises by MBC^B. Thus the net effect is to reduce the total cost of z to the firm. The marginal buyer cost curve for the firm, given that it can discriminate in this way, is the horizontal sum of MBC^A and MBC^B for $z > z_1^A$ and MBC^A for $z \le z_1^A$. This is drawn in part (c) of Fig. 6 as the curve MBC.

Part (c) also contains the firm's marginal revenue product curve MRP (we assume the monopsonist is also a monopolist) for the input and so profit is maximized where $MBC = MRP$, giving total purchases $z = z^*$.

Given the derivation of MBC we see that profit maximization implies

$$MBC^A = MBC^B = MRP \qquad\qquad [C.11]$$

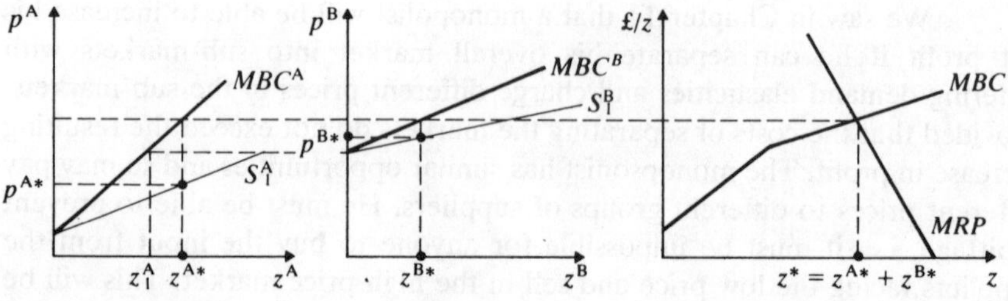

(a) (b) (c)

Fig. 6

In the figure total purchases of z^* are divided betwen the two groups of suppliers so that $z^{A*} + z^{B*} = z^*$ and [C.11] is satisfied. The prices set to the two groups are p^{A*}, p^{B*}. Using [C.8] and writing e^A, e^B for the supply elasticities of the two groups, the prices must satisfy

$$p^{A*}\left(1 + \frac{1}{e^A}\right) = p^{B*}\left(1 + \frac{1}{e^B}\right) \qquad [C.12]$$

Hence the group with the larger elasticity of supply will receive the higher price; in Fig. 6 this is group B.

Exercise 14C

1. Under monopoly there is no supply curve for the monopolized output in the sense of a one to one correspondence between market price and quantity produced. Show that under monopsony there is no market demand curve for the monopsonized input.
2. Analyse the monopsonist's cost minimization problem and the monopsonist's cost curves. (*Hint:* what does [C.1] imply about the isocost curves?) Show that at the monopsony equilibrium the input price ratio is not in general equal to the ratio of marginal products.
3. Suggest an index of monopsony power similar to the index of monopoly power mentioned in Chapter 11. How would you attempt to measure the losses imposed on input suppliers by monopsony (See Exercise 4C)?
4. Suppose that the two groups of suppliers in Fig. 6 were workers in different areas and that there was a cost of migration M between the two areas. How would this affect the determination of prices and purchases of z?
5. What is the effect of minimum wage legislation on the level of employment in (a) a competitive labour market (b) a monopsonized labour market?
6.* It is usually argued that for the 'same job':
        women are paid less than men;
        blacks are paid less than whites.
    If firms are profit maximizers, explain why this must require monopsony in the relevant labour markets, and discuss the implications for relative supply elasticities.
7.* What is the effect of equal pay legislation which makes it illegal for firms to pay men and women different wages for the same work? Do you think that women are paid less than men in the same jobs because of monopsonistic discrimination? If not what alternative explanations can you suggest for their wage differentials?

D. Monopoly in the input market

This section examines the determination of input prices when the buyers' side of the market is competitive but the supply is monopolized. If the input is non-human we can immediately apply the analysis of Chapters

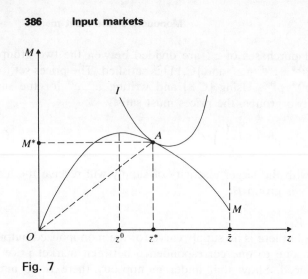

Fig. 7

11 or 13, depending on whether the single seller is interested in maximizing the profit from the sale of the input or has other objectives. We will therefore concentrate on monopoly in the supply of labour. The simplest case is that in which there is a single supplier of the labour because the labour he supplies is of a unique quality. An example of this would be a particularly talented musician or painter. He will face a downward sloping demand curve for his services because there is no perfect substitute for them. The individual's income is the total revenue he gets from the sale of his services and this is plotted as a function of the amount sold (z) in Fig. 7. Given the negatively sloped demand curve for z, the individual's income $M = pz$ (where p is the price of a unit of z) rises with z but then reaches a maximum at z^0 (where marginal revenue is zero) and then declines. $\bar{z}$ is the maximum feasible supply, set by the length of the period. The individual presumably prefers more income to less but his preferences as regards z (i.e. performing or painting) may be more complicated. He may like providing z but eventually as z increases with M fixed he will come to value his non-performing time more highly (even the most dedicated of artists will like to eat, sleep and argue). In this case, as in Fig. 7 his indifference curves will at first be negatively sloped, indicating that he prefers more of both M *and* z to less, but as z increases he starts to prefer less z to more, and the indifference curves become positively sloped.

In Fig. 7 the individual maximizes his utility at point A where he sells z^* of his services for an income of M^*, so that the price of his services (or fee) is M^*/z^*, the slope of the ray OA from the origin to A. In this case because of the individual's initial preference for work he is in equilibrium where his indifference curve is negatively sloped: he would be prepared to work more for the same income. However because at A his income curve OM is negatively sloped he would lose income by doing more work. At A the individual is doing more work than will maximize his income. This result depends on the individual's preferences and the demand for his services: the

reader can easily construct cases in which the individual either just maximizes his income or works less hard than will maximize M. We will leave
the comparative static properties of this model to the exercises and will
conclude by pointing out its resemblance to the Scitovsky model of the
entrepreneurial firm (section 13B). In both models the decision maker has a
utility function defined on income and work effort and there is a concave
relationship between income and effort. There is however one important
difference between the models: the individual of the model in this section
supplies a unique type of labour. This means that there is no possibility of
entry into the market for z and so, unlike the Scitovsky model of the firm,
the long-run equilibrium (after entry) is not one of profit maximization.

Unions as monopolists*

We will define a union as any association of the suppliers of a
particular type of labour which is formed with the aim of raising wages or
improving working conditions. A union need not, of course, be described as
such by its members: many professional associations (such as the British
Medical Association and the Law Society) act as unions. Not all unions
may be successful in raising the wages of their members above the competitive level. The union, like any would-be monopolist, must be able to control
the supply of labour offered to firms. One method of doing this is to ensure
that only union members can sell their labour in that particular market, a
device known as the 'closed shop'. The closed shop may, by itself, reduce the
supply of labour to the market if some potential workers dislike being union
members as such. In general, however, the closed shop must be coupled with
restrictions on the number of union members if all members are to be
employed, since higher wages will increase the number of workers wishing
to join the union, i.e. become employed at the higher wage.

If the union can act as a monopolist its behaviour will depend on the
objectives it pursues. By analogy with Chapter 13 it may be useful to
distinguish between the objectives of the officials who run the union and
those of the members. In the case of the firm, where conflicts of interest may
exist between shareholders and managers, the extent to which the managers
pursue the interests of the shareholders depends on the incentive system
which relates managerial pay to profits and on the threat of product or
capital market competition. Similar mechanisms may be at work in the case
of the union. Officials' salaries can be related to the pay of members of the
union. Unions which do not attend sufficiently closely to their members'
interests may start to lose members to rival unions. Officials may be
controlled directly through elections, but here the control mechanism may
be much weaker than in a firm. Each union member has only one vote and
so many members must cooperate to change the officials. Shareholders vote
in proportion to the numbers of shares held and so a relatively small group
of individual shareholders may exercise effective control.

We can use Fig. 8 to illustrate the implications of different union
objectives. D is the market demand curve for the type of labour

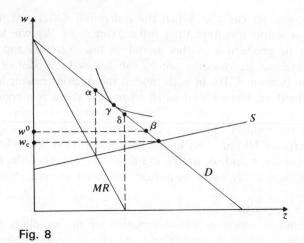

Fig. 8

monopolized by the union. *MR* is the corresponding 'marginal revenue' curve which shows the rate at which the total wage bill wz varies with z. S is the supply curve of z showing the minimum wage necessary to generate different supplies of labour. w_c is the competitive wage if there is no effective union. Economic rent is the surplus income that suppliers of an input receive over and above that necessary to induce them to supply the input (see exercise 4C). In Fig. 8 the total payment necessary to retain a given supply of labour z is the area under the S curve up to z, whereas the actual payment is wz. Hence economic rent is wz less the area under S up to the amount of z supplied. It is identical to the profit of a monopolist (if S is regarded as a kind of marginal cost curve). Hence, if the union wishes to maximize the economic rent of its members it will choose the point α on D: it will restrict supply to where MR cuts S, and so raise the wage above the competitive level.

If the union officials determine the objectives of the union the above policy may not be followed. The officials may for example prefer to maximize the size of the union because of the salary, political power and prestige associated with control of a large union. However, given the downward sloping demand curve for the labour of the union's members (and assuming a proportional relationship between z and numbers of members), a larger membership implies a lower wage. If the wage falls too low then members may assert themselves and remove the officials. Even if they do not the lowest wage that will be set by the union is w_c. If w is lowered below w_c the number of workers willing to supply labour will decline and so union membership will fall. Hence membership maximization will result in a wage equal to w_c or to some (larger) minimum level acceptable to members, such as w^0 in Fig. 8 where the union moves down D to β. Of course, by extending membership of one union to other types of workers the union leaders may mitigate this effect, in a manner analogous to product diversification by firms. Alternatively, the officials' preferences may be representable by a utility function of the form $U = U(w, z)$. They may prefer higher wages for their members to smaller, but also prefer a larger union to a smaller. In this case their preferences will give rise to indifference curves with the shape of those of section 3A. The officials are constrained by the market demand function for z and so the optimum position chosen on D is at γ where the indifference curve I is tangent to D. A special form of the above utility function is

$$U(w, z) = wz \qquad\qquad [\text{D.1}]$$

i.e. they wish to maximize the total wage bill. This may be because union membership fees are proportional to members' incomes or the wage rate. The total membership fees are the union's income and the officials' salaries or other benefits (pleasant working conditions, paid holidays, union conferences in exotic locations) may increase with the union's income. If [D.1] holds the indifference curves are rectangular hyperbolas (not shown in the figure) and the union chooses the point δ on D where MR is zero and so wz is maximized.

    We have assumed so far that the union consists only of workers actually in employment so that only the interests of the employed workers were considered. Suppose, however, that the union does not restrict membership to employed workers but extends membership to anyone who wishes to work in the industry, so that some members may be unemployed. The union can still enforce a closed shop on employers and can still fix the wage because it will expel members who work for less than the wage set by the union. We must distinguish between the wage w actually paid to members in work and the expected or average wage $\bar{w}$ of all members employed and unemployed.

    This average wage is given by

$$\bar{w} = \frac{wz_e + w_u z_u}{z_e + z_u} = \frac{wz_e + w_u z_u}{z} \qquad\qquad [\text{D.2}]$$

where z_e and z_u are the number of members employed and unemployed respectively, $z = z_e + z_u$ is total union membership and w_u is the wage received by union members without a job in the industry. w_u may be unemployment benefit or it may be the wage paid to members who have temporarily taken a job elsewhere, while waiting for a job in the unionized industry at the wage w. (For example 'resting' actors often take on temporary jobs while waiting for acting jobs.) If there is fairly frequent movement of workers between jobs so that a worker may expect to spend the proportion z_e/z of his time in work at the wage w and the proportion z_u/z unemployed (in the unionized industry) or 'resting' at the wage w_u, then the number of individuals wishing to work in the industry (z) will be determined by the average wage $\bar{w}$:

$$z = z(\bar{w}) \qquad\qquad [\text{D.3}]$$

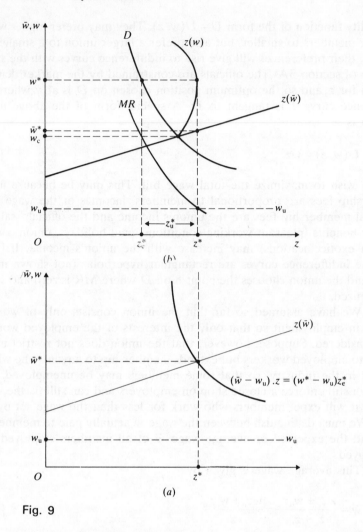

Fig. 9

The number of members actually in work is determined by the wage w set by the union and the market demand curve for workers:

$$z_e = D(w) \qquad \text{[D.4]}$$

Hence, once the union sets w, z_e is determined and from [D.2] and [D.3] the average wage and the number of members are also determined as functions of the wage set by the union. We can illustrate this in Fig. 9. In part (a) the $z(\bar{w})$ curve plots the number of members against the expected wage. If we rearrange [D.2] we get

$$\bar{w}z = wz_e + w_u z_u = wz_e + w_u(z - z_e)$$

and collecting terms we have

$$(\bar{w} - w_u)z = (w - w_u)z_e \qquad \text{[D.5]}$$

Now once w is fixed by the union z_e is also fixed (from [D.4]) and since w_u is assumed constant the righthand side of [D.5] is constant for given w. The lefthand side of [D.5] is the product of z and $(\bar{w} - w_u)$ and so if we plot the values of z and $(\bar{w} - w_u)$ satisfying [D.5] in Fig. 9(a) we will have a rectangular hyperbola. Since [D.2] (and hence [D.5]) and [D.3] must both be satisfied for a given w, the level of z for a particular value of w is shown by the intersection of the $z(w)$ curve and the relevant rectangular hyperbola generated by the particular w. Part (a) of Fig. 9 also shows the average wage for a given w, since there is only one value of $(\bar{w} - w_u)$ which satisfies both [D.2] and [D.3].

As w varies so will the position of the rectangular hyperbola in part (a) and hence z and $\bar{w}$ will also alter. The relationship between z, $\bar{w}$ and w is shown in part (b) of the figure. D and MR are again the market demand and 'marginal revenue' (or marginal wage bill) curves and $z(\bar{w})$ is reproduced from part (a). The curve $z(w)$ shows how z varies with w. Note that when $w \leq w_c$ all union members are employed and so $\bar{w} = w$ and $z(w)$ and $z(\bar{w})$ coincide. As w is raised above w_c the righthand side of [D.5] $(w - w_u)z_e$ rises at first, shifting the rectangular hyperbola in part (a) to the right and therefore raising z and $\bar{w}$. However as w is raised further $(w - w_u)z_e$ will reach a maximum and then decline. To see this expand $(w - w_u)z_e$ to give

$$wz_e - w_u z_e \tag{D.6}$$

The first term is the wage bill, shown by the area under the MR curve; the second term is the rectangular area under the w_u line in part (b). The difference between the two terms is maximized where the MR curve cuts the w_u line. Differentiating [D.6] with respect to w gives for a maximum (using [D.4]):

$$w\frac{dz_e}{dw} + z_e - w_u\frac{dz_e}{dw} = 0 \tag{D.7}$$

or

$$w + z_e\frac{dw}{dz_e} - w_u = 0 \tag{D.8}$$

The first term is the derivative of wz_e with respect to z_e (i.e. MR). Hence [D.6] is maximized where MR cuts w_u at a wage of w^* and from part (a) we see that w^* also maximizes z and $\bar{w}$. Any further rise in w will lower [D.6] and hence z so that the $z(w)$ curve bends back above w^*. Since z must also satisfy $z = z(\bar{w})$, the average wage $\bar{w}$ corresponding to any w is the height of the $z(\bar{w})$ curve at the level of $z(w)$ generated by the particular w.

We can now use Fig. 9(b) to examine the implications of the policy followed by the union. The members of the union may wish to maximize their average wage $\bar{w}$, in which case they will wish to see a wage of w^*, which leads to an expected wage of $\bar{w}^*$, and an unemployment rate amongst members of z_u^*/z^*. The union officials on the other hand may wish to maximize the size of the union z, in which case they will set the w which gives rise to the largest value of $z(w)$. But this is also w^*. In this model therefore the aims of members and officials differ but they can agree on an optimum wage rate.

It is possible to construct many models of the above kinds each of which may be appropriate to a particular union or industry. (The last model above may be useful in examining the behaviour of the actors' union, Equity.) The models are suggestive rather than exhaustive and they could be extended in a number of ways. A model of the way in which the union's objectives are determined is necessary in order to be able to predict what objectives will be dominant in what circumstances. This will require a detailed specification of the political constitution of the union, including the frequency and type of elections, whether officials are elected or are appointed and controlled by elected representatives and so on. In addition, the theory could be extended to take account of inter-union conflict or cooperation: will unions compete for new members? In what circumstances will unions merge or collude? It would be possible to approach these questions using the concepts of oligopoly theory developed in Chapter 12.

Exercise 14D
1. In Fig. 7 what will be the effects on the supply of the artist's services and the fee he charges of
    (a) shifts in the demand curve for his services
    (b) income taxes (proportional or progressive)
    (c) an alternative job (e.g. leaving music or painting) which pays a wage per hour which is independent of the hours worked
    (d) the development of cheap, good quality recordings or reproductions
    (e) state subsidies to opera houses, concert halls or modern art galleries?
2.* Why do the rules of many professional associations forbid or severely limit advertising by members? Why do some associations set their own examination and control their own pass rates, rather than being prepared to accept the results of the general educational system?
3.* What is the relevance of 'demarcation rules' and disputes to inter-union competition?

E. Bilateral monopoly

Bilateral monopoly is defined as a market in which a single seller of a good or input confronts a single buyer. A simple example is shown in Fig. 10. The seller S produces the input z which is required by the buyer B. S can produce z at a cost of $C(z)$ and this cost function for z gives rise to the average and marginal cost curves for z: $AC(z)$, $MC(z)$, which plot $C(z)/z$ and $C'(z)$ respectively. The single buyer B uses the input z to produce an output y subject to the production function $y = f(z)$. B monopolizes the market for y and the total revenue that B receives from the sale of y is

$$R = p(y)y = p(f(z)) \cdot f(z) = R(f(z)) \qquad [E.1]$$

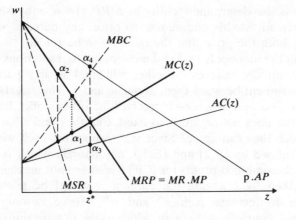

Fig. 10

(The analysis is essentially unchanged if y is sold in a competitive market.)
This total revenue function gives rise to the marginal revenue product curve
MRP which plots $dR/dz = R'f' = MR.MP$, using the notation of sections A
and C. The average revenue product curve ARP plots $R/z = py/z = pAP$,
where AP is the average product of $z : y/z$. The profits of B and S are

$$\pi^B = R(f(z)) - wz \qquad\qquad\qquad\qquad\qquad [\text{E.2}]$$
$$\pi^S = wz - C(z) \qquad\qquad\qquad\qquad\qquad\quad [\text{E.3}]$$

where w is the price of z.

If S treats w as a parameter and therefore produces where $MC(z) =$
w, then MC is the seller's supply curve. B would face the dashed marginal
buyer cost curve MBC and would choose a level of z where $MBC = MRP$.
The monopsony solution is at α_1 where B is off his demand curve for z
(MRP) and S is on his supply curve ($MC(z)$). Conversely, if B regards w as
a parameter and therefore wishes to purchase an amount of z where
$MRP = w$, then the MRP curve is B's demand curve for z. Hence the
marginal revenue curve facing the seller of z is the dashed MSR curve,
reflecting the fact that w must fall if more z is to be sold. The monopoly
solution is at α_2 where $MSR = MC(z)$ and the buyer is on his demand curve
(MRP) and the seller is off his supply curve ($MC(z)$).

It is rather unlikely however that the single-seller single-buyer
market will reduce to either monopsony or monopoly, since each party will
realize that he *can* affect w by his actions (i.e. the amount of z he wishes to
buy or sell). Since neither party will treat w as fixed, B will not be on his
demand curve and S will not be on his supply curve. This means that the
parties must agree on *both* w and z. In a market in which one party treats w
as fixed and adjusts the amount z he wishes to buy or sell accordingly, once

w is determined z is also determined (either by $MRP(z) = w$ or by $MC(z) = w$). If neither party adjusts his optimum z to price, any bargain between them must specify both the price *and* the quantity to be traded.

Comparing the monopoly (α_2) and monopsony (α_1) solutions we see that if each party initially believes the other will treat w as a parameter there will be disagreement between them about w and z. This situation will not persist however, because when each receives the other's offer both will realize that the other does *not* regard w as fixed. Can they find a bargain, a (w, z) pair, on which they can agree? Since we assume that each wishes to maximize profit (defined by [E.2] and [E.3]), any bargain which is struck must maximize their combined profits for if $\pi^S + \pi^B$ were not maximized by a (w, z) bargain then by changing the bargain it would be possible to increase either or to increase *both* π^S and π^B. Hence rational profit maximizers will not conclude a bargain which does not maximize their combined profits $\pi^S + \pi^B$. This will greatly reduce the set of bargains they will consider.

Let us examine separately the effect of the terms of the bargain (i.e. w and z) on the combined profits of S and B. Adding [$E.2$] to [E.3] gives

$$\pi^B + \pi^S = R(f(z)) - wz + wz - C(z) = R(f(z)) - C(z) \qquad [E.4]$$

We see that the wz term cancels and so $\pi^B + \pi^S$ is unaffected by the level of w agreed between the parties. Hence only z affects their combined profits and since the agreed bargain must maximize $\pi^B + \pi^S$ both B and S will agree on the level of z which maximizes [E.4]. A necessary condition for a maximum of [E.4] is

$$\frac{d(\pi^B + \pi^S)}{dz} = R'f' - C' = 0 \qquad [E.5]$$

Hence in figure [E.1] both parties will wish to trade z^* where $MRP = MC(z)$.

B and S can therefore agree on z^*, but what about the other term of the bargain, w? w does not affect the *sum* of the profits, but it does determine the *share* of combined profits which accrues to each party. Differentiating [E.2] and [E.3] with respect to w, with z (and therefore $\pi^S + \pi^B$) held constant, gives

$$\frac{\partial \pi^B}{\partial w} = -z \qquad [E.6]$$

$$\frac{\partial \pi^S}{\partial w} = z \qquad [E.7]$$

As w rises B's profit falls at the rate z and S's profit rises at the same rate. Hence B will wish to set w as low as possible and S will desire as large a w as possible. The upper and lower limits on w are set by the fact that neither party will agree to a bargain which results in his earning a profit less than the level he could get without concluding any bargain with the other party. In the model we are examining each party will earn zero profit if no bargain is made. Hence the bargain made must satisfy

$$\pi^B = R - wz = py - wz \geq 0 \qquad\qquad\qquad [E.8]$$
$$\pi^S = wz - C(z) \geq 0 \qquad\qquad\qquad\qquad\quad [E.9]$$

But [E.8] implies $w \leq py/z$ and [E.9] implies $w \geq C/z$ and so w must satisfy

$$AC(z) \leq w \leq pAP \qquad\qquad\qquad\qquad [E.10]$$

In Fig. 10 the bargain concluded must therefore, by [E.10], be on or below the pAP curve and on or above the $AC(z)$ curve. A bargain, i.e. a (w, z) point, in this area will, from [E.2], [E.3] determine π^S and π^B. Fig. 11 shows the combinations of π^B and π^S which result from these bargains $(w, z$ combinations). Since z^* maximizes $\pi^B + \pi^S$, any bargain on the vertical line at z^* will maximize $\pi^B + \pi^S$. The line π^* in Fig. 11 satisfies $\pi^B \geq 0$, $\pi^S \geq 0$ and

$$\pi^B + \pi^S = R(f(z^*)) - C(z^*) = \pi(z^*) \qquad\qquad [E.11]$$

and therefore shows the ways in which the maximum combined profit $\pi(z^*)$ can be divided between B and S. A point (bargain) on the vertical line at z^* in Fig. 10, not below $AC(z)$ and not above $p.AP$, will generate a particular division of $\pi(z^*)$ and will correspond to a point on π^* in Fig. 11. The larger is w the greater is π^S and the smaller is π^B, so that movements up the vertical z^* line in Fig. 10 correspond to movements along π^* from left to right in Fig. 11. For example the points α_3, α_4 in Fig. 10 map into the points (profit divisions) β_3, β_4 in Fig. 11. A bargain off the z^* line will imply less than maximum combined profits and therefore a (π^B, π^S) point in Fig. 11 below the π^* line. For example the points α_1, α_2 in Fig. 10 map into β_1, β_2 in Fig. 11. (Why is β_1 closer to the π^* line than β_2?)

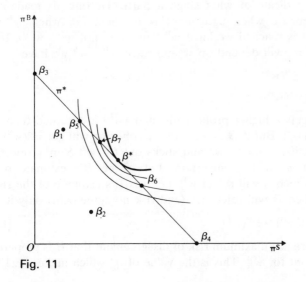

Fig. 11

Our assumption that B and S wish to maximize π^B and π^S respectively implies that, if they can agree on a bargain, the quantity traded will be z^*. The assumption is not however powerful enough to predict at what price w the trade will take place. All that we can predict is that w will satisfy [E.10]. In competitive, monopolistic or monopsonistic markets the assumption of profit (or utility) maximization, together with information on cost and demand conditions enables us to predict both the quantity traded and the price. If there is bilateral monopoly and neither side of the market takes the price as a parameter then our standard model is indeterminate. (Note that it is the model not the market which is indeterminate.)

Two ways out of this indeterminacy have been suggested. The first, associated with Nash, Shapley and other game theorists, lays down prior sets of conditions which a bargain may be expected to satisfy. These conditions will often be satisfied by only one bargain and this bargain is then the predicted solution. The alternative approach contrasts with the first in that it concentrates on the *process* of bargaining between the parties, while retaining the assumption of optimizing behaviour by the bargainers. Neither type of model is entirely satisfactory though each is at least suggestive. For reasons of space we will only consider the second, process-orientated approach.

Zeuthen's model of the bargaining process*

We will start by outlining the Zeuthen model of bargaining: it is the earliest and simplest of the models which focus on the process of bargaining. It is assumed that both B and S can agree to set z at its joint profit maximizing level, so that the parties bargain only about the price w at which z^* is to be traded. The process of bargaining consists of a sequence of offers and counter offers by B and S. w^B, w^S denote the offers of B and S at each stage in the process. (It is unnecessary in this simple model to index the w^B, w^S offers to indicate at what stage a particular offer is made.) The process will terminate when agreement is reached, i.e. when $w^B = w^S$. Before agreement is reached we have $w^B < w^S$ (why not $w^B > w^S$?). If z is fixed (at z^*) π^B, π^S will depend on w and since $w^B < w^S$ we have

$$\pi^B(w^B) > \pi^B(w^S)$$
$$\pi^S(w^S) > \pi^S(w^B)$$

For example, B gets a higher profit if his offer (w^B) is accepted than if he accepts S's offer (w^S). But if B accepts the w^S offer he will get $\pi^B(w^S)$ with certainty whereas if he rejects w^S and sticks out for w^B S may reject w^B. Hence the profit $\pi^B(w^B)$ is uncertain. Let q^S be B's estimate of the probability with which S will reject w^B, i.e. it is B's estimate of the risk of no agreement. Then B will reject w^S (and risk no agreement) only if

$$(1-q^S)\pi^B(w^B) > \pi^B(w^S) \qquad [\text{E}.12]$$

Given w^B, w^S there is a maximum risk of disagreement that B is prepared to bear by sticking out for w^B. This is the value of q^S which makes [E.12] an equation: at this value of q^S B is indifferent between sticking out for w^B and accepting w^S. Writing [E.12] as an equation and rearranging, we see that this critical value of q^S is given by

$$\frac{\pi^B(w^B) - \pi^B(w^S)}{\pi^B(w^B)} \qquad [E.13]$$

[E.13] can therefore be thought of as a measure of B's determination not to accept S's offer. Similarly we can measure S's determination not to accept w^B by

$$\frac{\pi^S(w^S) - \pi^S(w^B)}{\pi^S(w^S)} \qquad [E.14]$$

Zeuthen makes the intuitively appealing assumption that the party with less determination (i.e. with less willingness to risk no agreement) as measured by [E.13] and [E.14] will concede and adjust his offer. For example B will concede (i.e. raise w^B) if [E.14] exceeds [E.13]

$$\frac{\pi^S(w^S) - \pi^S(w^B)}{\pi^S(w^S)} > \frac{\pi^B(w^B) - \pi^B(w^S)}{\pi^B(w^B)} \qquad [E.15]$$

Rearranging [E.15] we get

$$\pi^S(w^S) \cdot \pi^B(w^S) > \pi^S(w^B) \cdot \pi^B(w^B) \qquad [E.16]$$

B concedes (raises w^B) if [E.16] holds and conversely S concedes (lowers w^S) if the inequality is reversed. But the two sides of [E.16] are merely the product of the profits of S and B evaluated at their two offers. B concedes if his last offer implies a lower value for the profit product $\pi^B \cdot \pi^S$ than S's last offer, and vice versa. Hence the sequence of offers by both parties will imply an increase in the value of $\pi^B \cdot \pi^S$. Will this process terminate, i.e. will agreement be reached? Referring to Fig. 11, the product of π^S and π^B is plotted as a series of rectangular hyperbolas, with the curves further from the origin corresponding to larger values of $\pi^B \pi^S$. Given that $z = z^*$, each offer w^B or w^S will imply a particular profit division on the line π^*. Suppose that at a particular stage in the bargaining B's offer corresponds to the point β_5 and S's offer to β_6. Then since β_6 is on a higher hyperbola than β_5 [E.16] holds and B will concede. He will therefore raise w^B and shift along π^* to β_7 say, where the inequality in [E.16] is reversed and S must now concede (lower w^S). This process will terminate at β^* where the highest parabola on π^* is reached and $w^B = w^S = w^*$. β^* is the mid-point of the line π^* (β^* maximizes $\pi^B \cdot \pi^S$ subject to $\pi^B + \pi^S = \pi(z^*)$). The bargain agreed (w^*) splits the combined profit equally between the two parties, so that

$$w^* = \frac{R(f(z^*)) + C(z^*)}{2z^*} \qquad [E.17]$$

(Show that [E.17] implies that $\pi^B = \pi^S$.)

The solution of the Zeuthen model (equal profit shares) is intuitively appealing but it and similar models (as well as the game-theory models) suffer from a number of difficulties. First, the model fails to explain why there may be failure to agree: there is always a bargain acceptable to both parties in the Zeuthen model, and so the observation that agreement is not achieved would refute the model. This is not an especially damaging criticism because bargainers usually do agree in the end. Secondly, and related to the first point, the model assumes certainty: both parties know the revenue $R(f(z))$ and cost $C(z)$ functions and hence the profit each will earn from any given bargain. This means that they can agree on the joint profit maximizing z and that they know (from [E.13], [E.14]) how willing the other party is to risk a failure to agree. Given this kind of information the parties need not go through a process of bargaining at all: they know how the process will end (at w^*), so they may as well agree to this bargain immediately. With full information a process of bargaining is merely a ritual.

Imperfect information and bargaining*
If there is imperfect information, in the sense that B only knows the revenue function $R(f(z))$ and S the cost function $C(z)$, the joint profit maximizing z will be chosen on the basis of information provided by B and S. This immediately raises the possibility that B and S may provide false information. Doing so may lead to an inefficient choice of z (i.e. $\pi^B + \pi^S$ will not be maximized) but the party providing the false information may find that his profit has increased.

Suppose, for example, that B only knows his revenue function and S his cost function but that S provides correct information on $C(z)$. Let $p = k - h(f(z))$ be the actual demand function for B's output so that the *actual* revenue function is

$$R = R(z, k) = pf(z) = [k - h(f(z))]f(z) \qquad [E.18]$$

(k is the intercept of the demand curve on the price axis). The revenue function which is *reported* by B however is

$$\hat{R} = R(z, \hat{k}) = [\hat{k} - h(f(z))]f(z) \qquad [E.19]$$

and since S does not know k, B may report an incorrect revenue function, i.e. the reported intercept $\hat{k}$ may differ from the actual intercept k. The level of z agreed by S and B is that which maximizes the reported joint profit

$$\hat{\pi} = \hat{\pi}^B + \pi^S = \hat{R} - C \qquad [E.20]$$

where $\hat{\pi}^B$ is B's reported profit, so that the agreed level of z depends on the *reported* k:

$$z^* = z(\hat{k}) \qquad [E.21]$$

Assuming that the agreed level of w is w^*, which divides the maximized $\hat{\pi}$ equally between B and S, we also have

$$w^* = \frac{\hat{R}(z^*, \hat{k}) + C(z^*)}{2z^*} = w^*(z^*\hat{k}) \qquad [E.22]$$

Hence the agreed w also depends on the reported $\hat{k}$. B's *actual* profit π^B is the difference between his actual revenue $R(k, z^*)$ and the cost of z^* to him

$$\pi^B = R(k, z^*(\hat{k})) - w^*(z^*, \hat{k}).z^*$$
$$= \pi^B(k, z^*, \hat{k}) \tag{E.23}$$

If B is honest, i.e. if $\hat{k} = k$, then

$$\pi^B(k, z^*, \hat{k}) = \pi^B(k, z^*, k) = \hat{\pi}^B \tag{E.24}$$

i.e. his actual and reported profit are equal. Varying $\hat{k}$ will alter π^B since it causes changes in both z^* (from [E.21]) and in w^* (from [E.22]):

$$\frac{d\pi^B}{d\hat{k}} = \frac{\partial \pi^B}{\partial z^*}\frac{dz^*}{d\hat{k}} + \frac{\partial \pi^B}{\partial \hat{k}}$$

$$= \frac{\partial \pi^B}{\partial z^*}\frac{dz^*}{d\hat{k}} + \frac{\partial \pi^B}{\partial w^*}\frac{\partial w^*}{\partial \hat{k}} \tag{E.25}$$

When B is honest $\pi^B = \hat{\pi}^B$ and since the agreed value of w splits $\hat{\pi} = \hat{\pi}^B + \pi^S$ equally between B and S we have $\pi^B = \hat{\pi}^B = \hat{\pi}/2$.

But z^* is chosen to maximize $\hat{\pi}$, and hence must satisfy $\partial \hat{\pi}/\partial z^* = 0$ and so when $\hat{k} = k$

$$\frac{\partial \pi^B}{\partial z^*} = \frac{\partial \hat{\pi}^B}{\partial z} = \frac{1}{2}\frac{\partial \hat{\pi}}{\partial z} = 0$$

Hence at $\hat{k} = k$ [E.25] reduces to

$$\frac{d\pi^B}{d\hat{k}} = \frac{\partial \pi^B}{\partial w^*}\frac{\partial w^*}{\partial \hat{k}}$$

which, from [E.23], [E.22] and [E.19], is

$$\frac{d\pi^B}{d\hat{k}} = z^*\frac{\partial w^*}{\partial \hat{k}} = \frac{-z^*}{2z^*}\cdot\frac{\partial \hat{R}}{\partial \hat{k}}$$

$$= -\frac{f(z^*)}{2} < 0$$

Hence honesty is not B's best policy: if $\hat{k} = k$, B can raise his actual profit by misinforming S about the revenue function and reporting a value of $\hat{k}$ *less* than the actual value. The total profit $\pi^B + \pi^S$ is reduced but because reporting a lower $\hat{k}$ lowers w, the reduction in the cost of z to B more than offsets the loss due to an inefficient choice of z. Similar results hold for the other parameters in the demand function.

If S does not cheat but reports $C(z)$ correctly and both parties agree on how w is to be determined, cheating by B does not destroy the determinacy of the model. It is not at all obvious however why S should accept B's reports of $\hat{k}$, nor why the information is so asymmetrically distributed. If B does not know $C(z)$ then S has exactly the same kind of incentive to cheat and the model is no longer determinate. Neither party will accept the other's statement on R and C at face value and there is scope for bluffing, and dissembling, and each party will attempt to learn what is the true position of the other party's cost or revenue function. The process of bargaining will not then be mere ritual: it will be a process whereby each party makes an offer, given his expectations of the other party's profit function and bargaining strategy, receives a new offer in the light of which he adjusts his expectations and makes a new offer and so on. The bargaining process in short is one of expectation formation, communication, learning and adjustment.

Exercise 14E

1. The solution to the monopsony situation in which the seller has no bargaining skill or power is rather implausible since the single buyer could exploit the single seller more effectively at another (w, z) point.
   (a) Where is the optimal solution for the monopsonist?
   (b) Why is this solution less likely to be achieved in a monopsonised market with many sellers?

2.* Compare the analysis of this section to that of the Edgeworth exchange model in Chapter 10. Explain why in the bilateral monopoly situation, the core consists of the set of points

   $$\{(z, w) \mid z = z^*, pAP \geq w \geq AC(z)\}$$

3.* How could the text model be extended to take account of the fact that z is an intermediate good, i.e. requires further costly processing by B before he can sell to the final consumers?

4.* Discuss the application of this section to the case in which B and S are divisions of the same firm, and managers' salaries depend on divisional profit.

References and further reading

There is an extensive discussion of the demand for inputs by the competitive firm in
   C. E. Ferguson. *The Neo-classical Theory of Production and Distribution*, Cambridge University Press, London, 1969, Chs. 6, 8, 9.
   J. Hicks. *Theory of Wages*, Macmillan, London, 1964
and the cost function is used to examine the competitive market input demand in
   W. E. Diewert. 'A note on the elasticity of derived demand in the n-factor case', *Economica*, May 1971, pp. 192–8.
The basic reference for human capital theory is
   G. S. Becker. *Human Capital: A Theoretical and Empirical Analysis*, National Bureau of Economic Research, New York, 1964.
The theory and evidence on the demand for labour, labour markets and the economics of unions is examined in
   B. M. Fleischer. *Labor Economics*, Prentice-Hall, Englewood Cliffs, N.J., 1970, Chs 6–12.
Bargaining theory is surveyed in
   A. Coddington. *Theories of the Bargaining Process*, George Allen and Unwin, London, 1968.
There is an attempt to provide a rational theory of bargaining in
   J. C. Harsanyi. *Rational Behavior and Bargaining Equilibrium in Games and Social Situations*, Cambridge University Press, Cambridge, 1977.

Chapter 15

Investment and consumption over time

A. Introduction

The theory of the consumer developed in Chapter 3 related to choice of consumption goods in a single, and, it was implied, fairly short time period. It took no account of saving and dissaving, or lending and borrowing, which we would normally expect to be an important aspect of consumer behaviour. Moreover, we know that the operation of the capital market – the market for borrowing and lending – influences the economy in important ways, and so it is useful to develop a theory of the operation of that market.

In the theory of the firm, the process of change in equilibrium scale in the long run can be viewed in a different way from that in which it was regarded in Chapter 8. The firm changes its scale by investing in new capacity, and so we could view the problem of determining long-run equilibrium output as the problem of choosing the most profitable amount of investment to undertake. Hence it would be instructive to construct a theory of how such investment decisions are taken. Section B examines the problem of optimal intertemporal consumption, section C the investment decision and section D the capital market. Section E shows how the two period model of previous sections may be generalised and considers some problems which arise.

B. Optimal consumption over time

We begin with the theory of the consumer. Assume that time is divided into equal discrete invervals – say into years. Given the consumer's annual income, we assume that the atemporal theory applies, and the consumer allocates this income optimally over goods. However, he also has a further choice, which is either to lend some of his income, or to borrow. Clearly, lending will imply a reduction in current consumption, but an increase in future consumption, and conversely for borrowing. Thus, the analysis of borrowing and lending decisions is essentially the analysis of the consumer's choice of a consumption pattern over time.

In analysing these decisions we find it convenient to make the following assumptions:

(a) Within each period of time prices are given and the consumer spends his consumption budget optimally, which implies that we can conduct the analysis entirely in terms of choices of values of the *total sum* of consumption expenditure in each period, rather than of quantities of particular goods and services.

(b) To reduce everything to two dimensions, we assume that only two time periods exist, time 0 (the present) and time 1 and denote the individual's total consumption expenditures in the two periods by M_0 and M_1 respectively. This assumption is largely for convenience of exposition.

(c) The consumer faces a perfectly competitive capital market. There is, therefore, a given price for borrowing and lending, which is usually expressed as an interest rate, r. Thus £100 borrowed at time 0 implies that £$100(1+r)$ must be repaid at time 1 (r is therefore defined as an *annual* interest rate), so $1+r$ can be thought of as the price paid for borrowing, or received for lending £1. Since the capital market is perfect, every borrower and lender can regard himself as being able to borrow or lend as much as he likes at the going rate of interest r.

Given these assumptions, we can immediately construct a model of choice of consumption over time. We assume that the consumer optimizes, so we can apply the theory of optimization. The elements of the optimization problem in this case are:

(a) The choice variables M_0 and M_1.

(b) We assume that the consumer has a preference ordering over combinations of current and future consumption expenditure (M_0, M_1), and that this ordering satisfies all the assumptions made in section 3A. Hence his preferences can be represented by the utility function $u(M_0, M_1)$ and his indifference curves have the usual shape. Note that since the consumer prefers more expenditure in one period to less, other things being equal, the marginal utility of current and future consumption is positive.

(c) The feasible set is defined as follows. The consumer will be initially endowed with an income timestream $(\bar{M}_0, \bar{M}_1)$, $\bar{M}_0, \bar{M}_1 \geq 0$. So that the problem is not trivial, we assume at least one of these is positive. Let A represent the amount the consumer borrows or lends in year 0, with $A > 0$ for borrowing, and $A < 0$ for lending. Then, the consumer's feasible consumptions will be constrained by:

$$0 \leq M_0 \leq \bar{M}_0 + A \qquad\qquad [\text{B}.1]$$

$$0 \leq M_1 \leq \bar{M}_1 - (1+r)A \qquad\qquad [\text{B}.2]$$

We can take it that the right hand equalities hold in [B.1] and [B.2], since from our earlier analysis we know that as a result of our non-satiation axiom the optimal point will be on a boundary of the feasible set. Then, solving for A in [B.2] and substituting into [B.1] gives:

$$(M_0 - \bar{M}_0) + \frac{(M_1 - \bar{M}_1)}{1+r} = 0 \qquad [B.3]$$

or:

$$M_0 + \frac{M_1}{1+r} = \bar{M}_0 + \frac{\bar{M}_1}{1+r} = V_0 \qquad [B.4]$$

Equation [B.3] should be compared with the consumer's budget constraint in section 3E; clearly, the present case is directly analogous with that analysed there, $(M_0 - \bar{M}_0)$ and $(M_1 - \bar{M}_1)$ representing net demands for consumption in the two periods, and $1/(1+r)$ the relative price. Equation [B.4] is known as the consumer's *wealth constraint*: it expresses the equality between the value of the consumer's chosen consumption time-stream and the value of his endowed income time-stream. These values are expressed in terms of income at time 0, i.e. they are *present values*, and hence V_0 can be defined as the present value of the consumer's endowed income time-stream, or in other words his wealth. The economic interpretation of [B.4] is as follows: by borrowing or lending the consumer may achieve a consumption time-stream which differs from his endowed time-stream, but in doing this he is constrained by the value of his wealth.

The assumption of a perfect capital market implies that r can be taken as constant by the consumer, and so the wealth constraint can be graphed as a straight line, known as a *wealth line*, such as V_0 in Fig. 1. The slope of this line referred to the M_0 axis, is:

$$\frac{dM_1}{dM_0} = -(1+r) \qquad [B.5]$$

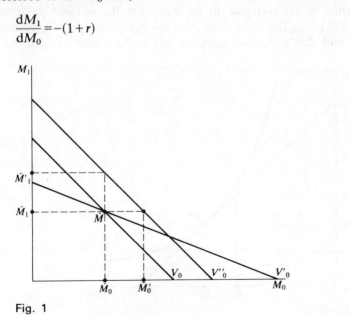

Fig. 1

since [B.4] implies the equation $M_1 = (1+r)V_0 - (1+r)M_0$. Note that it *must* pass through the initial endowment point $\bar{M} = (\bar{M}_0, \bar{M}_1)$, since this point always satisfies [B.4]. The wealth line V_0 represents the set of market exchange opportunities open to the consumer; by lending, he can move leftwards from $\bar{M}$ along the line; by borrowing, he moves rightward. Each point on V_0 represents simultaneously a consumption time-stream, an amount of borrowing or lending in year 0, and a corresponding repayment in year 1.

The absolute value of the slope of V_0 is determined by r. A reduction in r will therefore lead to a flatter line, such as V_0' in the figure. Note that this line must continue to pass through $\bar{M}$, since the initial endowment point continues to satisfy [B.4]. Hence, changes in r cause the line to rotate through $\bar{M}$. A change in an initial endowment, r remaining unchanged, will change the intercept of V_0 but not the slope of the line, and so the line shifts parallel to itself, for example to V_0''. This line corresponds to, say, an increase in $\bar{M}_0$ to $\bar{M}_0'$. or an increase in $\bar{M}_1$ to $\bar{M}_1'$, or intermediate increases in both. The new wealth line must pass through the new initial endowment point.

Consider now the solution to the consumer's optimization problem. Given our assumptions about preferences, we expect to obtain a tangency solution such as that in Fig. 2. (Why is it reasonable to assume that we would not have a corner solution in this case?) As drawn, we have a tangency solution at M^*, with the consumer's chosen consumption time-stream at (M_0^*, M_1^*). This is achieved by the consumer's borrowing an amount $M_0^* - \bar{M}_0$ in year 0, and having to repay $\bar{M}_1 - M_1^* = (1+r)(M_0^* - \bar{M}_0)$ in year 1. It would be quite possible for the indifference curves, initial endowments, or interest rate to be such that the optimal point implies lending (M^* to the left of $\bar{M}$ on V_0), or neither borrowing nor lending (M^* coincides with $\bar{M}$), and these cases are left to the reader to construct as an exercise.

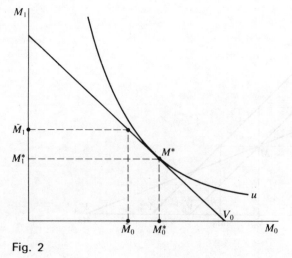

Fig. 2

Consider now the characterization of the optimum solution in terms of necessary conditions. At the optimum the slope of the indifference curve equals the slope of the wealth line. But the slope of the indifference curve is the negative of the ratio of marginal utilities, $-u_0/u_1$, where u_i is the marginal utility of period i consumption (see section 3A). At the optimum, therefore, using [B.5],

$$\frac{u_0}{u_1} = 1 + r \qquad \text{[B.6]}$$

Now a £1 reduction in M_0 reduces u by the marginal utility u_0. There will exist an increase in M_1 which will make the consumer just as well off as before the £1 reduction in M_0. This compensating increase in M_1 is $£(1+\rho)$ and is defined by

$$u_0(M_0, M_1) \equiv u_1(M_0, M_1)(1+\rho) \qquad \text{[B.7]}$$

where the notation emphasizes that the marginal utilities u_0 and u_1 depend on the consumption time-stream. In words, raising M_1 by £1 increases u by the marginal utility u_1 so that increasing M_1 by $£(1+\rho)$ will raise u by $u_1(1+\rho)$ and this just offsets the effect of the £1 reduction in M_0. Note that since $u_0 > 0$ and $u_1 > 0$ we must have $1 + \rho > 0$ so that $\rho > -1$. ρ can be interpreted as the consumer's *subjective rate of interest* since it shows how much *extra* consumption in period 1 is required to compensate for the loss of £1 of current consumption. ρ may be negative if less than £1 extra of M_1 is required. It is subjective because it depends on the consumer's preferences, not on observable market phenomena. Since u_0 and u_1 will depend on M_0 and M_1 so must ρ: $\rho = \rho(M_0, M_1)$. Rearranging [B.7], we get

$$\frac{u_0}{u_1} \equiv 1 + \rho \qquad \text{[B.8]}$$

and we see that as the consumer moves along an indifference curve from left to right substituting M_0 for M_1, ρ will decline since the slope of the indifference curve becomes flatter, and current consumption relatively less valuable. ρ is also known as the consumer's *rate of time preference*. We can use [B.8] to write the optimum condition in [B.6] simply as

$$\rho = \rho(M_0, M_1) = r \qquad \text{[B.9]}$$

The consumer is in equilibrium where his subjective rate of interest is equal to the market rate of interest. In other words, the consumer lends up to the point at which the market interest rate is just sufficient to compensate for the marginal reduction in current consumption. Alternatively, he borrows until he reaches the point at which the price he must pay (in terms of reduced consumption next period) is just sufficient to offset the value to him of the additional consumption this period.

Exercise 15B

1. (a) Explain in commonsense terms the inequalities in [B.1] and [B.2].

   (b) Draw diagrams analogous to Fig. 2, in which the consumer lends at the optimum, and in which he neither borrows nor lends.

   (c) Explain why a corner solution (with M_0^* or $M_1^* = 0$) would be intuitively unreasonable.

   (d) Explain why a constant time preference rate would be intuitively unreasonable

   (e) What would be implied by values of ρ equal, respectively, to -0.2, 0 and 0.2?

2.* Suppose that the interest rate at which the consumer can borrow exceeds that at which he can lend (though both are still invariant with the quantity borrowed or lent). Construct the feasible set in this case, and suggest the solution possibilities. Give, in terms of interest rates and the consumer's timé preference rate, the condition which holds at the optimal solution for a consumer who neither borrows nor lends.

C. The optimal investment decision

A 'firm' can be regarded for the moment as a single decision-taker who has available some specific set of *productive investment opportunities*, i.e. some means of transforming current income into future income, by means of production rather than exchange. The investment and production decisions taken by the owner of the firm will determine the cash flow he receives from the firm in each period. At the same time the owner has access to the capital market on which he can borrow or lend and so his consumption expenditure in each period need not equal the cash flow generated by his investment and production decisions. (We assume that the firm is the only source of income for the owner.) The owner of a firm with investment opportunities must therefore solve both the *investment and production decision problem*, which determines his firm's cash flow, and the *consumption decision problem*, which determines how his consumption expenditures differ from the income he receives from the firm.

We proceed by making the same two-period and perfect capital market assumptions as we did in the previous section in the case of the consumer. We also assume that the owner of the firm has a preference ordering over the consumption time-streams (M_0, M_1) and that we can represent this by indifference curves in the usual way. The only new element in the analysis is the feasible set, which now depends on the technological possibilities of production and investment as well as the terms on which the owner can borrow or lend in the capital market.

Production and investment possibilities

The cash flow or dividend D_t ($t = 0, 1$) received by the owner in each period from the firm is the firm's revenue less its expenditure. If labour is the only variable input, the expenditure in each period is the sum of the amount paid in wages and the outlay on purchases of additional physical capital, i.e. investment. Hence the cash flow is

$$D_0 = pf(L_0, K_0) - wL_0 - p_K(K_1 - K_0) = pf(L_0, K_0) - wL_0 - I \qquad [\text{C.1}]$$

$$D_1 = pf(L_1, K_1) - wL_1 \qquad [\text{C.2}]$$

where p, w and p_K are the competitive market prices of the firm's output, labour and physical capital; $f(L_t, K_t)$ is the firm's production function, L_t and K_t the labour and capital inputs, in period t. We assume for simplicity that all prices and the form of the production function are constant over time. K_0 is the stock of physical capital inherited at the start of period 0 and $I = p_K(K_1 - K_0)$ is the expenditure by the firm in period 0, for the purpose of increasing its capital stock to K_1 for use in production in period 1. Again for simplicity we assume that there is no depreciation of the capital stock. Note that there will be no investment in the second period since there is no third period, and also that if $K_1 < K_0$ the firm is disinvesting, i.e. selling off some of its capital to increase its cash flow in the first period.

The firm will always choose the labour input so as to maximize the cash flow in each period for given levels of the capital stock, since choice of L_t affects only the cash flow of that period and the owner will always prefer a larger cash flow to a smaller in a period given that the other period's cash flow is unaffected. Given the optimal choice of the variable input L_t in each period and the fixed initial capital stock K_0 the cash flows in each period depend only on the capital stock K_1 chosen for period 1:

$$D_0 = pf(L_0^*, K_0) - wL_0^* - p_K(K_1 - K_0) = D_0(K_1) \qquad [\text{C.3}]$$

$$D_1 = pf(L_1^*, K_1) - wL_1^* = D_1(K_1) \qquad [\text{C.4}]$$

where L_t^* is the optimal level of the labour input in period t. Since both periods' cash flows depend on K_1 we can derive a relationship between D_0 and D_1 by varying K_1, i.e. by investing (or disinvesting). L_0^* does not depend on K_1, since the marginal cash flow from variations in L_0 is $p\, \partial f(L_0, K_0)/\partial L_0 - w$, which does not vary with K_1. Hence increasing K_1 reduces D_0 at the rate p_K. L_1^* will however depend on K_1 since the marginal period 1 cash flow from variations in L_1 is $p\, \partial f(L_1, K_1)/\partial L_1 - w$, which is affected by changes in K_1. Hence

$$\frac{dD_1}{dK_1} = p\frac{\partial f(L_1^*, K_1)}{\partial K_1} + \left(p\frac{\partial f(L_1^*, K_1)}{\partial L_1} - w \right)\frac{dL_1^*}{dK_1} = p\frac{\partial f(L_1^*, K_1)}{\partial K_1} \qquad [\text{C.5}]$$

where we have used the fact that L_1^* maximizes D_1 for given K_1 and so the marginal period 1 cash flow from L_1 is zero at L_1^*. Increasing K_1 will therefore reduce D_0 and increase D_1 (as long the marginal product of capital is positive in period 1).

Figure 3 plots feasible combinations of cash flows that the owner of the firm can receive by varying his investment decision, i.e. by altering K_1 and so moving along the curve PP. $\bar{D} = (\bar{D}_0, \bar{D}_1)$ is assumed to be the cash

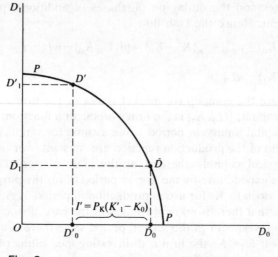

Fig. 3

flow time-stream the firm will generate if it neither invests nor disinvests, so that $K_1 = K_0$ and $I = 0$. By increasing K_1 say to K'_1 through investing $I' = p_K(K'_1 - K_0)$, the cash flow of the first period is reduced to $D'_0 = D_0 - I'$ and the next period's cash flow increased to D'_1. (The exercises at the end of this section ask you to investigate influences of the production function and p, w and p_K on the shape of curve PP.)

Borrowing and lending possibilities

The owner of the firm has access to a capital market on which he can borrow or lend at the interest rate r and so his consumption expenditure time-stream (M_0, M_1) may differ from the cash flow time stream (D_0, D_1) he receives from the firm.

Figure 4 combines wealth lines, similar to those of section B, with the curve PP from Fig. 3. It shows the feasible set when there are possibilities of altering the time pattern of consumption by both production and capital market activities, i.e. by moving along PP and along a wealth line (borrowing or lending).

By investing or disinvesting the owner of the firm can move along PP and achieve different combinations of cash flows. Given his investment decision (choice of D_0, D_1) the owner can then enter the capital market and trade (borrow or lend) to any point along the wealth line through his cash flow combination. For example if the owner does not invest or disinvest he will be at the point $\bar{D}$ on PP. He could then lend out some of his period 0 cash flow and move along the wealth line $\bar{V}$ to a point such as M' where he is better off (on a higher indifference curve than $\bar{u}$ through $\bar{D}$).

Higher wealth lines will present the owner with better consumption possibilities than lower wealth lines since there will always be some point on the higher wealth line which is on a higher indifference curve than *all* the points on the lower wealth line. Hence the firm's optimal investment decision (choice of K_1 or equivalently choice of D_0, D_1) will be that which maximises the owner's wealth. In Fig. 4 this is the cash flow combination D_0^*, D_1^* achieved by choosing a second period capital stock of K_1^* and investing $I^* = p_K(K_1^* - K_0)$ in the first period. V^* is the highest possible wealth line attainable by investment along PP and so by investing I^* the owner is put in the best possible position for engaging in borrowing or lending in the capital market along the wealth line V^*.

Given the optimal wealth maximizing investment and production decisions the owner chooses some combination of consumption expenditures in the two periods (M_0, M_1) along the maximum wealth line V^*.

In Fig. 4 are shown two possible final equilibrium positions. Given the pattern of preferences represented by indifference curve u^*, the overall optimum position is at $M^* = (M_0^*, M_1^*)$. We can think of the owner of the firm reaching this position in two steps: first, by investing I^* to get to D^*; and second, by *borrowing* the amount $M_0^* - D_0^*$, which implies that he will have to repay the amount $D_1^* - M_1^* = (1 + r)(M_0^* - D_0^*)$ out of cash flow in period 1. The first step is the solution to the *investment decision problem*, the second solves the *consumption decision problem*.

If, on the other hand, the pattern of preferences is represented by indifference curve u^{**}, then the overall optimal solution is at $M^{**} = (M_0^{**}, M_1^{**})$. This is again reached in two steps. First, the firm invests I^*; then the owner *lends* the amount $D_0^* - M_0^{**}$ on the capital market, implying that he will receive $M_1^{**} - D_1^* = (1 + r)(D_0^* - M_0^{**})$ in period 1, to add to period 1 cash flow. Thus, the solution to the investment decision problem is again to invest I^*, while the optimal consumption decision now involves further lending. There is a third kind of solution possibility, which would

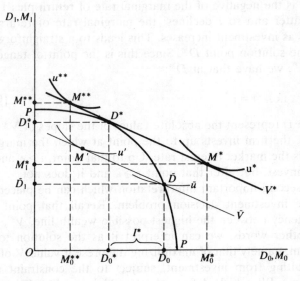

Fig. 4

arise if an indifference curve happened to be tangent to V^* at D^*, in which case I^* would still solve the investment decision problem, with no lending or borrowing on the capital market and $D^* = M^*$.

Thus we have three types of solution to the firm's problem of choosing an optimal consumption time-stream, one involving borrowing, one involving lending, and the third involving neither. The important point, however, is that in each case the solution to the optimal investment decision is the same, and is *independent* of the pattern of preferences, which determines the solution to the consumption decision. Thus there is a *separation* between the investment and consumption decisions because of the existence of a capital market, with the former requiring information only on investment opportunities – the curve PP – and the market interest rate. Let us examine further this solution to the optimal investment decision.

First note that as we move along PP and decrease D_0 by $-dD_0$, i.e. invest an additional increment $dI = -dD_0$, there is a corresponding increase in D_1 of dD_1, the gross return on the investment of dD_0. The net return is $dD_1 - dD_0$, and the *marginal rate of return* is the net return as a proportion of the additional investment:

$$ i \equiv \frac{dD_1 - dD_0}{dD_0} \qquad [C.6] $$

Rearranging gives

$$ \frac{dD_1}{dD_0} \equiv -(1+i) \qquad [C.7] $$

i.e. the slope of PP is the negative of the marginal rate of return plus 1. As D_0 falls PP gets flatter and so i declines: the marginal rate of return on investment declines as investment increases. This leads to a straightforward rationalization of the solution point D^*. Since this is the point of tangency between PP and V^*, we have that at D^*:

$$ 1 + r = 1 + i, \quad \text{i.e.} \quad r = i \qquad [C.8] $$

since $(1+r)$ and $(1+i)$ represent the absolute values of the slopes of V^* and PP. In other words, the firm invests up to the point at which the marginal rate of return equals the market interest rate. Up to that point, $i > r$, and so it pays the firm to invest, but after that point $r > i$, and it does not.

There is a second important interpretation which can be placed on the solution to the investment decision problem. Recall that point D^* corresponds to tangency between the highest possible wealth line, V^*, and the curve PP. In other words, we can interpret it as the solution to an optimization problem, namely that of maximizing the present value V of the income stream resulting from investment, subject to the constraint represented by the curve PP, which defines the feasible set of such income streams. Formally, we can write the problem as:

$$\max_{D_0, D_1} V = \frac{D_1}{1+r} + D_0 \quad \text{s.t.} \quad D_1 = P(D_0) \quad\quad\quad [C.9]$$

$$0 \le D_0$$

where the function P represents the curve PP. It will readily be verified that the solution to this problem implies (for $0 < D_0$) the necessary condition $dD_1/dD_0 = -(1+i) = -(1+r)$ at the optimal point (D_0^*, D_1^*). Thus, we have the important result that the optimal investment decision is solved by maximizing the present value of the income stream generated by investment, or equivalently the owner's wealth, over the available set of income streams. *For this, no information on preferences is necessary.* Note also that this solution will determine the capital stock, labour and output produced by the firm in period 1.

Shareholder-owned firms

The foregoing discussion was concerned with an 'owner-managed firm'. A single decision-taker controlled the firm, and chose an overall optimal consumption time-stream in the light of his own preferences (represented by indifference curves u^* or u^{**} in Fig. 4). Although the solution to the investment decision problem was independent of these preferences, it presupposed that the optimal finance decision would also be taken. In the case in which the firm is owned by two or more shareholders, while decisions are taken by a salaried manager, it may be thought that two kinds of problems would arise. First, the preferences of the shareholders are likely to differ, and so there appears to be the possibility of conflict. Second, how does the manager, to whom choice has been delegated, obtain information on shareholders' preferences, so as to make decisions in accordance with them?

We now establish an important proposition which shows that, if shareholders are able to borrow and lend on the capital market, neither of these problems arises. The proposition is: *if the capital market is perfect, then the manager of the firm acts in the best interests of the shareholders by choosing investment so as to maximize the present value of the firm's income stream.* We prove this proposition as follows.

The ith shareholder in the firm owns a proportion of the issued share capital, s_i, $i = 1, 2, \ldots n$, which entitles him to receive the share s_i in the income of the firm. Each shareholder will wish to choose a consumption time-stream which maximizes his utility, subject to his wealth constraint. But his endowed wealth depends at least in part on the income stream which will accrue from his ownership share in the firm, i.e.

$$V_i = V_a + s_i D_0 + s_i \frac{D_1}{1+r} = V_a + s_i V$$

where V_i is the ith shareholder's wealth, V_a that arising from sources other than the firm in question, and $V = D_0 + [D_1/(1+r)]$ the present value of the firm's income stream. Clearly, given V_a, maximizing V is in the interest of *every* shareholder, regardless of his particular preferences, since it puts him on the highest possible wealth constraint. Thus the firm's manager can choose optimal investment as before, and the only information he requires is the value of the market interest rate r. It is the *consumption decision* which changes for the shareholder-owned firm. There is now no single optimal solution to this, given $n(>1)$ shareholders with differing preferences. The most straightforward solution is for the firm to distribute to shareholders the net income stream resulting from the optimal investment choice, and shareholders are then able to adopt their own borrowing or lending policies in such a way as to attain their overall optimal positions.

We can view this result as an implication of the separation between investment and consumption decisions described earlier. If the optimal investment decision can be taken independently of preferences, then the existence of a number of shareholders with diverse preferences does not create problems. More light is cast on the role of the perfect capital market assumption if we adopt a slightly different interpretation of the proposition. Since all the shareholders can borrow or lend on the capital market at the same rate of interest, then each will be in equilibrium at the point at which his time preference rate equals the market interest rate. However diverse the general structure of their preferences therefore, each values a marginal increment of future income at the same rate in terms of current income, i.e. at the rate measured by the market interest rate r. In taking investment decisions on behalf of shareholders, the managers of the firm can use this interest rate to evaluate gains in future income against sacrifices in current consumption.

Present value and profit maximizing models

In this section we have outlined a model of the firm which chooses its variable input in each period and its capital stock for the next period so as to maximize the *present value of its cash flow*. In Chapter 9 we developed a model of the firm's choice of the same decision variables based on the assumption of *profit maximization*. We will now show that these two models are in fact equivalent.

The problem of maximizing the present value of the firm's cash flow is

$$\max_{L_0, L_1, K_1} V = D_0 + \frac{D_1}{(1+r)} \qquad \text{[C.10]}$$

where D_0 and D_1 are defined as in [C.1] and [C.2]. The first-order conditions are

$$\frac{\partial V}{\partial L_0} = \frac{\partial D_0}{\partial L_0} = p_0 f_L - w = 0 \qquad \text{[C.11]}$$

$$\frac{\partial V}{\partial L_1} = \frac{\partial D_1}{\partial L_1} \cdot \frac{1}{(1+r)} = \frac{1}{(1+r)} (p_1 f_L - w) = 0 \qquad \text{[C.12]}$$

$$\frac{\partial V}{\partial K_1} = \frac{\partial D_0}{\partial K_1} + \frac{\partial D_1}{\partial K_1} \frac{1}{(1+r)} = -p_K + \frac{1}{(1+r)} p_1 f_K = 0 \qquad \text{[C.13]}$$

where f_L, f_K are the marginal products of labour and capital and p_t is the price of output in period t and p_t may differ in the two periods. We see that the variable labour input is chosen in each period so that $p_t = w/f_L$. Since (from section 8C) w/f_L is short-run marginal cost, we have shown that, just like the profit maximizing firm of section 9B, the present value maximizing firm will always choose a variable input level (and hence output) where price is equal to short-run marginal cost.

From [C.13] the firm's investment decision (choice of K_1) satisfies

$$p_1 = \frac{p_K}{f_K} (1+r) = \frac{w}{f_L} \qquad \text{[C.14]}$$

An additional unit of capital bought in period 0 for use in period 1 costs p_K in cash flow forgone in period 0. Given the market rate of interest r, p_K forgone in period 0 is equivalent to $p_K(1+r)$ forgone in period 1, since a loan of p_K in period 0 would have to be repaid at a cost of $p_K(1+r)$ in period 1. Hence $p_K(1+r)$ is the opportunity cost of an additional unit of physical capital in terms of period 1 cash flow. The middle term in [C.14] is therefore the marginal cost in terms of period 1 cash flow of output in period 1 produced by installing more capital paid for in period 0. w/f_L is the marginal cost in terms of period 1 cash flow of producing output by hiring more labour (which must be paid for in that period). [C.14] expresses the requirement that when both inputs are variable, i.e. in *the long run*, the firm plans to produce where long-run marginal cost equals price and it chooses its fixed input on this basis. Actual output in period 1 is chosen by varying the labour input in period 1 so that short-run marginal cost is equal to price. If, as in this case, the firm accurately forecasts p_1, long-run marginal cost will also turn out to be equal to price. Thus maximizing the present value of the firm's cash flow and equating long-run marginal cost to price are equivalent formulations of the firm's investment decision.

We saw in Chapter 10 that for a competitive industry to be in long-run equilibrium every firm must have chosen the level of its fixed input so that price equals long-run marginal cost (so that it has no wish to alter its plant size) and every firm should just be breaking even, i.e. price equals long-run average cost (so that no firm wishes to enter or leave the industry).

We can restate these requirements in the equivalent terms of the present value-maximizing firm's investment decision.

Present value maximization requires that K_1 be chosen so that [C.14] holds and [C.14] can be rearranged to yield

$$r = \frac{p_1 f_K}{p_K} - 1 = \frac{p_1 f_K - p_K}{p_K} \qquad \text{[C.15]}$$

But the righthand side of [C.15] is merely i, the marginal rate of return. (To see this use [C.1] and [C.2] to substitute for D_0 and D_1 in [C.6] which defines i.) Hence, as we noted in discussion of [C.8], optimal investment implies that $r = i$ and this is the equivalent of the condition that price equals long-run marginal cost.

There will be no incentive for firms to enter the industry if the present value of the cash flows generated by starting production is non-positive. Since it takes one period to install new plant the present value of the cash flow from entry is

$$\frac{D_1}{(1 + r)} - p_K K_1 \qquad \text{[C.16]}$$

since the new firm will not be producing any output in period 0. [C.16] is also the present value of the *additional* cash flow to an existing firm which decides to continue in production i.e. to choose a positive K_1. [C.16] must therefore be non-negative for a firm which chooses to stay in the industry. Hence [C.16] must be zero if there is to be neither entry nor exit from the industry or

$$r = \frac{D_1 - p_K K_1}{p_K K_1} \qquad \text{[C.17]}$$

Now $D_1 - p_K K_1$ is the return from investing $p_K K_1$ in the industry so that $(D_1 - p_K K_1)/p_K K_1$ is the average rate of return, g. Hence if the industry is in long-run equilibrium the average rate of return being earned in the industry will be equal to the market rate of interest. This is an equivalent formulation of the price equals long-run average cost condition for long-run equilibrium in a competitive industry.

Thus we see that in long-run competitive equilibrium the rate of return on capital to *all* firms is equal to the market interest rate. The mechanism which brings this about can be explained as follows. If $g > r$ then capital is moved into the industry in search of an excess profit, while if $g < r$ capital is moved out because a higher profit can be earned elsewhere, e.g. by lending on the market. Thus the equalization of gross profit rates with each other and with the market rate of interest is a long-run tendency of a competitive economy.

Note, however, the assumptions necessary for this classical 'equalization of profit rate' result. Not only must there be no entry barriers.

Expectations of future prices and technologies must also be correct. If firms *overestimate* future price in a given market for example then *achieved* $g < r$, while if firms underestimate future price *achieved* $g > r$. Thus in an uncertain world persistent differences between g and r may exist in the long run, and those entrepreneurs who are better at guessing the future – or who are just plain lucky – can end up earning super-normal profits.

Exercise 15C

1. Examine the effects on the curve *PP* in Fig. 3 of
   (*a*) changes in the price of output, the capital good and labour;
   (*b*) the capital good depreciating at a constant % rate per period;
   (*c*) disinvestment being impossible.
2. How will the firm's investment and production decisions be affected by the changes in *PP* due to the factors listed in Question 1?
3. Show in Fig. 4 cases in which:
   (i) no investment would be undertaken
   (ii) D_1 would be maximized
   and state necessary and sufficient conditions for each of these.
4. Show that at an optimal solution to the firm's problem, $i = r = \rho$: where ρ is the owner's rate of time preference.
5.* Show that as long as the shareholder-owned firm makes the optimal investment choice (maximizes $D_0 + D_1/1 + r$), any borrowing or lending policy it then adopts leaves the shareholders' utility unaffected (provided of course that it distributes to shareholders all income flows resulting from investment, borrowing or lending). (*Hint:* consider the borrowing/lending policies which shareholders may then adopt in the perfect capital market.)
6.* Show the effects on the firm's investment and production decisions of a tax on operating profit (revenue less variable costs) when
   (*a*) interest payments are tax-deductible
   (*b*) interest payments are not tax-deductible.
7.* Generalize the model of this section to the case in which the firm is a monopolist in the output market. Will the monopolist's average and marginal rates of return be equal to or exceed r?
8.* What restrictions on the production function are necessary to ensure that *PP* is concave?
9.* Analyse the solutions to the optimal investment and consumption decisions problems when the interest rate at which the owner can borrow differs from that at which he can lend. State the implications for the separation of the two decisions discussed in this section. From that, suggest what difficulties confront a firm in which a salaried manager wishes to take decisions in the interests of n shareholders, where $n \geq 2$.
10.* Suppose that the firm could sell its capital equipment at the end of period 1. How would this affect Figs. 3 and 4?

D. Capital market equilibrium

In the previous sections, we took the market interest rate as given to consumers and firms. However the interest rate is a price and although the perfect capital market assumption implies that it can be taken as constant by each borrower and lender, its value will be determined by the overall interaction of the decisions of borrowers and lenders. The analysis is not complete, therefore, until this interaction is examined.

The capital market will be in equilibrium when supply, in the form of lending, equals demand, in the form of borrowing for investment and consumption. To see how this equilibrium is determined we proceed by deriving from the solutions to the optimization problems of consumers and firms the relation between the market interest rate and their borrowing or lending. Aggregation of the resulting relationships then leads to the determination of market equilibrium.

Consider first consumers. In section B above we analysed the consumer equilibrium; now we carry out some comparative statics. In Fig. 5 the consumer has an initial endowment $(\bar{M}_0, \bar{M}_1)$, and we observe how his equilibrium choices vary with changes in the interest rate. The line V_0 in (a) corresponds to interest rate r, and the consumer chooses current consumption of M_0^*. This implies lending $\bar{M}_0 - M_0^*$, shown as $A^*(<0)$ in (b) of the figure. The line V_0' corresponds to interest rate r', and yields an equilibrium current consumption choice at M_0^{**}. This implies borrowing of the amount $M_0^{**} - \bar{M}_0$, shown as $A^{**}(>0)$ in (b) of the figure. The curve A_c traces out the relation between the market interest rate and the consumer's lending $(A<0)$ or borrowing $(A>0)$. It can be thought of as corresponding to a sequence of equilibrium points in (a) of the figure, such as M^* and M^{**} (compare the analysis of the offer curve in section 3E). Figure 5(b) shows an intuitively appealing case: at sufficiently high interest rates, the consumer is a lender. Given his preferences and initial endowment, a falling interest rate causes a decrease in his lending until, after a point at which he neither lends nor borrows, he begins to borrow. Borrowing then varies inversely with the interest rate. Though appealing, this case is not inevitable, given the assumptions of the theory. A later exercise asks the reader to analyse other possibilities. In what follows, we shall take the case shown in Fig. 5 as typical.

Turning now to the case of the firm, which we assume initially to be owner-controlled, we have two sets of consequences following from a change in the interest rate, corresponding to the two decision problems the firm faces. In Fig. 6 there is an initial equilibrium at M^*, with V^* the highest present value line which can be reached, given the attainable set of points on PP. It is assumed that a borrowing solution obtains, with the firm investing $D_0^* - \bar{D}_0$, and borrowing $M_0^* - D_0^*$. If the interest rate now rises, there will be a family of parallel present value lines steeper than V^*, and V^{**} in the figure is the highest of these attainable. Hence, there is a new equilibrium at M^{**}, with investment at $D_0^{**} - \bar{D}_0$, and borrowing of

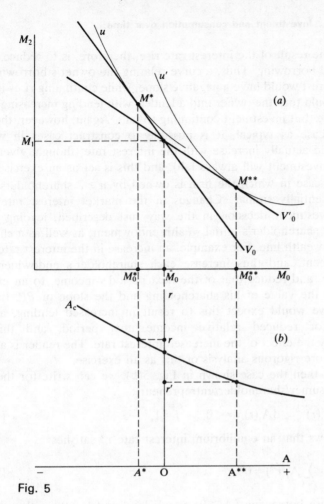

Fig. 5

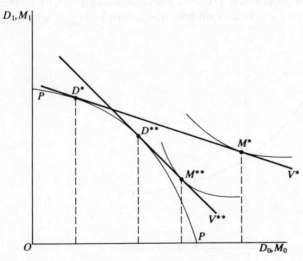

Fig. 6

$M_0^{**} - D_0^{**}$. The result of the interest rate rise, therefore, is to reduce both investment and borrowing. Thus, a curve relating the owner's borrowing to the rate of interest would have a negative slope, while continuing rises in the interest rate could turn the owner into a lender, with lending increasing with the interest rate (but investment continuing to fall). Again, however, though we take this case as typical, it is possible to construct cases in which borrowing could actually increase with the interest rate (though, given the shape of PP, investment will always fall), and this is set as an exercise.

In the case in which the firm is owned by $n \geq 2$ shareholders, the results are essentially similar. Changes in the market interest rate will change the investment decision in the way just described, leading to a change in each shareholder's initial wealth endowment, as well as a change in slope of the wealth line. For example, an increase in the interest rate will reduce investment, and thus increase each shareholder's endowment of current income, and reduce that of the next period's income, to an extent determined by the value of his shareholding and the slope of PP. In the normal case, we would expect this to result in increased lending, as he compensates for reduced relative income next period, and this is strengthened by the effect of the increased interest rate. The reader is asked to provide a more rigorous analysis of this as an exercise.

Taking then the case shown in Fig. 5(b), we can write for the jth individual (consumer/shareholder/entrepreneur):

$$A_j = A_j(r) \qquad dA_j(r)/dr < 0 \qquad j = 1, \ldots J \tag{D.1}$$

It follows that an equilibrium interest rate r^* satisfies

$$A(r^*) = \sum_{j=1}^{J} A_j(r^*) = 0 \tag{D.2}$$

since in that case borrowing ($A_j > 0$) equals lending ($A_j < 0$) in the aggregate, at interest rate r^*. This equilibrium is shown in Fig. 7, where the value

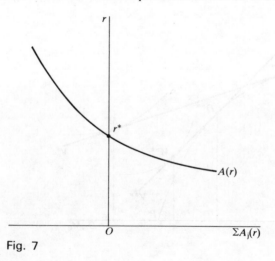

Fig. 7

$\sum_j A_j = 0$ corresponds to the interest rate r^*; the curve $A(r)$ can be regarded as the horizontal sum of all individual curves showing lending and borrowing as functions of the interest rate. (Compare the excess demand functions in Ch. 10, 16.)

Exercise 15D

1. Construct cases in which:
   (*a*) a consumer never borrows,
   (*b*) a consumer never lends,
   (*c*) the curve A_c in Fig. 5(*b*) has a positive slope over some range.
   By separating the effects of an interest rate change into substitution and wealth effects, formulate sufficient conditions under which the curve A_c will always have a negative slope.
2. Analyse the effects on a consumer's borrowing/lending behaviour of:
   (*a*) a windfall gain in next-period income;
   (*b*) the imposition of an income tax;
   (*c*) the imposition of a tax on the returns to lending.
3. Analyse the effects on the market interest rate of:
   (*a*) an increase in the price of output expected next period;
   (*b*) an increase in next period's expected wage rate;
   (*c*) a tax on returns to lending;
   (*d*) a profits tax (with loan interest not deductible).
4. Analyse the implications for the market interest rate of the changes listed in Question 2 above.
5. Construct a case in which the owner of a firm increases his borrowing following a rise in the interest rate. Explain the relation between the strength of the wealth effect and the curvature of *PP* in this case.

E. Generalizations and conclusions*

The analysis of the preceding sections has suggested that the equilibrium interest rate, levels of borrowing and lending and investment depend on patterns of consumers' preferences for consumption now as compared to consumption later, future production functions, and expectations about future prices and wage rates. Thus we see that at least in part, interest and investment are determined by the classical forces of 'productivity and thrift'. However, expectations about future prices and technology also play an important role and to investigate this further let us consider a generalization of the model analysed so far.

Suppose that there are $T > 2$ periods, indexed $t = 0, 1, \ldots T$, and consider first the consumer. He will face a sequence of budget constraints:

$$\sum_{j=1}^{m} p_{tj} x_{tj}^i + A_t \leq \sum_{j=1}^{m} p_{tj} \bar{x}_{tj}^i + A_{t-1}(1 + r_{t-1}) \qquad t = 0, \ldots T \qquad [\text{E.1}]$$

where p_{tj} is the price of good j *expected by the consumer* to prevail in year t, x_{tj}^i is his consumption of good j in year t, A_t is his bond-purchase or sale in that year, $\bar{x}^i_{tj}$ his initial endowment of good j in year t, and r_{t-1} is the interest rate which is expected to prevail in year $t-1$. Equation [E.1] simply says that in any year, the consumer's expenditure plus net bond purchases cannot exceed the value of his endowment of goods plus the net repayment of principal and interest on his bond purchase of the previous year. The difference from the constraints that were given in equations [B.1] and [B.2] is that now we explicitly incorporate *goods*.

In year 0, $A_{-1}(1+r_{-1})$ will be a given sum, determined by past decisions, and we denote this by R_0. In year T, $A_T = 0$, since in effect the economy ceases to exist after that time. Thus we have that in year T:

$$\sum_j p_{Tj}(x^i_{Tj} - \bar{x}^i_{Tj})/(1+r_{T-1}) = A_{T-1} \qquad [E.2]$$

from [E.1], where we have dropped the inequality on the premise that a boundary solution will always obtain. Substituting into the budget constraint for year $t-1$ gives:

$$\sum_j p_{T-1,j} x^i_{T-1,j} + \sum_j p_{Tj} \frac{(x^i_{Tj} - \bar{x}^i_{Tj})}{(1+r_{T-1})} = \sum_j p_{T-1,j}\bar{x}_{T-1,j} + A_{T-2}(1+r_{T-2})$$

$$[E.3]$$

and so solving for A_{T-2} gives:

$$\sum_j p_{T-1,j}(x^i_{T-1,j})/(1+r_{T-2})$$

$$+ \sum_j p_{Tj}(x^i_{T,j} - \bar{x}^i_{Tj})/(1+r_{T-2})(1+r_{T-1}) = A_{T-2} \qquad [E.4]$$

from which we could then substitute into the budget constraint for year $T-2$, and so on. Clearly, continuing this process, we would end up with the *single wealth constraint*:

$$\sum_j p_{0j}(x^i_{0j} - \bar{x}^i_{0j}) + \sum_j p_{1j}(x^i_{1j} - \bar{x}^i_{1j})/(1+r_0) + \ldots$$

$$+ \sum_j p_{Tj}(x^i_{Tj} - \bar{x}^i_{Tj})/(1+r_0)(1+r_1)\ldots(1+r_{T-1}) = R_0 \qquad [E.5]$$

This is the T-period counterpart of the wealth constraint in equation [B.3] earlier, again with the difference that it is written in terms of goods rather than generalized consumption. Now let us define:

$$p'_{tj} = p_{tj}/(1+r_0)(1+r_1)\ldots(1+r_{t-1}) \qquad t = 0, 1, \ldots T \qquad [E.6]$$

as the present value, at year 0, of the price of good j in year t. Then [E.5] can be rewritten as:

$$\sum_j \sum_t p'_{tj}(x^i_{tj} - \bar{x}^i_{tj}) = R_0 \qquad [E.7]$$

As a further notational simplification we can replace the double subscript tj by the single subscript s, i.e. we define:

$$s = 01, 02, \ldots 0J, 11, 12, \ldots 1J, \ldots TJ \qquad [E.8]$$

in which case the wealth constraint becomes simply:

$$\sum_s p'_s(x^i_s - \bar{x}^i_s) = R_0 \qquad s = 01, \dots TJ \qquad [\text{E.9}]$$

In other words, we simply use a single subscript to denote a given good at a particular date, so choice of a value of x^i_s is exactly equivalent to choice of consumption of that good at that date. Finally, we now define the consumer's utility function on goods rather than general consumption expenditure time-streams, so that:

$$u^i = u^i(x^i) \qquad i = 1, 2, \dots n \qquad [\text{E.10}]$$

where

$$x^i = (x_{01}, x_{02}, \dots, x_{TJ})$$

Then we can view the consumer's optimization problem as being that of choosing values of the goods x^i_s which maximize u^i subject to the wealth constraint in [E.9]. Clearly, provided the consumer knows the prices p_{tj} and interest rates $r_0, \dots r_{T-1}$, this problem is formally no different to that of consumption choices within a time period. Thus, if we characterize a good not only by its physical characteristics, but also by the date at which it is to be consumed, the earlier consumer analysis is directly applicable. In this case the equilibrium of the consumer determines not only a consumption pattern, but also a pattern of lending and borrowing over time. On the other hand, can we reasonably expect consumers to know future prices and interest rates? We shall consider this question further when we have generalized the model of the firm.

Let y^f_{tj} represent the fth firm's production of good j in year t. To simplify notation, let us assume that good J is the capital good, while $y^f_{t1}, y^f_{t2}, \dots y^f_{tJ-1}$ are outputs, if positive, or inputs, if negative, which are completely consumed in each period. A firm's acquisition of some amount y^f_{tJ} of the capital good increases its total capital stock by that amount, less depreciation of the capital goods previously acquired, so that at time t we have:

$$K^f_t = \sum_{k=0}^{t} (y^f_{t-k,J}(1-\delta)^k) + K^f_0(1-\delta)^t \qquad t = 1, \dots T \qquad [\text{E.11}]$$

where K^f_t is the fth firm's capital stock at time t, and $\delta < 1$ is the proportion of a unit of capital which wears out in one year, this proportion being assumed constant over time. K^f_0 is the amount of the capital good the firm has available at the beginning of period 0, as a result of past decisions. Equation [E.11] simply states that in any given year, the firm's capital stock is given by the sum of all previous years' investment, net of depreciation.

In each year t, the firm will have a production function:

$$g^f_t(y^f_t, K^f_t) = 0 \qquad t = 0, 1, 2, \dots T \qquad [\text{E.12}]$$

(where y_t^f is the vector of non-capital goods) which defines feasible input-output combinations. Its profit in year t is given by:

$$\pi_t^f = \sum_{j}^{J-1} p_{tj} y_{tj}^f \qquad \text{[E.13]}$$

(recalling that outputs are measured positively and inputs negatively). If the firm is acting in the best interests of its shareholders, it will wish to maximize:

$$V^f = \sum_{t=0}^{T} (\pi_t^f - p_{tJ} y_{tJ}^f)/(1+r_0)(1+r_1) \ldots (1+r_{T-1}) \qquad \text{[E.14]}$$

where V^f is given by the present value of the profit time-stream $(\pi_0^f \pi_1^f \ldots \pi_T^f)$, minus the present value of the investment expenditure time-stream $(p_{0J} y_{0J}^f, p_{1J} y_{1J}^f, \ldots p_{T-1J} y_{T-1,J}^f)$.

The firm will acquire none of the capital good in year T, since after that date the economy ceases to exist, and so $y_{TJ}^f = 0$, all f. Given the present value prices p_{tj}' defined as before, V^f can be written as:

$$V^f = \sum_{t} \sum_{j} (p_{tj}' y_{tj}^f - p_{tJ}' y_{tJ}^f) \qquad \text{[E.15]}$$

The firm will then choose outputs, inputs and investment in every period in such a way as to maximize V^f, given the $T+1$ production functions in [E.12] and the T capital stock equations in [E.11]. Thus, on the assumption that it knows future interest rates, prices, and technology, the firm can draw up at time 0 a 'production plan' specifying a net production of every good in every year, as well as a set of investment expenditures. Again, therefore, there is a formal similarity with the analysis of production and supply for a single period – if we characterize outputs and inputs by date as well as physical characteristics, and adopt the appropriate structure of production relationships, the assumption of a multi-period economy involves us in nothing essentially new. We could replace the double subscript tj with the single subscript s, and the firm's production plan represents a choice of values of the variables y_s^f, given prices p_s', in a way which has complete formal similarity with the atemporal case.

This discussion serves to emphasize the importance of the expectations of consumers and firms. We can envisage an extreme case, in which all consumers and firms expect the same prices p_s', and at these prices, all planned supplies and demands are consistent, so that the expected prices are the true equilibrium prices. In that case, all consumers' lending/borrowing and consumption plans will actually be realized, as will firms' production and investment plans. Equivalently, we could imagine that at year 0, markets are held in which are exchanged claims to specified goods at each future date, and claims to wealth at each date. In other words, there would be a market for every j and every t, held at year 0. In that case, the prices $p_{tj}' = p_s'$ would actually be established at that date, and consumers and firms would then spend the rest of time $(t = 1, 2, \ldots)$ honouring the commitments they made at year 0.

Neither of these cases appears to be an adequate description of the real world. Although some futures markets exist, most goods are traded on 'spot' markets, i.e. markets are held at every time t, including capital markets. Moreover, at any time, consumers may not know with certainty the tastes they will have at some future time, nor what their endowments of wealth will be. Similarly, firms may not know with certainty future technological possibilities. Expectations may differ about future prices and interest rates and the plans made by consumers and firms may be inconsistent, and so a given consumption or production plan may not be capable of realization at a given date. Firms and consumers are likely to be aware of this, and that awareness may influence the decisions they take at any one time. Thus, decisions over time can be handled without any change in the formal structure of analysis *if* we rule out uncertainty about future prices, tastes, and technology. But this means ignoring what appears to be an important and pervasive aspect of economic activity. Hence, in Chapters 19 and 20 below, we shall consider some elements of the economics of uncertainty.

Exercise 15E

1. Derive and discuss the necessary conditions for consumer and firm equilibrium in the T-period case. Discuss the consequences of assuming differences in expectations about future prices and interest rates among decision-takers.

References and further reading

The reader wishing to study questions of inter-temporal resource allocation in some depth should read:

J. Hirshleifer. *Investment, Interest and Capital*, Prentice-Hall, Englewood Cliffs, N.J., 1970;

C. J. Bliss. *Capital Theory and the Distribution of Income*, North-Holland, Amsterdam, 1975

and follow up the references given there.

Chapter 16

General equilibrium*

A. Introduction

The view of the economy with which we began this book is that of an interrelated system of markets through which one particular resource allocation is achieved out of infinitely many which are possible. Until now we have been considering the constituent elements of this system: households, firms, goods markets, and factor markets. We now have to synthesize all these elements into a model of the economy as a whole.

Our basic preoccupation is similar to that of the partial analyses carried out so far: we are concerned with the equilibrium position of a system, in this case a model of the market economy. This 'general equilibrium' is seen as providing us with the 'solution' to the system. The set of consumptions, input supplies and outputs, and the set of relative prices corresponding to this equilibrium are precisely the outcomes of the economic system in which we are interested. By examining the nature and determinants of this solution, we hope to increase our understanding of the way in which the market mechanism co-ordinates and makes consistent the separate decisions of all economic agents, each of whom acts independently in his own self-interest.

There are three broad points of interest in relation to the equilibrium resource allocation in a model of a market economy. First is the question of whether it exists: in other words, does the model of the economy, consisting of a system of interrelated markets of the kind we have been studying, have an equilibrium solution? For a long time it was assumed by economists that indeed it does, but this was actually proved only relatively recently. It should be obvious that such a proof is necessary from the point of view of the internal logical consistency of the model. We describe an economy by a general set of supply and demand relationships for goods and services and we imply that a resource allocation is determined when they hold simultaneously. But if there is no situation in which they can hold simultaneously, this suggests an inconsistency in our model and a failure to achieve its purpose. It is no use replying: 'The real world is such a dynamic place that it is unlikely that it is ever in equilibrium anyway.' Statements like that may lead us to look at the relevance of the premises and conclusions of the model, but are quite separate from its internal consistency.

The second point of interest relates to the stability and attainability of the equilibrium: we need to know not only the conditions under which an equilibrium exists, but also whether it will be reached by a system not already in it. As in the models of single markets, this is very relevant to our ability to make predictions of the consequences of change, based on comparison of static equilibria. At this point also we can consider the question of the uniqueness of an equilibrium position.

Finally, we are interested in the appraisal of the equilibrium resource allocation from the point of view of social welfare. This involves formulating some criterion of desirability on which alternative resource allocations may be compared and ranked in order of social preferences, and then the appraisal, on this criterion, of the equilibrium resource allocation. This forms part of the subject matter of 'welfare economics', that part of it which can best be treated from a general equilibrium point of view.

These topics will be considered in turn, in this chapter and the next two. But first we need to make more precise our model of the economy and our concept of equilibrium.

B. Characterization of an equilibrium of a competitive economy

The economy consists of households and firms trading goods and services in markets. We let x_{hj} be the *net* demand for the jth good of the hth household, $h = 1, 2, \ldots, H$, and x_{ij} the *net* supply of the good by the ith firm, $i = 1, 2, \ldots, M$. Recall from the analysis in Chapters 3, 7 and 9 that household net supplies of and firms' net demands for goods are measured negatively. The description of the economy now brings together the models of the household and firm set out in the earlier chapters.

Households possess *strictly* quasi-concave utility functions $u_h(x_h)$ where $x_h = (x_{h1}, x_{h2}, \ldots, x_{hn})$, which they maximize, given the budget constraints:

$$\sum_{j=1}^{n} p_j x_{hj} \leq 0 \qquad h = 1, 2, \ldots, H \qquad [\text{B.1}]$$

where p_j is the price of good j. This constraint represents simply the balance of household purchases of goods and services with household sales. Firms wish to maximize profit, defined as:

$$\Pi_i = \sum_{j=1}^{n} p_j x_{ij} \qquad i = 1, 2, \ldots, M \qquad [\text{B.2}]$$

subject to the production possibilities which satisfy:

$$f_i(x_i) \leq 0 \qquad i = 1, 2, \ldots, M \qquad [\text{B.3}]$$

where $x_i = (x_{i1}, x_{i2}, \ldots, x_{in})$. We assume that each production function, f_i, exhibits *strictly* diminishing returns.

From the analysis of Chapters 3 and 9, we can state the following: each household possesses net demand functions:

$$x_{hj} = D_{hj}(p_1, p_2, \ldots, p_n) \qquad h = 1, 2, \ldots, H$$
$$j = 1, 2, \ldots, n \qquad \text{[B.4]}$$

and each firm net supply functions:

$$x_{ij} = S_{ij}(p_1, p_2, \ldots, p_n) \qquad i = 1, 2, \ldots, M$$
$$j = 1, 2, \ldots, n \qquad \text{[B.5]}$$

where these functions possess the following properties:
- (a) for a given vector of prices, say $p' = (p'_1, p'_2, \ldots, p'_n)$, each net demand or supply is uniquely determined;
- (b) each net demand or supply varies continuously with prices;
- (c) if all prices change in the same proportion, each net demand or supply is unchanged.

Now consider, for good j, the sum:

$$z_j = \sum_{h=1}^{H} x_{hj} - \sum_{i=1}^{M} x_{ij} \qquad j = 1, 2, \ldots, n \qquad \text{[B.6]}$$

We refer to z_j as the *excess demand* for good j, since it represents the difference between demand and supply. Recalling the definitions of x_{hj} and x_{ij}, it is clear that if market demand exceeds supply, z_j will be positive, while if supply exceeds demand, z_j will be negative. It is also clear that we can write:

$$z_j = z_j(p_1, p_2, \ldots, p_n) \qquad j = 1, 2, \ldots, n \qquad \text{[B.7]}$$

and that, moreover, the three properties possessed by the individual D_{hj} and S_{ij} functions are also possessed by the functions z_j (see Question 1 of Exercise 16B). From now on, the analysis will be conducted entirely in terms of excess demands rather than the underlying individual demands and supplies. Figure 1 illustrates the derivation of the excess demand relationships.

In (a) we have the market demand and supply curves and in (c) the corresponding excess demand curve, given at each price by taking the horizontal distance between the two curves in (a).

In (b) is shown a case of interest, with the associated excess demand curve in (d). In (b), supply everywhere exceeds demand, and there is no positive price (such as p_j^* in (a)) at which excess demand is exactly zero. There is however, an equilibrium at a zero price and negative excess demand, since once this price is achieved there is no tendency to change. This is the case of a free good – it is not relatively scarce. If we assume it is possible to dispose of the excess supply costlessly, then we can quite easily incorporate this case into our model. In fact, there are strong reasons for

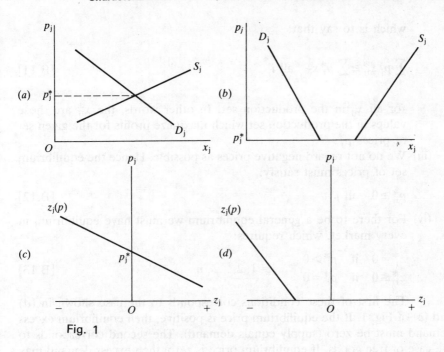

Fig. 1

doing so, since goods which may be free for some sets of relative prices may not be so for all; for example, very high prices for substitutes for the good shown in (c) (or high prices for goods which use it as an input) could lead it to have a positive price.

This completes our description of the economy. We can now describe exactly what we mean by an equilibrium of the economy: an equilibrium position consists of a vector of prices, $(p_1^*, p_2^*, \ldots, p_n^*)$, and a vector of excess demands, $(z_1^*, z_2^*, \ldots, z_n^*)$, which have the following properties:

(i) The individual household net demands, x_{hj}^*, corresponding to these z_j^* must be such that:

$$x_{hj}^* = D_{hj}(p_1^*, p_2^*, \ldots, p_n^*)$$ [B.8]

This amounts to saying that the x_{hj}^* must be the preferred quantities for the household, out of all those which are available to it for the given set of prices p_j^*; i.e.

$$u_h(x_h^*) \geq u_h(x_h) \quad \text{all } h$$ [B.9]

for all x_h satisfying: $\sum_j p_j^* x_{hj} \leq 0$ since this is the basis of the demand function.

(ii) Likewise, the individual firm's demands and supplies corresponding to these z_j^*, denoted x_{ij}^*, must be such that:

$$x_{ij}^* = S_{ij}(p_1^*, p_2^*, \ldots, p_n^*)$$ [B.10]

which is to say that:

$$\sum_j p_j^* x_{ij}^* \geq \sum_j p_j^* x_{ij} \quad \text{all } i \qquad \text{[B.11]}$$

for all x_{ij} in the production set. In other words, the x_{ij}^* are those values in the production set which maximize profits for the given set of prices p_j^*.

(iii) We do not regard negative prices as possible. Hence the equilibrium set of prices must satisfy:

$$p_j^* \geq 0 \quad \text{all } j \qquad \text{[B.12]}$$

(iv) For there to be a general equilibrium we must have equilibrium in every market, which requires:

$$\begin{aligned} z_j^* &= 0 \quad \text{if} \quad p_j^* > 0 \\ z_j^* &\leq 0 \quad \text{if} \quad p_j^* = 0 \end{aligned} \quad j = 1, 2, \ldots, n \qquad \text{[B.13]}$$

The first of these conditions corresponds to the case shown in (a) and (c) of Fig. 1. If the equilibrium price is positive, then equilibrium excess demand must be zero (supply equals demand). The second corresponds to the case of free goods. If equilibrium price is zero, then excess demand may be negative (supply exceeds demand at the zero price), or it may be that excess demand is zero at a zero price. A more succinct way of writing these conditions would be:

$$z_j^* \leq 0, \qquad p_j^* \geq 0, \qquad p_j^* z_j^* = 0. \qquad j = 1, 2, \ldots, n \qquad \text{[B.14]}$$

The reader should verify that [B.14] is implied by, and implies, [B.13].

As Fig. 1 showed, this corresponds to our usual idea of a market equilibrium, with supply equal to demand, but it also takes account of the possibility of free goods.

Taking conditions [B.9], [B.11], [B.12] and [B.14] as characterizing a general equilibrium, therefore, they can be summarized: a general equilibrium is a set of non-negative prices, and a set of demands and supplies of households and firms, such that each demand or supply is optimal for the corresponding household or firm at those prices (so that no decision-maker wishes to change his plans) and the resulting excess demands are all non-positive (so that all decision-makers' plans are compatible and can be realized). We now have to consider whether such an equilibrium could exist.

Exercise 16B
1. Show that continuity and invariance to equi-proportionate price changes of the net demand and supply functions implies the same properties for the excess demand functions.
2. Give examples of goods which have ceased to be free goods and have come to be sold at positive prices.

3. Draw the supply and demand curves for a good which could in principle be produced, but for which the quantity traded is zero.
4. Illustrate the case of a good whose supply is equal to demand, but whose price is zero.
5.* Explain why prices cannot be negative under the assumption of free disposal made in Section 7E. What are the consequences of replacing this with the assumption that disposal is costly?
6. Explain carefully why positive excess demand implies that some decision makers' optimal plans cannot be fulfilled but negative excess demand need not have the same implication.

C. Existence of general equilibrium†

One of the conclusions of the preceding section was that corresponding to each good and market in the economy is an excess demand function:

$$z_j = z_j(p_1, p_2, \ldots, p_n) \qquad j = 1, 2, \ldots, n \qquad [C.1]$$

which has the properties that it is continuous and invariant to equiproportionate changes in prices. In the language of Appendix 1 to this chapter, [C.1] defines a *mapping* from the set of price vectors into the set of excess demand vectors and, moreover, this mapping is *continuous* and *homogeneous of degree zero*.

In proving that an equilibrium, in the sense defined in the previous section, exists for this economy, we shall make use of the *fixed point theorem* set out in the appendix. Hence, we can regard our immediate task as that of making assumptions and definitions which allow us to bring this theorem into operation.

First consider the set of prices P, where an element of this set is a vector of prices $(p_1, p_2, \ldots, p_n)$. As it stands, this set is bounded below by the condition that $p_j \geq 0$, all j, but is not bounded above – we can in principle choose any price as high as we like. P is the set of all non-negative n-component vectors. In order to apply the fixed point theorem, we require the set of prices to be bounded and closed. P is closed, but is not bounded (Explain why). Hence, we adopt the following *normalization rule*. Given any price vector $(p_1, p_2, \ldots, p_n)$ in P we can form a new price vector $(p'_1, p'_2, \ldots, p'_n)$ by the normalization rule

$$p'_j = p_j \frac{1}{\sum p_j e_j} = p_j \cdot \frac{1}{pe} \qquad (j = 1, 2, \ldots, n) \qquad [C.2]$$

where $e = (e_1, e_2, \ldots, e_n) = (1, 1, \ldots, 1)$ is a vector whose jth component is one unit of good j. Hence $\sum p_j e_j$ is the cost in £ at prices p of a bundle of goods consisting of one unit of each commodity and $1/pe$ is the number of unit bundles that can be bought for £1. The effect of the normalization rule

† For the mathematics used in this section, see Appendix 1 to this chapter.

is, crudely, to increase the original price vector p proportionately if prices are low and to reduce p if prices are high.

The set of *normalized price vectors* P' defined by the normalization rule [C.2] is bounded, closed and convex. P' is bounded below since $p_j \geq 0$, all j, and all p' are positive multiples $(1/pe)$ of some p in P, thus $p'_j \geq 0$, all j. We can show that P' is also bounded above and hence bounded. From [C.2]

$$p'e = \sum_j p'_j e_j = \sum_j p_j e_j \frac{1}{pe} = \frac{1}{pe} \sum_j p_j e_j = 1 \qquad [\text{C.3}]$$

and since the normalized prices are non-negative this implies that $p'_j e_j \leq 1$, all j. But $e_j = 1$, all j, and so $p'_j \leq 1$, all j. We have therefore established

$$0 \leq p'_j \leq 1 \qquad (j = 1, 2, \ldots, n) \qquad [\text{C.4}]$$

and P' is indeed bounded. P' is also clearly closed. We leave the proof of the convexity of P' to Question 5 of Exercise 16C.

This normalization procedure can be readily illustrated for $n = 2$. In Fig. 2, we have the positive quadrant as the set P, since that corresponds to all pairs of non-negative price vectors (p_1, p_2). The line ab joins the price vectors $(0, 1)$ and $(1, 0)$, and so is the locus of price vectors satisfying the conditions in [C.3], [C.4] for $n = 2$. It has the equation:

$$p'_1 = (1 - p'_2 e_2)/e_1$$

(where e_1 and e_2 do not affect the numerical value of this expression but simply ensure that it is dimensionally correct). Thus it represents in two dimensions the set of normalized price vectors P'.

To illustrate the normalization rule, note first that every price vector (p_1, p_2) must lie on some ray through the origin in Fig. 2 and each ray must

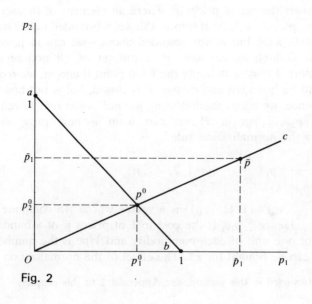

Fig. 2

intersect ab. Take for example the ray $0c$ in the figure. Given the price vector $p^0 = (p_1^0, p_2^0)$ on $0c$ and ab, any positive price vector along the ray can be written as:

$$p = kp^0 \qquad k > 0 \qquad\qquad\qquad [C.5]$$

for some number k. $\bar{p}$ in the figure is such a vector for a value of k, say $\bar{k}$. Note that $p^0 e = 1$. Now, applying the normalization rule to $\bar{p}$ gives the price vector:

$$\left(\frac{\bar{p}_1}{\bar{p}e}, \frac{\bar{p}_2}{\bar{p}e}\right) = \left(\frac{\bar{k}p_1^0}{\bar{k}p^0 e}, \frac{\bar{k}p_2^0}{\bar{k}p^0 e}\right) = \left(\frac{p_1^0}{p^0 e}, \frac{p_2^0}{p^0 e}\right) = p^0 \qquad\qquad [C.6]$$

and this will clearly be true for all values of k. Hence, we can regard the normalization rule as, in effect, 'collapsing' the infinite number of price vectors along any ray in the figure to a single point on the line, ab, which represents the set P'. It is easy to see that the set is bounded, closed and convex. Then [C.3] and [C.4] define the n-dimensional counterpart of the line ab.

Is it, however, permissible to restrict the possible price vectors to the set P'? Consideration of the zero degree homogeneity property of the excess demand functions shows that it is. Thus, this property implies that:

$$z_j = z_j(p_1, p_2, \ldots, p_n) = z_j(p_1', p_2', \ldots, p_n') \qquad\qquad [C.7]$$

provided that:

$$p_j' = \lambda p_j \quad \text{all } j, \qquad \lambda > 0 \qquad\qquad\qquad [C.8]$$

If we set: $\lambda = 1/pe$, it follows that the normalized prices p_j' lead to the same excess demand as the initial vector of prices. Hence we are justified in replacing the set P with, from our point of view, the 'more useful' set P'.

At this point we consider a problem which relates to the continuity of the mapping from prices to excess demands. It was asserted earlier that the excess demands are *continuous* functions of prices. This is true as long as all prices are positive, but a problem may arise when some prices are zero. For some households, this may mean that the prices of the goods and services they sell are positive, while those of the goods they buy are zero. It is therefore possible that their demands for these free goods are infinite, thus implying a discontinuity in the excess demand functions. In fact, the axiom of non-satiation as stated in Chapter 3 implies that this will be the case.

The possibility of discontinuity raises problems for the application of the fixed point theorem, since a condition in that theorem is that the mapping be continuous. We shall adopt the simple, but crude, solution here of assuming that this problem does not arise: *there is always a finite excess demand for a good whose price is zero.* This could be taken to be ensured by a modification of the non-satiation axiom: satiation levels, beyond which increments of consumption yield zero utility, exist for all goods, but there is always at least one good which the consumer buys at a positive price, and with which he is not satiated. The reason for this latter qualification will become clear when we derive *Walras' Law*, to which we now turn.

Recall that the x_h and x_i represent the *desired* or *planned* net demand and supply vectors of households and firms respectively. Then, each x_h must satisfy the budget constraint:

$$\sum_j p_j x_{hj} \le 0 \qquad h = 1, 2, \ldots, H \qquad\qquad [C.9]$$

But as long as each household is non-satiated with at least one good for each price vector, its budget constraint will be satisfied as an equality, and so summing [C.9] over h gives:

$$\sum_h \sum_j p_j x_{hj} = \sum_j p_j \sum_h x_{hj} = 0 \qquad\qquad [C.10]$$

Let us also make the assumption that at each price vector firms' output and input choices are such that each firm's maximized profit is exactly equal to zero,† i.e.

$$\sum_j p_j x_{ij} = 0 \qquad\qquad [C.11]$$

implying that if we sum over firms, we have:

$$\sum_i \sum_j p_j x_{ij} = \sum_j p_j \sum_i x_{ij} = 0 \qquad\qquad [C.12]$$

But then, subtracting [C.12] from [C.10] gives:

$$\sum_j p_j \sum_h x_{hj} - \sum_j p_j \sum_i x_{ij} = \sum_j p_j \left[\sum_h x_{hj} - \sum_i x_{ij} \right] = \sum_j p_j z_j = 0$$

In other words, at *any price vector* the total value of excess demands is exactly zero. This result is known as Walras' Law, and plays an important role in what follows.

We now present a proof of the existence of general equilibrium. The proposition can be stated formally as follows: given the continuity and zero-degree homogeneity of the excess demand functions $z_j = z_j(p)$, $p \in P'$, and Walras' Law, then there exists a price vector $p^* \in P'$, such that:

$$z_j^* = z(p^*) \le 0, \qquad p_j^* \ge 0, \qquad p_j^* z_j^* = 0 \quad \text{all } j \qquad\qquad [C.13]$$

where the excess demands correspond to utility maximizing choices by consumers, and profit maximizing choices by firms, at the price vector p^*.

We shall prove this proposition for the general case set out here, and then illustrate the proof in two dimensions.

† This could be thought of as resulting from a process of entry into markets with positive profits, and exit from markets with negative profits, in such a way that, for any price vector, firms always earn zero profits. This not quite satisfactory assumption can easily be dispensed with, however – see Question 4 of Exercise 16C.

First, in the terminology of the Appendix, we note that the excess demand functions define a continuous mapping from the set of normalized price vectors, P', to the set of excess demand vectors, which we call Z. That is:

$$Z = \{(z_1 z_2, \ldots, z_n) \,|\, z_j = z_j(p), p \in P', j = 1, 2, \ldots, n\} \qquad [C.14]$$

We can write this mapping as:

$$z : P' \to Z \qquad [C.15]$$

The strategy of the proof is to define a second continuous mapping, from the set Z of excess demands back into the set P'. Taking the composition of these two mappings, we then have a continuous mapping of the closed, bounded, convex set P' into itself, and so there exists a fixed point, i.e. a price vector p^* which, under the composite mapping, has itself as its image. By careful definition of the second mapping, we ensure that such a fixed point is also an equilibrium price vector. We shall then have proved that an equilibrium exists, on the stated assumptions.

Consider the mapping defined by the rule:

$$\hat{p}_j = \max [0, p'_j + k_j z_j(p')], \quad \text{for all} \quad p' \in P', \quad k_j > 0, \quad \text{all } j \quad [C.16]$$

where the righthand side is read: 'the greater of zero and $p'_j + k_j z_j(p')$'. This rule could be explained as follows. Choose some initial price vector $p' \in P'$, and consider separately each corresponding excess demand $z_j(p')$ and the associated price p'_j. We define a new price, $\hat{p}_j$, by the following rules:

If the excess demand $z_j(p')$ is positive, find the new price $\hat{p}_j$ by adding to the initial price p'_j some multiple k_j of the excess demand;

if the excess demand $z_j(p')$ is zero, set the new price $\hat{p}_j$ equal to the old price p'_j;

if the excess demand is negative, find the new price $\hat{p}_j$ by adding to the old price p'_j some multiple k_j of the excess demand (which means $\hat{p}_j < p'_j$ since z_j is negative), *unless* doing so would make the new price negative, in which case set it instead at zero.

The reader should verify that this set of verbal instructions, which defines a mapping from the set of excess demands to the set of *non-normalized* prices, is succinctly described in [C.16]. To define the mapping back into the set of *normalized* price vectors P', we re-apply the normalization rule† by multiplying each 'new' price $\hat{p}_j$ by $1/\hat{p}e$, where $\hat{p} = [\hat{p}_j]$. Thus we have defined the mapping

$$k : Z \to P' \qquad [C.17]$$

---

† This of course requires that $pe > 0$, i.e. that there will always be at least one strictly positive 'new' price. That this is so follows from Walras' Law, as will be shown below.

which, it can be shown, is continuous (see Question 3 of Exercise 16C). Hence, the composite mapping:

$$k \cdot z : P' \to P' \qquad \text{[C.18]}$$

is continuous, and maps the closed, bounded, convex set P' into itself. Given some initial $p' \in P'$, we find $z(p') \in Z$, and then $p = k[z(p')] \in P'$. But then, by the Brouwer fixed point theorem, we know that there exists a price vector $p^* \in P'$ such that:

$$p^* = k[z(p^*)] \qquad \text{[C.19]}$$

In words, when we:

(a) obtain the excess demands $z_j(p^*)$ by inserting p^* into the excess demand functions;

(b) obtain the (non-normalized) new prices $\hat{p}_j$ by applying the rule in [C.16];

(c) obtain the *normalized* new prices $p'_j = \hat{p}_j / \hat{p}e$

then for each j we have $p_j^* = p'_j$.

More concisely:

$$p_j^* = \frac{\max[0, \, p_j^* + k_j z_j(p^*)]}{\hat{p}e} = \frac{\hat{p}_j}{\hat{p}e} \qquad \text{[C.20]}$$

By examining [C.20] further, we can show that it implies that the vector of prices $[p_j^*]$ is an equilibrium price vector, and so the proof of existence of a fixed point effectively proves the existence of an equilibrium. This is done by first using [C.20] to prove (see Question 7 of Exercise 16C)

$$\sum_j \hat{p}_j z_j(p^*) = 0 \qquad \text{[C.21]}$$

Then, from the rule in [C.16], we know that either $\hat{p}_j = 0$, or:

$$\hat{p}_j = p_j^* + k_j z_j(p^*) > 0 \qquad \text{[C.22]}$$

Denote by p_j^+ those $\hat{p}_j$ which are non-zero (and therefore positive). For [C.21] to be satisfied, it must be the case that:

$$0 = \sum_j p_j^+ z_j(p^*) = \sum_j (p_j^* + k_j z_j(p^*)) z_j(p^*) \qquad \text{[C.23]}$$

But then expanding the brackets on the righthand side and using Walras' Law gives:

$$\sum_j k_j [z_j(p^*)]^2 = 0 \qquad \text{[C.24]}$$

This can only be satisfied if $z_j(p^*) = 0$, for each j for which $\hat{p}_j > 0$. Thus $\hat{p}_j > 0 \Rightarrow z_j(p^*) = 0$. Moreover, note from [C.20] that $\hat{p}_j > 0 \Leftrightarrow p_j^* > 0$ (since $\sum_i \hat{p}_i e_i > 0$), and so:

$$p_j^* > 0 \quad \Rightarrow \quad z_j(p^*) = 0 \qquad \text{[C.25]}$$

This equation then tells us that if, in [C.21], we have $z_j(p^*) \neq 0$, then its associated $\hat{p}_j = 0$, and from [C.20], $p_j^* = 0$ also.

Substituting the zero values for $\hat{p}_j$ and p_j^* in [C.16] gives:

$$0 = \max(0, 0 + k_j z_j(p^*)) \qquad \text{[C.26]}$$

In that case, the non-zero value of $z_j(p^*)$ cannot possibly be positive, but must be negative, and so:

$$z_j(p^*) < 0 \quad \Rightarrow \quad p_j^* = 0 \qquad \text{[C.27]}$$

Combining [C.25] and [C.27], we have

$$p_j^* \geq 0, \qquad z_j(p^*) \leq 0, \qquad p_j^* z_j(p^*) = 0 \qquad \text{[C.28]}$$

which is precisely the definition of the equilibrium. Thus we have shown that the fixed point under the composite mapping satisfies the definition of an equilibrium, and so under the stated assumptions an equilibrium exists.

In this proof, we assumed in the re-normalization that for every 'new' price vector $\hat{p}$ obtained by the rule in [C.16] $\hat{p}e > 0$. Since $\hat{p}_j \geq 0$, this implies that at least one $\hat{p}_j > 0$. We use Walras' Law to show that this must be so. Thus, assume to the contrary that $\hat{p}_j = 0$, every j. Then, from [C.16], this implies:

$$\max[0, p_j' + k_j z_j(p')] = 0 \quad \text{all } j. \qquad \text{[C.29]}$$

This means that for every $p_j' > 0$ (and there must be at least one) we must have $z_j(p') < 0$, because $p_j' + k_j z_j(p')$ must be negative. But then:

$$\sum_j p_j' z_j(p') < 0 \qquad \text{[C.30]}$$

which contradicts Walras' Law. It follows that at least one 'new' price must be positive, and so the normalization rule can be applied to take the new prices back into P'.

We now give a proof of the existence of an equilibrium price vector in two dimensions which, as well as being valid in its own right, allows us to illustrate the foregoing more general proof. In (a) of Fig. 3, the line ab again shows the set of normalized price vectors, and (b) of the figure shows the space of excess demand vectors (z_1, z_2). The point a in (a) is the price vector $(0, 1)$. Assume (since, after all, we are trying to prove the existence of an equilibrium) that this is not an equilibrium. Then the corresponding excess demand vector cannot be at the origin – the excess demand vector $(0, 0)$ – in (b) of the figure. From Walras' Law we must have:

$$0 \cdot z_1 + 1 \cdot z_2 = 0 \qquad \text{[C.31]}$$

implying $z_2 = 0$ and $z_1 > 0$. This latter follows because if $z_1 \leq 0$, then point a satisfies the definition of an equilibrium, which we have ruled out by assumption. Thus, corresponding to the price vector $(0, 1)$ in Fig. 3(a) must be an excess demand vector such as that at point α in Fig. 3(b), with $z_1 > 0$ and $z_2 = 0$. By a similar argument, point b in Fig. 3(a) must map into a point

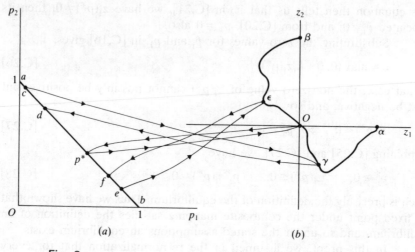

Fig. 3

such as β in Fig. 3(b). Now consider the set of excess demand vectors which will be obtained in (b) of the figure, as we choose successive price vectors along the line from a to b in (a) of the figure. Because of the continuity of the excess demand functions, the resulting excess demand vectors must lie along a continuous curve in the excess demand space, such as that shown joining α and β. Moreover, because of Walras' Law, the excess demands cannot *both* be in the positive quadrant (since then $p_1 z_1 + p_2 z_2 > 0$), or in the negative quadrant (since then $p_1 z_1 + p_2 z_2 < 0$). But then any continuous curve passing from α to β, and not passing through the positive or negative quadrants, *must* pass through the origin: that is, there must be a price vector which generates the excess demand vector $(0,0)$, and so this is the equilibrium price vector.

The more general proof can then be illustrated as follows. Take some point such as c in Fig. 3(a), and assume that under the mapping z, this yields point γ in (b). Then, under the mapping k, γ maps back into, say, point d, and so the composite mapping $k \cdot z$ maps c into d. Similarly, point e maps into point ε and then back into f. Then, given that this mapping of the line ab into itself is continuous, there must, by Brouwer's theorem, be a point such as p^* which maps into itself. But, by the way we have defined the mapping k from the set of excess demands back to the line, we know that p^* must, under the mapping z, yield the origin $(0,0)$, and must therefore be an equilibrium price vector.

Exercise 16C

1. Describe the roles played by the continuity and zero-degree homogeneity of the excess demand functions, and by Walras' Law, in the existence proofs of this section.

2. Why, in Fig. 3, is point d to the right of point c, and point f to the left of point e?

3.* (a) Show that the mapping:

$$p_j = \max (0, p'_j + k_j z_j)$$

for p'_j a given number, and z_j a variable number, is continuous. (*Hint:* draw a graph of the mapping.)

(b) Suppose that z_j is a linear function of p'_j, with all prices but the jth held constant. Draw the graph of the mapping:

$$p_j = \max (0, p'_j + k_j z(p'_j)).$$

in (p'_j, p_j) space.

4. Replace the zero-profit assumption in equation [C.10] by the assumption that household h owns a share θ_{hi} in the profits of firm i, and that $\sum_h \theta_{hi} = 1$, all i. Then, show that Walras' Law holds when firms' profits are positive or negative, as well as zero. (*Hint:* re-define the household's budget constraint and sum.)

5. Prove that the set P' of normalized price vectors is convex.

6. Illustrate the set of price vectors:

$$p' = \left\{ (p_1, p_2, p_3) \mid 0 \le p_j \le 1, \sum_j p_j e_j = 1, j = 1, 2, 3 \right\}$$

in three dimensions.

7.* Use equation [C.20] to prove [C.21]. (*Hint:* multiply through by z^*; sum, and apply Walras' Law.)

8. Why in defining the normalization rule in [C.2] do we insist upon introducing the vector e and not simply sum the prices, $\sum_j p_j$? (*Hint:* what would be the *dimension* of such a sum?) Prove that for the vector p^0 in Fig. 2, $p^0 e = 1$, and likewise for any other vector on ab.

D. Stability

It is of course not enough to know whether and under what conditions an equilibrium position of the system exists. We are also interested in the question of whether the system will tend to return to an equilibrium position when it is in disequilibrium. This is the problem of stability which was quite extensively discussed, in connection with single markets, in Chapter 10. It is useful to review some of that discussion here, as it applies to the system of interrelated markets.

First we distinguish between stability of some particular equilibrium position, and stability of the system as a whole. In the former case, we have a given equilibrium price vector, and we ask whether the actual price vector will tend to converge to it when away from it. In the latter case, we simply ask whether the system will converge to *some* equilibrium price vector, given that it is initially in disequilibrium. We shall be concerned with this latter question.

Secondly, we distinguish between local and global stability. An equilibrium position is locally stable if, given some price vector in a small neighbourhood of the equilibrium price vector, there is convergence to it. The equilibrium position is globally stable if there is convergence to it, however far away from it the initial price vector is. It follows, therefore, that global stability implies local stability, but not vice versa. Moreover, global stability of an equilibrium position must imply stability of the system, since the system tends to the globally stable equilibrium, and therefore to *some* equilibrium. Global stability of the system, on the other hand, does not imply global stability of any one particular equilibrium, since the system may converge to several different equilibria, none of which is globally stable, depending on its initial position. However, if we have global system stability, and a *unique* equilibrium, then this equilibrium must be globally stable.

The question of stability essentially involves analysis of the movement of prices through successive disequilibrium positions over time, and so it is best approached through an explicitly dynamic analysis. Thus, we take it that there exists at least one equilibrium price vector $p^* = (p_1^*, p_2^*, \ldots, p_n^*)$, and at an initial moment of time $t = 0$, there exists a price vector $p(0) \neq p^*$. We regard time as varying continuously, and so the price vector is a vector-valued function of time, $p(t) = (p_1(t), p_2(t), \ldots, p_n(t))$. The theory of the stability of general equilibrium is then concerned with the question: under what conditions will this time path of the price vector converge to an equilibrium price vector? We call the general equilibrium system *globally stable* if we can show that:

$$\lim_{t \to \infty} p(t) = p^* \qquad\qquad [D.1]$$

given any initial price vector $p(0)$, and an equilibrium price vector p^*.

To examine the question of stability we must have some hypothesis of the adjustment process which determines the time path of the price vector. Different adjustment processes could be postulated, with different dynamic behaviour, and so we have to discuss stability relative to a particular adjustment process. Here we shall consider the *tâtonnement process*, already discussed in relation to a single market, in Chapter 10. For the multimarket economy, the tâtonnement process can be described as follows: there exists an 'auctioneer', whose job it is to announce a price vector at each instant of time, to collect (instantaneously) the information on the resulting offers and demands for every good in the economy, and to decide whether or not to permit trading at those prices. He is bound to act according to the following rules:

(i) he announces a new price vector, if and only if the previous price vector is not an equilibrium, in the sense of the preceding section;

(ii) he permits trading only at equilibrium prices;

(iii) the rate at which he changes a given price, say the jth, $j = 1, 2, \ldots, n$, is proportionate to the excess demand for the corresponding jth commodity.

That is, given the prices $p_j(t)$ at time t, we may write:

$$\frac{dp_j(t)}{dt} = \dot{p}_j = \lambda_j z_j \qquad j = 1, 2, \ldots, n. \qquad \lambda_j > 0 \qquad \text{[D.2]}$$

where $\dot{p}_j$ is the rate of change of p_j over time, i.e. the speed with which p_j is changed by the auctioneer. [D.2] implies that if $z_j > 0$, p_j will be increased, since $\dot{p}_j > 0$, and the rate of increase will be greater, the greater the excess demand. Likewise, if $z_j < 0$, then p_j will be reduced, at a rate which is greater, the greater the excess supply. Finally, $z_j = 0$ implies that p_j is left unchanged.

The assumption that this adjustment process works in continuous time is not unduly restrictive – we could postulate that each stage of the process takes a finite amount of time and prices are adjusted discretely, with no real change in results. As usual, proceeding to the limit and taking derivatives rather than finite differences is a simplification. On the other hand, the assumption of no trading at disequilibrium prices is substantive rather than simplifying.

Walras' Law again holds for all price vectors, in and out of equilibrium. The reasoning is as before: since, for any announced price vector, consumers' net demands satisfy their budget constraints, and by assumption firms' profits are zero, aggregating over households and firms yields Walras' Law. Since trading does not take place out of equilibrium, the fact that plans are in aggregate inconsistent, and all consumers' *ex ante* demands *could not* be simultaneously satisfied if trade *did* take place, has no bearing on the analysis.

The adjustment rule defined in equation [D.2] is a generalization of that defined, in the context of a single market, in Chapter 10. It embodies the notion that goods in excess demand have their prices bid up, and those in excess supply have their prices bid down. It however specifies nothing beyond that about how markets actually work, and the criticisms of the tâtonnement process given in Chapter 10 apply equally here, and should be reviewed at this point.

For a single market, it was shown in Chapter 10 that the adjustment process in [D.2] in the presence of a negatively sloped excess demand curve, always generated a time-path of prices which converged to equilibrium. The problem now arises, however, that each excess demand depends on *all* prices, and so a negative slope for each excess demand curve is no longer sufficient. Thus, suppose all markets except those for goods 1 and 2 are in equilibrium, but $z_1 > 0$. Raising p_1 will cause increased excess demands for substitutes of good 1 and lower excess demands for its complements, and so the attempt to reach equilibrium in the first market may bring about disequilibrium in others. Moreover, if goods 1 and 2 are complements, the extent of the excess supply in market 2 will also have increased. Indeed, examples have been constructed in which the adjustment process defined in [D.2] is unstable, and so it alone cannot be sufficient for stability. This then raises the question: can we find conditions to impose upon the model of the economic system which ensure that the tâtonnement process is globally stable? The answer to this question is that there are several related but distinct cases in which sufficient conditions for global stability of the system can be formulated. An exhaustive treatment of these cases for the n-good economy is well beyond the limits of space of this book.† However, the following analysis will serve to give the flavour of the theory in this area.

To simplify proofs, we shall assume that there are only two goods, with excess demand functions $z_j(p_1, p_2)$, $j = 1, 2$. To begin with, the prices are *not* normalized in the sense of the previous section, so that the set of price vectors we are initially concerned with is the entire positive quadrant. We assume that there exists an equilibrium price vector $p^* > 0$ such that:

$$z_j(p_1^*, p_2^*) = 0 \qquad j = 1, 2 \qquad \text{[D.3]}$$

(thus ruling out the possibility of a free good.) The zero-degree homogeneity property of the excess demand functions implies that if p^* is an equilibrium price vector, so is μp^*, for any $\mu > 0$, which should be kept in mind in what follows. We shall now examine a central proposition in the area of stability theory, in the context of this two-good economy. This proposition can be stated:

Stability proposition: if all goods in the economy are *gross substitutes*, then the time path of prices, $p(t)$, determined by the tâtonnement adjustment process described in [D.2], converges to an equilibrium. That is:

$$\lim_{t \to \infty} p(t) = p^* \qquad \text{[D.4]}$$

for any initial price vector $p(0)$. Thus, the economic system is globally stable.

Before proving this theorem (for $n = 2$) we have to define 'gross substitutes'. The goods 1 and 2 are gross substitutes if

$$\frac{\partial z_1}{\partial p_2} > 0, \qquad \frac{\partial z_2}{\partial p_1} > 0 \qquad \text{[D.5]}$$

at all price vectors p. That is, the excess demand for one good increases with an increase in price of the other. In Chapter 3 we referred to gross substitutes in consumption. Here the term 'gross substitute' has a rather wider meaning since we are concerned with *excess* demand, i.e. with both supply and demand responses to price changes, rather than just demand responses as in Chapter 3. Note also that this restriction is placed on the excess demand functions not because of any great intuitive appeal, but because, as we shall see, it is sufficient to ensure stability. The extent to which real excess demand functions satisfy the restriction is an empirical matter on which it is hard to form *a priori* judgements.

† *Note:* See Arrow and Hahn (1971), Chs 9–13 for a comprehensive exposition. The treatment of the subject here draws heavily on the survey paper by T. Negishi (1962).

In proving the proposition, we find it useful first to use a device which effectively sets the 'speeds of adjustment' λ_1, λ_2, equal to unity. The price p_1 is measured as p_1 units of account ('money') per unit of good 1. Suppose we now define a new unit of good 1 as $1/\lambda_1$ of the old units. For example, if $\lambda_1 = 2$, then the new unit of good 1 is exactly $\frac{1}{2}$ the old unit. We are of course quite free to do this, since the units in which goods are measured are essentially arbitrary. It follows that the price of one unit of good j is now p_j/λ_j ($j = 1, 2$), e.g. if we halve the unit quantity then we halve the price. In addition, since λ_j is a constant, the rate of adjustment of the new price per unit of time is exactly $1/\lambda_j$ times the old, i.e. if $\hat{p}_j = (1/\lambda_j)p_j$, then

$$\frac{d\hat{p}_j}{dt} = \frac{1}{\lambda_j}\frac{dp_j}{dt}$$

But clearly from D.2, this is equivalent to dividing through the jth equation by λ_j. Thus the adjustment process becomes:

$$\frac{dp_1}{dt} = \dot{p}_1 = z_1(p_1, p_2)$$

[D.6]

$$\frac{dp_2}{dt} = \dot{p}_2 = z_2(p_1, p_2)$$

where the dimensions of all prices and excess demands are taken to be changed as just described.

Now, it is very simple to prove the above stability proposition using the special fetures of this two-good economy, and this is set as an exercise. (See Question 1 at the end of this section.) However, we shall work through the proof which holds for an n-good economy, making use of the two-good assumption just to simplify the algebra and to permit diagrammatic illustration.

In proving the stability proposition, we will first need three subsidiary propositions (which are also of interest in their own right):

(i) Given gross substitutability, the equilibrium price vector $p^* = (p_1^*, p_2^*)$ is unique (up to a scalar multiple).
That is, we can show that if there are two price vectors say p^* and p^{**}, such that $z_j(p^*) = z_j(p^{**}) = 0$, all j, then gross substitutability implies that $p^{**} = \mu p^*$, for μ some positive number. We proceed by assuming that p^* and p^{**} are equilibrium price vectors, but that no such μ exists. We then show that this leads to a contradiction. Consider Fig. 4.

The line through p^*, denoted by μp^*, shows the set of all price vectors which are scalar multiples of p^*. Because of the zero-degree homogeneity of the excess demand functions we know that if p^* is an equilibrium price vector, so must be μp^*, for any $\mu > 0$. If $p^{**} \neq \mu p^*$, then the line $0p^{**}$ must be distinct from $0p^*$, as shown in the figure. Again, from

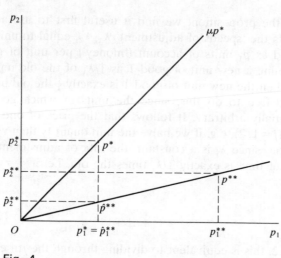

Fig. 4

the zero-degree homogeneity of excess demand functions, if p^{**} is an equilibrium price vector, so must be any point on the line $0p^{**}$, since such a point can be written as, say, $\hat{p}^{**} = \mu p^{**}$, for $1 > \mu > 0$. Consider in particular the point $\hat{p}^{**}$ shown in the figure. Comparing it to the vector p^{*}, we have:

$$\hat{p}_1^{**} = p_1^{*}$$

$$\hat{p}_2^{**} < p_2^{*}$$ [D.7]

Now, since p^{*} is an equilibrium, we must have:

$$z_1(p_1^{*}, p_2^{*}) = 0 = z_2(p_1^{*}, p_2^{*})$$ [D.8]

But, given gross-substitutability, [D.7] implies:

$$z_1(\hat{p}_1^{**}, \hat{p}_2^{**}) < 0$$

$$z_2(\hat{p}_1^{**}, \hat{p}_2^{**}) > 0$$ [D.9]

since $\hat{p}^{**}$ involves a lower price of good 2 than p^{*}. Hence, [D.9] implies that $\hat{p}^{**}$ is not an equilibrium, which in turn implies that $p^{**} = (1/\mu)\hat{p}^{**}$, cannot be an equilibrium. Hence, an equilibrium price vector can only lie along μp^{*}.

(ii) Gross substitutability, together with Walras' Law, implies that $p_1^{*}z_1(p_1, p_2) + p_2^{*}z_2(p_1, p_2) > 0$ for any *disequilibrium* price vector $p = (p_1, p_2)$.

In other words, we can show that the total value of disequilibrium excess demands, when valued at *equilibrium* prices, must always be strictly positive (the total value of equilibrium excess demands at equilibrium prices is of course zero, as is the total value of all excess demands when valued at the prices which generate them, from Walras' Law). First, we note again that, by the properties of the equilibrium:

$$z_1(p_1^*, p_2^*) = 0 = z_2(p_1^*, p_2^*)$$ [D.10]

Now define a new price vector, say $\hat{p}$ (which, because of (i), will be a disequilibrium price vector) as follows:

$$\hat{p}_1 < p_1^* \qquad \hat{p}_2 > p_2^*$$ [D.11]

Then, because of gross substitutability, we must have:

$$z_1(\hat{p}_1, \hat{p}_2) > 0 \qquad z_2(\hat{p}_1, \hat{p}_2) < 0$$ [D.12]

i.e. reducing p_1 from the equilibrium value, and raising p_2 above it, must result in a positive excess demand for good 1, and negative excess demand for good 2. Then [D.11] and [D.12] together imply:

$$(p_1^* - \hat{p}_1) \cdot z_1(\hat{p}_1, \hat{p}_2) + (p_2^* - \hat{p}_2) \cdot z_2(\hat{p}_1, \hat{p}_2) > 0$$ [D.13]

since each term in the sum must be positive. Rearranging gives:

$$p_1^* z_1 + p_2^* z_2 > \hat{p}_1 z_1 + \hat{p}_2 z_2$$ [D.14]

But by Walras' Law, the righthand side of this expression is zero. Hence the proposition is proved, at least for the directions of change in [D.11]. It is left to the reader to prove that it will also hold for all price vectors $\hat{p} = (\hat{p}_1, \hat{p}_2)$ such that $\hat{p}_1/\hat{p}_2 \neq p_1^*/p_2^*$ (see Question 2 of Exercise 16D).

(iii) Given an equilibrium price vector p^*, it is possible on the assumptions made to define a *distance function* $D(p(t), p^*)$, such that $dD/dt < 0$ for all $p(t) \neq \mu p^*$, while $p(t) = \mu p^*$, $\mu > 0$, implies $dD/dt = 0$.

An explanation of the concept of a distance function is given in Appendix 1 to this chapter. Here we note simply that a distance function assigns a real number D to each price vector $p(t)$, measuring its distance, in some sense, from an equilibrium vector p^*. This proposition then asserts that such a function can always be defined in the present case, and, given the tâtonnement process, Walras' Law, and the gross substitute assumption, its value falls monotonically through time. Moreover, it ceases to fall when $p(t)$ is either at the equilibrium vector p^*, or some scalar multiple of it, which must also be an equilibrium vector (given zero degree homogeneity of the excess demand functions). In other words, the time-path of the price vector is getting steadily closer to an equilibrium price vector, and if it reaches the equilibrium *price ray*, will cease to change. (In fact, as Appendix 2 shows, $p(t)$ must tend to one specific point on this ray, determined by the initial price vector $p(0)$.)

To prove proposition (iii), define the distance function:

$$D(p(t), p^*) = [p_1(t) - p_1^*]^2 + [p_2(t) - p_2^*]^2$$ [D.15]

which is clearly a differentiable function of t. Differentiating with respect to t we get:

$$\frac{dD}{dt} = 2[p_1(t) - p_1^*]\frac{dp_1}{dt} + 2[p_2(t) - p_2^*]\frac{dp_2}{dt}$$ [D.16]

Substituting for dp_1/dt and dp_2/dt from [D.16] and rearranging gives:

$$\frac{dD}{dt} = 2\{[p_1(t) - p_1^*]z_1(p_1, p_2) + [p_2(t) - p_2^*]z_2(p_1, p_2)\} \qquad [D.17]$$

$$= 2\{p_1 z_1 + p_2 z_2 - (p_1^* z_1 + p_2^* z_2)\} \qquad [D.18]$$

But, by Walras' Law, $p_1 z_1 + p_2 z_2 = 0$, while, from proposition (ii) above, $p_1^* z_1 + p_2^* z_2 > 0$, and so:

$$\frac{dD}{dt} = -2(p_1^* z_1 + p_2^* z_2) \lessgtr 0 \qquad [D.19]$$

If $p(t) = \mu p^*$, $\mu > 0$, then:

$$p_1^* z_1(\mu p_1^*, \mu p_2^*) + p_2^* z_2(\mu p_1^*, \mu p_2^*) = p_1^* z_1(p_1^*, p_2^*) + p_2^* z_2(p_1^*, p_2^*) = 0 \qquad [D.20]$$

using the zero degree homogeneity property, and Walras' Law, and so:

$$\frac{dD}{dt}(\mu p^*, p^*) = -2\{p_1^* z_1(p_1^*, p_2^*) + p_2^* z_2(p_1^*, p_2^*)\} = 0 \qquad [D.21]$$

These three propositions, and in particular proposition (iii), allow us to prove the stability proposition given earlier. Intuitively speaking, we might think that proposition (iii) provides us directly with the proof of stability, since if, as time passes, the distance between the price vector $p(t)$ and the equilibrium is steadily diminishing, we might feel that the time-path of price vectors must converge to p^*, while, because of [D.21] it would not over-shoot. However, there is an awkward possibility, which is that the price vector time-path may converge to a limit other than p^*, so that, even though it is always getting closer to p^*, it does not converge to it. If this seems counter-intuitive, consider the function:

$$y = \frac{1}{x} + a \qquad a, x > 0 \qquad [D.22]$$

As $x \to \infty$, y is becoming closer to zero – the distance between y and zero is decreasing monotonically – but $\lim_{x \to \infty} y = a \neq 0$, and so y does not converge to zero. We have to prove that in the present case no such possibility exists. It might be suspected that we can rule out this possibility, since, as [D.19] shows, the distance function continues to fall as long as $p(t) \neq p^*$, and, indeed, a proof can be constructed to show that no limit other than p^* is possible. This proof is somewhat technical, however, and so it is left for Appendix 2. Here, we take it as given, and go on to discuss the conclusions of the analysis.

To summarize this discussion of stability: given the assumptions underlying the form of the tâtonnement process, we have been able to find a set of conditions, namely the gross-substitutability conditions, under which the general system of interrelated markets will converge to an equilibrium, however far away from it the initial position is and whatever the speeds of adjustment λ_1, λ_2. Moreover, these conditions were also seen to imply uniqueness of the equilibrium price vector.

It would clearly have been damaging to the theory if no such conditions could have been found. Again, what is at issue is the internal consistency and coherence of the model of general equilibrium: if equilibrium in that model was found never to be stable, then this would severely limit the model's analytical scope. For example, the model could not be used for comparative statics analysis.

We have seen that the gross substitute condition is sufficient for stability of equilibrium. It is not, however, necessary – stability may exist when all goods are not gross substitutes. Thus, although it may seem something of a very special case, empirically speaking, that all goods should be gross substitutes, it may be that 'sufficient' gross substitutability exists for the stability proposition to be relevant. On the other hand, the question: 'What degree of gross substitutability must exist?' or, 'How closely must the conditions of the theorem be approximated?' is difficult to answer in *a priori* terms.

Finally, note that the entire analysis of this section relates to the tâtonnement process, which, as Chapter 10 has suggested, may not be a good description of real adjustment processes especially where *production* is involved. An essential feature is the 'no-trading out of equilibrium' assumption. If we permit trading at disequilibrium prices, then quantities which individuals and firms buy and sell in one 'round' of trading may differ from those expected, and the precise quantities which have been traded will affect trading in the next 'round'. Hence, the process of adjustment must take into account the time paths of quantities traded, and not only the time-paths of prices. This increased complexity has of course not prevented the analysis of so-called 'non-tatonnement' adjustment processes, but these cannot be examined here.

Exercise 16D

1. Show in a simple diagram that in a two-good economy, where the goods are gross substitutes, equilibrium is stable (*Hint:* set $p_2 = 1$ and draw the excess demand functions as functions of p_1/p_2 only, beginning with the equilibrium value).
2. Prove proposition (ii) for the case in which $p_1 > p_1^*$ and $p_2 < p_2^*$, and show that this, together with the case considered in equation [D.11] establishes the proposition for all possible price vectors.
3. Discuss in detail the meaning of gross-substitutability by:
   (a) distinguishing between supply and demand effects in the excess demand functions;
   (b) distinguishing between income and substitution effects in consumer demand functions.
   If two goods are gross substitutes are they also necessarily gross substitutes in consumption or Hicks–Allen substitutes?

E. Conclusions

In this chapter we have considered the existence, stability and uniqueness of a general equilibrium. We were usually concerned to frame conditions under which it can be shown that an equilibrium will exist and be unique and stable in some sense. The theories we have tried to introduce are not entirely satisfactory. They involve no market imperfections and no uncertainty; the analysis of stability rested heavily on the device of the tâtonnement process, which, as we saw in Chapter 10 may be very unsatisfactory as a representation of the real world.

On the other hand, the need for a general equilibrium analysis should be clear. To recall the intentions of microeconomics: our desire to gain some understanding of the determination of resource allocation in an economy leads us to consider the entire system of markets. The equilibrium methodology views a resource allocation as an equilibrium of the system. Hence we have to consider the problems of existence and stability of the equilibrium.

It is also worth noting that general equilibrium analysis is of considerable importance to empirical economic analysis. Any system with two or more interrelated markets can be viewed as a general equilibrium system. Once we wish to analyse such a system, allowing adjustments to take place in more than one market, then the considerations raised in this chapter become relevant. For example, suppose we were to conduct a 'realistic' analysis of the housing market. We would have to recognize a system of at least three markets: those for publicly-supplied rental accommodation, privately-supplied rental accommodation, and owner-occupied housing. In considering consequences of various policy measures, for example, changes in subsidies on mortgage interest rates or price control in the private rental market, an analysis which did not beg important questions would have to take account of interactions among the markets, and so would have to be conducted in general equilibrium terms. Problems would arise concerning the existence and stability of equilibria, which would be approached by the methods of this chapter. It therefore does not make any essential difference as to whether we consider an entire economy or a multi-market subsector of it, in terms of formal analysis. What matters is that there is more than one market.

Appendix 1

Mappings

Given two sets, X and Y, a mapping is a rule for associating one and only one element of the set Y with each element of the set X. The set X is called the *domain* of the mapping. The set of values in Y resulting from the mapping is called the *range*. A type of mapping which will already have been encountered by the reader is that defined by any of the elementary functions of mathematics. If we write, for example:

$$y = a + bx \qquad a, b \text{ and } x \text{ real numbers.} \qquad [A.1]$$

we are specifying a rule for associating a number y with each number x. By implication, the domain is the set of all real numbers, as is the range; the domain should always be specified for any mapping.

The concept of a mapping is, however, more general than that of an algebraic relation: it applies to any kind of rule for associating elements of sets of any kind.

The notation usually adopted for some mapping f, associating elements of a set Y with the elements of X, is:

$$f: X \to Y. \tag{A.2}$$

This reflects a terminology which is often used: the mapping f is said to map the set X into the set Y, in the sense that it picks out a subset of Y which corresponds to X under the mapping. The value $y' = f(x')$, $x' \in X$, is called the *image* of x' under the mapping.

Since the elements of the sets X and Y can be of any kind, this notion of a mapping is obviously of great generality. There are also many types and properties of mappings which are of interest. For our present purposes, however, we are interested only in particular types of sets and relatively few properties of mappings.

The sets in which we are interested are always sets of vectors of real numbers, where the number of components of the vectors will always be specified. Geometrically speaking, a vector has an interpretation as a *point* in a space of appropriate dimensions. Hence, we call sets of such vectors 'point sets'. Thus we could define X as the set of all three component vectors:

$$x = [x_1, x_2, x_3] \tag{A.3}$$

where each x is then a point in three-dimensional space. Given the mapping:

$$y = a_1 x_1 + a_2 x_2 + a_3 x_3$$
$$= ax \qquad a = (a_1, a_2, a_3), \qquad x \in X \tag{A.4}$$

this defines y as a scalar, and hence the set Y is the set of scalars or real numbers, points in one-dimensional space. It follows that this mapping $f: X \to Y$ maps points in three-dimensional space into points in one-dimensional space. In general, we may have mappings which map points in n-dimensional space (X is the set of vectors with n components) into points in m-dimensional space (Y is the set of vectors with m components), where $n \gtrless m$.

The particular kind of mapping with which we are concerned in Chapter 16 arises as follows. We have n functions of n variables:

$$y_1 = f_1(x_1, x_2, \ldots, x_n)$$
$$y_2 = f_2(x_1, x_2, \ldots, x_n)$$
$$\ldots \ldots \ldots \ldots \ldots \tag{A.5}$$
$$y_n = f_n(x_1, x_2, \ldots, x_n)$$

We can think of the n values of the variables $x_1, x_2, \ldots, x_n$ as a vector $x = [x_1, x_2, \ldots, x_n]$, a point in n-dimensional space. Let X be the set of these points. Given any x, and the functions $f_1, f_2, \ldots, f_n$, we obtain a set of values for the variables $y_1, y_2, \ldots, y_n$. Again, we can define the vector, $y = [y_1, y_2, \ldots, y_n]$, also a point in n-dimensional space, and Y can denote the set of these points. We could therefore think of the set of functions in [A.5] as giving a vector y for each vector x, so we write:

$$y = f(x) \tag{A.6}$$

f is called a *vector-valued function*, because for each vector $x \in X$ it gives a vector $y \in Y$. Alternatively, we could regard [A.5] as defining the mapping:

$$f : X \to Y \tag{A.7}$$

A property of mappings in which we are interested is continuity. Consider first the continuity of an algebraic function:

$$y = h(x) \tag{A.8}$$

where y and x are scalars. Continuity is defined for such a function in the following way: we consider a sequence of values of x, say $x^1, x^2, x^3, \ldots$, the limit of which is some specific value of x, say $\bar{x}$. This sequence defines a sequence of y values, $y^1 = h(x^1)$, $y^2 = h(x^2)$, $y^3 = h(x^3) \ldots$. We then define the function to be continuous at $x = \bar{x}$, if and only if the limit of the sequence $h(x^v)$ exists, $v = 1, 2, 3, \ldots$ and:

$$\lim_{x^v \to \bar{x}} h(x^v) = f(\bar{x}) \qquad v = 1, 2, 3, \ldots \tag{A.9}$$

A similar definition is used in the case of mappings in general. Thus, let $x^v \in X$ be a sequence of points in X, whose limit is $\bar{x}$. The image of x^v in Y is $y^v = f(x^v)$. Then the mapping is continuous at $x = \bar{x}$ if and only if the limit of the sequence $f(x^v)$ exists and:

$$\lim_{x^v \to \bar{x}} f(x^v) = f(\bar{x}) \qquad v = 1, 2, \ldots \tag{A.10}$$

To illustrate, consider Fig. 5. In (a) of the figure, the path of x^v values converging to $\bar{x} \in X$ gives rise to the image path in Y, as shown. If, as the path in X converges to $\bar{x}$, the image path converges to $f(\bar{x})$, the mapping is said to be continuous.

To return to the mapping represented by [A.5], and its more concise form [A.7], we can state the following proposition: if each of the functions in [A.5] is continuous, in the sense of the definition in [A.9], then the mapping in [A.7] is continuous in the sense of [A.10].

Fixed points and Brouwer's theorem

Consider first a mapping of a set into itself, which we could write as $f : X \to X$. For example, if X is the set of non-negative real numbers, the

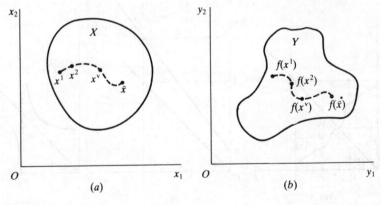

Fig. 5

mapping:

$$y = a + bx \qquad x \in X, \qquad a, b \geq 0 \tag{A.11}$$

gives a non-negative real number y for every x, and so maps the set of non-negative real numbers into itself.

A question which turns out to have considerable interest is the following: does there exist, for a given mapping of a set X into itself, a point x^* which is its own image, i.e. such that $x^* = f(x^*)$? Such a point is called a *fixed point*, because it remains unchanged under the mapping. Consider, for example, the mapping in [A.11]. If $a \neq 0$, and $b = 1$, there is clearly no fixed point, since $y \neq x$ always. If $a = 0$, then there is either one fixed point, at $x = 0$, or an infinite number, at every value of x, according to whether b is or is not equal to 1. If $a \neq 0$, and $b \neq 1$ there will be a fixed point at $x = a/(1 - b)$.

The existence of a fixed point depends both on the mapping and on the set X. It is of interest to have some general proposition about the circumstances under which a fixed point will exist. This is provided by the important *fixed point theorem* proved by the Dutch mathematician L. E. J. Brouwer (1881–1960) which can be stated as:

Brouwer's Fixed Point Theorem: a continuous mapping of a closed, bounded, convex set into itself, always has a fixed point.

The meaning of closedness, boundedness and convexity of a set should be recalled from Chapter 2. We have already considered the continuity property of mappings. A proof of this theorem is well outside the scope of this book. However, we shall try to illustrate the role which the various conditions of the theorem play, for a very simple case.

Let us take as the set X the closed interval of real numbers $0 \leq x \leq 1$, the *unit interval*. A mapping of this set into itself associates with *each* x in this interval one and only one value $f(x)$ which also lies in the interval. It is clear that X is closed, bounded, and convex. Whatever the mapping $f : X \to X$, the theorem assures us that, if it is continuous, at least one point, x^*, exists such that $x^* = f(x^*)$.

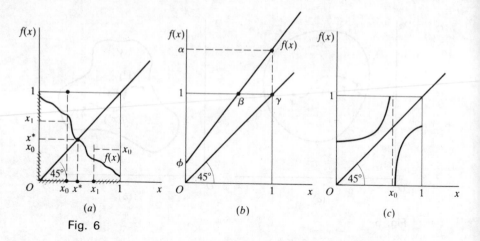

(a)   (b)   (c)

Fig. 6

To illustrate, consider Fig. 6. In (a) of the figure, the set X is shown as the unit interval on both axes. For emphasis, the unit square is drawn in. Consider the diagonal, which is a 45° line. Along this line, $x = f(x)$ and so to say that the mapping has a fixed point is to say that it contains at least one point on this line. Let the curve marked $f(x)$ in (a) be the graph of the mapping. Then, a point such as x^*, where the graph intersects the diagonal, is a fixed point. Now let us consider the roles played by the various conditions of the theorem:

(i) *Convexity of X*. Suppose that X were not convex. In the present case, this can only imply that it consists of two or more disjoint intervals on the real line. Suppose these were: $0 \leq x \leq x_0$, and $x_1 \leq x \leq 1$, as shown in (a) of the figure. X is then the union of these two subsets. The mapping in the diagram still maps X into itself, since each x in the two intervals has an image in one of the two intervals. However, there is no fixed point.

(ii) *Boundedness of X*. Consider (b) of the figure, and suppose that X consisted of all $x \geq 0$, so that it is unbounded above. Then the 45° line extending to infinity will still contain any fixed point which exists. Suppose the mapping were shown by the straight line $\phi\beta$ in the diagram, continued to $+\infty$. Then clearly no fixed point will exist, since there is no intersection with the 45° line.

An objection might be made at this point. Suppose that X is in fact the unit interval, as in (b). Then the mapping shown by $\phi\beta$ is continuous, the set is closed, bounded and convex, but there is still no fixed point. Hence, we seem to have a counter-example which disproves the theorem. This is however quickly resolved: in this case, the line $\phi\beta$ is not the graph of a mapping of a set into *itself*. The image set of the mapping is in fact 0α, as shown in (b), of which the unit interval is a proper subset. For the set to map into itself, we would have to have the mapping defined say by the kinked line $\phi\beta\gamma$, in which case a fixed point exists at γ.

(iii) *Closedness of X*. Suppose that the set X is defined as the half open interval $0 \leq x < 1$, and consider the mapping given by $\phi\beta\gamma$ in (b). The only point at which this meets the 45° line is at γ, where $x = 1$. But this point is not in the set X, and so there is no fixed point.

(iv) *Continuity of f.* Consider (c) in Fig. 6. There is a discontinuity in the mapping at $x = x_0$, and in this case no fixed point exists.

These various cases are meant to illustrate the possibility that when one of the conditions of the theorem is violated, a fixed point *may* not exist. It is quite possible that a fixed point will exist, when a condition is not satisfied, however. Thus the reader should, in each case (i)–(iv), draw a diagram on the lines of Fig. 6 in which a fixed point does exist. In other words, the theorem gives *sufficient* conditions for existence of a fixed point: if they are satisfied, we can be certain that a fixed point exists, and we cannot construct a counter-example where one does not.

We now consider briefly *composite mappings.* Given two mappings: $f : X \to Y$ and $g : Y \to Z$, we define the composite mapping $g \circ f : X \to Z$. In other words, taking some $x' \in X$, its image $y' \in Y$ has in turn an image $z' \in Z$. Hence we can take z' as the image of x' under the composite mapping $g \circ f = g[f(x)]$.

An example: X and Z are each the set of all real numbers, Y is the set of positive real numbers; the mappings are:

$$y = x^2 \qquad x \in X \tag{A.12}$$

$$z = a - by \qquad y \in Y \qquad a, b > 0. \tag{A.13}$$

and the composite mapping is:

$$z = a - bx^2 \qquad x \in X \tag{A.14}$$

Note that since X and Z are the same sets, the composite mapping is a mapping of a set into itself, though the mapping g is not. A proposition which is intuitively appealing and which can be proved is the following: if the mappings $f : X \to Y$ and $g : Y \to Z$ are continuous, then so is the composite mapping $g \circ f : X \to Z$

Distance functions

We conclude this Appendix by examining the concept of distance and *distance functions.* Intuitively, everyone knows what he means when he talks about the distance betweeen two points, but the mathematician is faced with the problem of defining a *measure* of distance between points in spaces of any number of dimensions – not just the one-, two-, or three-dimensional spaces of everyday experience. It can be agreed that the essential properties of a measure of distance between two points are the following:

(i) the measure should be zero if the two points coincide and positive if they are distinct;

(ii) it should be the same when measured from point a to point b, as when measured from b to a;

(iii) the distance from point a to point b *via* a third point, c, cannot be less than the distance from a to b directly.

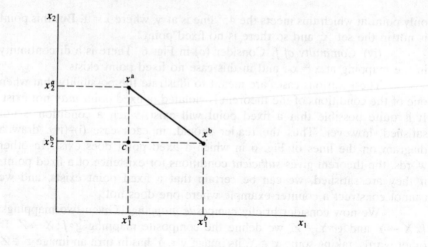

Fig. 7

These ideas can be formalized in the following way; given two points a and b in some space, a *distance function* is a function which assigns a positive real number $\delta = \delta(a, b)$ to each such pair of points and which satisfies the conditions:

(a) $\delta(a, b) \geq 0$ and $\delta(a, b) = 0$ if and only if $a = b$.

(b) $\delta(a, b) = \delta(b, a)$

(c) $\delta(a, c) + \delta(c, b) \geq \delta(a, b)$

It is left to the reader to confirm that these conditions embody the properties (i)–(iii), and in fact are formal statements of them.

The question of 'measuring the distance between points' then becomes that of defining an appropriate distance function. To illustrate one approach, consider Fig. 7. We take the two dimensional space of vectors $(x_1 x_2)$, and x^a and x^b are arbitrary points in this space. A natural way of measuring the distance between x^a and x^b is as the length of the line joining them, $x^a x^b$. To evaluate this length, consider the right-angled triangle $x^a c x^b$. From Pythagoras' theorem, we know that:

$$(\text{length of } x^a x^b)^2 = (\text{length of } x^b c)^2 + (\text{length of } x^a c)^2$$

Thus, if we define the length of $x^a x^b$ to be the value of the distance function $\delta(x^a x^b)$, the length of $x^b c$ by $x_1^a - x_1^b$, and the length of $x^a c$ by $x_2^a - x_2^b$, we can write:

$$\delta(x^a, x^b) = \sqrt{(x_1^a - x_1^b)^2 + (x_2^a - x_2^b)^2} \qquad [\text{A.15}]$$

Since x^a and x^b are arbitrary points, [A.15] defines a distance function which, it can be shown, possesses the three properties set out earlier. Moreover, this is true however many components x^a and x^b have (as long as they are points in the same space) and so we have a general distance function, known as the *Euclidian* distance function, for n dimensions:

$$\delta(x^a, x^b) = \sqrt{\sum_{j=1}^{n} (x_j^a - x_j^b)^2} \tag{A.16}$$

This distance function is not the only one possible. Consider the function:

$$D(x^a, x^b) = [\delta(x^a, x^b)]^2 = \sum_{j=1}^{n} (x_j^a - x_j^b)^2 \tag{A.17}$$

It can be shown that D possesses the three properties of a distance function, and so can be regarded also as giving a measure of the distance between two points. Because it does not involve the square root sign, this distance function is often more convenient to use. Direct use is made of it in section D of this chapter.

Appendix 2

Here we have to prove that under the assumptions of section D, the time-path of price vectors $p(t)$ does not converge to a price vector other than an equilibrium price vector. This proof is necessary because the demonstration that $dD/dt < 0$, for $p(t) \neq p^*$, is not sufficient to ensure that $\lim_{t \to \infty} p(t) = p^*$. The proof proceeds by contradiction. We suppose that $\lim_{t \to \infty} p(t) = \bar{p} \neq p^*$, and show that we obtain a contradiction, thus establishing the desired result.

First note that:

$$D(p(t), 0) = D(p(0), 0) = k \quad \text{all} \quad t > 0 \tag{A.18}$$

where $0 = [0, 0]$ is the origin. In words, the distance of every disequilibrium price vector from the origin is equal to a constant, k, defined by the distance of the initial price vector $p(0)$ from the origin. To prove this, note that by the definition of the distance function:

$$D(p(t), 0) = p_1^2(t) + p_2^2(t) \quad t \geq 0 \tag{A.19}$$

and therefore; for $t \geq 0$:

$$\frac{dD}{dt}(p(t), 0) = 2(p_1(t)\dot{p}_1 + p_2(t)\dot{p}_2)$$

$$= 2(p_1 z_1 + p_2 z_2)$$

$$= 0 \tag{A.20}$$

from Walras' Law. But this means that, for all $t \geq 0$, the distance of $p(t)$ from the origin is invariant with time, as asserted in [A.18]. (One implication of this is that the equilibrium price vector p^* should be regarded as a *normalized* price vector satisfying: $(p_1^*)^2 + (p_2^*)^2 = k$, since the price vector to which $p(t)$ tends must satisfy the condition in [A.18].)

Now we suppose that, contrary to the stability proposition;

$$\lim_{t \to \infty} p(t) = \bar{p} \neq p^* \qquad [A.21]$$

where it must also be the case that $\bar{p}_1^2 + \bar{p}_2^2 = k$. Since $\bar{p} \neq p^*$, we must have $D(\bar{p}, p^*) = \delta > 0$, and since $\bar{p}$ bounds the time-path of price vectors, $p(t)$, there must exist a set of price vectors $P_\delta = \{p \mid D(p, p^*) < \delta\}$. In other words, P_δ is a δ-neighbourhood of p^*, which does not contain, because of [A.21], any of the price vectors $p(t)$. Hence if we define the set $P_k = \{p \mid p_1^2 + p_2^2 = k\}$, it is clear that, given [A.21], the set $P = P_k - P_\delta$ (the complement of P_δ in P_k) must contain all the price vectors $p(t)$, and does not contain p^*. Moreover P is a bounded set, as a result of [A.18], and it is also closed, since it contains all its limit points (every price vector p, which contains in every open neighbourhood about itself, however small, a second price vector which is in P, is itself in P). Now the derivative dD/dt is a function of the price vectors $p(t)$, and moreover it is a continuous function. Thus we have a continuous function defined on a closed and bounded set of price vectors, and so, from Weierstrass' Theorem, we know that a maximum value of dD/dt exists on this set. Call this value s^*. Since we know dD/dt to be always negative, $s^* < 0$, and we have:

$$\frac{dD}{dt} \leq s^* < 0 \quad \text{all} \quad p(t) \in P \qquad [A.22]$$

Integrating over some interval $[0, \bar{t}]$ gives:

$$\int_0^{\bar{t}} \frac{dD}{dt} \, dt = [D(t)]_0^{\bar{t}} = D(\bar{t}) - D(0) \leq \int_0^{\bar{t}} s^* \, dt = s^* \bar{t} < 0 \qquad [A.23]$$

where $D(0) = D(p(0), p^*)$, and $D(\bar{t}) = D(p(\bar{t}), p^*)$, from the definition of the distance function D. [A.23] implies:

$$D(\bar{t}) \leq D(0) + s^* \bar{t} \qquad [A.24]$$

where, of course, $D(0)$ is constant while $s^* t$ is negative. It follows that we can find $\bar{t}$ sufficiently large that

$$D(0) + s^* \bar{t} < 0 \qquad [A.25]$$

implying:

$$D(\bar{t}) < 0 \qquad [A.26]$$

But the distance function D can never take on negative values: it must always be positive. Hence, the assertion that $p(t)$ tends to a limit other than p^* leads to a contradiction, and must be rejected. Thus the stability proposition is proved.

References and further reading

The leading references on general equilibrium theory are:

K. J. Arrow and **F. H. Hahn.** *General Competitive Analysis,* Oliver & Boyd, Edinburgh, 1971;

G. Debreu. *Theory of Value,* John Wiley, New York, 1959;

W. Hildenbrand and **A. Kirman.** *Introduction to Equilibrium Analysis,* North-Holland, Amsterdam, 1976,

all of which require a good background in mathematics. A less mathematical treatment can be found in:

J. Quirk and **R. Saposnick.** *Introduction to General Equilibrium Theory and Welfare Economics,* McGraw-Hill, 1968

though it must be said that if the reader wishes seriously to pursue general equilibrium theory, he should set about acquiring the mathematics required for the first three books. For this:

A. Takayama. *Mathematical Economics,* The Dryden Press, 1974 is an excellent text.

The central reference on the analysis of stability is:

T. Negishi. 'The stability of a competitive economy: a survey article', *Econometrica,* 30 Oct. 1962

Chapter 17

Welfare economics

A. Introduction

There is no reason for economists to confine themselves to a purely positive analysis of the economic system and to hold themselves back from an appraisal of the system from an ethical point of view. Indeed, it could be argued that because of their understanding of the workings of the system economists are particularly well qualified to contribute to such an appraisal, and it is certainly true that many people take up the study of economics because they want to do just this. In this chapter we shall be concerned with some aspects of welfare economics, which is that part of economic analysis concerned with the relation between the economic system and the well-being of individuals in society. We shall be mainly concerned with the following problem: out of the infinite number of resource allocations which are in principle possible, the market mechanism at a given point of time brings about one. We take this to be the equilibrium resource allocation, extensively discussed in the previous chapter. What then can be said about the *optimality properties* of this resource allocation: will it be the 'best' of those available to society, or not?

Attempts to answer this question have been made for as long as economics has existed. An alternative form of it could be phrased as follows: a market economy is essentially made up of individual decision-takers each pursuing his own narrow self-interest, subject to the stimuli and constraints of the price mechanism. No-one is concerned with the common good. Yet is it possible that this kind of economic organisation could bring about in some sense the 'best' state of economic well-being and, if so, under what conditions?

In order to answer the question, we need to know what we mean by the 'best' resource allocation. First of all, there can clearly be no objective sense in which we can interpret the word 'best'; each person may have his own view, based on his particular ethical position, about what constitutes a good resource allocation. Hence, any criterion upon which we compare resource allocations in terms of better or worse must be based on a specific set of ethical propositions or *value judgements*. The problem this then presents for our analysis is that of choosing a set of value judgements on which to base a criterion of comparison. We will first explore the implications of adopting one particular set of value judgements, which give rise to what is known as the Pareto criterion of optimality of resource allocations.

B. The Pareto criterion

Suppose that we adopt the following value judgements:
 (i) individuals are to be the sole judges of their own well-being, so that we regard an individual as better off after some change if he prefers the situation after it to that before it.
 (ii) resource allocation A is better than resource allocation B (and B is worse than A), if and only if at least one individual prefers A to B, and no-one prefers B to A. Another way of putting this is to say that if and only if a change from B to A makes someone better off, and no-one worse off, then A is better than B. Hence, a best or optimal resource allocation is one which does not have a better, in the sense just defined.

An explanation of these value judgements is best begun by showing what it is they avoid. (i) implies a refusal to adopt a paternalistic attitude and an espousal of an *individualistic* welfare criterion. We do not decide whether something is 'really' good or bad for the individual, or think that he ought to have more or less of something than he chooses, in 'his own best interests'.

The value judgement in (ii) expressly avoids making *interpersonal comparisons* of well-being. That is, it refuses to consider intensity of well-being or changes in it and to balance gains and losses of well-being of different people. If a change from allocation A to allocation B makes some people better off but others worse off, then B is considered neither better nor worse than A; it is in fact simply not ranked, in terms of this criterion: A and B are non-comparable. No attempt is made to ask: are those better off in B a very great deal better off, while those worse off only a little worse off? so that one may be tempted to conclude that the change is a good thing. Neither is it asked: are those who gain by the change deserving people, while those who lose by it are undeserving? so that again we might conclude that the change is a good thing. We rule out all such balancing out of individual gains and losses.

Although these value judgements are designed to be of very general appeal, it is possible that they would not be shared by many people. Most of us would think it justifiable to override individual preferences in consumption of some goods, for example heroin, and other hard drugs. The value judgements of some people extend to a much wider set of goods such as soft drugs, tobacco, alcohol in its various forms, some kinds of sexual gratification, opera and 'highbrow' music and drama. Laws, taxes and subsidies operate so as to lead people to consume less or more of these goods than would be the case in the absence of such paternalistic intervention. (Some, though in our view not all, of this could be explained by the existence of externalities: see the following chapter.)

Similarly, many of us would be willing to weigh up gains and losses of different individuals or well-defined groups, to arrive at a definite view of whether some change is good or not. Given that many real-world economic policies make someone worse off, policy-makers are in fact having to do this all the time. Note that it has also been argued that although ostensibly 'neutral' in its view of the distribution of well-being among individuals, the Pareto criterion has a bias toward the *status quo*. Since it cannot be used to justify an economic policy which makes some people worse off, it would not rule as 'good' a policy which made the 'very rich' a little worse off and the 'very poor' a lot better off.

It is therefore likely that many would feel that their value judgements were not completely described by the Pareto criterion. Why then should we adopt it as the basis of our present analysis? A reason for accepting the individualistic nature of the criterion is that, despite what was just said, this would be accepted as the general view in market economies. Although there may be paternalistic intervention in the case of some goods and services, people would be regarded as the best judges of their own self-interest in respect of the consumption of the vast majority of them. Hence it suffices as a first approximation to view resource allocation as entirely concerned with the latter kinds of goods and services.

There are two reasons for accepting the second value judgement. First, we can show that provided a certain plausible condition is met, the resource allocation which is optimal for some *explicit* set of interpersonal comparisons (i.e. some explicit evaluation of the relative desirability of gains or losses in the well-being of specific individuals), will always be a Pareto optimum. Of course, not *all* Pareto optimal resource allocations will be optimal for any *one* such explicit evaluation: but the set of all Pareto optimal allocations contains the set of all allocations which are optimal for all such explicit evaluations provided the condition is met. Thus, on grounds of generality, it seems useful to proceed by first analysing Pareto optimality, and then considering the consequences of applying some set of explicit interpersonal evaluations.

The condition just referred to can be stated as follows: under the set of value judgements defining the explicit set of interpersonal comparisons, it must be true that an increase in the well-being of any one individual is a good thing and a decrease a bad thing, *given that the well-being of no-one else changes*. Thus, the condition rules out 'soaking the rich', or 'grinding the faces of the poor', *for its own sake*, though it permits value judgements which would soak the rich in order to help the poor, or grind the poor to please the rich.

We can put this in a formal, though rather less general way as follows. Denote the level of well-being of individual h, $h = 1, 2, \ldots H$, by u_h, (where this is his own utility function, because of (i)). Suppose that a particular set of value judgements gives rise to a preference ordering over individual welfare levels, which can be represented by the *social welfare function* (assumed differentiable):

$$W = W(u_1, u_2, \ldots u_H) \qquad \text{[B.1]}$$

(the concept of a social welfare function will be examined at some length in section F below). Then the condition can be interpreted to imply that

$$\frac{\partial W}{\partial u_h} > 0 \quad \text{for every } h. \qquad \text{[B.2]}$$

We can use this formalization to prove that whatever the relative evaluations of the u_h (which will determine the specific form of the function W), a resource allocation which maximizes W (and therefore which is optimal for that set of value judgements) must be a Pareto optimum. Thus, take any resource allocation *not* a Pareto optimum, and assume that this generates individual levels of well-being u_h^*. Since this is not a Pareto optimum, we know that it is possible to change the resource allocation to make some individuals better off, i.e. to increase some u_h, and no-one worse off, i.e. no u_h decreases. Hence, given the condition in [B.2], the value of W must also increase by such a change. This proves that no resource allocation which is *not* a Pareto optimum can maximize W. If the set of all resource allocations can be partitioned into two subsets, namely the Pareto optima and the non-Pareto optima (which we take to be true), then since a resource allocation which maximizes W cannot lie in the latter, it must lie in the former.

Of course, it may be that the value of W may be increased by moving from one Pareto optimal allocation to another (by increasing u_h and reducing u_k, when $\partial W/\partial u_h > \partial W/\partial u_k$), or by moving from a Pareto optimal to a non-Pareto optimal allocation. But in this latter case, as we have just seen, it will then always be possible to increase W by moving to *some* Pareto optimal allocation. We can, therefore, think of the Pareto optimal allocations as an 'efficient set', from which someone with explicit value judgements concerning the distribution of well-being among individuals can choose.

The second reason for adopting value judgement (ii) and the Pareto criterion gives away the answer to the question posed in section A. We find in fact that under certain conditions, the equilibrium resource allocation attained by a market economy is a Pareto optimum. Hence, since we are interested in the optimality properties of the general equilibrium of a market economy, we have an answer: if an optimum is defined in a certain way, that is, with complete neutrality concerning the distribution of well-being among individuals, then the equilibrium resource allocation is optimal. Of course, if the value judgements of any one individual imply explicit preferences over distributions of well-being, then it is only by accident that he would find any *particular* market resource allocation optimal, but this is beside the point. By carefully defining the kind of optimum which the market economy can be shown to achieve (under certain conditions), we obtain a clear statement of precisely what its optimality properties are. No-one is thereby compelled to accept that the workings of the market economy are 'good', if he does not share the same value judgements.

C. Optimal resource allocation

In this chapter we are interested in describing the properties of a Pareto optimal resource allocation, i.e. a resource allocation which cannot be changed to make someone better off without also making someone worse off. As with any optimal position, we describe it in terms of the conditions which it satisfies, since in a general theoretical model we do not have information to solve for specific numerical values. We could think of a resource allocation as a 'list' of values of the following variables:

    (i) the consumption of each commodity by each individual in the economy;

    (ii) the consumption of each input by each firm;

    (iii) the production of each commodity by each firm in the economy;

    (iv) the supply of each input by each individual.

An economic system assigns values to each of these variables, i.e. determines a resource allocation. For ease of exposition, we will assume that the economy has only two consumers, two firms, two consumption goods, and two inputs. We place ourselves in the position of a 'central planner', who wishes to find the conditions which will be satisfied by a Pareto optimal allocation. He must take account of the following relationships in the economy:

    (a) *the utility functions:*

$$u_h(x_{h1}, x_{h2}, z_h) \qquad h = 1, 2. \qquad\qquad\text{[C.1]}$$

where x_{h1} and x_{h2} are quantities of the two goods consumed, and z_h is the quantity of input h supplied by household h. For simplicity, it is being assumed that one individual supplies one of the inputs, the other individual the other, and so inputs can be numbered according to which individual supplies them. The consumers' *initial endowments* of the inputs are denoted $\bar{z}_h$, $h = 1, 2$. The consumption goods yield positive marginal utility, while supply of the input yields negative marginal utility (cf. Ch. 3).

    (b) *the production functions:*

$$x_i = f_i(z_{i1}, z_{i2}) \qquad i = 1, 2. \qquad\qquad\text{[C.2]}$$

where x_i is output of good i, f_i the production function, and z_{i1}, z_{i2} the quantities of the two inputs used in producing good i. For simplicity, it is assumed that each firm produces just one of the goods.

As well as these four functions, which describe preferences on the one hand and technology on the other, the planner must realize that individuals cannot consume more than he arranges to produce, firms cannot use more inputs than he arranges to supply, and each consumer cannot supply more than his initial endowment of the input. Hence he must take into account the relationships:

$$\sum_{h=1}^{2} x_{h1} = x_1 \qquad \sum_{h=1}^{2} x_{h2} = x_2 \qquad\qquad \text{[C.3]}$$

$$\bar{z}_1 \geq z_1 = \sum_{i=1}^{2} z_{i1} \qquad \bar{z}_2 \geq z_2 = \sum_{i=1}^{2} z_{i2} \qquad\qquad \text{[C.4]}$$

where [C.3] expresses the equality of consumption and production, and [C.4] that of input supply and usage.

We wish to find the conditions which will be satisfied by a Pareto optimal resource allocation in this economy. We proceed by considering separately each of the four sets of variables described in (i)–(iv) above, taking values of the others as given. To begin with, take the values of all variables other than the x_{h1} and x_{h2} as given (and consistent with each other, in that they satisfy [C.2], and [C.4]). Thus, we wish to consider the question of the Pareto optimal distribution of the two outputs among individuals, given that their totals are fixed. It is convenient to introduce at this stage the Edgeworth box diagram, already used in the analysis of exchange situations in Chapter 10. Consider Fig. 1.

We choose as the length of the horizontal side of the box the quantity (assumed fixed) of x_1 available to the economy. Likewise, we choose as the length of the vertical side of the box, the (fixed) quantity of x_2 available to the economy. These are denoted $\bar{x}_1$ and $\bar{x}_2$ respectively. We can call 0_1 the origin for individual 1, and 0_2 the origin for individual 2. We measure x_{11} (1's consumption of good 1) horizontally from 0_1, and x_{12} (his

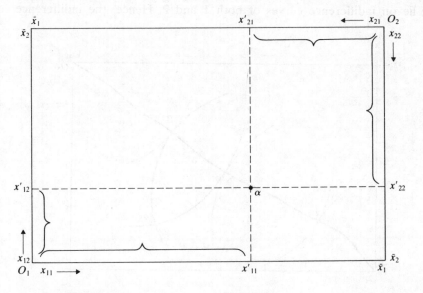

Fig. 1

consumption of good 2) vertically from 0_1. We measure x_{21} (2's consumption of good 1) horizontally from 0_2, and x_{22} (his consumption of good 2) vertically from 0_2. Consider therefore any point in the box, for example α in Fig. 1. This point corresponds to 1's consumption pair $(x'_{11}x'_{12})$ and 2's pair, $(x'_{21}x'_{22})$. Moreover, by construction, it must be true that:

$$x'_{11} + x'_{21} = \bar{x}_1 \qquad x'_{12} + x'_{22} = \bar{x}_2 \qquad\qquad [\text{C.5}]$$

Thus, any point in the box defines a set of four quantities – consumptions of each of the two goods by each individual – which, moreover, are such as just to satisfy the requirement imposed on the planner by equation [C.3]. It follows that the box (including its sides) defines the set of all *feasible* distributions of the goods, i.e. distributions which satisfy [C.3], for *given* total productions. (The reader should now prove for himself the following: (*a*) a point on a vertical side of the box implies no consumption of x_1 by one individual, and a point on a horizontal side implies no consumption of x_2 by one individual; (*b*) two distinct points, one showing 1's consumption pair, the other 2's imply violation of [C.3].)

From all these feasible distributions, the planner must choose one which is Pareto optimal. To analyse this, we incorporate information on consumers' preferences into the diagram. Taking 0_1 as the origin for consumer 1, we draw in some of his indifference curves, having the usual property of convexity to this origin. Likewise, taking 0_2 as the origin for consumer 2, we draw in some of his indifference curves, convex to *this* origin. The result is shown in Fig. 2. Note that 1 is made better off as we move rightward, and 2 is made better off as we move leftward in the figure.

Suppose the planner were arbitrarily to choose a distribution of the two goods at, say, α. Recalling the continuity property of utility functions, α must lie on indifference curves of both 1 and 2. Hence, the indifference

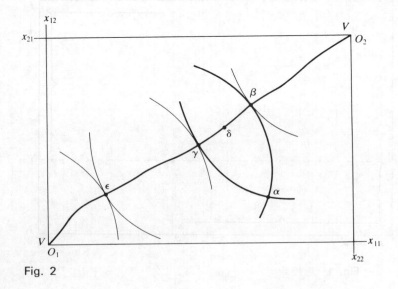

Fig. 2

curves must either be tangent, or intersect, at α. Let us assume that it is the latter, as shown in the figure. It is then easy to see that α cannot be a Pareto optimal point. By changing the distribution to that at point β, 1 is made better off and 2 no worse off. By moving to γ, 2 is better off and 1 no worse off. By moving to a point such as δ, *both* are better off.

Suppose, on the other hand, that the initial distribution had been at a point of tangency of the indifference curves, such as β, γ or ε. Moving rightward to a higher indifference curve for 1 *must* then make 2 worse off; moving leftward to a higher indifference curve for 2 *must* make 1 worse off. Moving along an indifference curve passing through one of these points makes one consumer worse off and the other no better off. The only other possible kind of change is one which makes *both* worse off. Hence, since no changes can be made from β, α or ε which satisfy the Pareto criterion for an improvement, these must be Pareto optimal allocations.

The property which points β, γ, ε possess, and α does not, is that of being at a tangency of 1's and 2's indifference curves. The curve vv in Fig. 2 is the locus of such points of tangency, and hence shows the set of Pareto optimal distributions. Recalling the terminology of Chapter 3, where the slope of an indifference curve was called the marginal rate of substitution, *MRS*, of one good for another, the property of the Pareto optimal points can be stated: for an allocation of the two goods between the two consumers to be Pareto-optimal, there must be equality of consumers' *MRS* at that allocation (strictly speaking this condition assumes that at all optimal points each good is consumed in positive amount by each consumer. See Question 1 of Exercise 17C). An arithmetical illustration can be given, equivalent to the geometry but helping intuition in a different way. Suppose, at an initial allocation, 1's *MRS* had the value 3, and 2's had the value 5. This means that 1 would be happy to give up one unit of x_1 for anything more than 3 units of x_2, while 2 would be happy to give up anything less than 5 units of x_2 for one unit of x_1. It follows that if 1 were given 4 units of x_2 and deprived of one unit of x_1, while 2 were given the unit of x_1 and deprived of 4 units of x_2, they would both be better off. As long as the *MRS* were unequal, the planner could make such reallocations. Hence equality of *MRS* is a necessary condition for a Pareto optimal allocation of goods among consumers.

We have defined the curve vv in Fig. 2 as the locus of tangency points, or set of allocations at which *MRS* of the two consumers are equal, and so it shows the set of Pareto optimal allocations. The allocations in this set differ in their distribution of well-being as between the two individuals: as we move along vv from ε to β, 1 is made better off at the expense of 2. Note that, on the Pareto criterion, we cannot say that *any one* point on vv is better than *any one* point off it. For example, we cannot say that point ε represents a better allocation than point α; they are non-comparable on the Pareto criterion, since a move from α to ε (or *vice versa*) makes one individual better off and the other worse off. What we can say, however, is that given any point *not* on vv, there always exists a better point on it.

We can relate this directly to the following question: suppose our 'central planner' does have explicit preferences over distributions of welfare. For example, suppose that the economy is at point ε in Fig. 2, and that the planner would prefer an allocation where 1 was better off, even if that meant making 2 worse off. He may, in fact, prefer α to ε, on the basis of his distributional preferences. However, provided that he does not actually prefer to make 2 worse off, he would clearly prefer any point on vv, between β and γ, to α, since he can make at least one of them (only consumer 1, if he so chooses) better off by moving there. This implies that a planner with explicit distributional preferences can view his problem as one of 'moving along' the curve vv, or, alternatively, choosing from the set of Pareto optimal allocations. This is of course a re-iteration of the point made in the previous section, and will be further developed in section E below.

We now consider the second element of the resource allocation, the consumption of inputs by firms. Again, we proceed by taking as fixed everything but the variables with which we are concerned. In this case firm 1's inputs z_{11}, z_{12}, and firm 2's inputs, z_{21}, z_{22}, are the variables of direct concern, but since variations in these in general imply variations in outputs x_1 and x_2, we take as fixed only total input supplies. If we denote the fixed input supplies by $\hat{z}_1$ and $\hat{z}_2$ respectively, then the planner is subject to the constraints:

$$\sum_{i=1}^{2} z_{i1} = \hat{z}_1 \quad \sum_{i=1}^{2} z_{i2} = \hat{z}_2 \qquad \text{[C.6]}$$

We can again use the Edgeworth box diagram to good effect. In Fig. 3, the horizontal side has length $\hat{z}_1$, the vertical has length $\hat{z}_2$, firm 1's input consumptions are measured from 0_1, and firm 2's from 0_2. Again, any point in the box (or on its sides) represents a particular input allocation which

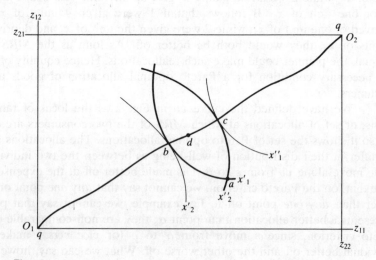

Fig. 3

satisfies the constraint in [C.6]. The analysis here closely parallels that for the allocation of goods among consumers, and so will be dealt with more briefly. We draw in the isoquants representing firm 1's production function with origin 0_1, and those representing firm 2's production function with origin 0_2. Again, given the continuity of production functions, every point in the box will be on an isoquant of firm 1 and an isoquant of firm 2. Given an arbitrary initial allocation of inputs, say at a, it is clearly possible to reallocate inputs between the two firms in such a way as to increase output of at least one firm. Thus, a move from a to c increases firm 1's output leaving that of firm 2 unchanged; a move from a to b increases firm 2's output leaving that of firm 1 unchanged; and a move from a to a point such as d, lying between b and c on the curve qq, increases output of *both* firms. Since we assume that consumers are never satiated with the two goods, such changes must allow at least one consumer to be better off, and none worse off, and so points b, d, c, are better than a on the Pareto criterion. If the initial allocation had been at b, d or c, no such improvements could be made, and so these points are Pareto optimal. The property which distinguishes these points from a is that of *tangency* of the isoquants, which, recalling the terminology of Chapter 7, can be expressed as equality between firms' marginal rates of technical substitution, *MRTS*, of one input for another (the reader is invited to apply the previous arithmetical example to this case also). The curve qq is the locus of such tangency points, and so represents the set of Pareto optimal allocations of inputs. A particular point on qq implies a particular pair of outputs of x_1 and x_2 in the economy, given our assumption that firm 1 produces all of x_1 and firm 2 all of x_2. Hence, we know that if the planner wishes to achieve a Pareto optimum (or some specific resource allocation which is in the Pareto optimal set), then for any particular pair of outputs x_1, x_2 he may choose, he should choose the input allocation at the corresponding point on the curve qq.

We now consider the third aspect of resource allocation, the choice of outputs of the two goods to be produced by the two firms. In this, we first have to determine the set of outputs which are attainable by the economy, given the technological possibilities (represented by the production functions) and the availability of inputs. Again, we proceed by taking the total input availabilities as fixed, at $\hat{z}_1$ and $\hat{z}_2$.

A procedure for determining the feasible set of outputs (for fixed input supplies) is to take a given level of one output, say x_1, and find the maximum level of the other output which can be achieved by the economy. By repeating this, varying x_1 over all its possible values, we then generate the set of possible output pairs (x_1, x_2). Thus consider again Fig. 3. Taking the output of x_1 corresponding to the isoquant labelled x_1', we find the maximum output of x_2 is that corresponding to the isoquant labelled x_2', the isoquants being tangent at b. Thus one feasible output pair is (x_1', x_2'). Likewise, taking output x_1'', the maximum output of x_2 is that corresponding to the isoquant labelled x_2'', the isoquants being tangent at c, so another feasible output pair is (x_1'', x_2''). And so on. Clearly, for any output of x_1, the maximum output of x_2 is found from the point of tangency. Hence, the curve qq can be regarded as the locus of output pairs (x_1, x_2) having the property that one is the maximum output achievable for the given value of the other. We call such output pairs 'efficient'. Given the appropriate numerical information, we could read off the values of the efficient output pairs as we move along qq. An obvious implication is that in these output pairs, x_1 and x_2 vary inversely (e.g. $x_1'' > x_1'$ and $x_2'' < x_2'$). In the absence of numerical information, we can only hope to place general qualitative restrictions on this relation between x_1 and x_2 along qq. In doing this, it is useful to develop a different geometrical analysis.

First, note that the curve qq in Fig. 3 gives us two kinds of information: it shows, as just suggested, the set of efficient output pairs; and it also shows the Pareto optimal input allocations. Thus, at each point on qq, we have a pair of outputs, (x_1, x_2), and four input quantities, $z_{11}, z_{12}, z_{21}, z_{22}$, which are the optimal values for these outputs. If we denote these input quantities by $z_{11}^*, z_{12}^*, z_{21}^*, z_{22}^*$, then the outputs along qq are given by:

$$x_1^* = f_1(z_{11}^*, z_{12}^*) \qquad x_2^* = f_2(z_{21}^*, z_{22}^*) \qquad \text{[C.7]}$$

where f_1 and f_2 are the production functions. From the constraints in [C.6], we can write:

$$z_{21}^* = \hat{z}_1 - z_{11}^* \qquad z_{22}^* = \hat{z}_2 - z_{12}^* \qquad \text{[C.8]}$$

and therefore we can write firm 2's production function in terms of z_{11}^* and z_{12}^* as

$$x_2^* = f_2(\hat{z}_1 - z_{11}^*, \hat{z}_2 - z_{12}^*) = \phi_2(z_{11}^*, z_{12}^*) \qquad \text{[C.9]}$$

Thus, because the inputs devoted to production of x_1 must be taken out of production of x_2, we can regard output of x_2 as determined by the levels of inputs into x_1. The function ϕ_2 expresses this. Note that x_2^* must vary *inversely* with z_{11}^* and z_{12}^*, as is clear from Fig. 3.

The pairs of values $(z_{11}^* z_{12}^*)$ can be read off the curve qq in Fig. 3, and corresponding to each are values of x_1 and x_2. Let us associate with each pair (z_{11}^*, z_{12}^*) on qq a real number, say k. For convenience, we could set $k = 0$ when $(z_{11}^*, z_{12}^*) = (0, 0)$ i.e. when the entire quantities of the inputs are used in producing x_2; and we could set $k = 1$, when $(z_{11}^*, z_{12}^*) = (\hat{z}_1, \hat{z}_2)$, i.e. when the entire quantities of the inputs are used in producing x_1. As the pair (z_{11}^*, z_{12}^*) varies continuously along qq, so k varies continuously from zero to 1 taking on a value in that interval for every pair. We can therefore express the outputs as functions of k, i.e. we can write:

$$x_1^* = f_1(k) \qquad x_2^* = \phi_2(k) \qquad \text{[C.10]}$$

where k is simply an index representing pairs (z_{11}^*, z_{12}^*). An intuitive interpretation of this would be to regard a particular input pair as a 'dose' of the two inputs, where these 'doses' must be chosen so as to lie along qq, and k is simply a number representing a particular *scale* of dose (but note that increasing the scale of dose need not imply increasing the two inputs

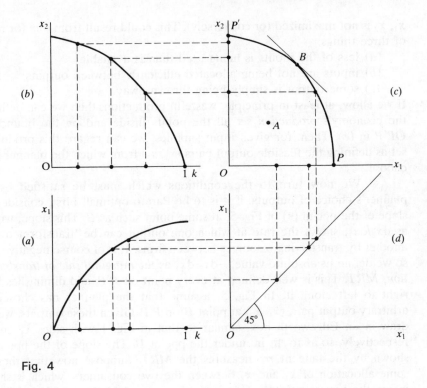

Fig. 4

proportionately, as was done in the discussion of returns to scale in Chapter 7).

We can now use the expressions in [C.10] to derive the relation between x_1^* and x_2^*. Thus, in Fig. 4, (a) shows how x_1 varies as k (the scale of optimal input dose) varies, and (b) shows how x_2 varies as k varies. Both can be thought of as being read off the curve qq in Fig. 3. It is assumed that as the scale of input in x_1 or x_2 increases, the outputs increase at a diminishing rate, i.e. there are diminishing returns to scale of the 'optimal dose'. When $k = 0$, x_2 is at its maximum, as shown in (b) and (c). As k increases (implying diversion of the optimal amounts of inputs from x_2 into x_1), x_1 increases at a diminishing rate, x_2 decreases at an increasing rate, each as a result of the assumption of diminishing returns to scale of dose. By taking the values of x_2 directly across to the vertical axis in (c), and taking the values of x_1, (via the 45° line in (d)), to the horizontal axis in (c), we derive the curve $P'P$ in (c). This curve is the economy's *production possibility curve*, ppc, which can be defined as follows: for given total input supplies, the ppc shows the maximum amount of one output which can be obtained for given amounts of the other, when inputs are optimally allocated between firms. The shape of the curve $P'P$ results directly from the assumption of diminishing returns to scale of dose, as should be clear from the figure.

Consider now the meaning of a point below $P'P$ in (c), such as A. It clearly represents 'wasteful production', in the sense that for a given level of

x_1, x_2 is not maximized (or conversely). This could result from one (or more) of three things:

  (a) less of the inputs is being used than is available;
  (b) inputs are not being allocated efficiently between outputs;
  (c) some output is simply being thrown away.

If we allow, at least in principle, wasteful production, then we can define as the economy's *production set* all the points inside and on the boundaries $OP'P$ in (c). Then, for given input supplies, we can regard this production set as defining the feasible output pairs (x_1, x_2) from which the planner must choose.

   We now turn to the conditions which must be satisfied by the planner's choice of outputs, if it is to be Pareto optimal. First, consider the slope of the ppc in (c) of Fig. 5, at some point such as B. This slope, written as dx_2/dx_1, shows the rate at which one output can be 'transformed' into another by transferring resources between firms. It is of course negative, and so we define its absolute value, $-dx_2/dx_1$ as *the marginal rate of transformation, MRT*. This is well-defined at every point on $P'P$, and diminishes from right to left along it. In Fig. 5, assume that the planner has chosen an arbitrary output pair, $(\bar{x}_1, \bar{x}_2)$ at point B on $P'P$. Given these outputs, we can draw in an Edgeworth box, similar to that in Fig. 1 with sides $\bar{x}_1$ and $\bar{x}_2$ respectively, so as to 'fit in' under the ppc at B. The slope of the ppc at B, shown by the tangent rr, measures the MRT. Suppose now that there is some allocation of x_1 and x_2 between the two consumers, which is shown inside the box at point α. This is on the curve VV, the locus of points of equality of MRS of consumers, and we assume their common MRS at point α is shown by the slope of the line ss, tangent to both indifference curves at α. The line $s's'$ is drawn through B, parallel to ss. Hence, rr at B represents the MRT, at the output pair $(\bar{x}_2, \bar{x}_2)$ and $s's'$ the MRS of each consumer, at the allocation among consumers shown by α. This is reproduced in an enlarged form in Fig. 6.

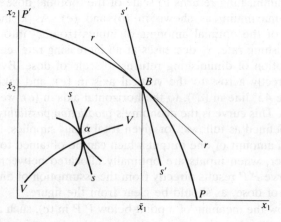

Fig. 5

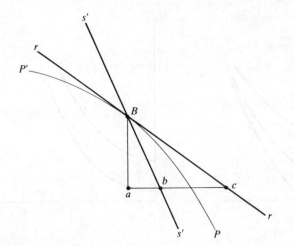

Fig. 6

Now the slope $s's'$, equal to each consumer's *MRS*, has the interpretation that it shows the minimum rate at which each consumer would require to be compensated for reductions in one good, by increases in the other. Thus, in Fig. 6, for a small reduction in x_2 the consumers must each be compensated at the rate ab/Ba. The *MRT* has the interpretation that it shows the rate at which reductions in one good can be 'transformed' into increases in the other. Thus, in the figure, x_2 can be transformed into x_1 at B at the rate ac/Ba. Hence, there is clearly a gain in reducing x_2 and increasing x_1, since the rate at which the transformation can take place is more than sufficient to compensate either of the consumers for the change.

To use an equivalent numerical illustration, suppose that each *MRS* is 1/3, implying that each consumer is happy to give up 1 unit of x_2 in exchange for at least 3 units of x_1; and that the *MRT* is 1/5, implying that for one unit of x_2 given up, 5 units of x_1 can be produced. Then, clearly, the allocation of outputs can change, in the direction of increased x_1, with an improvement for either or both of the consumers. The possibility of varying the composition of output in such a way as to make everyone better off, whenever $MRS \neq MRT$, implies that such a situation cannot be Pareto optimal. At an optimum we must have that $MRS = MRT$, which is therefore a necessary condition for Pareto optimality.

Finally, we consider the planner's choice of quantities of inputs to be supplied by each consumer. Recall that we assumed for simplicity that consumer 1 supplied only z_1 and consumer 2 only z_2. If we allow z_1 and z_2 to vary, then we must also of course allow x_1 and x_2 to vary, according to the production functions $f_i(z_{i1}, z_{i2})$, $i = 1, 2$. It follows, therefore, that consumptions of the two will also vary. In terms of the analysis in Fig. 5 above, increasing the amounts of z_1 and z_2 will lead to outward shifts in the ppc, thus permitting consumption of both goods to be increased. However, the cost of this is measured by the *disutilities* incurred by individual 1 when z_1 is

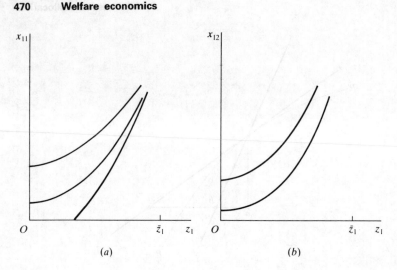

Fig. 7

increased and by 2 when z_2 is increased. Hence, the planner must weigh up these utility losses against the utility gains of increased consumption, in choosing a Pareto optimal position. In what follows, we assume that given any total input pair (z_1, z_2), the planner chooses allocation of the inputs between firms' total outputs, and allocation of these outputs between households, in such a way as to satisfy the Pareto optimality conditions already described above.

First consider the input z_1, and its supplier, consumer 1. His utility function was earlier written as $u_1(x_{11}, x_{12}, z_1)$. We assume that this utility function satisfies the axioms set out in Chapter 3; hence, if we hold x_{12} fixed, we can draw indifference curves as in (a) of Fig. 7; and if we hold x_{11} fixed, we can draw indifference curves as in (b) of Fig. 7.

The shapes of these indifference curves reflect the fact that z_1 yields disutility: in order to compensate the consumer for an increase in input supply, more of the consumption good has to be given; while the axiom of convexity (see Ch. 3) here implies the convex curvature of the indifference curves, which could be expressed as: the more of the input the consumer supplies, the bigger the increment of the consumption good which is required to induce him to supply a little more.

We can first state, and then explain, the conditions for Pareto optimal choice of z_1. It must be true at the optimum that:

(a) the MRS between x_{11} and z_1 is equal to the marginal product of z_1 in producing x_1 (call this MP_{11});

(b) the MRS between x_{12} and z_1 is equal to the marginal product of z_1 in producing x_2 (call this MP_{21}).

To explain condition (a), consider Fig. 8, which reproduces the indifference map of Fig. 7(a).

Suppose that at the amount z_1' of z_1, consumer 1 receives the amount x_{11}^* of good x_1, so that (given his consumption of x_2) he is at point a on indifference curve $\bar{u}_1$. The MRS between x_{11} and z_1 is equal to the slope of $\bar{u}_1$ at a, which is shown by the tangent uu at that point. Suppose that the marginal product of z_1 in producing x_1, i.e. MP_{11}, is shown by·the slope of the line mm, which passes through a. Now, if we consider a very small increase in z_1, from point a, then to leave the consumer's utility unchanged, we would have to compensate him at a rate shown by the slope of uu. On the other hand, an increase in z_1 would increase output of x_1 at a rate shown by the slope of mm, i.e. the rate of increase in output is greater than that required to compensate consumer 1. Hence, it would be possible to change z_1 in such a way as to make one or both of the consumers better off. (The reader should show that if mm were flatter than uu at a, it would be possible to reduce z_1 and make one or both consumers better off). Such a possibility would not exist if mm and uu had the same slope at a, but this is precisely the condition that $MP_{11} = MRS$ between x_{11} and z_1. Hence, this equality is a necessary condition for a Pareto optimal choice of z_1.

By exactly similar reasoning, it could be shown that a necessary condition relating to optimal choice of z_1 is that $MP_{12} = MRS$ between z_1 and x_{12}. Moreover, precisely the same arguments can be used for the input supplies of consumer 2. Hence we have the necessary conditions for Pareto optimal input choice.

To illustrate this analysis numerically, suppose that consumer 1's MRS between x_{11} and z_1 is 2, implying that in order to supply 1 more unit of the input, he requires 2 more units of good x_{11}. Suppose the marginal product of z_1 in producing x_1 is 3. Then, by using the extra unit of z_1, consumer 1 can be compensated by 2 units, leaving 1 unit to be allocated in such a way as to make one or both consumers positively better off.

A further, intuitively appealing, interpretation can be given to these conditions. As shown in Chapter 3, we can express a marginal rate of

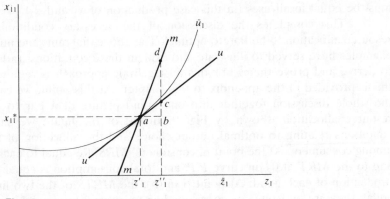

Fig. 8

substitution as a ratio of marginal utilities; that is, we can for example write:

$$MRS \text{ between } x_{11} \text{ and } z_1 = \frac{(-)MU(z_1)}{MU(x_{11})} \qquad [C.11]$$

where the negative sign in brackets is required to make the expression positive. Hence, we can write the condition (a) above as:

$$\frac{(-)MU(z_1)}{MU(x_{11})} = MP_{11} \qquad [C.12]$$

or, as:

$$(-)MU(z_1) = MU(x_{11}) \cdot MP_{11} \qquad [C.13]$$

Now, we can regard the lefthand side of [C.13] as the marginal cost of the input z_1 to the economy, expressed in terms of disutility, rather than money: that is, the cost of an increment of the input z_1 is essentially the loss of utility suffered by the supplier of that increment. Likewise, we could regard the righthand side of [C.13] as giving the 'value of the marginal product' of z_1 in producing x_1, again in utility terms, since it gives the marginal product MP_{11} 'valued' at consumer 1's marginal utility of x_1. Hence, [C.13] expresses the optimality condition as the equality of the input cost with the value of its marginal product, all expressed in terms of the utility of consumer 1. In a similar way, we could obtain the expression:

$$(-)MU(z_1) = MU(x_{12}) \cdot MP_{21} \qquad [C.14]$$

which gives the condition for optimal supply of z_1 in terms of the second good, as the equality of marginal cost with value of marginal product, expressed in terms of consumer 1's utility. Exactly similar expressions could be derived for consumer 2's supply of z_2.

Finally, note that from [C.13] and [C.14] we have:

$$MU(x_{11}) \cdot MP_{11} = MU(x_{12}) \cdot MP_{21} \qquad [C.15]$$

In words: the values of marginal products of a given input (in this case z_1) must be equal in all uses (in this case production of x_1 and x_2).

This completes the discussion of the necessary conditions for a resource allocation to be Pareto optimal. The above diagrams and numerical examples have served to illustrate and explain these conditions, rather than to derive and prove them. For this an algebraic approach is required, and this is provided in the appendix to this chapter. At this point, we can bring the whole discussion together into one grand picture of a Pareto optimal resource allocation, shown by Fig. 9. In (a) of the figure we show the conditions relating to optimal output choice and the allocation of outputs among consumers. At the point α, consumers' MRS are equal to each other, and to the MRT at 0_2 on curve $P'P$, and total consumption is equal to total production of each good. At point β in (b), the MRTS of the two firms are equal, they are on isoquants corresponding to optimal total productions x_1^*,

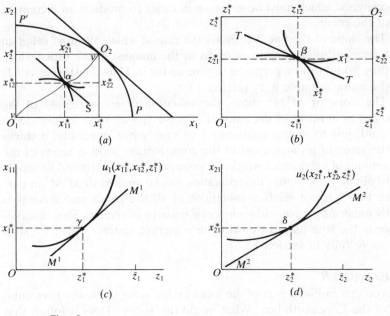

Fig. 9

x_2^*, and their input allocations sum to the amounts of the inputs made available by households, z_1^* and z_2^*. In (c) and (d), we see the conditions relating to optimal choice of these input quantities: at point γ in (c), the *MRS* between x_{11} and z_1, which are respectively consumer 1's consumption of good 1 and supply of input 1, must be equal to the marginal product of input 1 in producing good 1. This could also have been expressed in terms of good 2. Likewise, at point δ in (d), the *MRS* between x_{21} and z_2, respectively consumer 2's consumption of good 1 and supply of input 2, must be equal to the marginal product of input 2 in producing good 1. Again, this could also have been expressed in terms of good 2.

The coordinates of all four points $\alpha\beta\gamma\delta$ are meant to be consistent with each other, in that they satisfy the relations in [C.2], [C.3] and [C.4] above. They represent a specific Pareto optimal resource allocation. An important feature of this resource allocation should be noted.

Associated with the choice of physical quantities – consumptions and input supplies, productions and input usage – is a set of marginal rates of substitution and transformation, indicated by the slopes of the lines: *SS* in (a), *TT* in (b), M^1M^1 in (c), and M^2M^2 in (d). These constitute a set of *relative valuations* of the physical quantities at the optimum point. Thus:

(a) The slope of the line *SS* shows the rate at which all consumers value an increment of one good, in terms of the amount of the other good which they would just be prepared to give up for it. It also measures (since it is equal to the slope of *PP* at 0_2) the *opportunity cost* of one good in terms of the other, since it shows the amount of one good which must be given up in order to produce an increment of the other.

(b) The slope of the line TT shows the rate at which all firms value an increment of one input, in terms of the amount of the other which they would just be prepared to give up for it. Thus the steeper is TT, the more valuable is z_1 relative to z_2.

(c) The slope of M^1M^1 shows the valuation of an increment of the input z_1 in terms of the amount of good x_1 which would have to be 'paid' just to induce consumer 1 to supply it. Conversely, it shows the value of an increment of the consumption good in terms of the amount of extra input which the consumer is just prepared to supply to obtain it. A similar interpretation can be applied to M^2M^2 in (d).

So we see that a set of relative valuations of all the goods and services is *necessarily implied by a particular choice of resource allocation*. This observation suggests the role played by prices in a market system, which we shall consider more fully in section E.

Exercise 17C

1.* Suppose that in Fig. 2 part of the locus vv lay along the lower horizontal side of the Edgeworth box. What would this imply? Does it follow that the consumers' marginal rates of substitution must always be equal at a Pareto optimum? Formulate true necessary conditions for a Pareto optimum which take account of this case (If necessary refer back to Chapter 2).

2. Why is unemployment not Pareto optimal?

3.* Show that the slope of the ppc is equal to the ratio of the marginal products of each input in the two firms, i.e.

$$\text{slope of ppc} = \frac{MP_{11}}{MP_{21}} = \frac{MP_{12}}{MP_{22}}$$

(*Hint:* use [C.15] to show that the two marginal product ratios must be equal. Then note what follows from writing MP_{ij} as dx_i/dz_j, i, $j = 1, 2$).

4.* Explain what is meant by the proposition that a given Pareto optimum can be *sustained* by an appropriate set of relative prices. (*Hint:* what do the lines SS, TT, M^1M^1 in Fig. 9 remind you of?)

6.* Explain why 'diminishing returns to scale of dose' is not the same as the concept of diminishing returns to scale introduced in Chapter 6. Show that constant returns to scale in each industry, in the latter sense, may yet imply diminishing returns to scale of dose. Under what conditions would constant returns in the first sense imply constant returns in the second, and what are the implications for the ppc?

D. The market economy

The preceding section was concerned with deriving the conditions which must be fulfilled by a Pareto optimal resource allocation. In addition, we noted that associated with any resource allocation will be an implied set of relative values of outputs and inputs. We now examine the relation between an equilibrium resource allocation in a competitive market economy and the Pareto optimality conditions. To facilitate comparison, we will do this for the same economy considered in the previous section, except that instead of a 'central planner' markets now exist for each input and output. Consumers wish to maximize their utility, where:

$$u_h = u_h(x_{h1}, x_{h2}, z_h) \qquad h = 1, 2 \tag{D.1}$$

is again the utility function of consumer h, subject to the budget constraint:

$$p_1 x_{h1} + p_2 x_{h2} - w_h z_h = R_h \qquad z_h \le \bar{z}_h \qquad h = 1, 2 \tag{D.2}$$

where p_1 and p_2 are the output prices, w_h is the price of input h, and R_h is the *wealth* of consumer h. This wealth could be made up of initial endowments of the two goods together with shareholdings in the profits of the two firms. In this model we have assumed the former to be zero, for simplicity, and so we have:

$$R_h = \beta_{h1} \pi_1 + \beta_{h2} \pi_2 \qquad 0 \le \beta_{hi} \le 1, \qquad h, i = 1, 2 \tag{D.3}$$

where β_{hi} is consumer h's ownership share in firm i and so $\beta_{1i} + \beta_{2i} = 1$. π_i denotes firm i's profit:

$$\pi_i = p_i x_i - w_1 z_{i1} - w_2 z_{i2} \qquad i = 1, 2 \tag{D.4}$$

and each firm seeks to maximize this subject to its production function $x_i = f_i(z_{i1}, z_{i2})$. All consumers and firms are assumed to take prices as given and outside their control – *the competitive market assumption*.

Drawing on the analyses of earlier chapters, we can immediately write down the conditions which will be fulfilled at the equilibrium resource allocation in the market economy:

(*a*) *Consumers:* we know that the equilibrium choices of consumers will have the properties that:

(i) $MRS_{12}^h = p_1/p_2 \qquad h = 1, 2 \tag{D.5}$

i.e. the equality between the hth consumer's *MRS* for the two goods and the price ratio

(ii) $MRS_{ih}^h = w_h/p_i \qquad h = 1, 2 \qquad i = 1, 2. \tag{D.6}$

This is the condition that the *MRS* between good i, and the input z_h, will be equal to the ratio of the input price to price of the good (cf. the analysis of Ch. 3), for consumer h.

(*b*) *Firms:* We know that the equilibrium choices of firms will have the properties that:

(i) $p_i = \dfrac{w_1}{MP_{i1}} = \dfrac{w_2}{MP_{i2}} \qquad i = 1, 2 \tag{D.7}$

where MP_{i1} is the marginal product of input 1 in producing good i, while MP_{i2} is that of input 2. This is effectively the 'price = marginal cost' condition (see Ch. 8).

$$\text{(ii)} \quad MRTS_{12}^i = \frac{MP_{i1}}{MP_{i2}} = \frac{w_1}{w_2} \quad i = 1, 2. \quad [\text{D.8}]$$

This is the condition for optimal input choice, and states that the marginal rate of technical substitution between the 2 inputs in production of good i (which is equal to the ratio of their marginal products) must equal the ratio of input prices.

Finally, we know that in equilibrium, total consumption of each good is equal to total production (we assume no free goods), and total input supply is equal to total input usage. Moreover, firms' input-output choices satisfy their production functions.

It remains to show that these conditions which are satisfied at the equilibrium of a competitive economy imply satisfaction of the conditions for Pareto optimality.

First, from [D.5], since the price ratio p_1/p_2 is, in a competitive economy, the same for all consumers, we must have that;

$$MRS_{12}^1 = MRS_{12}^2 \quad [\text{D.9}]$$

i.e. consumers' MRS between the two goods are equal to each other. This meets the first condition for Pareto optimality.

Second, from [D.8], since all firms face the same input prices, we must have that:

$$MRTS_{12}^1 = \frac{MP_{11}}{MP_{12}} = \frac{MP_{21}}{MP_{22}} = MRTS_{12}^2 \quad [\text{D.10}]$$

i.e. firms' marginal rates of technical substitution between the two inputs are equal. This meets the second condition for Pareto optimality.

Next, from [D.7], taking the ratio of the two goods prices gives:

$$\frac{p_1}{p_2} = \frac{w_1/MP_{11}}{w_1/MP_{21}} = \frac{MP_{21}}{MP_{11}} = \frac{\text{marginal product of input 1 in good 1}}{\text{marginal product of input 1 in good 2}}$$

$$= \frac{w_2/MP_{12}}{w_2/MP_{22}} = \frac{MP_{22}}{MP_{12}} = \frac{\text{marginal product of input 2 in good 1}}{\text{marginal product of input 2 in good 2}}$$

$$[\text{D.11}]$$

But each of these ratios of marginal products is equal to what we, in section C, called the 'marginal rate of transformation', MRT; i.e. the slope of the production possibility curve at a point (See Question 3 of Exercise 17C). Hence, putting together [D.5], [D.9] and [D.11] gives:

$$MRS_{12}^1 = MRS_{12}^2 = \frac{p_1}{p_2} = \frac{MP_{21}}{MP_{11}} = \frac{MP_{22}}{MP_{12}} = MRT \quad [\text{D.12}]$$

i.e. consumers' *MRS* between the two goods are equal to the marginal rate of transformation between the two goods in production. Hence the third condition for optimality is satisfied.

To show that the fourth and last condition is also satisfied, take the case of consumer 1 and good 1. Then [D.6] becomes:

$$MRS^1_{11} = w_1/p_1 \qquad\qquad\qquad [D.13]$$

where the lefthand side is the *MRS* between consumption of good 1 and supply of input 1. Now for this case, from [D.7] we have:

$$p_1 = w_1/MP_{11} \qquad\qquad\qquad [D.14]$$

Hence, [D.13] and [D.14] imply:

$$MRS^1_{11} = w_1/(w_1/MP_{11}) = MP_{11} \qquad\qquad\qquad [D.15]$$

which is precisely the fourth condition for this case.

Thus we see that an equilibrium resource allocation in a competitive market economy satisfies the necessary conditions for a Pareto optimal resource allocation. It would not in general be strictly valid to jump to the conclusion that the competitive equilibrium resource allocation *is* therefore a Pareto optimum, because we have only examined *necessary* conditions. In other words a resource allocation which *minimized* one consumer's utility for a given utility level of the other would also satisfy these conditions. However, on the assumptions made – indifference curves and isoquants strictly convex to the origin, diminishing returns to scale in both industries – the necessary conditions are also sufficient: every allocation satisfying them is a Pareto optimum.

This proof of the optimality of competitive equilibrium in terms of a comparison of sets of necessary conditions has a number of drawbacks. As well as being lengthy, it requires that all utility and production functions are differentiable everywhere so that the marginal rates of substitution and transformation are well-defined, and moreover appears to require convexity assumptions to ensure sufficiency as well as necessity. It is not even fully general, since the forms of the conditions, in terms of *equalities*, implicitly assume that all goods and inputs take on strictly positive values at the optimum (Refer back to Question 1 of Exercise 17C and Ch. 2). This may seem reasonable for a two-output, two-input model but hardly describes reality.

In fact there is a far simpler proof which works in terms of the logic of the properties of competitive equilibrium and Pareto optima, and shows that we can dispense with assumptions of differentiability *and even convexity*. We shall present the proof (which closely resembles the proof given in Chapter 10 showing that the competitive equilibrium lies in the core) for the particular economy that has been considered here.

Recalling the discussion at the beginning of section C, we can denote a resource allocation as $[x_{hi}, x_i, z_{ih}, z_h]$, $i, h = 1, 2$, i.e. a list of values of consumptions, outputs, inputs used and inputs supplied. To be feasible a resource allocation must satisfy the conditions:

$$F. \sum_{h=1}^{2} x_{hi} = x_i = f_i(z_{i1}, z_{i2}) \qquad \sum_{i=1}^{2} z_{ih} = z_h \leq \bar{z}_h \qquad i, h = 1, 2$$

In words, it must be capable of being produced by the technology at the economy's disposal and consumptions of goods and inputs must equal the amounts of them made available.

Denote a Pareto optimal allocation by $[x_{hi}^*, x_i^*, z_{ih}^*, z_h^*]$. It must first of all be feasible, i.e. satisfy F, and also, from the definition, satisfy the optimality condition:

P. there exists *no* feasible resource allocation $[\hat{x}_{hi}, \hat{x}_i, \hat{z}_{ih}, \hat{z}_h]$ such that $u_h(\hat{x}_{h1}, \hat{x}_{h2}, \hat{z}_h) \geq u_h(x_{h1}^*, x_{h2}^*, z_h^*)$, $h = 1, 2$, with the strict inequality holding for at least one h. In words, no other feasible resource allocation exists which makes one consumer better off and the other at least no worse off.

In the same vein, consider the properties of a competitive market equilibrium allocation denoted $\{[p_1', p_2', w_1', w_2'][x_{hi}', x_i', z_{hi}', z_i']\}$ (Note that the equilibrium price vector is an essential part of the description of the market allocation). First, it will clearly be feasible, i.e. satisfy condition F, since supply will equal demand on each market and the firms will be 'on' their production functions. Moreover, we know that:

C. *Consumer optimality:* $u_h(x_{h1}', x_{h2}', z_h') \geq u_h(x_{h1}, x_{h2}, z_h)$ for all consumptions satisfying the budget constraints

$$p_1' x_{h1} + p_2' x_{h2} - w_h' z_h = R_h \qquad h = 1, 2$$

The consumptions in the market equilibrium are those preferred by consumers over all those which satisfy their budget constraints given the equilibrium prices.

M. *Firms' optimality:* $p_i' x_i' - w_1 z_{i1}' - w_2' z_{i2}' \geq p_i' x_i - w_1' z_{i1} - w_2' z_{i2}$, $i = 1, 2$ for all outputs and inputs satisfying the production function constraint:

$$x_i = f_i(z_{i1}, z_{i2})$$

The outputs and inputs which enter into the market equilibrium are those which maximize the firms' profits at the given equilibrium prices.

We now show that possession of properties C and M by the market allocation implies that it possesses property P of a Pareto optimal allocation. We proceed by assuming that the market equilibrium is not a Pareto optimum and then establish a contradiction. Thus suppose there exists a feasible resource allocation $[\hat{x}_{hi}, \hat{x}_i, \hat{z}_{ih}, \hat{z}_h]$ such that:

$$u_1(\hat{x}_{11}, \hat{x}_{12}, \hat{z}_1) > u_1(x_{11}', x_{12}', z_1') \tag{D.16}$$

and

$$u_2(\hat{x}_{21}, \hat{x}_{22}, \hat{z}_2) \geq u_2(x_{21}', x_{22}', z_2') \tag{D.17}$$

so that the market allocation is not Pareto optimal. From the property C, it must follow that:

$$p_1'\hat{x}_{11} + p_2'\hat{x}_{12} - w_1'\hat{z}_1 > p_1'x_{11}' + p_2'x_{12}' - w_1'z_1' \tag{D.18}$$

$$p_1'\hat{x}_{21} + p_2'\hat{x}_{22} - w_2'\hat{z}_2 \geq p_1'x_{21}' + p_2'x_{22}' - w_2'z_2' \tag{D.19}$$

because, if [D.16] were true, then at the prices p_1', p_2' and w_1' the values $(\hat{x}_{11}, \hat{x}_{12}, \hat{z}_1)$ could not have been feasible for consumer 1, or he would have chosen them. By the same argument [D.17] implies [D.19]. Summing [D.18] and [D.19] then gives:

$$p_1'(\hat{x}_{11} + \hat{x}_{21}) + p_2'(\hat{x}_{12} + \hat{x}_{22}) - w_1'\hat{z}_1 - w_2'\hat{z}_2$$

$$> p_1'(x_{11}' + x_{21}') + p_2'(x_{12}' + x_{22}') - w_1'z_1' - w_2'z_2' \tag{D.20}$$

From the equalities in condition F we can replace [D.20] by:

$$p_1'(\hat{x}_{11} + \hat{x}_{21}) + p_2'(\hat{x}_{12} + \hat{x}_{22}) - w_1'\hat{z}_1 - w_2'\hat{z}_2$$

$$> p_1'x_1' + p_2'x_2' - w_1'(z_{11}' + z_{21}') - w_2'(z_{12}' + z_{22}') \tag{D.21}$$

But the righthand side of [D.21] is the sum of the firms' profits in the market equilibrium resource allocation, and we know moreover that these profits are the maximum possible at the given prices for all input-output combinations which satisfy the production functions. In particular:

$$(p_1'x_1' - w_1'z_{11}' - w_2'z_{12}') + (p_2'x_2' - w_1'z_{21}' - w_2'z_{22}')$$

$$\geq (p_1'\hat{x}_1 - w_1'\hat{z}_{11} - w_2'\hat{z}_{22}) + (p_2'\hat{x}_2 - w_1'\hat{z}_{21} - w_2'\hat{z}_{22}) \tag{D.22}$$

Profits in each firm are at least as high at (x_1', z_{11}', z_{12}') as at $(\hat{x}_i, \hat{z}_{i1}, \hat{z}_{i2})$ and so the same must be true of the sums of firms' profits. But then combining [D.21] with [D.22] and rearranging gives:

$$p_1'(\hat{x}_{11} + \hat{x}_{21} - \hat{x}_1) + p_2'(\hat{x}_{12} + \hat{x}_{22} - \hat{x}_2)$$

$$- w_1'(\hat{z}_1 - \hat{z}_{11} - \hat{z}_{21}) - w_2'(\hat{z}_2 - \hat{z}_{12} - \hat{z}_{22}) > 0 \tag{D.23}$$

Given that all prices are positive, this can only hold if at least one of the bracketed terms is non-zero. This then implies that the feasibility condition is violated, and so we have a contradiction. There can be no other resource allocation which is both feasible and Pareto-superior to the market equilibrium allocation. Note that the crucial parts of this proof are [D.18] and [D.22], which follow directly from the properties of consumers' and firms' equilibrium choices. Nowhere did we require assumptions of differentiability or convexity to prove the Pareto optimality of the competitive market equilibrium. Thus this optimality property holds under very general assumptions.

This proof could be regarded as a rigorous demonstration of the existence of Adam Smith's 'invisible hand'. There are, however, two reservations which must be made concerning the applicability of the result to any real-world market economy. First, it can be shown that the result no longer holds when certain central assumptions on which the model of the economy was based are relaxed:

  (i) the assumption that all consumers and firms act as price-takers – the competitive assumption;

 (ii) the assumption, *implicit* in the formulations of utility and production functions in the model, that all the variables in his utility or production function are directly under the economic agent's control. If some were actually the choice variables of another agent then we would have 'external effects' or 'externalities' – direct economic interactions among agents which are not mediated through markets;

(iii) again an implicit assumption was that consumption of a unit of a good by one consumer reduced the available supply of the good to the other also by one unit. There is a class of goods, called *public goods*, for which this is not true: for example my consumption of a broadcast on my radio set does not reduce the amount of it you can consume on yours. If such goods are at all significant in an economy the proposition, demonstrated in the following chapter, that a market mechanism would *not* lead to an optimal allocation of resources to them, is a serious limitation on the result just derived.

Relaxation of these assumptions leads to instances of 'market failure', the failure of a market economy to achieve a Pareto optimum given its available resources and technology, and this will be examined at some length in the next chapter.

There are also important features of real economies which are not captured in static models such as that examined in this chapter, chief among which are changes over time in tastes, technology, resource endowments, the size and identity of the set of consumers and firms, and the prevalence of uncertainty in decision-taking. We cannot yet say whether a market economy characterized by these features achieves a Pareto optimum, since this requires major revisions to the economic models themselves, and these are still at the forefront of research.

Thus one reason for treating the Pareto optimality proposition with reserve is doubt about the realism of the assumptions which underlie the model. Note that this runs counter to the methodological position: models should be assessed on how well the hypotheses deduced from their assumptions conform to reality, rather than on the *a priori* 'realism' of the assumptions themselves. This position is not really tenable in welfare economics because welfare propositions are not *practicably testable*. How would you *in practice* test the proposition that a competitive resource allocation achieves a Pareto optimum in a modern economy? How would you present alternatives to individual consumers, collect information on whether they prefer one allocation to another, and what weight could you attach to the information assuming you had it? Given the non-testability of welfare propositions we have to rely on analysis of assumptions. We ask: on what assumptions does the proposition rest; how might we have to vary an assumption to reflect reality more closely; does this variation in assumptions invalidate the proposition? Even if one accepted the Paretian value judgements therefore, one might doubt the optimality of a real market economy on the empirical grounds that market imperfections, externalities and public goods are significant real phenomena.

The second source of hesitation about the optimality conclusion concerns the distribution of welfare. On the given assumptions the market equilibrium allocation is just one member of the entire set of Pareto optimal resource allocations, which vary greatly in the distribution of welfare (We shall examine the nature of this set from the point of view of welfare distribution in some detail in the next section). Thus consider again our two-person model. Consumer h's budget constraint can be written:

$$p_1 x_{h1} + p_2 x_{h2} = w_h z_h + [\beta_{h1} \pi_1 + \beta_{h2} \pi_2] \qquad h = 1, 2$$

The distance of the budget constraint from the origin, and therefore the level of consumption the consumer finally enjoys, will be greater, *other things being equal:*

    (a) the greater his shareholdings in company profits β_{h1}, $i = 1, 2$; with which he is initially endowed;

    (b) the higher are profits π_i, $i = 1, 2$;

    (c) the higher the price w_h at which he sells his input;

    (d) the lower the prices of the goods he buys.

Some of these of course conflict, for example (c) with (b) and (d), and (d) with (b). The only one of these factors exogenous to the model is (a), the initial endowment of shareholdings (which results perhaps from inheritance or past saving). Prices, profits and input supplies are determined within the model and so reflect the basic data of preferences of the two consumers and the technological conditions in the two firms. Clearly, if consumer 1 had no initial shareholdings and a low marginal productivity of his input supplied only to a good with low demand, then in the market equilibrium consumer 2 will end up with most of the consumption. But this result is still Pareto optimal. As A. Sen (1970, p. 22) has remarked: 'A society or an economy can be Pareto-optimal and still be perfectly disgusting'.

Someone who shared the neutrality towards income distribution inherent in the Paretian value judgements could not make this kind of comment, but it is probable that few people are so neutral (though someone opposed to income redistributions which make himself worse off may well find a convenient rationalization in Pareto optimality). We now turn therefore to an explicit analysis of the question of welfare distribution.

Exercise 17D

1.* Suppose that in the two-person economy examined in this section the consumers have the identical utility functions:

    $u_h = x_{h1} x_{h2}^{1/2} / z_h$

while the firms have the production functions:

    $x_1 = z_{11}^{1/2} z_{12}^{1/4} \qquad x_2 = z_{21}^{1/2}$

The shares in both firms are held equally by the consumers.

(a) Solve for the market equilibrium prices and resource allocation.

(b) Show that this is Pareto optimal.

(c) Comment on the resulting utility values of the two consumers, stating carefully the assumptions you may make in doing so.

(d) Show the effects on the utility distribution of giving consumer 2 all the shares in firm 1.

(e) Derive the general relationship between the utilities of the two consumers traced out as we redistribute initial shareholdings between them, and comment on its shape.

[*Hint:* first derive the individual demand and supply functions as functions of prices and initial shareholdings. Insert these into the demand = supply conditions. Set one price = 1 and eliminate the corresponding market condition (Walras' Law). Then solve for equilibrium prices and quantities.]

2. Discuss the assertion that welfare propositions are not testable and the consequences of this.

3. Discuss the similarities in the proof given here of the optimality of competitive equilibrium to the proof given in Chapter 10 that the competitive equilibrium allocation lay in the core.

E. The distribution of welfare

First we must decide what we mean by a 'distribution of welfare'. A natural definition would be, in the two-consumer economy considered in this chapter, a pair of utility values (u_1, u_2). This is unambiguous as long as we want to talk only about *directions of change*; it must always be remembered that the utility functions are simply ordinal indicators of preferences and do not measure the 'amount' of welfare or well-being in any sense. We cannot, for example, conclude that a high value for u_1 and a low value for u_2 implies unequal welfare or that equal values imply an egalitarian distribution, since exactly the same distribution of consumption bundles is consistent with a completely different relationship between the u-values, as we apply positive monotonic transformations to the utility functions. Nevertheless, holding to the given u-functions throughout the analysis, we shall still be able to clarify some important issues concerning welfare distribution.

Now consider the welfare distributions – set of (u_1, u_2) pairs – available to the two-person economy examined in the previous two sections. Refer back first to Fig. 2. If we hold constant all outputs and input supplies, the locus vv in the figure shows the set of Pareto optimal distributions of the two consumption goods between the two consumers. At each point on vv there is a pair of indifference curves – and so a (u_1, u_2) pair – for which it is a point of tangency. The curve uu' in Fig. 10 shows therefore the (u_1, u_2) values we read off as we move along vv. For example, u shows the pair of values at 0_2 in Fig. 2, and u' shows that at 0_1. There is nothing unique about the shape or location of the curve uu' – by transforming one or both of the

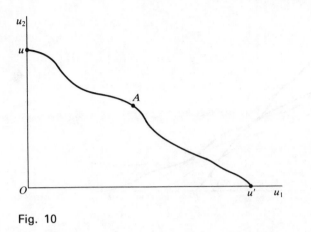

Fig. 10

utility functions we can shift it in just about any way we please, *except that an essential characteristic is its negative slope*. This expresses the fact that as we re-distribute the consumption goods from one consumer to the other *through the set of Pareto optimal consumption distributions* one consumer is necessarily worse off as the other is better off (but see Question 1 of Exercise 17E).

The curve uu' shows the possible welfare distributions *given the constraint* that all variables in the resource allocation other than the consumption quantities must be held constant and we refer to it as the *utility possibility curve*, upc. By referring back to Fig. $9(a)$ we can see that we can do better than this. At α in the figure we have that each MRS is equal to the MRT at 0_2 (slope of $P'P$). If we hold outputs constant and reallocate consumptions along vv away from α, we will in general move to points at which the common MRS of the consumers is unequal to the MRT – i.e. we violate the necessary conditions for optimal pattern of production even though we still satisfy that for optimal distribution of consumption. In addition we will in general shift the indifference curves relating to combinations of z_h and x_{hi} (explain why) and so distort the input supply conditions also. Thus if, in Fig. 10, point A is the utility pair corresponding to point α in Fig. $9(a)$, we know that in general at points on uu' other than A we could make *both* consumers better off by a change in outputs and input supplies. Therefore if we relax the constraint of fixed outputs and inputs we should be able to achieve a set of feasible welfare distributions which will in general lie above uu' except at A.

In Fig. 11 we show, as the curve FF', the *utility frontier* for the economy. This is derived by maximizing consumer 2's utility at each value of consumer 1's utility on the interval OF', allowing all outputs, inputs and consumptions to vary. Each point on FF' is therefore a full Pareto optimum – the set of tangencies shown in Fig. 9 will hold at each point, though naturally with different values of the variables in the resource allocation. The utility frontier depicts the Pareto optimal set of utility pairs

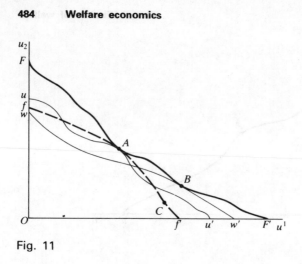

Fig. 11

given the technology and resources available to the economy. The previous upc uu' touches the welfare frontier at A because at this welfare distribution the output pattern corresponding to uu' satisfies the full optimality conditions. At other welfare distributions on uu' the fixed production and input supplies violate the necessary conditions and so at any given u_1, u_2 must generally be lower than the corresponding point on the utility frontier (we cannot rule out the possibility that uu' might happen to coincide with FF' at some other points – see Question 2 of Exercise 17E). The curve labelled ww' in Fig. 11 is also a upc. At point B it happens that the pattern of production and input supplies with respect to which ww' is drawn satisfies the full set of necessary conditions, while at other points, although the distribution of consumptions is Pareto optimal, the pattern of outputs and input supplies is not. To each point on FF' a curve similar to uu' and ww' could be drawn, none of which can lie above FF', and so the utility frontier can be regarded as the envelope of the infinity of upc's possible in this economy.

We have described the derivation of the utility frontier in terms of our fictitious 'central planner' who generates the Pareto optimal set of utility pairs by choosing a sequence of optimal resource allocations. What relevance does this have for the market economy, however, and, in particular, how might the concept of the utility frontier be useful to a policy-maker in such an economy?

First of all, we know that under the conditions stated, a market equilibrium will result in a utility-pair or point on FF', since it is a Pareto optimum. As we saw in the previous section the precise utility pair (for *given* utility functions) is determined, at least partly, by the initial wealth distribution, which in the model considered here consists of shareholdings in firms. Suppose that the policy-maker in the market economy is able to change the initial wealth distribution (he has the right, or the power, to abrogate individual property rights and transfer property without compensation, something which all governments in all market economies in fact possess within limits) by transferring shareholdings form one consumer to the other.

Such a transfer is called *lump-sum* because, in the context of the present model, the amount of the transfer does not affect any consumer's or firm's choices *at the margin*: each will still seek to equate *MRS* to the market price ratio; each firm will equate marginal cost to the market price and *MRTS* to the market price ratio of inputs. As a result the *new* resource allocation produced by the market economy after the lump-sum redistribution will continue to be Pareto optimal and so will also generate a utility pair on *FF'*. The market resource allocation will of course be changed because the change in their initial wealths – shifts in their budget constraints – will cause the consumers to revise their demands and input supplies, and hence firms will have to revise their production plans. For example, a transfer of shareholdings from consumer 2 to 1 will improve consumer 1's position and worsen that of consumer 2, and so if the utility pair was initially at *A* then the new position will be something like point *B* on *FF'* in Fig. 11.

This then suggests a very attractive possibility for economic policy in a market economy, which could be put as follows. The market mechanism can be thought of as an efficient 'black box' or resource allocation machine: feed in an initial wealth distribution, the mechanism churns away and out comes a Pareto-optimum, a point on *FF'*. A policy-maker who dislikes the welfare distribution implied by a given market equilibrium can best improve things *not* by interfering with the market mechanism – the works of the black box – but rather by changing the wealth distribution directly. He may, by intervening in the market mechanism, achieve a resource allocation which he regards as distributionally superior to that of *A* in Fig. 11, say that at *C* in the figure. But then there always exists a feasible resource allocation which makes *both* individuals better off, such as that at *B*. Therefore, *in terms of the policy-maker's own value judgements* (assuming they have the Pareto property and concern only the welfare distribution, not the allocation mechanism *as such*) the policy of lump-sum redistribution together with unfettered operation of the market mechanism is superior.

It is possible to prove the following proposition: *every Pareto optimal resource allocation can be achieved as a competitive market equilibrium given an appropriate initial distribution of wealth* (for a proof, see Takayama (1974), pp. 185–201. See also Question 4 of Exercise 17E). In the present case, this means that *every* point on *FF'* can be achieved by choosing an appropriate set of lump-sum wealth transfers and then allowing the market mechanism to work. This proposition therefore gives formal expression to the approach to economic policy in the market economy just described.

An intuitive feeling for the meaning of this proposition can be obtained by referring back to Fig. 9. The lines *SS*, M^1M^1, and M^2M^2 which show the relevant consumer marginal rates of substitution are analogous to budget lines: the *slope* of each defines a price ratio and the *position* of each an amount of wealth just enough to give the correct intercepts on the axes. Thus if the implied wealths and relative prices were specified to each consumer they would face the resulting budget constraints and so continue to choose the quantities shown in the figure – the resource allocation would be *sustained* by the wealth distribution and relative prices in question. The formal proposition then shows that such a wealth distribution and set of relative prices can be found to sustain every possible Pareto optimum in the economy.

The applicability of the proposition, which underlies a 'laissez-faire' approach to economic policy, is, however, subject to three limitations. First is the problem already mentioned and later considered in some detail in Chapter 18, of whether the 'black box' does work efficiently, i.e. of whether the market mechanism as it actually exists does in fact produce a Pareto optimum. Secondly, the proof of the proposition that any Pareto optimum is attainable as a market equilibrium, given an appropriate initial wealth distribution *does* require convexity assumptions both for consumers and firms. In the former case the assumption – that the better set for any consumption bundle is a convex set (recall Chapter 3) – is reasonably palatable. In the case of firms however the assumption rules out increasing returns to scale in the aggregate production of each commodity, and this is far less acceptable an assumption.

Finally, in reality it is not in general possible to devise *lump-sum* redistributive measures on a sufficient scale. Virtually every measure we can think of for redistributing wealth will cause violation of the necessary conditions for optimality and so the valuable *separation of redistribution from resource allocation*, which was the central element of the proposition being considered, breaks down. If, therefore, redistribution necessarily involves violation of the optimality conditions it is no longer obviously true that direct intervention in the market mechanism is counter-productive. We are forced to compare two *second-best* forms of policy in terms of their effects on welfare distribution and optimality of resource allocation and it is no longer obvious on *a priori* grounds that one is better than the other.

Take, for example, the redistribution of shareholdings, which is, relative to the model considered here, truly lump-sum. A more complete model would, however, include the intertemporal savings decisions of consumers and investment decisions of firms, coordinated through a capital market. Saving would constitute buying shares in firms, and it is straightforward to extend the analysis of Pareto optimality to this economy. However, a policy of redistributing shareholdings from say, the consumer with the greater shareholdings to the consumer with the smaller shareholdings is effectively a tax on saving which will drive a wedge between the relevant marginal rate of substitution (consumption now for consumption in future) and price ratio (determined by the rate of dividend on shareholdings). Thus the redistribution leads to violation of the Pareto optimality conditions in this economy.

To see how taxation leads to violation of Pareto optimality in more detail, suppose that in our simple model of the economy income is redistributed by imposing a proportionate tax, t on the income consumer 1 receives from supplying his input, and paying the proceeds to consumer 2. Consumer

1's budget constraint then becomes:

$$p_1 x_{11} + p_2 x_{12} - (1-t)w_1 z_1 = R_1 \qquad \text{[E.1]}$$

where $(1-t)$ is the proportion of income left after tax. The utility maximizing choice of consumption and input supply will now satisfy the condition:

$$MRS_{11}^1 = (1-t)w_1/p_1 \qquad \text{[E.2]}$$

i.e. the relevant wage rate is the after-tax wage rate. However, each firm still pays the price w_1 for the input z_1. Hence, for example, the choice of input z_1 by firm 1 still satisfies the condition:

$$p_1 = w_1/MP_{11} \qquad \text{[E.3]}$$

Hence, from [E.2] and [E.3] we have:

$$MRS_{11}^1 \neq MP_{11} \qquad \text{[E.4]}$$

in other words, non-satisfaction of one of the necessary conditions for a Pareto optimum. As we have already seen, this implies that we could make a change in resource allocation which would make both consumers better off. For example, if $MP_{11} > MRS_{11}$, we could increase z_{11}, compensate consumer 1 with at least enough to leave him no worse off, and give all the excess to consumer 2. However, as long as we operate through prices, there is no way we can do this without removing the tax t.

A similar proposition can be shown for any attempt to redistribute well-being by taxes or subsidies which lead different consumers or firms in the economy to face different prices.

If, then, true lump-sum redistributions are not feasible, the set of welfare distributions actually available to the economy is *not* the utility frontier FF' in Fig. 11. Rather it will be a locus such as the dotted curve ff' in the figure, which is drawn on the assumption that, given the prevailing initial wealth distribution, the market equilibrium results in point A. If then it is desired to change the welfare distribution non-lump-sum policies must be used which, as we have seen, violate the optimality conditions and so define the *utility feasibility* curve ff'. If we are interested in the question of the choice of welfare distribution then it is *this* utility feasibility curve which is relevant. An important problem in applied economics is that of finding the *best* such curve, i.e. one which lies as close to FF' as possible. This involves finding the redistribution policy which minimizes the loss in allocative efficiency (the reduction in u_2 for each given value of u_1) while achieving the desired welfare distribution.

The idea of *choice* over welfare distributions raises the question of preferences and the social welfare function, which was briefly introduced in section A and will be discussed more fully below. First, however, we consider the application of the utility feasibility curve concept to the discussion of the so-called *compensation principle* first formulated by N. Kaldor (1939).

The Kaldor compensation principle

In the 1930s and early 1940s, largely as a result of an influential essay by L. Robbins (1932), a number of economists looked for a way of assessing the desirability of economic policy which was as far as possible free of value judgements or particular ethical views. The Pareto criterion seemed very attractive (the mildness and apparent neutrality of its value judgements even gave some the impression that they were not value judgements at all) but as we have seen could not be applied to policies which made some individuals better off and others worse off, i.e. most policies of interest in the real world. In an attempt to extend the criterion, N. Kaldor suggested that social welfare could be said to have been increased by a policy if the gainers could compensate the losers to leave them exactly as well off as before and still retain some benefit from the change. Note that this compensation is purely hypothetical: if it were *actually* paid then the combination of the policy and compensation is approved on the Pareto criterion and no extension is necessary. All that is required by Kaldor's principle is that gainers *could* 'overcompensate' losers. Fig. 12 illustrates the operation of the principle. Suppose that the welfare distribution is initially at A in the figure, but the introduction of the policy would result in point B, where 1 is better off and 2 worse off. The curve f_B is the utility feasibility curve through B. It represents the set of feasible welfare distributions which can be attained from B. Then Kaldor's principle can be interpreted as saying: if f_B passes through a point such as C, where 2 is as well off as at A and 1 is still better off, then the move to B should be made (although the subsequent move to C will *not* be made; C is a purely hypothetical point for the economy).

It was not long before T. Scitovsky (1941/2) pointed out a logical difficulty with the Kaldor principle. It is quite possible that the principle will recommend that a move from A to B is a good thing, and also that a move from B to A is a good thing. Thus suppose in Fig. 12 that the move to B has been made, and someone now proposes a policy reversal which will take us back to A:f_A is the utility feasibility curve through A and shows the set of welfare distributions attainable from A. Then clearly, since f_A passes

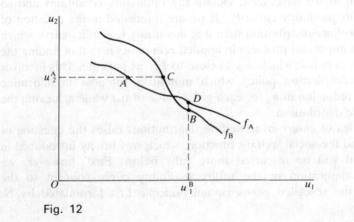

Fig. 12

through point D at which 1 is as well off as at B and 2 is better off, the Kaldor principle would recommend the move to A. Thus the economy could oscillate indefinitely between A and B *as long as compensation is never actually paid*. This makes the principle virtually useless for policy purposes.

In the case in which f_B lay everywhere above f_A this logical difficulty with the compensation principle would not arise. There is nothing to suggest that this must generally be the case for economic policies however. The intersection of the utility feasibility curves simply reflects the fact that the set of institutions, resource endowments and technological conditions following the policy make one consumer better off over one range of welfare distributions and worse off over another for each given utility level of the other. It is an empirical question whether some particular policy has this effect but it would certainly be heroic to assume that all relevant policies would make all consumers either strictly better or strictly worse off at all possible welfare distributions.

Apart from the logical difficulty, the compensation principle is open to the objection that its attempt to avoid value judgements is bound to fail. Thus suppose an economic policy made the very rich very much richer and the poor a little poorer. The rich gainers *could* overcompensate the poor losers and so the Kaldor criterion says, accept the policy. No compensation is of course paid. Would most people agree that social welfare had increased? Explicitly or implicitly value judgements about welfare distribution are held by individuals and governments alike. A far more fruitful approach therefore would be to find some explicit and systematic way of incorporating these into the analysis rather than to attempt something which is neither possible nor desirable, a 'value-free' welfare economics. In the next section we examine the concept of the social welfare function which results from this approach.

Exercise 17E

1. Suppose that the utility function for consumer 1 is written:

$$u_1 = u_1(x_{11}, x_{12}, x_{22}, z_1) \qquad \frac{\partial u_1}{\partial x_{22}} > 0$$

i.e. we have a consumption externality in that 1's utility depends on 2's consumption of good 2. In this case explain why the upc could have a *positive* slope over some range.

2. Use the Edgeworth box diagram to explain the conditions under which a upc may touch the utility frontier at more than one point.

3. Explain fully why, in the model of this section, a redistribution of shareholdings is lump sum.

4.* Take a two-good, two-consumer pure exchange economy, with given initial endowments of the two goods to the consumers. Using the Edgeworth box diagram, show that if the indifference curves are convex, any Pareto optimum can be achieved by appropriately redistributing initial endowments and then allowing trade at given equilibrium prices

(*Hint:* for any point of tangency of indifference curves what would the budget lines have to be to ensure that that point is *chosen* by both consumers?). Now suppose that one of the consumers has indifference curves concave to his origin. Show that the proposition no longer holds.

5.* Examine the types of taxes levied by governments (purchase taxes, income taxes, value added taxes, motor vehicle licence fees, wealth taxes etc). How many of these will not alter the marginal rewards of different activities by individuals and firms, i.e. are lump-sum taxes? Can there be lump sum taxes if individuals can emigrate?

F. The social welfare function

The main purpose of the attempt to exclude specific value judgements from economics was to further the analysis of the workings of the economy – what would now be called 'positive economics'. Quite simply, if we are to understand how the system works it is likely to be more productive to set to one side preconceived notions about it. Likewise empirical tests of hypotheses about the workings of the system need to be conducted in a reasonably objective way if any general credibility is to attach to the results. Such total 'scientific objectivity' is, of course, rarely achieved in practice but the norms of twentieth century scientific method require that it at least be aimed for. It would however be a good example of babies being poured away with bathwater if it were then held that there is no place for value judgements when we wish to appraise economic policies and the optimality of economic systems. The concept of the social welfare function (*swf*) formulated by A. Bergson (1938) is designed to allow value judgements to be introduced into welfare economics in a systematic and objective way. It therefore resolves the dilemma arising out of the impossibility of excluding value judgements on the one hand and on the other the impossibility of saying anything in general if at the outset one specific set of value judgements is adopted. It permits an objective analysis of the implications of different sets of value judgements including, quite possibly, our own.

As a starting point in construction of the *swf* we take *as given* a set of value judgements – they could belong to a political party, a well-defined ideology, a government, or an individual. We assume that these value judgements will define a preference ordering over all relevant states of the economic system, where a 'state of the economic system' is a list of variables which are held to determine the well-being of members of society. The consequences of a set of value judgements can then be evaluated by constructing the preference ordering over states of the economic system to which they give rise and applying it to the set of alternatives under consideration.

To illustrate, suppose we have the following value judgements relating to the two-person, two-output economy considered in this chapter, where the relevant states of the economic system are the bundles of goods (x_{h1}, x_{h2}, z_h), $h = 1, 2$ consumed by the two individuals:

(i) Individual preferences are to count in the sense that the *social* preference ordering over bundles consumed by one individual coincides exactly with that of the individual concerned (in other words this is the first of the two Paretian value judgements).

(ii) A well-defined social preference ordering exists over pairs of consumption bundles for the two individuals, i.e. for any two such pairs $\{[x'_{11}, x'_{12}, z'_1], [x'_{21}, x'_{22}, z'_2]\}$ and $\{[\hat{x}_{11}, \hat{x}_{12}, \hat{z}_1], [\hat{x}_{21}, \hat{x}_{22}, \hat{z}_2]\}$, one is always either preferred or indifferent to the other, and moreover such choices are transitive and reflexive (recall Chapter 3).

(iii) A social state A, in which one individual has a preferred bundle and the other no worse a bundle than in social state B, will always be socially preferred to B (the Pareto property).

These value judgements extend the Paretian ones by introducing in (ii) explicit interpersonal comparisons of well-being. They are sufficient to allow choice to be made among Pareto optimal allocations and indeed between *any* two allocations which are non-comparable on the Pareto criterion.

Recall from Chapter 3 that if we wish to represent the preference ordering by a numerical function some sort of continuity axiom is required to rule out cases, such as that of the lexicographic ordering, where no such function can exist. We thereby add nothing to the *solvability* of the problem, but may find it a more convenient mode of analysis. Assuming we have made such an axiom, we can conveniently write the *swf* for our two-person economy as:

$$W = W[u_1(x_{11}, x_{12}, z_1), u_2(x_{21}, x_{22}, z_2)]$$
$$= W(u_1, u_2) \qquad W_h > 0, \qquad h = 1, 2$$

which associates, with each pair of utility numbers (u_1, u_2), a real number W. Value judgement (iii) is effectively a 'non-satiation' axiom given that non-satiation also characterizes the individual utility functions. Adopting further axioms of differentiability and convexity means that W can be treated very much like an individual utility function, with the difference that it is drawn in the space of utility pairs or welfare distributions rather than consumption bundles (Question 2 of Exercise 17F asks you to pursue the implications of this in some depth).

What exactly does it mean, however, to define a social welfare function on individual utility functions which are themselves purely ordinal – i.e. can be made subject to arbitrary positive monotonic transformations? What kind of function is W? We can answer these questions by noting the restrictions which the value judgements (i)–(iii) place on W:

(a) Because of value judgement (i), the *social MRS* between two consumption goods for a *given* consumer must be the same as that of the consumer himself, i.e.

$$\frac{\partial W}{\partial x_{h1}} \bigg/ \frac{\partial W}{\partial x_{h2}} = \frac{\partial u_h}{\partial x_{h1}} \bigg/ \frac{\partial u_h}{\partial x_{h2}} \qquad h = 1, 2$$

If this were not true, an individual might be regarded as socially better or worse off when he would regard himself as neither.

(b) Also because of (i), W must increase when the individual moves to a preferred bundle and remain constant when he moves to an indifferent one.

Both these requirements are met when W is made an increasing function of the individual utility functions, as the reader can quickly verify.

(c) The value of W must remain the same over pairs of consumption bundles (one for each consumer) which are indifferent in the social preference ordering, and increase over pairs which are preferred. Hence W need only be an *ordinal* numerical representation of social preferences. Since each pair of consumption bundles determines a pair of individual utility numbers (u_1, u_2), the numerical ordering can be applied to these utility pairs just as well. However, once we express W as a function of (u_1, u_2) pairs it becomes dependent on the precise specifications of the individual utility functions. If one of these is transformed then the social welfare function W must be changed in order that it goes on providing an accurate representation of the underlying social preference ordering over pairs of consumption bundles for the two consumers.

Thus the social welfare function W is an ordinal function defined on utility pairs, which must be changed if one of the underlying utility functions is transformed. As long as we hold these utility functions constant throughout the analysis however it allows us to determine an overall social optimum.

The possibility of a social welfare function

The Bergson *swf* is a useful conceptual device for analysing a wide range of problems in theoretical welfare economics, but how in fact is it formulated? Some economists, most notably P. A. Samuelson, would regard this question as beside the point, belonging properly to political science rather than to economics. What is important is that once we have it we can set to work conducting analyses of its implications. In reality however matters are not so clearcut. Economists, when analysing economic policy, are virtually *never* handed a well-defined *swf* but in fact are often themselves involved in articulating social preferences and trade-offs. Cost-benefit analysis is a good example: far from having well-defined social preferences concerning, say, alternative combinations of expenditure on road schemes, lives saved through accident reductions and travelling time saved, economists in this area have worked out monetary values of the latter two kinds of benefits which *become* the social marginal rates of substitution. Though cloaked in apparent scientific objectivity which may conceal the fact that value judgements are being made, the value judgements are there nevertheless. Thus economists are frequently involved in the process of formulation of the *swf*. Closely allied to this point is the further argument that as a result of a considerable expansion in the scope of state economic activity, the processes of decision-taking and policy-making inside the government apparatus have become important aspects of the resource allocation process. They are therefore legitimate areas of study for economists.

For these two reasons, the subject of 'social choice' is a large and growing one in economics. Much of it has originated in the work of K. J. Arrow (1951), which is concerned with the question: how is Bergson's *swf* in fact derived? The remainder of this section will be concerned with Arrow's analysis.

Arrow's impossibility theorem

Recall that the expression of the *swf* as a differentiable function of individual utilities is in a sense optional – what matters is the existence of the underlying preference ordering over social states. Arrow's analysis is then concerned with the question of the existence of a complete, transitive and reflexive social preference ordering, the conditions for which are less restrictive than those for the existence of a numerical function since no continuity axiom is required (Recall the discussion of Chapter 3).

The analysis relates to a society which is individualistic: each member of the society has his own (complete, transitive, reflexive) preference ordering over social states, and somehow these individual orderings become 'aggregated' into a set of social choices. One way in which this might be done for example is by a voting procedure: alternative social states are put up to the vote, there is some rule which determines a social choice from a particular voting pattern, and individual preferences will determine the voting pattern.

A modern political system is of course much more complex than this 'direct democracy' but ultimately it is a process for translating the set of individual preference orderings into choices among social states. Moreover this is true of the 'rules' or 'constitutions' of many other social organizations, such as clubs, committees, trades unions, joint-stock companies (shareholders are the 'social group') and worker cooperatives.

The level of abstraction of Arrow's analysis therefore gives it a very wide field of application. A 'social state' is defined very generally as being whatever set of variables enters into the individual preference orderings of the given social group. So, for an economy this might be an allocation of resources; for a joint-stock company it could be the level of dividends and remuneration of directors, and for the committee of a social club it might be the price of beer. Note also that the preference ordering of an individual relates to entire social states and not simply to the values of his own individual choice variables within them. In other words the preference ordering reflects the individual's views of what the social state ought to be and not simply preferences over, say, his own consumption bundles (They are thus what has been called his *ethical* preferences rather than his *individual* preferences).

A *sufficient* condition for a social choice to be made from a given set of alternatives is that there exists a social preference ordering (underlying the Bergson *swf*) which can be applied to it. Arrow called the *process* or constitution by which individual preferences are transformed into a social preference ordering a social welfare function. As a number of authors have noted, this is unfortunate because it invites confusion with Bergson's *swf* which is the outcome of the process. To avoid this, we adopt A. Sen's convention of denoting Arrow's social welfare function by *SWF*. Then Arrow's *SWF* is a rule (a process, a constitution) which associates with each set of individual preference orderings a social preference ordering.

The first requirement of a *SWF* therefore is that it produces a social preference ordering from the orderings of the individual members of the group. It is easy to find an example of a *SWF* which does not do this, and the presentation of this example will be a useful means of introducing the notation we shall use throughout the analysis. We consider a group of three individuals, labelled 1, 2, 3. There are also three possible social states, labelled a, b, c. It is assumed that preferences over states are *strict* – no individual is indifferent between any two states. These assumptions are of course purely simplifying. A particular preference ordering for individual $i = 1, 2, 3$ is written $(a, b, c)_i$, which means that i prefers a to b and b to c. This implies the three pairwise orderings $(a, b)_i$, $(a, c)_i$, and $(b, c)_i$. A particular *social* preference ordering is denoted $[a, b, c]$, which means that a is socially preferred to b and b to c. This implies the three pairwise social orderings $[a, b]$, $[b, c]$ and $[a, c]$.

Consider now a *SWF* consisting of the simple *majority voting* rule in this three-person three-state society. The individual preference orderings are assumed to be $(a, b, c)_1$, $(b, c, a)_2$, and $(c, a, b)_3$. (The pattern is simply that $i+1$'s ordering is derived from i's by taking the first alternative and putting it last, $i = 1, 2$.) The individuals vote on each pair of alternatives, and the social ordering is to be determined by the majority outcomes of the votes. We assume that individuals vote exactly in accordance with their preference orderings, i.e. there is no 'strategic voting'.

Taking first the pair (a, b), from the above preference orderings we have:

$$(a, b)_1 \text{ and } (b, a)_2 \text{ and } (a, b)_3 \Rightarrow [a, b]$$

i.e. 2 is outvoted by 1 and 3. Taking the pair (b, c) we have:

$$(b, c)_1 \text{ and } (b, c)_2 \text{ and } (c, b)_3 \Rightarrow [b, c]$$

i.e. 3 is outvoted by 1 and 2. Finally taking the pair (a, c) we have:

$$(a, c)_1 \text{ and } (c, a)_2 \text{ and } (c, a)_3 \Rightarrow [c, a]$$

i.e. 1 is outvoted by 2 and 3. The result of the voting is that a is socially preferred to b and b is socially preferred to c but c is socially preferred to a. This is an intransitive result and so rules out the existence of a social ordering over the three states. Thus the majority voting *SWF* does not produce a social ordering (and so a Bergson *swf*).

This so-called 'paradox of voting' has been known for many years, but is useful in introducing the main concern of Arrow's theorem. A natural response to the paradox might be to set about trying to design a *SWF* which yields transitive social choices. Indeed, the majority voting *SWF* would have done so if the individual preferences had been $(a, b, c)_i$, $\forall i$, since then we would have had complete unanimity on $[a, b, c]$. In designing a *SWF* however, we would want it to possess some desirable attributes other than simply that it results in a social ordering (though Stalin was a tyrant he certainly got things done!). Arrow suggested four *minimal* and apparently rather mild attributes that the *SWF* should possess (the presentation here follows closely that of Sen (1970)):

(i) *U: the condition of unrestricted domain:* we saw that the majority voting rule failed for one pattern of individual preference orderings but gave a social ordering for another. If we are designing a *SWF* 'in advance' of its particular application we would presumably want it to 'work' *whatever* the pattern of individual preferences. Thus, within the brackets $(.)_i$ we would wish to allow any of the six possible permutations of the three alternatives a, b, c, and each of these can be combined with any of the six possible permutations for each of the others. Thus there are $6^3 = 216$ possible patterns of individual preferences. This condition then says that the *SWF* must 'work' for them all. In other words the domain of the function which maps a set of individual preferences $\{(.)_1, (.)_2, (.)_3\}$ into a social preference ordering $[.]$ is unrestricted.

(ii) *D: non-dictatorship:* a dictator could be defined formally as someone whose choice between all pairs of alternatives is *decisive*, i.e. determines the social choice regardless of the preferences of all other members of the group. Thus for example if, given $(a, b\,c)_1$, we had $[a, b]$, $[a, c]$ and $[b, c]$ regardless of the preferences of 2 and 3, then 1 would be a dictator. It seems a plausible reflection of the values of liberal Western democracies that this be ruled out in the *SWF*.

(iii) *P: Pareto principle:* we have earlier emphasized the reasonableness of the Paretian value judgement, which here takes the form: suppose $(a, b)_i$ for all i; then $[a, b]$. In words, if *everyone* prefers a to b then a should be preferred to b in the social ordering.

(iv) *I: independence of irrelevant alternatives:* this is a condition whose appeal is *technical* rather than *ethical* and, as is often the case with such conditions, is suggested by the requirements of the proof of a theorem. Suppose we have $[a, b]$. Now let the individual orderings $(.)_i$ change in a way which *leaves unchanged* each i's preferences between a and b. Then $[a, b]$ should continue to hold. Thus a change only of c's position in the individual preference orderings would not of itself change the social ordering of a and b (c is the irrelevant alternative in a pairwise choice between a and b).

The position adopted by Arrow is then that although one may be able to think of further desirable properties of a constitution or *SWF*, one could hardly be content with less. And though these conditions form a minimal set, they are in fact sufficient for Arrow's result, which is the general impossibility theorem: *no* SWF *exists which satisfies the four conditions* U, P, I *and* D, *and which can produce a transitive preference ordering over social states.*

Thus an attempt to draw up a constitution which transforms individual into social preference orderings and satisfies these four reasonable conditions is doomed to failure. Moreover any existing process which does this must violate at least one of the conditions.

Proof of Arrow's theorem *

The proof of the theorem (which is that given by Sen [1970]) will be given here for our three-person, three-state society. (For the generalization see Sen, Chs 3 and 3*.)

First we define the concepts of an *almost decisive individual or group* and a *decisive individual or group*. Suppose we have that $(a, b)_1$, $(b, a)_2$ and $(b, a)_3$, but the *SWF* produces $[a, b]$. 1's preference becomes the social preference despite strict opposition by 2 and 3. 1 is then called *almost decisive* for the pair (a, b), and we use the notation $A(a, b)$ to denote this. Suppose alternatively we have $(a, b)_1$ and $[a, b]$ *whatever* the preferences of the other two. Then 1 is called *decisive* for (a, b) and we denote this by $D(a, b)$. Clearly $D(a, b) \Rightarrow A(a, b)$ since if 1 is decisive whatever the others' preferences he is decisive if they are strictly opposed to his own. The ideas of almost decisive and decisive could be applied to a group – the group's pairwise ordering becomes the social ordering despite strict opposition, or whatever the orderings, of the rest of society. The notation $A(.)$ and $D(.)$ will in what follows always refer to 1's decisiveness however (nothing is lost by this since the numbering of the individuals is arbitrary).

We now prove Arrow's theorem, in two steps. First we prove that if 1 is almost decisive for any one pair of alternatives, then under a *SWF* satisfying conditions *U*, *I* and *P* and producing a transitive social preference ordering he must be a dictator. We then prove that if the *SWF* does satisfy *U*, *I* and *P* there must be an individual (whom we can number 1) who is almost decisive over at least one pair of alternatives, and therefore, by the first step, is a dictator. Thus the requirements that a *SWF* produce a transitive preference ordering and that it satisfy Arrow's four conditions are mutually inconsistent: no *SWF* can exist which does so.

To prove the first step, suppose $A(a, b)$. Then:

1. If the pattern of preferences is such that $(a, b, c)_1$, $(b, a)_i$, $(b, c)_i$, $i = 2, 3$:
   (a) the fact that 1 is almost decisive over (a, b) implies $[a, b]$.
   (b) the Pareto principle *P* implies $[b, c]$.
   (c) therefore transitivity of the social preference ordering implies $[a, c]$. Nothing was specified about 2 and 3's preferences over the pair (a, c), and yet we have $[a, c]$. Moreover, condition *I*

says that if 2 and 3's stated preferences above were changed to $(a, b)_i$ and $(c, b)_i$, $i = 2, 3$, the social ordering $[a, c]$ cannot change. Thus $[a, c]$ has been obtained independently of the orderings of this pair by 2 and 3, so that 1 must be decisive over (a, c). We have therefore:

$$A(a, b) \Rightarrow D(a, c) \qquad\qquad\qquad\qquad\qquad\qquad [F.1]$$

1 is decisive over the pair (a, c) if he is almost decisive over (a, b).

2. If the preference pattern is such that $(c, a, b)_1$, $(c, a)_i$, $(b, a)_i$, $i = 2, 3$:

(a) $P \Rightarrow [c, a]$ (b) $A(a, b) \Rightarrow [a, b]$ (c) transitivity   implies $[c, b]$.

Again, 1 is decisive over (c, b) since $[c, b]$ must follow whatever the preferences of 2 and 3 (I rules out a change if we were to have $(a, c)_i$ or $(a, b)_i$, $i = 2, 3$). Thus:

$$A(a, b) \Rightarrow D(c, b) \qquad\qquad\qquad\qquad\qquad\qquad [F.2]$$

3. Suppose now that 1 is almost decisive over (a, c), i.e. $A(a, c)$. Then given the preference pattern $(b, a, c)_1$, $(c, a)_i$, $(b, a)_i$, $i = 2, 3$:

(a) $P \Rightarrow [b, a]$ (b) $A(a, c) \Rightarrow [a, c]$ (c) transitivity $\Rightarrow [b, c]$

By exactly similar reasoning as before therefore we have:

$$A(a, c) \Rightarrow D(b, c) \qquad\qquad\qquad\qquad\qquad\qquad [F.3]$$

4. Suppose now that $A(b, c)$. Then given the preference pattern $(b, c, a)_1$, $(c, b)_i$, $(c, a)_i$, $i = 2, 3$:

(a) $P \Rightarrow [c, a]$ (b) $A(b, c) \Rightarrow [b, c]$ (c) transitivity $\Rightarrow [b, a]$

and so, by the usual reasoning:

$$A(b, c) \Rightarrow D(b, a) \qquad\qquad\qquad\qquad\qquad\qquad [F.4]$$

5. Suppose that $A(b, a)$. Given $(c, b, a)_1$, $(a, b)_i$, $(c, b)_i$, $i = 2, 3$:

(a) $P \Rightarrow [c, b]$ (b) $A(b, a) \Rightarrow [b, a]$ (c) transitivity $\Rightarrow [c, a]$

and so in the usual way:

$$A(b, a) \Rightarrow D(c, a) \qquad\qquad\qquad\qquad\qquad\qquad [F.5]$$

6. Suppose $A(c, b)$. Given $(a, c, b)_1$, $(a, c)_i$, $(b, c)_i$, $i = 2, 3$:

(a) $P \Rightarrow [a, c]$ (b) $A(c, b) \Rightarrow [c, b]$ (c) transitivity $\Rightarrow [a, b]$

and so:

$$A(c, b) \Rightarrow D(a, b) \qquad\qquad\qquad\qquad\qquad\qquad [F.6]$$

This first step in the proof is now virtually complete. Recall that by definition $D(.) \Rightarrow A(.)$ for any pair of alternatives. Therefore, putting together [F.1], [F.3]–[F.5] gives the chain of implications:

$$\underbrace{A(a,b) \Rightarrow D(a,c)}_{[F.1]} \Rightarrow \underbrace{A(a,c) \Rightarrow D(b,c)}_{[F.3]} \Rightarrow$$

$$\underbrace{A(b,c) \Rightarrow D(b,a)}_{[F.4]} \Rightarrow \underbrace{A(b,a) \Rightarrow D(c,a)}_{[F.5]}$$

while putting together [F.2] and [F.6] gives the chain:

$$\underbrace{A(a,b) \Rightarrow D(c,b)}_{[F.2]} \Rightarrow \underbrace{A(c,b) \Rightarrow D(a,b)}_{[F.6]}$$

But these chains of implications mean that if 1 is almost decisive over one pair, *he is decisive over all six pairs of choices* and is therefore a dictator. In other words, if the design of the *SWF* meets the conditions *U*, *P* and *I*, and allows one individual to override the opposition of all others on just *one* pairwise choice, then it effectively allows him to have his way on *all* pairwise choices whatever the preferences of the others. This might perhaps be taken as a salutary warning not to allow an almost decisive individual in design of the *SWF*, if it were not for the second part of the proof, which shows that there is *always* such an individual for any *SWF* with properties *U*, *P* and *I*.

First, note that taking any pair of alternatives, say (a, b), the set of all three individuals $\{1, 2, 3\}$ must be decisive for this pair since by *P*, if $(a, b)_i$, $i = 1, 2, 3$, then $[a, b]$. Thus for every pair of alternatives at least one decisive set of individuals exists, namely $\{1, 2, 3\}$. It may be that for some pairs a smaller decisive set of individuals exists, e.g. if $(b, c)_i \Rightarrow [b, c]$ for $i = 1, 2$, then $\{1, 2\}$ is a decisive set for this pair. Moreover any decisive set must be almost decisive. What we have to prove is that for some pair there exists an almost decisive set containing just one individual.

The proof proceeds by contradiction: suppose any almost decisive set has more than one member. Given that for each pair of alternatives there is at least one almost decisive set, we take the almost decisive set with fewest elements – it must contain either two or three individuals. For concreteness suppose it is the set $\{1, 2\}$, and let $(a, b)_i$, $i = 1, 2$. *Because of condition* U, we are free to assume the following pattern of preferences: $(a, b, c)_1$, $(c, a, b)_2$, and $(b, c, a)_3$. Since $\{1, 2\}$ is almost decisive for (a, b) we must have $[a, b]$. Only individual 2 prefers *c* to *b*, and so if $[c, b]$, he would be an almost decisive individual which is ruled out by assumption. Therefore we can take it that $[b, c]$ (strictly, *b* and *c* could be socially indifferent but this turns out not to matter). Therefore the transitivity of the social ordering implies $[a, c]$. But looking again at the individual orderings we see that $(a, c)_1$, $(c, a)_2$, $(c, a)_3$, and so individual 1 is almost decisive over (a, c). But this contradicts the assertion that there is no almost decisive individual, which is therefore false.

Consequences of the theorem

The method of proof of the theorem was to show that a *SWF* producing a transitive social preference ordering and satisfying conditions *U*, *P* and *I* must allow for the existence of a dictator. It would be wrong however to interpret this as implying that 'dictatorship is inevitable' or indeed that there is any *particular* difficulty in defining a *SWF* which meets condition *D*. Rather it is the *full set* of requirements, including that of a transitive social ordering, which has been proved to be *mutually* incompatible. The impossibility result can be made to disappear by relaxing an appropriately chosen requirement. For example, the consequence of dropping *U*, the unrestricted domain condition was discussed earlier (see also Question 7 of Exercise 17F). It might be argued that in a given social group it is unreasonable to allow all possible logical combinations of individual orderings. The nature of social relationships may be such as to suggest certain patterns of orderings, and *SWF*s may exist satisfying conditions *P*, *I* and *D* for such patterns.

Alternatively it has been suggested that the requirement that the *SWF* produce a *transitive* social preference ordering is unnecessarily stringent (see Sen (1970) Ch. 4). If what we want is a definite choice of an alternative out of a given set, then transitivity is sufficient but not necessary. A somewhat weaker condition of *acyclicity*, which, in terms of the social ordering means that if $[a, b]$ and $[b, c]$ then we do not have $[c, a]$, is all that is required for social choice. Moreover, Sen shows that *SWF*s exist which satisfy conditions *U*, *P*, *I*, *D* and yield acyclic orderings.

In fact each of Arrow's conditions has been closely examined to see if more scope can be found for the possibility of the existence of a *SWF* and therefore, ultimately a Bergson *swf*. The reader is referred to Sen (1970) for an exhaustive treatment of the literature.

As helpful as the concept of the Bergson *swf* has been at the general level of *theoretical* welfare economics therefore, the view that in applied welfare economics all we need do is analyse the implications of a given *swf* is increasingly open to doubt. Not only is there empirical evidence of the rarity of statements of well-defined social preferences; there is also a powerful theoretical argument which we have just examined, to the effect that if our political process possesses certain properties we like to think it possesses, no such *swf* is in fact possible.

Exercise 17F

1.* Show the consequences for the *SWF* in the two-person economy of replacing value judgement (iii) at the beginning of this section by:

   (*a*) the value judgement that any social state in which consumer 1 is better off is preferred to one in which he is worse off; the social preference between two states between which 1 is indifferent is determined by 2's preferences.

   (*b*) Only consumer 1's preferences are to count – the social preference ordering is to reflect his own preferences over consumption bundles $[x_{11}, x_{12}, z_1]$.

2. Given the axioms which allow the *swf* to be treated like a consumer's utility function on the space of (u_1, u_2) pairs, use it in conjunction with the welfare frontier and utility feasibility curve of the previous section to answer the following questions:

    (a) Assuming lump-sum redistribution is feasible, solve for the overall optimal allocation of resources. What significance attaches to the fact that the welfare frontier cannot be regarded generally as strictly convex to the origin?

    (b) Show that if lump-sum redistribution is not feasible, a resource allocation which is not Pareto optimal may be preferred to one which is, even when the latter is available.

    (c) Show the implications for the indifference curves of the *swf*, and for the solution of problem (a), of assuming cases (a) and (b) in Question 1.*

3.* *Maximin swf.* Suppose that value judgement (iii) is replaced by the *maximin value judgement:* society must seek to maximize the well-being of its worse off members. Show the consequences for the *swf*'s indifference curves (What assumptions do you make about individual utility functions?) and for the solution to the resource allocation problem.

4. Explain why value judgement (ii) implies that the *swf* can be expressed as a function of the individual utility functions.

5. Discuss whether economists should be interested in the question of how the *swf* is formulated.

6. Explain clearly the distinction between Bergson's *swf* and Arrow's SWF.

7. Construct examples where three individuals' preference orderings over three social states are all different, but the majority voting rule yields a transitive social preference ordering.

8.* Suppose, in the second step in the proof of Arrow's theorem, that the smallest almost decisive set was $\{1, 2, 3\}$. Show that the proof carries through nevertheless. (*Hint:* partition the set into $\{1\}$, $\{2, 3\}$, assume $(a, b, c)_1$, $(c, a, b)_i$, $i = 2, 3$, and show that if 1 is not almost decisive over (a, c), $\{1, 2\}$ must be almost decisive over (b, c).)

9. Explain the difference between transitivity and acyclicity. Why is the latter a weaker requirement?

Appendix

In this appendix we derive the necessary conditions for Pareto optimality, which were described at some length in section C of this chapter. The model of the economy is again:

utility functions: $u^h(x_{h1}, x_{h2}, z_h)$ $h = 1, 2$ [A.1]

production functions: $x_i = f^i(z_{i1}, z_{i2})$ $i = 1, 2$ [A.2] market clearing conditions: $\displaystyle\sum_{h=1}^{2} x_{hi} - x_i = 0 \qquad i = 1, 2.$ [A.3]

$$z_h - \sum_{i=1}^{2} z_{ih} = 0 \qquad h = 1, 2.$$ [A.4]

We wish to find necessary conditions for a resource allocation which satisfies these constraints, and which maximizes one consumer's utility function subject to a given level of the other's. Mathematically, this can be expressed by defining the problem:

$$\max u^1(x_{11}, x_{12}, z_1)$$ [A.5]

$$\text{s.t. } \bar{u}^2 = u^2(x_{21}, x_{22}, z_2)$$ [A.6]

and the constraints 2–4. On certain assumptions (see Ch. 2), we can associate Lagrange multipliers μ_i, λ_i, ω_h and ρ with constraints 2, 3, 4, 6, respectively, and write the necessary conditions for a Pareto optimal resource allocation as:

$$\left.\begin{aligned} u_i^1 - \lambda_i &= 0 \\ u_3^1 - \omega_1 &= 0 \\ \rho u_i^2 - \lambda_i &= 0 \\ \rho u_3^2 - \omega_2 &= 0 \end{aligned}\right\} \quad \begin{array}{l} i = 1, 2 \\[4pt] \text{allocation of inputs and outputs} \\ \text{among consumers.} \end{array}$$

$$-\mu_i + \lambda_i = 0 \quad i = 1, 2 \quad \text{total output condition}$$

$$\mu_i f_h^i - \omega_h = 0 \quad h = 1, 2 \quad \text{input allocation among firms}$$

together with constraints [A.2], [A.3], [A.4], [A.6].

Then, we can verify the conditions set out in section C by taking the appropriate ratios. Thus:

$$\frac{u_1^1}{u_2^1} = \frac{\lambda_1}{\lambda_2} = \frac{u_1^2}{u_2^2} \quad \begin{array}{l} \text{is the condition of equality of} \\ MRS \text{ in consumption} \end{array}$$

$$\frac{u_3^h}{u_i^h} = \frac{\omega_h}{\lambda_i} = f_h^i \quad \begin{array}{l} h = 1, 2 \quad i = 1, 2, \text{ is the condition of equality of} \\ MRS \text{ in input supply} \end{array}$$

$$\frac{f_1^1}{f_2^1} = \frac{\omega_1}{\omega_2} = \frac{f_2^1}{f_2^2} \quad \begin{array}{l} \text{is the condition of equality of} \\ MRTS \text{ in production} \end{array}$$

$$\frac{u_1^1}{u_2^1} = \frac{u_1^2}{u_2^2} = \frac{\lambda_1}{\lambda_2} = \frac{\mu_1}{\mu_2} = \frac{\omega_h}{f_h^1} \bigg/ \frac{\omega_h}{f_h^2} = \frac{f_h^2}{f_h^1} = MRT$$

is the condition of equality of MRS with MRT. These conditions then are the counterpart to Fig. 9. Note that we can interpret the ratios λ_1/λ_2, ω_1/ω_2, as the slopes of the tangents to the indifference curves, and isoquants, in those diagrams, and hence as the appropriate 'shadow price ratios'. Note finally that to solve these conditions for a particular resource allocation involves assigning a *specific* value for $\bar{u}^2$, i.e. the fixed level of consumer 2's utility. By varying $\bar{u}^2$, we trace out the whole set of Pareto optimal allocations, and hence the welfare frontier shown in Fig. 11.

References and further reading

The starting point for further study of the kind of welfare economics discussed in this chapter is:

J. de V. Graaff. *Theoretical Welfare Economics*, Cambridge University Press, London, 1963.

while:

I. M. D. Little. *A Critique of Welfare Economics*, Clarendon Press, Oxford, 1957, (2nd ed.)

is also important. Useful historical background is provided by:

H. Myint. *Theories of Welfare Economics*, Harvard University Press, 1948.

For applications of welfare theory to specific areas of economic policy, see:

J. E. Meade. *Trade and Welfare: The Theory of International Economic Policy*, Oxford University Press, Oxford, 1955.

R. Rees. *Public Enterprise Economics*, Weidenfeld, London, 1976.

P. A. Diamond and **J. Mirrlees.** 'Optimal taxation and public production' I and II, *American Economic Review*, 1971.

A. P. Lerner. 'The concept of monopoly and the measurement of monopoly power', *Review of Economic Studies*, 1933/4.

E. J. Mishan. *Cost-Benefit Analysis*, George Allen & Unwin, London, 1971.

On the Bergson social welfare function see:

A. Bergson. 'A reformulation of certain aspects of welfare economics', *Quarterly Journal of Economics*, 52, 1938.

P. A. Samuelson. *Foundations of Economic Analysis*, Harvard University Press, 1948.

For anyone wishing to pursue the theory of social choice, indispensable works are:

K. J. Arrow. *Social Choice and Individual Values*, John Wiley, New York, 1951, (2nd ed. 1963).

A. K. Sen. *Collective Choice and Social Welfare*, Holden-Day, 1970.

On the compensation principle see:

N. Kaldor. 'Welfare propositions of economics and interpersonal comparisons of utility' *Economic Journal*, 49, 1939.

T. Scitovsky. 'A note on welfare propositions in economics' *Review of Economic Studies*, 9, 1941–2.

An influential contribution is:

L. Robbins. *An Essay on the Nature and Significance of Economic Science*, London, 1932.

Chapter 18

Market failure and the second best

Introduction

In the previous chapter it was shown that the resource allocation associated with the equilibrium of a competitive market system will be Pareto optimal. In this chapter we consider the circumstances under which markets may fail to allocate resources optimally and the questions of whether and how government action can correct this market failure.

The conventional approach to market failure is to list the types of situations in which resource misallocation may occur: monopoly, interdependence of economic agents external to the market mechanism, public goods, common access resources and so on. However, a deeper analysis of these *instances* of market failure suggests that underlying them all is a common set of fundamental *causes* which have much to do with property rights, information and transactions costs. For example, the existence of a single seller is not in itself *sufficient* to lead to a market outcome in which there are unexploited gains from trade, i.e. in which there is market failure. Examination of these causes gives a great deal of insight into the nature of the market mechanism as well as a better understanding of particular instances of market failure and the means of their correction. Accordingly in section A we consider the causes of market failure and, in section B, the specific instances of resource misallocation.

The observation that markets may fail has been a major factor in supporting microeconomic activity by governments. In the last two sections of the chapter, therefore, we consider the theory of the second best, which is concerned with government policy in an economy characterized by market failure, and the concept of 'government failure', which stems from the observation that it is misleading to assume an omniscient and altruistic central policy-maker if we wish to discuss economic policy in practice.

A. The causes of market failure

We begin by taking a deeper view than hitherto of the nature of market exchange. A market is an institution in which individuals (or firms) exchange not just commodities, but the *rights* to use them in particular ways for particular lengths of time. For example, when a consumer buys a motor car, he buys not just a physical asset but the rights to use that asset in certain specified ways. He acquires the right to drive on public highways, at certain speeds, carrying specified numbers of passengers. He may have the rights to park on the public highway without payment, to prevent other individuals using the car without his consent, and so on. When an employer hires a worker he buys the right to direct the worker to perform certain tasks at certain times for a specified period. What is exchanged for these rights to use the car or direct the worker in specified ways is not just a quantity of finely engraved paper money, but the right to use that paper in order to settle debts incurred in the purchase of other bundles of rights to use assets. These rights, which define the uses to which the assets may be put, are known as *property rights*. Markets are institutions which organise the *exchange of control* of commodities, where the nature of the control is defined by the property rights attached to the commodity.

Inefficiency and exchange

We saw in the previous chapter that if marginal rates of substitution between two goods are not equal for two consumers, an inefficient allocation would exist: it would be possible by rearranging consumption vectors to make at least one individual better off and no-one worse off. In such a situation there is the possibility of mutually advantageous trade between the two individuals. The reader should refer to the numerical example quoted in section C of the previous chapter and satisfy himself that a contract by which individual 1 agreed to exchange, with individual 2, one of his units of x_1 for 4 of individuals 2's units of x_2 would make both parties better off. Alternatively a middleman could make contracts with each individual whereby the middleman traded $3\frac{1}{2}$ units of x_2 for one unit of x_1 with individual 1, and 1 unit of x_1 for $4\frac{1}{2}$ units of x_2 with individual 2. As a result both individuals are better off, and the middleman makes a profit of one unit of x_2.

This example is an illustration of a general rule which follows from the very definition of Pareto optimality. If there is inefficiency it is possible, by exchange or production, to make at least one person better off without making anyone else worse off. Inefficiency implies the existence of potentially mutually advantageous trades or profitable production decisions. Hence the question of why a particular resource allocation mechanism is inefficient can be rephrased as the question of why such advantageous or profitable exchanges or production decisions do not occur. Given that individuals would wish to make themselves better off by trade or production, inefficiency can only persist: (*a*) if individuals do not have sufficient control over commodities (including productive assets) to effect profitable or advantageous exchanges and production; (*b*) if individuals do not have sufficient information to seek out such profitable or advantageous opportunities; or (*c*) if the individual parties to a trade cannot agree on how to share the gains from their mutually advantageous exchange. We consider these fundamental causes of market failure in turn.

(a) *Insufficient control.* An individual's control over commodities is defined by the system of property rights, and a system of property rights can be incomplete, from the point of view of efficiency, because of *imperfect excludability* or because of *non-transferability.*

Imperfect Excludability.   Imperfect excludability arises when effective control of a commodity is not conferred on a single individual but rather on a (possibly very large) group of individuals. Control of a commodity or asset means the ability to determine who shall use it, in what circumstances, for what length of time and under what terms. When control is vested in a group, an individual who wishes to acquire that control must enter into contracts with all the individuals in the group, and this may be so difficult or costly (for reasons examined below) that no individual can acquire exclusive control. Consider the example of the level of traffic on a public road which, as the name suggests, is an asset 'owned' by all, in the sense that everyone with a valid driving licence, insurance certificate and roadworthy vehicle has the right to drive on the road. An individual who wished to acquire control of the level of traffic on the road would have to enter into contracts with every actual or potential road user, whereby the road user agreed, in return for some suitable consideration, to limit his use of the road in some specified fashion. The difficulties of this procedure indicate why there is no market for the control of the use of public roads. Commodities or assets with this characteristic are described variously as *non-exclusive, common-property* or *free access* resources because all the joint owners (which may be every individual in the economy) have the right to use them in particular ways. Further examples are common grazing lands, ocean fishing grounds, beaches, public parks and rivers.

Control may be equivalently defined as the ability to *exclude* any individual, i.e. to determine who shall *not* use the commodity. The first requirement for excludability, as we have seen, is one of legality: the property rights attached to a commodity must allow exclusion by one individual of all other individuals from use of the commodity. The legal *right* to exclude must also be supported by the *ability* to enforce that right. In many cases enforcement of the right to exclude is simple and inexpensive. The consumer who purchases a loaf of bread has a very good chance, in a reasonably law-abiding society, of getting it home and consuming it himself without incurring significant costs of excluding others from consuming it. The supermarket which sells him the loaf has a more difficult task of preventing consumers who have not paid from removing goods, and it has to incur the expense of hiring check-out and security staff. Similarly the owner of a piece of land, i.e. the individual who has the legal right to exclude others from using the land, may have to fence and guard the land to enforce his legal right. Cinemas, theatres and football grounds will have to install box offices and turnstiles, print tickets and employ staff to ensure that all who enjoy the entertainment provided have paid and that those who have paid for low-priced seats do not occupy high-priced seats. In addition to attempting to prevent unauthorized use of his property, the individual may also have to devote resources to the detection and punishment of such unauthorized use as does occur. These costs of preventing, detecting and punishing unauthorized use are known as *exclusion costs*. They will depend on the legal and social framework of the economy and on the state of technology. For example if the maximum punishments for unauthorized use of some assets are reduced, this will tend to increase the resources which must be devoted to prevention and detection. Alternatively, inventions such as barbed wire or better burglar alarms will tend to reduce exclusion costs.

Hence potentially advantageous trades or exchanges may not take place because of imperfect excludability. It may be impossible for an individual to acquire effective control or exclusive use of the good or asset in question, either because of the lack of a legal right to exclude, or because high exclusion costs will more than outweigh the gains from trade. Similarly, potentially beneficial production may not occur if individuals making production decisions cannot exclude other individuals from the benefits of the decision. Farmers will have little incentive to plant crops if the law permits anybody to harvest the crops without the consent of the farmer. The lack of exclusion dissipates the benefits of the increased output amongst many individuals and hence reduces any single individual's incentives to bear the costs necessary to produce the extra output.

Non-transferability. Even when the legal right to exclude is vested in a single individual and exclusion costs are low, so that the individual in question is the owner of the asset or good, he may not have the legal right to *transfer* use or ownership to just any individual on just any terms. Lack of transferability may take the extreme form of a complete absence of the right to transfer any of the property rights associated with the good or asset on any terms to anybody. For example squatters who occupy land or property without the consent of the owner of the land may have the right to uninterrupted use and enjoyment of the property, but they do not have the right to sell it; tenants may hold property on leases which do not permit subletting; land may be entailed i.e. owned by an individual in the sense that he can exclude others, but he cannot sell the land to anyone. Less extreme is the case of the labour market: individuals own their labour and can sell it for limited periods, but the law does not permit permanent transfer of control over a man's labour: slavery is illegal. Still milder forms of reduced transferability exist when individuals are constrained in the terms on which they can conclude an exchange, as for example when maximum or minimum prices are fixed by law; or when the hours during which trades may take place are prescribed; or when trade must be carried on in specified locations. There may also be restrictions on *which* individuals may trade: minors under 18 years cannot buy alcohol from licensed premises, but they can consume it; gunsmiths cannot sell arms to people who do not have a firearms licence; taxis cannot ply for hire unless licensed by the local authority. Thus, restrictions on the terms of exchange may prevent or inhibit trades which the parties themselves perceive to be mutually advantageous.

(b) *Information costs.* A further reason for non-occurrence of some exchanges is that exchange requires information: the identity and location of potential buyers and sellers must be known; the terms on which they are prepared to trade must be ascertained; and the quality of the goods or services to be exchanged and the validity of the property rights attached to them must be checked. Information is not a free good (see section 5E) and in some cases the costs of acquiring the necessary information may be larger than the gains to be had from the exchange.

(c) *'Small numbers' and the indeterminacy of bargaining.* Finally, a mutually advantageous trade may not be concluded because of the failure of the trading parties to agree upon the terms of the trade. For example, in Chapter 17, Fig. 2, *any* bargain by which individual 1 exchanges some of his endowment of good x_1 for some of individual 2's x_2, such that there is a movement from $\dot{\alpha}$ to a point between γ and β on *CC*, will make both individuals better off. There is an infinite number of different bargains with the above property; they differ in the final utility levels achieved by the individuals. Individual 1 will obviously prefer to trade at a low price of x_2 in terms of x_1 since he is buying x_2 with his x_1; individual 2 prefers to trade at a higher price. Both will gain from the trade but the division of the gains from trade will depend on the precise terms of the bargain. This may lead to lengthy and costly bargaining and in some cases the parties may not be able to reach agreement at all.

This failure to agree stems from the *multiplicity* of possible terms on which the exchange could take place so as to leave both parties better off. If the only alternatives open to the parties were to trade at some fixed terms or not at all, then there is nothing for them to bargain about: if the prescribed terms make both parties better off they will trade; if the terms make either party worse off they will not trade. Both parties treat the prescribed terms as parameters which cannot be altered by their actions. This is just the situation which prevails at the equilibrium of a competitive market: there is a single price which is taken as given by every trader, and so there is no scope for bargaining and no failure to conclude mutually advantageous trades because of lack of agreement on terms. In equilibrium no seller will ask and no buyer would pay a price exceeding the market price, because any buyer confronted with a higher price will buy from another seller at the market price. Similarly no seller will offer, or buyer ask for, a price below the market price because every seller knows he can sell his goods at the market price to other buyers.

Our discussion in section 10E of the concept of the core suggests that a failure to agree on how to split the gains from trade is more likely the fewer the number of potential contractors.

B. Instances of market failure

We now examine some of the ways in which market failure manifests itself, and relate them to the underlying causes of such failure just discussed.

Monopoly

As we have seen in Chapter 11, a monopolist will aim to maximize his profit by producing an output at which marginal revenue equals marginal cost. The monopolist's equilibrium is shown in Fig. 1, where q_m and p_m are the monopoly output and price, and we have assumed constant average and marginal costs for simplicity. This situation is Pareto inefficient. The consumers would be prepared to pay up to p_m for an additional unit of output, and the cost of an additional unit is the monopolist's marginal cost MC. Since $MR = MC$ and $p_m > MR$ it follows that $p_m > MC$: consumers are willing to pay more for an extra unit than its cost of production. If consumers actually paid something less than p_m but more than MC for the additional unit, *while continuing to pay $p_m \cdot q_m$ for the units already produced*, both monopolist and consumers would be better off: the monopolist's profit increases, while consumers obtain extra consumption at a price which is less than its value to them.

The Pareto optimal output of the good is at the point where consumer's willingness to pay for an extra unit, measured by the height of the demand curve, is equal to the cost of the extra unit. This is the output q^* where the demand curve cuts the marginal cost curve. Since the monopoly price and output are inefficient there are potential gains to both consumers and monopolist if output is increased from q_m to the level q^*. One contract between monopolist and consumers which would lead to the optimal output is for the monopolist to agree to sell output q^* at a price p^* equal to marginal cost. Since his profit on his sales would fall by $(p_m - p^*) \cdot q_m$ (explain why) the consumers would have to agree to pay him a lump sum of at least this magnitude. They could do so and still be better off since the gain to them of a fall in price is measured by the area $p_m b a p^*$ (Recall the discussion of consumer's surplus in Chapter 4). This area exceeds $(p_m - p^*) \cdot q_m$ by G, which is the gain available for division between the monopolist and consumers.

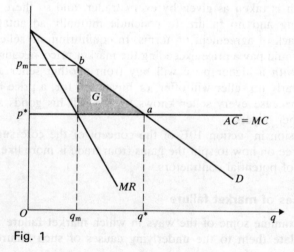

Fig. 1

Why then do monopolists price at above marginal cost? The answer must be that for the reasons outlined earlier, consumers and the producer fail to conclude a mutually satisfactory bargain. They may not be able to agree on the division of the gain from the increase in output. There may be very high costs associated with locating and organizing consumers. They may not be able to agree on how the burden of the lump-sum payment should be shared out. It may be impossible to prevent consumers who do not contribute to the lump-sum payment from enjoying the benefits (lower price) from the contract with the monopolists (This type of failure through inability to exclude is known as the *free rider problem*). The monopolist therefore may be forced to make individual contracts with consumers. If he cannot prevent resale amongst them, he will have to set the same price in each contract, and so we have the normal, inefficient monopoly situation, in which the monopolist confronts a downward sloping demand curve and sets $MR = MC$. Consumers will treat price as a parameter, since an individual consumer cannot persuade the monopolist to lower his price, because of the monopolist's inability to prevent resale.

Externality

An externality is said to exist if some of the variables which affect one decision-maker's utility or profit are under the control of another decision-maker. For example a brewery sited downstream from a chemical works which pumps noxious effluent into the stream will find that the cost of producing beer depends on its choice of output level and input combinations *and* on the amount of effluent which has to be removed from the water before it can be used in beer production. In this case the externality is *detrimental*, but in other cases there may be *beneficial externalities*, as for example when a bee-keeper is located next to an apple grower. The bees will cross-pollinate the apple trees, benefiting the orchard owner, and feed off the apple blossom, benefiting the bee-keeper. This is also an example of a *reciprocal externality*: the bee-keeper's output of honey depends on the number of apple trees, the output of apples depends on the number of beehives. In addition to these producer-producer externalities there may be consumer-consumer externalities (my utility depends on, amongst other things, your use of your record player) producer-consumer externalities (residential areas sited downwind of a smoky or odorous factory) and consumer-producer externalities (fires started as a result of family outings in wooded areas).

To see why the existence of externalities may lead to a Pareto inefficient allocation of resources, suppose that individual 2 inflicts an external detriment on individual 1. Now, in determining the level of his activity, we take it that individual 2 will be concerned only with the value of his own objective function (the *private* welfare), rather than with the values of his own *and* individual 1's objective function (the *social* welfare). He will thus set the activity at the level at which its marginal net benefit to himself is zero. But at this level, individual 1 may be prepared to pay individual 2 to reduce the activity level, the maximum amount of this payment being the value of the marginal detriment which is imposed upon him. If this payment exceeds the maximum amount which individual 2 requires to induce him to make the change, then there are obviously 'gains from trade'. Thus, the initial situation is inefficient. Clearly, the essence of this argument is unaffected by changing the detriment to a benefit, or by switching the roles of the individuals.

To express all this more formally, let $B_1(x_1, x_2)$ be the objective function of the first decision-maker, where x_1 is the activity he controls and x_2 the activity controlled by the second decision-maker. $B_2(x_2)$ is the second individual's objective function, which is maximized by setting x_2 at the level x_2^* for which

$$MB_2(x_2^*) = 0 \qquad\qquad\qquad [\text{B.1}]$$

where MB_2 is marginal benefit of x_2 to individual 2. Individual 1 maximizes $B_1(x_1, x_2)$ by choice of x_1 and treats x_2 as given, since he cannot control it. Then x_1^*, the optimal level of x_1, will depend on the level of x_2, i.e. $x_1^* = x_1(x_2)$; and so B_1^*, the maximized value of B_1 depends on x_2:

$$B_1^* = B_1(x_1^*, x_2) = B_1(x_1(x_2), x_2) = B_1^*(x_2)$$

Variations in x_2 will therefore cause changes in B_1^*. We let $MB_1^*(x_2)$ be the marginal benefit to individual 1 of individual 2's activity. For simplicity MB_2 and MB_1^* are in monetary units, so that they measure the amount of money each individual would pay for a marginal increase in x_2. Given that the externality is detrimental, $MB_1^*(x_2^*)$ is negative (individual 1 would have to be paid to compensate for a bit more of x_2).

Figure 2 plots MB_2 and $-MB_1^* = MD_1$ against x_2. The negative of MB_1^* is the marginal damage MD_1 suffered by individual 1 from x_2, and is

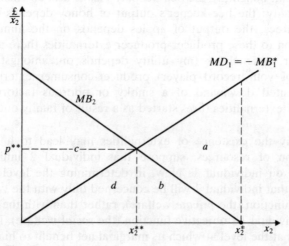

Fig. 2

the sum of money individual 1 would pay for a one unit reduction in x_2. The marginal social benefit of x_2 is the sum of the private marginal benefit MB_2 and the marginal externality MB_1^*. Optimality requires that the marginal social benefit MSB be zero or

$$MSB = MB_1^* + MB_2 = 0 \qquad \text{[B.2]}$$

which in turn implies

$$MB_2 = -MB_1^* = MD_1 \qquad \text{[B.3]}$$

Hence marginal social benefit is zero at x_2^{**}. This level is Pareto optimal because it is impossible to alter x_2 in a way which makes one individual better off, and the other no worse off, when $x_2 = x_2^{**}$. A one-unit rise in x_2 leads to $MB_2 < MD_1$, and the gainer (individual 2) cannot compensate the loser (individual 1), since the former's gain is less that the latter's loss. The reader should apply a similar argument to the case of a unit decrease in x_2 to prove that the gainer (individual 1) cannot compensate the loser (individual 2). Since individual 2 ignores the effect x_2 has on individual 1, x_2 is set at x_2^*, where $MB_2 = 0$. Since $MB_2^*(x_2^*) < 0$ we have:

$$MSB(x_2^*) = MB_1^*(x_2^*) + MB_2(x_2^*) < 0 \qquad \text{[B.4]}$$

and there is inefficiency in that too large a level of x_2 is chosen.

This situation arises because individual 1 cannot control x_2, a variable which affects his objective function but which is under the control of another decision-maker. We argued above that markets are institutions which facilitate the exchange of property rights or the rights to control certain activities. This suggests that externalities exist because markets do not. If there were a market in x_2 the two individuals would enter into a mutually advantageous contract to regulate the level of x_2. Consider a contract whereby individual 2 agrees to reduce x_2 from the privately optimal x_2^* to the Pareto optimal x_2^{**}. The gain to individual 1 would be measured by $a + b$: the area under MD_1 between x_2^* and x_2^{**}. The loss to individual 2 would be b: the area under MD_2 between x_2^* and x_2^{**}. Hence there is a net gain of $(a + b) - b = a$ available to make both parties better off, and the result of the contract is an optimal output.

Alternatively, individual 1 may buy reductions in x_2 below x_2^* from individual 2, at some fixed price per unit. If this price is set at p^{**}, the height of the MB_2 and MD_1 lines at x_2^{**}, an efficient level of x_2 will result. Define x_2^b as the level of x_2 individual 1 (the buyer) wishes to have when faced with a fixed price per unit reduction in x_2. x_2^s is the level of x_2 the seller (individual 2) wishes to have when he faces a fixed price per unit reduction. With a fixed price of p^{**} individual 1's objective function (after optimal choice of x_1) is:

$$B_1^*(x_2^b) - p^{**}(x_2^* - x_2^b)$$

where $x_2^* - x_2^b$ is the reduction in x_2 he wishes to buy at a total cost of $p^{**}(x_2^* - x_2^b)$, and he sets x_2^b so that its marginal effect is zero:

$$MB_1^* + p^{**} = 0 \qquad\qquad\qquad [\text{B.5}]$$

(Remember MB_1^* is negative.) Since p^{**} is the height of $MD_1 = -MB_1^*$ at x_2^{**}, individual 1 sets $x_2^b = x_2^{**}$. Individual 2's objective function when there is a fixed market price p^{**} is:

$$B_2(x_2^s) + p^{**}(x_2^* - x_2^s)$$

where $p^{**}(x_2^* - x_2^s)$ is the return from selling a reduction of $x_2^* - x_2^s$ in x_2. Individual 2 sets x_2^s so that its marginal effect on his new objective function is zero:

$$MB_2 - p^{**} = 0 \qquad\qquad\qquad [\text{B.6}]$$

Since p^{**} is also the height of the MB_2 curve at x_2^{**}, x_2^s is set equal to x_2^{**}. Hence at p^{**} both parties wish to see the same Pareto optimal level of x_2: $x_2^s = x_2^b = x_2^{**}$ and from [B.5] and [B.6]

$$p^{**} = -MB_1^* = MB_2 \qquad\qquad\qquad [\text{B.7}]$$

The existence of a market in x_2 means that individual 1 can, if he wishes, control all the variables in his decision problem by contracting with individual 2 over the level of x_2. Individual 2 will take account of *all* the effects of his actions, including their effect on individual 1, because the existence of a market in x_2 means that individual 1 can influence the marginal benefit accruing to individual 2 by suitable payments related to the level of x_2. The market therefore *internalizes* the externality and ends the divergence between private and social marginal benefits.

Externalities persist because of inadequacies in or non-existence of the relevant markets. In 'small number' externality situations, there may be failure to agree on the division of the gains from a move to a more efficient allocation. In 'large number' externality cases (as for example when a factory pollutes over a large area) the absence of contracting between polluter and victims may arise from any of the reasons mentioned at the end of our discussion of monopoly. The free rider problem, for example, is likely to be important, because it will be difficult for the polluter to control the pollution level for a particular victim. Reductions in pollution will tend to benefit all victims in the area. Hence individual victims will have a reduced incentive to contract individually with the polluter, since they will benefit from contracts made between the polluter and other victims, to which they are not party. The same argument applies to a contract between the polluter and a voluntary association of victims; it will be difficult to exclude those who do not pay for a reduction in pollution from benefiting from such a contract. In addition the legal situation may not be well defined, so that it is not clear whether the polluter has the legal right to pollute, or his victims the legal right to protection from his pollution. Establishing through the courts who has the ownership of 'the right to pollute' may be very costly. Even if the market is established it may not be competitive; a single polluter confronting many victims may act like a monopolist with respect to changes in the level of pollution. Thus failure by monopoly compounds the failure by externality.

Common property resources

A common property resource is an asset whose services are used in production or consumption and which is not owned by any one individual. Examples include ocean fisheries (anyone may fish outside territorial waters), common grazing land (anyone satisfying certain requirements, such as residence in a particular area, may graze as many cattle as he wishes on the land) and public roads (any motorist with a valid driving licence may drive a roadworthy insured vehicle on public roads). We suggested earlier that common ownership can cause inefficiency and we will now show this a little more rigorously. We take the case of a lake in which all members of a community have the right to fish. For simplicity we assume that the total catch (the 'output' of fish from the lake) depends only on the total time spent fishing by all individuals:

$$q = f(L) = f(\sum L_i) \tag{B.8}$$

where q is the total catch, L_i is time spent fishing by the ith individual and $L = \sum L_i$ is total time spent fishing. The total catch increases with L up to $\hat{L}$ and decreases thereafter, i.e. the marginal product f' is positive for $L < \hat{L}$ and negative for $L > \hat{L}$. The marginal product declines with L : $f'' < 0$. There are, in other words, diminishing returns to fishing in the lake. The ith fisherman's catch q_i is

$$q_i = (L_i/L) \cdot f(L) \tag{B.9}$$

The assumptions underlying [B.9] are that all fishermen are equally skilful, can fish anywhere in the lake, and the fish can swim anywhere in the lake. Hence the proportion of the total catch made by the ith fisherman is simply the proportion of total fishing effort accounted for by his labour input: $q_i/q = L_i/L$. Alternatively, output per unit of labour input is q/L and so L_i hours spent fishing yield a catch of $L_i q/L$.

We will assume for convenience that variations in total fish output from the lake have no effect on the price of fish p and similarly that variations in the total labour input to fishing in the lake have no effect on the wage rate w. The fishermen each wish to maximize their individual profit

$$\pi_i = pq_i - wL_i \tag{B.10}$$

where π_i is fisherman i's profit. Hence each sets L_i so that:

$$\frac{d\pi_i}{dL_i} = \frac{d}{dL_i} \left(\frac{pL_i \cdot f(L)}{L} - wL_i \right)$$

$$= p[q/L + (L_i/L)(f' - q/L)] - w = 0 \tag{B.11}$$

When [B.11] is satisfied each fisherman is maximizing profit and is in fact earning a positive profit. To see this write profit π_i as

$$pq_i - wL_i = (p \cdot q/L - w) \cdot L_i$$

which is positive, for $L_i > 0$, if and only if

$$p \cdot q/L - w > 0$$

Now by our assumption that marginal product is declining ($f'' < 0$) marginal product f' is less than average product q/L. Hence, from [B.11],

$$p \cdot q/L - w = p(L_i/L)(q/L - f') > 0$$

and positive profits are made. These positive profits will attract more fishermen to the lake since there are no restrictions on entry to a free access resource. Entry will continue until each individual fisherman provides a very small share of the total labour input and π_i tends to zero with L_i/L. The full equilibrium will therefore be characterized by an arbitrarily large number of fishermen, each earning zero profit and hence with total industry profits of zero:

$$pq - wL = 0 \tag{B.12}$$

This is illustrated in Fig. 3 where $p \cdot q$ shows the total value of fish produced and wL the cost of the labour employed. The free access equilibrium is at L^0 where $pq = wL$ and [B.12] is satisfied.

The equilibrium total labour input L^0 in Fig. 3 has the property that a reduction in total fishing effort, say to $\hat{L}$, would actually increase total output. This occurs because the wage rate is low enough for an intersection to take place in the range of negative marginal products. The outcome in this case will clearly be inefficient as long as the output of fish has a positive value and labour devoted to fishing has a negative value. In order to

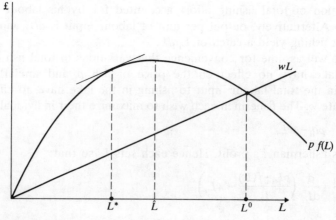

Fig. 3

generalize this result (e.g. to cover cases in which an intersection might take place where marginal products are positive), we have to make some assumptions about the marginal social value of fish and the marginal social cost of labour. We will assume that these are in fact measured by the market prices of fish (p) and labour (w) respectively. Hence the net social benefit from fishing in the lake is:

$$pq - wL \qquad\qquad [B.13]$$

which is maximized when

$$pf' - w = 0 \qquad\qquad [B.14]$$

In terms of Fig. 3 the efficient level of L is L^*, where the vertical distance between the pq and wL curves is greatest. Notice that by comparing [B.14] and [B.12] L^* is always less than L^0 since $f' < q/L$: free access always leads to overfishing if there are diminishing returns. Diagrammatically, this means that the intersection of wL and $pf(L)$ in the figure always occurs at a value of L greater than that at which their slopes are equal.

The optimal outcome could be achieved if all the individuals with fishing rights can agree to reduce their total labour to L^*. Such an agreement may not be very likely if there are a large number of individuals with fishing rights or if it is difficult to police such an agreement. Any individual fisherman will always find it profitable to break the agreement. The marginal profit from extra L_i is (see [B.11])

$$p[q/L + (L_i/L)(f' - q/L)] - w \qquad\qquad [B.15]$$

and at L^* we have $pf' = w$ from [B.14]. Substituting for w in [B.15] and rearranging gives:

$$d\pi_i/dL_i = p(q/L - f')(1 - L_i/L) > 0 \qquad\qquad [B.16]$$

and so there will always be an incentive for an individual fisherman to increase his labour input. One solution is to divide the lake amongst the fishermen and give each of them exclusive fishing rights to his part of the lake. These rights will however require policing and enforcing and this may be costly. An alternative solution which might not require so large an expenditure on exclusion, would be to vest ownership of the lake in one individual. He could then organize the fishing of the lake himself and, since on our assumptions total profit from fish production from the lake is the net social benefit, maximization of profit leads to the efficient labour input (*provided the final fish market remains competitive*). Note, however, that in this example, the fishing is viewed as production rather than consumption – no-one derives utility from fishing itself. For a variation of this assumption, see Question 6 of Exercise 18B.

Unrestricted access leads in this simple example to overly intensive use, but it may also lead to other kinds of inefficiency because it weakens the incentive to individual decision makers to invest in improvements to the productivity of the resource, or to pay regard to the possibility of extinction of the fish stock through overfishing. Since a single individual cannot prevent others from using the resource, the benefits from investment or voluntary restraint will be spread over all other users, rather than being appropriated by himself. As a result it will not pay any single decision maker to undertake the investment (for example improving the fish stock), or to restrict his catch, even though the total benefits to all users exceed the cost. Even if the share of the benefits accruing to a single individual exceed their cost, the investment may not be undertaken, if each individual believes that he will benefit from the investment of other users. Because of non-excludability, investment by other users is a substitute for investment by any particular individual and if all individuals realise this, no investment may occur.

The market fails in this case because no market can exist in the absence of well-defined and easily enforceable rights to exclude by any *single* individual. There is nothing, in other words, which can be exchanged and no means by which individuals can capture or be made to bear *all* the results of their actions.

Public goods

The defining characteristic of a public good is that consumption of it by one individual does not actually or potentially reduce the amount available to be consumed by another individual. Examples include radio and television broadcasts and national defence. Any individual can listen to or watch the output of a broadcasting station, without preventing any other individual who possesses a radio or television receiver from consuming the same output. Any individual can increase his consumption of television broadcasts, up to the total number of hours broadcast, without reducing any other individual's actual or potential consumption. Broadcasts are an example of an *optional* public good in that one can choose to consume any amount of the output produced, including zero. Defence, which is the protection of civil and property rights against external threats, is on the other hand a *non-optional* public good, in that all inhabitants of the country consume the total quantity provided, and if one inhabitant is to be defended all will be.

In the case of non-optional public goods, if we denote the total quantity produced by Q_p, the total quantity consumed by Q_c, and the quantity consumed by the ith individual by q_i, we have

$$q_1 = q_2 = \ldots = q_n = Q_p$$

and

$$Q_c = n \cdot Q_p \qquad \text{[B.17]}$$

On the other hand, for an optional public good we have:

$$Q_p \geq q_1 \geq 0 \qquad Q_p \geq q_2 \geq 0 \ldots Q_p \geq q_n \geq 0$$

and

$$nQ_p \geq Q_c \geq 0 \qquad \text{[B.18]}$$

By contrast, private goods are the goods we have been using in our analysis in the rest of the book and have the characteristic that with a given output, an increase in one individual's consumption of a private good reduces the amount *available for consumption* by other individuals. Note that an increase in one individual's consumption of a private good need not actually reduce the level of consumption by any other individual, but only the amount *available* to be consumed by others. For example, if I occupy a seat in an empty railway compartment my consumption of the railway journey does not reduce that of anyone else but it reduces the *availability* of consumption to one other since I have occupied one seat. In the case of private goods the relationship between individual and total consumption and output is:

$$x_1 + x_2 + \ldots + x_n = X_c \leq X_p \qquad [B.19]$$

where x_i is the ith individual's consumption of the private good, X_c its total consumption, and X_p its total output.

Let us now derive the conditions necessary for optimality in an economy with public goods. Public goods enter utility functions just as do private goods, and so an individual's marginal rate of substitution between a public good and a private good is the amount of the private good he would be willing to give up for an additional unit of the public good. It is in other words his *marginal valuation* of public good q in terms of the private good. We will denote it by v_i^q. Public goods also enter production functions in the same way as private goods, and so we can interpret the marginal rate of transformation between a public good q and a private good as the marginal cost of q in terms of the private good, and denote it by C^q.

An additional unit of the public good will, since it is available for consumption by *all* individuals, be valued at $\sum_i^n v_i^q$: we must *sum* the marginal valuations. $\sum_i^n v_i^q$ is therefore the marginal social value of an additional unit of the public good in terms of a particular private good. The marginal social cost of the extra unit is the amount of the private good which must be forgone to produce the additional unit of q, i.e. C^q. Hence efficiency requires that

$$v_1^q + v_2^q + \ldots + v_n^q = C^q \qquad [B.20]$$

Suppose, for example, that $\sum v_i^q > C^q$; then the individuals would be prepared to give up, in total, $\sum v_i^q$ units of the private good for one unit of the public good, and in fact they would only have to give up C^q units. Hence $\sum v_i^q \neq C^q$ is incompatible with Pareto optimality.

By contrast, referring back to Chapter 17, we see that for private goods all individuals' marginal rates of substitution between two private goods should be equal to the marginal rate of transformation, or in terms of marginal valuations and marginal cost:

$$v_1^x = v_2^x = \ldots = v_n^x = C^x \qquad [B.21]$$

where v_i^x is the ith individual's marginal valuation, and C^x the marginal cost, of private good x in terms of some other private good. Notice the 'duality' of the relationship between [B.17] and [B.20], and [B.19] and [B.21]: public goods are defined (in the non-optional case) by an *equality* of consumption levels and the efficiency condition involves a *summation* of marginal valuations; private goods are defined by *summation* of consumption levels and the efficiency condition involves *equality* of marginal valuations.

'Market failure' in respect of public goods may take one of two forms. First, a public good might not be supplied at all in a competitive market economy, even though there exist scales of output at which the total benefit to consumers exceeds the total cost. Secondly, even if it is supplied in a market economy, the optimality condition in [B.20] may not be satisfied. Since this means that, though positive, the public good's output is non-optimal, the case of a (non-optimally) zero output of the public good can be viewed as a special, extreme case of geneal failure of the competitive market system to achieve an optimal allocation of resources to supply of the public good.

There are two reasons for this market failure. First, many public goods are non-excludable, for example defence; or excludable only at a high cost. In the case of broadcasting it is technically possible but expensive to make television or radio broadcasts excludable by scrambling the transmissions so that they can be received in intelligible form only by those who have metered descrambling devices fitted to their televisions or radios. However, this is not unique to public goods, and indeed is not shared by all public goods (Suggest examples).

The second reason market failure occurs with public goods arises out of their essential characteristic as defined in [B.17] or [B.18]. Suppose that a good is excludable, transferable, there are low information costs, many producers and many consumers. Then, as we have suggested in section A, if the good is private the resulting market equilibrium allocation will be optimal. Competition amongst producers will ensure that all consumers face the same price, which will be equal to the marginal cost of the good in each of the firms. Consumers will compete for a given output of the good and, since the opportunity cost of a unit sold to one consumer is the sale of that unit at the market price to some other consumer, no consumer will be offered or be able to force a sale at less than the market price. By contrast if the good is public, even though excludable, the opportunity cost of a unit sold to one customer *when output Q_p is given* is zero. Because the good is public, an additional unit consumed by one individual does not reduce the amount available for consumption by any other individual. This means that no consumer is competing against any other consumer for the units *he* consumes, *and so the market is not competitive*, despite the large numbers of buyers and sellers. If a consumer realizes that the marginal cost of his own consumption is zero, he may offer to the producer a very low payment for the right to consume the producer's output. If all consumers act in this way the amount offered by consumers will be insufficient to cover the costs of production and a zero output will result. In a market for a private good consumers realize that they cannot affect the market price and hence they adjust their consumption until their marginal valuation of the private good is equal to its price. Hence all consumers' marginal valuations are equal to the price, and in a competitive market price is equal to marginal cost, and [B.21] will be satisfied. In a market for a public good consumers' marginal valuations of the good will generally differ and so each should be charged a different price equal to his marginal valuation. The sum of these prices should then be equated to the marginal cost of the public good. Consumers, however, have no incentive *to reveal correctly* their marginal valuations of the public good since they do not regard the prices as unalterable, and so [B.20] will not be satisfied.

For example, suppose a number of farms are located in a river valley, and it is thought that the existing defences against flooding are inadequate. A local construction company, scenting business, asks each farmer how much he would be prepared to pay for an improvement in the flood defence. An individualistically rational farmer will reason as follows: 'I'm going to be asked to pay what my valuation is, and so I'll say something pretty small, certainly well below what I really think it's worth'. The problem is that if each farmer adopts this strategy, the construction company will find that it cannot cover the costs of the improvement, and so it is not made. The public good, flood prevention, is supplied at less than the optimal level because of the understatement of valuations of increments to it. This example then suggests the point: why doesn't 'the government' step in, undertake the construction, and then tax the farmers to finance it, possibly in proportion to the value it thinks each will benefit? This raises the general question of government action, to which we turn in the next two sections.

Exercise 18B

1.* Lack of information may prevent potentially advantageous exchanges occurring so that information is valuable and there will be a demand for it from potential traders. What characteristics of information as a commodity make it unlikely that it will be efficiently supplied (a) by the market (b) by the state?

2. Compare, from the point of view of the determinacy of bargaining in the sense of this section, an Eastern bazaar where haggling is commonplace, and a Western department store where prices are fixed.

3. Mr Brown has a beautiful unwalled garden, freely visible to all passers by. He decides to recoup some of the costs of his gardening by charging onlookers a price for the view. What kinds of exclusion costs must he incur?

4.* A monopolist may choose to supply an inefficient quality as well as quantity. Do there exist contracts between a monopolist and the consumers of his output which would remedy his inefficient choice of quality?

5.* (a) Show that free access to the fishing ground in the model in the text gives rise to a detrimental externality (i.e. $\partial \pi_i / \partial L_j < 0$) if and only if there are diminishing returns.

(b) Reformulate the diagrammatic analysis of free access resources in terms of average and marginal revenue product and cost curves. Derive the lake's supply curve of fish as a function of the relative price of fish in terms of labour (p/w) under free access and private ownership.

(c) Examine the implications of free access and private ownership respectively when the lake is the only source of supply for the type of fish in it, so that $p = p(q)$ and $p' < 0$.

6.* Discuss the implications for the fishing example of assuming that fishermen derive pleasure from fishing.

7. Is 'cable television' a public good?

8. Give examples of
(a) public goods which are supplied by private enterprise;
(b) private goods which are supplied by public enterprise.
Relate these examples to the discussion of public goods in this section.

9.* *Coase Theorem*: using the analysis of externalities and market failure given in this section, explain why the following propositions (the 'Coase Theorem') must hold:

(a) If property rights are well-defined, so that either a polluter has a clear right to pollute or the individual suffering the pollution has the clear right to stop him, and if costs of reaching an agreement are zero, the pollution externality will always be internalized;

(b) the Pareto optimal solution which will be reached is unique regardless of the distribution of property rights as long as income effects can be ignored.

C. The theory of the second best

The theory of the second best is directed towards the question of government policy formation in an economy in which there is market failure. We can distinguish three broad aims of government policy in its *microeconomic* aspects (that is, ignoring macroeconomic policy):

1. The correction of market failure itself: for example, the nationalization or regulation of monopolies, correction of externalities, provision of public goods.

2. The adjustment of the outcomes of competitive markets in the light of value judgements which differ from those underlying the Pareto criterion: for example it might be thought that some drugs and certain kinds of sexual activity are bad for people, or that education and the consumption of classical music are good, and so government intervenes to change the market outcome (Note that for this to differ from the first aim, there must be an element of paternalism and not simply a desire to correct for the externalities which consumption of these goods might generate).

3. The achievement of what would be regarded as a desirable distribution of real income.

The theory of the second best in general ignores the second of these aims and is concerned with the formulation of policies designed to correct market failure and change income distribution. We shall adopt that not entirely satisfactory restriction here.

Conceived of in the most general way, an economic policy is a rule for associating with each member of a given set of economic agents (consumers and firms) values of the elements of a given set of policy instruments. For example, we could think of a policy which seeks to correct the external detriment created by a firm which pollutes the atmosphere as specifying the optimal amount of the tax (the instrument) to be charged to the polluter (the economic agent), with a zero tax to all other economic agents in the economy.

Now if there were no restrictions whatsoever on the two sets involved in policy formulation – the set of economic agents to whom the instruments can be applied and the set of instruments and their values which can be adopted – then the policy-makers can achieve a Pareto optimum which is 'first best', i.e. a resource allocation which cannot be improved upon, in the Paretian sense, *given only* the constraints on resource availability and technology in the economy. In terms of Chapter 17, Fig. 11, the economy can be moved to a point such as B on the welfare frontier from a point such as C below it (at which there is market failure) or from a point such as A also on it (which let us say involves an 'undesirable' welfare distribution). If the sets are unrestricted then any policy of lump-sum redistributions is possible and so, as we saw in section 17E, income distributional goals can be achieved without losses of allocative efficiency – the economy can be moved around the welfare frontier. Likewise any specific instance of market failure can be corrected if the two sets are unrestricted. A monopolist can be forced to price at marginal cost (or can be subsidized to do so) and lump-sum redistributions used to correct whatever undesirable effects on income distribution follow from this. Public goods can be provided in optimal quantities by pricing their supply separately to each individual, externalities can be corrected by appropriate taxes and subsidies, and so on. Clearly, an important restriction which must be absent is that on the availability of information to the policy-maker. He must be assumed to know the values of the parameters in the functional relationships which the analyses in this chapter and the last show to be involved in the various kinds of policy problem.

The policy problem is regarded as one of seeking the 'second best' when *non-trivial restrictions* exist on one or both of the set of policy instruments and the set of economic agents whose behaviour can be directly influenced. Usually we would place severe restrictions on the possibility of lump-sum redistributions and as a result the income distribution would have to be varied by taxes and subsidies on incomes and outputs which create divergences between marginal rates of substitution and marginal rates of transformation. The second best policy problem is then to find the values of the taxes and subsidies which achieve the optimum trade-off between distributional equity and allocative efficiency. As we saw in section 17E, the problem can be represented as one of maximizing a Bergsonian social welfare function subject to a utility feasibility frontier, where the latter shows the available set of utility distributions *given* the restriction on policy instruments and will in general lie inside the first best welfare frontier.

In formulating a problem designed to find the optimal policy for correcting some form of market failure, a crucial first step is the specification of the restrictions on the set of policy instruments and their values and on the set of economic agents whose behaviour can be directly influenced, i.e. for whom values of the instruments can be chosen. Differences in these specifications will in general have important consequences both for the methods of analysis and for the form of policy prescriptions which result. Obviously, since the policy analysis is intended to be relevant to the real world, the restrictions on the two sets which are adopted should reflect those which exist in reality, *even if to the logical mind these latter may seem illogical.* This point is central to the controversy over 'piecemeal second best' policy (See P. Bohm (1967) and M. McManus (1967) for one side of the argument and R. G. Lipsey and K. Lancaster (1956/7) and O. Davis and A. Whinston (1965), (1967), for the other).

Thus, suppose the government has nationalized a monopoly and so can directly determine its pricing policy (nationalization is an element in the set of instruments). However, for some reason it has not nationalized a second monopoly whose output is a close substitute to that of the first (this in itself may seem illogical if we ignore the political realities of market economies). Now if the government can directly influence the behaviour of the private monopolist, for example by imposing a combination of a subsidy per unit of output and a lump-sum profits tax, it can ensure that its output is set where price equals marginal cost. If it also equates price to marginal cost in the nationalized monopoly, we have the 'first best' outcome with all consumers' marginal rates of substitution between the two outputs equal to the marginal rate of transformation (ratio of marginal costs). If, on the other hand, the government *cannot* tax or subsidize the private monopolist directly, or indeed alter its behaviour in any way *except through the demand interdependence with the nationalized monopoly*, we have to exclude the private monopoly from the set of economic agents for whom values of policy instruments can be directly prescribed. The policy problem is then to choose a price for the nationalized monopoly when this is *the only instrument* determining the resource allocation in both monopolies. Given this extremely strong restriction, we would expect the optimal policy for the nationalized monopoly to differ from that when the first best is available, and this can be shown to be true (Perhaps the simplest such demonstration is given in R. Rees (1976), Ch. 6).

The first type of policy just described, where the monopolist can be directly influenced, is clearly more powerful than the second, which would

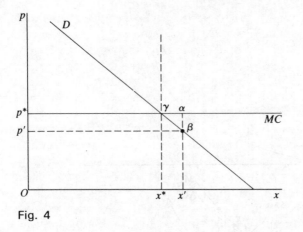

Fig. 4

be called 'piecemeal second best policy'. However, the question of which is the more appropriate approach to adopt in modelling the problem cannot be resolved at the purely logical level (illogical though it may appear that a government uses only a piecemeal policy) but requires a specification of the constraints on agents and instruments which are *actually* in force. Such 'illogicalities' in government policies do exist, at least in part because policies are carried out by a range of different agencies with differing goals and amongst which communication and coordination are imperfect. The real world of economic policy is far removed from the idealized 'central planner' of economics text books.

We can illustrate these ideas about the theory of the second best with a specific example. Suppose that a public agency is planning to construct a road bridge across an estuary, on which a toll will be charged. The demand curve in Fig. 4 shows the estimated relation between the toll, p, and the desired number of trips per day across the bridge. For simplicity it is assumed that the demand curve is constant over time – there is neither long-term growth nor seasonal variation. Trips across the bridge are also assumed to take place at a constant rate throughout the day – there are no 'peak-load' problems. The *LMC* curve in the figure reflects the assumption that total costs per day increase proportionately with the capacity of the bridge. The optimal solution in an economy without market failure would be to set a toll of $p^* = LMC$ and construct a bridge of capacity x^* – this is the 'marginal cost price solution'.

Suppose however that there is market failure in the economy. A road already exists around the estuary, *on which no toll is charged* and which is severely congested. The nature of the market failure here is similar to that of the fishery problem analysed in the previous section – overutilization of a common access resource. Thus (*a*) in Fig. 5 shows how the total costs per day to the users of the estuary road increase with the number of trips. These costs include not only petrol and vehicle wear and tear costs, but also maintenance costs of the roadway and the cost of the time spent by

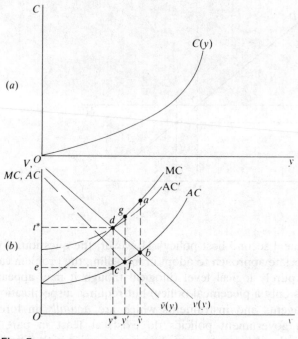

Fig. 5

motorists in making the trip (we assume we know the value of motorists' time). The curvature of the total cost function $C(y)$ reflects the fact that as traffic flow increases journey time lengthens and so time and petrol costs increase more than proportionately with total trips, y. In (b) of the figure the marginal and average cost curves corresponding to $C(y)$ are shown, with of course *MC* everywhere above *AC*.

Let v denote the 'full price' a motorist pays to make a trip on the road, i.e. the cost to himself in terms of petrol, vehicle wear and tear and time, *plus* any toll which may be charged. Then $v(y)$ shows the demand curve for trips on the road–the lower the full price the greater the number of trips. Moreover, at any level of y, say $\hat{y}$, the marginal trip along the road has a value to the motorist who makes it of exactly $v(\hat{y})$.

In the absence of a toll on the road, each motorist would take as the cost to himself of making a trip along the road the *average cost, AC*, since this is the actual cost incurred by each motorist who makes the trip. Hence, $\hat{y}$ is the resulting equilibrium number of trips along the road – the value of the marginal trip is just equal to the *perceived cost* to the motorist who makes it, at b in the figure. However at this equilibrium the true cost of the marginal trip is *MC* at a: in costing his trip at the *average* cost the marginal user is ignoring the extra costs he imposes through longer journey times on all other users by his decision to make the trip, and this is measured by ab. There is therefore a resource misallocation. The Pareto optimal solution would be to impose a toll of $et^* = cd$ in the figure, since this would result in the *perceived* average cost curve AC' and an equilibrium at y^*, where marginal cost MC is equal to marginal value $v(y^*)$. This solution is, however, ruled out by the absence of a pricing mechanism in the market for trips along the road. The *marginal welfare loss* – the excess of social cost over value of the marginal trip – is given by $MC - v(\hat{y}) = ab$.

Returning now to the bridge, clearly it will be a substitute for the estuary road. Assume that the equilibrium position for the road shown in Fig. 5(*b*) is that which would obtain if the bridge were built at capacity x^* and a toll of p^* charged – the two Figs. 4 and 5(*b*) are in a consistent equilibrium relationship with each other. We can now show that the optimal second best solution *given the restriction that no toll can be charged on the road* involves a departure from marginal cost pricing on the bridge. Thus suppose the bridge toll were reduced from p^* to p', and capacity increased from x^* to x'. *In terms of the bridge alone* there is an apparent resource misallocation since the value of the extra resources absorbed by the bridge – area $x^*\gamma\alpha x'$ – exceeds the value of the extra trips to those who make them – area $x^*\gamma\beta x'$. At toll p' the *marginal* welfare loss on the bridge is $p^* - p' = \alpha\beta$. However, the reduction in bridge toll will have caused a fall in the demand for road trips, say to $\bar{v}(y)$ in Fig. 5(*b*). As a result there is a reduction in net welfare losses ('congestion costs') on the estuary road which may more than offset the welfare losses on the bridge, since the marginal welfare loss on the road fg exceeds the marginal welfare loss on the bridge $\alpha\beta$. In other words, the savings in social costs on the road could be used to meet the excess of the value of resources absorbed by the additional bridge trips over their value to those who make them, and there would still be a net gain. Thus the toll of p^* on the bridge cannot be Pareto optimal. The necessary condition for the (second best) Pareto optimal bridge toll p^0 is:

$$(p^* - p^0)\frac{\partial x}{\partial p} = (-)(MC - v(y))\frac{\partial y}{\partial p} \qquad \text{[C.1]}$$

or: marginal welfare loss on bridge = marginal welfare gain on road. Only if these two marginal welfare changes, the first imposed by the extra trip made across the bridge, the second saved on the marginal trip not made on the road, as a result of the bridge toll reduction, are equal will it not be possible to change the bridge toll further and achieve a net welfare gain.

Quite clearly we see in [C.1] that either:

(*a*) $MC = v(y)$, i.e. no marginal welfare loss on the road, or
(*b*) $\partial y/\partial p = 0$, i.e. a change in the bridge toll has no effect on road demand,

is sufficient for $p^* = p^0$, the 'first best' solution. The former will only be satisfied if resource allocation on the road can be optimized directly, which is ruled out by assumption.

We therefore see the characteristic solution to 'piecemeal second best' problems. This was expressed by R. G. Lipsey and K. Lancaster in the following way: even when the policy-maker is able to implement the first best solution ($p = p^*$) in the sector he controls (the bridge) this solution will not in general be correct (Pareto optimal) when that sector is interdependent with one in which the first best condition $(MC = v(y))$ does not hold and *cannot directly be achieved.*

The second best solution is in general inferior to the first best (explain why), and so we may be led to question the logic of the constraint which rules out some economic agents (the road users) from the set to whom an instrument (a toll) can be applied, leaving bridge users as the only economic agents who can be *directly* influenced and the bridge toll as the only instrument. The argument that a road toll would cost 'too much' to administer looks dubious if the bridge toll would not be ruled out on these grounds. Certainly, in reality many major river bridges carry tolls while, in the United Kingdom, virtually no roads do so. The illogicality must stem from an inconsistency in the way in which transport policy is formulated and applied, for which in turn there may well exist *rational* grounds in terms of the preferences of politicians and bureaucrats. This is a suitable point at which to consider a generalization of these ideas, in the concept of 'government failure'.

Exercise 18C

1. Discuss possible explanations for the fact that a new bridge may carry a toll while use of an existing road would remain unpriced.
2.* Adapt the analysis of this section to the problem of formulating a second-best pricing policy for a nationalized monopoly which produces an output strongly complementary in demand to a private monopoly output.

D. Government action and government failure

Types of government action

As we have just seen, the possibility, indeed the probability, of market failure raises the question of action by the political authorities in an economy as a means of rectifying departures from the (first best) Pareto optimality conditions. This inefficiency is, of course, not the only reason for government intervention. An allocation may be Pareto optimal but, according to one's value judgements, distributionally inequitable. It might also be argued that in some cases individuals are not the best judges of their own actions so that the Pareto conditions cease to have any force even as necessary conditions for an optimal allocation. We will, however, again concentrate in this section on government action directed towards increasing the efficiency of resource allocation.

Firstly, the government can legislate to modify the system of property rights governing the exchange of goods and services. Common access resources can be transformed into private property by vesting the right to exclusive use and disposal in a single individual, as, for example, in the acts by which the commons were enclosed in England. The ability to exclude can be strengthened by changes in the criminal law. The terms on which exchanges can be made may be restricted by legislation. Regulatory bodies can be established to mitigate the market power of monopolies by limiting their prices or profits. Minimum levels of consumption of goods, such as education, generating beneficial externalities, may be laid down. Public bodies may be set up to regulate common access resources, as an alternative to vesting ownership in private individuals.

Second, the prices at which exchanges take place may be varied by the imposition of taxes or subsidies to reduce the production and consumption of commodities which give rise to detrimental externalities and to increase those of commodities causing beneficial externalities. Effluent taxes equal to the marginal damage caused by firms' discharge of effluent may be levied so that private and social costs of effluent discharge are equated. Subsidies may be paid to increase the output of monopolized goods.

Thirdly, the state may intervene in the allocation mechanism directly by producing goods and services itself. Monopolies may be nationalized and their outputs sold at marginal cost. Education may be produced at zero price to encourage its consumption. The government will provide police and legal services to determine and enforce individual property rights.

Government failure

The government has a variety of policy instruments which it can use in the attempt to improve the efficiency of resource allocation. We cannot, however, conclude that government action will necessarily lead to Pareto optimality, even of the second best, because it must first be established that the government will be both willing and able to act in the required way. We need therefore a *positive* theory of government decision-making in the same way that prediction of consumer or firm behaviour requires a positive theory of consumer or firm decision-making. We cannot here construct such a theory but we can mention two propositions which have been advanced in support of the argument that, to put it no higher, it is not obvious that government intervention in the economy will fully correct for market failure.

First, the policies pursued by the state result from the actions and interactions of voters, politicians, civil servants, bureaucrats and managers and workers in public firms. We cannot assume that any of these individuals are completely altruistic in the sense that they are motivated solely by the desire to achieve a Pareto optimal resource allocation. Voters may be concerned about the effect of policies on their tax bills; politicians about their chances of re-election; managers of public firms may prefer not to devote a large amount of time and effort to producing output at least cost; bureaucrats may adopt the size of their bureau's budgeted expenditure on its staff as a measure of their status.

Secondly *information is required* for policy making and control, both in deciding what policy should be adopted, and in ensuring that it has in fact been implemented and the desired result achieved. But information is not a free good: it is often dispersed over many individuals, it is costly to acquire and to transmit.

These two factors – non-altruism and information costs – mean that in order to predict the ways in which government will intervene in the economy we must examine the institutions in the public sector. The institutions will constrain the actions of individuals in the public sector and provide incentives for particular sorts of behaviour and the production, processing and transmission of particular kinds of information. An examination of the way in which institutional frameworks structure the rewards and penalties for different types of individual behaviour is required, in order to decide whether a particular institutional setting will induce efficient behaviour. Consider the following examples.

Majority voting and public goods

Suppose that the output of a public good q is to be determined by majority vote of the n consumers in the economy, with the total cost of the public good $C(q)$ being covered by a tax levied equally on all consumers. The ith consumer has a marginal valuation of the public good of $v_i(q)$ which declines with q. Each consumer pays a tax of $C(q)/n$, and so the marginal tax cost to consumer i of the public good is $C^q(q)/n$, where C^q is the marginal cost of the public good. If the ith consumer could choose the output of the public good he would set q so that its marginal value was just equal to its marginal cost to him in extra taxes:

$$v_i(q) = C^q(q)/n \qquad \text{[D.1]}$$

If the political system were a dictatorship and i the dictator, [D.1] would determine the output of the public good. Comparison with [B.20] indicates that the output of q is rather unlikely to be optimal since $n \cdot v_i(q)$ may be greater or less than $\sum_i v_i(q)$. However we are assuming that there is a majority voting on the public good rather than dictatorship. Since different individuals may have different preferences and hence different marginal valuations, they will disagree on the best level of q. Suppose that there are five individuals, all of whom wish for different q, i.e. the q satisfying [D.1] differs for each i. Label the consumers in ascending order of their desired q. Hence individual 1 desires a smaller q than individual 2, who desires a smaller level than individual 3 and so on. Fig. 6 illustrates, with q_i^* the desired q for individual i. All five consumers will vote in favour of increasing q from zero to q_1^*. Four consumers will vote for increasing q from q_1^* to q_2^* and one will vote against; three will vote for an increase to q_3^* and two will vote against; and two consumers will vote for an increase from q_3^* to q_4^* and three against. Hence the level of q determined by majority voting in this five consumer economy is q_3^* since a majority of votes are cast against an increase or a decrease from q_3^*. The q chosen in this particular institutional setting is determined by

$$v_3(q) = C^q/5 \qquad \text{[D.2]}$$

which is not likely to satisfy [B.19] since $5 \cdot v_3(q)$ may be larger or smaller than $\sum_{i=1}^{5} v_i(q)$.

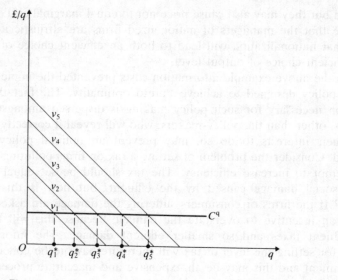

Fig. 6

Efficiency in nationalized industries

As a second example of the way in which non-market allocation mechanisms may fail consider the problem of ensuring that a nationalized industry is run optimally by its managers. Even if the political authorities to whom the managers are responsible have the inclination, they will lack the necessary knowledge to verify that the particular output level chosen is the optimal one. They could instruct the managers to produce where price equals marginal cost, but they would be unable to confirm that the particular marginal cost curve on which the nationalized firm operates is that derived from a least cost choice of production techniques. There will be no incentive for the managers to minimize production cost, since political authorities' ignorance of production conditions means that no workable system of pecuniary incentives could be devised. The gains from lower cost production will accrue to managers in a very attenuated form in their role as consumers or taxpayers when the gains are spread over *all* taxpayers or consumers.

There will probably be little product market competition for the firm so that a failure to minimize costs and consequently higher prices will not lead to the firm being unable to sell its product. Finally, by definition, there is no external incentive from the threat of takeover, such as may lead managers of private firms to aim at maximizing profits and hence minimizing costs.

Alternatively, the managers could be set minimum profit targets, since profit figures are easily obtainable from the firm's accounts, in an attempt to imitate the constraints on the managers of private firms when there are active and informed owners, product market competition or the threat of takeover. Such targets may lead to a lowering of the cost of production but they may also cause price not to equal marginal cost. Unless we assume that the managers of nationalized firms are altruistic it seems unlikely that nationalization will lead to both an efficient choice of inputs and an efficient choice of output level.

In the above example information costs prevented the implementation of a policy designed to achieve Pareto optimality. The fact that the information necessary for such policy making is dispersed amongst many individuals, other than the policy-makers, who will reveal it correctly only if it is in their interests to do so, may prevent an optimal policy being formulated. Consider the problem of setting a tax on firms polluting a river in an attempt to increase efficiency. The tax should be set equal to the marginal social damage caused by the effluent, but how is this to be measured? If the firms or consumers suffering the damage are asked, they will have an incentive to overstate the damage because this will lead to higher effluent taxes and so smaller effluent damage. The information necessary for setting the level of tax will therefore have to be collected by the government and this may be an expensive and inaccurate process.

A comparative institutions approach to policy-making

A demonstration of the ways in which one particular institutional framework may fail to satisfy the marginal conditions for Pareto optimality does not in itself provide a conclusive argument in favour of adopting an alternative framework. Market failure does not in itself imply the necessity for government action, and likewise government failure does not in itself imply that the scope of market allocation should be extended. Since both institutional frameworks may fail to satisfy the Pareto optimality conditions, a move from one to the other is justified on such grounds only if one institutional framework is more efficient than the other. This will depend on the particular cases being considered: what is required is a comparison of the way different institutions allocate resources in each case.

As an illustration of the kind of analysis which might be conducted, consider again the case of the proposed construction of a bridge which we now, however, assume *can only be built in one size*, with high costs of construction and low constant marginal running costs. In Fig. 7 D is the demand curve for trips across the bridge, MR the corresponding marginal revenue curve, the marginal cost of trips across the bridge is r, the capacity of the bridge is q_{max} trips per year and the annuitised construction cost of the bridge is K. Two interdependent decisions must be made: (*a*) if the bridge is built what is the optimal number of trips per annum across it (or alternatively what toll should be charged)? (*b*) should the bridge be built at all? Assuming that the rest of the economy satisfies the conditions for Pareto optimality, a consumer's marginal valuation of a trip is equal to the price he pays for it. Optimal use of the bridge requires that each consumer's marginal valuation be equal to the marginal cost of extra trips (from condition [B.21]). Hence the optimal price p^* is equal to r and there should be q^* trips across the bridge. There is spare capacity in that $q^* < q_{max}$ and

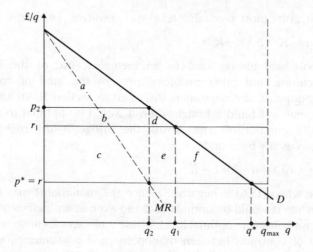

Fig. 7

consumers could be induced to use the bridge fully by a reduction in p. This however would be inefficient since their marginal valuation of these additional trips is less than the extra cost incurred.

The second decision, whether to build the bridge, is made by comparing the total cost of providing the bridge with the total benefit to consumers *at its actual rate of use*. If the bridge is used optimally at q^* the total benefit to consumers is the total amount they would be prepared to pay for q^*. This willingness to pay $W(q^*)$ is measured by the area under the demand curve up to q^*:

$$W(q^*) = a + b + c + d + e + f + p^*q^* \qquad [D.3]$$

The total cost of supplying q^* is the construction cost plus the running costs:

$$C(q^*) = K + rq^* \qquad [D.4]$$

The difference between the benefit [D.3] and the cost [D.4] is the net social benefit when the bridge is used optimally:

$$W - C = a + b + c + d + e + f - K \qquad [D.5]$$

Where we have used the fact that $p^* = r$. The bridge should be built or not as [D.5] is positive or negative.

Now let us compare the ways in which the two decisions on construction and use of the bridge would be made by a private monopolist on the one hand and by a public sector decision-taker on the other. Assuming that the monopolist wishes to maximize his profits he will, if the bridge is built, set $MR = r$ and charge a price p_2 so that $q_2 < q^*$ trips are made. He will base his decision on whether to build the bridge or not on a comparison of the construction cost with the excess of his revenue $(p_2 q_2)$ over the running costs rq_2. He will build the bridge if his profit from doing so and operating it at its most profitable level q_2 is positive, i.e. if:

$$(p_2 - r)q_2 - K = b + c - K > 0 \qquad\qquad [\text{D}.6]$$

Private monopoly will always lead to an inefficient use of the bridge ($q_2 < q^*$) if exclusion and other problems prevent the kind of contract between the monopolist and consumers discussed in section B. In addition the monopolist may not build a bridge when it would be optimal to do so. Note that if the number of trips across the bridge is q_2, consumers' willingness to pay is $a + b + c$ and:

$$W(q_2) - C(q_2) = a + b + c - K \qquad\qquad [\text{D}.7]$$

may be positive when [D.6] is negative. Hence the monopolist may fail to build a bridge when it would be optimal to do so even at an inefficient price which restricts use below the optimal level. These inefficiencies arise because the feasible set of contracts between monopolist and consumers does not permit consumers to bribe the monopolist to act optimally.

The inefficiencies resulting from monopoly would not arise with an ideally functioning public sector: the decision to build would be made by reference to consumers' willingness to pay rather than their actual payments (the revenue from the bridge). The toll would be set at its efficient level p^* and the resulting losses

$$C(q^*) - p^*q^* = K + rq^* - p^*q^* = K \qquad\qquad [\text{D}.8]$$

(i.e. the construction costs) could be financed out of general taxation. We cannot, however, conclude that optimality dictates that the bridge ought to be supplied by the state until we have examined how public supply would *actually* operate. There are a number of reasons for supposing that public sector decision-making about the construction and use of the bridge may not be optimal either.

For example:

(*a*) The political authorities may not use the sign of [D.5] as the criterion for building the bridge. They may instead be motivated by the effect of the bridge on their chances of retaining office. The bridge may, for example, be situated in a marginal constituency, and even if the benefits were less than the costs, the benefits will accrue to the voters in the constituency and may be substantial enough to secure their votes. The construction cost will be spread across all taxpayers in all constituencies and may therefore not hit each taxpayer hard enough to influence his vote adversely. The same circumstances may lead to an inefficiently low price being charged for use of the bridge.

(*b*) A decision to build the bridge must be based on an estimate of the demand curve for the bridge made before the bridge is actually built. This problem faces both the monopolist and the public sector decision makers. It is not at all clear which institutional setting will lead to more accurate estimates. A private firm bears the cost of any erroneous demand estimates. An erroneous decision to build will result in irreversible losses. A mistaken decision not to build however may not be so easily identified and in any case may be rectified later. Managers in a private firm, particularly if risk-averse, may therefore underestimate rather than overestimate demand, thus further increasing the possibility of an inefficient decision not to build. In the case of public supply, losses do not necessarily indicate a mistaken decision to build since a loss would be incurred in any case if $p = r$. A mistaken decision to build could only be identified by a deliberate *ex post* comparison of the estimated demand with the actual demand. Since the public sector decision makers have no incentive to audit past decisions, and *individual* taxpayers only a very diluted one, mistakes may not be discovered. Given the factors mentioned under point (a), this may lead to a tendency to build the bridge when it would not be warranted by an objective comparison of costs and benefits, via a tendency to take an optimistic view of future demand.

(c) A publicly supplied bridge may have a higher than minimum construction cost because of the lack of incentives for public officials to ensure that costs are minimized. If we denote the construction cost under public supply by K_1, the net benefits from the bridge under public supply and efficient pricing can be written:

$$a + b + c + d + e + f - K_1 \qquad\qquad \text{[D.9]}$$

Under private supply the net social benefits are:

$$W(q_2) - C(q_2) = a + b + c - K \qquad\qquad \text{[D.10]}$$

and hence public supply may be less efficient than private supply if [D.9] is less than [D.10] or

$$K_1 - K > d + e + f \qquad\qquad \text{[D.11]}$$

Private supply leads to a loss in net social benefit due to inefficient pricing of $d + e + f$, against which must be set the loss in net social benefit under public supply, due to non-minimized construction costs, of $K_1 - K$.

(d) Similarly, a publicly operated bridge may have marginal running costs of r_1 rather than the minimum marginal running cost of r under a profit maximizing (and hence cost minimizing) private supplier. If the public bridge is priced at actual marginal running cost so that $p = p_1 = r_1$ then net social benefit is:

$$W(q_1) - r_1 q_1 - K = a + b + d - K \qquad\qquad \text{[D.12]}$$

(Why is p_1 the optimal price under public supply *in these circumstances*?) Comparing [D.12] and [D.10], we see that public operation is preferable if

$$d > c \qquad\qquad \text{[D.13]}$$

The choice is between private supply at q_2 and public supply of q_1 with higher running costs. c is the additional running costs incurred on output up to q_2 with public operation. This must be compared with the net gain resulting from the higher output of a public bridge compared with private operation. The benefit to consumers of the additional $q_1 - q_2$ units is the area under the demand curve between these two points and the cost of producing it is $r_1(q_1 - q_2)$. The net gain from the increased output is therefore d. [D.13] will hold provided the public managers of the bridge are not 'too inefficient'. If they are very inefficient then we may have $q_2 > q_1$ and a larger output under monopoly than with public operation.

Exercise 18D

1.* Analyse the implications of the following possible policies towards monopoly:
   (a) maximum price control;
   (b) special 'excess' profits taxes;
   (c) maximum rate of return control;
   (d) nationalization;
   (e) competitive tendering for the right to monopolize an industry, whereby potential monopolists buy the right from the state.

2.* Show that in general with n consumers (n is odd) the output of the public good under majority voting is that desired by the median $((n-1)/2$ th) consumer. How would you expect the results of majority voting on the supply of a public good to differ if the cost of the public good is covered by a proportional income tax and consumers' marginal valuations of the public good are (a) positively (b) negatively correlated with their income?

3.* Suppose the output of a public good is determined by asking consumers what their marginal valuations are and then equating the sum of the stated marginal valuations to the marginal cost of the public good. Would there be too large or too small an output if the cost of the good was covered by
   (a) equal taxes on consumers
   (b) a proportional income tax
   (c) consumption taxes on the public good equal to the stated marginal valuations?

4.* How would the comparison of monopoly and public supply of the bridge in the text be affected if it is assumed that the monopolist's objective function is not profit but one of the alternatives discussed in Chapter 13?

References and further reading

A good summary of the traditional approach to market failure is:

   F. M. Bator. 'The anatomy of market failure', *Quarterly Journal of Economics*, August 1958.

The approach to market failure in this chapter is based on:

   R. Coase. 'The problem of social cost', *Journal of Law and Economics*, October 1960;

   H. Demsetz. 'The exchange and enforcement of property rights', *Journal of Law and Economics*, October 1964;

K. J. Arrow. 'The organisation of economic activity: issues pertinent to the choice of market versus non-market allocation', in R. H. Haveman and J. Margolis (eds.), *Public Expenditures and Policy Analysis*, Markham, Chicago, 1970;

and examples of its application are:

S. N. Cheung. 'The fable of the bees: an economic investigation', *Journal of Law and Economics*, April 1973;

T. L. Anderson and **P. J. Hill.** 'The evolution of property rights: a study of the American West', *Journal of Law and Economics*, April 1975.

A useful book of readings on the economic implications of property rights is

E. G. Furubotn and **S. Pejovich** (eds), *The Economics of Property Rights*, Ballinger, Cambridge, Massachusetts, 1974.

On the theory of the second-best, see:

R. G. Lipsey and **K. Lancaster.** 'The general theory of the second best', *Review of Economic Studies*, 1956/7;

O. A. Davis and **A. Whinston.** 'Welfare economics and the theory of the second best', *Review of Economic Studies*, 1965;

O. A. Davis and **A. Whinston.** 'Piecemeal policy in the theory of second best', *Review of Economic Studies*, 1967;

R. Rees. *Public Enterprise Economics*, Weidenfeld and Nicholson, London, 1976, Chs. 3, 6;

P. Bohm. 'On the theory of second best', *Review of Economic Studies*, 1967;

M. McManus. 'Private and social costs in the theory of second best', *Review of Economic Studies*, 1967.

For one solution to the second best problem of achieving an optimal distribution of income when lump sum taxes are impossible, see:

P. A. Diamond and **J. A. Mirrlees.** 'Optimal taxation and public production', *American Economic Review*, March and June 1971.

Some positive theories of decision making in the public sector are surveyed in:

D. C. Mueller. *Public Choice*, Cambridge University Press, Cambridge, 1979.

Chapter 19

Choice under uncertainty*

A. Introduction

The analysis of much of the preceding chapters has assumed that all decisions are taken in conditions of certainty. That is, any decision would result in one and only one outcome. When a firm chooses a set of input quantities, there is only one level of output which will result, and it knows 'for certain' the profit which it will receive from the sale of each output. This is held to be true, no matter how far in the future the production and selling will take place. Likewise, in planning their purchases of goods and services, and borrowing or lending decisions, households are assumed to know with certainty the expenditure and utility associated with each consumption vector.

This obviously does not realistically describe the world. There may be *technological uncertainty*, whereby the firm may not be able to predict with certainty the output level which would result from a given set of input quantities. This may arise, for example, from the possibility of variation of exogenous variables which affect the outcome but which are outside the firm's control, e.g. weather conditions. There may also be *market uncertainty*: a single household or firm may not be able to predict with certainty the market prices at which it will buy or sell, though it has to take decisions in advance of acquiring this information. This uncertainty will be very much associated with disequilibrium and change: if an economy were permanently in long-run static equilibrium, then firms and households would expect to trade at equilibrium prices, which, by experience, become known. If, however, changes are taking place through time which change equilibrium positions, the individual agents in the markets cannot know the new equilibria in advance, and can only form expectations of prices which they know may be wrong.

Extension of the theory to take account of uncertainty has two main aims. It should first of all tell us something about the usefulness and validity of the concepts and propositions already derived. What becomes of the conclusions about the workings of a decentralized price mechanism, for example? Can we still establish existence and optimality of competitive equilibrium? Are the predictions about households' and firms' responses to changes in parameters affected qualitatively? The answers are important from both positive and normative points of view. Secondly, it is clear that many important aspects of economic activity cannot adequately be analysed, if at all, without explicit recognition of uncertainty. For example, the joint-stock limited liability company, the basic institutional form of the firm in capitalist economies, has no real rationale in a world of certainty, and so neither has the stock market. Insurance, futures markets and speculation are forms of economic activity which cannot be understood except in the context of uncertainty, and relaxation of the certainty assumption would give us new insights into many other areas, for example investment decisions. Hence the second aim of the economics of uncertainty is to extend economic analysis to take account of a class of problems which cannot otherwise be satisfactorily treated.

Our procedure in developing some aspects of the economics of uncertainty will parallel that adopted in the first part of this book. We begin with the optimization problem of a single decision-taker and construct a theory about how he solves it. The nature of this solution then provides a basis for generalization to markets and to the economy as a whole. The optimization problem under uncertainty can be thought of as having the same basic structure as under certainty: objects of choice; objective function; and constraints defining a feasible set of choice objects. The main interest centres on the first two of these, and, in particular, the construction of a set of axioms which allows us to define a preference ordering, representable by a 'utility function', over the objects of choice.

B. A formalization of 'uncertainty'

Our view of uncertainty is that it arises because the consequence of a decision is seen to be not a single sure outcome but rather a number of possible outcomes. Our first task in developing a theory of choice under uncertainty is to set out a precise formalization of the decision-taking situation under uncertainty. We can begin by distinguishing three kinds of variables which play a part in an economic system. These are:

(i) The choice variables of the decision-taker, those variables whose values are directly under his control. Such variables are not only endogenous to the model of the economic system, but are also endogenous to the model of the individual economic agent. Examples abound in earlier chapters including firms' output levels and consumers' purchases.

(ii) Variables whose values are determined by the operation of the economic system, i.e. by the interaction of the choices of individual economic agents, and which are regarded as parameters by them. For example, in a *competitive* economy prices are such *determined variables*. These variables are endogenous to the model of the economic system, but exogenous to the model of the individual economic agent.

(iii) *Environmental variables*, whose values are determined by some mechanism outside the economic system, and which can be regarded as parameters of the economic system. They influence its outcome, but are not in turn affected by it. The weather is an obvious example.

Now let us suppose that the economy operates over only two periods, period 1 (the present) and period 2 (the future). In period 1, the environmental variables all take on specific values which are known to all economic agents, and we can assume that the economy works in such a way as to produce a resource allocation and a set of relative prices, as has been analysed in earlier chapters. Now if there were complete independence between the decisions made in period 1 and those to be made in period 2, then the state of knowledge existing at period 1 about the environmental variables at period 2 is irrelevant. In this case, decisions for period 2 can be left for then, and need not impinge on decision-taking at period 1. However, we take it to be the case that this kind of *temporal separability* of decision-taking does not exist. At period 1, economic agents will have to choose values of variables such as investment (purchase of durable goods), financial assets (bonds and shares), and money balances, all of which have significance for period 2. For that reason, agents' *plans* for the values of variables they will choose at period 2, influenced by their *expectations* about the values of variables outside their control at period 2 – determined variables such as prices, and environmental variables like the weather – will condition their choices at period 1. We therefore need a theoretical framework within which to analyse the formation of plans and expectations, and their influence on current choices.

We proceed as follows: suppose there exists a vector of environmental variables $(e_1, e_2, \ldots, e_n)$, where each environmental variable is capable of taking on a *finite number of values*. Let E_j denote the set of values which can be taken by environmental variable e_j, $j = 1, 2, \ldots n$. For example, e_1 could be the average temperature over period 2, measured to the nearest degree centigrade, and E_1 would be the set $\{e_1 \mid 50°\text{C} \geq e_1 \geq -80°\text{C}\}$, which includes all values with non-zero probabilities (given non-catastrophic climatic conditions), and has a finite number of elements (since the temperature is measured in units of $1°\text{C}$). Then, we define *a state of the world* as a specific combination of values of the environmental variables, i.e. as a specific value of the vector (e_j). For convenience, denote such a specific value by s. Since each e_j can take on only a finite number of values, the number of possible values of s, which we can denote by S, is also finite, but possibly large. We can thus use $s = 1, 2, \ldots S$ as an index, to denote a value of any choice variable or determined variable in the state of the world s (the set of possible states of the world, $\{s\}$, is the *Cartesian product* of the E_j, i.e. $\{s\} = E_1 \times E_2 \times \ldots \times E_n$).

From this discussion, the three fundamental properties of the set of states of the world should be clear:

(i) the set is *exhaustive*, in that it contains *all* the states of the world which could possibly obtain at period 2;

(ii) members of the set are *mutually exclusive*, in that the occurrence of any one rules out the occurrence of any other;

(iii) the states of the world are *outside the control* of any decision-taker, so that the occurrence of any one of them cannot be influenced by the choice of any economic agent, or indeed by any coalition of agents.

The definition and properties of these 'states of the world' are basic to all subsequent analysis. They can be regarded as an attempt to eliminate the elements of doubt, apprehension, and muddle which are part of the every-day meaning of the word 'uncertainty', and to give the situation a precise formalization, for purposes of the theory. Three further assumptions we shall make, which are important in the analysis of the following chapter, are:

(*a*) All decision-takers have in their minds the same sets of states of the world – they classify the possible combinations of environmental variables in the same way.

(*b*) When period 2 arrives, all decision-takers will be able to recognize which state of the world in fact exists, and will all agree on this.

(*c*) At period 1, each decision-taker is able to assign a probability to the event that a particular state of the world will occur at period 2; these probabilities may differ for different decision-takers, but all probability assignments satisfy the basic probability laws: the probability associated with the sth state by decision-taker i, denoted p_s^i, lies on the interval $1 \geq p_s^i \geq 0$, with $p_s^i = 1$ implying that i regards state s as certain to occur, and $p_s^i = 0$ implying that he regards state s as certain *not* to occur; the probability of one or another of several states occurring is the sum of their probabilities (with the probability of their simultaneous occurrence of course zero), and, in particular, one of the S states *must* occur, i.e. $\sum_{s=1}^{S} p_s^i = 1$, all i.

Each of these assumptions is quite strong, and plays an important part in what follows. The first would appear to be necessary if we are to portray decision-takers as making agreements in *state-contingent* terms: in order for one to agree with another that 'if state 1 occurs I will do x, in return for your doing y if state 2 occurs', it is necessary that they should understand each other's references to states.

The second assumption is also required for the formation and discharge of agreements framed in state-contingent terms. If parties to an agreement would differ about which state of the world exists *ex post*, they are unlikely to agree *ex ante* on some exchange which is contingent on states of the world. The assumption also rules out problems which might arise from differences in the information which different decision-takers may possess. Suppose, for example, that A cannot tell whether it is state 1 or state 2 which actually prevails at period 2, while B does know. Then A is unlikely to conclude an agreement with B under which, say, A gains and B

loses if state 1 occurs, while B gains and A loses if state 2 occurs, because of course A could be exploited by B.

The assumption that decision-takers assign numerical probabilities to states of the world, where these probabilities obey the usual probability laws, is a strong one. It seems perfectly reasonable to suppose that most people, when faced with a decision under uncertainty, form explicitly or implicitly some judgement of the relative likelihoods of the various outcomes and act in accordance with them. These judgements tend to be broadly qualitative, however, and probably fall far short of the precise numerical assignment assumed here. For purposes of the theory, we are assuming far more precision in probability judgements than they are likely to possess

The literature on the philosophical meaning of 'probability' is large and often controversial, and there is also considerable debate on the possibility of turning someone's qualitative perceptions of relative likelihood into numerical probabilities. Following on the work of F. P. Ramsey (1931), it is possible to construct a set of axioms which imply the existence of numerical probabilities with the desired properties. If, therefore, these axioms could be taken to hold for a given individual, it would be possible to construct for him a set of numerical probabilities over states of the world, and to predict his choices among uncertain prospects on the basis of them. The axioms have much in common with those we shall be considering in the next section, in connection with the measurement of utility. Since our main concern is with the utility theory, we shall have to ignore the question of probability measurement, and simply *assume* the existence of the required probabilities. The interested reader is referred to K. J. Arrow (1970) and H. Raiffa (1968) for thorough, though technical, discussions of the probability axioms, and of their relation to the theory to be set out in the next section.

C. Choice under uncertainty

We now consider the question of optimal choice under uncertainty. First, we need to define the objects of choice, and then we can consider the question of the decision-taker's preference ordering over these choice objects.

Initially, we assume that there exists a single good, which is measured in units of account, and which can be thought of as 'income'. Let x_s, $s = 1, 2, \ldots S$, denote an amount of income which the decision-taker will have if and only if state s occurs (in this section we shall be concerned only with a single 'representative' decision-taker, and so do not need to burden ourselves with a notation which distinguishes among decision-takers). We assume that our representative individual assigns a probability p_s to state of the world s, and we denote the vector of these probabilities by $p = [p_1, p_2, \ldots, p_S]$, while $x = [x_1, x_2, \ldots, x_S]$ is the corresponding vector of state-distributed incomes. We now define a *prospect*, P, as a given income vector with an associated probability vector, i.e.

$$P = (p, x) \tag{C.1}$$

We could define a new prospect by changing the probability vector p, or the income vector x (or both). Another term for a prospect would be a *probability distribution of incomes*, but we shall use the more convenient term, prospect.

We take the choice objects of our theory to be prospects such as P. That is, any decision has as its *only* and *entire* consequence some prospect P, and so choice between alternative actions or decisions is equivalent to choice between alternative prospects, and a preference ordering over decisions can only be derived from a preference ordering over their associated prospects.

For example, consider the decision of a market gardener to insure or not against loss of income through sickness or poor weather – such as severe frost. Decision A is the decision *not* to insure, decision B is to insure. Then associated with A is a prospect, $P^A = (p, x^A)$ where x^A is an income vector, the components of which will vary across states of the world. In the subset of states in which he is sick, income will take on one value; in the subset of states in which there is frost, income takes on another value; in the subset in which he is sick and there is frost, there will be a third value; and when he is not sick and there is no frost, there will be a fourth (and presumably the highest) value. Associated with B is a *certain prospect* (assuming that compensation for loss of income through sickness or frost is complete) $P^B = (p, x^B)$, where x^B is equal to what income would be in the absence of sickness and frost, *minus* the insurance premium, which must of course be paid in all states of the world. Then the choice between A and B, i.e. the decision whether or not to insure, will depend on whether P^A is or is not preferred to P^B. To analyse choice under uncertainty therefore requires us tc construct a theory of the preference ordering over prospects.

Note that in this example we could have achieved a useful simplification of prospect P^A, in the following way. We had four subsets of states of the world corresponding to the events: (1) only fall sick; (2) only frost; (3) fall sick *and* frost; (4) neither. This forms a *partition* of the set of states of the world, in that every state falls into one and only one of these subsets. Within each subset, income is the same, while between subsets, it may differ. We could therefore use events (defined as subsets of states of the world) rather than states as the basic way of describing prospects, so that the vector of incomes could be written as (x_1, x_2, x_3, x_4), and the probability vector as (p_1, p_2, p_3, p_4), where any p_v, $v = 1, 2, 3, 4$, is the sum of the probabilities of the states corresponding to event v. This formulation is commonly adopted in the literature, especially in the more advanced analysis. However, it is a refinement which will not really be required in what follows, and so we shall continue to describe prospects in terms of states of the world, the reader having been made aware that other possibilities exist.

We are now in a position to construct a theory of the preference ordering over prospects. The formulation of this is basically due to J. von Neumann and O. Morgenstern (1947), but the presentation here follows that of R. Luce and H. Raiffa (1957). The view we adopt is this: if certain assumptions (axioms) concerning a decision-maker's preferences are taken to be satisfied, then we are able to represent those preferences – i.e. the principle on which he takes his choices – in a simple and appealing way. A test of the appropriateness of the assumptions would be to show that we can correctly predict choices not yet observed, on the basis of observation of choices already made. It should be emphasized that our theory is a device for permitting such predictions, rather than for describing whatever thought process a decision-taker goes through when making choices. The objects of choice consist of a set of prospects, which we can denote by $\{P^1, P^2, \ldots P^n\}$. The first axiom is:

1. Ordering of prospects

Given any two prospects, the decision-taker can always say that he prefers one to the other, or is indifferent between them, and moreover, these relations of preference and indifference are *transitive*. Thus, in the notation of Chapter 3, we have that for any two prospects P^j, P^k, exactly one of the statements: $P^j > P^k$, $P^j < P^k$, $P^j \sim P^k$, is true, while

$$P^j > P^k \quad \text{and} \quad P^k > P^l \Rightarrow P^j > P^l, \qquad [C.2]$$

and similarly for the indifference relation $\sim$. This axiom therefore associates with the preference ordering over prospects the same desirable properties of completeness and consistency which were attributed to the preference ordering over bundles of goods in Chapter 3.

Before stating the second axiom, we need to introduce the concept of a *standard prospect*. Given the set of prospects under consideration we can take all the income values which appear in them, regardless of the state and the prospect to which they belong, as defining a set of values of the variable, income. Since there is a finite number of states and prospects, there is a finite number of such income values (*at most,* $n \cdot S$ of them), and so there will be a greatest income value, and a smallest income value. Denote these values by x_u and x_L respectively. It follows that all income values lie on the interval $[x_u, x_L]$, and we can construct our theory so as to apply to this entire interval on the real line. Now we define a standard prospect, P_0, as a prospect involving only the two outcomes x_u and x_L, with probabilities u and $1 - u$ respectively, where $1 \geq u \geq 0$. Given a specific standard prospect, P_0^1, written as:

$$P_0^1 = (u^1, x_u, x_L) \qquad [C.3]$$

(where for convenience we do not bother to write the second probability $1 - u^1$), we obtain a second standard prospect, P_0^{11}, by changing u, the probability of getting the better outcome, to u^{11}, so that

$$P_0^{11} = (u^{11}, x_u, x_L) \qquad [C.4]$$

We can then state the second axiom.

2. Preference increasing with probability

Given any two standard prospects P_0^1 and P_0^{11}, then:

$$P_0^1 > P_0^{11} \Leftrightarrow u^1 > u^{11} \qquad [C.5]$$

$$P_0^1 \sim P_0^{11} \Leftrightarrow u^1 = u^{11} \qquad [C.6]$$

This axiom simply states that the decision-taker would always prefer a standard prospect which gives the better chance of getting the higher-valued outcome, while two standard prospects with the same chance of getting the better outcome would be regarded as equivalent.

3. Equivalent standard prospects

Given any *certain* income value x^1 such that $x_u \geq x^1 \geq x_L$, there exists one and only one value u^1 such that:

$$x^1 \sim P_0^1 = (u^1, x_u, x_L) \qquad [C.7]$$

where P_0^1 will be called the *equivalent standard prospect* for x^1.

This axiom is saying the following: we can take a value of income in the given interval, and always find a probability of getting the better outcome in the standard prospect, such that the decision-taker would be indifferent between getting the income for certain, and having the standard prospect. We know this is true for two values of income, namely x_u and x_L. We must have:

$$x_u \sim P_0^u = (1, x_u, x_L) \qquad [C.8]$$

$$x_L \sim P_0^L = (O, x_u, x_L) \qquad [C.9]$$

since P_0^u and P_0^L correspond to the *certain* receipt of x_u and x_L respectively. Axiom 3 then is asserting that we could choose any income between x_u and x_L, and always find a unique u value to define an equivalent standard prospect. But then [C.7] is defining a *function* from the income domain $x_u \geq x^1 \geq x_L$ to the range of probability values $1 \geq u \geq 0$, which we could write as $u(x^1)$, in the usual notation. On the plausible assumption that more income is preferred to less, axiom 2 also implies that the value of u must increase as x^1 increases, in order to maintain indifference between x^1 and the standard prospect, while, as long as $x^1 < x_u$, its corresponding $u^1 < 1$. Hence $u(x^1)$ will be an increasing function. *Given x_u and x_L*, axiom 3 implies that this function is uniquely defined. However, it should be clear that the values of x_u and x_L are essentially arbitrary and can be changed without affecting the basic nature of the theory. For example, if we define a new standard prospect, $P_{\circ 0}^1$, by choosing a better outcome $x_u^1 > x_u$, then we could apply axiom 3 to find the u values in P_0^1 corresponding to each x value, and we would expect them to be different – in particular, we would now have $u(x_u) < 1$. Similarly, we could choose $x_L^1 < x_L$, to define a new standard prospect, and again we would expect to obtain a different relationship between u and x. Thus the function $u(x)$ cannot be unique in a general sense, but only relative to a specific choice of outcomes for the standard prospect. We shall return to this point later, when we take up again the properties of the function $u(x)$.

In order to describe the fourth axiom, we need to introduce yet another type of prospect, known as a *compound prospect*. In general, a compound prospect P_c is one which has, for at least one of its outcomes, another prospect, rather than a single value of income. A commonplace example of a compound prospect is a so-called 'accumulator' bet which one may place on horse-racing. If one places a 'double', one puts a stake on a horse in race 1, and specifies that if it wins, the resulting payout will be used as a stake on a horse in race 2. The possible outcomes of the prospect are therefore to lose the original stake, t, with probability p_1, or to gain a further gamble, on the second race, with probability $1 - p_1$. This second gamble, or prospect, has the possible outcomes of losing the stake with probability p_2, and winning the payout on the 'double', W_2. Hence, the 'double', as a compound prospect, can be written:

$$P_c^d = [p_1, x - t, (p_2, x - W_1, x + W_2)] = (p_1, x - t, P^1) \qquad [\text{C}.10]$$

where $P^1 = (p_2, x - W_1, x + W_2)$ is the gamble on the second race, W_1 is the payout on winning the first race and x is income without the bet. (As with the notation for the standard prospect, whenever a prospect involves only two outcomes, only the probability of the first outcome will be written, since the probability of the second is simply 1 *minus* the probability of the first.)

How should a rational decision-taker evaluate a compound prospect? Take our accumulator bet, the 'double', as an example. The punter may lose in one of two mutually exclusive ways: losing on the first race, with probability p_1; and losing on the second race, with probability p_2, *given* that he has won on the first race, with probability $1 - p_1$. Applying standard probability laws, the overall probability that he will lose on the second race is $p_2(1 - p_1)$ (probability of joint event 'win on first race *and* lose on second', where the separate probabilities are independent), and so the probability that he will lose on either the first or second race is $p_1 + p_2(1 - p_1) = \hat{p}$. The probability that he will win the payout W_2 is the probability of winning the second race *and* winning the first, i.e. $(1 - p_1)(1 - p_2) = (1 - \hat{p})$. Now if the punter loses, his actual income loss is $-t$, the loss of the stake money. That is, although, strictly speaking, winning on the first race and losing on the second means he loses W_1, this was never available to him as income, under the terms of the bet, and so is in the land of might-have-beens. Looking at the net income difference brought about by the bet, he ends up *either* with having lost the stake t, with probability $\hat{p}$, or having won the payout W_2, with probability $1 - \hat{p}$, and so we can define the *simple* prospect P^d, which summarizes the *overall* net income represented by the *compound* prospect P_c^d, as:

$$P^d = (\hat{p}, x - t, x + W_2) \qquad [\text{C}.11]$$

We could argue that P^d is *equivalent* to P_c^d, in that a rational gambler, working out the final possible income positions, and their associated probabilities, would conclude that the compound prospect 'boils down' to this simple prospect. However this is not quite the same as saying that any decision-taker would be *indifferent* between the compound prospect P_c^d and its *rational equivalent* P^d. We might feel that a rational individual *ought* to be indifferent between the two, but it is not hard to find punters who prefer to go for a double even when exactly the same payouts are available with separate bets on the two races (Question 4 of Exercise 19C asks you to discuss this further).

Now let us generalize from this example. We shall be interested in a particular kind of compound prospect, namely one which has as its outcomes *standard prospects*. That is, compound prospects of the kind:

$$P_c^1 = [p^1, (u^1, x_u, x_L), (u^2, x_u, x_L), \ldots (u^S, x_u, x_L)]$$
$$= (p^1, P_0^1, P_0^2, \ldots P_0^S) \qquad \text{[C.12]}$$

where p^1 is a vector of probabilities, $p^1 = [p_1^1, p_2^1, \ldots, p_S^1]$, and u^s, $s = 1, 2, \ldots S$, is the probability of getting the better outcome x_u in the sth standard prospect. Thus, the first 'gamble' involves obtaining a standard prospect with probability p_1^1, while p_s^1 is the probability of getting the sth standard prospect. Clearly, the compound prospect P_c^1 simply involves S different ways of getting either x_u or x_L. It follows that the probability of getting x_u overall is:

$$\bar{u} = p_1^1 u^1 + p_2^1 u^2 + \ldots + p_s^1 u^s + \ldots + p_S^1 u^S = \sum_{s=1}^{S} p_s^1 u^s \qquad \text{[C.13]}$$

since x_u may be won by winning prospect P_0^s with probability p_s^1 and then winning x_u with probability u^s, so that the probability of winning x_u in *this particular way* is $p_s^1 u^s$, and that of winning x_u in one or another of these S mutually exclusive ways is $\bar{u} = \sum_{s=1}^{S} p_s^1 u^s$. In a similar way it can be shown that the overall probability of winning x_L is $1 - \bar{u}$. Thus, we can define as the *rational equivalent* of P_c^1 in [C.12] the standard prospect:

$$P_0^1 = (\bar{u}, x_u, x_L) \qquad \text{[C.14]}$$

since P_0^1 yields x_u with probability $\bar{u}$, and x_L with probability $1 - \bar{u}$. We can now state the axiom.

4. Rational equivalence

Given any compound prospect P_c^1, having as outcomes only standard prospects (as in [C.12]), and given its rational equivalent P_0^1 (as in [C.14]), then $P_c^1 \sim P_0^1$.

In other words, axiom 4 is asserting that the decision-taker does indeed rationally evaluate the probabilities of ultimately obtaining the two outcomes, and is not affected by the two-stage nature of the gamble – we could perhaps say that he does not suffer from '*risk illusion*'. Clearly, this axiom incorporates a strong assumption about the rationality and computational ability of the individual decision-taker.

Axiom 3 stated that for any income value x^1 we can find an equivalent standard prospect P_0^1 by suitable choice of a value u^1. Take now any one of the prospects $P^1, P^2, \ldots P^n$, which form the original set of objects of choice for the decision-taker, with:

$$P^j = (p, x^j) \qquad j = 1, 2, \ldots n \tag{C.15}$$

where p is the vector of probabilities and $x^j = [x_1^j, x_2^j, \ldots, x_S^j]$ is the vector of state-contingent incomes. Applying axiom 3, we can find for each x_s^j, $s = 1, 2, \ldots S$, the equivalent standard prospect P_0^{js} such that:

$$x_s^j \sim P_0^{js} = (u^{js}, x_u, x_L) \tag{C.16}$$

where, consistent with our earlier notation, we have:

$$u^{js} = u(x_s^j) \qquad j = 1, 2, \ldots n \qquad s = 1, 2, \ldots S \tag{C.17}$$

Now consider the *compound prospect*, P_c^j, which is formed from P^j by replacing each component of the income vector by its equivalent standard prospect, i.e:

$$P_c^j = (p, [P_0^{j1}, P_0^{j2}, \ldots, P_0^{jS}]) \tag{C.18}$$

where each $P_0^{js}, s = 1, 2, \ldots S$, satisfies [C.16]. Thus, whereas the outcomes in P^j are amounts of income, the outcomes in P_c^j are the equivalent standard prospects. Then the fifth and final axiom can be stated.

5. Context independence

$$P^j \sim P_c^j, \quad \text{all} \quad j = 1, 2, \ldots n.$$

In words: the decision-taker will be indifferent between a given prospect, on the one hand, and a compound prospect formed by replacing each value of income by its equivalent standard prospect, on the other. For example, suppose that the decision-taker is in turn indifferent between: (*a*) £70 for certain, and a 50–50 chance of £200 or £10; (*b*) £100 for certain, and a 75–25 chance of £200 or £10; then axiom 5 asserts that he would then be indifferent between a 50–50 chance of £70 or £100, on the one hand, and a 50–50 chance of obtaining one of two further gambles: (*a*) a 50–50 chance of £200 or £10, and (*b*) a 75–25 chance of £200 or £10 on the other. The fact that values of income, and their equivalent standard prospects, may be included in prospects, does not change their basic relation of indifference (which is what the term 'context independence' tries to convey). We could represent this example as:

$$([0.5\ 0.5], [£70\ £100])$$

$$\sim ([0.5\ 0.5][(0.5, £200, £10)(0.75, £200, £10)]) \tag{C.19}$$

Thus, an attribute of rationality is taken to be that equivalent standard prospects can be substituted for incomes, without changing the place of a prospect in the preference ordering.

Given this set of axioms, we now show that they lead to an appealing way of representing the decision-taker's preference ordering.

Axiom 5 implies that given any set of prospects $\{P^1, P^2, \ldots P^n,\}$ we can replace each by the corresponding compound prospects $P_c^1, P_c^2, \ldots P_c^n$, where each P_c^j, $j = 1, 2, \ldots n$, satisfies [C.18]. In other words, we can express each of the 'primary' prospects as a compound prospect involving *only* various chances of obtaining standard prospects. This is an important step, since it puts the individual prospects on to a common basis of comparison – *they become simply different ways of winning one or other of the same two outcomes*. Moreover, axiom 4 tells us that each of the P_c^j will be indifferent to its rational equivalent, i.e. a standard prospect involving only outcomes x_u and x_L, with probabilities derived in a straightforward way from those appearing in the P_c^j. Thus, we can write:

$$P^j \sim P_c^j \sim P_0^j \tag{C.20}$$

or more fully:

$$(p, x^j) \sim (p, [P_0^{j1}, P_0^{j2}, \ldots, P_0^{jS}]) \sim (\bar{u}^j, x_u, x_L) \tag{C.21}$$

where $P_0^{js} = (u^{js}, x_u, x_L)$, and:

$$\bar{u}^j = \sum_{s=1}^{S} p_s u^{js} = \sum_{s=1}^{S} p_s u(x_s^j) \tag{C.22}$$

Now, from axiom 2, we have that $P_0^j > P_0^k$, if and only if $\bar{u}^j > \bar{u}^k$, and that $P_0^j \sim P_0^k$ if and only if $\bar{u}^j = \bar{u}^k$. It follows that the rational equivalent standard prospects $P_0^1, P_0^2 \ldots P_0^n$ can be completely ordered by the values of $\bar{u}$ which appear in them. The preferred rational equivalent standard prospect will be that with the highest $\bar{u}$ value. Thus, we can say, for purposes of the theory, that the decision-taker chooses among the prospects P_0^j in such a way as *to maximize the value of $\bar{u}$*, that is, he acts *as if* his intention is to make $\bar{u}$ as large as possible. But, from axiom 1, the preference ordering over all prospects (including standard prospects) is transitive, so that:

$$P^j \sim P_0^j \quad and \quad P^k \sim P_0^k \quad and \quad P_0^j > P_0^k \Rightarrow P^j > P^k \tag{C.23}$$

Thus, because of [C.20], the preference ordering over the rational equivalent standard prospects P_0^j, represented by the values of the $\bar{u}^j$, is identical to the preference ordering over the initial prospects, P^j, $j = 1, 2, \ldots n$. It follows that choice among these initial prospects can be represented as the attempt by the decision-taker to maximize $\bar{u}$, and we predict that if a prospect P^j is actually chosen, and if we were to carry out the measurements implied by the axioms of the theory, then we would find that it yielded the greatest value of $\bar{u}$.

The axioms, then, can be regarded as providing us with a procedure for predicting the choices among prospects of a decision-taker to whom they apply. We might proceed as follows: by a large number (in principle an infinity) of paired comparisons between certain income values on the interval $[x_u, x_L]$, and standard prospects P_0, we could find the function $u(x)$. We could then take two prospects, say P^1 and P^2, and, by inserting the values of the incomes x_s^1, x_s^2, $s = 1, 2, \ldots S$, into this function, we obtain the values $u_s^1 = u(x_s^1)$, $u_s^2 = u(x_s^2)$. Then we can calculate $\bar{u}^1 = \sum_s p_s u_s^1$, and $\bar{u}^2 = \sum_s p_s u_s^2$ and predict that the prospect with the higher of these two values will be chosen.

　　In theoretical analysis, of course, we do not have specific functions $u(x)$. Rather, we have to work only with certain general properties of this function. In the next section, we shall consider the most important of these properties in some detail. We conclude this section with a note on terminology. It is usual to call the function $u(x)$ a utility function, since it is a real-valued numerical representation of a preference ordering. It should be clear from the way in which this function is derived that 'utility' is not to be interpreted as a quantity of satisfaction, well-being or other psychic sensation concerned with ownership of income, but simply as a name for the numbers which result when we carry out a series of paired comparisons. Now, given a discrete probability distribution of some variable, say z, we define the *expected value* of this variable, $\bar{z}$, as:

$$\bar{z} = \sum_{s=1}^{S} p_s z_s \qquad\qquad [\text{C.24}]$$

where p_s is the probability of occurrence of the value z_s. It follows that we refer to the value $\bar{u}^j = \sum_{s=1}^{S} p_s u_s^j$ as the *expected utility* of prospect P^j, and we can interpret the axioms to mean that the decision-taker chooses among projects as if to maximize this expected utility. For this reason, the theory based on these assumptions is often called the expected utility theory of choice under uncertainty.

　　In this section we have been concerned to set out the axioms underlying the expected utility theory. In the next section, we go on to discuss some properties which can be attributed to the utility function $u(x)$. Following that, we shall consider some objections to and criticisms of the axioms, directed mainly at their *a priori* reasonableness as properties of the choice behaviour of individual decision-takers.

Exercise 19C

1. Mr A has a utility function given by: $u = \sqrt{x}$, where x is income. He is asked to enter a business venture, which involves a 50–50 chance of an income of £900, or £400, and so the expected value of income from the venture is £650.

   (a) If asked to pay a 'fair price' of £650 in order to take part in the venture, would he accept?

   (b) What is the largest sum of money he would be prepared to pay to take part in the venture?

   (*Hint:* find the *certainty equivalent* of the prospect defined by the venture, i.e. the income which, if received for certain, has a utility equal to the expected utility of the prospect.)

2. Now suppose Mr A has the utility function: (i) $u = ax$ where $a > 0$; or (ii) $u = x^2$. How would your answers to Question 1 change?

3.* *St. Petersburg Paradox*　Suppose we define the following gamble: we toss a coin, and if it lands heads, you receive £2, and if it lands tails, we toss it again; if on the second toss it lands heads, you receive £4 ($= £2^2$), and if it lands tails, we toss it again; if on the third toss it lands heads, you receive £8 ($= £2^3$), and if it lands tails, we toss it again ... and so on *ad infinitum*. Thus on the nth toss, a head wins you £2^n, while a tail leads to a further toss. Now, assuming the coin is fair, the probability of a head on the first toss is $\frac{1}{2}$; the probability of a head on the second toss (the sequence, a tail then a head) is $(\frac{1}{2})^2$; and the probability of a sequence of $n-1$ tails and then a head on the nth toss is $(\frac{1}{2})^n$. Therefore, the expected value of the game is:

$$E = (\tfrac{1}{2})£2 + (\tfrac{1}{2})^2£4 + (\tfrac{1}{2})^3£8 + \ldots + (\tfrac{1}{2})^n£2^n + \ldots$$

$$= 1 + 1 + 1 \ldots$$

which is infinite, assuming nothing prevents us playing the game forever. It has been noticed, however, that the maximum amount one would pay to take part in the game is, for most people, finite. Discuss possible explanations of this, and, in particular, what it might imply about the utility function $u(x)$.

4.* Consider an accumulator bet on horse-racing, known as a treble: the punter specifies three horses in successive races, and places a stake on the horse on the first race; if it wins, the winnings become the stake on the horse on the second race; if this wins, the winnings become the stake on the horse in the third race. Write down this 'treble' in the notation for prospects introduced in this section, assuming the punter assigns probabilities to the events of each horse winning its race. Now derive the rational equivalent of this prospect. How many outcomes does it have? Suppose that the punter also has the option of making three separate bets on each of the races, the bet on the second race being laid after the result of the first is known, and the bet on the third race being made after the result of the second is known. Describe this option as a prospect, and compare it to the treble. Discuss possible reasons for a punter's having a preference for the treble.

5.* Choose someone with enough patience, and try to construct his utility function for incomes over the range £0–£100 a week, in the manner suggested by this section. Note the problems you encounter, and relate them to the axioms set out above.

D. Properties of the utility function

The axioms set out in the previous section already imply certain important properties of the utility function $u(x)$. They imply that it increases with income, x; that it is uniquely defined *relative to* the values x_u and x_L; and that it is bounded above by the value 1 and below by the value 0. Moreover, as we shall see, the fact that the decision-taker can be assumed to act as if he maximized expected utility implies a further very important property of the function. On the other hand, there are certain properties of the function which we would like it to have, but which are not implied by the axioms set out so far, and so further assumptions have to be made to endow it with them. We shall consider these assumptions first and then look at the properties already implied by the axioms of the previous section.

For the kinds of analysis we wish to carry out, it is useful if the utility function is differentiable at least twice in its entire domain, that is, if the derivatives $u'(x)$ and $u''(x)$ exist for all x in the interval $[x_u\ x_L]$. Thus we make the assumption of differentiability.

1. Differentiability

The utility function is at least twice differentiable, at all income levels in the given domain. Consistent with the usual terminology, we call $u'(x)$ the *marginal utility of income*, and so $u''(x)$ is the rate at which marginal utility of income changes with income. Note that this differentiability assumption implies that the utility function is continuous.

The second assumption we shall make concerns the attitude of the decision-taker towards risk. Thus, suppose he is confronted with a prospect $P = (p, x_1, x_2)$. The expected value of the outcomes is then $\bar{x} = px_1 + (1-p)x_2$. We define the *certainty equivalent* of the prospect, $\tilde{x}$, as that value of income which satisfies:

$$\tilde{x} \sim P \tag{D.1}$$

or equivalently:

$$u(\tilde{x}) = \bar{u} = pu(x_1) + (1-p)u(x_2) \tag{D.2}$$

That is, $\tilde{x}$ is the amount of income which, if received for certain, would be regarded by the decision-taker as just as good as the prospect P. [D.1] says that $\tilde{x}$ is indifferent to P, and [D.2] that its utility must equal the expected utility of P, which, in the light of the analysis in the previous section, is an equivalent statement. Now a great deal of interest centres on the relation between this certainty equivalent, $\tilde{x}$, and the expected value of the outcomes, $\bar{x}$. Consider the three possible cases:

(a) $\tilde{x} = \bar{x}$. In this case, the decision-taker values the prospect at its expected value. For example, offered a bet that if a fair coin lands heads he will receive £6, and if it lands tails he must pay £4, he would certainly accept the bet. To see this, note that when his original income is x the choice is between the prospect $P^1 = (0.5, x + £6, x - £4)$, and the prospect $P^2 = (1, x, x)$ since to refuse the bet is to accept the certainty of no income gain. Then, the expected value of the prospect P^2 is $\bar{x}^2 = x$, while that of P^1 is $\bar{x}^1 = £1 + x$. But since certainty equivalents equal expected values, and $u(x+1) > u(x)$, he must prefer P^1 and so will take the bet. Indeed, he would be prepared to pay anything up to £1 for the opportunity to engage in the bet, since the expected value of his winnings, £1 *minus* what he pays, will still be positive. In general terms we can characterize this case as one in which the following equation holds:

$$pu(x_1)+(1-p)u(x_2)=\bar{u}=u(\tilde{x})=u(\bar{x}) \qquad [D.3]$$

A preference ordering over alternative prospects can then be based entirely on the expected values of the outcomes of the prospects, with higher expected value always being preferred to lower.

(b) $\tilde{x}<\bar{x}$. In this case, the decision-taker values the prospect at less than its expected value. For example, given the above example of the prospect $P^1=(0.5, x+\text{\pounds}6, x-\text{\pounds}4)$ we can no longer be sure that it will be accepted in preference to the prospect $P^2=(1, x, x)$, and the decision-taker would certainly pay less than £1 for the opportunity to take it. In general terms we have:

$$pu(x_1)+(1-p)u(x_2)=\bar{u}=u(\tilde{x})<u(\bar{x}) \qquad [D.4]$$

where $\bar{x}=px_1+(1-p)x_2$. In this case a preference ordering over alternative prospects could *not* be based on the expected values of outcomes, since these overstate the values of the prospects. To predict the ranking we would need to know the utility function, or the certainty equivalents.

(c) $\tilde{x}>\bar{x}$. In this case, the decision-taker values the prospect at more than its expected value. In our previous example, he would certainly accept the prospect P^1, since $\tilde{x}^1>\bar{x}^1>x$, while he would actually be prepared to pay more than $\tilde{x}^1-x=\text{\pounds}1$ for the opportunity to take the gamble. In general terms, we have:

$$pu(x_1)+(1-p)u(x_2)=\bar{u}=u(\tilde{x})>u(\bar{x}) \qquad [D.5]$$

where $\bar{x}=px_1+(1-p)x_2$. Again, a preference ordering over prospects could not be based on the expected values of outcomes, since these now *understate* the values of the prospects. To predict the ranking we would again need to know the utility function or certainty equivalents.

These three cases provide us with a way of classifying attitudes to risk, based on a comparison of the certainty equivalent, on the one hand, and expected value, on the other. It is usual to call the first kind of attitude, where prospects are valued at their expected values, *risk neutral*; the second, where prospects are valued at less than their expected values, *risk-averse*; and the third case, *risk-attracted*. As we shall see later, there are strong arguments for regarding risk-aversion as typical.

We consider now the implications of these three cases for the nature of the utility function $u(x)$. First recall from Chapter 2 the definitions of convex and concave functions. Given some function $f(x)$, defined on a convex set X, the function is said to be concave if and only if:

$$f(\bar{x})\geq kf(x_1)+(1-k)f(x_2) \qquad 0\leq k\leq 1$$

$$x_1, x_2 \in X \qquad [D.6]$$

where $\bar{x}=kx_1+(1-k)x_2$. A linear function satisfies [D.6] as an equality, while a *strictly* concave function satisfies it as a strict inequality. But in equations [D.3], [D.4] and [D.5], if we replace k by the probability p (defined on precisely the same interval), and replace f by u, we see that case (a), risk neutrality, must correspond to a linear utility function (at least over the range $[x_1, x_2]$), while case (b) risk aversion, corresponds to a strictly concave utility function (over the range $[x_1, x_2]$). Moreover, the function $f(x)$ is strictly convex if $-f(x)$ is strictly concave, and so we see that case (c), risk attraction, corresponds to a strictly convex utility function. Figure 1 illustrates these propositions. In (a) of the figure, the utility function $u(x)$ is drawn strictly concave. Corresponding to the income levels x_1, x_2 are the utility values $u(x_1), u(x_2)$, at points a and b respectively. Given a value of p, the expected value $\bar{x} = px_1 + (1-p)x_2$ will lie somewhere between x_1 and x_2, such as at the point shown in the figure. Consider the straight line ab, whose end points are at the values $u(x_1)$ and $u(x_2)$ respectively. It can easily be shown that the expected utility of the prospect $P = (p, x_1, x_2)$, can always be found at a point such as c, i.e. the point on the line ab directly above the expected value of the prospect, $\bar{x} = px_1 + (1-p)x_2$. Thus, since the slope of the straight line ab is $[u(x_2) - u(x_1)]/(x_2 - x_1)$, letting $f(x)$ denote its height at x, we have

$$f(x) = u(x_1) + \frac{[u(x_2) - u(x_1)](x - x_1)}{x_2 - x_1} \qquad [D.7]$$

In particular the height of the line at c above $\bar{x} = px_1 + (1-p)x_2$ is

$$f(x) = u(x_1) + \frac{[u(x_2) - u(x_1)][px_1 + (1-p)x_2 - x_1]}{x_2 - x_1}$$

$$= u(x_1) + \frac{[u(x_2) - u(x_1)](1-p)(x_2 - x_1)}{x_2 - x_1}$$

$$= u(x_1) + [u(x_2) - u(x_1)](1-p)$$

$$= pu(x_1) + (1-p)u(x_2) = \bar{u} \qquad [D.8]$$

which gives $\bar{u}$ as point c in the figure.

From this we can immediately find the certainty equivalent of the prospect P. We have to find the income value $\tilde{x}$ which satisfies:

$$u(\tilde{x}) = \bar{u} \qquad [D.9]$$

and this is clearly given by $\tilde{x}$ in the figure since, at point d, the utility of $\tilde{x}$ if it is received for certain, is just equal to the expected utility of the prospect. Thus, we see the equivalence between the inequality $\tilde{x} < \bar{x}$, and the strict concavity of the utility function. Each can therefore be taken to represent the assumption of risk aversion.

In (b) of the figure, $u(x)$ is drawn strictly convex. $\bar{x}$ again shows the expected value of income, for a particular choice of p, and, in exactly the same way as before, the expected utility $\bar{u}$ can be shown to be given by g in the figure. Now, however, the certainty equivalent is $\tilde{x} > \bar{x}$, since $u(\tilde{x}) = \bar{u}$ at h. Thus, risk attraction is equivalently described as corresponding to a

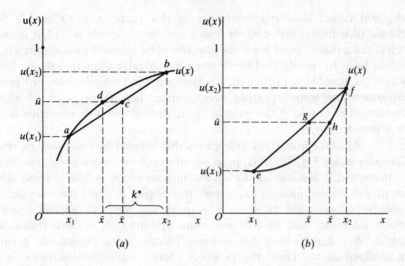

Fig. 1

strictly convex utility function, or a certainty equivalent in excess of expected value of income.

The case of risk neutrality could be illustrated in either part of the figure. Take (a), and suppose now that the utility function *is* the line drawn between a and b. Then clearly $\bar{u} = u(\bar{x})$ (whereas in the strictly concave case of course $u(\bar{x}) > \bar{u}$), and $\bar{x}$ is the certainty equivalent of the prospect P. Hence, risk neutrality corresponds to the case of a linear utility function.

As yet another way of describing the decision-taker's attitude to risk, note that the differentiability assumption allows us to express convexity and concavity in terms of derivatives of the utility function. Thus marginal utility $u'(x)$ measures the slope, at a point, of a curve in Fig. 1, while the second derivative, $u''(x)$, is determined by the curvature. Thus, strict concavity over the range of x values implies that at every point, $u''(x) < 0$, i.e. there is diminishing marginal utility of income; strict convexity implies $u''(x) > 0$, increasing marginal utility of income, and linearity implies $u''(x) = 0$, constant marginal utility of income. We can therefore say that a decision-taker will be risk averse, risk attracted or risk neutral, according as his marginal utility of income is diminishing, increasing or constant, respectively.

So far, we have been simply considering some logical possibilities. Nothing in the axioms implies any one shape for the utility function, or indeed, that its curvature is uniform over a range of incomes. However, we now make assumption 2.

2. Risk aversion

All decision-takers are risk-averse, so that their utility functions $u(x)$ are strictly concave.

Part of the reason for making this assumption is empirical: it appears to be the case that people behave in ways consistent with risk aversion rather than risk neutrality or risk preference. Offered a 50–50 chance of winning, say, £50, or losing £49, most people would, it is argued, reject the gamble, or at least not pay 50p to be allowed to undertake it. (We would have to specify that there was no particular attraction in the form in which the gamble is presented, e.g. as something which would enhance the enjoyment of some sporting event, since then there is an element of consumption in taking the gamble, quite distinct from its objective features as a prospect.)

Another important example is that offered by insurance behaviour. Consider again Fig. 1(a). Suppose we interpret the figure as follows: in state of the world 2, income will be x_2, but in state of the world 1, some adverse event will reduce income to x_1 with probability p. Thus the decision-taker already *possesses* the prospect $P^1 = (p, x_1, x_2)$. Suppose he can insure, by which we mean that he will pay some premium, k, in both states of the world, in order to have his income (before deduction of the premium) maintained at x_2. Thus, the prospect corresponding to insurance is $P^2 = (p, x_2 - k, x_2 - k)$, i.e. the certain income $x_2 - k$. Clearly, whether P^2 is or is not preferred to P^1 depends on the expected utility $\bar{u} = pu(x_1) + (1 - p)u(x_2)$, on the one hand, and $u(x_2 - k)$, on the other. The *largest* premium that would be paid is the value, k^*, which satisfies:

$$u(x_2 - k^*) = \bar{u} \tag{D.10}$$

because any $k < k^*$ leaves the decision-taker with a certain income which is preferred to P^1. Since, by definition of the certainty equivalent, $\bar{u} = u(\tilde{x})$, we must have:

$$k^* = x_2 - \tilde{x} > x_2 - \bar{x} \tag{D.11}$$

which can easily be confirmed from the figure. But since:

$$x_2 - \bar{x} = p(x_2 - x_1) < k^*$$

this implies that the risk averse decision-taker is prepared to pay a premium greater than the expected value of the loss he may incur. It has been observed that insurance premiums are often in excess of the expected value of loss to the insured, and this tends to confirm the assumption of risk aversion (but see Question 3 Exercise 19D). Finally, as we shall see in the next chapter, the preference people seem to show for *diversification of risks* suggests risk aversion. For example, suppose someone was indifferent between a 50–50 chance of £100 in state of the world 1, and nothing in state 2, on the one hand; and a 50–50 chance of nothing in state 1 and £100 in state 2, on the other. If offered some linear combination of these prospects, for example the certainty of £50 (representing the combination of one-half of each prospect), it is suggested that most people would prefer it to each of them – almost literally, 'a bird in the hand is worth two in the bush'. But this implies that the utility of the expected value is greater than the expected utility of each prospect, implying in turn risk aversion.

However, such 'empirical evidence' as this is somewhat casual, and behaviour which contradicts it can sometimes be found. A further reason for making the assumption of risk aversion is analytical convenience. We thereby obtain a 'well-behaved' representation of the decision-taker's preferences, for which sufficiency conditions for optimal solutions are satisfied, and local maxima are always also global maxima (recall the discussion of concave functions in Ch. 2). This will become clear in the analysis in the next chapter.

The question now arises: is it in fact valid to ascribe a particular shape to the utility function $u(x)$; or, equivalently, to place restrictions on the sign of the second derivative $u''(x)$? Recall the discussion of the ordinal utility function in Chapter 3. We argued there that the utility function was unique only up to a positive monotonic transformation, implying that it could not be specified as 'convex' or 'concave', since functions of both kinds could be permissible representations of the preferences satisfying the axioms stated in the chapter. Indeed, this provided the motivation for the introduction of the concepts of quasi-concavity and quasi-convexity in Chapter 2. If $u(x)$ *were* an ordinal utility function, we could not place a sign restriction on its second derivative. For example, if $u = \sqrt{x}$ were a permissible ordinal utility function, with $u''(x) = -\frac{1}{4}x^{-\frac{3}{2}} < 0$, so would be $v = u^2$, or $w = u^4$, which have zero and positive second derivatives, respectively. The implicit assumption in the preceding discussion that it is meaningful to place sign restrictions on $u''(x)$ hints that the utility function $u(x)$ is not an ordinal utility function. We now have to consider this further.

First of all, as already suggested, the utility function $u(x)$ *is not a unique* representation of the decision-taker's preferences. By changing one or both of the outcomes in the standard prospect we would obtain, for each certain income x, a different probability u at which the decision-taker would be indifferent between the certain income and the standard prospect. Figure 2 illustrates. In (a) of the figure, we assume first that $u(x)$ is measured against a standard prospect containing x_L and x_u, and then we replace x_L by $x'_L < x_L$. We then obtain the new utility function, denoted $v(x)$, for which we must have $v(x'_L) = 0$, $v(x_u) = 1$ and $v(x) > u(x)$ for $x_L < x < x_u$ (Explain why).

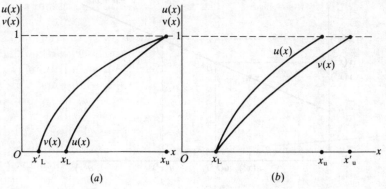

Fig. 2

Thus $v(x)$ and $u(x)$ must bear the general relationship to each other shown in the figure. In (b) of the figure, we assume $u(x)$ is as before, while $v(x)$ is obtained by replacing x_u with x'_u in the standard prospect. Here, we must have $v(x_L) = 0$, $v(x'_u) = 1$ and $v(x) < u(x)$ for $x_L < x < x_u$ (explain why), and so the general relationship between the two functions is as shown in the figure.

Although the utility function clearly cannot therefore be unique in any absolute sense, we can show that the relationship among all possible utility functions, of which $u(x)$ and $v(x)$ are examples, is much more restricted in the present theory than that among the ordinal utility functions which represent consumer preferences under certainty. We can show that any two utility functions $u(x)$ and $v(x)$ calibrated for a decision-taker whose choices conform to our axioms must bear to each other the linear relationship:

$$v(x) = a + bu(x) \qquad b > 0 \qquad\qquad [D.12]$$

In other words, as we vary the level of certain income, the utility numbers we obtain by use of one standard prospect must vary linearly with those we obtain by use of a different standard prospect. Figure 3 illustrates. A given income level, x, implies a pair of values (u, v) (such as that at α), and, as the income value varies, through x^1 to x^3, the pair of utility values varies along the line through β to γ. This is obviously a strong restriction on the class of permissible utility functions, and can be expressed by the statement: the utility function $u(x)$ is unique up to a *positive linear* transformation (cf. the ordinal utility function's property of uniqueness up to a *positive monotonic* transformation). This restriction provides the justification for attaching significance to the sign of $u''(x)$, since, if $v(x)$ must satisfy [D.12], $v''(x)$ must have the same sign (Prove; see also Question 4, Exercise 19D).

This important property of the utility function can be shown to be implied by our axioms. Thus, take three income values $x^1 < x^2 < x^3$, and

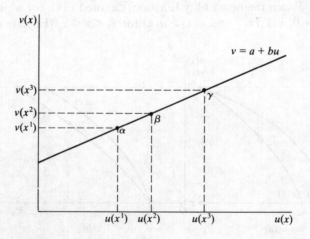

Fig. 3

suppose that we observe for some probability p:

$$x^2 \sim (p, x^1, x^3) \qquad\qquad [D.13]$$

i.e. the decision-taker is indifferent between x^2 for certain and a prospect involving x^1 and x^3. Then, from our utility theory we can write:

$$u(x^2) = pu(x^1) + (1-p)u(x^3) \qquad\qquad [D.14]$$

$$v(x^2) = pv(x^1) + (1-p)v(x^3) \qquad\qquad [D.15]$$

for two permissible utility functions $u(x)$ and $v(x)$. Given that the decision-taker conforms to our axioms, [D.14] and [D.15] are equivalent ways of expressing [D.13]. Writing these two equations in vector notation gives:

$$[u^2, v^2] = p[u^1, v^1] + (1-p)[u^3, v^3] \qquad 0 \le p \le 1 \qquad [D.16]$$

where $u^2 = u(x^2)$, $v^2 = v(x^2)$, and so on. But [D.16] is stating that the pair of utility values (u^2, v^2) must lie on the line joining the pair (u^1, v^1) with the pair (u^3, v^3), since it is equivalent to the standard expression for a convex combination of two vectors. Since x^1 and x^3 can be taken as *any* two income values, we have established the result that any two permissible functions $u(x)$ and $v(x)$ must be linearly related.

Possession of the property of uniqueness up to a positive *linear* transformation implies that the utility function $u(x)$ provides a *cardinal* rather than an ordinal measure of utility, since this is the defining property of cardinal measures in general. Thus the von Neumann–Morgenstern axioms provide us with a measure of utility comparable to the commonly used measures of temperature – since the Fahrenheit and Centigrade scales are similarly linearly related. If the theory holds, utility is cardinally measurable. However, it is important to stress that this does *not* mean that we have succeeded in 'measuring utility' as if utility were a physical magnitude in the same sense as weight or height. Nothing has been said about the 'amount' of intrinsic pleasure which the decision-taker receives from various amounts of income, and the word 'utility' as it is used here does *not* refer to this. The basis of the theory is still the ordering relation of preference or indifference, and the decision-taker's ability to compare and rank is the only aspect of his psychology in which we are interested. What we have shown is that if his ranking behaviour satisfies a number of conditions of rationality and consistency, then he can be represented as acting *as if* he maximized the expected value of a numerical function which must therefore be cardinal. The word 'utility' is used, perhaps unfortunately, in describing this function, but nothing is implied about the measurability of sensations of pleasure or satisfaction.

Exercise 19D

1. Someone is offered a 50–50 chance of winning £21 or losing £20, and he rejects it. Which of the following reasons for his rejection are

consistent with the expected utility theory:

(i) he never gambles, because he believes gambling to be morally wrong;

(ii) he is sure he will lose, because he is always unlucky at gambling;

(iii) the £20 he might lose is worth more to him than the £21 he might win;

(iv) he cannot afford to risk £20;

(v) he has better ways of risking £20;

(vi) he does not have £20.

2.* Under the expected utility formulation of this chapter, the utility number associated with a given income is independent of the state of the world in which that income is to be received. Give reasonably plausible examples which suggest that the utility of income could depend on the state of the world in which it will be received. What part of the axiom system implicitly ruled out such dependence? (See the reference to J. Hirshleifer (1970) given at the end of this chapter).

3.* It has been observed that an individual will, in insuring himself against loss, pay a premium greater than the expected value of his loss; and, at the same time accept a gamble whose expected value is negative (for example by buying a premium bond). Explain why this appears to contradict the assumption of risk aversion. Suggest ways in which the observation of such behaviour could be made consistent with the analysis (See the reference to M. Friedman and L. J. Savage (1948)).

4.* Given the relation between utility functions: $v(x) = a + bu(x)$, $a, b > 0$, use the definition of concave functions to prove that if u is concave, so must be v. Extend this to show that any function $\bar{u}(x)$, which is a linear combination of concave functions, u_s, of the form:

$$\bar{u}(x) = \sum_{s=1}^{S} p_s u_s(x_s) \qquad 1 > p_s > 0 \qquad \sum_s p_s = 1$$

is itself a concave function.

5. Give an explanation of why, in Fig. 2(a), $v(x)$ lies above $u(x)$, and in Fig. 2 (b), $v(x)$ lies below $u(x)$, in terms of the choice between each income value and each of the standard prospects.

6. In Alexander Pushkin's short story 'Queen of Spades', Herrman explains his refusal to gamble by the statement: 'I am not in a position to sacrifice the essential in the hope of acquiring the superfluous'. Rationalize this in terms of expected utility theory.

7. Construct a numerical example to show that if the utility function $u(x)$ were an *ordinal* function, i.e. unique up to a positive monotonic transformation, then two permissible utility functions could be found, such that with one of them prospect P^1 is preferred to prospect P^2, and with the other, the converse is true.

8. Show that the Centigrade, Fahrenheit and Réaumur temperature scales are indeed linearly related. Is it sensible to say that one cup of tea is twice as hot as another, one prospect has twice the expected utility of another or that one output level is twice as profitable as another?

E. Criticisms of the expected utility theory

The hypothesis that a decision-taker chooses among risky alternatives in such a way as to maximize expected utility has come to dominate the
economic theory of resource allocation under uncertainty. As we shall see in
the next chapter, it has become the mainspring of models which analyse
insurance and stock markets and general equilibrium under uncertainty, as
well as a host of other topics (e.g. the output and pricing decisions of a
monopolist faced with demand uncertainty) not covered here. A large part
of the reason for this is the simplicity and power of the hypothesis. It neatly
replaces the objective function – the ordinal utility function – in optimization
problems, without requiring a change in the basic structure of the problem,
or in the mode of analysis. Using the same relatively simple techniques of
constrained maximization, further hypotheses can be generated about
economic behaviour under uncertainty, so that in their analysis of the
economy economists can take the existence of uncertainty in their stride. It
is therefore as well to be aware of the criticisms which can be made of the
hypothesis: an understanding of the possible flaws in the foundations helps
us to form a view of the likely stability of the vast edifice erected upon them.

There are three main lines of criticism, which we can consider in
order of increasing generality. First, one may have reservations about the
descriptive realism of the axioms themselves. Although axioms 1 (ordering
of prospects), 2 (preference increasing with probability) and 3 (existence of
equivalent standard prospects) may seem more or less plausible, axioms 4
(rational equivalence) and 5 (context independence) appear to assume a
good deal of rationality and objectivity in the face of risky decisions, which
may in *a priori* terms seem rather strong. Now, one response to this may be
to adopt the argument suggested by M. Friedman (1953), which says that
the realism of the axioms (assumptions) themselves is irrelevant, and that
what matters is the truth of the further hypotheses (predictions) which are
deduced from the axioms. But, as T. Koopmans (1957) has pointed out, this
position is not really tenable, since the axioms themselves are direct
hypotheses (or predictions) about the behaviour of decision-takers, and so
cannot escape being found either true or false. For example, axiom 5
'predicts' that *if* for a given decision-taker:

$$£70 \sim (0.5, £200, £10) = P^1 \tag{E.1}$$

and:

$$£100 \sim (0.75, £200, £10) = P^2 \tag{E.2}$$

then that decision-taker will consider:

$$(0.5, £70, £100) \sim (0.5, P^1, P^2) \tag{E.3}$$

as explained in section C. This prediction can be directly tested, and if it were
not true for a given decision-taker, then we have to conclude that the
hypothesis contained in the axiom is refuted for the decision-taker.

We can perhaps capture the spirit of Friedman's objection, while
not falling foul of Koopmans' criticism, if we argue as follows: what is

essential to the theory is the hypothesis that decision-takers choose as if to maximize expected utility, and not the particular set of axioms which generates that hypothesis. A given axiom may be *sufficient* to generate the hypothesis, but not *necessary*, and so to show that it does not hold does not refute the hypothesis. There are several sets of axioms which generate the expected utility hypothesis: those given here were chosen for their clarity and because they allow us to show how the expected utility function is actually *constructed* (i.e. they provide a *constructive proof* of the existence of the utility function), but they are by no means the only ones possible. For example, the axioms originally given by von Neumann and Morgenstern were different in several respects and far more concise, not containing, incidentally, axiom 5. If our interest, therefore, is in the validity of the expected utility theory, rather than in the merits of the different axiom systems which generate it, we should be more concerned with testing that theory itself, rather than the individual axioms.

How, then, should we test the hypothesis that decision-takers choose as if to maximize expected utility? At a very early stage in their training, economists are taught that 'controlled experiments' or laboratory tests in economics are virtually impossible, and so the inclination of economists faced with this question would be to look for observations of market behaviour to see whether this provides a refutation of the hypothesis. Psychologists, however, perhaps as a result of *their* training, appear to have no such inhibitions, and a number of very interesting controlled experiments have been carried out, to see whether people, when choosing under conditions of uncertainty, act in accordance with the expected utility hypothesis. Thus, Mosteller and Nogee (1951), Davidson, Suppes and Siegel (1955), and Tversky (1967), have carried out controlled experiments of decision-taking under uncertainty.

A general conclusion which can be drawn from these studies is that where relatively simple choices are involved decision-takers will conform to the expected utility hypothesis, while in more complex situations they tend to depart from it. It may then be argued that the hypothesis may have primarily a *normative* use: it could be used to 'correct mistaken choices' in complex situations. This suggestion has in fact been made by a prominent advocate of the hypothesis, and we shall return to the discussion of it in a moment. For now, we note that the experimental evidence gives only limited support for the hypothesis that decision-takers choose among prospects as if they were maximizing expected utility.

The second line of criticism is based upon introspection rather than experiment. M. Allais (1953) has formulated an example in which what appear to be reasonable choices rule out the existence of a utility function. Thus, suppose that you are offered a choice between $£\frac{1}{2}$m for certain and the prospect:

$$P^1 = ([0.1, 0.89, 0.01], [£2.5m, £0.5m, 0])$$ [E.4]

It will help matters if at this point you write down which you prefer. Let us suppose you chose the £½m for certain. Then, in terms of the expected utility theory, this implies:

$$u(\tfrac{1}{2}) > 0.1u(2\tfrac{1}{2}) + 0.89u(\tfrac{1}{2}) + 0.01u(0) \qquad [E.5]$$

Subtracting $0.89u(\tfrac{1}{2})$ from both sides gives:

$$0.11u(\tfrac{1}{2}) > 0.1u(2\tfrac{1}{2}) + 0.01u(0) \qquad [E.6]$$

Suppose now that you are offered a second choice. (You have not acquired the £½m, and everything about you is assumed the same as before.) You have to choose one of the prospects:

$$P^2 = ([0.11, 0.89], [£\tfrac{1}{2}m, 0]) \qquad [E.7]$$

$$P^3 = ([0.1, 0.9], [£2\tfrac{1}{2}m, 0]) \qquad [E.8]$$

Again, record now which you would choose. To many people, P^3 would seem preferable to P^2, since it involves a slightly increased chance of nothing but a much larger favourable outcome. Let us suppose that you also chose P^3 Then again, in terms of expected utility theory:

$$0.1u(2\tfrac{1}{2}) + 0.9u(0) > 0.11u(\tfrac{1}{2}) + 0.89u(0) \qquad [E.9]$$

and so, subtracting $0.89u(0)$ from both sides gives:

$$0.1u(2\tfrac{1}{2}) + 0.01u(0) > 0.11u(\tfrac{1}{2}) \qquad [E.10]$$

But [E.10] directly contradicts [E.6]. There can be no utility function which satisfies both inequalities, and so someone who prefers £0.5m for certain to P^1, and P^3 to P^2, cannot be behaving in a way consistent with the expected utility hypothesis. But, Allais argues, many people would find it perfectly reasonable to choose in this way, and so, by introspection, we must reject the expected utility hypothesis.

    L. J. Savage (1954), on whose discussion of this example the present exposition is based, wishes to support the expected utility hypothesis, but cannot reject the *a priori* reasonableness of the choices Allais postulates – in fact he apparently made them himself when first confronted with these alternatives. However, the fact that these choices conflict with the hypothesis alerts us to the possibility of some inconsistency or irrationality as between the two choices. Let us try to expose this inconsistency.† First, define three events, E_1, E_2, E_3, the occurrence of which is determined by some randomizing device, with probabilities 0.01, 0.1 and 0.89 respectively. Then we can express the prospects in terms of these events as follows:

    (a) *the certainty*: in each of the events E_1, E_2, E_3 you receive £½m;
    (b) P^1: in E_1 you receive £0, in E_2 £2½m, in E_3 £½m;
    (c) P^2: in E_1 you receive £½m, in E_2 £½m, in E_3 £0;
    (d) P^3: in E_1 you receive £0, in E_2 £2½m, in E_3 £0.

It is easy to confirm that this generates the probabilities given in equations [E.6]–[E.8].

† The following discussion is based on that of Savage (1954), pp. 91–104.

Now consider Table 1:

		E_1 (0.01)	E_2 (0.1)	E_3 (0.89)
Situation 1	Certainty:	$\frac{1}{2}$	$\frac{1}{2}$	$\frac{1}{2}$
	P^1	0	$2\frac{1}{2}$	$\frac{1}{2}$
	Difference	$\frac{1}{2}$	-2	0
Situation 2	P^2	$\frac{1}{2}$	$\frac{1}{2}$	0
	P^3	0	$2\frac{1}{2}$	0
	Difference	$\frac{1}{2}$	-2	0

The table shows the alternatives in the two situations, their outcomes in the specified events, and the *differences* in these outcomes. These differences give the answers to the question: what is the net gain or loss, in each event, of choosing the certainty rather than P^1 in situation 1, and P^2 rather than P^3 in situation 2. Choosing the certainty rather than P^1 implies a net gain of £$\frac{1}{2}$m in E_1, a net loss of £2m in E_2, and nothing in E_3. We can therefore surmise that choice of the certainty implies that one is prepared to risk the loss of £2m with probability 0.1, (given that one will have £$\frac{1}{2}$m in that event anyway) to avoid the risk of losing £$\frac{1}{2}$m with probability 0.01, and having nothing in E_1. The outcomes in E_3 are irrelevant to this choice, since they are the same for both options. When we look at situation 2, we see that choice of P^3 rather than P^2 implies *exactly the reverse*. Choosing P^3 implies that one is prepared to take the risk of losing £$\frac{1}{2}$m and having nothing with probability 0.01, in exchange for the chance of being £2m better off with probability 0.1. Again, what happens in E_3 is irrelevant to the choice because the outcomes are then the same. Thus, interpreted in this way, the choices which Allais suggests are reasonable if the two situations are inconsistent, because they imply an exact reversal of the very same evaluation of outcomes (it is easy to show that someone who chooses as if to maximise expected utility would always choose consistently in the two situations: see Question 1 of Exercise 20E).

Once he has identified the inconsistency, Savage is prepared to modify his original choice – he sees the inconsistency of his initial preferences, and reverses his 'mistake'. This therefore suggests a *normative* role for the expected utility hypothesis: it can be used to check the rationality of decisions, and to work out the 'best' course of action in a more or less complex situation of choice under uncertainty. However, not everyone may be prepared to accept this: one may continue to prefer the certainty of £$\frac{1}{2}$m to P^1, and P^3 to P^2, even after one's 'inconsistency' in doing so is pointed out. Moreover, as we have stressed all along, from the point of view of economic theory we wish to use the expected utility hypothesis to derive propositions about real economic behaviour, and so we are concerned with the way in which choices are actually made. Hence, we still require the hypothesis to have positive, and not simply normative, content. Thus, if the 'inconsistent' response to examples such as Allais' is at all widespread, this must lead to doubts about the empirical validity of the theory.

The third line of criticism is rather more general than those considered so far, in that it goes beyond the expected utility hypothesis as such and attacks the basic conceptual framework of rational choice in economics. However, since the requirements of rationality in the expected utility theory seem particularly strong, the criticism bears particularly heavily on this theory.

Over two decades, H. A. Simon has developed a critique of the concept of rationality in economics which takes the following form. The economic theory of rational behaviour sees the decision-taker as faced with an externally given set of constraints which define a possibly very large set of alternatives. The decision-taker applies a preference ordering to this set of alternatives and chooses the best alternative. However, Simon argues that in reality there is an important limitation on the computational and information-processing capabilities of the decision-taker which creates a constraint arising out of the nature of the decision-taker himself, and this constraint makes possible only a limited degree of rationality, which Simon terms *bounded rationality*.

Simon believes that theories which do not regard rationality as bounded are likely to ignore important aspects of reality and to provide rather inadequate accounts of actual decision-taking. He suggests that bounded rationality can be incorporated into two types of decision model.†
The first proceeds by adopting a highly simplified description of reality, so that the environment is reduced to a degree of complication which the decision-taker can handle. Given the much-reduced set of alternatives which result, a preference ordering is applied and the best alternative chosen. Thus, this is a type of optimization model.

In the present case, this suggests that a very small number of very broad states of the world would be defined, a small number of alternative prospects considered, and the best of these chosen. For example, instead of considering all possible portfolios of all possible financial assets and their returns in all possible states of the world, an investor might simply choose between putting his money into a unit trust or into a building society, and might classify states of the world according to whether the inflation rate will rise, fall or stay the same. Thus he replaces a potentially very complex decision situation with a rather simple one. Simon emphasises that the 'best' decision in this framework is only *approximately* optimal. It may in fact be a long way away from the optimal solution in the absence of information-processing limitations. At the same time, it is worth noting that the theory set out in this chapter is directly applicable to this 'approximate optimization

---

† The present discussion is based on H. A. Simon (1972), though the issues are also considered at some length in Simon (1957).

problem', since there is still the basic framework of alternatives, states of the world, and an outcome for each alternative in each state of the world (it is of interest in this connection that the controlled experiments discussed earlier tended to involve choices between two alternatives with only two states of the world).

The conclusion therefore cannot be that the theory of this chapter is inapplicable to *any* situation involving bounded rationality, since it can be applied in this 'approximate optimization model', but that (*a*) it ignores the important question of the way in which the complex environment is simplified, and therefore cannot assess the degree of approximation to the 'true optimum' which the approach will achieve; (*b*) it is no longer obvious that the approach yields the best solution *given the limitations on information processing which exist* – that is, as a kind of 'second best' proposition, the best way to approach decision problems in the case of bounded rationality may not be that which we would adopt when information-processing capacity is unlimited.

This latter point is brought out by the second type of decision model which Simon suggests can be used to incorporate the notion of bounded rationality. This is the so-called *satisficing model*. Instead of applying a given preference ordering to a given (possibly highly simplified) set of alternatives and outcomes, Simon suggests that a decision-taker may begin with an *aspiration level* of the value of the outcome, which defines what he regards to be a satisfactory or acceptable outcome. Of course, for this to represent a separate model, this aspiration level must be below the *optimum* value of the outcome (there is a suggestion that over time, in a stable environment, with repeated choices, the aspiration level would tend to be revised upward towards the optimum, so the theory must be concerned with decision-taking in a changing and unstable environment). Then, the decision-taker considers a broader set of alternatives and a fuller set of possible outcomes than under the 'approximate optimization' model just discussed, but stops searching when he has found a satisfactory solution, rather than the best solution. In terms of our earlier example, an investor may be prepared to consider the alternatives of entering directly into the stock market to buy shares, investing in a unit trust, saving with a building society, buying government bonds, or some mixed portfolio of all these. He may also be interested in their returns not only in the light of possible inflation rates, but also of the likely development of economic activity and changes in the tax structure. However, rather than computing the possible outcomes of each alternative portfolio in each possible state of the world and finding the best portfolio (as envisaged in the expected utility theory), he will examine the alternatives in turn, and stop once he has found one which offers him, say, a 'satisfactory' level of return with an 'acceptable' degree of risk, even, if, for example, this were the very first alternative he considered.

Clearly, as a theory of decision-taking, the satisficing model leaves a great deal to be specified, in particular the determinants of the aspiration level, of the sets of alternatives and states of the world to be considered, and of the sequence in which elements of these sets will be searched. However, it is clear that the model provides a definite alternative to the expected utility theory, and one which some economists have found very appealing (see for example Cyert and March (1963)).

The conclusion of this line of criticism, therefore, is that the model of decision-taking under uncertainty set out earlier in this chapter, of which the expected utility theory is a part, unreasonably assumes unlimited computational and information-processing capabilities on the part of the individual. He is supposed to be able to define the entire set of states of the world, to assign an outcome for each decision alternative to each state, a probability to each state, and then to apply a complete consistent preference ordering over the entire set of prospects. This seems to eliminate from the situation all the doubt, ignorance and incompleteness of information which we commonly associate with the term uncertainty, and Simon argues that this achieves too much. Acknowledgement that rationality is bounded leads to a qualitatively different approach to decision-taking in general, and choice under uncertainty in particular.

It is of course possible to construct a defence of the expected utility theory against the lines of criticism which have been set out in this section. One could argue that the evidence from the controlled experiments, using students, national guardsmen and prison inmates may not be applicable to the areas of economic decision-taking with which the theory is ultimately concerned. The same may be said of Allais' 'armchair examples'. The 'behaviourist' approach which follows from Simon's ideas has failed to provide models which displace the neo-classical models based on unbounded rationality (cf. the discussion in Ch. 1), and there are doubts as to whether models which seek to replicate *processes* of decision-taking can be very useful in the *a priori* analysis of the *outcomes* of decision-taking.

However, we do not propose here to discuss at length the relative merits of the various arguments. It is clear that the expected utility theory has become part of the mainstream of economic analysis and it has proved fruitful in the development of a theory of resource allocation under uncertainty. As the subject develops, and theories are confronted with facts, it should become clear whether actual economic behaviour is consistent with the implications of the theory. If there is a gradual accumulation of evidence which runs counter to the theory, it is probable that some part of the explanation, and perhaps also the remedy, will lie in the contributions discussed in this section.

Exercise 19E

1. Show, in relation to Table 1, that someone who chooses between prospects in such a way as to maximize expected utility, will always choose *either* the certainty in situation 1 and P^2 in situation 2, *or* P^1 in situation 1 and P^3 in situation 2. (*Hint*: replace the money value x by the utility value $u(x)$ in the table, and then take the expected values of utility differences.)

2.* By examining the structure of Table 1, construct 5 numerical examples of the Allais type. Then confront someone with the five pairs of choice situations, and observe how many times he violates the expected utility hypothesis. Note his reaction when you point out any inconsistencies in his choices.

3.* How well do you think Simon's concept of bounded rationality, and the associated models of 'approximate optimization' and 'satisficing' provide a realistic description of actual decision-taking behaviour?

F. Conclusions

In this chapter, we first formalized the situation of 'decision-taking under uncertainty', the essential features of this formalization being a set of states of the world, a set of alternative decisions, a set of outcomes of each decision in each state of the world, and a set of probabilities, one for each state of the world. A vector of outcomes with a vector of probabilities defines for each alternative a prospect, and choice among alternatives reduces to choice among prospects. Thus we are led to consider a theory of the preference ordering over prospects.

We examined a set of axioms which imply the existence of a utility function defined on values of the outcome, and unique up to a positive linear transformation. We saw that any decision-taker whose choices would conform to our axioms can be regarded as choosing *as if* he sought to maximize the expected utility of the prospects, and so this gives us a straight-forward principle on which to base predictions of his choices among prospects. It therefore also provides us with an objective function which can be used to solve optimization problems under uncertainty. In essentially the same way as in the microeconomic theory set out earlier in this book, we can then go on to formulate models of individual economic behaviour, based on the optimization approach. However, we should note reservations concerning the expected utility theory. Controlled experiments carried out by a number of psychologists give only partial support for the theory, and in particular suggest that it may not perform well in relatively more complex situations. Simple examples can be devised in which apparently reasonable choices preclude the existence of a utility function. And finally it is argued that the theory requires unlimited computational and information processing abilities, whereas in reality rationality is necessarily bounded, and recognition of this would lead to different models. The response that the expected utility theory may still have an important normative role to play does not resolve these difficulties, since we are concerned with using the theory to generate positive hypotheses about actual decision-taking behaviour. Despite these criticisms, the dominant approach to the economics of uncertainty is based on the expected utility theory. In the next chapter we examine some models which illustrate the usefulness of the theory in analysing economic behaviour.

References and further reading

On the general question of theoretical approaches to decision-taking under uncertainty, see:

K. J. Arrow. 'Alternative approaches to the theory of choice in risk-taking situations', *Econometrica*, Vol. 19, 1951.

K. Borch. *The Economics of Uncertainty*, Princeton University Press, Princeton, N.J., 1968.

Expositions of and comments on the von Neumann–Morgenstern axioms are given by:

J. Hirshleifer. *Investment, Interest and Capital*, Prentice-Hall, 1970, Ch. 8.

J. von Neumann and **O. Morgenstern.** *Theory of Games and Economic Behaviour*, John Wiley, New York, 1964 ed., Ch. 3.

R. D. Luce and **H. Raiffa.** *Games and Decisions*, John Wiley, New York, 1966, Ch. 2.

K. Borch. *op. cit.*, Chs. III, IV, VI.

J. H. Dreze. 'Axiomatic theories of choice, cardinal utility and subjective probability: A Review' in J. H. Dreze (ed.): *Allocation under Uncertainty*, Macmillan, London, 1974.

K. J. Arrow. 'Exposition of the theory of choice under uncertainty' and 'The theory of risk aversion' in his *Essays in the Theory of Risk-Bearing*, North-Holland, Amsterdam, 1970.

M. Friedman and **L. Savage.** 'The utility analysis of choices involving risk', *Journal of Political Economy*, 1948.

H. Raiffa. *Decision Analysis*, Addison-Wesley, 1968.

Reports on the experimental tests of the expected utility theory are given in:

F. Mosteller and **P. Nogee.** 'An experimental measurement of utility', *Journal of Political Economy*, 1951.

D. Davidson, S. Siegel and **P. Suppes.** 'Some experiments and related theory on the measurement of utility and subjective probability', *Applied Mathematics and Statistics Laboratory*, Technical Report 1, Stanford University, 1955.

A. Tversky. 'Additivity, utility and subjective probability', *Journal of Mathematical Psychology*, 1967.

For a discussion of the 'Allais Paradox', see:

M. Allais. 'Le comportement de l'homme rationnel devant le risque: critique des postulats et des axiomes de l'école américaine', *Econometrica*, 1953.

L. J. Savage. *The Foundations of Statistics*, John Wiley, New York, 1954, pp. 100–104.

For a dissenting opinion see:

H. A. Simon. 'Theories of Bounded Rationality', Ch. 8 of C. B. McGuire and R. Radner (eds): *Decision and Organisation*, North-Holland, Amsterdam, 1972.

H. A. Simon. 'Theories of Decision-Making in Economics and Behavioural Science', *American Economic Review*, Vol. XLIX, No. 3, 1959.

For a critique of M. Friedman's methodological position see:

T. Koopmans. *Three Essays on the State of Economic Science*, McGraw Hill, 1957, Ch. 2.

F. P. Ramsey. *The Foundations of Mathematics and Other Logical Essays* (ed. R. B. Braithwaite), Routledge & Kegan Paul, London, 1931.

Chapter 20

Exchange under uncertainty*

A. Introduction

In the previous chapter we developed a theory of individual choice under uncertainty. We now go on to apply that theory to the analysis of exchange. We begin with an analysis of the insurance decision which, as well as introducing some useful diagrammatic tools, gives a good deal of insight into the nature of insurance markets and the role they play in the economy. With the same objective we examine a model of the stock market. Finally, we generalize these analyses of specific markets to consider some aspects of the theory of general equilibrium under uncertainty.

B. The insurance decision

This was already discussed in Chapter 19, in connection with the definition of risk-aversion, but here we shall recast and extend the analysis. Consider first the representation of a decision-taker's preferences. Suppose there can exist only two states of the world, and x_s, $s = 1, 2$, again denotes the decision-taker's income in state s. To begin with, he has a given endowment of income, $\hat{x}_s$, in state s, where in general $\hat{x}_1 \neq \hat{x}_2$, so that his income endowment is uncertain. Given that our axioms apply, the decision-taker's preferences are represented by the expected utility function:

$$\bar{u}(x_1, x_2) = pu(x_1) + (1-p)u(x_2) \qquad [\text{B.1}]$$

where p is the probability he assigns to state 1. We assume, as before, that the decision-taker is risk-averse, which implies not only that $u(x_s)$ is strictly concave, but also that $\bar{u}(x_1, x_2)$ is strictly concave (see Question 4 of Exercise 19D). Consider now a contour of the expected utility function:

$$\bar{u}(x_1, x_2) = \bar{u}^0 = pu(x_1) + (1-p)u(x_2) \qquad [\text{B.2}]$$

where $\bar{u}^0$ is some fixed value of utility. The graph of this contour is an indifference curve, showing pairs of values (x_1, x_2) which yield the same expected utility, $\bar{u}^0$. Figure 1 illustrates such an indifference curve, labelled

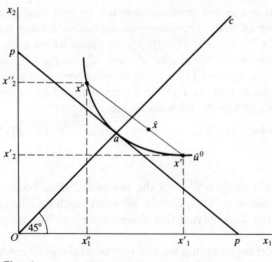

Fig. 1

$\bar{u}^0$. It bears a striking resemblance to those which we encountered in the theory of the consumer, and this can be explained in the following way:

(i) *its slope is negative:* differentiate the equation in [B.2] totally (the differentiability assumption of the previous chapter allows us to do this) to obtain:

$$d\bar{u}^0 = 0 = pu'(x_1)\,dx_1 + (1-p)u'(x_2)\,dx_2 \qquad [B.3]$$

implying that the slope of the indifference curve:

$$\frac{dx_2}{dx_1} = \frac{-pu'(x_1)}{(1-p)u'(x_2)} < 0 \qquad [B.4]$$

since probabilities and marginal utilities are all strictly positive. Intuitively, we would expect the slope to be negative since marginal utility of income is positive. Note in addition that, since the utility function does not depend on the state of the world (see Question 2 of Exercise 19D):

$$x_1 = x_2 \Rightarrow u'(x_1) = u'(x_2) \Rightarrow \frac{dx_2}{dx_1} = \frac{-p}{1-p} \qquad [B.5]$$

Thus, in Fig. 1, the point at which the 45° line Oc intersects the indifference curve, point a, has its coordinates equal to each other, and so the slope of the indifference curve at that point is equal to $-p/1-p$. Thus the straight line pp drawn tangent to the indifference curve at a in the figure has this slope;

(ii) *it is convex to the origin:* any strictly concave function is also strictly quasi-concave (see Question 1 of Exercise 20B), and so $\bar{u}(x_1, x_2)$ is strictly quasi-concave and has indifference curves which are convex to the origin. This property can be used to illustrate one of the aspects of

risk-aversion pointed out in the previous chapter, namely that of a preference for diversification of risks. Thus, suppose the decision-taker has available two prospects $P' = (p, x')$, and $P'' = (p, x'')$, between which he is indifferent. These are represented by points x' and x'' in Fig. 1, with their
co-ordinate vectors (x_1', x_2') and (x_1'', x_2''), as shown. Now any point on the
straight line joining them, such as $\bar{x}$ in the figure, is found as a combination
or mixture of the two prospects, with the income vector;

$$(\bar{x}_1, \bar{x}_2) = \bar{x} = kx' + (1-k)x'' = (kx_1' + (1-k)x_1'', kx_2' + (1-k)x_2'')$$

$$0 \le k \le 1 \qquad\qquad\qquad\qquad\qquad\qquad\qquad\qquad\qquad\qquad\text{[B.6]}$$

and so can be regarded as a *portfolio* of the prospects, since both prospects
are held in given proportions. Then clearly, all points such as $\bar{x}$ lie on higher
indifference curves than $\bar{u}^0$, implying that diversified portfolios are preferred
to 'extreme' ones.

　　This discussion suggests that we can represent the preferences of the
decision-taker by a family of indifference curves of the usual shape, all of
which have slopes of $-p/1-p$ at their points of intersection with the line Oc.
It is convenient to refer to Oc as the *certainty line*, since it shows the points
at which $x_1 = x_2$ (if the decision-taker will receive the same income in each
state, his income is certain).

　　Note that there is an important difference in the meaning of a point
such as x' or x'' in Fig. 1, from that of a point representing a consumption
vector in the theory of the consumer under certainty. In the latter, *all* the
components of the vector were available *ex post* as well as *ex ante* – the
consumer would end up with the entire vector he chose. In the present case,
however, one and only one state of the world can occur, and so *ex post* the
decision-taker receives only one element of the vector. In discussing choices
of points in the (x_1, x_2) space, therefore, we must always be talking in *ex
ante* terms. We can best think in terms of choice of *claims* to incomes, made
before the state of the world is known, with only one income claim actually
being 'valid' or 'enforceable' in the event, namely the claim for income in
that state which actually occurs. For this reason, we can regard the points in
(x_1, x_2) space as representing vectors of *state-contingent income claims*, the
term 'state-contingent' emphasizing that the value of a claim is zero if any
state occurs other than the one to which it corresponds. The expected utility
function $\bar{u}(x_1, x_2)$ is then regarded as a function of these state-contingent
income claims.

　　Let us turn now to an analysis of the insurance decision. In Fig. 2,
the point $\hat{x}$ represents the decision-taker's initial endowment of state-
contingent income claims, and I, the indifference curve passing through it,
shows all pairs of income claims which yield the same expected utility as $\hat{x}$.
In particular, point a, corresponding to the income vector (x_1^*, x_2^*), with
$x_1^* = x_2^*$, shows the certain income which is indifferent to the uncertain initial
endowment (in other words x_s^* is the certainty equivalent to the prospect
corresponding to point $\hat{x}$). Recall that the line pp through a has slope equal

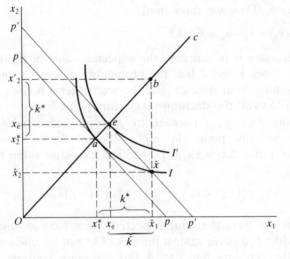

Fig. 2

to $-p/1-p$. Now suppose the decision-taker can enter into an insurance contract which will, in state 2, raise his income to equal that in state 1 (it 'compensates' for whatever event in state 2 causes the income reduction). Then, before payment of the insurance premium, this would put him at point b on the certainty line. This is clearly superior to point $\hat{x}$, as indeed is any point on the certainty line above point a. We can regard the payment of the insurance premium, k, as an equal subtraction from income in each state, and so it can be thought of diagrammatically as causing a movement along the certainty line back towards a, since it implies the *certain* income pair $(\hat{x}_1 - k, x'_2 - k)$, where $\hat{x}_1 = x'_2$. The maximum premium the decision-taker would be prepared to pay is found easily from the figure: if, after insuring, the decision-taker is left at any point to the right of a on the certainty line, he is better off, and so the largest premium he would be prepared to pay is, from the figure:

$$\hat{x}_1 - x_1^* = x'_2 - x_2^* = k^* \qquad [B.7]$$

In Chapter 19 we showed that this maximum premium, k^*, was greater than the expected value of the 'loss of income' against which the decision-taker is insuring. This can also be shown in the present case, and the demonstration will be useful in suggesting a generalization of the analysis. Consider point e in Fig. 2, whose (equal) co-ordinates are denoted by x_e. Point e is found as the point at which the certainty line, Oc, intersects $p'p'$, which is a line parallel to pp, and passing through the initial endowment point, $\hat{x} = (\hat{x}_1, \hat{x}_2)$. We shall show that if the decision-taker were to pay a premium exactly equal to the expected value of loss, this would put him at point e, and so the fact that e is to the right of a establishes the excess of k^* over this 'expected value' premium, or, as it is sometimes called, the 'fair premium', which we denote by $\bar{k}$. Thus, we show that:

$$(1-p)(\hat{x}_1 - \hat{x}_2) = \hat{x}_1 - x_e = \bar{k} < k^* \qquad \text{[B.8]}$$

where the first expression is in this case the expected value of the income difference between states 1 and 2 (i.e. the probability of state 2 *times* the 'loss of income' resulting from state 2), and the second term is the value of the premium which 'moves' the decision-taker from point b to e.

Consider the line $p'p'$, parallel to pp and hence with slope $-p/(1-p)$. Let x be any point on $p'p'$, different from $\hat{x}$, so that $x = [\hat{x}_1 - \Delta x_1, \hat{x}_2 + \Delta x_2]$ and $\Delta x_2 = \Delta x_1 p/(1-p)$. The expected value of x is

$$p(\hat{x}_1 - \Delta x_1) + (1-p)\left(\hat{x}_2 + \Delta x_1 \cdot \frac{p}{1-p}\right) = p\hat{x}_1 + (1-p)\hat{x}_2 \qquad \text{[B.9]}$$

Hence all points on $p'p'$ have the same expected value. Now an insurance contract which provides full cover against the risk of loss of income must put the individual on the certainty line Oc. A fair insurance contract is one which does not change the expected value of his income, i.e. leaves him on the line $p'p'$ through his original endowment. A full cover, fair, insurance contract must therefore leave the individual at the intersection of Oc and $p'p'$ at e.

The fair premium for this full insurance contract is $\bar{k}$, which, from Fig. 2, is

$$\bar{k} = \hat{x}_1 - x_e \qquad \text{[B.10]}$$

But since $p'p'$ is a constant expected income line we have

$$px_e + (1-p)x_e = x_e = p\hat{x}_1 + (1-p)\hat{x}_2 \qquad \text{[B.11]}$$

and substituting the r.h.s. for x_e in B.10 yields

$$\bar{k} = \hat{x}_1 - [p\hat{x}_1 + (1-p)\hat{x}_2] = (1-p)(\hat{x}_1 - \hat{x}_2) \qquad \text{[B.12]}$$

as the fair premium for full cover insurance which moves the individual from his original risky endowment $\hat{x}$ to the certainty line at e.

If the fair premium $\bar{k}$ were to be charged, the decision-taker would clearly choose to insure, since point e lies on a higher indifference curve than does point $\hat{x}$. Fig. 2 then suggests an alternative way of regarding the 'move' from $\hat{x}$ to e: effectively, the decision-taker is giving up a claim to income in state 1 of the amount $\hat{x}_1 - x_e$, *in exchange for* a claim to income in state 2 of the amount $x_e - \hat{x}_2$. That is, the fair insurance contract can be viewed as an agreement *to exchange state-contingent income claims*, at a rate which is determined by the slope of the line $p'p'$. But this suggests an immediate analogy between the line $p'p'$ and the *budget line* of the consumer in Chapter 3. Rewriting the equation for the line $p'p'$, from [B.9], as:

$$px_1 + (1-p)x_2 = p\hat{x}_1 + (1-p)\hat{x}_2 \qquad \text{[B.13]}$$

this could be interpreted as constraining the *expected value* of the chosen pair of state-contingent income claims to equal the expected value of the initial state-contingent income claim endowment.

However, on the assumptions made so far, the analogy with the consumer's budget constraint is not strictly valid; if the insurance contract is framed in terms of a *fixed* compensation, exactly equal to loss of income which occurs in state 2, with an associated *fixed* premium $\bar{k}$, then in fact only *two* points on the line $p'p'$ are available to the decision-taker, namely points $\hat{x}$ and e, and the remaining points on the line are unattainable.

Suppose, however, that the insurance contract were framed in terms of a *variable* premium $k \geq 0$, and a corresponding variable 'compensation', $\tilde{x}_2 - \hat{x}_2$, where the two are related by the equation:

$$k = (1-p)(\tilde{x}_2 - \hat{x}_2) \qquad k \geq 0 \qquad\qquad\qquad\qquad [\text{B}.14]$$

That is, the decision-taker is free *to choose* any premium and will receive, if and only if state 2 occurs, the compensation implied by [B.14], so that $\tilde{x}_2$ is his state 2 income, if insured, before payment of the insurance premium k. In the special case of fixed compensation we had ([B.8]) $\tilde{x}_2 = \hat{x}_1$. Then it is easy to show (see Question 4 of Exercise 20B) that this makes available *the whole* of the line $p'p'$ to the left of point $\hat{x}$, and so equation [B.13], for $x_1 \leq \hat{x}_1$, and $x_2 \geq \hat{x}_2$, does become a true analogue to the budget constraint in consumer theory. In other words, by choosing a suitable value of k, the decision-taker can move leftward along $p'p'$ for any distance he likes.

At the same time (postponing for the moment the question of its reasonableness on empirical grounds), this generalization does not appear to be an important one since even if the entire line $p'p'$ were available to the decision-taker, we know he would choose point e, because at that point the line is tangent to an indifference curve, as the figure shows. Thus the decision-taker will pay a premium k and hold the certain income claim x_e.

This suggests a further generalization. Suppose that the variable premium $k \geq 0$, and the associated compensation $\tilde{x}_2 - \hat{x}_2$, are related by:

$$k = (1-q)(\tilde{x}_2 - \hat{x}_2) \qquad 0 < q < 1 \qquad\qquad\qquad\qquad [\text{B}.15]$$

where $q \gtreqless p$. In other words, the insurance contract may contain a different *implied probability* of state of the world 2. The 'budget constraint' then becomes:

$$qx_1 + (1-q)x_2 = q\hat{x}_1 + (1-q)\hat{x}_2 \qquad x_1 \leq \hat{x}_1 \qquad\qquad [\text{B}.16]$$

$$x_2 \geq \hat{x}_2$$

(Prove this). We can then distinguish three possible cases, each of which is illustrated in Fig. 3:

(a) $q = p$. In this case, the slope of the 'budget line' is again equal to $-p/1-p$, and we have the case just analysed: whatever the possibilities, point e is chosen and the premium $\bar{k}$ is paid.

(b) $q > p$. In this case, the slope of the budget line, in absolute

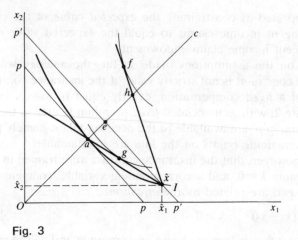

Fig. 3

value, is $q/1-q > p/1-p$, and so the line will be steeper than $p'p'$, while still passing through point $\hat{x}$. It will therefore look like the line $\hat{x}hf$ in Fig. 3.

In this case, we know that point h, on the certainty line, cannot be the optimal point for the decision-taker, since the indifference curve passing through that point has a slope of $-p/1-p$ at h. The tangency point must be at some point such as f in the figure, where the indifference curve is steeper than at its intersection with Oc. Thus, in this case, the decision-taker does not choose a point on the certainty line, but rather chooses a pair of state-contingent claims with the claim in state 2 actually greater than that in state 1, essentially because the probability p which *he* associates with state 1 is smaller than that of the 'insurer'. He is in fact gambling on the occurrence of state 2.

(c) $q < p$. In this case, the absolute value of the slope of the budget line is $q/1-q < p/1-p$, and so the line will be flatter than $p'p'$, while passing through point $\hat{x}$. For example, take the line $\hat{x}ga$ in Fig. 3. Clearly, point g rather than point a will be chosen by the decision-taker, and so he retains some uncertainty since he still incurs a loss of income if state 2 occurs. However, note that in this case, since points a and $\hat{x}$ are indifferent to each other, he may not have insured at all if a were the only point, other than $\hat{x}$, available, while he certainly insures if he can make an insurance contract at the terms implied by the slope of the line $\hat{x}ga$.

Markets in state-contingent income claims

Consideration of Fig. 3 then suggests a way of regarding a market in insurance of this 'flexible' kind. It is *as if*, before the state of the world is known, two markets were set up. On one of them can be bought or sold state-contingent income claims for state 1: that is, a contract can be made which specifies that some amount of income will be delivered if and only if state 1 occurs. At the time of concluding the contract, a price, say π_1, is paid, per unit of income to be delivered in state 1. Likewise, on the other market, one can enter into contracts for state-contingent delivery of income in state 2, paying a price π_2 per unit of the income claim. Then an individual can engage in transactions in these markets, subject to the budget constraint:

$$\pi_1 x_1 + \pi_2 x_2 = \pi_1 \hat{x}_1 + \pi_2 \hat{x}_2 \qquad [B.17]$$

which says that the value of his final holding of state-contingent income claims must equal the value of his initial endowment. Any one of the 'budget lines' $\hat{x}e$, $\hat{x}hf$ and $\hat{x}ga$ in Fig. 3 can then be thought of as corresponding to this budget constraint, with slope $-\pi_1/\pi_2$, the relative price ratio. Moreover, the equilibrium solution, such as points f, e or g, can be characterized in a familiar way. The decision-taker chooses his optimal holding of state-contingent income claims *as if* he maximized his expected utility function in [B.1] subject to the budget constraint in [B.19], yielding as a necessary condition:

$$\frac{p}{(1-p)} \frac{u'(x_1)}{u'(x_2)} = \frac{\pi_1}{\pi_2} \qquad [B.18]$$

where the lefthand side is the *MRS* between state-contingent income claims. Thus we have the usual *MRS* = price ratio condition. From these conditions, we can also determine *demand functions* for state-contingent income claims:

$$x_s = D_s(\pi_1, \pi_2) \qquad s = 1, 2 \qquad [B.19]$$

which relate to the decision-taker's trading in the markets for state-contingent claims before the state of the world is known. The condition in [B.18], incidentally, makes clear that only when $\pi_1/\pi_2 = p/1 - p$, will the optimal point lie on the certainty line.

It should be stressed that this formulation of markets in state-contingent income claims is an interpretation we can place, for theoretical purposes, on the way in which competitive markets in 'flexible' insurance contracts work. Its usefulness is that *it immediately establishes a formal identity between the analysis of insurance markets, and the whole body of neo-classical price theory which we have previously considered*, since a state-contingent income claim becomes formally identical with a good or commodity in that theory. We can then apply the results of that theory to the analysis of insurance markets, with a considerable economy of effort and gain in insight.

Forms of insurance contract

We can summarize the discussion so far in this section in the following way: there are two types of insurance contract, one of which restricts compensation to the difference between state 2 and state 1 income, and charges a fixed premium; the other of which allows the buyer of insurance to choose the amount of compensation and associated premium. The first type, therefore, offers the buyer a point on the certainty line and, as long as the premium is less than k^*, the buyer will choose to insure. The second type offers the buyer, in effect, a 'budget line' with an implicit relative price ratio, along which he can move, and from which he can choose his preferred holding of state-contingent income claims. Only in the case in which the 'budget line' happens to coincide with $p'p'$, i.e. in which the 'implied probability of state 2' in the insurance contract equals the decision-taker's own probability of state 2, will a point on the certainty line be chosen. In all other cases, the optimal choice will imply income uncertainty, in the sense that the chosen state-contingent income claims will not be equal. This allows us immediately to conclude that from the point of view of consumer welfare, the second type of insurance contract is superior to the first, since under it buyers cannot be worse off and may be better off than if they were constrained always to choose a point on the certainty line. In other words, the 'flexible terms' insurance policy *permits a wider set of exchange possibilities* than the 'fixed terms' insurance policy, and so the decision-taker cannot do worse and may do better with the former type of policy.

In practice, both kinds of insurance policy, as well as intermediate versions, appear to exist. For example under a life insurance contract one can choose the amount of compensation payable upon death, and the associated premium: compensation is not restricted to payment to dependants of the income which would have been earned by the deceased if he had lived. Similarly, one may insure against loss of a limb, an eye, etc in variable terms.

On the other hand, the form of insurance contract for medical care entered into with the state in the United Kingdom is an example of a fixed insurance policy. One pays a fixed insurance premium (which may also embody an element of income taxation), and receives free of charge (for most types of care) certain medical services on falling ill. The extent and nature of these services is determined by the physician and the rules of the National Health Service, rather than by the individual (unless he chooses to become a private patient and thereby opts out of the state system). We can regard the insurance contract therefore as consisting of a fixed premium and a fixed amount of compensation equal to the costs of the medical care incurred in the event that one falls ill.

Intermediate types of contract also exist. For example, on taking out motor insurance against accidental damage, a fixed premium is paid (determined by certain characteristics of the driver and the car, which are supposed to determine the probability of an accident), and compensation is limited to the actual cost of an accident. So, on the face of it, the motor insurance contract is in fixed terms. However, it is often possible to incorporate a 'deductible' or an 'excess' into the policy. That is, a discount on the premium is received, in return for an undertaking to pay the first £x of the assessed repair cost, where several values of x, and associated discounts, are available. In effect therefore, in terms of Fig. 3, a *discrete* number of separate points on the 'budget line' are available, up to the point at which it meets the certainty line. For example, several points on the line $\hat{x}ga$ in Fig. 3 might be available, other than $\hat{x}$ and a, and so the decision-taker might be able to get fairly close to his optimal point g, depending on the exact locations of the available points. Such a 'discretely variable' insurance contract will clearly be superior to a *fixed* policy, in the sense that the decision-taker may be better off and cannot be worse off under the former than under the latter; but, in exactly the same sense, the discretely variable policy is inferior to a fully flexible one.

A question which naturally arises is: why should different types of insurance contract exist and in particular, why should they not all be completely flexible? The above examples may suggest possible answers. Suppose, in the case of motor insurance, one could name any sum as compensation, and pay a corresponding premium which is some stated fraction of this sum. Then if buyers of insurance behave in an individually rational way, selling insurance cannot be profitable. The rational individual would pay the largest possible premium he and his creditors could raise and find a safe and apparently accidental way of crashing his car. He is less likely to do this with life or limb (and in any case suicide often invalidates a life insurance contract). In other words, the probability of occurrence of states of the world or events upon which contracts are contingent may be capable of being influenced by the decision-taker, and if insurance is to be made available at all, it may have to be accompanied by constraints which limit the type of contract available. This is an aspect of *moral hazard*, which we shall discuss at some length at the end of this section.

The question of why an insurance contract may be only *discretely* and not *fully* flexible may perhaps be explained by *transactions costs*. If, for example, the costs of drawing up and concluding contracts, administering claims, etc, increases with the number of types of contract; while it is found from experience that buyers do not vary uniformly in the precise terms of contract which they would choose, but rather 'cluster' around particular points, then discretely flexible contracts may on balance be the most economical way of organizing insurance. We shall return to this question at the end of this section.

Insurance as exchange

We have so far discussed the insurance decision of an individual in isolation and showed that an insurance contract could be regarded, for theoretical purposes, as defining a price ratio at which state-contingent income claims could be exchanged. Exchange implies the existence of other individuals with whom trade can take place, and our analysis is incomplete until it is extended to take account of the way in which decisions of two or more individuals interact to determine the price ratio. In carrying out this analysis we assume that insurance contracts may be fully flexible. Thus we can proceed *as if* there existed markets in state-contingent income claims, the significance of this being that we can directly apply the framework of analysis already used in Chapter 10.

Suppose that there are just two individuals; $\hat{x}_s^i$ is the initial endowment of individual $i = 1, 2$ in state $s = 1, 2$, and x_s^i the corresponding state-contingent income claim. The expected utility functions are:

$$\bar{u}^i(x_1^i, x_2^i) = p^i u^i(x_1^i) + (1-p^i)u^i(x_2^i) \qquad i = 1, 2 \qquad [B.20]$$

where p^i is the probability assigned to state 1 by decision-taker i. Note that we permit $p^1 \gtreqless p^2$, i.e. we do not assume that the decision-takers have identical probability beliefs. We do assume however that the utility functions u^i are strictly concave, implying once again indifference curves convex-to-the-origin.

The situation is taken to be one of pure exchange: the total amounts of income available to the economy are given by the sums of initial endowments:

$$\sum_i \hat{x}_s^i = \hat{x}_s \qquad s = 1, 2 \qquad [B.21]$$

and we are interested in the question of the equilibrium of exchange involving state-contingent income claims x_s^i, where we must have:

$$\sum_i x_s^i = \hat{x}_s \qquad s = 1, 2 \qquad [B.22]$$

as an equilibrium condition. In Fig. 4, we present an analysis of the situation in terms of an Edgeworth box diagram. The horizontal sides of the box correspond to the total initial endowment of income in state 1, $\hat{x}_1$, and the vertical sides to the total initial endowment of income in state 2, $\hat{x}_2$. From the origin at the south-west corner, denoted O_1, we measure, for decision-taker 1, his income in state 1, x_1^1, in the horizontal direction, and his income in state 2, x_2^1, in the vertical. Likewise, from the origin at the north-east corner, denoted O_2, we measure 2's state 1 income leftwards, and his state 2 income downwards. Any point in the box represents *four* income values

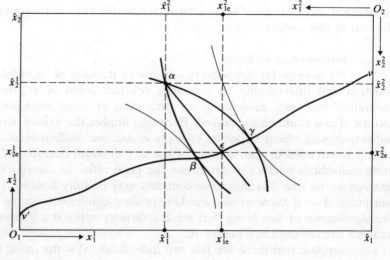

Fig. 4

$(x_1^1, x_2^1, x_1^2, x_2^2)$, such that the equilibrium conditions in [B.21] are exactly satisfied. 1's indifference curves are drawn convex to the origin at O_1, and 2's are drawn convex to the origin at O_2. Special interest attaches to the locus of points of tangency of the indifference curves, here shown as vv'. Given that 1's initial endowments are $(\hat{x}_1^1, \hat{x}_2^1)$, and 2's are $(\hat{x}_1^2, x_2^2)$, we can regard this two-person economy as being initially at point α in the box.

Let us now adopt the Edgeworth assumption, as we did in Chapter 10, to the effect that: the decision-takers will carry out any exchange which makes at least one of them better off and the other no worse off. By exact analogy with the earlier analysis of two-person exchange, we would then predict that they will end up somewhere on the contract curve, shown by the locus $\beta \, \varepsilon \, \gamma$ in Fig. 4. The reasoning is as before: at point α, there is clearly scope for at least one of them to become better off. For example, if they carried out the exchange which would move them to the incomes corresponding to point β, 1 is no worse off, 2 is better off, and indeed has appropriated all the gains from trade. If they moved to point γ, 2 would be no worse off and 1 would have all the gains from trade. Assume instead that they agree on exchanges which result in point ε, corresponding, since it is on vv', to a point of tangency of indifference curves (not drawn). In this case they share the gains from trade. Given the Edgeworth assumption, they must end up somewhere on the locus of points of tangency of the indifference curves, vv', since at any point off that locus, indifference curves intersect and there is scope for further gains from trade. However, they clearly will not move to a point on the locus other than in the interval $\beta \, \varepsilon \, \gamma$ since this would make one of them strictly worse off than at α. Hence the curve $\beta \, \varepsilon \, \gamma$ represents the set of possible equilibrium outcomes to the exchange process, or, in the terminology of Chapter 10, it represents *the core* of this exchange process.

If we assume that the exchange process results in point ε, then we can regard the decision-takers as having traded at a price ratio given by the slope of the line $\alpha\varepsilon$. The first decision-taker has given up $(\hat{x}_2^1 - x_{2e}^1)$ of x_2, in exchange for $(x_{1e}^1 - \hat{x}_1^1)$ of x_1 and so the ratio of these quantities determines the equilibrium rate of exchange, or price ratio, for the two quantities. Thus, there is a very close analogy with the earlier analysis of exchange in Chapter 10. However, the specific interpretation of the exchange here is rather different. Here, the parties are exchanging *claims*, rather than specific quantities of goods. The first decision-taker is undertaking to pay the second the amount of income $(\hat{x}_2^1 - x_{2e}^1)$ *if and only if state of the world 2 occurs*, in exchange for 2's undertaking to pay $(x_{1e}^1 - \hat{x}_1^1)$ *if and only if state 1 occurs*. Such a contract, in state-contingent terms, would only be entered into *before* the state of the world is known because, of course, in this one-good world, once the state of the world is known, there are no gains from trade – the economy ends up on a *side* of the box. In *ex ante* terms, however, before the state of the world is known, both decision-takers can make a gain in *expected utility* by exchanging state-contingent income claims, enforceable in only one state of the world.

We can of course interpret the equilibrium of exchange in Fig. 4 in terms of an insurance contract. As it stands the analysis of exchange is quite neutral as to the identities of the insurer and the insured, so let us take it that 1 sells insurance to 2. If, in their bargaining about an insurance contract, they end up at point ε, we can deduce the terms of this 'equilibrium insurance contract' in the following way. Since 2 has a net reduction of income in state 1 of the amount $(\hat{x}_1^2 - x_{1e}^2)$ this is the amount of the premium he pays. Call this k_e. In exchange for the undertaking to pay k_e in *each* state of the world, 2 receives a *net* compensation in state 2 of the amount $(x_{2e}^2 - \hat{x}_2^2)$, implying a *gross* compensation of the amount $(x_{2e}^2 - \hat{x}_2^2 + k_e)$. Thus, the insurance contract will specify a premium k_e payable for certain, and a gross compensation $C = (x_{2e}^2 - \hat{x}_2^2 + k_e)$, which will be paid if and only if state 2 occurs. Note that in general, given dissimilar preferences and probability beliefs, there is no reason for point ε in Fig. 4 to lie on a certainty line, either for individual 1 or 2 (as long as $\hat{x}_1 \neq \hat{x}_2$ the two certainty lines will not meet. Explain why.). The only essential point is that as a result of agreeing on an insurance contract, that is, on making an exchange of state-contingent income claims, both decision-takers can make gains from trade and end up better off.

The optimality properties of the outcome of the exchange process shown in Fig. 4 are essentially familiar from the analysis in Chapter 17. We know that any point on the locus vv' is a Pareto optimum; given an allocation on the locus, there is no way in which one consumer can be made better off and the other no worse off. Hence the equilibrium of the exchange process is a Pareto optimum. This property of the outcome follows directly from the Edgeworth assumption. However it is interesting to note the meaning which must be attached to Pareto optimality in this context. At a point on vv', no individual can be made better off and the other worse off *in terms of his own expected utilities*, which depend, *inter alia*, on his probability beliefs. This is clearly seen if we recall from [B.4] the definition of the marginal rate of substitution between income claims, and note that, since they are equal along vv', we must have:

$$\left(\frac{p^1}{1-p^1}\right)\frac{u_1'(x_1^1)}{u_1'(x_2^1)} = \left(\frac{p^2}{1-p^2}\right)\frac{u_2'(x_1^2)}{u_2'(x_2^2)}$$

implying that, as long as $p^1 \neq p^2$, the locus of Pareto optimal points vv' is *not* independent of the probability assignments made by the decision-takers. This adds in this case another dimension of 'individualism' to the value judgements underlying the Pareto criterion. If we are to propose the Pareto criterion as a basis for *social* optimality, this implies that we respect not only individual preferences, but also individual probability beliefs. An individual is regarded as better off, if and only if he experiences an increase in his expected utility, which incorporates his own probability beliefs. Thus, we would have to reject paternalism, not only in respect of tastes, but also in respect of the views people take of the relative likelihoods of future states of the world, even where these may differ from our own. It is an interesting question, of whether tolerance of other people's tastes is or is not more reasonable than tolerance of their probability beliefs, though one which will not be pursued here.

General equilibrium with state-contingent income claims

As we know from Chapter 10, corresponding to this analysis of two-person exchange along the lines laid down by Edgeworth is a Walrasian formulation which works in terms of organized markets and market prices. In fact this formulation is implicit in the earlier analogy we drew between markets in 'flexible' insurance contracts and markets on which state-contingent income claims could be bought and sold at prices π_s, $s = 1, 2$. Thus, we showed that we could derive demand functions for state-contingent income claims, which, for individual i, can be written as:

$$x_s^i = D_s^i(\pi_1, \pi_2) \qquad i, s = 1, 2 \qquad \text{[B.23]}$$

We then say that an equilibrium exists when we have prices π_s^* and demands x_s^{i*} such that:

$$\sum_i x_s^{i*} = \sum_i D_s^i(\pi_1^*, \pi_2^*) = \sum_i \hat{x}_s^i \qquad s = 1, 2 \qquad \text{[B.24]}$$

i.e. when supply equals demand in each market. We could analyse the existence and stability of such an equilibrium in precisely those terms adopted in Chapter 16. We could, for example, show that the demand functions in [B.23] are continuous and homogeneous of degree zero in prices, and also that Walras' Law will hold. We could then apply essentially the same existence proof. Similarly, we could prove global stability on the basis of the gross substitute assumption, or one of its equivalents. We already have a conclusion on the optimality properties of the solution. Since all decision-takers face the same prices, their marginal rates of substitution between the pair of state-contingent income claims will all be equal, and so the market equilibrium satisfies the necessary conditions for a Pareto optimum.

Thus, we conclude that when 'flexible' insurance contracts exist, we can apply directly the entire framework of the earlier analysis of competitive equilibrium. However, the condition on the flexibility of insurance is necessary, as well as sufficient: as we have seen, when 'compensation' is strictly confined to the value of income lost, choice is restricted to the certainty line, and only in the case in which the price ratio, π_1/π_2, corresponds to the decision-taker's probability ratio, $p_1^i/1 - p_1^i$, will this satisfy the necessary condition for an optimal choice. If we now think of an economy with a large number of decision-takers, facing the *same* insurance terms, then differences in their probabilities p^i must imply that at least some of them are not at points of tangency, and the condition for Pareto optimality will be violated. Thus, an economy without flexible insurance contracts presents us with a case of market failure.

It is of course an empirical question as to whether insurance contracts have sufficient flexibility to allow us to conclude that the real economy achieves an optimum. There appear to be two respects in which real-world insurance markets do not correspond to the theoretical ideal we have just been examining:

(*a*) The assumption of just two states of the world is of course a simplification and in reality many states exist. There appear to be many events against which it is not possible to insure and which adversely affect income or utility, and so it is not possible to exchange income between any state of the world corresponding to such an event, and any other state. In terms of the state-contingent income claim concept, it is as if markets in some claims did not exist.

(*b*) The fact that many insurance contracts may be in fixed or at best discretely variable terms implies restrictions on the set of possibilities for exchange: the set consists of a fairly small finite number of points. Thus restrictions on insurance contracts imply that exchange possibilities do not extend across all states of the world and where exchange between states is possible, only a small number of state-contingent income vectors may be available.

Transactions costs and moral hazard

As we have already suggested, there are two sets of factors which are usually put forward to explain the restrictions on insurance possibilities: transactions costs and moral hazard. However it is not at all clear that a rigid separation between these two categories of explanation can be maintained, for the reason that moral hazard is essentially due to the cost of obtaining information, which is one important element in what are usually termed 'transactions costs'. For that reason, we shall not try to force explanations into this rigid and imperfect dichotomy, but will simply consider the main types of explanation which have been put forward.

In operating a market, it is necessary to incur certain costs of an administrative nature. Contracts have to be drawn up, buyers and sellers have to be brought into contact, transactions registered, a system of rules devised and enforced, and so on. Ultimately, these costs must fall on the parties to the transactions (except to the extent that they are borne out of taxation, e.g. as in administration of the legal system, because of the general social advantages of maintaining the exchange system), and will be met out of their gains from trade. If, therefore, the gains from trade were insufficient to finance the costs of operating the market, a market will not exist. For example, a rail commuter cannot take out insurance against the event that his train is late, even though it is an event with a well-defined probability and one which imposes costs on him and his employers. Presumably the costs of organizing this kind of insurance, assessing compensation, etc would be large relative to the losses in income and utility which the commuters experience – the required premiums would exceed their willingness to pay. On the other hand, it used not to be possible to insure against being unable to take a planned holiday, but now, with the advent of mass tourism, hotel overbooking, strike-prone air transport and precariously-financed travel agents, a market in such insurance does exist.

A second major cost in operating an insurance market is the cost incurred by the seller in assessing the degree of risk presented by a potential buyer, i.e. the probability that the event against which the individual is insuring will in fact occur. There are two cases here which can be distinguished. First, the probability of the event may depend on a number of *objective* factors which vary across individuals, where by 'objective' we mean that they are independent of any decisions or actions which the individual might take. For example, in the case of life insurance, a major objective factor would be the age of the prospective buyer of insurance. Secondly, the probability of the event may depend on decisions or actions within the individual's control. To continue the example of life insurance, an important factor would be the smoking habits of the buyer and the extent to which he takes exercise. In motor insurance, the care exercised by the driver is a factor within his control. In the case of property insurance, the extent of the householder's investment in security devices such as locks and burglar alarms, fireproofing, quality of electrical installation, etc. will determine the likelihood of the events of loss of property through fire or theft.

Acquisition of 'objective' information is usually carried out in a straightforward way. On the basis of a statistical analysis, it is often possible to find the most important factors which determine the probability of the event and the buyer of insurance then has to provide the relevant information about himself. (The so-called 'proposal form' which a buyer of insurance must complete before an insurance contract is concluded is designed expressly to provide this sort of information, and also always carries the warning that deliberate provision of false information will nullify the contract.) Individuals in the different objective risk classes thus identified can then be offered insurance at premia related to their different risks.

It may be very costly or impossible for insurers to identify which risk class individuals belong to. They will then be forced to offer the same premium to individuals who have different probabilities of the insured event occurring. This premium will be based on the insurer's experience with all the insured individuals and will therefore be higher than the fair premium for good (i.e. low) risk individuals and lower than the fair premium for bad (i.e. high) risk individuals. Some of the good risk individuals may choose not to insure because the unfair averaged premium will exceed the maximum amount they are willing to pay to be relieved of their risk. If some good risks do not insure the actual losses of the insurer will be worse than he anticipated when setting the averaged premium and he will be forced to raise his premium. This may force more of the good risks out of his insurance pool and the process may continue until only the most risk averse of the good risks remain insured. This process is known as *adverse selection* in that the averaged premium which is unfair for the good risks will discourage them, but not the bad risk individuals.

It is the second kind of information which presents the greatest difficulty, the crux of the problem being the *endogeneity* of the probability of the event to the buyer's behaviour. The buyer may adjust his choice of action, in the light of the terms of the insurance contract, in a way which is advantageous to him but disadvantageous to the insurer. The earlier example of the apparently accidental car crash was a case in point: if any amount of compensation can be paid in exchange for a premium which is a fraction of it, then the buyer of insurance has the incentive to set the probability of an accident equal to 1. A similar example would be provided by the case in which a merchant about to go bankrupt takes out a huge insurance on his warehouse and then discreetly sets fire to it. In a less extreme way, the fact that a property owner would be fully compensated for the damage done by a fire might lead him to minimize his expenditure on fire-prevention devices, thus increasing the probability of the event against which he is insuring. The problem the insurer faces is to design an insurance contract which takes account of the action chosen by the buyer and which has a relation between premium and compensation which correctly reflects the probability of the event determined by the specific action chosen by the buyer.

Thus suppose it were possible to ascertain *without cost* the action of the buyer (e.g. our bankrupt arsonist is sure to be found out at zero cost). Then the corresponding probability of the event conditional on the action of the buyer could be calculated, and the insurer could offer a fully flexible insurance contract based on this (ignoring other transactions costs). He could offer a different contract for each possible action of the buyer (a lower premium the greater the expenditure on fire prevention, for example) and the buyer could then weigh up the cost of his action against the cost of the premium and choose his optimal contract.

However, information on the actions of the buyer is not usually costless and may be inaccurate. Companies which sell insurance against loss of property through fire and theft, for example, commonly employ investigators, inspectors and assessors to provide them with this kind of information. It may then be possible that the costs of acquiring the information may be so great as to outweigh gains from trade. Or, in trading off the gains from trade against information cost, insurers find it optimal to place restrictions on the insurance contract.

One such restriction is the inclusion of *coinsurance*. Coinsurance takes place when the insurer pays as compensation *only some proportion* of the actual loss incurred by the buyer of the insurance. The fact that some of the loss will be borne by himself will then induce the buyer to incur costs to reduce the probability of the event. From our present point of view, coinsurance, which arises out of the costliness of information, represents a severe restriction of the exchange possibilities open to the buyer, since it is now not only the case that no available point lies *beyond* the certainty line, but also no point *on* the certainty line is available, since some amount of loss is always carried by the buyer. In terms of Fig. 3 above, the lines $\hat{x}hf$, $\hat{x}e$ or $\hat{x}ga$ would have to be truncated at some point below Oc, the precise point being determined by the degree of coinsurance. Thus we see that costliness of information, in the presence of dependence of the probability of the event insured against on the action of the buyer, leads to a severe restriction on the set of possibilities of exchange of state-contingent income claims.

The type of informational problem just discussed is often referred to as a form of 'moral hazard'. We could more fruitfully view the problem as that of a conflict between individual and group rationality. Given the nature of an insurance policy (in the absence of coinsurance) each individual finds it in his own interests to choose the action which maximizes his gain; this may then cause modifications in the nature of insurance contracts which make everyone worse off than if they had chosen initially in a 'socially responsible way'. The individually rational choice leads to a worse outcome for everyone than the socially rational choice. The structure of the situation is that of the 'prisoners' dilemma' game, and occurs in many other areas of economic behaviour – see for example the discussion of cheating in oligopolies in Chapter 12 and of public goods in Chapter 18.

Another aspect of 'moral hazard' which may lead to restrictions on the set of exchange possibilities is the dependence of the *amount of compensation*, (rather than the probability of occurrence of the event insured against) on the actions of the buyer of insurance, and again the problem may arise that the buyer adjusts to an insurance contract in ways which are advantageous to him and disadvantageous to the insurer. A frequently cited example is that of medical care. Suppose there were no medical insurance. In the event that an individual fell ill, he would have to buy medical care at the market rate. Given his illness, income and preferences, he will at the given price choose a particular amount of medical care. In general the lower the price, the greater the quantity of medical care he will choose. (This simple proposition about the nature of demand curves may appear out of place in this context, but there is no reason for it to be. The number of physicians' visits, the amount and type of medication, the duration and nature of hospital services, the degree of eminence of the doctor, even the type of surgery, if any, carried out, can all in general be varied, at a price, for a specific type of illness). Suppose now that it becomes possible to insure against ill-health and that the insurer undertakes to cover all the costs of medical care, *whatever they turn out to be*. Effectively, therefore, the price of medical care to the individual falls to zero, and he will increase his demand accordingly – he will choose the 'best' treatment, the 'best' doctors, etc, regardless of cost.

The cost of medical care in this case will determine the premium to be paid. Thus, let us suppose that we have a population of identical individuals, with p the probability that an individual will contract a particular illness, C_1 the cost of the medical services each would buy *in the absence of insurance*, and $C_2 > C_1$ the cost of the services each will buy when the insurance company pays. Then pC_1 represents the expected value of each person's loss without insurance, while pC_2 represents the 'fair premium' which the insurer might charge (if there exist a large number of these identical individuals, then charging each of them pC_2 will mean that the insurer will just about break even, assuming the illness is non-contagious and ignoring administrative costs). Given that the individual is risk-averse, he will be prepared to pay a premium greater than pC_1, but he may not be prepared to pay the premium pC_2. If not, then he does not insure, but instead carries the risk himself. Because, therefore, everyone, when insured, treats medical care as a free good, we have that people will not insure; if everyone restricted their demands to the cost level C_1, on the other hand, then a premium of pC_1 would be offered, and everyone could insure and be better off, since they are risk-averse. The problem is that *given* the existence of insurance, no one individual has any incentive to restrain his demand for medical care, and so again we have a divergence between individually and socially rational actions. More generally, if individuals differ in their incomes and tastes, some may be prepared to pay the premium pC_2 and some not, but again the latter group are losing out because of the 'zero price effect' which insurance may have.

Sellers of insurance may meet this difficulty by again imposing restrictions on insurance contracts. The most obvious restriction is on the amount of expenditure and types of medical treatment for which compensation will be paid. By incorporating such restrictions into contracts, and at the same time offering a *range* of contracts with varying amounts of treatment and corresponding premiums, quite a wide range of possibilities could be made available, and the restrictions on the set of exchange possibilities may not be very severe. Under the National Health Service in the United Kingdom, the insurer, the state, also controls the supply of medical services, and so is able to determine the medical services, and their cost, which the 'buyer' of insurance will receive.

To conclude: in this section we have discussed at some length, though by no means exhaustively, the economics of insurance. We saw that where markets in 'flexible' insurance contracts exist it is as if there was a complete market in state-contingent income claims and we can apply the standard tools of price theory to analyse the equilibrium of this system. In particular, on 'standard assumptions', we are able to show that a Pareto optimum is achieved, with all consumers at least as well off as they could be under any other system of insurance contracts, since each has available a full range of exchange possibilities. In reality however, constraints exist on the set of exchange possibilities open to an individual, because some events cannot be insured against, or because insurance contracts are not fully flexible. We saw that this arises from the existence of: transactions costs; information costs, which are especially important when the probability of the event insured against can be influenced by the buyer; and variability of the amount of compensation with the actions of the buyer. We now turn to an analysis, in somewhat similar terms, of another type of market which may permit exchange of state-contingent income claims, the stock market.

Exercise 20B

1. Prove that any strictly concave function $f(x)$, defined on a convex set X, is strictly quasi-concave. (*Hint:* choose the vectors x' and x'' such that $f(x') = f(x'')$.)

2. Show that the indifference curves relating to state-contingent income claims are:
   (a) straight-lines with slope $-p/1-p$, for a risk-neutral decision-taker;
   (b) concave-to-the-origin curves for a risk-attracted decision-taker.
   Explain why, in each of these cases, we would *not* observe diversification of risks.

3. Explain in intuitive terms why, at a point on the certainty line, the marginal rate of substitution between state-contingent income claims should equal $-p/1-p$ (*Hint:* to start with, take $p = 0.5$).

4. Show that the relationship in equation [B.16] is equivalent to the constraint: $px_1 + (1-p)x_2 = p\hat{x}_1 + (1-p)\hat{x}_2$, $x_1 < \hat{x}_1$, $x_2 > \hat{x}_2$.

5. Point out the similarities and the differences between the 'budget constraint' in the previous question, and the wealth constraint of the individual consumer in the analysis of the borrowing/lending decision in Chapter 15.

6.* Suppose that a buyer of insurance can take out:
   (a) a policy which pays him a fixed compensation, $\hat{x}_2 - \hat{x}_1$, in exchange for a premium $\bar{k} = (1-p)(\hat{x}_1 - \hat{x}_2)$;
   (b) a policy which allows him to choose the amount of compensation, $x_2 - \hat{x}_2$, he is paid, provided he pays the premium $k = (1-q)(x_2 - \hat{x}_2)$, (the notation is that used in the first half of this section). Using a diagram along the lines of Fig. 3, show that he would never choose policy (b), if $q < p$, but would always choose policy (b) if $q > p$.

7.* The following table shows the terms of an insurance contract, offered by Thos. Cook & Son, London, in 1974, to cover medical expenses incurred by a traveller aged between 1 and 70 years, on a holiday of up to 1 month, anywhere in the world:

Premium £	Compensation £
1.41	100
1.93	200
2.44	300
2.95	400
3.46	500

Calculate the implied value of $1-q$. The policy covers only expenses actually incurred. Why might this be? Discuss explicitly the considerations you would take into account in choosing an insurance policy (or none), and relate them to the analysis of this section.

8.* Suppose, in a two-person two-state economy the expected utility functions are identical, both decision-takers believe the two states equally likely, and decision taker 1 has the initial endowment vector $(\hat{x}_1^1, 0)$ and 2 the vector $(0, \hat{x}_2^2)$, with $\hat{x}_1^1 = \hat{x}_2^2$. In an Edgeworth box diagram, find the exchange equilibrium in this economy, and discuss its characteristics. Interpret the exchange in terms of an insurance transaction. Will the equilibrium $\pi_1/\pi_2 = p_1/1 - p_1$? Suppose $\hat{x}_1^1 > \hat{x}_2^2$. What effect will this have on the equilibrium price ratio π_1/π_2?

9.* Discuss the feasibility of introducing markets which sell insurance:
  (a) to rail commuters, against the event of their being late for work;
  (b) to road commuters, against the same event;
  (c) to married couples, against the event that they get divorced;
  (d) to companies, against the event that they will go bankrupt.

10.* Discuss, in terms of the analysis of this section, the argument against unemployment insurance which pays as unemployment benefit 100% of income when employed.

11.* Prove that if it is possible for insurance companies in a competitive insurance market costlessly to distinguish good and bad risk individuals then such individuals will be offered different premiums related to their risks. Will this risk rating of premiums occur if the insurance market is monopolized?

12.* In what sense do adverse selection and moral hazard lead to market failure? Are there any feasible alternative institutions which might achieve a better allocation of risk bearing?

C. Stock markets

A stock market is a market on which are exchanged shares in the profits of companies (we ignore for present purposes fixed interest securities; see Question 1 of Exercise 20C). Since the companies are engaged in production, a full analysis of stock markets would require a model of production decisions under uncertainty. This would take us rather further afield than we are able to go here. We limit the analysis, therefore, to the pure-exchange aspects of stock markets. The only fact about a company which we take to be relevant is the amount of profit which will be available for distribution to shareholders in each state of the world. We are then interested in the question: what possibilites for exchange of state-contingent income claims are made available by a market in company shares? In particular, we shall try to find conditions under which a stock market provides a set of exchange possibilities equivalent to those generated by markets in state-contingent income claims, as discussed in section B.

We begin by again taking a single decision-taker, and two states of the world. Suppose also that there are two companies: let y_s^j denote the jth company's profit in state $s = 1, 2$ and $y^j = (y_1^j, y_2^j)$ $j = 1, 2$, the jth company's vector of state-contingent profits, with $y_1^j \neq y_2^j$. Company j has issued N_j shares, and if the price of one share on the stock market is v_j, then the *stock market value* of the company is $V_j = v_j N_j$. Now suppose that our decision-taker initially owns $\hat{n}_j$ shares in company j. He can buy or sell shares on the market, to end up with a shareholding n_j, but such transactions must be subject to the budget constraint:

$$v_1 n_1 + v_2 n_2 = v_1 \hat{n}_1 + v_2 \hat{n}_2 \qquad [\text{C.1}]$$

which states simply that the market value of his shareholding must equal the value of his initial endowment of shares. In (n_1, n_2)-space, this budget constraint would be drawn as a straight line (given that the stock market is competitive), with slope $-v_1/v_2$, passing through the initial endowment point $(\hat{n}_1, \hat{n}_2)$, and bounded by the constraints $n_j \leq N_j$, $j = 1, 2$.

A question of some importance, as we shall see, is whether we restrict n_j to be non-negative: in other words, can we permit a negative shareholding? It may appear nonsensical to own a negative number of shares, until we realize that a negative number can be thought of as a debt: our decision-taker could sell more shares than he in fact possesses, relying on being able to buy the shares he needs on the market when the time comes to meet his obligations. Such a possibility certainly exists in reality and is known as 'selling short'. Initially, we shall assume that 'short sales' are not permitted, so that we constrain $n_j \geq 0$. However, we shall later introduce the possibility of short sales and note the consequences of this.

Given a holding of n_j shares in company j, this entitles the individual to a share of:

$$\beta_j \equiv n_j/N_j \qquad [\text{C.2}]$$

in the profits of company j, in each state of the world. If N_j is very large, we can regard β_j as taking any value on the interval $(0,1)$. Permitting short sales would make the lower bound of this interval -1. If $\hat{\beta}_j = \hat{n}_j/N_j$, we can therefore write the shareholder's initial endowment of state-contingent incomes as:

$$\hat{x}_s = \hat{\beta}_1 y_s^1 + \hat{\beta}_2 y_s^2 \qquad s = 1, 2 \qquad [\text{C.3}]$$

that is, the initial income endowment in state s is simply the sum of the shares in profits of the two companies in that state. Figure 5 illustrates. In (a) of the figure, y^1, with coordinate vector (y_1^1, y_2^1), is the profit vector of company 1; and $y^2 = (y_1^2, y_2^2)$ that of company 2. Then, $\hat{\beta}_1 y^1$, on the line Oy^1, shows the income vector $(\hat{\beta}_1 y_1^1, \hat{\beta}_1 y_2^1)$ which the decision-taker owns by virtue of his shareholding in company 1; and $\hat{\beta}_2 y^2$, on Oy^2, shows the income vector $(\hat{\beta}_2 y_1^2, \hat{\beta}_2 y_2^2)$ which he owns through his shareholding in company 2. His initial income endowment vector, therefore, shown as point $\hat{x}$, is the sum of these two vectors, i.e. it has the coordinate vector $(\hat{\beta}_1 y_1^1 + \hat{\beta}_2 y_1^2, \hat{\beta}_1 y_2^1 + \hat{\beta}_2 y_2^2)$ (and so is found by the 'parallelogram law' of addition of vectors). Clearly, as long as $\hat{\beta}_1, \hat{\beta}_2 > 0$, $\hat{x}$ lies within the space bounded by Oy^1 and Oy^2. The lines Oy^1 and Oy^2 are distinct from each other, and this implies the assumption that y^1 and y^2 are *linearly independent vectors*. In (b) of the figure, on the other hand, it is assumed that the profit vectors are linearly dependent: that is, they lie along the same straight

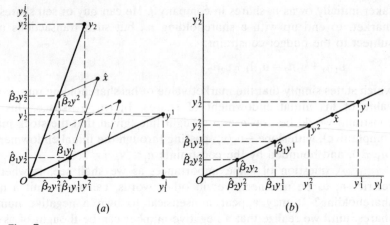

Fig. 5

line, and so a scalar μ can be found such that $y^1 = \mu y^2$. In this case, the initial endowment point $\hat{x}$ must also lie on this line.

Consider now the consequence of exchange of shares. A rough idea of this can be gathered from Fig. 5. Since the decision-taker holds shares only in these two companies, an increase in one shareholding must be accompanied by a reduction in the other, according to the budget constraint in equation [C.1]. Then, in (b) of Fig. 5, this implies a move *along* Oy^1 since variations in β_1 and β_2 simply lead to new income vectors on the line.

In fact, since the profit vector of company 1 is simply μ times that of company 2, we would expect the share price of company 1 to be μ times that of company 2 and, as can be shown (see Question 2 of Exercise 20C), this implies that no movement from point $\hat{x}$ is possible. Thus, in the case where company profit vectors are *linearly dependent*, the shareholder cannot, by buying and selling shares, exchange claims to income in one state of the world for those in another.

Suppose however that company profit vectors are linearly independent, as in (a) of the figure. Then we can see that, say, reducing β_2 from $\hat{\beta}_2$, and increasing β_1, will (using the parallelogram law) generate a point which has more state 1 income, and less state 2 income, than at $\hat{x}$. Thus, in effect, exchange of state-contingent income claims appears to be possible through share transactions.

Let us now make this more precise. If he sold his entire shareholding in company 2 and bought with the proceeds shares in company 1, the shareholder would own $n_1^0 = (v_1\hat{n}_1 + v_2\hat{n}_2)/v_1$ shares in company 1, thus giving him the shareholding $\beta_1^0 = n_1^0/N_1$. His income in state s would then be:

$$x_s^1 = \beta_1^0 y_s^1 \qquad s = 1, 2 \qquad [C.4]$$

Alternatively, if he sold his shares in company 1 and bought company 2 shares, he would own $n_2^0 = (v_1\hat{n}_1 + v_2\hat{n}_2)/v_2$ shares in company 2, giving him the shareholding $\beta_2^0 = n_2^0/N_2$, and state-contingent income:

$$x_s^2 = \beta_2^0 y_s^2 \qquad s = 1, 2 \qquad\qquad [C.5]$$

These two points, $x^1 = (x_1^1, x_2^1)$ and $x^2 = (x_1^2, x_2^2)$ are shown in (a) of Fig. 6.

Figure 6 is designed to show the relationship between variations in shareholdings and consequential variations in state-contingent income claims. Part (b) of the figure shows the initial share endowment point $\hat{\beta} = (\hat{\beta}_1, \hat{\beta}_2)$, and the intercepts β_1^0 and β_2^0 which correspond to exclusive holdings in company 1 and company 2 respectively. In (a) of the figure the initial endowment of state-contingent claims at point $\hat{x}$ corresponds to the initial endowment of shareholdings at $\hat{\beta}$, while x^1 corresponds to point β_1^0 and x^2 to point β_2^0.

Now as the decision-taker sells shares in company 2 and uses the proceeds to buy shares in company 1 he moves *rightward* along the 'share-budget line' in (b) of the figure, towards β_1^0, and this causes a

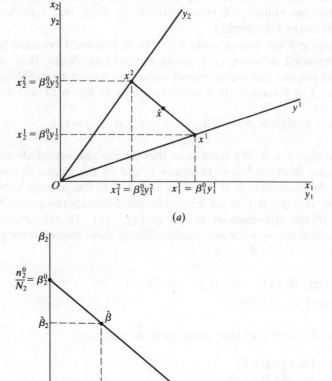

(a)

(b)

Fig. 6

consequent rightward move towards x^1 along the 'income-budget line' in (a) of the figure. Similarly, as he trades shares in company 1 for shares in company 2 to move *leftward* towards β_2^0 in (b), he moves leftward towards x^2 in (a). Thus the 'income-budget line' in (a) is generated by movements along the 'share-budget line' in (b). What we have to prove of course is that the two budget constraints *are* in fact straight lines.

Intuitively, the reason for the linear relationship is easy to see: giving up, say, one extra share in company 2 reduces income in each state by given amounts, and allows an increase in the shareholding in company 1 and hence an increase in income in the two states. The *net* income change in each state is then the difference between the gain in income from company 1 and the loss in income from company 2. Since a share in company 1 yields more state 1 income and less state 2 income than a share in company 2, there will always be a net increase in state 1 income and net decrease in state 2 income by selling company 2 shares and buying company 1 shares. The net increase in state 1 income and decrease in state 2 income, which result from selling a share in company 2 and buying a share in company 1 do not vary with the number of shares bought or sold, and this therefore generates the linear relationship.

We can put the matter more formally as follows. Given the budget constraint expressed in terms of absolute numbers of shares, it is easy to show that this implies the *linear* budget constraint among shareholdings β_j, (see Question 3 of Exercise 20C) which is drawn in Fig. 6(b) and written:

$$V_1\beta_1 + V_2\beta_2 = V_1\hat{\beta}_1 + V_2\hat{\beta}_2, \qquad 1 \geq \beta_j \geq 0 \qquad j = 1, 2 \qquad \text{[C.6]}$$

where $V_j = v_j N_j$, $j = 1, 2$. We have seen that (in the absence of short sales) β_1^0 is the largest shareholding in company 1, and β_2^0 the largest in company 2, which the decision-taker is able to buy. From [C.6] the possible vectors of shareholdings, $\beta = (\beta_1, \beta_2)$ lie on a straight line between the points $(\beta_1^0, 0)$ and $(0, \beta_2^0)$, in (β_1, β_2)-space as shown in Fig. 6(b). Therefore any such vector can be written as a convex combination of these two extreme points, of the form:

$$\beta = \lambda(\beta_1^0, 0) + (1-\lambda)(0, \beta_2^0) \qquad 0 \leq \lambda \leq 1 \qquad \text{[C.7]}$$
$$= (\lambda\beta_1^0, (1-\lambda)\beta_2^0)$$

We can write the vector of state-contingent incomes as:

$$\begin{bmatrix} x_1 \\ x_2 \end{bmatrix} = \begin{bmatrix} \beta_1 y_1^1 + \beta_2 y_1^2 \\ \beta_1 y_2^1 + \beta_2 y_2^2 \end{bmatrix} \qquad \text{[C.8]}$$

and so substituting for β_1 and β_2 from [C.7] gives

$$\begin{bmatrix} x_1 \\ x_2 \end{bmatrix} = \begin{bmatrix} \lambda\beta_1^0 y_1^1 + (1-\lambda)\beta_2^0 y_1^2 \\ \lambda\beta_1^0 y_2^1 + (1-\lambda)\beta_2^0 y_2^2 \end{bmatrix} \qquad \text{[C.9]}$$

But recalling from [C.4] and [C.5] the definitions of x_s^1 and x_s^2, $s = 1, 2$, and substituting into [C.9] gives:

$$\begin{bmatrix} x_1 \\ x_2 \end{bmatrix} = \begin{bmatrix} \lambda x_1^1 + (1-\lambda)x_1^2 \\ \lambda x_2^1 + (1-\lambda)x_2^2 \end{bmatrix} \qquad\qquad \text{[C.10]}$$

or in more concise vector notation

$$x = \lambda x^1 + (1-\lambda)x^2 \qquad 0 \le \lambda \le 1 \qquad\qquad \text{[C.11]}$$

Thus any state-contingent income vector x attainable through share transactions must lie on the straight line between x^1 and x^2 in Fig. 6(a). (Confirm that $\hat{x}$ must lie on this line.)

This analysis then suggests the conclusion: if, in this two-state, two-company case, the companies' profit vectors are linearly independent, then possibilities for the exchange of state-contingent income claims do exist. However, these possibilities are not in general equivalent to those generated by markets in state-contingent income claims. As is clear from Fig. 6(a), the exchange possibilities are bounded by the lines Oy^1, Oy^2, and do not extend right to the axes. The greater the angle between these lines, the wider the set of exchange possibilities; conversely, the smaller the angle, the narrower the exchange possibilities, until, as we have seen, when the lines coincide, none exist. The widest set of exchange possibilities exists when the companies' profit vectors are:

$$y^1 = (y_1^1, 0) \qquad y^2 = (0, y_2^2) \qquad\qquad \text{[C.12]}$$

since then the lines Oy^1 and Oy^2 coincide with the axes. In this extreme case shares in the companies are securities yielding purely state-contingent income claims: a share in company j pays off if and only if state $s = j$ occurs. Thus, what may appear as a 'riskier' world actually offers greater possibilities of exchange of incomes across states of the world.

The significance of the restriction on the set of exchange possibilities illustrated in Fig. 6 depends on the nature of the decision-taker's preferences. Given his expected utility function $\bar{u}(x_1, x_2)$, if its indifference curves were such that a tangency of an indifference curve and the line x^1x^2 occurred, then the restriction is clearly irrelevant: such a tangency would determine the optimal income vector (x_1^*, x_2^*), and the optimal shareholdings (β_1^*, β_2^*), or, in other words, the optimal share portfolio. On the other hand, such a tangency need not exist, in which case either x^1 or x^2 would be chosen, and the restriction on exchange possibilities is binding. A general conclusion we can draw is that an expansion of the exchange possibilities shown in Fig. 6 cannot make the decision-taker worse off (since the line x^1x^2 is still available) and may make him better off (if a tangency would occur outside the range x^1x^2).

This proposition can be amplified if we now consider the possibility of short sales. Figure 7 shows the consequence of permitting short sales. The positive quadrant of the figure shows the profit vectors y^1 and y^2, and the set of exchange possibilities in the absence of short sales, given by the line

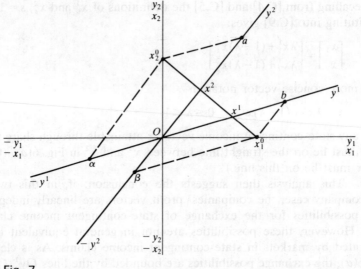

Fig. 7

x^1x^2. In the negative quadrant are shown the vectors $-y_1$ and $-y_2$. We now prove the proposition that, if short sales are permitted, the whole of the line $x_1^0x_2^0$ becomes available, so that the exchange possibilities correspond to those which would obtain if markets existed in state-contingent income claims. As an illustration, consider point x_1^0. This is given by the sum of the positive vector Ob, and the negative vector $O\beta$ (Confirm, using the parallelogram rule). The shareholder achieves these income vectors by selling company 2's shares short, until he reaches the point $O\beta$, and using the proceeds to buy company 1's shares, reaching the point Ob. That is, for every company 2 share he sells short, the decision-taker moves some distance along the line Oy^2, since he effectively *owes* the income vector corresponding to the share he has sold short. This then has to be subtracted from the increment in income he gains when he purchases an additional shareholding in company 1 with the proceeds of his short sales. The net result, in state-contingent income terms, is to move him along the line $x^1x_1^0$. By a similar argument the point x_2^0 is reached by selling company 1 shares short up to point $O\alpha$, and using the proceeds to buy company 2 shares up to point Oa. The sum of these two income vectors, one positive the other negative, then gives point x_2^0. Thus, a policy of selling company 1 shares short in effect moves the decision-taker along the line $x^2x_2^0$.

A formal proof that short sales make available the entire line $x_1^0x_2^0$ can be given on much the same lines as before. The relation in [C.6] still holds, with, however, the constraint $1 \geq \beta_j \geq -1$ replacing that of non-negativity of shareholdings. Defining β_1^0 and β_2^0 in the same way as before, any vector of shareholdings on the line defined by [C.6] can now be written as a linear combination:

$$\beta = (\beta_1, \beta_2) = \lambda_1(\beta_1^0, 0) + \lambda_2(0, \beta_2^0) \qquad \lambda_1, \lambda_2 \neq 0 \qquad \text{[C.13]}$$

for suitably chosen numbers λ_1, λ_2. Hence, just as before, state-contingent income can be written as:

$$x_s = \lambda_1 x_s^1 + \lambda_2 x_s^2 \qquad s = 1, 2 \qquad [C.14]$$

implying that the state-contingent income vectors x are a linear combination of the two vectors x^1, x^2:

$$x = \lambda_1 x^1 + \lambda_2 x^2 \qquad \lambda_1, \lambda_2 \neq 0 \qquad [C.15]$$

where the line now extends beyond x^1 to the right and x^2 to the left. To ensure that x_1^0 and x_2^0 in Fig. 7 are in fact attainable, however, requires us to assume that at those points, the constraint $1 \geq \beta_j \geq -1$ is not violated: in other words, they do not imply selling short or buying more than the total shareholding of a company. This is implicitly assumed in the figure, where a and b lie below y_2 and y_1. The economic significance of the assumption is that the individuals' initial endowments of shares, and thus the attainable shareholdings, must be 'small' in relation to the total outstanding share issues. This will be satisfied if there is a large number of shareholders in each company, with a low degree of concentration of shareholdings, which is consistent with the idea of competitive markets in shares.

The conclusions of the analysis can therefore be stated as follows: in an economy with two states of the world and with two companies which have linearly independent profits vectors, a competitive stock market, in which shares can be traded at given prices and with short sales permitted, is equivalent to a system of markets in state-contingent income claims, in the sense that the full set of exchange possibilities exists. It follows that we can apply the framework of analysis of exchange of state-contingent income claims to the analysis of exchange in stock markets. In particular, we can use it to establish conditions for the existence and stability of stock market equilibrium and to examine the optimality properties of this equilibrium.

Moreover, the assumption of only two states of the world is not restrictive in a formal sense. We can show, in essentially the same way as for the two-state case, that if there are $S > 2$ states of the world, then the above conclusion still holds if and only if there are S companies with linearly independent profits vectors (and short sales are allowed): the set of possibilities for exchanging income claims between states will be equivalent to those available when S markets exist for trade in state-contingent income claims. Thus, from the point of view of the formal analysis the value of S is not crucial. However, this value, in relation to the number of firms in the economy, is important for the *empirical relevance* of the conclusion, since, for example, if it exceeds the number of firms, then it is impossible to find S profit vectors, and so the stock market is not equivalent to a system of markets in state-contingent income claims. Furthermore, if the number of firms is at least as great as the number of states of the world, we cannot conclude that the stock market is necessarily equivalent to the system of markets in state-contingent claims, because of course there may not be S

linearly independent profits vectors: if the profits of companies are significantly correlated with each other across states of the world, then they will be linearly related, and it may not then be possible to find S linearly independent profits vectors. The question of whether sufficient independence of profits vectors exists, in reality, for the analysis of this section to be applied, requires an empirical investigation which, to our knowledge, has not been carried out. Thus, in our theoretical discussion, we shall have to assume that both cases are possible.

Exercise 20C

1.* Show that a fixed interest security allows exchange of income claims over time but not across states of the world. What is the significance of bankruptcy in this context?

2. Show that if $y^1 = \mu y^2$, and $v_1 = \mu v_2$, in the notation of this section, then no point other than the initial endowment point $\hat{x}$ is available to the decision-taker.

3.* Show that the budget constraint in terms of numbers of shares:

$$v_1 n_1 + v_2 n_2 = v_1 \hat{n}_1 + v_2 \hat{n}_2$$

   implies the budget constraint in terms of proportionate shareholdings:

$$V_1 \beta_1 + V_2 \beta_2 = V_1 \hat{\beta}_1 + V_2 \hat{\beta}_2$$

   where $V_j = v_j/N_j$, $j = 1, 2$. Draw graphs of the latter budget constraint, on the assumption:
   (a) each β_j must lie on the interval $1 \geq \beta_j \geq 0$;
   (b) each β_j must lie on the interval $1 \geq \beta_j \geq -1$.

4.* Using Fig. 7 introduce the shareholder's indifference curves and illustrate the case in which:
   (a) he holds positive amounts of both shares;
   (b) he 'goes short' in shares of company 2. Then consider the consequence of a fall in the price of company 1 shares relative to those of company 2.

5.* Assume a two-state, two-shareholder, two-company economy. Given that the company profits vectors y^1, y^2 are linearly independent, and that short sales are permitted, construct an Edgeworth box diagram in terms of state-contingent income claims, and analyse the determination of the equilibrium price ratio of these claims. Then, translate this analysis into terms of the stock market, showing how it implies equilibrium share portfolios, share prices, and stock market valuations of the two companies (given the number of shares each has issued). Then analyse the consequences of the imposition of a proportionate profits tax on the profits of company 1 only.

D. State-contingent commodities

The previous two sections have applied the expected utility theory to the analysis of exchange under uncertainty, in the rather restrictive context of a one-good, two-state economy. The purpose of the analyses was threefold: first, to gain some insight into the roles played by insurance and stock markets in resource allocation under uncertainty; secondly, to introduce the concept of a system of markets in state-contingent income claims, which allows us to apply the formal framework of the neo-classical analysis to the case of an economy under uncertainty; and finally to raise and partially answer the important question: to what extent do insurance and stock markets provide exchange possibilities which are equivalent to those made available by a system of markets in state-contingent income claims?

In this section we shall generalize the analysis by assuming any finite numbers of goods, states and decision-takers. The conclusions of the preceding two sections will be useful when we come to consider the problems of resource allocation in this case.

Let $x_s^i = [x_{s1}^i, x_{s2}^i, \ldots, x_{sn}^i]$ denote a vector of n commodities which individual i may consume in state $s = 1, 2, \ldots, S$. That is, before the state of the world is known, individual i can plan to consume the vector of commodities x_s^i, if and only if state s occurs, and so he may plan S such commodity vectors. As in the theory of the consumer under certainty commodities are distinguished by their physical characteristics and possibly the location at which they will be made available. Thus, x_{38}^5 is the quantity of commodity 8 which consumer 5 plans to consume if and only if state 3 occurs. Also, let $\hat{x}_s^i = [\hat{x}_{s1}^i, \hat{x}_{s2}^i, \ldots, \hat{x}_{sn}^i]$ be a vector of initial endowments of commodities which the ith consumer will have if and only if state s occurs. The commodity vectors x_s^i and $\hat{x}_s^i$ are then the counterparts here of the state-contingent income claims of the previous two sections. We now assume that the expected utility functions are expressed in terms of these state-contingent commodity vectors, i.e. that:

$$\bar{u}^i = \bar{u}^i(x_s^i) = \sum_{s=1}^{S} p_s^i u^i(x_{s1}^i, x_{s2}^i, \ldots, x_{sn}^i) \qquad i = 1, 2, \ldots, I \qquad \text{[D.1]}$$

An axiom system for this representation of the utility function could be constructed by replacing, in Chapter 19, the *incomes* x_s, by the *commodity vectors*, x_s^i, and no formal change in the axioms presented there needs to be made (see Question 1 of Exercise 20D), provided the properties of the preference ordering over consumption vectors which are *certain*, are first specified (thus recall that in Chapter 19 we assumed that more income was always preferred to less: when we replace the scalar, income, by a vector of commodities, this assumption has to be extended to that of a complete, transitive preference ordering over commodity vectors, with more of any one commodity always being preferred to less). Without going through the requisite axiomatization, we simply assume that the utility functions in [D.1] exist, are differentiable, strictly concave and increasing in all their arguments.

We now describe the counterpart, in this n-good economy, of the system of markets in state-contingent income claims discussed earlier. Suppose it is possible to make a contract which specifies an amount of the jth good, $j = 1, 2, \ldots, n$, which the seller will deliver to the buyer, if and only if state s occurs. That is, the contract is enforceable if and only if state s occurs, and otherwise is void. Suppose also that there is an organized market for these contracts. Thus, on the market for delivery of the jth good in the sth state the buyer will pay the seller a price π_{sj}, for each unit of the good which will be delivered if and only if state s occurs. The price is paid at the time of concluding the contract, which is of course before the state of the world is known. Markets in which a price is paid in return for a promise of future delivery are known as *futures markets,* and so we are supposing that a futures market exists for every good and every state, i.e. there are $n \cdot S$ futures markets. Then, any one decision-taker can buy and sell on these markets, subject only to the budget constraint:

$$\sum_j \sum_s \pi_{sj} x_{sj}^i = \sum_j \sum_s \pi_{sj} \hat{x}_{sj}^i \qquad [D.2]$$

in words: the value of his state-contingent claims to commodities must equal the value of his initial endowments of them. We could then represent the consumer as choosing state-contingent consumption vectors x_s^i in such a way as to maximize expected ultility, $\bar{u}^i$, and subject to the budget constraint in [D.2]. We could then derive demand functions for state-contingent claims to commodities, and discuss the determination of equilibrium market prices π_{sj}, and the question of the existence, stability, and optimality properties of a general equilibrium of the system of futures markets. It should be clear that, once again, the whole framework of analysis developed for the competitive economy under certainty becomes directly applicable. The *state-contingent commodity,* defined not only according to physical characteristics and location, but also according to the state of the world in which it will be made available, becomes the analogue of the commodity under certainty and given a price and a market for each state-contingent commodity, each consumer has a full set of exchange possibilities. The analysis of individual consumer equilibrium and the nature and properties of general equilibrium then becomes formally identical to that carried out for the competitive economy under certainty. Question 2 of Exercise 20D asks you to show this.

Again, we are faced with the fact that a complete system of futures markets in state-contingent commodities does not exist in reality. Some futures markets exist, particularly in primary products such as tin, copper, cotton, wheat, etc. However, they fall a long way short of providing markets for all goods and services in all states in that delivery is certain at a future date, not contingent on a particular state occurring at that date. The reasons for the absence of markets may again be ascribed to moral hazard and transactions costs (refer to the discussion in section B above). Thus, the complete market system just outlined is to be regarded as an 'ideal type', a point of reference against which the real market economy can be examined and evaluated.

Economies without markets in state-contingent commodities

To clarify the consequences of *not* having a complete system of futures markets in state-contingent commodities, let us suppose that *no* such markets exist. Instead, we assume that there exist only *spot markets*, i.e. markets which will be held in whatever state of the world occurs, and on which quantities of each commodity are bought and sold *for immediate delivery*. Consider the position of a consumer before the state of the world is known, contemplating what his choices will be. He can now of course only *plan* his future choices in each state, in the light of his *expectations* about what the future spot prices will be. Thus, let $\bar{x}^i_{sj}$ be the quantity of good j that consumer i *plans* to purchase in state s, and let $\bar{\pi}^i_{sj}$ be the spot price he *expects* to prevail for good j in the market in state s. The superscript i indicates that the expectation may be specific to the consumer. Then, he knows that in state s, he will face the *state-contingent budget constraint*

$$\sum_j \bar{\pi}^i_{sj} \bar{x}^i_{sj} = \sum_j \bar{\pi}^i_{sj} \hat{x}^i_{sj} \qquad s = 1, 2, \ldots, S \qquad \text{[D.3]}$$

where $\hat{x}^i_{sj}$ is again his initial endowment of good j in state s. This says simply that the value of his planned consumption must equal the value of his endowment, at the prices he *expects* to prevail in state s. There are S such budget constraints, one for each state. Moreover, as the system stands, there is no way of transferring income between states, and so each constraint must stand as a separate constraint on the consumer's planned choices in state s. Given the expected utility function in [D.1], defined on planned consumption choices, maximization of the expected utility function subject to the budget constraints in [D.3] yields as necessary conditions:

$$\frac{\partial \bar{u}^i}{\partial \bar{x}^i_{sj}} - \lambda^i_s \bar{\pi}^i_{sj} = 0 \qquad s = 1, 2, \ldots, S; \qquad j = 1, 2, \ldots, n \qquad \text{[D.4]}$$

where λ^i_s is the ith consumer's marginal expected utility of income in state s. Now, for a given state s, planned choices between goods j and k will satisfy:

$$\frac{\partial \bar{u}^i}{\partial x^i_{sj}} \bigg/ \frac{\partial \bar{u}^i}{\partial x^i_{sk}} = \frac{\partial u^i}{\partial x^i_{sj}} \bigg/ \frac{\partial u^i}{\partial x^i_{sk}} = \frac{\bar{\pi}^i_{sj}}{\bar{\pi}^i_{sk}} \qquad \text{[D.5]}$$

i.e. we have the equality between marginal rate of substitution and ratio of *expected* prices. However, for a given good j and different states s and t, we have:

$$\frac{\partial \bar{u}^i}{\partial x^i_{sj}} \bigg/ \frac{\partial \bar{u}^i}{\partial x^i_{tj}} = p^i_s \frac{\partial u^i}{\partial x^i_{sj}} \bigg/ p^i_t \frac{\partial u^i}{\partial x^i_{tj}} = \frac{\lambda^i_s \bar{\pi}^i_{sj}}{\lambda^i_t \bar{\pi}^i_{tj}} \qquad \text{[D.6]}$$

i.e. the *MRS* between goods in different states of the world will in general differ from the price ratio, because in general $\lambda^i_s \neq \lambda^i_t$: marginal expected utilities of income may differ across states, since there is no mechanism by which income may be transferred across states to equalize them (see Question 4 of Exercise 20D).

For example, suppose the initial endowment of goods in state s is very small, while that in state t is very large. Then, other things being equal (especially the probabilities of the two states), we would expect the consumer to have a higher marginal expected utility of income in state s than in state t, given that marginal utility diminishes with consumption. Then, if $\bar{\pi}^i_{sj} = \bar{\pi}^i_{tj}$ the marginal rate of substitution between $\bar{x}^i_{sj}$ and $\bar{x}^i_{tj}$ will not be unity, since $\lambda_s > \lambda_t$. Only when two commodities can effectively be exchanged for each other, *via* market transactions, can we expect that the optimal position will be characterized by equality of marginal rate of substitution with the market rate of exchange (= price ratio). In the present case, no exchange between goods in different states of the world is possible, and so the price ratios $\bar{\pi}^i_{sj}/\bar{\pi}^i_{tk}$, $s, t = 1, 2, \ldots, S, t \neq s$, are essentially meaningless – they do not represent rates at which one good can be exchanged for another (or is *expected* to exchange for another) *via* market transactions. Moreover, a change in one expected price, $\bar{\pi}^i_{sj}$, will leave unaffected the planned demands for goods in states $t \neq s$, since:

(a) the budget constraints for states $t \neq s$ are unaffected by the change in $\bar{\pi}^i_{sj}$;

(b) the marginal expected utilities of goods $\bar{x}^i_{tj}$, $t \neq s$, are unaffected by changes in the $\bar{x}^i_{sj}$ which may result from the change in $\bar{\pi}^i_{sj}$, because of the separability of the expected utility function $\bar{u}^i$.

In other words, given the consumer's preferences over consumption plans, and the budget constraint in a given state of the world, the optimum choice of consumption plans for that state will not be affected by a change in price of a good in some other state, since neither the preference ordering nor budget constraint are changed for the first state. It is as if, therefore, the consumer is simply anticipating the choices he will make once he knows which state of the world prevails (given that he has correctly guessed the prices), where these choices are quite independent of what *might* have happened in some other state.

The question then arises: why does the consumer formulate such plans at all; why not simply wait and see what state of the world occurs, and make choices in the light of the prices which actually prevail? Recall the discussion of the nature of decision-taking under uncertainty with which we began Chapter 19: such postponement of decision-taking is not possible as long as some decision variables, e.g. investment and asset holdings, must be chosen before the state of the world is known, and have repercussions for the period which is uncertain. In that case, plans must be formed now of the decisions one will make in the future and rationally, these plans will be formed in state-contingent terms.

This point will be developed more fully in a moment. First let us consider the situation from the point of view of the economy as a whole. The conditions in equations [D.5] and [D.6] will hold for each of the I consumers in the economy. However, remember that the quantities $\bar{x}^i_{sj}$ are *plans* and not actual transactions, while the prices $\bar{\pi}^i_{sj}$ are *expectations* held by consumers before the states of the world are known and markets held. Now there is no mechanism in the model to ensure the overall equilibrium of these plans, since no market transactions take place in them. They are simply mental constructs of consumers, which may not be realized in the event. Likewise, the price expectations $\bar{\pi}^i_{sj}$ may well differ among consumers, so that, even for planned transactions within a given state, there is nothing to guarantee that marginal rates of substitution between planned quantities of two goods will be equal (the righthand sides of equation [D.5] may differ for different consumers). Hence it does not seem possible to postulate that in general our propositions about the existence and optimality of equilibrium, in respect of these planned state-contingent consumption quantities, can be applied. It might of course be argued that such an attempt to apply these propositions to consumer *plans* is unnecessary: at each period, in whatever state of the world occurs, markets will be held and a resource allocation established, and it is these *realized* resource allocations which are the subject of analysis. However, in *intertemporal* models of the economy, we are often concerned with the optimality of investment and saving decisions, which involves the optimality of consumption *plans*, and so the conclusions we have just reached have important applications in this case. To argue this fully would however take us well beyond the scope and intentions of this book.

Markets in Arrow-securities

Let us return to the question of exchange of income across states of the world. In an economy in which only spot markets in goods exist, there are, as we have just seen, no possibilities of such exchange. However, in reality insurance and stock markets exist which permit some degree of exchange, and so it is of interest to see how this affects the analysis. To fix our ideas, therefore, let us suppose that the economy possesses not only spot markets in goods, but also a complete system of markets in state-contingent *income* claims. That is, before the state of the world is known, one may buy or sell a security, which promises to pay one unit of income if and only if a specified state of the world occurs. Such a security is called an *Arrow-security*, since its form was first defined by K. J. Arrow (1964). Let A_s^i denote the number of such securities, contingent on state s, held by individual i, with $A_s^i > 0$ if he will *receive* that amount of income in state s, and $A_s^i < 0$ if he will have to pay it. In addition, let q_s be the price, payable before the state of the world is known, at which one security, paying one unit of income contingent on state s, can be traded. Then the ith consumer's budget constraint relating to transactions in the markets for Arrow-securities is:

$$\sum_s q_s A_s^i = 0 \qquad i = 1, 2, \ldots, I \qquad [\text{D.7}]$$

which states that the value of his purchases of state-contingent income claims must equal the value of his sales. His *state-contingent budget constraints* now become:

$$\sum_j \bar{\pi}_{sj}^i \bar{x}_{sj}^i = \sum_j \bar{\pi}_{sj}^i \hat{x}_{sj}^i + A_s^i \qquad s = 1, 2, \ldots, S \qquad [\text{D.8}]$$

implying that the value of his planned consumption is constrained by the value of his initial endowment plus (or minus) his receipts (or payments) on the state-contingent securities relating to state s. From [D.8] we have that:

$$A_s^i = \sum_j \bar{\pi}_{sj}^i (\bar{x}_{sj}^i - \hat{x}_{sj}^i) \qquad \text{[D.9]}$$

and so substituting into [D.7] for A_s^i gives:

$$\sum_s q_s \sum_j \bar{\pi}_{sj}^i (\bar{x}_{sj}^i - \hat{x}_{sj}^i) = 0 \qquad \text{[D.10]}$$

If we now define 'prices':

$$\bar{q}_{sj}^i = q_s \bar{\pi}_{sj}^i \qquad \text{[D.11]}$$

then [D.10] becomes:

$$\sum_s \sum_j \bar{q}_{ij}^i \bar{x}_{sj}^i = \sum_s \sum_j \bar{q}_{sj}^i \hat{x}_{sj}^i \qquad \text{[D.12]}$$

which is a single budget constraint, restricting the value of planned state-contingent consumptions, across *all* states of the world, to equal the value of initial endowments, at the 'prices' $\bar{q}_{sj}^i$. These 'prices' are clearly composites of, on the one hand, the expected price of a specific good in a specific state and, on the other, of the general price q_s of a unit of income in that state.

The fact that [D.10] is a single budget constraint implies that *in effect* state-contingent commodities *can* be 'exchanged' across states of the world: for example good j in state s can be exchanged for good j in state t at the price ratio $\bar{q}_{sj}^i / \bar{q}_{tj}^i = q_s \bar{\pi}_{sj}^i / q_t \bar{\pi}_{tj}^i$. The intuitive explanation of this is as follows: by reducing, say his planned consumption $\bar{x}_{sj}^i$ by one unit, the consumer 'saves' the amount $\bar{\pi}_{sj}^i$. He can then *sell* $\bar{\pi}_{sj}^i$ units of income contingent on state s, by selling an Arrow-security which will require him to pay an amount $\bar{\pi}_{sj}^i$ in state s. Since the price of one unit of income contingent on state s is q_s, this sale yields him the proceeds $q_s \bar{\pi}_{sj}^i$. He can use this to *buy* an Arrow-security, and the amount of income contingent on state t that this will bring him is equal to $q_s \bar{\pi}_{sj}^i / q_t$, since this is the number of Arrow securities he can buy at price q_t. Thus, he can plan to increase his expenditure on $\bar{x}_{tj}^i$ by the amount:

$$\bar{\pi}_{tj}^i \Delta \bar{x}_{tj}^i = q_s \bar{\pi}_{sj}^i / q_t \qquad \text{[D.13]}$$

where $\Delta \bar{x}_{tj}^i$ is his increased planned consumption of $\bar{x}_{tj}^i$. This implies:

$$\Delta \bar{x}_{tj}^i = \frac{q_s \bar{\pi}_{sj}^i}{q_t \bar{\pi}_{tj}^i} = \bar{q}_{sj}^i / \bar{q}_{tj}^i \qquad \text{[D.14]}$$

i.e. the increased planned consumption of good j in state t which can be achieved by reducing planned consumption of good j in state s by one unit, is found by the price ratio $\bar{q}_{sj}^i / \bar{q}_{tj}^i$. Clearly, this could apply to any pair of goods. Thus, the combination of n spot markets in commodities and S

markets in Arrow-securities, or state-contingent income claims yields to each consumer as full a set of exchange possibilities as would be available under a complete system of markets in state-contingent commodities. It could therefore be argued that the former system 'economizes' on the number of markets, since under it we need only $n + S$ markets, as opposed to $n.S$ in the state-contingent commodity system.

We make two remarks upon this conclusion. First, since markets in Arrow-securities do not exist in reality, we require that the system of insurance and stock markets be such as to work *as if* they were equivalent to a complete system of markets in state-contingent income claims. This issue was discussed in the previous two sections, where we saw that because of moral hazard and transactions costs this may well not be the case. Thus, we have here found circumstances under which a market economy *may* permit as wide a set of exchange possibilities as when complete markets in state-contingent commodities exist, but we cannot necessarily conclude that the real economy does so.

Secondly, note that even if the full set of exchange possibilities is available, there is still no mechanism by which consumers are informed of the 'true' prices which will prevail on spot markets in each state of the world – the $\bar{\pi}^i_{sj}$ remain individual guesses. Consequently the composite prices $\bar{q}^i_{sj}$ may also differ among consumers and so our previous comment about the non-Pareto optimality of the planned state-contingent consumptions $\bar{x}^i_{sj}$ continues to hold. Although, in effect, exchange can take place between states, by appropriate choice of Arrow-security holdings, the marginal rates of substitution between a pair of planned consumption goods will differ for any two consumers with different price expectations and so a necessary condition for Pareto optimality will not be satisfied.

Exercise 20D

1.* Redefine the axiom system given in Chapter 19, with state-contingent commodity vectors $x_s = [x_{s1}, x_{s2}, \ldots, x_{sn}]$ in place of state-contingent income claims. Show in the same way as before that the resulting utility function is unique up to a positive linear transformation.

2.* Given that a complete system of futures markets exists for state-contingent commodities:
   (a) write down the conditions for consumer equilibrium implied by maximization of the expected utility function in [D.1], subject to the budget constraint in [D.2];
   (b) set out the conditions which must hold at a general equilibrium of this market system (cf. Ch. 16);
   (c) give a proof of the existence of a general equilibrium of this economy;
   (d) show that the equilibrium resource allocation in this economy is Pareto optimal, in terms of the expected utility functions of the decision-takers.

3. Given a general equilibrium as in Question 2, what is the cost to a

consumer of ensuring that he will have a unit of the jth commodity whatever the state of the world turns out to be?

4.* Explain why a consumer would want to exchange income across states of the world, whenever marginal expected utilities of income in different states are unequal.

5.* Show that if all consumers have identical price expectations, and a complete system of markets in state-contingent income claims exists, the planned state-contingent consumption choices of consumers will satisfy the conditions for Pareto optimality.

6.* In an economy in which a complete system of markets in Arrow-securities exists, show that the choice of an optimal set of planned consumptions $\bar{x}_{sj}^i$ can be broken down into:

(a) choosing quantities within each state of the world in such a way as to equalize marginal rates of substitution with expected price ratios;

(b) allocating income between states in such a way as to equalize the ratios of marginal expected utilities of income, λ_s/λ_t, to the price ratios of Arrow-securities, q_s/q_t.

E. Conclusions

This chapter has been concerned with the application of the expected utility theory to analysis of resource allocation under uncertainty. An important concept introduced was that of the state-contingent income claim, and we saw that in an economy which possesses a complete system of markets in these claims, resource allocation can be analysed by a direct application of the theory developed for a competitive economy under certainty. The state-contingent income claim is the analogue of a commodity in that theory, and all the propositions on existence, stability and optimality of an equilibrium resource allocation can be directly applied.

It is then of interest to consider the extent to which insurance and stock markets provide exchange possibilities equivalent to those existing in an economy with a complete system of markets in state-contingent income claims. We were able to frame conditions under which this would be the case, and considered how information and transactions costs and 'moral hazard', in insurance markets, and linear dependence among company profit vectors in stock markets, might lead these conditions not to be met in reality. We then went on to generalize the analysis to any finite number of goods and states of the world, and were led to the definition of the 'state-contingent commodity'. Again, an economy with a complete system of markets in state-contingent commodities could be analysed by a direct application of the theory developed for a competitive economy under certainty.

It is clear that such a system of markets does not in fact exist, and so we considered to what extent an economy with only spot markets and markets in Arrow-securities, or state-contingent income claims, would yield the same results. The element in this analysis which differs from that of insurance and stock markets is the role of *price expectations*. Given the markets in Arrow-securities, income and goods can in effect be exchanged between states. However, since consumers' plans depend on *expected* prices, and since there is no mechanism by which expected price ratios may be equalized over all consumers and made correct, an equilibrium in this economy will not satisfy the conditions for Pareto optimality. Moreover, in order to discuss the questions of existence and stability of equilibrium, we should have to specify the process by which expectations are formed and revised in response to the current operation of markets. This brings us very close to the present frontiers of economic theory.

References and further reading

There is an excellent survey of many aspects of uncertainty in:

J. **Hirshleifer** and J. **G. Riley.** 'The analytics of uncertainty and information – an expository survey', *Journal of Economic Literature*, December 1979.

On the concept of state-contingent claims and use of the indifference curve analysis, see:

K. **J. Arrow.** 'The role of securities in the optimal allocation of risk-bearing', *Review of Economic Studies*, 1964.

J. **Hirshleifer.** 'Investment decision under uncertainty: choice theoretic approaches', *Quarterly Journal of Economics*, 1965. 'Investment decision under uncertainty: applications of the state preference approach', *Quarterly Journal of Economics*, 1966. *Investment, Interest and Capital*, Prentice-Hall, Englewood Cliffs, N.J., 1970, Chs. 8, 9.

On the economics of insurance, moral hazard, etc. see:

K. **J. Arrow.** 'Insurance, risk and resource allocation', 'Uncertainty and the welfare economics of medical care', 'The economics of moral hazard; further comment', all in his *Essays in the Theory of Risk-Bearing*, North-Holland, Amsterdam, 1970.

R. **Kihlstrom** and M. **V. Pauly.** 'The role of insurance in the allocation of risk', *American Economic Review*, Papers and Proceedings, 1971.

M. **Spence** and R. **Zeckhauser.** 'Insurance, information and individual action', *American Economic Review*, Papers and Proceedings, 1971.

G. **Akerlof.** 'The market for lemons: qualitative uncertainty and the market mechanism', *Quarterly Journal of Economics*, 1970.

M. **V. Pauly.** 'Over-insurance and public provision of insurance: the roles of moral hazard and adverse selection', *Quarterly Journal of Economics*, 1974.

The approach adopted here to the economics of stock markets is developed more generally and rigorously in:

J. **Hirshleifer.** *Investment, Interest and Capital*, Prentice-Hall, Englewood Cliffs, N.J., 1970, Ch. 9.

P. **A. Diamond.** 'The role of a stock market in a general equilibrium model with technological uncertainty', *American Economic Review*, 1967.

J. **Dreze.** 'Investment under private ownership: optimality, equilibrium and stability' in J. Dreze (ed.), *Allocation under Uncertainty*, Macmillan, London, 1974.

L. **Gevers.** 'Competitive equilibrium of the stock exchange and pareto efficiency' in J. Dreze, *op. cit.*

Models of resource allocation under uncertainty are developed and analysed in:

K. Borch. *The Economics of Uncertainty*, Princeton University Press, 1968, Ch. VIII.

R. Guesnerie and **T. de Montbrial.** 'Allocation under uncertainty: a survey', in J. Dreze, *op. cit.*

J. Dreze. 'Market allocation under uncertainty', *European Economic Review*, Vol. 11, 1971.

G. Debreu. *Theory of Value*, John Wiley, New York, 1959, Ch. 7.

An alternative approach to the problem of uncertainty is examined in a seminal work:

A. M. Spence, *Market Signalling*, Harvard University Press, 1974.

Index

SURVEYS IN ECONOMICS
Series editors: Robert Millward, Michael T. Sumner and George Zis

This new series surveys the primary literature on selected economic topics for intermediate and advanced undergraduate students. The surveys have been written for those who are studying or have completed intermediate courses in economic theory and quantitative methods. They guide the reader through the professional literature explaining the major issues, and directing attention towards the most useful sources for further study.

By providing a comprehensive overview of its subject, each survey enables users to pursue particular aspects of the topics in greater depth through the medium of primary sources.

Series titles
Economics of Empire
Industrial Economics
International Economics
Labour Economics
Macroeconomics
Microeconomics
Monetary Economics
The Public Sector

WHY ECONOMISTS DISAGREE
The political economy of economics
Ken Cole, John Cameron and Chris Edwards
First published 1983

Many people call themselves 'economists' and thus apparently
accept some shared identity. It is obvious, however, that there
are major areas of disagreement between them, and while they
may agree on 'where' they disagree, they will rarely agree on
'why'. This book has been written for the benefit of students
who are aware of this situation, especially as it concerns
current political and economic debates, but can find no
satisfactory explanation of it in standard courses and
textbooks.

Why Economists Disagree provides a rigorous, non-
mathematical analysis of the theory and politics of each school
and brings the subject alive by showing the links between
economic theory and political practice. Extensive use is made
of flow diagrams to help explain the logic of the theories and
notes on further reading are given for additional guidance.

ISBN 0 582 29546 7